D1299886

PRINCIPLES OF INFORMATION TECHNOLOGY

by

Kathleen M. Austin
Lorraine N. Bergkvist

Publisher
The Goodheart-Willcox Company, Inc.
Tinley Park, Illinois
www.g-w.com

Introduction

As you prepare for college and career, you will likely find that information technology (IT) is unavoidable. Workplace correspondence, payroll, banking, and countless other activities associated with everyday life are all done primarily on a mobile device or in front of a personal computer. In *Principles of Information Technology*, you will learn basic principles and concepts about information technology to help you become a more valuable employee, a better citizen, and a knowledgeable consumer.

This text is laid out in a logical, conceptual progression. You begin by learning about the basic ins and outs of information technology, progress to applications that will likely be used in the workplace, and finish by learning about the interconnectivity that runs in daily life. Each chapter is laid out in a manner that is easy to read, easy to follow, and easy to understand. Figures, photos, and illustrations help provide clarity, understanding, and comprehension. Hands-on activities featured in the chapters allow you to practice the topics discussed in an easy and intuitive manner.

Certification

Whether you are new to IT or experienced, *Principles of Information Technology* affords an opportunity to build and refine your knowledge and skills in the IT world. This text will help you prepare for college and career. It will also help you prepare for and pass Certiport IC3 Digital Literacy Certification. The three areas of IC3 certification are Computing Fundamentals, Key Applications, and Living Online. For more information on IC3 certification, please visit Certiport at www.certiport.com.

About the Authors

Kathleen M. Austin was a senior lecturer in the School of Information Arts and Technologies at the University of Baltimore. She has participated in the development of many educational multimedia projects. She has authored, coauthored, or contributed to several textbooks, including *Consumer Mathematics* and *Mathematics of the World of Work*. She holds a Master of Science degree in Computer Science from Johns Hopkins University and a Doctor of Communications Design from the University of Baltimore as well as IC3 certification.

Lorraine N. Bergkvist is an Adjunct Professor at the University of Baltimore providing instruction in Visual Basic programming, database implementation, and web-page creation. She is also the owner of Federal Hill Résumé Center, which provides professional résumé-writing services as well as consulting and editing in the information technology field. She developed the curriculum and taught the Introduction to Technology course at the University of Baltimore and the College of Notre Dame of Maryland. She holds a Master of Education degree from Towson University and IC3 certification and has received several scholarships and grants in the technology field.

Reviewers

Goodheart-Willcox Publisher would like to thank the following people who reviewed selected chapters and contributed valuable input to this edition of *Principles of Information Technology*.

Lorie S. Atkinson
Technology Teacher
Elgin High School
Elgin, TX

J. Burton Browning
Business, Engineering, and Technology
    Department Chair
Brunswick Community College
Supply, NC

Kevin J. Grump
CTE Teacher
Oceanside High School
Oceanside, CA

Austin Guiswite
Senior Software Developer
CGI Federal
Fairfax, VA

Karn Gustafson
Digital Film Product, CAD Architecture, CAD
    Engineering Teacher
Volcano Vista High School
Albuquerque, NM

Madison Holloman
Business Education Teacher
Irmo High School
Columbia, SC

Sandra Jaworski
Business Department Chair
Jeffersontown High School
Louisville, KY

Tammy G. Neil
Computer Applications and Game Design &
    Simulations Teacher
Branford High School
Branford, FL

Erin L. Wasson
Science and Technology Instructor/STEAM
    Coordinator
Jackson Heights Middle School
Oviedo, FL

CONTENTS IN BRIEF

EXPANDED TABLE OF CONTENTS

Unit 2 Key Applications 210

Unit 3
Living Online 506

HANDS-ON EXAMPLES

PREPARE FOR YOUR FUTURE

As you prepare for college and career, an important key to success will be the fundamentals and foundations of information technology. Understanding the basics of computing, applications, and online technology is the first step toward personal success. By studying *Principles of Information Technology*, you will have an opportunity to learn about the three elements of IT and how to make them work for you.

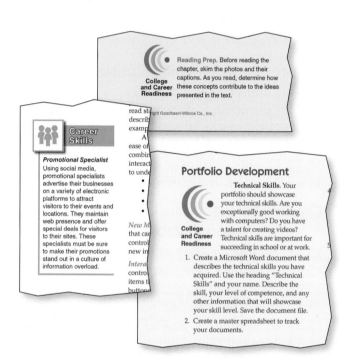

It is all about getting ready for college and career. College and career readiness activities address literacy skills to help prepare you for the real world.

- English/Language Arts standards for reading, writing, speaking, and listening are incorporated in **Reading Prep** activities as well as in end-of-chapter applications.
- **Career Skills** features present information about potential career opportunities in the Information Technology career cluster. By studying these, you can explore career possibilities for your future.
- **Portfolio Development** activities provide guidance to create a personal portfolio for use when exploring volunteer, education and training, and career opportunities.

Practical information helps you prepare for your future. Special features add realism and interest to enhance learning.

- **Ethics** offers insight into ethical issues with which you will be confronted in the workplace.
- **Green Tech** illustrates the importance of respecting the environment in the workplace.
- **STEM** illustrates the importance of science, technology, engineering, and mathematics skills in the workplace.

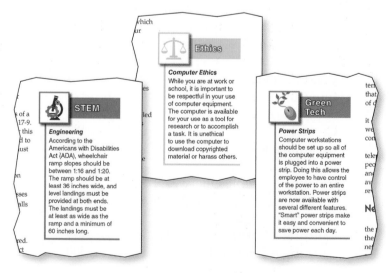

AMPLIFY YOUR LEARNING

Content is presented in an easy-to-comprehend and relevant format. Activities relate everyday learning to enable you to experience real-life situations and challenges.

- IC3 objectives covered in the chapter are outlined at the beginning. This provides an overview of the certification material covered in the chapter.

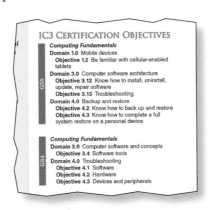

- IC3 objectives are called out within the chapter where the material is covered. This allows you to focus learning on specific certification content.

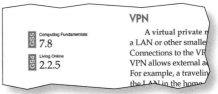

- Each chapter opens with a **pretest**. The pretest will help you evaluate your prior knowledge of the chapter content.

- Each chapter also concludes with a **posttest**. The posttest will help you evaluate what you have learned after studying the chapter.

- The **Essential Question** at the beginning of each section will engage you as you uncover the important points presented in the content.

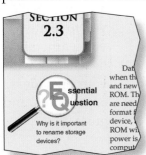

- Research skills are critical for success in college and career. **Internet Research** activities at the end of each chapter provide opportunities to put them to work.

Internet Research

History of the Internet. Research the history of the Internet using various resources. Why was the Internet first developed? When did the Internet become standardized? Write several paragraphs describing what you learned. Use correct punctuation as you write and edit your document.

- **Event Prep** presents information to use when preparing for competitive activities in career and technical student organization (CTSO) competitions.

ASSESS YOUR PROGRESS

It is important to assess what you learn as you progress through the textbook. Multiple opportunities are provided to confirm learning as you explore the content. *Formative assessment* includes the following.

- **Check Your Understanding** questions at the end of each major section of the chapter provide an opportunity to review what you have learned before moving on to additional content.
- An **IC3 Certification Practice** question in each section review presents a question designed to help you prepare for IC3 Digital Literacy Certification.
- **Build Your Vocabulary** activities review the key terms presented in each major section. By completing these activities, you will be able to demonstrate your understanding of communication terms.

11.1 SECTION REVIEW

CHECK YOUR UNDERSTANDING

1. What does each function in Microsoft Excel begin with?
2. Which dialog box is used to add a function to a spreadsheet in Microsoft Excel?
3. What three values are needed to calculate loan payments using the **PMT** function in Excel?
4. What does a logical function test for?
5. Which logical function is used to test the values of two expressions?

IC3 CERTIFICATION PRACTICE

The following question is a sample of the types of questions presented on the IC3 exam.

1. The formula =SUM(G7:G25) calculates the sum of the range G7:G25. Modify this formula to instead find the largest value in the same range.

BUILD YOUR VOCABULARY

As you progress through this course, develop a personal IT glossary. This will help you build your vocabulary and prepare you for a career. Write a definition for each of the following terms and add it to your IT glossary.

arguments
function
logical functions
principal
term

- **Communication Skills** activities provide ways for you to demonstrate the literacy and career readiness skills you have mastered.

- **Teamwork** activities encourage a collaborative experience to help you learn to interact with other students in a productive manner.

and terminology as you write.

Teamwork

Working with your team, conduct an audit of the hardware in your computer lab. What items are common to all computers? What items are found on only some computers?

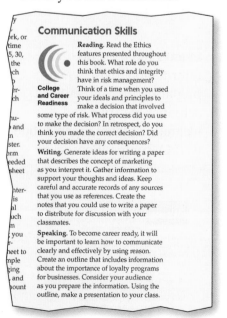

Communication Skills

College and Career Readiness

Reading. Read the Ethics features presented throughout this book. What role do you think that ethics and integrity have in risk management? Think of a time when you used your ideals and principles to make a decision that involved some type of risk. What process did you use to make the decision? In retrospect, do you think you made the correct decision? Did your decision have any consequences?

Writing. Generate ideas for writing a paper that describes the concept of marketing as you interpret it. Gather information to support your thoughts and ideas. Keep careful and accurate records of any sources that you use as references. Create the notes that you could use to write a paper to distribute for discussion with your classmates.

Speaking. To become career ready, it will be important to learn how to communicate clearly and effectively by using reason. Create an outline that includes information about the importance of loyalty programs for businesses. Consider your audience as you prepare the information. Using the outline, make a presentation to your class.

Application and Extension of Knowledge

1. Research common locations of embedded computers. Make a list of devices you use each day that contain embedded computers. Bring your list to class for discussion.
2. Identify three emerging technologies. List one positive and negative effect of each. Be prepared to defend your position in a class discussion.
3. Identify five new information technology careers that were created as a result of the advent of social media.
4. Research the practice of data mining, and develop an opinion on the practice. Write a one-page paper stating your view of the advantages and disadvantages of data mining with regard to personal privacy.
5. Write a one-page paper describing why you feel an information technology worker must keep his or her skills up to date.

- **Application and Extension of Knowledge** activities challenge you to relate what you learned in the chapter with your own ideas, experiences, and goals.

MAXIMIZE THE IMPACT

G-W Learning Companion Website

Technology is an important part of your world. So, it should be part of your everyday learning experiences. G-W Learning for *Principles of Information Technology* is a study reference that contains activity files, vocabulary exercises, interactive quizzes, and more.

Visit www.g-wlearning.com.

G-W Learning provides you with opportunities for hands-on interactivity so you can study on the go. Look for the activity icon in the text next to the following activities.

- Chapter **pretests** and **posttests** allow you to assess what you know before you begin the chapter as well as evaluate what you have learned at the completion of your study.

- **E-flash cards** and **matching activities** for every key term in each chapter will reinforce vocabulary learned in the text and enable you to study on the go.

- **Certification practice tests** help you prepare for IC3 Digital Literacy Certification by answering the types of questions found on the certification exams.

Goodheart-Willcox QR Codes

This Goodheart-Willcox product contains QR codes*, or quick response codes. These codes can be scanned with a smartphone bar code reader to access the chapter pretests and posttests. For more information on using QR codes and a recommended QR code reader, visit G-W Learning.

www.g-wlearning.com

An Internet connection is required to access the QR code destinations. Data-transfer rates may apply. Check with your Internet service provider for information on your data-transfer rates.

G-W INTEGRATED LEARNING SOLUTION

The G-W Integrated Learning Solution offers easy-to-use resources for both students and instructors. Digital and blended learning content can be accessed through any Internet-enabled device such as a computer, smartphone, or tablet. Students spend more time learning, and instructors spend less time administering.

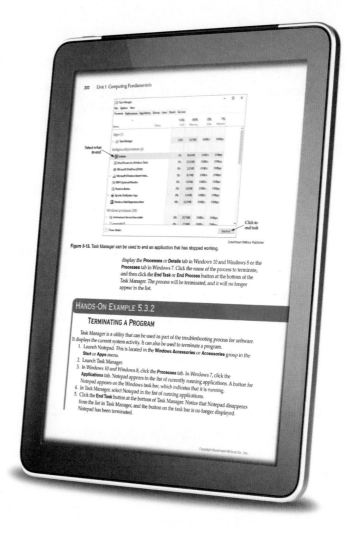

G-W Learning Companion Website/Student Textbook

The G-W Learning companion website is a study reference that contains e-flash cards, vocabulary exercises, interactive quizzes, and more! Accessible from any digital device, the G-W Learning companion website complements the textbook and is available to the student at no charge.

Visit www.g-wlearning.com.

Online Learning Suite

Available as a classroom subscription, the Online Learning Suite provides the foundation of instruction and learning for digital and blended classrooms. An easy-to-manage shared classroom subscription makes it a hassle-free solution for both students and instructors. An online student text along with rich supplemental content brings digital learning to the classroom. All instructional materials are found on a convenient online bookshelf and are accessible at home, at school, or on the go.

Online Learning Suite/Student Textbook Bundle

Looking for a blended solution? Goodheart-Willcox offers the Online Learning Suite bundled with the printed text in one easy-to-access package. Students have the flexibility to use the print version, the Online Learning Suite, or a combination of both components to meet their individual learning style. The convenient packaging makes managing and accessing content easy and efficient.

Online Instructor Resources

Online Instructor Resources provide all the support needed to make preparation and classroom instruction easier than ever. Available in one accessible location, support materials include Answer Keys, Lesson Plans, Instructor's Presentations for PowerPoint®, ExamView® Assessment Suite, and more! Online Instructor Resources are available as a subscription and can be accessed at school or at home.

G-W Integrated Learning Solution

For the Student:

Student Textbook (print)
G-W Learning Companion Website
  (free)
Online Learning Suite (subscription)
Online Learning Suite/Student
  Textbook Bundle

For the Instructor:

Instructor's Presentations for
  PowerPoint® (CD)
ExamView® Assessment Suite (CD)
Instructor Resources (CD)
Online Instructor Resources
  (subscription)

UNIT 1
COMPUTING FUNDAMENTALS

Olga Lipatova/Shutterstock.com

This unit provides a background in the subjects needed to begin understanding computing, including the efficient and thoughtful use of computer hardware, software, and operating systems. Skills covered include solving basic digital-literacy problems, using common production applications, and describing current technologies. This acquired knowledge can then be applied in new circumstances.

Information gathered in this unit will support your learning in the final two units: Key Applications and Living Online. It will provide a foundation for further learning in the field of information technology. The material in this textbook, from provided information to acquired skills and activities, supports the objectives for the IC3 Digital Literacy Certification. Learning and studying this material will help to prepare for taking this certification exam.

 While studying, look for the activity icon for:

- Pretests and posttests
- Vocabulary terms with e-flash cards and matching activities
- Formative assessment

INTRODUCTION TO INFORMATION TECHNOLOGY

SECTIONS

1.1 COMPUTERS ARE EVERYWHERE

1.2 COMPUTERS IN THE WORKPLACE

1.3 CHALLENGES OF A DIGITAL SOCIETY

Most young adults have been using computers since they could read and write or, in many cases, even before then. Computers are used to complete school assignments, conduct business, and—most of all—communicate. Most people are computer *users*; they know how to *operate* these devices. After completing this course, you will become computer *literate*. That is, you will understand more than just how to operate computers. You will understand the details of how computers work and the impact computers have on your life and career.

This chapter provides an overview of the field of information technology (IT). You may already know some of the facts, but some facts will likely be new to you. You will learn about emerging technologies as well as the arithmetic that computers use. Additionally, information is included about future career opportunities. Other topics are discussed to start you thinking about issues faced by information technology professionals and society as a whole. Perhaps you will be able to solve some of these problems yourself.

IC3 CERTIFICATION OBJECTIVES

Computing Fundamentals

Domain 1.0 Mobile devices
Objective 1.1 Understand cellular phone concepts
Objective 1.3 Be familiar with smartphones
Domain 2.0 Hardware devices
Objective 2.8 Know platform considerations and implications
Objective 2.11 Understand concepts regarding connecting to the Internet
Domain 6.0 Cloud computing
Objective 6.1 Understand "cloud" concepts
Objective 6.2 Know the benefits of using cloud storage
Objective 6.3 Access and use of the cloud
Objective 6.4 Web apps vs. local apps
Objective 6.5 Understand web app types

Living Online

Domain 6.0 Communication
Objective 6.1 Know the best tool for the various situations and scenarios
Domain 9.0 Digital principles/ethics/skills/citizenship
Objective 9.1 Understand the necessity of coping with change in technology

Computing Fundamentals

Domain 2.0 Computer hardware and concepts
Objective 2.2 Types of devices
Domain 4.0 Troubleshooting
Objective 4.4 Backup/restore

GS5

GS4

Reading Prep. As you read this chapter, determine the point of view or purpose of the author. What aspects of the text help to establish this purpose or point of view?

College and Career Readiness

COMPUTERS ARE EVERYWHERE

Essential Question

How has the digital revolution changed communication?

Look around. There are computers everywhere! They can be found on desks, in people's pockets, under people's arms, in offices, in stores, in banks, and in movie theaters. Some computers are located where you cannot look: inside other devices. The average person operates more than 20 computerized devices every day. Most people take computers for granted because this technology has become an integral part of our lives. The integration of computer technology into daily life is why our society is referred to as a *digital society*.

Understanding where computers are and how they function is a necessity for social and professional success. Computers are used for communication, social connections, business, industry, research, recreation, and navigation, among other applications. The demand for better and new digital devices continues to grow.

This section explores the widespread use of computers and other digital devices in today's world.

Lisa F. Young/Shutterstock.com

TERMS

augmented printing

augmented reality (AR)

bandwidth

cloud computing

computer

digital revolution

e-mail

embedded computers

emerging technologies

information technology (IT)

quick response (QR) codes

interactive books

smartphone

software as a service (SaaS)

software-defined storage

LEARNING GOALS

After completing this section, you will be able to:

- List the phases of the digital revolution.
- Describe embedded computers.
- Identify communication technologies.
- Discuss emerging technologies.

Digital Revolution

The field of **information technology (IT)** includes all work done with computers, from the design and installation of hardware and software to the maintenance of these systems. Many changes have occurred over time in the IT field. The state of the art of computing today is ever-changing with new and innovative additions, such as shown in Figure 1-1. These changes are part of the digital revolution. The **digital revolution** is the ever-expanding progression of technical, economic, and cultural changes brought about by computers. It has gone through four phases:

- giant computers
- personal computers
- networked computers
- cloud computing

A **computer** is a device that handles input, processes data, stores data, and produces usable output according to sets of stored instructions. Computer categories are covered in detail in Chapter 2.

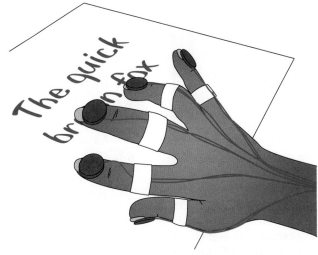

Goodheart-Willcox Publisher

Figure 1-1. An innovative method for data input to a computer uses sensors on the fingers to determine input.

Giant Computers

The first phase of the digital revolution occurred from the 1940s through the 1960s and is characterized by the use of giant computing machines. These machines were physically so large that they had to be located in special facilities, as shown in Figure 1-2. These computers required highly skilled technicians to run even simple reports. Programs had to be small and extremely efficient.

At first, only one program could be run at a time. Computer time had to be scheduled because there were so few computers. Later, workstations were connected to the main computer. These workstations, or terminals, allowed many people to connect to the computer and share computing time. However, these workstations were called "dumb" terminals because they were not able to do anything on their own. They just connected to the giant machines.

Personal Computers

The second phase of the digital revolution began with the advent of personal computers (PCs) in the 1970s and lasted through the early 1990s. PCs were small and inexpensive enough to be used in households and businesses. They were not dumb

US Army Photo

Figure 1-2. Programmers Elizabeth (Betty) Jean Jennings and Frances (Fran) Bilas preparing for the public unveiling of ENIAC. ENIAC was the first electronic digital computer.

Green Tech

Power Strips
Computer workstations should be set up so all of the computer equipment is plugged into a power strip. Doing this allows the employee to have control of the power to an entire workstation. Power strips are now available with several different features. "Smart" power strips make it easy and convenient to save power each day.

terminals connected to a main computer. They were complete computers that could run programs all by themselves. The first PCs were only capable of displaying one color on the monitor screen against a black background.

The software had a text-based interface, and many people found it difficult to use. Word processing and business spreadsheet programs were the most popular business applications. Games were the most used computer programs at home.

Communication from computer to computer was performed over telephone lines. Computer hobbyists set up programs that allowed other people to connect to a software program called a bulletin board to leave and retrieve messages. What became known as the Internet was not available to the general public until late in the second phase of the digital revolution, and the World Wide Web did not exist.

Networked Computers

The popularity of personal computers only gradually increased until the mid-1990s. It was at this time when software became what most of the population could consider user-friendly. Also at this time, computer networks became interconnected, as shown in Figure 1-3. Both businesses and the general public alike could access these networks. This marks the beginning of the third phase of the digital revolution, which would last through the early 2000s.

Arjuna Kodisinghe/Shutterstock.com

Figure 1-3. Computer networks can be very large and may contain many servers to manage data.

Networks were invented around 1970, but they became easier to use with the evolution of personal computers. The computers were connected in a limited area, such as within a business, school, or house. These were called local area networks (LANs).

Networks allowed for great expansion in the use of electronic mail (e-mail). **E-mail** is communication sent to a computer address where the message is stored to be read at a later time by the recipient. E-mail became popular in the general public through companies such as AOL (formerly called America On-Line) and CompuServe. These were two early commercial Internet service providers (ISPs). Many people today use web-based e-mail, such as Google or Yahoo! mail, and a wide variety of ISPs.

Internet

The Internet began as a project in the 1960s called ARPANET. This project was funded by the US Department of Defense and produced a network of computers for efficient transmission of data between different geographic locations. The network was known as the wide area network (WAN). It was connected to the National Science Foundation network (NSFNET) in 1990, and in 1995 the last restrictions on its commercial use were eliminated.

World Wide Web

The World Wide Web (WWW), or the web, is a part of the Internet. The web *uses* the Internet, but the Internet and the web are not the same thing. There are other parts of the Internet, such as e-mail, file transfers, and news feeds, that are not part of the web. The World Wide Web was launched in 1991.

The World Wide Web was conceived and developed by Sir Tim Berners-Lee. He found that locating the proper document on the Internet, transmitting it to his computer, and trying to figure out how to open the document was inefficient and time-consuming. He created the World Wide Web as an easy way to find and read documents.

At the beginning, the web was one web page on one website. The web grew slowly at first, staying very small and containing few pages and documents. Today, the web extends all over the world and contains trillions of pages and documents.

Mobile Computers

Mobile devices are commonplace today. These are small, typically handheld digital devices that rely on satellite, microwave, and cellular transmissions for data transfer. Examples of mobile devices are cellular telephones and smartphones, tablet computers, e-book readers, and global positioning system (GPS) devices. The distinctions between types of computers begin to blur now that a smartphone can perform the same actions as desktop computers plus telephone communication.

Mobile devices are often capable of using Wi-Fi to minimize other forms of more costly transmissions. Wi-Fi is a local area network in which the network connection is provided wirelessly. Wi-Fi is available in many public places, sometimes provided as part of a purchased data plan or provided for free by a business, school, or municipality as a public service. Many people have a Wi-Fi network within their homes as well. The name *Wi-Fi* is a play on the phrase used to describe high-quality sound reproduction. High fidelity was called *hi-fi* for short.

GS4 Computing Fundamentals
2.2.4, 2.2.5, 2.2.6

Cloud Computing

The fourth and current phase of the digital revolution began in the early 2000s when cloud computing became popular. **Cloud computing** involves storing and retrieving data from Internet-based spaces. Collectively, these spaces are called *the cloud*. The cloud is useful for backing up and sharing data, but it also makes it possible to run a program not installed on the local computer. The cloud involves sharing resources among computers.

In a sense, it can be said that information technology is back at the giant computers phase. The cloud is like the giant computer, and personal computing devices are like the terminals. However, the cloud is more powerful because the terminals are "smart" and portable.

FYI

The concept of cloud computing dates to the 1950s. Functional precursors to the cloud began appearing in the 1990s.

GS5 Computing Fundamentals
6.1.1

GS4 Computing Fundamentals
4.4.3

Embedded Computers

Embedded computers are small digital computers found inside other devices. They are not readily visible, nor do they look like familiar desktop, laptop, or tablet computers. Embedded systems are found in digital cameras, mobile phones, home appliances, music players, special IT hardware, and even automobiles. Embedded systems must be reliable because they are programmed to perform the same tasks over and over.

Location

A remarkable characteristic of embedded computers is that they can be easily incorporated into many devices that did not previously contain them. For example, automobiles have become increasingly computerized over the last few decades. Embedded computers can be found in very visible devices, such as navigation and entertainment systems. But they are also being used to affect the fundamental functioning of the vehicle: metering fuel flow, monitoring emissions levels, controlling braking systems, and even diagnosing functional problems.

Embedded computers can be found in a wide variety of devices. In an average living room, embedded computers are found in televisions, DVD players, game consoles, and all of the remotes that control them. Programmable home thermostats contain them, as shown in Figure 1-4. Medical devices, business and industrial equipment, and even many washers, dryers, ovens, and stoves may contain embedded computers. Any device that is programmable likely contains an embedded computer.

Steve Cukrov/Shutterstock.com

Figure 1-4. Most programmable home thermostats contain embedded computers.

Continuous Operation

Embedded computers often reside in machines that are expected to run continuously for years without errors. Sometimes these embedded computers must recover by themselves if a system error occurs. As a result, the software and hardware are thoroughly tested and run flawlessly.

Imagine a situation where the system cannot be shut down for repair or is too inaccessible to reach. The systems on NASA space probes and the Mars rover Curiosity are impossible to access except through data communication. Other examples of remote applications include undersea cables, navigational beacons, and control systems for boreholes that carry fluids hundreds of feet underground.

Sometimes systems that include embedded computers must be kept running for safety reasons. Such devices handle aircraft navigation, nuclear reactor control systems, chemical factory controls, and train signals.

Other systems containing embedded computers demand high reliability because of the potential for significant disruptions to business or loss of large amounts of money when shut down. Examples are telephone switches, factory controls, bridge and elevator controls, and automated trains and trams.

Communication Technologies

Computer technology has made it possible for those with access to digital communication devices to stay in touch with others 24 hours a day. As a result, communication methods are changing at a rapid pace. A notable innovation in communication technology is the smartphone. The **smartphone** is a handheld computer that contains a telephone, software applications commonly called apps, and the ability to quickly connect to the Internet. The impact of having a smartphone is the increased speed of communication and the breadth of geographic reach. There are advantages and disadvantages to the advances in communication technology.

GS5 Computing Fundamentals
1.1.1, 1.3.1

Speed

In the past, a person had to wait days for the post office to carry written communication in the form of a letter. Even in the last decade of the 20th century, fast written communication meant waiting minutes to send a fax. The Internet has reduced waiting time for written communication to milliseconds. Even spoken communication is carried over the Internet in nearly real time.

GS5 Computing Fundamentals
2.11.2

Bandwidth is a measure of the amount of data that can travel on a communication system. Just as a large artery can carry more blood cells than a small capillary, a high-bandwidth Internet connection can carry more data at one time than a low-bandwidth connection. The demand for greater bandwidth is growing. Multiuser networks, music and movie streaming, and the ever-growing number of Internet users all increase the need for greater bandwidth. Use of high bandwidth is also referred to as *broadband communication*.

Ethics

Reach

Communication programs that share video, voice, and data are accessible to anyone with a computer or smartphone and an Internet connection. In developing countries, people who may have never owned a radio or television now often have smartphones. These devices allow global communication, which opens a wide view of world culture.

Sourcing
Factories in which products are created should be clean and safe for its workers. Most electronic devices are manufactured overseas. Manufacturers in other countries may have different work safety standards than the United States. It is important to remember that purchasing products at the expense of others to save money is unethical, even if the working conditions are deemed legal.

Advantages

The amount, intimacy, and power of computer-based communication have been enormously affected by social media through innovations such as Facebook, Twitter, Tumblr, and LinkedIn, as shown in Figure 1-5. Participation in Facebook has been described as an ongoing virtual reality show where the users are the entertainers as well as the audience.

Pieter Beens/Shutterstock.com

Figure 1-5. Smartphones have been a key part of the growth of social media, which itself greatly affected computer-based communication.

FYI

Google Flu Trends is www.google.org/flutrends/. Click a country on the map to see its statistics.

The speed and reach of social media have had enormous consequences in giving the users significant power to access information and participate in global discussions. News and opinions spread quickly. For example, when Britain's Prince George was born in July of 2013, the initial announcement received over 13,000 retweets and nearly 4,000 favorites in the first few minutes after its posting. Additionally, the Royal Family made the official birth announcement through its account on Instagram. When Princess Charlotte was born in 2015, the Royal Family's first announcement was on Twitter, not the traditional posting of a physical note on the palace gates.

When the first cases of swine flu (H1N1) were detected in the spring of 2009, postings on Twitter were numerous. Researchers from leading search engine providers like Google and Yahoo found that certain search terms were good indicators of flu activity. As a result, Google launched Google Flu Trends to estimate flu activity. Researchers at the University of Iowa found Twitter could not only track the reaction to H1N1, but also track the disease itself by using the comments in tweets not available in search terms. Twitter could become an innovative scientific tool for epidemiologists. Epidemiologists are scientists who study the cause and spread of disease.

Global communication has allowed small businesses in developing countries to have a worldwide marketplace. In many developing countries, a majority of workers have low incomes, limited job security, and no social protection. Technology allows these workers to participate in the global market. In turn, there is the potential they can raise their welfare and improve economic outcomes.

Starting up businesses requires money. Many businesses borrow money from banks to get going. Smartphones have made it possible for very small businesses in developing countries to have access to banks and money. Microfinancing is providing small loans to businesses in developing countries. Providing microfinance services is made possible by direct interaction between lenders and borrowers via the Internet rather than physical offices.

There are many other advantages of communication technologies. There is a greater use of online health care services. Medical diagnosis one day may be done by an online artificial intelligence. There is more transparency in pricing online education. This has lead to more competition, resulting in lower costs for many students.

Disadvantages

Internet-based communication is so fast that the expectation is a message must be sent or replied to as quickly as possible. As a result, often people do not take time for reflection before sending the message. This can end in embarrassing situations when an inappropriate message is sent. If the communication is part of work functions, the inappropriate message may even result in the worker being fired.

Internet-based communication has also led to an epidemic of crime, including fraud, and unethical behavior, such as cyberbullying. In many cases, cyberbullying can be a crime, but it is always unethical behavior. E-mail scams such as phishing seek to steal a person's identity and use it to commit fraud, which is a form of theft. Computer viruses and other malware can also be transmitted by Internet-based communication.

The privacy and security of personal and business information as well as the ownership of that information are at risk. The ease of obtaining digital information through communication technologies leads many to believe the information is not owned by anybody. This is incorrect. Almost everything on the Internet, from text to streamed videos and music downloads, is copyrighted and owned by somebody. This means it is intellectual property protected by law. It is illegal to copy and use the information without permission.

Emerging Technologies

Evolving and emerging technologies can have a great impact on the exchange of information. Evolving technologies are those that change over time, such as how cell phones rapidly advanced over a short period of time into the smartphones of today. **Emerging technologies** are innovations that represent significantly new fields or technologies. Companies are finding new ways to use technology to make money. However, emerging technologies can also be found in education and other industries that are not driven by profit.

One emerging technology that is a new field is electronic textiles, or e-textiles. E-textiles are fabrics with embedded computers that react to sensors in the fabric. Currently available is a belt with an embedded performance monitor that is worn around the torso. The company that manufactures this product predicts additional products in the future, such as a touch screen fitness tracker embedded in the fabric of an exercise shirt.

Visual Displays

Another example of an emerging technology is augmented reality. **Augmented reality (AR)** is a view of the live world that has been enhanced with computerized graphics, sound, or other outputs. A form of AR is **augmented printing**. The user holds a mobile device over a printed page, and instantly associated videos or other content appears on the screen. In this way, the printed page is connected to the virtual world.

Currently available AR systems include Google Glass and smartphone apps that overlay data on the phone's video display, as shown in Figure 1-6. Other possible applications include computer-linked glasses or bionic contact lenses that can be used for facial recognition. For example, while attending a meeting or convention, the wearer could enter a voice or eye-movement command to activate facial-recognition software, and then the computer would display profile information about the speaker the user is engaging.

Medical Technology

Evolving and emerging technologies have led to amazing advances in medical diagnosis and treatment. Diagnosis can be done remotely, including collecting and analyzing blood samples. Ultra-high-resolution

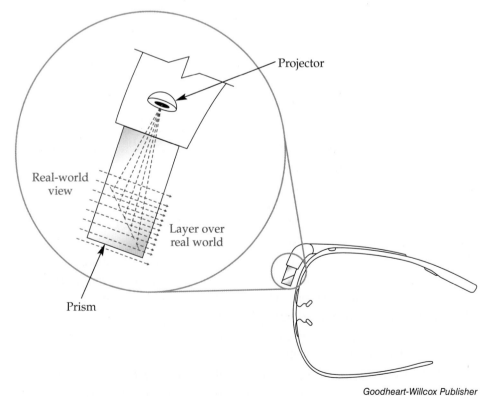

Goodheart-Willcox Publisher

Figure 1-6. An augmented-reality device provides a view of the real world enhanced with computerized elements.

graphics allow physicians to visualize the detail and activity of functioning hearts and brains. With feedback systems under development, they can even feel the organs without actually touching the patient.

Three-dimensional (3D) printing, which is itself an emerging technology, has led to emerging technology in the area of organ-transplant surgery. Researchers are working on eliminating the need for an organ donor by using the patient's own living cells to create a 3D-printed kidney. About 98% of patients on the organ waiting lists need kidneys.

Interactive Books

Most electronic books (e-books) offer limited interaction with the material. The reader can turn the pages, search for content, or highlight words to view a dictionary definition. Additionally, visually impaired readers benefit from the ability to increase the size of the text. E-book technology is evolving to allow interactive books that offer many improvements over standard e-books.

Interactive books are enhanced e-books that contain integrated multimedia features such as audio, video, pop-up graphics, 3D images, and animations. This technology offers consumers upgraded works of fiction and nonfiction that incorporate movies, videos, photographs, illustrations, and maps. It also leads to enhanced educational opportunities when publishers offer interactive digital textbooks.

New and Emerging Classes of Software

The basic fact of emerging technologies is that they will continue to multiply at a very quick pace. Keeping current is the way of life for an IT professional. Some of the technologies that did not exist just a few years ago are software as a service, software-defined storage, QR codes, and software-defined networking.

Software as a Service

Software as a service (SaaS) is software that resides in the cloud and is accessed by users without downloading or installing it on their local computers. Another name for this software is *on-demand software*. Some of the software is free to use, while other software is for-purchase that the user typically pays a monthly subscription fee to access. The advantage is that users do not need to purchase expensive licenses to own the software and the software is always up to date. Google Apps, which includes Calendar, Gmail, and Docs, is an example of free SaaS. An example of a subscription SaaS is Adobe Creative Cloud, which includes Adobe Photoshop, Adobe Illustrator, and Adobe InDesign. Microsoft Office 365 is another example of a subscription SaaS.

Software-Defined Storage

Software-defined storage is cloud-based file storage. Sharing of files such as photos or documents can be permitted, or the files may be stored privately. Examples of free software-defined storage are Dropbox,

FYI

The distinction between apps and e-books can be confusing. Both are digital files, but apps are computer applications and e-books are documents. Generally, an app is needed to read an e-book.

GS5 Computing Fundamentals
6.5.1, 6.5.2

GS5 Computing Fundamentals
2.8.1, 6.1.1, 6.4.1

GS5 Computing Fundamentals
6.1.1, 6.2, 6.3.1, 6.3.2, 6.3.3, 6.3.4

GS4 Computing Fundamentals
4.4.3

TITANS OF TECHNOLOGY

While computing has been a human need for thousands of years, electronic digital computers have existed for less than a century. Starting in 1945 with the development of the Electronic Numerical Integrator and Computer (ENIAC), the digital age was born. The leaders of the design team for this first programmable digital computer were J. Presper Eckert and John Mauchly at the University of Pennsylvania. They conceived the idea for using vacuum tubes to represent the on-off digital values. The calculations required 36 vacuum tubes to represent a single digit. Once the ENIAC was completed and tested, it was used at Aberdeen Proving Ground in Maryland to perform ballistics calculations. The first programmers were Kay McNulty, Betty Jennings, Betty Snyder, Marlyn Wescoff, Fran Bilas, and Ruth Lichterman.

Apple iCloud, Google Drive, and Amazon Cloud. For-purchase software-defined storage is also available, which typically offers benefits not found in the free options.

To access or store files on the cloud, an account must be created. There is a process for signing up for an account during which a user name and password will be assigned to the account. To access the files stored in this account, you must log into the account with the name and password.

Most cloud-based storage applications allow the user to synchronize, or sync, files between the cloud and a personal device or computer. To sync files is to make sure the same file exists in each location. However, this process usually does not compare the content of files, so it is possible to lose content when syncing files.

There are several advantages to storing files in the cloud. Where a local disk drive may fail, resulting in loss of files, cloud storage has redundancies to prevent data loss. Restoring files from the cloud is easier and faster than restoring files from an inventory of physical media.

HANDS-ON EXAMPLE 1.1.1

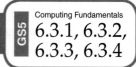
GS5 | Computing Fundamentals
6.3.1, 6.3.2, 6.3.3, 6.3.4

SOFTWARE-DEFINED STORAGE

Google Photos is a cloud-based storage application for photographs and videos. It is able to sync effortlessly with all devices, such as your desktop computer, laptop, tablet, and smartphone. It allows control for building albums, collages, and videos. To use Google Photos, you must have a Google account.

1. Navigate to the student companion website at www.g-wlearning.com, download the data files for this chapter, and save them in your project folder. The file Bison.jpg will be used in this example.

2. Launch a web browser, and navigate to www.google.com.

HANDS-ON EXAMPLE 1.1.1 (CONTINUED)

Google
Apps

3. Click the **Google Apps** button on the web page to display a drop-down menu, as shown.

4. Click **Photos** in the drop-down menu to launch Google Photos. If a splash screen appears, click **Go to Google Photos** or a similar link to continue to the application.
5. If you are not signed in to your Google account, you will be asked to sign in. If you do not have an account, you can sign up for one at this time.
6. The first time you launch Google Photos, you may be asked to set up parameters. Select the high resolution option instead of the original option. This option allows unlimited storage. After the parameters are set, the main Google Photos interface appears, which is what you normally see when launching the application.
7. To upload a photograph, click the **Upload photos** button along the top of the web page. A standard **Open** dialog box is displayed.

Upload
photos

8. Navigate to your working folder, select the Bison.jpg file, and click the **Open** button.
9. If a dialog box appears asking which quality setting to use for the image, click the **High Quality** radio button and then the **Continue** link. The image is uploaded to Google Photos.
10. Move the cursor over the image, and click the check mark in the upper-left corner to select the image. Once an image is selected, it can be deleted, downloaded, or shared.

HANDS-ON EXAMPLE 1.1.1 (CONTINUED)

Download

11. Click the **Download** button in the bar at the top of the web page, as shown. The image file is downloaded to the web browser's default location. From there, the file can be copied or moved to another location.

Click to download the selected image

Click to select

QR Codes

Quick response (QR) codes are two-dimensional bar codes. The traditional one-dimensional bar code, or zebra stripe, contains information that can be read only in one direction. The universal product code (UPC) symbols found on all product packaging and scanned at the cash register are examples of one-dimensional bar codes. QR codes contain information that can be read in two directions. A comparison of a QR code and a traditional zebra stripe is shown in Figure 1-7.

QR codes are used to facilitate the exchange of information. They typically contain an encoded web or e-mail address, but may contain information in one of four data types: numeric, alphanumeric, binary, and kanji. QR codes can be scanned using a smartphone and the proper app. Many QR code reader apps are free.

FYI

Kanji are characters in the Japanese written alphabet. QR codes were invented in 1994 for use in the Japanese automotive manufacturing industry.

Software-Defined Networking

Some areas of networks used to be controlled by hardware, but are now under software control. Until recently, all modifications to the network architecture had to be made at the network source. New technology allows programming of the network by external applications. This technology slightly modifies the Open System Interconnection (OSI) model. This is the long-standing model for network architecture. The shift to software control also allows network administrators to centrally control and view the network. This provides better flexibility for network administrators and more secure networks.

Goodheart-Willcox Publisher

Figure 1-7. A QR code (left) is a two-dimensional bar code, while a UPC zebra stripe (right) is a one-dimensional bar code.

1.1 SECTION REVIEW

CHECK YOUR UNDERSTANDING

1. List the four phases of the digital revolution.
2. Name three items that currently are enhanced due to embedded computer technology.
3. Use of high bandwidth is also referred to as _____.
4. What functions of e-book technology make it an evolving technology?
5. List four new and emerging classes of software.

IC3 CERTIFICATION PRACTICE

The following question is a sample of the types of questions presented on the IC3 exam.

1. Perform this simulation.
   Demonstrate how to safely back up and restore data and software to the cloud.

BUILD YOUR VOCABULARY

As you progress through this course, develop a personal IT glossary. This will help you build your vocabulary and prepare you for a career. Write a definition for each of the following terms and add it to your IT glossary.

augmented printing
augmented reality (AR)
bandwidth
cloud computing
computer
digital revolution
e-mail
embedded computers
emerging technologies

information technology (IT)
interactive books
quick response (QR) codes
smartphone
software as a service (SaaS)
software-defined storage

COMPUTERS IN THE WORKPLACE

Essential Question

How does changing technology affect current and future employment?

Computers have greatly changed work. In the beginning days of electronic computers, computers were single-purpose machines. For example, the ENIAC was used at Aberdeen Proving Ground in 1946 to calculate ballistics information.

With the advent of operating systems in the 1960s, computers could be used for many different purposes. New ideas were quickly implemented. The uses spanned data processing, spreadsheet generation, word processing, and desktop publishing. Soon almost every office worker had a desktop computer. Productivity soared. Output improved. Some jobs began to be replaced by computers, but new jobs were created for people who could work with computers. This section discusses how computers have affected worker productivity as well as what jobs are available.

wavebreakmedia/Shutterstock

LEARNING GOALS

After completing this section, you will be able to:
- Explain how advances in information technology have affected productivity.
- Describe the use of information technology in current employment.
- Discuss the future outlook for employment in information technology.

TERMS

telecommuting
worker productivity

Worker Productivity

Worker productivity is a measure of how efficiently and quickly a person completes tasks. Using computers in the workplace has increased the efficiency, speed, level of detail, and overall progress of many types of jobs. The workplace is responding to the exponential growth in technology. Use of computers and the Internet have revolutionized how and where people work. See Figure 1-8. The new world of work has changed peoples' values and created a global economy.

Changing Tools

Workers are becoming loyal to their skills, not to their employers. Work used to be somewhere people went. Now it has become something people do. People used to read books and manuals to learn things. Now they use the Internet and search engines such as Google. There are over six million searches conducted on Google each day.

Eliminating Distance

People can work from anywhere. Distance does not matter. Thomas Friedman, well-known journalist and author, has said:

> "It has become possible for more people to collaborate and compete in real time, with more other people on more different kinds of work from more different corners of the planet, on a more equal footing than any previous time in the history of the world."

For example, the authors of this textbook live and work in different states and the publisher is located in a third state. Working together is

FYI

The US Department of Labor predicts that today's high school students will have held between 10 and 14 jobs by the time they are 38 years old.

LDprod/Shutterstock.com

Figure 1-8. Computer-based communication technologies have changed how and where work can be done.

not bound by nearness anymore. Employees can communicate with colleagues around the world.

Many workers have offices in their homes. This can result in significant savings of time and money since they do not have to travel to an office. **Telecommuting** is working for a company from home using information technologies. Telecommuters can spend more time working instead of driving. They can save money on transportation costs.

Technical Knowledge

The number of Internet devices in use around the world in 1984 was only one thousand. That number grew to one million by 1994. In 2008, it exceeded one billion. Employers expect workers to have an increasing grasp of software, such as project management, spreadsheet, and database software, and the Internet. Employers also expect a solid foundation in use of hardware, including networked computers and cloud computing.

The amount of available information is overwhelming. This exponential rate of exploding information will have significant effects on the lives of students starting a four-year technical degree. It is possible that what they learn in their first year will be outdated by their third year. Educators have the daunting task of preparing students for jobs that do not currently exist.

Corepics VOF/Shutterstock.com

Figure 1-9. Package delivery workers use personal digital assistants to track deliveries.

Current Employment

Most jobs today require that employees have at least a basic understanding of how to use computers. Law enforcement officials use the Internet to find lost children, track and apprehend suspects, and connect to national and global databases. Educators work with computer programmers to develop software that allows autistic children to speak. Medical personnel use computers to research diseases and maintain complex health records. Package delivery workers carry personal data assistants (PDAs), also called personal digital assistants, to track the progress of a package from its origin to its destination, as shown in Figure 1-9.

Advances in technology have changed the types of jobs people do. Many jobs have disappeared or changed as technology has advanced. Typewriter repair is a job that has all but disappeared. The number of photographers at major newspapers has declined in part due to the prevalence of digital cameras on mobile devices in the hands of the public. The publishing industry is undergoing a revolution from creating printed products to digital products, so the jobs involved in creating the final product are changing.

On the other hand, many new types of careers have been created. Somebody has to program the software and hardware to make augmented reality and other emerging technologies work. Continued growth in the use of the Internet and communication technologies means technicians must design, install, and maintain new systems. Additionally, customer support is needed for new technology, and there is an increased demand for sales associates.

Future Employment

The field of research in digital applications is rapidly growing. Emerging technologies grow from this research. What inventions do you think have yet to be created? Perhaps you will have a career that uses some new form of information technology to improve the lives of people around the nation or across the globe.

In addition to careers in the digital arena, other fields are emerging as a good source of rewarding employment. The use of computers and the Internet will be essential to success in these fields.

It is safe to anticipate that many new jobs will emerge as time goes on. Keeping current is the top educational goal for an IT professional. IT careers are discussed in detail in Chapter 17.

Advanced Medical Research

A current trend in the medical field is to move from treating and curing diseases to preventing diseases. Using the results of research projects such as decoding the human genome can be coupled with the ability to track detailed personal health. IT is vital here because of the enormous amount of data that need to be processed. More personalized health care will create more jobs. Patients will have their own private web pages established by their physicians. Their medical histories will be instantly available. This will lead to more personalized health care, thus creating more jobs. More laboratory analysis jobs will appear. Examples could be a gene splicer or DNA information specialist.

Automotive Industry

Vehicles are becoming more energy efficient. Hybrid and electric cars are more common than they were just a few years ago. More complex embedded computer systems are being developed. This has prompted changes in urban planning, including new infrastructure to accommodate new vehicle models. New jobs would include designing these new streets and electrical-charging stations. These jobs will require knowledge of 3D mapping and computer-aided design software.

Finance

The world of money will include a look at gathering more real-time data in an effort to model future growth. This will help corporations to better invest their assets. Individuals will need more help from personal financial advisors or rely on computer programs to perform that function.

Career Skills

Architect
An architect uses information technology in every phase of design and presentation. The use of 3D modeling software to design and develop structures, as well as the use of databases to identify the proper materials for strength and stability, is an ongoing process for architects. Architects often use word processing software to create documents that will serve as communication with the clients and the building contractors. They may also communicate using e-mail, the Internet, and by smartphones.

Home Health Care

The health care industry has found it is more affordable and beneficial for patients to recuperate at home than in a hospital. As a result, hospitals discharge patients as soon as it is medically appropriate to do so. But the patients must have specialized, individual, and intermittent care. The home health care field increased in size by around 50 percent over the past few years. Employees in this field can have direct contact with the patients or act in an advisory capacity at a remote location. Networks and the Internet make this possible. Knowledge on how to set up and maintain these systems will require proficiency with hardware and software.

Green Collar Jobs

Green collar jobs are those involved in designing, manufacturing, selling, installing, and maintaining environmentally friendly technologies. As interest in this area continues to grow, there will be a need for more investigation and implementation of renewable energy sources such as wind and solar. Initiatives in urban planning will lead to changes in the management of the electrical grid. Examples of new jobs might be supervising energy-management systems, tracking and managing a community green space or garden project, or engineering soil replenishment. All of these systems will require knowledge of hardware to track the statistics and skills in software usage to interpret the data.

1.2 SECTION REVIEW

CHECK YOUR UNDERSTANDING

1. What are four ways in which the use of computers has impacted the workplace?
2. How does telecommuting improve productivity?
3. How have advances in technology changed the types of jobs people do?
4. How will continued growth in the use of the Internet and communication technologies create new careers?
5. What are green collar jobs, and how is IT needed in them?

IC3 CERTIFICATION PRACTICE

The following question is a sample of the type of questions presented on the IC3 exam.

1. People who certify in IC3 include:
   A. beginning professional
   B. student
   C. average user
   D. All of the above.

BUILD YOUR VOCABULARY

As you progress through this course, develop a personal IT glossary. This will help you build your vocabulary and prepare you for a career. Write a definition for each of the following terms and add it to your IT glossary.

telecommuting
worker productivity

CHALLENGES OF A DIGITAL SOCIETY

michaeljung/Shutterstock.com

All of the major technical advances over the past 150 years were impressive when they first appeared. But soon society absorbed them, and the innovations became commonplace and moved into the background of people's lives. Examples include automobiles, washing machines, radios, landline and cellular telephones, televisions, microwaves, personal computers, and home computer printers.

Digital devices were once remarkable innovations, too, but now are commonplace. The number of homes with digital devices has grown, but the situation is not uniformly good. Some people have no or limited access to computers. People without access to digital devices are placed at a disadvantage. This section discusses the challenges faced by society as digital devices become more and more integrated.

Essential Question

Why is it important to close the digital divide?

TERMS

cybersecurity
data mining
digital divide
digital middle class

LEARNING GOALS

After completing this section, you will be able to:
- Identify cultural and social issues related to information technology.
- Discuss ways to close the digital divide.

Cultural and Societal Issues

The first computers were used mostly as electronic typewriters or calculators with memory. For most people, computers were not easy to use. Before the Internet, computing was primarily a local and individual endeavor. At about the same time that personal and commercial connections to the Internet began in the 1990s, consumers began demanding that computers be easier to use and more powerful. As a result, computers became more popular. This had a profound effect on society and culture.

Digital Middle Class

The **digital middle class** is the group of people who extensively use digital devices and embrace the newest digital technologies. These users expect more capability to be available to maximize access to the Internet and all it offers, including social media and the cloud. Small businesses will drive the movement because they will need to create distinct markets all over the world. People without computers are at a disadvantage and denied entry into the digital middle class.

Data Mining

Data mining is the method of searching through huge amounts of data to find patterns. See Figure 1-10. Data mining is an enormous asset to a business. Owners can know how much and when to stock inventory

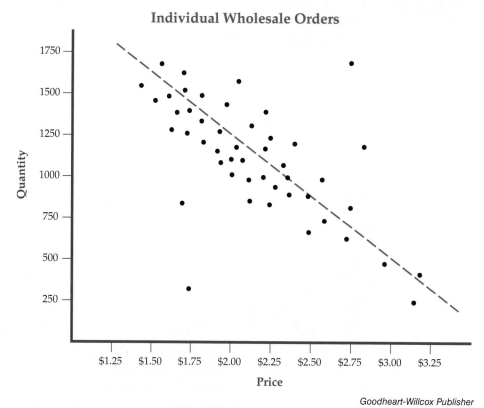

Figure 1-10. Data mining allows businesses to find patterns that can be used to improve sales, services, or products.

and what items to put on sale. Because of the use of data mining, the buying behavior of customers is analyzed and trends are made visible. These results translate into valuable marketing data.

When an online movie source recommends what movies a client would probably enjoy, it is not just guessing. Similarly, online retailers can suggest new purchases that will probably appeal to a customer. These predictions are based on hard facts obtained through data mining. Online search engines also engage in data mining, and then place advertisements on the screen in response to a user's search. Supermarkets actually reward their customers for donating information. Many stores give out discounts to cardholders so that the store is able to track customers' purchases.

Data mining presents concerns about what data are being collected. Many people express concern over the amount of data about themselves that companies mine. Many others may not even be aware of how much data about them are being collected.

Cybersecurity

Individuals, companies, and governments have enormous quantities of information on the Internet, much of it confidential. With so much data available and easily transmittable, security of this information is a great concern to society. There are many software programs, safety procedures, and protective methods to aid users in maintaining their privacy. See Figure 1-11.

Figure 1-11. Cybersecurity protects computer systems. It is important to many aspects of life, such as online shopping.

A career in cybersecurity is a path an IT professional may choose to pursue. **Cybersecurity** is the branch of IT that protects computer systems. The prefix *cyber* means relating to computers or computer networks. Cybersecurity is more fully discussed in Chapter 16.

Closing the Digital Divide

GS5 Living Online 9.1.1

The **digital divide** is most commonly defined as the gap between those individuals, communities, and countries having access to the information technologies that transform life and those who do not have this access. A more technical definition is an educational, social, and economic disparity across socioeconomic status, race, and gender caused by unequal contact with computing resources. The digital divide was created when people became classified as *computer users* or *not computer users*.

Educational

Many initiatives are directed at closing the digital divide in education. Access to technology and learning how to use it are important for preparing students for future careers and civic duties. Many schools provide tablet computers for students. This ensures equal access to the technology. The students access digital textbooks or use productivity tools such as word processing. A critical step is providing computer literacy for all students. In addition, many schools offer access to computers before and after school.

Social

Access to information is necessary for promoting good citizenship. There are many sources for free access to computing. Most public libraries provide access to computers. Free Wi-Fi is offered in many public locations. This helps people who may have access to a mobile device, but do not have Internet service in their homes.

More and more governmental agencies have websites to assist the citizens in getting problems resolved. Libraries and community colleges often have free training sessions on how to use these sites.

Economic

The economic impact of the digital divide is most obvious in developing countries. Many developing regions do not have a dependable source of electricity. Among other things, that means access to radios, televisions, or computers is limited or missing. Those who do not have access to this technology are not as able to improve their economic situations as those who have access. Therefore, in these countries, technologies are being invented to operate without an electrical power grid. Use of solar power or windup generators provides the ability to power computers or mobile devices.

An important step to a good economy is access to money. The growth of smartphone use is narrowing the digital divide. With smartphones,

STEM

Technology

In June 2009, the United States transitioned its television broadcasts from analog to digital. The benefits of digital are better quality pictures, higher resolution pictures, high-definition broadcasts, less bandwidth usage, and multicasting. The downside is that digital channels either work or they do not; there is no gray area. Additionally, older televisions cannot receive digital signals, which may be a socioeconomic issue that widens the digital divide.

remote areas can have a way to obtain financial services. MasterCard developed a smartphone-based service to allow users to make payments, deposits, and transfers as well as purchase prepaid credit cards. As a result, funds can be exchanged over smartphones even though the financial institution is in another country. Visa allows smartphone companies and banks to create their own customized mobile financial services. This service has been set up in both a very large developing country (India) and a very small developing country (Rwanda).

In Nigeria, farmers use their smartphones to receive vouchers for seed and fertilizer. The Nigerian government uses the phones and biometrics to match the exact locations of registered farmers. This method eliminated a centuries-old tradition of corruption, thus ensuring materials actually reach the farmers who need them. In turn, the farmers are able to improve their economic situations.

1.3 | SECTION REVIEW

CHECK YOUR UNDERSTANDING

1. What is the meaning of a digital society?
2. Searching through huge amounts of data to find patterns describes what aspect of information technology?
3. Which field of IT is involved in keeping computer systems protected?
4. What is the digital divide?
5. What are the three areas of the digital divide that define the gap?

IC3 CERTIFICATION PRACTICE

The following question is a sample of the type of questions presented on the IC3 exam.

1. A search engine is used to:
   A. store data in a database.
   B. generate reports from a database.
   C. mine data in a database.
   D. None of the above.

BUILD YOUR VOCABULARY

As you progress through this course, develop a personal IT glossary. This will help you build your vocabulary and prepare you for a career. Write a definition for each of the following terms and add it to your IT glossary.

cybersecurity
data mining
digital divide
digital middle class

1 REVIEW AND ASSESSMENT

Chapter Summary

Section 1.1
Computers Are Everywhere

- The digital revolution is the ever-expanding progression of technical, economic, and cultural changes brought about by computers. It has gone through four phases: giant computers, personal computers, networked computers, and cloud computing.

- Embedded computers are small digital computers found inside of other devices, such as digital cameras, mobile phones, home appliances, music players, special IT hardware, and even automobiles.

- Computer technology has made it possible for those with access to digital communication devices to stay in touch with others 24 hours a day. Advances in this technology have increased the speed of communication and the breadth of geographic reach, but there are advantages and disadvantages to the technology.

- Emerging technologies are innovations that represent significantly new fields or technologies. Visual displays, medical technology, interactive books, and new and emerging classes of software are all areas in which emerging technologies play an important role.

Section 1.2
Computers in the Workplace

- Using computers in the workplace has increased the efficiency, speed, level of detail, and overall progress of many types of jobs. The tools used in the workplace have changed due to computers,

computer technology has eliminated distance as a restriction, and technical knowledge of workers has increased.

- Most jobs today require that employees have at least a basic understanding of how to use computers. Advances in technology have changed the types of jobs people do, and many new types of careers have been created.

- There are many careers in the digital arena and in other fields as well that are related to information technology. Due to rapid growth in the IT field, many new jobs will emerge as time goes on.

Section 1.3
Challenges of a Digital Society

- Computers have had a profound effect on society and culture. The digital middle class has been created, data mining has evolved as an important tool for business, and cybersecurity has become a critical issue.

- The digital divide is the gap between those who do and do not have access to the information technologies that transform life. The digital divide can be closed by addressing the educational, social, and economic aspects that cause the divide.

Now that you have finished this chapter, see what you know about information technology by scanning the QR code to take the chapter posttest. If you do not have a smartphone, visit www.g-wlearning.com.

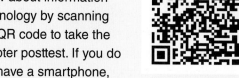

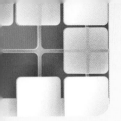

Chapter 1 Test

Multiple Choice

Select the best response.

1. Which event is not a major phase of the digital revolution?
   A. Giant computers.
   B. The Industrial Revolution.
   C. Cloud computing.
   D. Personal computers.

2. The Internet began as:
   A. the World Wide Web
   B. NSFNET
   C. ARPANET
   D. WWW

3. Which of the following does *not* describe or identify an evolving technology?
   A. Medical technology allowing remote diagnosis.
   B. E-books becoming interactive books.
   C. Cell phones becoming smartphones.
   D. Digital middle class.

4. An emerging technology can be described or identified as a(n):
   A. innovation that represents a significantly new field or technology.
   B. technology that was invented at the beginning of the information age.
   C. way in which workers apply information technology in the workplace.
   D. alternative to perform the same tasks as existing technologies.

5. What defines the digital middle class?
   A. Casual use of the Internet.
   B. Extensive use of digital devices and adoption of the newest digital technologies.
   C. Ownership of a smartphone.
   D. Online gaming.

Completion

Complete the following sentences with the correct word(s).

6. A(n) _____ is a device that handles input, processes data, stores data, and produces usable output according to sets of stored instructions.

7. _____ measures how efficiently and quickly a person completes tasks.

8. _____ is working for a company from home using information technologies.

9. Data mining is the method of searching through huge amounts of data to find _____.

10. The gap between those countries that have access to computer technology and those without is the _____.

Matching

Match the correct term with its definition.

A. emerging technology
B. data mining
C. evolving technology
D. digital revolution
E. digital divide

11. Ever-expanding progression of technical, economic, and cultural change brought about by computers and the Internet.

12. The changes of technology over time.

13. Technologies that represent a new field or technology.

14. Process of extracting useful information in the form of relationships and patterns from stored information from purchases.

15. An educational, social, and economic disparity across socioeconomic status, race, and gender caused by unequal contact with computing resources.

REVIEW AND ASSESSMENT

Application and Extension of Knowledge

1. Research common locations of embedded computers. Make a list of devices you use each day that contain embedded computers. Bring your list to class for discussion.
2. Identify three emerging and three evolving technologies. List one positive and negative effect of each. Be prepared to defend your position in a class discussion.
3. Identify five new information technology careers that were created as a result of the advent of social media.
4. Research the practice of data mining, and develop an opinion on the practice. Write a one-page paper stating your view of the advantages and disadvantages of data mining with regard to personal privacy.
5. Write a one-page paper describing why you feel an information technology worker must keep his or her skills up to date.

Online Activities

Complete the following activities, which will help you learn, practice, and expand your knowledge and skills.

Certification Practice. Complete the certification practice test for this chapter.

Vocabulary. Practice vocabulary for this chapter using the e-flash cards, matching activity, and vocabulary game until you are able to recognize their meanings.

Communication Skills

College and Career Readiness

Reading. Read a magazine, newspaper, or online article about the importance of effective communication for teens, especially when using social media. Determine the central ideas of the article and review the conclusions made by the author. Take notes to identify its purpose and intended audience. Demonstrate your understanding of the information by summarizing what you read.

Writing. Rhetoric is the study of writing or speaking as a way of communicating information or persuading someone. Describe a rhetorical technique that a writer can use to provide information or persuade someone about a digital device. Write an example of the technique you chose.

Speaking. Create a one-act play for two persons that depicts both a positive and a negative interaction between a computer salesperson and a customer. Include notes to the actors about body language and facial expressions. What is the essential difference between the two interactions? How does body language influence whether the message will be received negatively or positively? Write several paragraphs describing your opinion about the impact of body language in the workplace.

Internet Research

Digital Citizenship. Research digital citizenship using various Internet resources. List and analyze specific elements of digital citizenship that users of technology should understand when using the Internet. What are the day-to-day effects of digital citizenship on society? Summarize your findings.

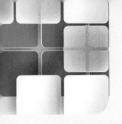

Teamwork

With your team, create a list of long or complex words or phrases that might be used in technical writing related to information technology. List each of the words and phrases on a dry-erase board or flip chart. As a team, work together to think of simpler words or phrases to replace each list item. Use a thesaurus if one is available.

Portfolio Development

College and Career Readiness

Portfolio Overview. When you apply for a job, community service, or college, you will need to tell others why you are qualified for the position. To support your qualifications, you will need to create a portfolio. A *portfolio* is a selection of related materials that you collect and organize to show your qualifications, skills, and talents to support a career or personal goal. For example, a certificate that shows you have completed lifeguard and first-aid training could help you get a job at a local pool as a lifeguard. An essay you wrote about protecting native plants could show that you are serious about eco-friendly efforts and help you get a volunteer position at a park. A transcript of your school grades could help show that you are qualified for college. A portfolio is a *living document*, which means it should be reviewed and updated on a regular basis.

Artists and other communication professionals have historically presented portfolios of their creative work when seeking jobs or admission to educational institutions. However, portfolios are now used in many professions.

Two types of portfolios commonly used are print portfolios and digital portfolios. A digital portfolio may also be called an *e-portfolio*.

1. Use the Internet to search for *print portfolio* and *digital portfolio*. Read articles about each type.
2. In your own words, compare and contrast a print portfolio with a digital one.

CTSOs

Student Organizations. Career and technical student organizations (CTSOs) are a valuable asset to any educational program. These organizations support student learning and the application of the skills learned in real-world situations. Competitive events may be written, oral, or a combination of both. There is a variety of organizations from which to select, depending on the goals of your educational program. To prepare for any competitive event, complete the following activities.

1. Go to the website of your organization to find specific information for the events. Visit the site often because information changes quickly. If the organization has an app, download it to your digital device.
2. Read all the organization's guidelines closely. These rules and regulations must be strictly followed, or disqualification can occur.
3. Communication plays a role in all the competitive events, so read which communication skills are covered in the event you select. Research and preparation are important keys to a successful competition.
4. Select one or two events that are of interest to you. Print the information for the events and discuss your interest with your instructor.

2

HARDWARE

The hardware components of a computer are easy to see. Most desktop computers have external devices attached to them in addition to components internal to the case, or box. Each hardware component has a specific job in storing, retrieving, and displaying information. Being familiar with hardware terminology helps the user follow directions in assembling a computer system and visualizing how it will function. Knowledge of the technology of each component helps the user in knowing what steps to take to make the parts work together. It also helps to diagnose problems when they do not.

Understanding the operation of a computer makes a person a more-effective user. This can help anyone select the right systems to match his or her needs. In addition, an understanding of how a computer functions will help a person get the most out of the machine in terms of use and performance. In this chapter, you will study the different types of computers and how information is entered, displayed, processed, and stored.

College and Career Readiness

Reading Prep. Read the chapter title and tell a classmate what you have experienced or already know about the topic. Write a paragraph describing what you would like to learn about the topic. After reading the chapter, share two things you have learned with the classmate.

IC3 CERTIFICATION OBJECTIVES

GS5

Computing Fundamentals

Domain 1.0 Mobile devices
  Objective 1.2 Be familiar with cellular-enabled tablets
  Objective 1.3 Be familiar with smartphones
Domain 2.0 Hardware devices
  Objective 2.1 Types of devices
  Objective 2.2 Know the impact of memory and storage on usage
  Objective 2.3 Know how to connect different peripherals
  Objective 2.8 Know platform considerations and implications
  Objective 2.9 Know platform compatibility, device limitations
  Objective 2.12 Understand common hardware configurations
  Objective 2.14 Understand the pros and cons of touch screens vs. non-touch screen devices
Domain 3.0 Computer software architecture
  Objective 3.7 Document management

Key Applications

Domain 5.0 Presentations
  Objective 5.2 Understand how to connect to external/extended monitors to display presentation

GS4

Computing Fundamentals

Domain 2.0 Computer hardware and concepts
  Objective 2.1 Common computer terminology
  Objective 2.2 Types of devices
  Objective 2.3 Computer performance
Domain 3.0 Computer software and concepts
  Objective 3.3 Software usage
Domain 4.0 Troubleshooting
  Objective 4.2 Hardware

TYPES OF COMPUTERS AND COMPONENTS

Essential Question

How has the evolution of computers impacted your life?

The term *computer* covers a wide variety of multipurpose devices that handle input, process data, store data, and produce usable output according to sets of stored instructions. Computers vary extensively according to size, use, cost, and capability.

The path of computer development from the 1940s forward has been to increase processing speed, increase storage capacity, decrease energy consumption, decrease component size, and invent devices to solve a wider variety of problems. A popular description of the trend to smaller, better, and faster computers was created by Gordon Moore. In 1965, he noticed that the number of components on a computer chip had doubled every two years since 1958. The trend, now known as Moore's law, can be applied to many aspects of computing, from processor speed to computer price and the resolution of monitors.

auremar/Shutterstock.com

TERMS

arithmetic/logic unit (ALU)
booting
central processing unit (CPU)
clock speed
computer system
control unit
firmware
floating point operations per second (FLOPS)
hardware

input
input device
mainframe computers
memory
millions of instructions per second (MIPS)
motherboard
operating system (OS)
output
peripheral devices

personal computer
port
processing
random-access memory (RAM)
read-only memory (ROM)
server
storage
supercomputers
universal serial bus (USB)

LEARNING GOALS

After completing this section, you will be able to:
- List the categories of computers.
- Identify basic parts and functions of a computer.
- Explain the purpose of an operating system.

Categories of Computers

Historically, computers were grouped in one of three categories based on size: mainframes, minicomputers, or microcomputers. A mainframe is a very large, high-processing computer that is used for big computing needs. A minicomputer is a computer of midrange size and performance between a microcomputer and a mainframe. A microcomputer is a computer based on a microchip for the central processing unit (CPU).

The distinctions between the historical categories have become blurred so much that the term minicomputer is rarely used today. This is because the capability of microcomputers, smallest of the three, has significantly expanded. Today, computers are usually categorized based on usage and cost as well as size:

- supercomputers
- mainframes
- servers
- personal computers and mobile devices

Note that these are the categories of computers, which should not be confused with the four phases of the digital revolution discussed in Chapter 1.

FYI

There are many ways to classify computers. Other classifications or applications include the SETI project, ROCKS clusters and cluster computing, and the DWave quantum computer.

Supercomputers

Supercomputers have processing power that can handle complex jobs beyond the scope of other computer systems. Supercomputers are the fastest computers. Examples of projects undertaken by supercomputers include breaking codes, molecular modeling, atmospheric modeling, and climate predictions. The tasks analyze enormous amounts of data. Supercomputers can be used to simulate global weather patterns, results from earthquakes, and consequences from nuclear explosions. Scientists and engineers are the primary users of supercomputers.

The speed of supercomputers is usually measured in **floating point operations per second (FLOPS).** *Floating point* means numbers containing decimal fractions. Figure 2-1 shows the constantly increased capability of supercomputers over the years.

The Chinese have built one of the fastest supercomputers in the world. The Tianhe-2 (Milky Way-2) computer operates at a speed of 38.6 petaFLOPS. The prefix *peta* means 10^{15}, so this is 38,600,000,000,000,000 FLOPS. The number of calculations this system can perform in one hour would require 300 years if every person on earth contributed to the project using a calculator. The current listing of the world's fastest supercomputers can be found on the Top 500 website (www.top500.org).

Mainframes

Mainframe computers provide centralized storage, processing, and overall management of large amounts of data. While supercomputers are used for crunching data and numbers, mainframes are used to process

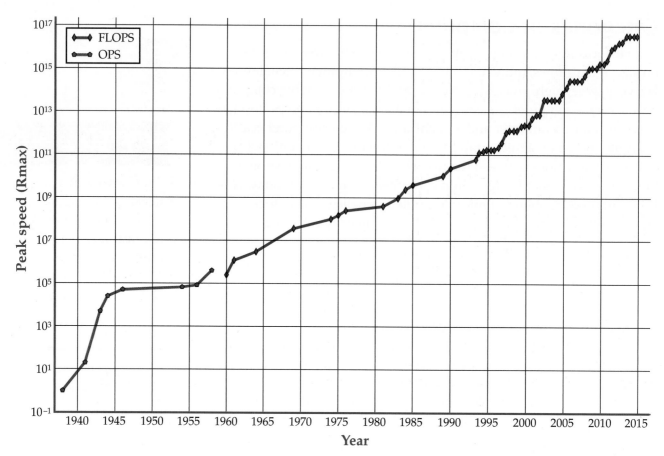

Goodheart-Willcox Publisher

Figure 2-1. The capability of supercomputers has constantly increased over the years.

and store business transactions. The speed of mainframes is measured in **millions of instructions per second (MIPS)**.

Mainframes are built to tackle data-intensive, detailed transactions in the business world. Typical business operations include updating a database for inventory control of supplies, scheduling airline reservations, or managing bank transactions.

GS5
Computing Fundamentals
2.1.1

GS4
Computing Fundamentals
2.2.1

Servers

A server is a special type of computer found on a network. A **server** stores data and responds when requested by other computers in the network. It allows other computers on the network to share programs and data. Sharing data makes it possible for many users on the network to see and access each other's information. A server generally handles backing up the stored data for all users so that data can be retrieved if a part of the system malfunctions. Network administrators are specially trained to manage the functions of servers and are employed by many businesses, schools, and organizations.

GS4
Computing Fundamentals
2.2.2, 2.2.3, 2.2.4, 2.2.5, 2.2.6

Personal Computers and Mobile Devices

A **personal computer** is a processing device designed to meet the needs of an individual user, whether in the home, a business, or a school.

It has a screen, a mouse, and a keyboard and is generally connected to the Internet, as shown in Figure 2-2. Personal computers vary in their speed, size, and portability. They come in the forms of desktop models, laptops and related models, and mobile devices.

Desktop Computers

Desktop computers are larger than other personal computers and are intended to be used as a stationary device because they need a constant source of electricity. Their components include a box that holds the CPU, the memory, and the cards that communicate with other devices; a keyboard; a monitor; and usually a

Figure 2-2. A personal computer has a screen, mouse, and keyboard in addition to the CPU unit.

mouse. Many are also equipped with network capabilities. Additional devices may support external media, such as DVDs, or a printer. A wide range of devices may be added to a desktop computer by means of adapter ports, such as the universal serial bus (USB). Because of the tall box containing the CPU and expansion cards, desktop computers are sometimes called tower computers. Desktop computers are found everywhere, from offices to schools, homes, and manufacturing plants.

GS5   Computing Fundamentals

2.1.3

FYI

Some desktop computers combine the monitor with the box that holds the CPU and devices. These are called all-in-one computers.

Laptop Computers

Laptop computers are single-unit, portable devices that run on a battery. Laptop computers are light enough to carry and small enough to fit on a lap. Ultimately the battery must be recharged at an electrical outlet. Typical users of laptops are people who need to have constant access to computers and use them in places other than a fixed location.

The single unit contains a keyboard, a pointing stick or touch pad, a monitor, the CPU, and the memory. Internal chips may control USB ports and wireless network support. Additional devices may be connected to a laptop.

Depending on the size, the model may be a laptop, notebook, or netbook computer. Other terms are used for various configurations in this category, such as subnotebook and convertible. The convertible is a cross between a laptop computer and a tablet mobile device.

GS5   Computing Fundamentals
2.1.2

Mobile Devices

Mobile devices are smaller and lighter than laptop computers. They are battery-operated like a laptop, but limited to the number of devices that can be connected to them. Another difference is mobile devices use a touch screen for input instead of a keyboard or touchpad. Mobile devices rely on wireless transmission of data to printers or to other users. Mobile devices vary in configuration, from tablet computers to smarthpones.

Cellular telephones, or cell phones, make and receive calls using radio waves transmitted to and from geographic areas known as cells. Each cell contains a tower, and these towers form the cellular network.

GS5   Computing Fundamentals
1.2.1, 1.2.2, 1.2.3,
1.2.4, 1.3.1, 1.3.2,
1.3.3, 1.3.4, 1.3.5

Most cell phones can send text messages and many can also receive e-mail and have limited Internet capabilities.

A smartphone is a computer and a cellular telephone in one device. The smartphone is able to wirelessly connect to the Internet for expanded capabilities such as streaming movies, downloading music, finding locations using GPS, demonstrating ticket and coupon purchases, and using the World Wide Web. These functions are limited by the user's location. The phone must be in an area that is Wi-Fi enabled. Also, the screens on smartphones are smaller than a display found on a laptop or desktop computer. The size limits the amount of a web page that can be viewed at one time.

An advantage of smartphones over standard cell phones is the use of apps. These computer programs are written to run on mobile devices and accommodate the small displays. Apps provide weather updates, e-mail and messaging, social networking, games, and more. Many businesses provide apps to allow the user to conduct transactions from the smartphone. For example, banks provide apps to allow the depositing of checks. Many apps are free, while others must be purchased. An app must be written for the operating system used by the smartphone.

Tablet computers are roughly the height and width of a textbook, as shown in Figure 2-3. However, there are many variations in size. There are over 70 tablets on the market. Tablets use mobile operating systems similar to smartphones. Their features consist of touch screens, long battery life, similar apps to smartphones, and Internet connectivity. Many tablets can access cellular networks. This allows connection to the Internet where there is no Wi-Fi service, but a cellular data plan must be purchased. There may be a data limit on a cellular data plan, whereas a Wi-Fi plan usually does not have a data limit.

michaeljung/Shutterstock.com

Figure 2-3. A tablet computer is usually the size of a textbook, but thinner.

Other mobile devices are developed to meet special needs. Some are used by service technicians to communicate to their offices while they are working in your home. Packages shipped by commercial carriers are scanned and tracked by a PDA. Other devices include wearable computers, portable media players, e-book readers, and GPS.

Basic Parts and Functions of a Computer

No matter the size or use for a computer, all computers contain the same basic types of components. **Hardware** is the physical components of the computer. Generally speaking, there are four main hardware components to a computer:

- input device
- memory
- processor
- output device

This is the minimum hardware for a computer. If a device does not have all four components, it is not a computer.

All computers are also basically the same in terms of functions, which are parallel to the basic hardware. A computer is defined by these four basic capabilities or functions:

- accept data input
- store data
- process data
- produce output

This is the minimum functional definition of a computer. If a device does not have all four functions, it is not a computer. A computer with its attached devices is called a **computer system**.

Attached devices that are not critical to computer operation are called **peripheral devices**, or *peripherals*. For example, a peripheral can be used to provide Wi-Fi access. Without the hardware to provide Wi-Fi access, the computer will not be able to connect to Wi-Fi. Each peripheral has its own methods for connection and for handling input or output. There is no universal standard for all peripherals on how they handle input or output. For this reason, the manufacturer of each device must supply code called a driver that communicates with the operating system. Device drivers are discussed in Chapter 3.

Input

The **input** function translates data from the human world into computer data. Input can be described as data that are entered, scanned, or otherwise sent to a computer system. The data can originate from a person, the environment, or another computer. Examples of input are:

- adding words and numbers into documents;
- setting the temperature in a thermostat containing an embedded computer;
- activating a sensor in a computerized house alarm system;
- scanning a photograph;
- recording a video with a camcorder;
- loading an MP3 file; and
- sending an e-mail or tweet.

An **input device** provides the computer with data on which it can act, as shown in Figure 2-4. The input device is the basis of interaction with a computer. Data can be entered from a keyboard, keypad, touch pad, mouse, scanner, camera, microphone, or game controller. These are all input devices. Users can see and feel many input

Computer Ethics
While you are at work or school, it is important to be respectful in your use of computer equipment. The computer is available for your use as a tool for research or to accomplish a task. It is unethical to use the computer to download copyrighted material or harass others.

GS5   Computing Fundamentals
2.9.2

Sheftsoff Women Girls/Shutterstock.com

Figure 2-4. This musician is using several input devices, including a mouse, computer keyboard, and MIDI music keyboard.

devices, but how the computer uses the data input is more mysterious because that takes place inside the box itself without any visible moving parts.

An input device can be human-operated, an environmental trigger, another computer, or one of many other devices. For example, a sensor may detect changes in the environment, such as an increase in temperature, and provide that as data to a computer system, which in turn regulates the temperature of a room. The sensor in this example is an input device.

Storage

GS4 Computing Fundamentals
2.1.2, 2.3.2

Storage is where data are kept by the computer so the information can be viewed, played, or otherwise used. The most familiar storage locations are the computer system's memory and hard disk drive, but flash drives and other forms of external storage devices are also common.

GS5 Computing Fundamentals
2.2.3

Additionally, certain types of files require large amounts of storage. For example, movies and photos can quickly fill up the storage capacity of a hard drive. Most mobile devices, such as smartphones and tablets, have limited storage. Devices with traditional operating systems, such as desktop and laptop computers, have larger storage capacities.

GS5 Computing Fundamentals
2.2.1, 2.2.2

Memory is the part of the computer that stores information for immediate processing. It stores the code for the computer programs, data used for the programs, results from executing the programs, and much more. Some memory is *involatile*, which means it is kept even when the computer is turned off. The basic startup program in a computer is stored in persistent memory. Other memory is *volatile*, which means it is erased when the power is off. There are two types of memory.

- random-access memory
- read-only memory

Radu Bercan/Shutterstock.com

Figure 2-5. The green board is a RAM unit, which holds many RAM chips. The RAM chips are black in this example. The metal feet are hidden because the chips are surface mounted.

Random-Access Memory

Random-access memory (RAM) is memory that can be changed. This hardware holds instructions that the processor can immediately use. RAM is what most users think of when the word *memory* is mentioned.

As various programs are used, the constantly changing instructions are loaded into RAM. When the computer is turned off, all data and instructions that were stored in RAM are erased. Therefore, RAM is volatile memory. It is just a temporary holding area for data and instructions.

The physical chips that hold RAM look like small black rectangles with many pairs of metal feet, as shown in Figure 2-5. If a computer needs more memory, additional chips can be easily installed. The more RAM a computer has installed, the more programs it can be running simultaneously. If a program requires more RAM than the system possesses, it will not run. An insufficient amount of RAM can cause the system to crash.

Read-Only Memory

Read-only memory (ROM) is memory that cannot be changed. ROM contains static information the computer will always need to operate. This information cannot be subject to variation. This includes the instructions that tell the system what steps to take during start-up. ROM holds its information even if the computer is turned off, which means it is involatile memory.

Measuring Memory

The capacity of memory is measured in how many bytes it can hold. One byte holds enough information for one character. Figure 2-6 describes the prefixes for various quantities of bytes and the approximate data storage capacity.

Processing

Processing of the data takes place between the input and the output. **Processing** is the transformation of input data and acting on those data.

Computing Fundamentals
2.1.1, 2.3.2

Metric Symbols	Number of bytes*	Equivalent sizes
byte	1	One character.
kilobyte (KB)	1 thousand bytes	One short letter or memo.
megabyte (MB)	1 million bytes	A typical high-resolution photo is about 2.5MB. The information in 40 paperback books (a stack about three feet high) is about 50MB.
gigabyte (GB)	1 billion bytes	One hour of a feature film is about 1.5GB. The information in 800 paperback books (a stack about 650 feet high) is about 20GB.
terabyte (TB)	1 trillion bytes	The information in 800,000 paperback books (a stack about 10 miles high) is about 1TB. Library of Congress archives contain 160TB.
petabyte (PB)	1,000 terabytes	Seventy-seven million CDs each containing 700MB is 50PB.
exabyte (EB)	1,000 petabytes	All words ever spoken by human beings are about 5EB.
zettabyte (ZB)	1,000 exabytes	The information in 174 newspapers received daily by every person on Earth is about 4ZB.

*Note: there are actually 1024 bytes in a kilobyte, so these values are rounded.

Goodheart-Willcox Publisher

Figure 2-6. Quantities of bytes and approximate storage capacity.

In principle, processing is very simple: additions and decisions. These two instructions are used to load programs and data, to follow instructions, and to produce output. More complex actions are developed using these two basic functions. The result is called *the instruction set* for a central processing unit. The basic instruction set is different for each central processing unit.

Central Processing Unit

The **central processing unit (CPU)** is the device that fetches coded instructions, decodes them, and then runs or executes them. The CPU is also called a *microprocessor* or *chip*. Although it is about the size of a thumbnail, the CPU contains billions of circuits. See Figure 2-7. Many computers contain multiple CPUs. The CPU often has a large heat sink installed on top of it to cool the circuits. A heat sink looks like a bunch of metal fins.

The CPU controls all jobs performed by the computer's other parts. When the user runs a program, the program's instructions set the CPU's list of jobs. The CPU has two primary components: the arithmetic/logic unit and the control unit.

The **arithmetic/logic unit (ALU)** temporarily holds data that are being processed and handles all arithmetic operations such as addition and subtraction. It also performs logic tasks, such as comparing values to see which is greater or where bits do not match up. Because it can combine these types of operations, the ALU can perform complex tasks that make it possible to run programs requiring fast action, such as video games.

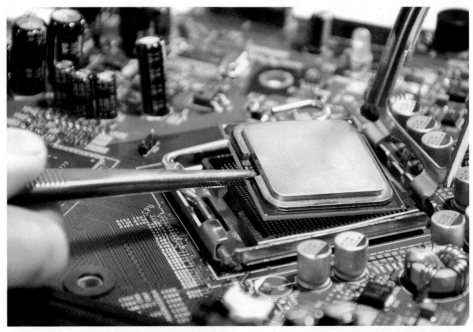

RomboStudio/Shutterstock.com

Figure 2-7. A CPU being inserted into a socket on the motherboard.

The **control unit** fetches each instruction from the list directed by the program being run. It then decodes the instruction and executes it. Finally, the control unit places the result in the ALU.

Fetching, decoding, and running one instruction is one cycle. CPU speeds are measured in how many cycles can be performed in one second. The speed rating of a CPU is also called **clock speed**. Currently, clock speeds are in the range of gigacycles, or gigahertz (GHz). The prefix *giga* means billions. Hz is the symbol for hertz, which is a unit of measure for frequency. One hertz is one cycle per second. Therefore, 1GHz is one billion cycles per second. A 1GHz processor can fetch, decode, and run one billion instructions every second. Most current CPUs can perform 3.5 billion tasks per second without error.

Motherboard

The CPU and memory are both mounted on a larger printed circuit board called the motherboard or the *system board*. The **motherboard** connects all of the hardware in the computer. It provides the electrical connections through which all data are transferred between hardware devices. In addition to connecting the on-board hardware, such as the CPU and memory, the motherboard also contains expansion ports or slots to connect external devices, such as hard drives and video cards. The three main components on the motherboard are the processor, memory, and expansion ports/slots.

For data to travel to and from the motherboard, the motherboard must be connected to the input and output devices. The most common connection is the USB port. A **port** is a point of interface between the motherboard and external devices. **Universal serial bus (USB)** is an industry standard for communication between devices and the computer. Many keyboards, printers, and pointing devices are USB-connected devices.

A computer may have many other types of ports. These ports are usually connected to the motherboard by device-interface cards contained in expansion slots on the motherboard. Audio ports connect headphones, microphones, and speakers. Some devices, such as cameras, speakers, and printers, may be connected using Bluetooth or infrared technologies. The computer must be equipped with Bluetooth or infrared cards in order to use these technologies.

There are three kinds of video ports. The video graphics array (VGA) port is used by older LCD monitors. More recent models as well as televisions, DVD players, and projectors connect to digital video interface (DVI) ports. The third type, high-definition multimedia interface (HDMI), is used for HD-television and gaming setups. It carries HD video and uncompressed digital audio on one cable.

To add additional ports to a laptop, special expansion cards can be used. An express card adapter fits into a slot on the side of a laptop. The card may provide a network port, USB port, FireWire ports, or other type of connection.

FYI

Many stand-alone monitors contain USB ports on the side so peripherals can be attached without needing to reach to the computer box.

Computing Fundamentals
2.3.1, 2.3.2, 2.3.3, 2.3.4, 2.3.5, 2.3.6
Key Applications
5.2.1, 5.2.2

GS5

Output

Output is data provided to the user. An output device produces an action based on the instructions from the CPU. The most common output device is a computer monitor. This device formats the 1s and 0s the CPU uses into human-readable material. Speakers output audio based on the 1s and 0s generated by the CPU. Data can also be output to a printer; an internal or external storage device such as a hard drive, flash drive, CD, or DVD; another computer; a mechanical system such as a relay or switch; or a number of other devices.

HANDS-ON EXAMPLE 2.1.1

COMPONENT IDENTIFICATION

Using the image shown, identify the computer hardware components labeled by number.

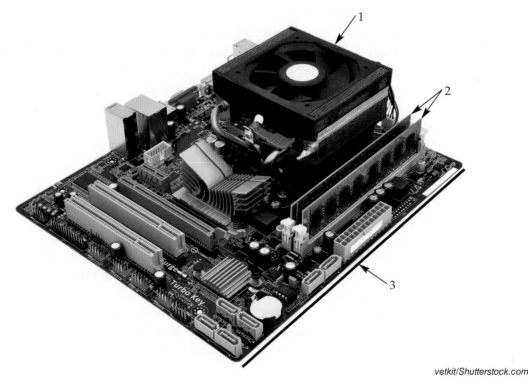

vetkit/Shutterstock.com

1. Object number 1 is called a(n) ____.
2. Objects number 2 are ____.
3. Assembly number 3 is called a(n) ____.

Operating System

The **operating system (OS)** is software that manages all of the devices, as well as locates and provides instructions to the CPU. It is specific to the type of the computer. The various versions of Windows, Mac OS, and GNU/Linux are all examples of computer operating systems.

General-use computers, such as a PC or tablet, must have an OS to work. Single-use computers, such as those in satellites and space probes, do not require an operating system. Operating systems are discussed in detail in Chapter 3.

Before the operating system can run, the computer must go through boot procedures to get the basic functions started and the OS loaded. **Booting** or *bootstrapping* describes using a small program to get the computer running and the OS loaded. This program is stored in ROM on the motherboard. It contains circuitry and software, sometimes referred to as **firmware**, that hold instructions for initializing the hardware and loading the main OS. In PCs, firmware is generally used to remember how to boot the computer. On smartphones, the entire OS and bundled application suites are stored in firmware.

Six events take place when a computer running the Windows operating systems boots up, starting with the power being turned on:

1. The power light comes on, the fan starts up, and electricity is sent throughout the hardware components.
2. The CPU follows the instructions set up in ROM.
3. The CPU performs tests on the computer's critical internal systems.
4. The CPU finds all connected peripheral devices, checks their settings, and alerts the user if there is a problem.
5. The CPU loads the OS from the hard drive into RAM.
6. The OS reads a file that contains configuration data to tell it what windows to open, icons to display, or programs to run.

When the main screen appears on the computer monitor, the system is ready to follow the user's directions.

Computing Fundamentals
GS5 2.8.1

Computing Fundamentals
GS4 3.3.1

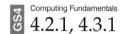
Computing Fundamentals
GS4 4.2.1, 4.3.1

FYI

When people wore big, heavy boots, they had trouble pulling them on. Shoe manufacturers included a small strap across the heel so the wearer could pull on the boot without any help. This is the origin of the computer term *booting*.

HANDS-ON EXAMPLE 2.1.2

BASIC COMPUTER COMPONENTS

Locate a computer to use for this activity. Do not open the computer box unless directed to do so by your instructor.

1. Click the **Apps** button or the **Start** button.
2. In Windows 10, click **File Explorer** in the **Start** menu, and then click This PC in the tree on the left-hand side of File Explorer. In Windows 8, click **This PC** in the **Windows System** group of the **Apps** menu. In Windows 7, click **Computer** in the right-hand column of the **Start** menu. A list of hard drives and devices with removable storage is displayed, as shown. Name them.

HANDS-ON EXAMPLE 2.1.2 (CONTINUED)

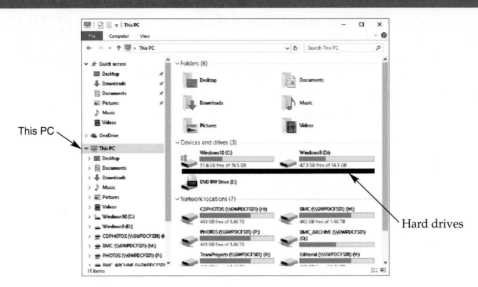

This PC

Hard drives

3. Click **System Properties** at the top of the window.
4. List the Windows version that the computer is using.
5. Identify the type of processor.
6. Identify the amount of installed memory (RAM).

2.1 SECTION REVIEW

CHECK YOUR UNDERSTANDING

1. What are four main categories of computers?
2. What are the four functions of a computer?
3. What does an input device provide to the computer?
4. Why are device drivers needed when attaching peripherals to a computer?
5. What is the purpose of the operating system?

IC3 CERTIFICATION PRACTICE

The following question is a sample of the types of questions presented on the IC3 exam.

1. The processing speed of a computer is measured in:
   A. bytes
   B. gigabytes
   C. hertz
   D. gigaseconds

BUILD YOUR VOCABULARY

As you progress through this course, develop a personal IT glossary. This will help you build your vocabulary and prepare you for a career. Write a definition for each of the following terms and add it to your IT glossary.

arithmetic/logic unit (ALU)
booting
central processing unit (CPU)
clock speed
computer system
control unit
firmware
floating point operations per second (FLOPS)
hardware
input
input device
mainframe computers
memory

millions of instructions per second (MIPS)
motherboard
operating system (OS)
output
peripheral devices
personal computer
port
processing
random-access memory (RAM)
read-only memory (ROM)
server
storage
supercomputers
universal serial bus (USB)

INPUT AND OUTPUT DEVICES

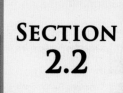

KPG_Payless/Shutterstock.com

To enable processing, information must reach the CPU inside the computer system. There are many input devices for entering data, from the common keyboard to a complex voice- or retinal-recognition system. Input tasks require the most work by the user. For users to "see" the results, the information must be output in the form of text, pictures, sounds, or video.

The earliest computers relied on punched cards for input and output on the large machines. Soon thereafter, a freestanding machine similar to a typewriter called a teleprinter, often sold under the trade name Teletype, was used for both input and output. Thanks to teleprinters, for the first time reports on paper were available to let programmers know what the calculations were producing. Users soon identified their growing needs for entering data more easily. Engineers have since designed and implemented a very large variety of input and output devices.

Essential Question

Why is it important for input and output devices to be accessible to people with disabilities?

LEARNING GOALS

After completing this section, you will be able to:

- Discuss input devices and their functions.
- Describe output devices and their functions.

TERMS

audio-input devices
audio-output device
data projector
image-input devices
keyboard
monitor
mouse
optical-character
   recognition (OCR)

output device
pointing device
printer
ripping
stylus
text-input devices
touch screen
user interface (UI)
webcam

GS5   Computing Fundamentals
2.12

GS4   Computing Fundamentals
2.1.1, 3.3.1

Input Devices and Their Functions

An input device makes it possible for the user to provide communication to the computer. The means by which the user enters data and receives feedback is called the **user interface (UI).** The UI is a combination of hardware and software. There are many input devices available to the user, including keyboards, pointing devices, touch screens, image-input devices, text-input devices, audio-input devices, and devices to assist persons with disabilities.

Keyboards

The **keyboard** is a device for inputting textual and numeric data. It is the most basic input device for user interface. The keyboard is used for creating documents and spreadsheets, navigating windows in the operating system, playing games, controlling functions of the computer, and many other purposes.

Actions of Keyboards

The keys on a keyboard trigger switches inside the device. When a switch is triggered, an electrical signal is sent to the CPU. The CPU then processes the signal and provides the data to whatever software is running. The software in turn acts on the data.

Types of Keyboards

The placement of the alphabetic and numeric characters is fairly standard on keyboards. This is important because people who learn how to touch-type expect the keys to be in the same positions on any keyboard. The most common arrangement of keys on a keyboard in the United States is referred to as the *QWERTY layout*, as shown in Figure 2-8. This name comes from the positions of the first six keys on the left in the top row of letters. The letters in the Latin alphabet are in the middle of the keyboard, and a row of Arabic numerals appears above the letters. The QWERTY layout was designed to avoid the jamming of keys on early mechanical typewriters.

> **FYI**
>
> Some keyboards, especially on laptop computers, support fingerprint recognition to prevent unlawful use.

> **FYI**
>
> The ability to use a keyboard without looking at the keys is an important skill to develop.

BonD80/Shutterstock.com

Figure 2-8. The most common keyboard layout in the United States is the QWERTY layout.

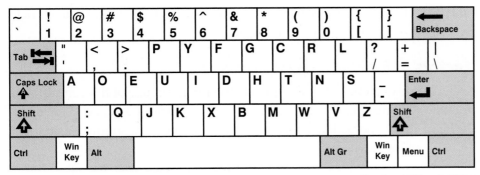

Goodheart-Willcox Publisher

Figure 2-9. The layout of a Dvorak keyboard.

Other schemes for key placement have been proposed. For example, the *Dvorak keyboard*, shown in Figure 2-9, was invented in the 1930s. In this layout, the characters of the Latin alphabet most commonly used in English are the "home keys" in the middle of the keyboard. The Dvorak keyboard is designed to allow for faster finger movement. However, the traditional QWERTY layout remains the most popular.

Standard QWERTY keyboards have 12 function keys along the top, labeled [F1] through [F12]. These keys are used to immediately execute a function. Windows keyboards also have two alternate keys, labeled [Alt], and two control keys, labeled [Ctrl]. These keys are used in combination with other keys to execute shortcuts and commands. Standard keyboards also have a set of arrows for navigation and sometimes an extra numeric keypad. The numeric keypad allows for faster entry of numeric data than is possible with the row of number keys above the letter keys.

Keyboards on laptop computers are smaller than the keyboards for desktop computers. Additionally, they do not have a separate numeric keypad, but several of the keys have dual functions to make up for this. The secondary purpose is activated with the function key, labeled [Fn].

Wireless keyboards eliminate the need to have the keyboard close to the system's processing unit. In fact, wireless keyboards can be located from six to 30 feet away from the system, depending on the keyboard. The data are transmitted to the computer via radio signals.

Some keyboards are *virtual keyboards*, which means they do not physically exist. One form of virtual keyboard is projection-based. An image of the keyboard is projected on a flat surface and sensors detect when the user's fingers touch the images of the keys. A sound can be played to provide feedback to the user since there is no physical feedback provided to the fingers. Figure 2-10 depicts a projection keyboard in use. Other virtual keyboards are displayed on-screen.

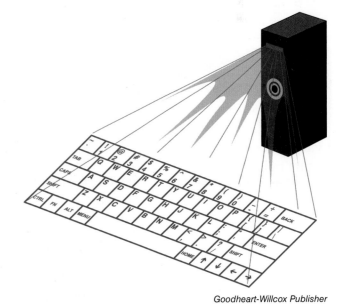

Goodheart-Willcox Publisher

Figure 2-10. A projection keyboard is a type of virtual keyboard.

The user clicks the keys with the pointing device or, in the case of a touch screen, touches the keys with a finger.

Factors in Evaluating Keyboards

GS4 Computing Fundamentals
2.3.1

Choose a keyboard that supports the intended use of the computer. If much of the input is numeric, ensure that the numeric keypad is included. If the primary user is left-handed, the numeric keypad should be on the left side of the keyboard.

Consider how far from the computer system the user will sit. If the computer box is across the room, a wireless keyboard may be required. Wireless keyboards are powered by batteries, which may be a concern. A rechargeable unit eliminates the need to replace batteries. However, a wired keyboard may need to be kept as a backup for when the batteries run out.

How your body is positioned when using the keyboard is a concern. Choose a keyboard that will maintain a straight wrist during typing. Several of these are available and are discussed in Chapter 16.

Pointing Devices

The **pointing device** allows the user to control the movement of the cursor, or pointer, on the screen. There are many types of pointing devices that can be used with a computer, but a mouse is the most common type, as shown in Figure 2-11. Most pointing devices have at least two buttons and many have a wheel. Some pointing devices may have three or more buttons to allow for specialized functions.

wavebreakmedia/Shutterstock.com

Figure 2-11. This student is using a computer that has not only a mouse, but a graphics tablet.

Actions of Pointing Devices

The basic actions of a pointing device include:
- pointing;
- clicking;
- dragging; and
- double-clicking.

Pointing is moving the cursor to a particular screen location. *Clicking* is pressing the primary button once, which is done to activate a command button, set the insertion point in a document, or otherwise interact with the system. *Dragging* is clicking and holding down the primary button while moving the pointing device to highlight text or move an object on the screen. *Double-clicking* is quickly pressing the primary button twice, which is usually done to select a word or to initiate an option.

The left button on the pointing device is the primary button and used for most standard operations. Generally, the right button displays a shortcut menu containing commands and options. The functions of the buttons can be reversed for a left-handed setup.

FYI

It is often possible to use associated software to vary the options when using pointing devices.

The wheel on the pointing device allows the user to scroll through a document or web page. Games often make use of the wheel for zooming as well as allowing the user to scroll through an inventory of items.

Types of Pointing Devices

A basic or traditional **mouse** is a device with one or more buttons that can be moved on a flat surface to control the cursor. A *mechanical mouse* has a rollerball on the bottom surface. As it rolls on a flat surface, it sends signals to the system unit. It requires a mouse pad to run smoothly. An *optical mouse* uses a laser instead of a rollerball to track the mouse's movements. It does not require a mouse pad and has fewer moving parts than a mechanical version. This is the most common type of mouse. A *touch mouse* is an optical mouse with a touch-sensitive top surface in place of buttons and a wheel.

A *trackball mouse* is similar to a mechanical mouse, but the rollerball is located on the top or side of the device. When the user wants to move the pointer on the screen, the mouse remains stationary while the user rolls the ball.

Laptop computers contain an integrated pointing device, either a touch pad or a pointing stick, and two buttons below the keyboard. A *touch pad* is a touch-sensitive area, usually below the keyboard, that the user can tap or slide fingers across. A *pointing stick* is a small joystick in the middle of the keyboard. The buttons below the keyboard correspond to the left and right mouse buttons.

A *graphics tablet* is a form of touch pad, but is a separate device that is larger than what is found on a laptop. A graphics tablet is usually connected to a desktop computer. A stylus is used to interact with the graphics tablet. A **stylus** is a pen-like pointer, but without ink. Graphics tablets are most commonly used for applications such as computer-aided design (CAD), photo editing, and other graphics work.

A pointing device may be wired or wireless. The wireless versions send data to the computer via radio signals and are powered by batteries.

Factors in Evaluating Pointing Devices

Choose a pointing device that supports the intended use of the computer. If the user is required to do a great deal of Internet browsing or reading of long documents, a pointing device with a wheel will make these tasks easier. If most of the work is text input where the pointing device is not often used, then a basic mouse without a wheel may provide enough function. Also consider where the pointing device will be used. If there is not a flat surface on which to operate a mouse, a trackball mouse may be the best option.

Some applications may be able to take advantage of a pointing device with more than two buttons. Many intensive graphics applications, such as CAD, have options for using multibutton pointing devices.

A wireless pointing device is encouraged for places where the wire will impede the movement of the device. Often, a desktop computer box

Technology
A battery is an electrical device consisting of electrochemical cells. These cells convert chemical energy into electrical energy. Single-use batteries are discarded after the electrode materials are discharged. Rechargeable batteries, such as electric car batteries and lithium-ion batteries in electronic devices, can be recharged through electrical outlets.

Computing Fundamentals
2.3.1

cristovao/Shutterstock.com

Figure 2-12. A touch screen serves as both output and input.

is placed on the floor. The wire for the pointing device may not be long enough to provide free movement. A wireless pointing device will not have this issue.

Touch Screens

A **touch screen** is a device that senses applied pressure and sends signals to the CPU. A touch screen makes it easy to input data if a keyboard or traditional pointing device is impractical. Unlike the touch pads found on laptops, touch screens also provide display output. A touch screen provides the functions of a pointing device and the computer monitor, as shown in Figure 2-12.

Actions of Touch Screens

A finger or a stylus is used to apply the pressure to the touch screen. The touch screen provides the four basic functions of a pointing device: pointing, clicking, dragging, and double-clicking.

Types of Touch Screens

The following devices all have touch screens: tablets, smartphones, and portable gaming devices. Many desktop computers have touch-screen monitors. Additionally, many devices with embedded computers have touch screens, such as music players, thermostats, and automotive diagnostic tools.

Interactive kiosks usually have touch screens. A kiosk is a stand-alone computerized device placed in a public space to provide information, sales, or entertainment. The ease of use of a touch screen allows an intuitive interface to be designed for these devices. Many automated teller machines (ATMs) have touch screens for the same reason.

Factors in Evaluating Touch Screens

A consideration in touch screen use is the accuracy of the pressure response. A touch screen should have a quick and accurate response. Often the size of areas for touching is controlled by software. For devices with small touch screens, a stylus may be required if icons and other interface items are too small and close together for a human finger to individually touch.

Touch screens have limited usefulness when precision is a factor. If the tasks are heavily text oriented, a standard keyboard will be the most efficient way to enter the text. For applications that require precise movement of the cursor, a standard mouse will perform better than a touch screen.

Image-Input Devices

Image-input devices are used to digitize images so they can be used by the computer. To *digitize* means to convert from a physical form, such

GS5 Computing Fundamentals
2.14

GS4 Computing Fundamentals
2.3.1

GS5 Computing Fundamentals
3.7.1, 3.7.2

as a photograph, into data the computer can use. These images can be in the form of still pictures or video clips, as shown in Figure 2-13.

Actions of Image-Input Devices

White light consists of all colors of the visible spectrum: red, orange, yellow, green, blue, indigo, and violet. As light strikes an object, the object absorbs some of the light and reflects some of it. What you see as the color of an object is really the part of light that the object reflects. So, when you see a red apple, you are seeing the red portion of white light reflected off the apple. All other portions of white light are absorbed by the apple.

Figure 2-13. A cell phone camera is a type of image-input device.

Image-input devices are digital devices that use electronics to create electrical signals to represent data. Scanners and digital cameras digitize images based on light. In the case of a scanner, a light inside the device it used. In the case of a camera, the light in the environment is used, sometimes with additional light provided by a flash. Both scanners and cameras contain sensors that detect which colors are hitting them. The position of each sensor in the group determines where that color is placed in the final image.

Types of Image-Input Devices

In addition to making phone calls and texting, most cell phones also function as digital cameras. A digital camera is a handheld image-input device that captures still or motion images. The camera digitizes the actual image and stores it in a file of 1s and 0s in the camera. Video cameras, also called camcorders, generally only capture motion video. However, the capture is performed in exactly the same manner as a digital camera.

A **webcam** is an image-input device that can be mounted on top of a monitor or may be built into a laptop computer. The webcam transfers live video over the web. Skype is a popular application that uses a webcam to allow users to see each other from distant locations.

Scanners also create visual images. They can digitize an image and save the data in a graphic file format. Scanned images are stored as raster images in which the image consists of many dots, each representing a separate color. This is discussed in more detail in Chapter 3.

Computing Fundamentals
GS5 3.7.1

Factors in Evaluating Image-Input Devices

The greater number of pixels in a digitized image, the better the representation of the real object. Higher pixel density or pixels per inch produce better quality images. Some digital cameras also provide a video capture option.

Computing Fundamentals
GS4 2.3.1

A webcam is a simple video and still camera that is attached to a computer. Its purpose is to facilitate video communication. Focus is available, but mobility is not its strength. A handheld video camera provides more flexibility in taking video. Not only is it mobile, but it provides the ability to change focus. Some video cameras provide editing capability on the camera itself. A higher-end cell phone provides video capture, but the capability is limited in quality.

A wide range of scanners is available for purchase. Even the very inexpensive models provide a range of resolutions for the final image. Almost all also provide a cropping feature to limit the portion being scanned. If the primary task is scanning pages, then a page feeder is recommended. If the primary use is scanning business cards or photo slides, buy a specialized small scanner for that task.

LoloStock/Shutterstock.com

Figure 2-14. OCR software can be used with a scanner to input text from a hard copy, such as a book.

Text-Input Devices

Text-input devices are generally image-input devices used with software to convert the image to text that can be used by the computer, as shown in Figure 2-14.

Actions of Text-Input Devices

The basic feature of a scanner digitizes the original document as an image. An image of a text page is fine for reading; however, the text is pixels, not characters that can be edited. To be able to edit a scanned document, the image must be transformed into a text document. **Optical-character recognition (OCR)** software can be used with image scanners to digitize text so the computer understands it as text characters. Much of the reliability of OCR software depends on the quality of the original printed page. Proofread the document to make sure it has been properly scanned.

Banks use OCR software to scan the numerical information on checks. Businesses scan old typewritten documents to convert them into computer-usable text files. In some cases, handwritten notes can be scanned into text files.

Types of Text-Input Devices

Text can be entered using a scanner if there is a feature for converting the scanned image into text. Many scanners produce a PDF output. There are third-party software packages that will perform the step of converting a PDF file into a text document. The more reliable method is to use OCR software with the scanner.

Many smartphones use a variety of methods to enter text. The most often used is the virtual keyboard that appears on the display. To enter text, use your fingers to tap the keys. This is the basis of texting. The text also can be sent to another phone user or entered into a file to be saved on the smartphone. In addition, voice can be used to speak into the phone and speech recognition software converts the sounds to text. Some smartphones have an additional hardware component of a physical keyboard that slides out for use.

Factors in Evaluating Text-Input Devices

Choose a scanning device that supports the intended use. For scanning multiple loose pages, select a scanner with an automatic document feeder. For scanning pages in a bound document, select a scanner that can automatically turn pages as it scans.

Scanner resolution and speed are important considerations. Fast or low-resolution scans are generally not as clear as slow or high-resolution scans. However, there needs to be a balance between how long a job will take and the cleanliness of the resulting text document. Depending on your needs, a high-end scanner may be required to quickly scan at a high resolution.

If considering a smartphone as a scanning device, look at the resolution of the phone's camera and the effectiveness of the autofocus feature. These will impact the quality of the scan. Also, be sure OCR software is available for the smartphone.

An additional aspect to evaluate is the OCR software that will be used. Be sure the capability of the software will meet your needs. For example, if you plan to scan handwritten notes, look for software that supports handwriting recognition. Also be sure the software can save text in a file format that you will be able to use.

Audio-Input Devices

Audio-input devices convert sounds into data that can be used by the computer. Digitized sound can be used for audio playback or voice commands. Inputting sound into the computer requires the use of a microphone. Many laptops and mobile devices have embedded microphones.

Voice input allows the user to issue computer commands and enter text without using a keyboard or pointing device. Directory assistance on the telephone and search functions on a smartphone are examples of voice input.

Voice-recognition software must be installed to enable voice input. Early versions of voice-recognition software had to be "taught" to understand the user. Current versions of voice-recognition software understand most voices and accents found in the general public without prior preparation by the user.

Actions of Audio-Input Devices

To capture sound for computer use, it must be digitized. In nature, sound is continuous. The digital world works in individual bits or binary digits. Audio-input devices use a process called sampling. Sampling is capturing data at very small and regular intervals, as shown in Figure 2-15. The input device assigns a number to each sample and saves

Computing Fundamentals
GS4 2.3.1

Green Tech

Environmentally Friendly Electronics
It is important to purchase environmentally friendly devices. Some manufacturers use recycled materials in the construction of their products. Additionally, some companies offer electronics recycling services. They often partner with recyclers who use best practices to repair, repurpose, or recycle the equipment. These products send the message that the company values preserving the environment.

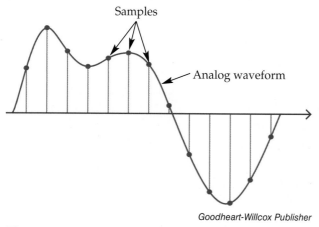

Samples

Analog waveform

Goodheart-Willcox Publisher

Figure 2-15. To convert sound into digital form, it must be sampled at regular intervals.

these numbers in an audio file. Playback devices use the numbers to replicate the sound. Sampling is discussed in more detail in Chapter 14.

The smaller the interval, or the higher the sampling rate, the better the representation of the original sound will be. Increasing the sampling rate also increases the file size. Fortunately, there are many very good audio compression-decompression schemes (codecs). A typical sampling rate for CD quality audio is 44,100 times per second. This is often enough to fool the human ear into thinking the playback is a continuous sound and not a stream of samples played back-to-back.

Types of Audio-Input Devices

Many computers have an imbedded microphone. If not, external microphones can be used by way of the microphone jack on the audio card. The better the quality of the microphone, the better the quality of the audio capture will be. Care must be taken using an external microphone because touching it or moving it adds extra noise to the captured file. A headset eliminates this problem.

A headset is a device that sits securely on the user's head and holds a microphone near the user's mouth. This keeps the microphone steady and at the same distance from a user's mouth even if the head turns. Many headsets are a combination of microphone and earphones.

Ripping audio is another method for getting audio into the computer. **Ripping** is the process of extracting audio from a CD, DVD, or video file. The audio in this format is not directly playable using a computer-based media player. Ripping converts it to a computer-based format.

Certain electronic musical devices can be connected to a computer by way of the musical instrument digital interface (MIDI). A MIDI device may be able to stream data to a computer for capture of a real-time performance. MIDI software also can be used to create music using the computer keyboard.

Factors in Evaluating Audio-Input Devices

Computing Fundamentals
2.3.1

Choosing an audio-input device for a system depends on the user's needs. Microphones can sit on the desk, be clipped onto the user's clothing, or be part of a headset or webcam. Smartphones also have microphones. Select the type of microphone that will work best for your needs.

The intended input is also a consideration in selecting an audio-input device. For voice input, a simple microphone is usually fine. However, for conversations online, a headset is recommended so that there is no feedback from the audio output. Feedback occurs when the microphone picks up the output from the speakers and feeds it back into the computer. This produces, at best, an echo or, at worst, a screeching sound.

For capturing high-quality audio, the tonal qualities of the microphone must be considered. High-quality audio may be needed for a movie or video soundtrack, musical recordings, or other application. The quality of the captured sound will be only as good as the capabilities of the input device.

Input Devices for Users with Disabilities

Just about everybody relies on computers, and people with disabilities are no different. Special input devices make computers accessible to those facing challenges related to mobility, visual impairment, and motor control.

Actions of Accessible Input Devices

Many adaptive devices are available to support people with disabilities. The actual input device for a person with a disability depends on the nature of the disability and the input to be captured. For example, a person unable to control a computer mouse by hand may use a device controlled by the head to point and click at a computer screen. The purpose of an accessible device is the same as a noncompliant device: to enter data that can be digitized.

Types of Accessible Input Devices

Many adaptive devices are available to support people with disabilities. The types of accessible input devices include keyboards, pointing devices, touch screens, image-input devices, text-input devices, and audio-input devices. Following are some examples.

Voice-recognition technology has made it possible for disabled people to command wheelchair movement. This technology also allows commands to be entered into the computer, as shown in Figure 2-16. Data can be entered using this technology as well.

Enlarged keyboards and touch-screen devices help visually challenged users input data. The larger size allows for characters on the keys or screen to be easier to see.

Special trackballs and head-mounted pointing devices can be used if arm movement is impaired. One example is a light pen attached to a headset or eyeglasses that directs a laser beam at the monitor. The monitor uses a reader to interpret where the beam is pointing, which takes the place of mouse input.

> **FYI**
>
> The Americans with Disabilities Act provides guidelines for accessible devices. Devices that do not meet these guidelines are considered *noncompliant*.

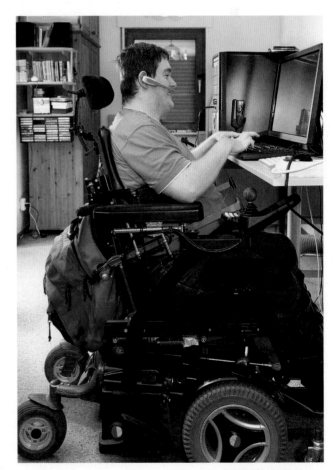

Belushi/Shutterstock.com

Figure 2-16. This person is using a headset with his computer that allows him to input commands using his voice.

GS4 Computing Fundamentals
2.3.1

Factors in Evaluating Accessible Input Devices

While there is a wide range of assistive devices available, there are a few key assessments for all of them. Check that the device is simple and intuitive to use for the person who will operate it. See that the input is easy to accomplish. Be sure the device will function within any space constraints where it will be used. Ensure that the effort required to operate the device is within the normal range of the person who will use the device.

Another important consideration is the error rate for input. This is a measure of how accurately the user can achieve the intended result. The error rate should be as low as possible to ensure an efficient computer-operating experience.

GS5 Computing Fundamentals
2.12

GS4 Computing Fundamentals
3.3.1

Output Devices and Their Functions

An **output device** makes it possible for the user to receive communication from the computer. To see, hear, save, or send the results of the computer's processor, the information must be transformed by an output device. Information can be output to the user as video (text and images), sound, or in physical form (printed). There are thousands of output devices, the most common ones are discussed here.

Monitors

The most common output device is the monitor. A **monitor** is a device that provides a display output. Most of the output from a computer is provided to the user through the monitor. This is the device where the user can see the graphical interface of the operating system and software applications.

Actions of Monitors

Monitors operate by displaying the video output from the computer as a collection of pixels. One *pixel*, or picture element, is the smallest point a monitor can display. Each pixel is a tiny point of light made of a combination of red, green, and blue, as shown in Figure 2-17. A fluorescent panel is illuminated at the back of the screen. When an electrical current is applied, which comes from CPU via the video card, how much and what color light passes through each pixel is set.

Types of Monitors

The most common type of monitor is a liquid crystal display (LCD). It is also called a *flat-panel monitor*. LCDs are popular because they are light, inexpensive, and energy efficient.

A newer type of flat-panel monitor is the LED monitor. This monitor uses light-emitting diodes (LEDs) to create the light instead of an LCD. An LED monitor is even more efficient and has better color representation than an LCD monitor.

> ## FYI
>
> The pixels in a monitor can be clearly seen by holding a magnifying glass to the screen.

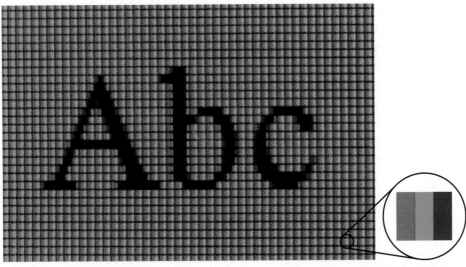

Figure 2-17. One pixel on the monitor is a combination of red, green, and blue light.

Older monitors were cathode-ray tubes (CRTs). These are the large monitors that looked like an old-style television. CRT monitors have been almost completely replaced by LCD and LED monitors, but may still be found in applications such as automated teller machines.

Connecting a monitor is usually as simple as plugging it into the graphics card on the computer. A desktop computer will have at least one monitor, but, in many cases, two monitors are used to extend the working area. Use of two monitors is called a *dual-monitor setup*. In some specialized applications, more than two monitors may be connected to a computer. In order to use more than one monitor, the graphics card must be capable of supporting the setup.

GS5
Computing Fundamentals
2.3.6

Most modern laptops are automatically equipped to connect to an external monitor in addition to the laptop's own display. To add the external monitor, locate the VGA port on the laptop and plug in the monitor. The additional monitor can be used with the laptop's display or as the only display.

Factors in Evaluating Monitors

The efficiency of monitors is measured by:

GS4
Computing Fundamentals
2.3.1

- screen size;
- contrast ratio;
- dot pitch;
- resolution; and
- viewing angle.

The *screen size* is a diagonal measurement, in inches, from corner to corner. This is the physical size of the screen in the monitor. Common standard desktop monitors are usually between 17 and 28 inches. Laptop screens are usually between 10 and 15 inches. Smartphone screens are usually between 4.5 inches and 6 inches.

FYI

The actual displayed screen resolution is a function of the video card, but the monitor screen determines what screen resolutions are supported.

The number of pixels on the screen is referred to as *screen resolution*. The more pixels there are in a given space, the more precise the image that can be displayed. A 21-inch monitor typically can display a maximum of 1680 pixels horizontally and 1050 pixels vertically.

The *contrast ratio* is the difference in light intensity between the brightest white and the darkest black. The higher the ratio, the greater the intensity difference between white and black. A high contrast ratio will make the images on screen easier to see in a well-lighted room.

The *dot pitch*, also called the *pixel pitch*, is the distance, in millimeters, between pixels. The smaller the distance between the pixels, the sharper the display appears. A dot pitch between 0.22 and 0.28 mm is typical.

The *resolution* of a monitor is the density of the pixels displayed on the screen. The higher the resolution, the clearer the display is. Resolution is measured in horizontal and vertical pixels. A resolution of 1024 × 768, for example, means 1,024 pixels are displayed in the horizontal direction and 768 are displayed in the vertical direction. The resolution settings are determined by the graphics card and the monitor itself.

The *viewing angle* is how far the user can move to the side before the image can no longer be seen. Most LCD monitors have a viewing angle of 150°. This means the user can move 75° to either side of center and still see the images on screen.

bikeriderlondon/Shutterstock.com

Figure 2-18. A data projector is like a computer monitor, except the graphic output is projected onto a separate screen.

Projectors

A **data projector** is an output device that collects video data from a computer or other media player and projects the images onto a separate screen, as shown in Figure 2-18. Projectors are most commonly used in educational and business settings to show images, lessons, and presentations. It is also common to find these output devices in sports and entertainment venues where large audiences attend and it is difficult to see the performers.

Actions of Projectors

A projector is a light-based device that collects data intended for the monitor and displays it elsewhere. In general, these devices accept a signal from the computer and pass it through a prism or spinning color wheel to break up the signal into the three basic computer colors of red, green, and blue (RGB). Then each of these colors is separately projected into another component within the device, such as another prism. This combines the three colored beams of light into a single beam that is then projected onto a screen.

Often, a laptop with a video projector is used for showing a presentation to a group of people. To connect the laptop to a video projector, connect the projector's video cable to the VGA port on the laptop just as you would for connecting an external monitor. If audio is to be part of the presentation, the audio cable from the projector must be plugged into the laptop's audio-out port as well.

Types of Projectors

There are several different types of projects, including LCD, DLP, LCoS, and LED. A liquid crystal display (LCD) projector uses a prism to split a white light signal into RBG display. A digital light processing (DLP) projector uses a rotating color wheel to split a white signal into RBG display. A liquid crystal on silicone (LCoS) projector uses a combination of prisms and silicone panels to provide a display that is as easy to see close up as well as far away. A light emitting diode (LED) projector creates the projected image based on light emitted from the diode array. This type eliminates the heat and warm-up time of other projector types. The result is greater image clarity and less power consumption.

Factors in Evaluating Projectors

Computing Fundamentals
GS4 **2.3.1**

Two factors to consider when selecting a projector are its size and weight. If the device is to be stationary, weight and size are not as important as if the device is to be carried to presentations in other places. For portability, a small size and light weight are best. If portability is important, size and weight may have a greater influence in selection than other factors.

A key feature of quality that increases with the cost is the number of lumens, which is a measure of brightness. If the presentations are to be given in a lighted room, the projector must have a greater lumens rating than if the session is in a darkened room.

Resolution may be a concern. If the projected display needs to show fine details, such as when demonstrating photographic or illustrative work, a high-resolution projector may be needed. However, basic projectors are capable of a resolution suitable for most uses.

The distance the projector will be from the screen should be considered. This distance determines the size of the projected image. Moving the projector closer to the screen will reduce the size of the image. Moving the projector farther from the screen will increase the size of the image.

Printers

The second most common output device is a printer. The **printer** transforms computer information into a physical form, most commonly an image or text on paper, as shown in Figure 2-19.

Chuck Rausin/Shutterstock.com

Figure 2-19. This large-format ink-jet printer is typical of the type of computer printer used in the graphics industry.

Actions of Printers

The true action of a printer occurs in the printer driver. It is this software program that formats the printed page from the printer based on the output from another software program, such as Microsoft Word or Adobe Photoshop. Once the page is formatted, instructions are sent to the printer. The printer then creates the printed page by depositing ink or toner onto the paper based on the instructions from the printer driver.

Types of Printers

Two types of printers are currently widespread: ink-jet and laser. However, other types of printers exist, such as solid-ink and 3D.

Ink-jet printers are common for home use and small businesses. They are affordable and can produce high-quality color printouts quickly and quietly. Ink-jet printers spray tiny drops of ink through a nozzle onto the paper to form the output. This type of printer uses the cyan, magenta, yellow, key (CMYK) color model. Most ink-jet printers have four ink cartridges, one for each color with black being the key color. Some ink-jet printers have two cartridges, one that contains cyan, magenta, and yellow and one for black.

Laser printers use the same principle as photocopiers. A laser beam creates a charge of static electricity on a drum. The toner, which is a fine powder, is attracted to the charge and sticks to the drum. As the drum is rotated, paper moves past it and the toner is transferred to the paper. Heat is then applied to fuse the toner to the paper. Laser printers are popular in offices and schools because they produce high-quality text and are generally faster than ink-jet printers. The majority of laser printers output in black only, but color laser printers are available.

Solid-ink printers use wax-like sticks of solid ink to create an image on paper. In function, these printers are similar to ink-jet printers. The solid ink is melted and then sprayed onto the paper. However, the melted ink solidifies very quickly once it is on the paper. The liquid ink in an ink-jet printer must dry for a few seconds before becoming permanent. Solid-ink printers generate less waste because there are no ink or toner cartridges. The per-page operating cost of solid-ink printers is much lower than other printers. Solid-ink printers are not common, usually found only in some businesses and schools.

Ink-jet, laser, and solid-ink printers produce an image on a flat surface. This is a two-dimensional (2D) output. However, 3D printers produce a three-dimensional (3D) output. These printers create 3D output by building up material in very thin layers. Most 3D printers create the output in plastic, but printers that output in metal and other materials have been created.

Factors in Evaluating Printers

When evaluating an ink-jet or laser printer, consider:
- speed;
- resolution;
- duty cycle; and
- cost.

FYI

With the proper paper, the output from an ink-jet printer can look like a traditional continuous tone photograph.

FYI

Impact printers, which create an image by pressing ink into the paper, are no longer common in general use, but still have specialized uses.

Computing Fundamentals
GS4 2.3.1

The speed of ink-jet and laser printers are measured by pages per minute (ppm). Printer speeds are typically in the 8 to 38 ppm range. Color output generally takes longer than black output.

The resolution of a printer is measured in dots per inch (dpi). The greater the dpi, the higher the resolution the printer can output. For most applications, 1,200 dpi is sufficient. For photographic-quality output, the resolution should be at least 2,400 dpi.

The *duty cycle* is the manufacturer's estimate for how long a machine can print before a failure occurs. This is generally expressed in the number of pages produced on a monthly basis. A personal laser printer has a duty cycle of about 3,000 pages per month. A good ink-jet printer may be rated at 1,000 pages per month. A printer for business use should be rated much higher.

Printers themselves are very inexpensive compared to the cost of using them. In addition to the initial cost of the printer, ink or toner is used up as pages are printed. It is important to consider the cost of replacing these items. The capacity of these cartridges varies, so be sure to check the output rating when comparing prices. With ink-jet printers, a model having a separate cartridge for each color instead of colors combined in a single cartridge can be more economical. The type of paper required by the printer is also a variable expense. Photo-quality paper is generally more expensive than the paper used for printing text.

> ## FYI
>
> Some printers are capable of duplex printing, which is the ability to print on both sides of the page. This can save paper and the associated cost.

Audio-Output Devices

An **audio-output device** converts data in the computer into sounds, as shown in Figure 2-20. The computer uses sounds to alert the user about the status of the system. Additionally, many applications use sounds to communicate with the user. Sound is an integral part of most video games as well.

Actions of Audio-Output Devices

An audio-output device uses the decompression instructions of the codec used to create the file. The device takes the digitized sound file, decompresses it, and uses its hardware to play it. The digitized sound is replicated by the hardware of the device.

Kzenon/Shutterstock.com

Figure 2-20. This audio technician has speakers and earphones as output devices from his computer.

Types of Audio-Output Devices

Almost all personal computers are equipped with internal speakers. These speakers are sufficient for the basic audio communication from the computer. They are sufficient to play basic audio, such as sound clips and videoconferencing.

To play high-quality audio, such as music, movie soundtracks, and game sound effects, external speakers may be required. External speakers are connected to the computer through an audio jack in the sound card. There are many variations in external speakers, from small units that sit on the desk in front of the user, to surround-sound systems with large speakers that sit in the corners of the room and a subwoofer that sits under the desk.

For privacy, headphones or earbuds can be used. These devices generate sound directly at the user's ears, so the sounds cannot be heard by anyone other than the user.

In some cases, the audio-output device is a storage device such as a hard drive or DVD. For example, if the computer is used to compose and mix music, the audio output may be recorded directly on a DVD.

Factors in Evaluating Audio-Output Devices

Computing Fundamentals
2.3.1

The intended use of the audio output will determine the type of device. For music, movie playback, or gaming, high-quality external speakers are needed, but the specific quality and other features of the speakers are largely a personal decision. If the playback is for a performance, then size of the venue and connection to the venue's sound-amplification system are key factors.

Cost is a consideration. Generally, as the physical size and the quality of the speakers increase, so will the price. There is a wide range of prices for audio-output devices.

HANDS-ON EXAMPLE 2.2.1

AUDIO OUTPUT

The Windows operating system has several events with which a sound can be associated. It is easy to change these sounds.

1. In Windows 10, right-click on the **Start** button, and then click **Control Panel** in the shortcut menu. In Windows 8 and Windows 7, click the **Apps** or **Start** button, and click **Control Panel** in the menu.
2. The Control Panel window is displayed.
3. Click **Hardware and Sound**. Note: if you do not see this option, click the **View by:** link at the top of the dialog box, and click **Category** in the drop-down menu.
4. Under the **Sound** heading, click **Adjust System Volume**. The **Volume Mixer** dialog box is opened, which provides volume control of the unit's sounds. Drag the slider for **System Sounds** upward to increase the volume. To mute, or silence, the system sounds, click the speaker icon below the **System Sounds** slider. This is a toggle, which means clicking it turns it on or off. For this activity, make sure the system sounds are on.
5. Close the **Volume Mixer** dialog box by clicking the standard close button, which is the X in the upper-right corner.
6. Click **Change System Sounds** in the **Hardware and Sound** view of the Control Panel window. The **Sound** dialog box is displayed, as shown. If the **Sounds** tab is not already active, click it.

HANDS-ON EXAMPLE 2.2.1 (CONTINUED)

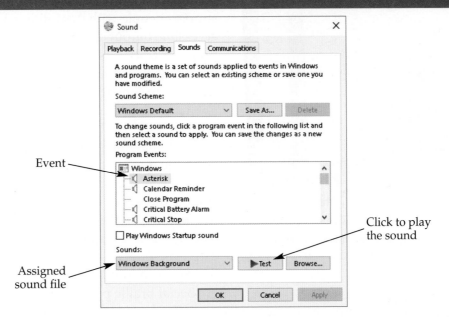

Event

Click to play the sound

Assigned sound file

7. One by one, highlight each of the events in the **Program Events:** window, and click the **Test** button to hear the sound. Only those events with a speaker icon next to it currently have an associated sound.
8. Highlight an event that currently does not have a sound associated with it. Then, click the **Browse...** button. A standard Windows open dialog box is displayed.
9. Navigate to a folder containing WAV files. The Windows\Media folder should contain several. WAV files are sound wave files.
10. Open a WAV file from the folder to associate the sound with the event.
11. Click the **Test** button to play the sound associated with the event.
12. Click the **Save As...** button in the **Sound** dialog box. In the dialog box that is displayed, enter *YourName_*Sounds, and click the **OK** button. The sound scheme is saved under this name and can be restored.
13. Close the **Sound** dialog box by clicking the **OK** button, and close the Control Panel window by clicking the Windows close button (X).

Output Devices for Users with Disabilities

People with disabilities rely on computers as much as those who do not have disabilities. Computers are made accessible to those facing challenges related to mobility, visual impairment, and motor control through special output devices, as shown in Figure 2-21.

Actions of Accessible Output Devices

Many adaptive devices are available to support people with disabilities. The actual output device for a person with a disability depends on the nature of the disability and the output to be created. For example, a person unable to view a computer screen in the default resolutions may use a device that magnifies the content on the screen. The purpose of the device is the same: to output data in a format the person can use.

Goodheart-Willcox Publisher; Denis Tabler/Shutterstock.com

Figure 2-21. A screen magnifier can make a computer accessible for someone with impaired vision.

FYI

A correctly designed website will contain the information needed by screen readers. Web accessibility is an important aspect of website design.

Computing Fundamentals
2.3.1

Types of Accessible Output Devices

Many adaptive devices are available to support people with disabilities. The types of accessible output devices include monitors, projectors, printers, and audio-output devices. Following are some examples. Other output devices are similarly made accessible.

Larger monitors with a lower-resolution setting can assist those with impaired vision. This, in effect, magnifies the screen display. If this is not an adequate accommodation, there are software solutions. A screen-magnification program will enlarge the screen display, often with a scrolling function to pan the view. A screen reader is software that reads text aloud or describes what is displayed on the screen.

For printing, text can be enlarged in software or special Braille printers can be used to make the output accessible to the visually impaired. Braille is a code of raised dots in which English can be written. Braille printers are impact printers that emboss the page so those who are blind can read with their fingertips.

Closed captioning should be provided for video content. This allows the content to be accessed by those with hearing impairments. Closed captioning can be provided through software. Additionally, many software programs that use sound as a communication feature have settings that allow a visual cue to be used instead of the sound. For example, software that plays a sound when a new e-mail message is received may have an option for the cursor to flash instead of playing a sound.

Factors in Evaluating Accessible Output Devices

While there is a wide range of assistive devices available, there are a few key assessments for all of them. Check that the device is simple and intuitive to use for the person who will use it. Check that the output will be easy to use. Be sure the device will function within any space constraints where it will be used. Ensure that the device produces an output within the normal range of the person who will use the device.

Cost is a consideration for some assistive output devices. Larger monitors generally cost more than smaller monitors. Braille printers are expensive. The cost is in the range of $2,000 for personal printers to $80,000 for large-scale printing operations. These printers are also noisy to operate and much slower than ink-jet and laser printers.

HANDS-ON EXAMPLE 2.2.2

ACCESSIBILITY ASSESSMENT

This checklist covers recommendations from the University of Washington to increase accessibility for all users in a computer lab. Complete this assessment to see if any of these

HANDS-ON EXAMPLE 2.2.2 (CONTINUED)

recommendations are provided in your school's computer lab. Be prepared to discuss with the class how to implement any missing accommodations or additional accommodations that could be included.

Accommodation	✓
Printed resources placed so that a wheelchair user can reach them.	
At least one adjustable workstation provided.	
Keyboard guards and wrist rests provided.	
Trackball, joystick, or other mouse alternative available.	
Lab signs printed in high contrast and large print.	
Key documents available in large print or Braille formats.	
Screen-reading software and a speech-output system provided.	
Braille conversion programs and a Braille printer available.	
Large-print key-top labels, screen-enlargement software, and a large monitor (at least 17 inches) available.	
Key documents state the school's commitment to access and provide procedures for requesting disability accommodations.	
Staff is familiar with the adaptive technology and trained in disability issues.	

2.2 SECTION REVIEW

CHECK YOUR UNDERSTANDING

1. What is the function of the user interface?
2. Which input device senses applied pressure and sends signals to the CPU while providing the function of a computer monitor?
3. How does the purpose of an input device for users with disabilities differ from the purpose of a noncompliant device?
4. What is the most common output device?
5. What are the four factors to consider when evaluating an ink-jet or laser printer?

IC3 CERTIFICATION PRACTICE

The following question is a sample of the type of questions presented on the IC3 exam.

1. Which is the most common type of computer monitor in use today?
   A. LCD
   B. CRT
   C. LED
   D. HD

BUILD YOUR VOCABULARY

As you progress through this course, develop a personal IT glossary. This will help you build your vocabulary and prepare you for a career. Write a definition for each of the following terms and add it to your IT glossary.

audio-input devices
audio-output device
data projector
image-input devices
keyboard
monitor
mouse
optical-character recognition (OCR)
output device
pointing device
printer
ripping
stylus
text-input devices
touch screen
user interface (UI)
webcam

STORAGE DEVICES

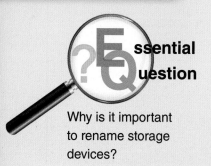

Data stored in RAM disappears when the computer is turned off, and new data cannot be saved in ROM. Therefore, storage devices are needed to keep data in digital format for reuse. Without a storage device, all data not stored in ROM will be erased as soon as power is disconnected from the computer. Storage devices also allow for portability of data between computers and keeping data in a location other than inside the computer.

Different types of storage devices have different ways in which data are saved on the device. However, all storage devices save data in the forms of on and off (1s and 0s). The amount of data held by storage devices is measured in bytes, the same way as the capacity of RAM is measured. The capacity of storage devices varies by type. Some types of storage devices are available in a range of capacities, while other types are a fixed size.

Goodluz/Shutterstock.com

LEARNING GOALS

After completing this section, you will be able to:
• Identify types of storage devices.
• Assign names to storage devices.

TERMS

flash drives
hard disk drive
magnetic media
optical storage
solid-state drives (SSDs)
volume label

Types of Storage Devices

There are a variety of storage devices that may be used with a computer. The most popular storage devices are hard drives, CDs and DVDs, and flash drives. These devices fall into three basics types of storage media: magnetic media, optical storage, and solid-state devices.

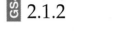

GS4 Computing Fundamentals
3.3.1

Magnetic Media

Magnetic media are made of iron oxide–coated disks that can be selectively magnetized to store on-off signals (1s and 0s). The computer's internal hard disk drive is the most common example of a magnetic medium. It converts the electronic signals from RAM into stored data by orienting the iron components based on their magnetic properties.

GS4 Computing Fundamentals
2.1.2

A **hard disk drive**, or *hard drive*, is a sealed unit that contains a stack of individual disks, or platters, which are magnetic media that rotate at a very high speed, as shown in Figure 2-22. Each platter has a large number of concentric circles on it, and data are stored in these rings. A hard drive also contains fixed read-write heads that move across the surface of the platters to store and retrieve patterns of magnetism. Hard drives can have enormous storage capacities. Commonly available hard drives can hold over 5 terabytes of data. That is more data than can be found in all printed books in an average school library.

External hard drives are commonly used to provide additional storage. They are very useful as back-up devices. Data from the internal hard drive can be copied to an external drive in case a problem arises in the internal drive. External hard drives are also portable and can be used to share data between computers. Common external hard drives currently have capacities of between 2 and 4 TB.

FYI

Although personal computers are expected to have hard drives, a hard drive is not essential to the basic operation of a computer.

Hellen Sergeyeva/Shutterstock.com

Figure 2-22. A hard disk drive consists of multiple platters. The unit is enclosed, but the cover has been removed in this photo.

Special care should be taken to protect a hard drive from any damage. Hard drives are sensitive to dust and dirt, which is why they are sealed units. Hard drives are also sensitive to high temperature, jarring, and external magnetic fields.

Optical Storage

Optical storage involves saving data as tiny pits in foil on a plastic disc. These pits are read with a laser. The optical discs come in the form of a compact disc (CD), digital versatile disc (DVD), and Blu-ray discs (BD). These discs are the same physical size, but each type holds a different amount of data. The capacity of each type is fixed.

Optical discs are more resilient than hard disks. They can tolerate dirt because they can be cleaned with a soft cloth. They are immune to normal temperature changes and extraneous magnetic fields. However, care must be taken to avoid scratches and prolonged exposure to ultraviolet (UV) light.

CD

The CD was first developed for audio recordings as a replacement for tapes and records. However, the format was quickly adapted for use in computers as the CD-ROM. A CD offers 700 MB of storage. There are several types of CDs:

- compact disc digital audio (CD-DA)
- compact disc read-only memory (CD-ROM)
- compact disc interactive (CD-i)
- compact disc recordable (CD-R)
- compact disc rewritable (CD-RW)

There are two basic types of recordable and rewritable discs: minus (–) and plus (+). The minus discs, such as CD-R and CD-RW, are single-session discs. All data must be added in one session. The plus discs, such as CD+R and CD+RW, are multisession discs. Data can be added at different times.

DVD

The DVD format is more advanced than the CD format. It was initially developed for video recordings as a replacement for video tapes. However, like the CD format, the DVD format was quickly adapted for use in computers. The wavelength of the laser used in the DVD format is shorter than that used in the CD format. As a result, a DVD can hold more data than a CD. A DVD can store 4.5 GB. That is enough capacity to store 4.5 hours of high-definition video. DVD drives can read CDs.

Blu-ray

The Blu-ray disc format is designed to replace the DVD format. Blu-ray is so named because the technology uses a blue laser instead of the infrared laser for CD and red laser for DVD. The wavelength of the blue laser is shorter. This allows for more information to be stored on a Blu-ray disc than on a DVD or CD. A Blu-ray disc typically holds 25 GB. Blu-ray drives can read DVDs and CDs.

TITANS OF TECHNOLOGY

Intel Corporation was founded in 1968 by Gordon Moore and Robert Noyce under the name NM Electronics. Intel Corporation is a semiconductor company responsible for the most popular CPUs used in personal computers. Moore's law is based on an observation made by Gordon Moore that the number of transistors incorporated in a chip double about every 24 months. Even though this observation was made over 50 years ago, it holds today. Robert Noyce coinvented the integrated circuit. This device now exists in every digital device. Each integrated circuit is a collection of electronic circuits on a chip made of silicon. Developers have decreased the distance between transistors, making the chips smaller and smaller. This continual miniaturization accounts for part of the increase of processing speed because the signals have to travel shorter and shorter distances. The continued miniaturization of chips is what allows Moore's law to remain current.

Solid-State Drives

Solid-state drives (SSDs) are similar to RAM, but they have an integrated circuit to store data as involatile memory rather than volatile memory. **Flash drives**, also known as thumb or jump drives, are removable peripheral devices and the most recognizable examples of SSDs. However, SSDs are also used in place of traditional hard drives in many portable devices, such as netbooks and tablets.

Flash drives are physically small, extremely portable, provide quick access to data, and use very little power. They are so small and portable that it is very easy for students to forget about them and leave them in the computer lab. Flash drives are available in different sizes, from as small as 2GB to as large as 256GB.

Naming Storage Devices

Storage devices are usually automatically named by the operating system. The device drive name is a letter followed by a colon. For example, C: is the primary hard drive, and it is referred to as the "C drive." Additionally, the name of the device itself is called the **volume label** or *volume name*. The volume label can be more descriptive than the device drive name. The volume label can usually be changed for rewritable media, such as hard disks, flash drives, and rewritable optical discs.

There is a pattern for how drive names are assigned to devices. Internal disk drives are named first, followed by optical drives. Removable drives are named after optical drives. All of these letters are usually automatically assigned by the operating system. Network drives are named after all other drives. The user can usually select the drive letter when network drives are connected. Network drive letters conventionally are selected from letters at the end of the alphabet.

The volume label for a device is usually given a name by the manufacturer of the device. In the case of CDs, DVDs, and Blu-ray discs, the volume label is added to the disc when the disc is manufactured. Rewritable discs and other rewriteable media generally can be renamed by the user.

FYI

The device drive names A: and B: are designated for floppy disk drives, which is obsolete technology. These drive letters are reserved to maintain backward compatibility.

HANDS-ON EXAMPLE 2.3.1

STORAGE DEVICE NAMES AND VOLUME LABELS

The device drive name for installed storage devices can be easily identified using Windows Explorer. Rewritable storage media, such as a flash drive, can have its volume label changed.

1. Open Windows File Explorer. This can be done by double-clicking the **Computer** icon on the desktop or by right-clicking on the **Start** menu button and clicking **Open Windows Explorer** or **File Explorer** in the shortcut menu.
2. Locate the left-hand pane in Windows Explorer. This contains a tree that shows the devices, folders, and files accessible to the computer, as shown.

Folder tree —→

3. In the left-hand pane, locate the primary hard disk drive. What letter is assigned to this storage device?
4. Are there any other storage devices attached to the computer? Notice the icon in the tree for each attached device represents the type of device. What are the letters assigned?
5. Insert your course flash drive into one of the USB ports on the computer.
6. In Windows 10, click the slide-in alert that indicates to choose what happens with removable drives. The autoplay dialog box is displayed. In Windows 8 and Windows 7, the autoplay dialog box should automatically appear. Make note of the drive letter for the flash drive shown in the dialog box.
7. Click **Open folder to view files** in the autoplay dialog box. Windows Explorer is launched.
8. Locate the flash drive in the left-hand pane. It will have the same drive letter that was displayed in the autoplay dialog box.
9. Right-click on the flash drive in Windows Explorer, and click **Rename** in the shortcut menu. The volume label for the drive becomes editable. Notice the current name is highlighted in blue. This means the text is selected.
10. Using the keyboard, enter the name PRINC-OF-IT.
11. Press the [Enter] key to rename the volume label. This flash drive will hold your notes from this course.

2.3 SECTION REVIEW

CHECK YOUR UNDERSTANDING

1. What is the most common example of a magnetic storage medium in a personal computer?
2. What type of storage media are CDs, DVD, and Blu-ray?
3. What type of storage device is a flash drive?
4. Describe a volume label for a storage device.
5. Which type of drive is named first when names are assigned?

IC3 CERTIFICATION PRACTICE

The following question is a sample of the type of questions presented on the IC3 exam.

1. An external device connected to a computer is called a:
   A. processor device
   B. CPU
   C. peripheral device
   D. driver device

BUILD YOUR VOCABULARY

As you progress through this course, develop a personal IT glossary. This will help you build your vocabulary and prepare you for a career. Write a definition for each of the following terms and add it to your IT glossary.

flash drives
hard disk drive
magnetic media
optical storage
solid-state drives (SSDs)
volume label

2 REVIEW AND ASSESSMENT

Chapter Summary

Section 2.1
Types of Computers and Components

- Historically, computers were grouped in one of three categories based on size: mainframes, minicomputers, or microcomputers. Computers today are usually categorized based on usage and cost as well as size: supercomputers, mainframes, servers, and personal computers and mobile devices.

- All computers contain the same basic types of components: input device, memory, processor, and output device. If a device does not have all four components, it is not a computer.

- The operating system (OS) is software that manages all of the devices, as well as locates and provides instructions to the CPU. General-use computers, such as a PC or tablet, must have an OS to work, but single-use computers do not require an operating system.

Section 2.2
Input and Output Devices

- An input device makes it possible for the user to provide communication to the computer. Input devices include keyboards, pointing devices, touch screens, image-input devices, text-input devices, audio-input devices, and devices to assist persons with disabilities.

- An output device makes it possible for the user to receive communication from the computer. Information can be output to the user as video, sound, or in physical form.

Section 2.3
Storage Devices

- There are three basics types of storage media: magnetic media, optical storage, and solid-state devices. The most popular storage devices are hard drives, CDs and DVDs, and flash drives.

- The volume label is the name of the device. The volume label can usually be changed for rewritable media, such as hard disks, flash drives, and rewritable optical discs.

Now that you have finished this chapter, see what you know about information technology by scanning the QR code to take the chapter posttest. If you do not have a smartphone, visit www.g-wlearning.com.

Chapter 2 Test

Multiple Choice
Select the best response.

1. Which of the following is *not* a current computer classification?
   A. supercomputers
   B. personal computers
   C. miniframes
   D. mainframes

2. The four major hardware components of a computer are:
   A. Computer programs, input, processing, and joysticks.
   B. Phones, Internet, apps and social networks.
   C. Input device, memory, processor, and output device.
   D. Personal computers, tablets, smartphones, and video cameras.

3. Which of the following is not one of the basic capabilities of a computer?
   A. produce output
   B. store data
   C. process data
   D. operate peripherals

4. Which of the following computer peripherals provides input?
   A. mouse
   B. touch pad
   C. keyboard
   D. All of the above.

5. Which of the following computer peripherals provides output?
   A. printer
   B. RAM
   C. microphone
   D. All of the above.

Completion

Complete the following sentences with the correct word(s).

6. The _____ is the device that fetches coded instructions, decodes them, and then runs or executes them.

7. The two types of memory are _____, which is permanent, and _____, which is erased when the power is turned off.

8. In the United States, the most common keyboard is the _____ layout.

9. The _____ is the most common output device.

10. The three major technologies for storage devices are _____, _____, and _____.

Matching

A. output device
B. input device
C. volatile memory (RAM)
D. processing
E. storage device

11. Loads programs and executes them.

12. Gives information to a computer.

13. Records the results of computer processing.

14. Permanently saves information.

15. Temporarily saves information.

Application and Extension of Knowledge

1. Look at your home computer or a computer in the school's computer lab. Make a list of all peripherals attached to the computer. Write one sentence for each device explaining why you think it is a peripheral. Be prepared to discuss your list with the class.

2. Complete the following table by converting the given information into the missing information.

Unit	byte	kilobyte	megabyte	gigabyte	terabyte
500 bytes	—				
2058 kilobytes		—			
50.4 megabytes			—		
5.7 gigabytes				—	
2.5 terabytes					—

3. Examine your school's computer lab or visit your local library and examine the computers for public use. What accommodations have been made for people with disabilities? Look for both accessible input and output devices. What other accommodations have been made, such as for wheelchair access? Be prepared to discuss your findings in class.

4. Select a type of printer to research. Locate information regarding its cost of operation. Most manufacturers provide this information in sales or technical literature. Identify the specific ink or toner cartridge(s) the printer uses, and price the replacements from three different stores.

5. Visit a local computer store, and examine the storage devices offered. Compare the type of storage device, whether it is internal or external, the storage capacity, and the prices. Make a table to summarize your research.

Online Activities

Complete the following activities, which will help you learn, practice, and expand your knowledge and skills.

Certification Practice. Complete the certification practice test for this chapter.

Vocabulary. Practice vocabulary for this chapter using the e-flash cards, matching activity, and vocabulary game until you are able to recognize their meanings.

Communication Skills

College and Career Readiness

Reading. Skimming means to quickly glance through an entire document. Skimming will give you a preview of the material to help comprehension when you read the chapter. You should notice headings, key words, phrases, and visual elements. The goal is to identify the main idea of the content. Skim this chapter. Provide an overview of what you read.

Writing. Generate ideas for writing a paper that describes the concept of technology as you interpret it. Gather information to support your thoughts and ideas. Keep careful and accurate records of any sources that you use as references. Create the notes that you could use to write a paper to distribute for discussion with your classmates.

Speaking. Career-ready individuals understand that demonstrating leadership qualities is a way to make a positive contribution to the team. Identify leadership

characteristics that you believe all members of a technology team should possess. Use a graphic organizer to record your ideas. Share with the class.

Internet Research

Hard Disk Drives. Research the evolution of the hard disk drive (HDD) using various Internet resources. Write several paragraphs that describe how HDDs have developed since their inception. Did the hard disk drive replace any technology when it was developed? Has new technology begun to replace the hard disk drive? Use correct grammar, punctuation, and terminology as you write.

Teamwork

Working with your team, conduct an audit of the hardware in your computer lab. What items are common to all computers? What items are found on only some computers?

Portfolio Development

College and Career Readiness

Objective. Before you begin collecting information for your portfolio, write an objective for the finished product. An *objective* is a complete sentence or two that states what you want to accomplish.

The language in your objective should be clear and specific. Include enough details so you can easily judge when you have accomplished it. Consider this objective: "I will try to get into college." Such an objective is too general. A better, more detailed objective might read: "I will get accepted into the communications program at one of my top three colleges of choice." Creating a clear objective is a good

starting point for beginning to work on your portfolio.

1. Decide the purpose of the portfolio you are creating, such as short-term employment, career, community service, or college application.
2. Set a timeline to finish the final product.
3. Write an objective for your portfolio.

CTSOs

Performance. Some competitive events for CTSOs have a performance component. The activity could potentially be a decision-making scenario for which your team will provide a solution and present to the judges.

To prepare for the performance component of a presentation, complete the following activities.

1. On your CTSO's website, locate a rubric or scoring sheet for the event.
2. Confirm whether visual aids may be used in the presentation and the amount of setup time permitted.
3. Review the rules to confirm whether questions will be asked or if the team will need to defend a case or situation.
4. Make notes on index cards about important points to remember. Use these notes to study. You may also be able to use these notes during the event.
5. Practice the performance. You should introduce yourself, review the topic that is being presented, defend the topic being presented, and conclude with a summary.
6. After the performance is complete, ask for feedback from your instructor. You may also consider having a student audience listen and give feedback.

3

SOFTWARE

In the previous chapter, you learned about computer hardware. Software is what makes the hardware work. Without software, a computer waits for instructions. Although the user cannot see, hear, or feel it, the software contains all of the instructions to operate the hardware. A set of instructions that tells the computer what to do is called a software program. Programs tell a computer to do specific jobs. These jobs include, among others, creating a document, scanning a photo, editing a video, and connecting to the Internet.

There are two basic types of software: system software and application software. System software works to help the CPU find programs, assign memory, run the devices, and provide utility programs. Application software is the software that performs the user's work. Applications include Microsoft Office, video games, phone apps, and web browsers. Users have a wide choice of software. Program selection is limited by what type of hardware is connected to the computer. Other choices depend on what tasks the user wants to perform. This chapter investigates many types of software, as well as discussing the language of computers.

College and Career Readiness

Reading Prep. Before you begin reading this chapter, consider how the author developed and presented the information. How does it provide the foundation for the next chapter?

IC3 CERTIFICATION OBJECTIVES

GS5

Computing Fundamentals

Domain 2.0 Hardware devices
  Objective 2.6 Understand power management and power settings
  Objective 2.7 Understand driver concepts as well as their device compatibility
  Objective 2.8 Know platform considerations and implications
  Objective 2.9 Know platform compatibility, device limitations

Domain 3.0 Computer software architecture
  Objective 3.1 Understand operating system versioning and update awareness
  Objective 3.2 Know concepts surrounding applications vs. operating system vs. global settings
  Objective 3.3 Have a general understanding of operating systems and software settings
  Objective 3.5 Users and profiles
  Objective 3.8 Menu navigation
  Objective 3.9 Searching for files
  Objective 3.12 Know how to install, uninstall, update, repair software

Domain 6.0 Cloud computing
  Objective 6.5 Understand web app types

Domain 7.0 Security
  Objective 7.1 Know credential management best practices

Key Applications

Domain 6.0 App culture
  Objective 6.1 Understand how to obtain apps
  Objective 6.2 Identify different app genres
  Objective 6.3 Understand strengths and limits of apps and applications

Living Online

Domain 1.0 Internet (navigation)
  Objective 1.1 Understand what the Internet is

GS4

Computing Fundamentals

Domain 1.0 Operating system
  Objective 1.1 What is an OS and what does it do?
  Objective 1.2 Manage computer files and folders
  Objective 1.3 Manage computer configuration, Control Panel, OS drivers

Domain 3.0 Computer software and concepts
  Objective 3.1 Software management
  Objective 3.2 Licensing
  Objective 3.3 Software usage
  Objective 3.4 Software tools

Domain 4.0 Troubleshooting
  Objective 4.1 Software
  Objective 4.3 Devices and peripherals

Key Applications

Domain 1.0 Common application features
  Objective 1.3 Navigating

Living Online

Domain 4.0 Digital citizenship
  Objective 4.2 Legal and responsible use of computers

SECTION 3.1

LANGUAGE OF COMPUTERS

Essential Question

How is a strong understanding of math important to computer programmers?

At the core of computers is the notion of two states: on-off, true-false, or yes-no. This two-state relationship is the key to how all information is stored and processed in the computer and has not changed since the concept of computers was developed. In electronic computers, which were first developed in the mid-20th century, the two states can be represented by 1s and 0s, giving rise to the use of the binary number system. A code was developed to represent alphabetic and special characters using patterns of binary numbers.

Knowledge of numbering systems, especially the numbering systems used by computers, is important to fully understanding how computers function. Information for use by the computer is encoded using these numbering systems. This section will describe how a language of binary numbers is used to store programs and data.

Dean Drobot/Shutterstock.com

TERMS

American Standard Code for Information Interchange (ASCII)
assembly language
bit
byte
bytecode
code
compiler
computer algorithm
data type
encoding
high-level programming language
interpreter
low-level programming language
machine language
object-oriented languages
procedural languages
programs
unicode

LEARNING GOALS

- Compare mechanical and electronic computers.
- Explain various number systems.
- Discuss computer programming languages.

Electronic Computers

The difference between mechanical and electronic computers is that the processor in an electronic computer has no moving parts. However, in both types of computers, the communication inside the computer is conducted through a series of on-off signals. In an electronic computer, each piece of information is kept in the form of a tiny amount of electricity. The electricity is either on (5 volts) or off (0 volts). These on and off signals are represented by the digits 1 and 0. The binary digit or **bit** is the basic building block for communication in an electronic computer. A bit can be only one of two values, which in an electronic computer is 1 or 0. Eight bits equal one **byte**.

All information in a digital computer is represented by the digits 0 and 1. Computer programs are developed in various programming languages and then decoded, or compiled, into 1s and 0s. All text, sounds, videos, and images are composed of 1s and 0s. Even numbers are ultimately combinations of 1s and 0s.

GS5 Living Online
1.1.1.5

FYI

Electronic computers date from the 1940s when the Electronic Numerical Integrator and Calculator (ENIAC) was in development at the University of Pennsylvania.

Number Systems

The most widely used number or counting system in the world is the decimal system. It is based on ten digits, 0–9, and was invented by Indian mathematicians between the first and fourth centuries. Arab mathematicians adopted the system in the ninth century, and the digits became known as Arabic numerals or Hindu-Arabic numerals. European societies adopted the system in the tenth century.

However, the decimal system is not the only counting or number system. Binary and hexadecimal number systems are used in certain applications, such as computer technology. Other number systems also exist.

Decimal Numbers

The decimal number system is a *positional* system. The position that a digit holds in a number indicates its value, as shown in Figure 3-1. In the number 2,587, the 5 indicates 500, but in the number 2,857 it indicates 50. Ten is the basis for the decimal system, which is why it is called a base-10 system. This means counting and arithmetic are done in groups of ten. It also means that the individual digits of a decimal number are represented by a power of 10. Recall from math class that the number 2,587 as an expanded number is:

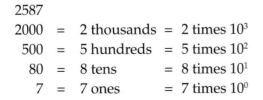

$$2587$$
$$2000 = 2\ \text{thousands} = 2\ \text{times}\ 10^3$$
$$500 = 5\ \text{hundreds} = 5\ \text{times}\ 10^2$$
$$80 = 8\ \text{tens} = 8\ \text{times}\ 10^1$$
$$7 = 7\ \text{ones} = 7\ \text{times}\ 10^0$$

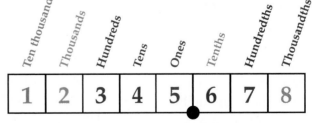

Goodheart-Willcox Publisher

Figure 3-1. In the decimal system, the position of a digit determines its value.

Binary Numbers

It became clear early in the development of computers that trying to represent ten different digits could make the computer too slow and bulky. The developers decided to use binary numbers to represent everything.

The binary number system is also a positional system. It is a base-2 system, so each individual digit of a binary number is represented by a power of 2. This is a sample binary number: 1111. As an expanded number, it is:

$$
\begin{aligned}
1111 & \\
1000 &= 1 \text{ eights} &= 1 \text{ times } 2^3 \\
100 &= 1 \text{ fours} &= 1 \text{ times } 2^2 \\
10 &= 1 \text{ twos} &= 1 \text{ times } 2^1 \\
1 &= 1 \text{ ones} &= 1 \text{ times } 2^0
\end{aligned}
$$

The binary number 1111 is the same value as 15 in the decimal system. Verify this by adding 1 eight + 1 four + 1 two + 1 one. The sum is 15.

The decimal number 2,587 converted to binary is 1010 0001 1011. This binary number can be expanded as:

$$
\begin{aligned}
1010\ 0001\ 1011 & \\
1000\ 0000\ 0000 &= 1 \text{ two thousand forty-eights} &= 1 \text{ times } 2^{11} \\
000\ 0000\ 0000 &= 0 \text{ one thousand twenty-fours} &= 0 \text{ times } 2^{10} \\
10\ 0000\ 0000 &= 1 \text{ five hundred twelves} &= 1 \text{ times } 2^9 \\
0\ 0000\ 0000 &= 0 \text{ two hundred fifty-sixes} &= 0 \text{ times } 2^8 \\
0000\ 0000 &= 0 \text{ one hundred twenty-eights} &= 0 \text{ times } 2^7 \\
000\ 0000 &= 0 \text{ sixty-fours} &= 0 \text{ times } 2^6 \\
00\ 0000 &= 0 \text{ thirty-twos} &= 0 \text{ times } 2^5 \\
1\ 0000 &= 1 \text{ sixteens} &= 1 \text{ times } 2^4 \\
1000 &= 1 \text{ eights} &= 1 \text{ times } 2^3 \\
000 &= 0 \text{ fours} &= 0 \text{ times } 2^2 \\
10 &= 1 \text{ twos} &= 1 \text{ times } 2^1 \\
1 &= 1 \text{ ones} &= 1 \text{ times } 2^0
\end{aligned}
$$

To verify the conversion, add 2048 + 512 + 16 + 8 + 2 + 1. The sum is 2,587, which is the original decimal number.

Hexadecimal Numbers

Some of the numbers needed for output diagnostic procedures, memory management, and identification of network adapters and other hardware are very large. Large binary numbers can be easily misread by people because there are so many digits. For example, the binary number 1010 0001 1011 could be difficult for people to quickly interpret. Hexadecimal notation came to the rescue as a way to balance the ability for a human to read the number with a number system that could be easily read by a computer.

Hexadecimal notation, or hex, is a base-16 number system. When counting in base-16, new symbols are required to represent digits higher than 9. The 16 digits in the hexadecimal number system are: 0, 1, 2, 3, 4, 5, 6, 7, 8, 9, A, B, C, D, E, and F.

FYI

The binary number equivalent of a decimal number usually has more digits, but the computer arithmetic is much faster using binary numbers than decimal numbers.

FYI

Another number system used in programming, although less frequently than binary and hex, is octal. The octal number system, or oct, is a base-8 number system that uses the digits 0 through 7.

In hexadecimal notation, binary digits are grouped into units of four, each represented by another symbol. Four binary digits hold 16 different numbers, 0 to 15 or 0000 to 1111. Therefore, it is easy to write each group of four binary digits as one hex digit, which means fewer digits are needed to represent the number. This is why hex was adopted in computing.

Figure 3-2 compares initial values of the decimal, binary, and hexadecimal number systems. The binary number 1010 0001 1011 can be converted into hexadecimal using this table. Because each hex digit represents four binary digits, first break the binary number into groups of four digits starting from the right. Next, look up the corresponding hex digit for each group.

    1010   0001   1011
    1010 = A
                0001 = 1
                        1011 = B

The hex conversion of 1010 0001 1011 is A1B. To avoid confusion with other number systems, it is a convention to write hex numbers with the 0x prefix. Therefore, the hex representation of the binary number 1010 0001 1011 is 0xA1B.

Decimal	Binary	Hex
0	0000	0
1	0001	1
2	0010	2
3	0011	3
4	0100	4
5	0101	5
6	0110	6
7	0111	7
8	1000	8
9	1001	9
10	1010	A
11	1011	B
12	1100	C
13	1101	D
14	1110	E
15	1111	F
16	1 0000	10

Goodheart-Willcox Publisher

Figure 3-2. A comparison of values in the decimal, binary, and hexadecimal number systems.

HANDS-ON EXAMPLE 3.1.1

CONVERTING BETWEEN NUMBER SYSTEMS

The Windows operating system has a calculator accessory. When the calculator is used in the programmer view, changing between number systems is as easy as clicking radio buttons.

1. In Windows 10, launch the calculator by clicking the **Start** button followed by **All apps** and then **Calculator**. In Windows 8, launch the desktop calculator by clicking the **Apps** button and then **Calculator** in **Windows Accessories** group. Do not use the calculator app located in the **Apps** group. It has limited features. In Windows 7, launch the calculator by clicking the **Start** button followed by **Accessories** and then **Calculator**.

2. In Windows 10, click the button in the upper-left corner of the calculator, and then click **Programmer** in the drop-down menu. In Windows 8 and Windows 7, click the **View** pull-down menu, and click **Programmer** in the menu. The display should look like the one shown.

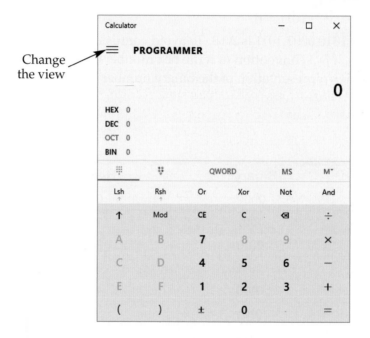

Change the view

3. Click the **Dec** label or radio button. This specifies the entry will be in decimal units.
4. Enter the number 365 using the keyboard or by clicking the number buttons.
5. Click the **Hex** label or radio button. The decimal number is converted to the hexadecimal equivalent and displayed, which is 16D.
6. Click the **Bin** label or radio button. The hexadecimal number is converted to the binary equivalent and displayed, which is 1 0110 1101 (without spaces).
7. Click the **Dec** label or radio button. The binary number is converted to the decimal equivalent, which is the original number entered.

Code

It is important for an IT professional to be able to understand and use number systems. Number systems represent more than numbers in the computer. They are used to convert media instructions, make programming codes, identify memory locations, identify peripherals, and many other tasks. Besides using binary numbers for calculations, computers use them to represent data and run computer programs.

Encoding Instructions

The process of converting human-readable data and computer programs into a computer-readable format is called **encoding**. The result of this process is called **code**. IT professionals often call computer programs *code*, referring to the end result rather than the program they are writing.

Different CPUs have different ways of interpreting code. This makes it impossible for one program to work on all computers. An example of code that tells a certain CPU to add two numbers is:

    EB GB 00

Fortunately, most information technology professionals do not need to worry about this. There are many layers between what the CPU understands and what computer programmers write. Cross-platform tools allow a programmer to write a program once and then encode it for different CPUs.

Encoding Data

Programmers must know how computers translate data that the user may enter. Some agreements have been made by industry professionals to make sharing data among different computers easier than sharing programs. These agreements are called *standards*. The **American Standard Code for Information Interchange (ASCII)** is a standard for representing text that most computers support. The acronym ASCII is usually pronounced *askee*.

ASCII is a system for encoding the characters in the English alphabet and text for the digits 0–9. It also includes basic punctuation symbols and a blank space. There are 32 nonprinting characters used to control processes such as a hard return for the end of a paragraph.

Figure 3-3 shows an ASCII code chart for several text characters, also called symbols or *glyphs*. Notice that each ASCII character is defined by an eight-place binary number. This means eight bits are required to represent each ASCII character. Since eight bits equal one byte, each ASCII character uses up one byte of storage.

A curiosity that the ASCII table points out is the number 1 and the text character 1 are represented two different ways in a computer although they look the same when displayed on the monitor. The byte that represents the number 1 is the binary pattern 0000 0001 or hex 01. However, the byte that represents the text character 1 is the binary pattern 0011 0001 or hex 31. This is a source of concern for computer programmers. Text-character digits must be converted to binary numbers so the input can be used in a calculation.

STEM

Mathematics
The order of operations is a set of rules stating which operations in an equation are performed first. This order is often stated using the acronym *PEMDAS*. PEMDAS stands for parentheses, exponents, multiplication and division, and addition and subtraction. This means anything inside parentheses is computed first. Exponents are computed next. Then, any multiplication and division operations are computed. Finally, any addition and subtraction operations are computed to find the answer to the problem.

Binary	Dec	Hex	Symbol	Binary	Dec	Hex	Symbol	Binary	Dec	Hex	Symbol
0010 0000	32	20	(space)	0100 0000	64	40	@	0110 0000	96	60	`
0010 0001	33	21	!	0100 0001	65	41	A	0110 0001	97	61	a
0010 0010	34	22	"	0100 0010	66	42	B	0110 0010	98	62	b
0010 0011	35	23	#	0100 0011	67	43	C	0110 0011	99	63	c
0010 0100	36	24	$	0100 0100	68	44	D	0110 0100	100	64	d
0010 0101	37	25	%	0100 0101	69	45	E	0110 0101	101	65	e
0010 0110	38	26	&	0100 0110	70	46	F	0110 0110	102	66	f
0010 0111	39	27	'	0100 0111	71	47	G	0110 0111	103	67	g
0010 1000	40	28	(	0100 1000	72	48	H	0110 1000	104	68	h
0010 1001	41	29	)	0100 1001	73	49	I	0110 1001	105	69	i
0010 1010	42	2A	*	0100 1010	74	4A	J	0110 1010	106	6A	j
0010 1011	43	2B	+	0100 1011	75	4B	K	0110 1011	107	6B	k
0010 1100	44	2C	,	0100 1100	76	4C	L	0110 1100	108	6C	l
0010 1101	45	2D	-	0100 1101	77	4D	M	0110 1101	109	6D	m
0010 1110	46	2E	.	0100 1110	78	4E	N	0110 1110	110	6E	n
0010 1111	47	2F	/	0100 1111	79	4F	O	0110 1111	111	6F	o
0011 0000	48	30	0	0101 0000	80	50	P	0111 0000	112	70	p
0011 0001	49	31	1	0101 0001	81	51	Q	0111 0001	113	71	q
0011 0010	50	32	2	0101 0010	82	52	R	0111 0010	114	72	r
0011 0011	51	33	3	0101 0011	83	53	S	0111 0011	115	73	s
0011 0100	52	34	4	0101 0100	84	54	T	0111 0100	116	74	t
0011 0101	53	35	5	0101 0101	85	55	U	0111 0101	117	75	u
0011 0110	54	36	6	0101 0110	86	56	V	0111 0110	118	76	v
0011 0111	55	37	7	0101 0111	87	57	W	0111 0111	119	77	w
0011 1000	56	38	8	0101 1000	88	58	X	0111 1000	120	78	x
0011 1001	57	39	9	0101 1001	89	59	Y	0111 1001	121	79	y
0011 1010	58	3A	:	0101 1010	90	5A	Z	0111 1010	122	7A	z
0011 1011	59	3B	;	0101 1011	91	5B	[	0111 1011	123	7B	{
0011 1100	60	3C	<	0101 1100	92	5C	\	0111 1100	124	7C	l
0011 1101	61	3D	=	0101 1101	93	5D	]	0111 1101	125	7D	}
0011 1110	62	3E	>	0101 1110	94	5E	^	0111 1110	126	7E	~
0011 1111	63	3F	?	0101 1111	95	5F	_				

Figure 3-3. ASCII characters (symbols) and their binary, decimal, and hexadecimal codes.

Note that the table shows the binary, decimal, and hexadecimal code for each symbol. To store the characters in the word *Book*, these hex codes are used:

B	42
o	6F
o	6F
k	6B

That means the word *Book* is encoded in hex as 0x426F6F6B. No calculations are performed on these hex patterns. They are used only to represent the letters.

Because of a need to represent more than 256 characters, the Unicode system was developed. **Unicode** is a system for encoding text characters in which two bytes are assigned to each character. This allows for a much greater number of characters, as well as support for other features. ASCII is incorporated into the Unicode scheme. Unicode is gaining wide acceptance.

HANDS-ON EXAMPLE 3.1.2

ENCODING TEXT STRINGS

Encode the text string *Hello World!* using hex notation. Use the ASCII chart shown in Figure 3-3 to locate the correct symbols.
1. Locate the codes for the characters in the word *Hello*.
2. Locate the code for a space.
3. Locate the codes for the characters in *World*.
4. Locate the code for the exclamation point.
5. Write the codes in order from left to right to form the code for the entire text string. Use the 0x prefix.

Computer Programming Languages

Programs are the sets of instructions that carry out the tasks of the user. Writing computer code using 1s and 0s was the original way to program a computer. Today, computer programmers use programming languages to write instructions that appear similar to English. There are two basic levels of programming languages: high and low.

High-Level Languages

Most software programmers use high-level languages. A **high-level programming language** contains instructions that are far removed from the instructions the computer CPU uses. High-level languages contain a limited set of near-to-English words, so they are easy for a person to read. Instructions may be commands such as **PRINT**, **IF**, **NEXT**, and **GET**. Programming in a high-level language can also be like algebra. For example, to add 42 to another number that is stored in the variable named JerseyNumber, write JerseyNumber + 42. Examples of high-level programming languages are Visual Basic, C++, Java, and COBOL.

The programming software contains a **compiler** that converts the programmer's code into code the CPU can understand. The compiled code is then linked with operating system–specific code to make the executable program. Examples of languages that are compiled and linked are C, C++, Fortran, and COBOL.

Some languages are not compiled and linked, rather they are *interpreted*. In an **interpreter**, the instructions are converted to code the CPU can understand as the program is executing. This has two basic effects. First, the execution is slower than linked code because time must be taken to do the conversion for each instruction every time the program is run. Second, interpreted programs provide an opportunity to rapidly modify the code. Examples of interpreted languages are Smalltalk, Python, and some versions of BASIC.

A happy medium between a fully compiled language and an interpreted language is the bytecode. **Bytecode** is a set of instructions composed of compact numeric codes, constants, and references that can be efficiently processed by an interpreter. At run time, a software program called the *runtime engine* or the *virtual machine* interprets the bytecode for the target CPU. The advantage of bytecode is that high-level programs can be written for a wide range of CPU instruction sets and the interpretation does not take as long as fully interpreted code. Java and C# are two languages that partially compile their code so that they are more portable between operating systems and CPUs. In the case of Java, this step is performed every time the application is run. In C#, on the first execution of the program, the final linked code for the current computer is created and the resulting program is stored on the computer. Further running of the program is from the fully executable program and does not require interpreting.

Procedural languages are computer programming languages in which instructions are gathered into collections called procedures or functions. Each function contains a list of instructions for the computer to execute step-by-step. Examples of procedural languages are BASIC, C, Perl, and HTML.

Object-oriented languages contain data structures, called objects, and actions that can be performed on those structures, called methods. In addition to what can be accomplished using a procedural language, programmers are able to create programming objects to protect data related to the object. Examples of object-oriented languages are C++, C#, Java, and ActionScript.

Low-Level Languages

Once a program is written in one of the high-level languages, it must be converted into a digital format that the computer CPU can process. A **low-level programming language** is one that is very close to the instruction set used by the CPU. **Machine language,** or *machine code*, is a low-level language composed of the 0s and 1s the computer CPU uses. It is the only language that a CPU can directly understand. **Assembly language**, or *assembly*, is very close to machine language, but the CPU cannot directly understand it. An *assembler* is used to convert the program into machine code.

Programs in low-level languages are difficult for a person to read and write. For example, to store the number 42 into a register so that it can be used in a calculation, the command in assembly is MOV AL 2A. The benefit of assembly is that the code is written for a specific machine. This can make the execution of the program faster. The disadvantage of assembly programs is that they are generally not transportable to other CPUs.

Data Types Used in Computer Programming

In arithmetic, different types of numbers are used, such as counting numbers, fractions, and decimals. In a similar manner, computer languages distinguish among a variety of types of data, or data types. In computer programming, a **data type** is the description of values or information that can be accepted. Because data types are so different from each other, they are all stored in different ways.

- Integers are the positive and negative counting numbers and zero.
- Floating point numbers are decimal numbers.
- Boolean types only hold values for true or false.
- Characters are single letters, digits, or other symbols.
- Strings hold alphabetic and numeric data, along with special symbols.
- Date types hold time and date information.

Programmers can also create their own data types. For example, if a programmer wants to use fractions, he or she could create a custom data type to represent the numerators and denominators of fractions.

Algorithms

A **computer algorithm** is a series of steps used to perform an action. An algorithm is not a programming language or programming code. Rather, it is a map of what needs to be done, and programmers write the code to activate the algorithm. At a basic level, this is the **IF**… **THEN** statement used in computer programming. For example, **IF** the user presses the [Ctrl][Z] key combination, **THEN** undo the last command.

A linear algorithm is processed once and the solution is output. An iterative algorithm is repeated, or looped, until a condition, called the terminating condition, is met. An algorithm may have both linear and iterative parts. For example, calculating an average of grades includes both types of algorithm. The program loops to keep adding grades until all are included (iterative) in the sum and then divides the sum by the number of grades (linear). A flowchart can be used to map out the steps in an algorithm, as shown in Figure 3-4.

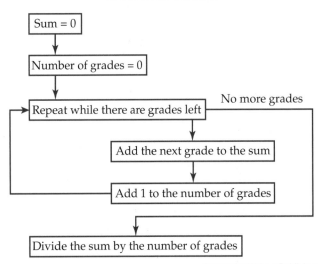

Algorithm to Find the Average of a Set of Grades

Sum = 0

Number of grades = 0

Repeat while there are grades left — No more grades

Add the next grade to the sum

Add 1 to the number of grades

Divide the sum by the number of grades

Goodheart-Willcox Publisher

Figure 3-4. A flowchart can be used to map out the steps in an algorithm.

3.1 SECTION REVIEW

CHECK YOUR UNDERSTANDING

1. Convert this hex code into its binary equivalent: 0xF6A9
2. Convert this binary code into its hex equivalent: 1101101010011
3. What is the name of a program that converts higher-level programming language into machine language?
4. What is the difference between a compiler and an interpreter?
5. What is the basic diffference between a linear algorithm and an interative algorithm?

IC3 CERTIFICATION PRACTICE

The following question is a sample of the type of questions presented on the IC3 exam.

1. A memory address is stated as 0x14DE. What is the binary equivalent?

BUILD YOUR VOCABULARY

As you progress through this course, develop a personal IT glossary. This will help you build your vocabulary and prepare you for a career. Write a definition for each of the following terms and add it to your IT glossary.

American Standard Code for Information Interchange (ASCII)
assembly language
bit
byte
bytecode
code
compiler
computer algorithm
data type
encoding

high-level programming language
interpreter
low-level programming language
machine language
object-oriented languages
procedural languages
programs
unicode

SYSTEM SOFTWARE

lightwavemedia/Shutterstock.com

There are similar tasks common to most applications, such as saving data, retrieving documents, and printing. This is why operating systems were created. The operating system, or OS for short, sits between the hardware and the applications to handle all common tasks in one way. For a visual metaphor, think of a road as the hardware. The cars driving on the road are the applications. The drivers are the users, and the crossing guard is the operating system. It is the operating system that keeps all of the applications running smoothly and connected with the CPU and the peripherals.

System software contains the operating system, utilities, device drivers, and programs. Utilities help with housekeeping tasks. Device drivers provide instructions for how the operating system is to use peripheral devices. Programs are the applications that users run to complete the desired tasks.

Essential Question

Which operating system is the best to use?

LEARNING GOALS

- Explain operating systems.
- Identify system utility programs.
- Describe device drivers.
- Discuss programs.

TERMS

accessibility options
check box
desktop theme
device driver
drop-down menu
hibernation
language packs
platform

power down
power options
power states
radio button
sleep
system software
user account
utility programs

Operating Systems

GS5 Computing Fundamentals
2.8.1, 3.2

GS4 Computing Fundamentals
1.1.1, 1.1.2, 1.1.3

System software includes four types of software: the operating system, utility programs, device drivers, and programs. All computers that run more than one program must have an operating system. The operating system (OS) performs communication with the user and the hardware. See Figure 3-5. The OS works behind the scenes. Most of the time it is silently working in the background to monitor system activity and optimize its own efficiency.

Figure 3-6 shows a photograph of the Apollo Guidance Computer on a display at the Smithsonian Institution. This computer used a real-time operating system. Astronauts entered simple commands as pairs of nouns and verbs. These commands were used to control the spacecraft. Today, operating systems are advanced software that must communicate with the user, multiple hardware devices, and multiple software programs as well as manage all of the interactions and functions of the computer system.

Some tasks performed by the OS are powering on and off the system; logging in, logging out, or switching users; and locking and unlocking the interface. The OS also controls the order of processing events, manages the movement of files to and from storage devices, and interacts with the peripheral devices such as the keyboard and the printer. The OS manages the allocation of memory for programs and data as well as system security through the use of passwords.

The OS is generally preinstalled on a computer when the hardware is purchased. A computer's processor determines what operating systems can be used. For example, Microsoft Windows operating systems work with processors in the Intel family. The computer **platform** is the combination of the operating system and the processor. Figure 3-7 shows

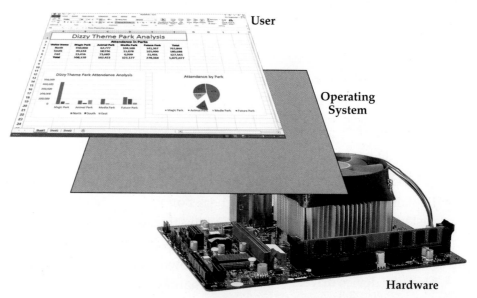

Goodheart-Willcox Publisher; Denis Dryashkin/Shutterstock.com

Figure 3-5. The operating system sits between the hardware and the software providing communication between them, facilitating the execution of the software programs, and managing the hardware resources.

a comparison of operating systems currently in use.

Reduced-instruction chips called ARM microprocessors, produced by ARM Holdings, power most mobile devices. These chips allow processing speeds that could support a desktop or laptop. The idea is that the fewer instruction types to process, the faster a chip can run. Windows 8 is an OS that runs on the ARM chip.

Operating systems changed with the introduction of a graphical user interface (GUI), which is usually pronounced *goo-ey*. Users did not have to behave like programmers and enter commands. With a GUI, users could use a mouse to select options from menus. Personal computers then became very popular. The Apple Macintosh was the first commercially successful computer with a GUI OS. The OS for this computer was called System Software, which was eventually changed to Mac OS. GUI versions of Windows soon followed the introduction of the Macintosh computer.

GNU 1.2/Creative Common 3.0 (Tamorlan)

Figure 3-6. This is the user interface of the Apollo Guidance Computer on display in the Smithsonian National Air and Space Museum in Washington, DC.

Windows Operating System

The operating system contains all directions for working with the hardware. As new hardware is introduced, the OS must be updated.

Operating System	Platforms	Distinctions
Windows	PCs, Microsoft phones, and tablets Apple products in a Windows partition	Most widely used OS Multiple versions Proprietary
iOS	Apple mobile products, iPhone, iPad, iTouch, etc.	Proprietary Distribution of apps limited to Apple App Store
Mac OS	Macintosh computers	Proprietary
Unix	PCs, large mainframe computers, supercomputers, web servers	Open source Free to use Stable, less downtime than Windows Better security Greater processing power Generally found on networked systems
Linux	PCs, several mobile devices, large mainframe computers, web servers	Open source, based on Unix Free to use Low resource requirements High security level Generally found on networked systems
Android	Google mobile OS based on Linux	Open Source Open distribution of apps via Internet

Goodheart-Willcox Publisher

Figure 3-7. Several operating systems are available. The platforms on which each is used varies by application.

Microsoft Windows has gone through several versions since it was introduced. For example, a very old version, Windows 3.1, did not know how to tell a CD to play or how to read data from a USB port. Newer versions have most of the functionality of the older versions plus more.

There are many computers that still run on older versions of Windows, such as Windows XP or Windows Vista. However, Windows 7, Windows 8, and Windows 10 are more common. The functions described here are specific to Windows, but most operating systems have similar settings.

Windows Interface Overview

The Windows desktop is a virtual workspace for the operating system. Program icons and document files can be placed on the desktop for easy access. In Windows 10 and Windows 7, the desktop is automatically displayed when the OS starts up. In Windows 8, you are automatically switched to the desktop when a program is launched. You can also manually display the desktop by clicking **Desktop** in the main menu.

When something is placed on the desktop, it appears as an icon. An icon contains a definition of what to launch when it is double-clicked. It appears as a small graphic on the desktop. The icon for a document file will launch the program associated with the file type and load the file in the program. The icon for a program will launch the program.

One of the keys to the Windows OS is the ability to have multiple programs running at the same time. The user sees each program in a frame called a window. Each program window appears as a tab in the task bar. To switch between windows, either click the tab on the task bar or use the [Alt][Tab] key combination.

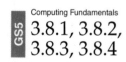

Computing Fundamentals
3.8.1, 3.8.2,
3.8.3, 3.8.4

Interface Controls

Systems that are based on a graphical user interface (GUI) have many efficient ways to allow the user to enter choices. These include radio buttons, check boxes, and drop-down menus.

A **radio button** is an interface control that looks like a small circle next to a selection choice. Radio buttons let the user choose only one option from the list of choices. Only one radio button can be on at a time.

A **check box** is an interface control that looks like a small square. When the user selects one option, the box is filled in with an X. The user can select one or many check boxes at the same time. It is a multi-select interface. Another interface option is a drop-down menu.

A **drop-down menu** is an interface control that presents command choices in a list once displayed. It is displayed by clicking the small downward-facing arrow next to a text box.

Starting Programs in Windows

Computing Fundamentals
3.9

There are several ways to start, or *launch*, a program in Microsoft Windows. The most common ways are to use an icon in the **Apps** or **Start** menu or a desktop icon. If the program appears as an icon on the desktop, double-click the icon to launch the program.

In Windows 10, click or tap the **Start** button on the taskbar at the bottom of the screen. Next, click **All apps** in the menu. An alphabetical listing of applications and programs is displayed, as shown in Figure 3-8. Scroll through the list to find the correct program, and click or tap it to launch the program.

In Windows 8, click or tap the **Apps** button at the bottom of the **Start** screen. The screen changes to display icons for installed programs, which are listed by categories. Locate the icon for the program to launch, and click or tap it.

In Windows 7, click the **Start** button on the taskbar at the bottom of the screen. Some program icons may be displayed in this portion of the menu, or you may need to click **All Programs** in the menu and browse to the icon of the program. Once the program icon is located, click it to launch the program.

Another way to launch a program is to double-click the icon for a document file, either on the desktop or in a file folder. Most documents are associated with a program based on the file extension of the document. Double-clicking on a document file will launch the associated program and load the document.

One more way to start a program is to click the **Start** or **Apps** button or press the Windows key on the keyboard. The search box at the bottom of the **Start** menu is automatically active, and you can begin entering the name of an application. In Windows 10, you can also click in the search box on the task bar. In a Mac environment, the [Cmd] + spacebar key combination is used.

For example, once the search box is active, enter the letters cmd. The Command Prompt application (or cmd.exe) appears as an option in the

FYI

If a document file extension is not associated with a program, Windows will ask you to select a program to use to open the program.

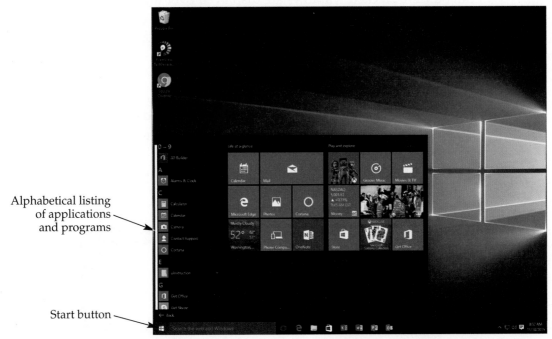

Alphabetical listing of applications and programs

Start button

Goodheart-Willcox Publisher

Figure 3-8. In Windows 10, clicking the **Start** button followed by **All apps** displays an alphabetical listing of all installed applications and programs.

Start menu. Since this is the only option, it is highlighted, and pressing the [Enter] key will launch the program. You can also click the entry to launch the program. Any program or application installed on the computer can be located using this method.

Common Tasks Using Windows

GS5   Computing Fundamentals
3.3.2

GS4   Computing Fundamentals
1.2.2

There are several key combinations and mouse clicks that behave in the same manner no matter what program windows are open. As discussed in Chapter 2, these are clicking, double-clicking, dragging, and right-clicking. There are standard key combinations as well.

The [Ctrl][A] key combination is used to select all items in the current view, such as all words in a document or all files in a folder. The [Ctrl][C] key combination copies the current selection to the system clipboard. The [Ctrl][X] key combination removes, or cuts, the current selection and places it on the system clipboard. The [Ctrl][V] key combination pastes the contents of the system clipboard in the current location. The [Ctrl][Z] key combination reverses the last operation, which is called an *undo*.

GS4   Key Applications
1.3.4

The [Alt][Tab] key combination is used to navigate through open program windows. Holding down the [Alt] key while repeatedly pressing the [Tab] key selects which window will be made active, as shown in Figure 3-9. When the correct icon is highlighted, release the [Alt] key to make that window active. The desktop is treated as a window in this navigation.

All open windows can be arranged for better viewing and use. Right-click on the taskbar, but not on an icon, to display a shortcut menu. This menu contains choices to **Cascade windows**, **Show windows stacked**, and **Show windows side by side**. Cascading windows are displayed one on top of another offset slightly so a small portion of each window underneath can be seen. Stacked windows are displayed over the width of the desktop and top to bottom, but the windows do not overlap. Side-by-side windows are displayed over the height of the desktop and side-by-side, but the windows do not overlap. See Figure 3-10.

Starting and Exiting the OS

GS4   Computing Fundamentals
1.1.2

Unlike a light switch that can be instantly turned on or off, a computer must perform an orderly power up and shut down.

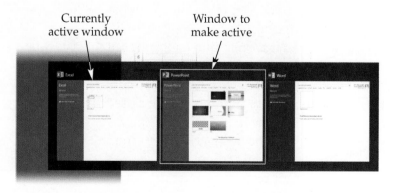

Currently active window

Window to make active

Goodheart-Willcox Publisher

Figure 3-9. The [Alt][Tab] key combination is used to switch between windows.

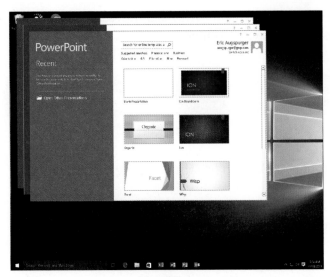

Cascading

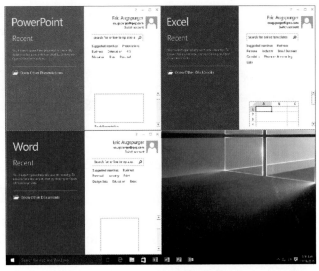

Side-by-Side or Stacked

Goodheart-Willcox Publisher

Figure 3-10. Windows can be displayed full-screen, cascading, side-by-side, or stacked. In Windows 10, side-by-side and stacked may appear identical.

Additionally, different users may work on a computer. The Windows OS has some functions for allowing these actions:

- power on and off
- log on and off
- switch user
- lock and unlock

When the computer is powered on, the boot process starts the OS. Software programs are loaded and run before the user can begin to input requests or data. When the computer is powered off, or powered down, programs must be closed according to their programming, and the OS must perform shut-down procedures. Always use the OS shut-down function to turn off the computer. Do not use the computer's power button to power off the computer. Computer programs need to follow a sequence to close all files.

When there is more than one user for a computer, each user should have a separate account. This maintains a level of security and privacy between users. Logging on is the process of a user signing into his or her account on the computer. Once logged on, the user has access to all of the software and files that have been made available to that account. Logging off closes any programs that are running and signs out the user, but the computer remains on with the OS is functioning in the background.

Switching a user is similar to logging off. The current user is signed out, however programs that are running are not closed. This allows a different user to log on and use the system, but the work session of the original user is maintained. The original user can continue where he or she stopped once logged on again.

Locking the computer prevents another person from using it without requiring the current user to log off. The user's current work session remains running, but only the current user or an administrator can unlock

Ethics

Code of Ethics
Most companies establish a set of ethics that employees must follow. The code of ethics outlines acceptable behavior when interacting with coworkers, suppliers, and customers. Some businesses even post their code of ethics on their websites. Employees must be familiar with the code in order to make correct decisions on behalf of the company, including those related to using the company's computers and other technology.

and use the computer. For security reasons, the machine should be locked whenever the current user steps away from it.

HANDS-ON EXAMPLE 3.2.1

LOCKING THE COMPUTER

To prevent somebody else from using a computer, lock it. To use the computer again, unlock it with a password.

1. In Windows 10, press the [Ctrl][Alt][Delete] key combination. In Windows 8, click or tap the user name in the upper-right corner of the **Start** screen. In Windows 7, click the **Start** menu button, and click the arrow next to the **Shutdown** button.
2. Click **Lock** in the menu that appears. The screen displays a message indicating the computer is locked along with the name of the account that locked it.
3. In Windows 10 and Windows 8, swipe up from the bottom of the screen or press any key to terminate the lock screen. In Windows 7, press the [Ctrl][Alt][Delete] key combination.
4. Enter the password to unlock the computer. The computer must be unlocked by the account that locked it. The user account cannot be changed in Windows 8, but can be changed in Windows 10 and Windows 7.

User Accounts

Computing Fundamentals
GS5
3.5, 7.1.1, 7.1.2, 7.1.3

Computing Fundamentals
GS4
1.3.6

User accounts are assigned for privacy and system security. A **user account** is a set of privileges for allowed actions. A user may be allowed to install and delete applications, read and write files, change attributes for files and folders, create other user accounts, or may be prevented from any of these actions.

Setting up a user account assigns a user ID and a password to the account. The user ID is a series of characters that becomes a unique identifier. This allows the system to know who the user is. The password is another series of characters that verifies the user's ID. It allows the user to actually use the hardware or software. The user account can be personalized, such as changing the screen colors or system sounds. In some cases, software can be installed in such a way that only certain user accounts can access it.

A *group policy* provides the ability for the IT administrator to change permissions and configurations of all or some user accounts for the devices within a group of devices. The devices may be desktop, laptop, or mobile computers. For example, an IT administrator may determine that a change to the access permission for a file or new folder should be made. This can be applied to a group of user accounts through a group policy.

Basic Desktop Configuration

Computing Fundamentals
GS5
3.3.1

Computing Fundamentals
GS4
1.3.1

The OS provides a wide range of configurations that can be used to customize a user's experience. Some of these choices include which language is used, the time zone, how the computer display appears, and which accessibility options are used. Most of these options are accessed via the Windows Control Panel.

Languages

Windows supports a wide range of languages. The language setting is used for the text and instructions, displayed on the desktop. The keyboard can also be set for a different language. The default language is set at the factory based on where the computer or operating system will be sold.

Normally, the language used in the interface is set during the Windows OS installation. It is not easy to change after the OS has been installed. However, **language packs** can be downloaded from Microsoft and installed to change the language of the OS interface.

Date and Time

The date and time are calculated in Coordinated Universal Time (UTC) and distributed to 24 time zones around the world. UTC is the standard by which countries around the world regulate time. Windows provides an option to configure the time zone where the user resides. In addition, synchronization can be configured so that the time automatically updates to match the UTC value.

Visual Options

The display can be configured in one of the resolutions available with the combination of the computer's graphics card and monitor. The screen resolution controls how large the text and images appear on the display.

In Windows, a **desktop theme** sets the colors used for window borders, the desktop background, and other visual qualities, as shown in Figure 3-11. A user can select a desktop background image from one of several defaults or from a file. The size of the icons displayed in the Windows taskbar is also an option.

Accessibility Options

Windows provides a set of **accessibility options** to assist users with vision, mobility, or hearing impairment. Options include optimizing the visual display, replacing sounds with visual cues, changing how the mouse works, changing how the keyboard works, and enabling speech-recognition input. The accessibility options are set in the Control Panel window. Click the **Ease of Access** heading to review and change the settings.

Power Configuration Options

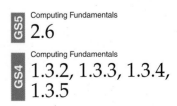

GS5 Computing Fundamentals
2.6

GS4 Computing Fundamentals
1.3.2, 1.3.3, 1.3.4, 1.3.5

Windows offers several **power options** for managing how the computer uses electricity. This is important for computers that run on a battery, such as a laptop or mobile computer. Conserving power is a tradeoff with computer performance. By lowering performance, the electrical charge in the battery can be extended.

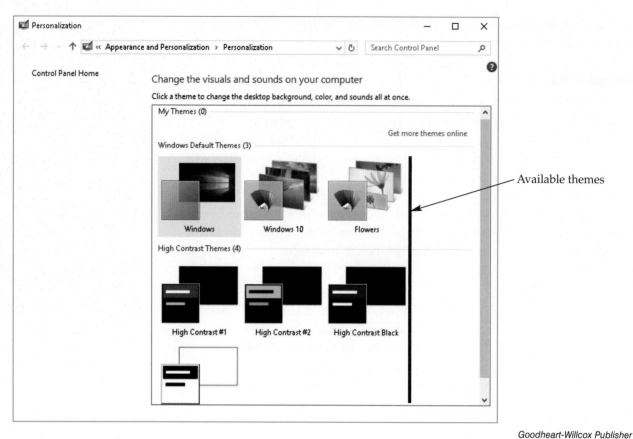

Available themes

Goodheart-Willcox Publisher

Figure 3-11. A desktop theme controls the visual qualities of the desktop, such as color, background image, and sounds.

There are three **power states**, or *power plans*, for conserving the power consumed by the CPU:

- power saver
- balanced
- high performance

The power use is low, medium, and high, respectively. Programs such as Microsoft Word or other Microsoft Office applications usually do not require high performance from the CPU. When running these programs, the power saver setting is often acceptable. However, programs such as video editing, graphic manipulation, and video games require high performance from the CPU. When running these programs, the computer should be set to high performance. Power conservation will be minimal with this setting.

The OS can be configured to **power down** the computer when it is idle for a period of time. The display may simply dim, the computer may go into a sleep or hibernation mode, or it may power off. When the display is dimmed, all programs continue to run, but the display consumes less power. When the computer is powered off, all programs are closed and the computer is turned off.

Sleep saves all settings and running programs in memory using just a small amount of power. Think of sleep mode as like pausing a DVR. The computer will wake from sleep mode very quickly, often in one or two seconds.

Hibernation saves all settings and running programs to the hard disk drive. The computer consumes no power in this state. When the computer is powered up, all programs that were running are returned to their previous state.

Laptop computers often run on battery power. There are many factors that can contribute to battery performance, including the age of the battery, processor usage, and temperature of the room. To prolong laptop-battery life, turn off Wi-Fi if it is not needed. Close programs not being used instead of letting them run in the background. Another tip is to dim the screen since it is the largest energy user of the system. If taking a break from work, turn off the screen and place the computer in sleep mode. The system should not be turned on and off frequently since booting the system uses power.

FYI

There may be a hybrid power-down option, which is a combination of sleep and hibernation.

Computing Fundamentals 2.6

HANDS-ON EXAMPLE 3.2.2

POWER-MANAGEMENT SETTINGS

Windows will automatically place the computer in sleep mode after a set amount of time to conserve power. The amount of time of inactivity can be changed.

1. In Windows 10, right-click on the **Start** button, and then click **Control Panel** in the shortcut menu. In Windows 8 and Windows 7, click the **Apps** or **Start** button, and click **Control Panel** in the menu. The Control Panel window is displayed.
2. Select **System and Security** and then **Power Options**. Note: if you do not see this option, click the **View by:** link at the top of the window, and click **Category** in the drop-down menu.
3. In the list of power-management plans, the radio button next to the current plan is on. Click the **Change plan settings** link next to this plan.
4. In the new Control Panel view, click the drop-down arrow next to **Turn off the display:**, and click **1 minute** in the drop-down menu. This sets the amount of idle time before entering sleep mode to one minute.
5. Click the **Save Changes** button, and close the Control Panel window.

Handheld Device Operating Systems

Operating systems have been specially created for handheld devices such as smartphones and tablets. These operating systems are simpler because they are designed to work on smaller devices. The OS of these devices can run limited sets of programs, allow input from a touch screen, and facilitate communication functions, as shown in Figure 3-12.

The OS for a handheld device is unique to the device. For example, an iPhone will not run the Android operating system. When a smartphone is purchased, its specific OS is preinstalled. Examples of operating systems for handheld devices are:

- Android for Google Nexus Phone and other devices;
- iOS for Apple iPhone, iPad, and other Apple devices;

Georgejmclittle/Shutterstock.com

Figure 3-12. The operating system on a mobile device is simpler than one designed for a desktop or laptop computer due to the fact it is designed to run on a smaller device.

- Windows Phone for Nokia, HTC, and Samsung smartphones and other devices; and
- BlackBerry for BlackBerry smartphones and tablets.

The Android OS accounts for the largest portion of the handheld device market, about 85 percent. This is because the Android OS runs on devices manufactured by many companies, including Samsung, Motorola, and HTC. There are different versions of the Android OS just as there are different versions of other operating systems. The iOS represents about 10 percent of the market. The Windows Phone OS represents about 3 percent of the market. The BlackBerry OS represents about 1 percent of the market. The rest of the handheld market is made up of several, mostly open-source operating systems.

System Utility Programs

GS4
Computing Fundamentals
3.4.3

In terms of system software, **utility programs** assist in managing and optimizing a computer's performance. These programs can add extra protection against viruses and malware, assist in installing or removing software, find files, and speed up communication.

An example of a Windows system utility is the disk defragmenter. The disk defragmenter, or *defrag*, reorganizes the files stored on a disk so, as much as possible, files are not divided among different storage locations. Each time the file is saved, a new piece of the file is stored. This new piece, or segment, may not be stored next to all of the other segments of the file. Segments of the file are stored in free space throughout the hard drive. As a result, the file may not be one piece in a single location on the disk. As files are deleted, space is freed between files and segments. When segments are scattered, it takes the disk drive longer to read and use the files. This scattering of file segments is called fragmentation.

HANDS-ON EXAMPLE 3.2.3

WINDOWS SYSTEM UTILITIES

Many of the Windows system utilities are accessed via the Control Panel window. Other system utilities are accessed through the **Start** screen or menu.
1. In Windows 10, right-click on the **Start** menu button. In Windows 8, click the **Apps** button at the bottom of the **Start** screen. In Windows 7, click the **Start** menu button.
2. Click **Control Panel** in the menu to display the Control Panel window.

HANDS-ON EXAMPLE 3.2.3 (CONTINUED)

3. Hover the cursor over a category. A tool tip will appear to identify what the utilities in that category can do. Help is available at every step to explain the process.
4. Click the **Uninstall a program** link below the **Programs** category. A list of the currently installed programs is displayed in the Control Panel window. Review the list to see what programs are installed. Do *not* uninstall any programs without permission.
5. Close the Control Panel window.
6. Display the **Start** screen or menu.
7. In Windows 10, click in the search box on the taskbar. In Windows 8, move the cursor to the upper-right corner and click **Search** when the menu appears. In Windows 7, the search box is located at the bottom of the **Start** menu.
8. Enter cttune.exe.
9. In the search results, click the cttune.exe program file. The **ClearType Text Tuner** dialog box is displayed, as shown. This is a wizard to adjust the clarity of the text display.

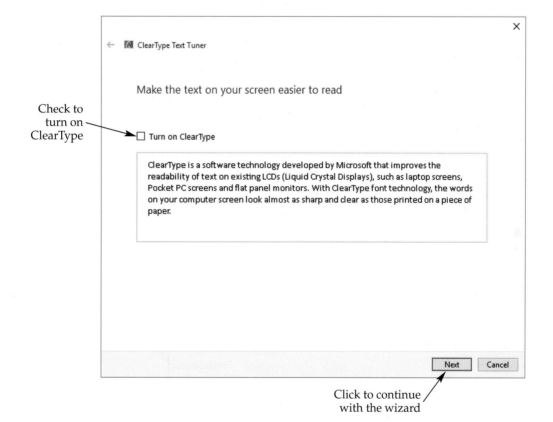

Check to turn on ClearType

Click to continue with the wizard

10. Check the **Turn on ClearType** check box, and click the **Next** button to move to the next page of the wizard.
11. The next four pages of the wizard give you a choice of sample text. Click the sample text that appears best to you, and click the **Next** button.
12. The final page of the wizard indicates it is finished. Close the program by clicking the **Finish** button.

GS5 Computing Fundamentals
2.7.1, 2.7.2, 2.9.1

GS4 Computing Fundamentals
1.1.3, 4.3.3

Device Drivers

A **device driver** is a special software program that provides instructions to the operating system for how to use a specific peripheral. All peripherals require this type of system software, including printers, monitors, graphics cards, sound cards, and scanners, as shown in Figure 3-13. The use of device drivers makes it possible for software developers to write code that lets the user choose from a wide range of peripheral devices. Hardware developers write the device driver to a set of specifications. Software developers write programs that address those specifications. This simplifies the writing of application software because specific instructions do not need to be included to address every device that the software may possibly use.

For example, consider printing a document from a word processing program. The programmers of the word processor only need to write instructions for how to print, not how to communicate with every possible printer. When the user selects which printer to use, the operating system calls up the device driver for that printer. The OS then conducts the communication between the word processing software and the printer hardware to finish the print job.

When installing a new peripheral device, the Windows OS will detect new hardware. In many cases, the driver is automatically installed. However, in some cases Windows will run a wizard to help install the new device. Installing the device driver sets up the communication between the CPU and the new hardware.

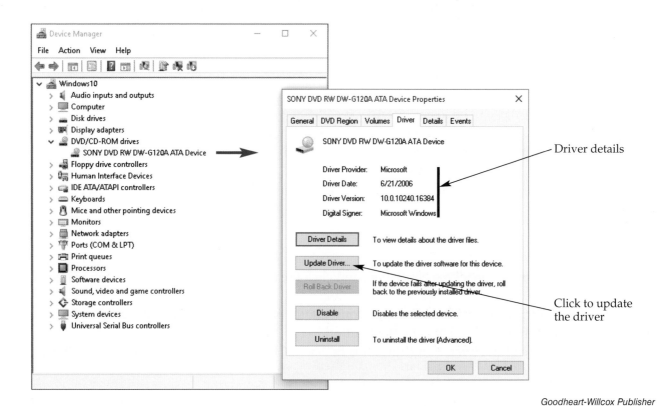

Goodheart-Willcox Publisher

Figure 3-13. All peripherals have device drivers that provide instructions to the operating system on how to use the device.

TITANS OF TECHNOLOGY

Grace Murray Hopper made many key contributions to software development in the early stages of digital computers. Formerly an instructor at Vassar College, Hopper earned her PhD in mathematics from Yale University. She joined the Naval Reserve during World War II. Because of her high intelligence and innovative spirit, she was tapped to work on the Mark series of digital computers at Harvard. She rose to the rank of Rear Admiral in the US Navy, the first woman to reach that rank. Her programming career started by rearranging wires on circuit planes to provide instructions for the Mark I computer. After tiring of rewiring the same set of instructions and then having to move them to accommodate new instructions, Dr. Hopper invented relocatable code. This provided for her inventions of compilers and human-readable code. She wrote the first compiler, which was B-O for the Univac. It was created to accept human-readable code and translate it into computer code. Eventually, she coauthored the COBOL language, which is still used in some business applications to this day. Her most far-reaching contribution was the standardization of compilers. She directed teams at the Navy to develop procedures and eventually automated the process for validation of COBOL compilers. Often called the Grand Lady of Software, Dr. Hopper's impact on the field of software development is still felt today.

Peripheral devices often include a CD containing the device driver. The installation wizard may ask you for the location of the device driver. If this happens, specify the CD as the location. However, there may have been updates to the driver since the CD was created. It is best to download device drivers from the manufacturer's website. During the installation process, specify the folder that contains the downloaded driver as the location of the driver.

Video cards require video drivers. When installing one from the manufacturer, the user will have to specify the exact model and the operating system of the computer. Mobile devices also require drivers. Smartphones can communicate with a PC only if proper drivers are installed.

A peripheral only has to be installed once on a given system. The hardware can be moved between systems, but a device driver must be installed on each system. If the correct device driver already exists on the system, the hardware should be ready to use once it is attached. If a driver is not installed, the system will treat the device as new hardware.

Programs

Personal computers make it possible to organize, create, and modify documents, spreadsheets, slide shows, digital images, music, videos, and many other types of data. For example, with the appropriate software, an image can be captured from a smartphone or digital camera. This image then can be opened in other software and combined with other images or text and exported. The exported file can be placed in a newsletter, added to a slide show, enhanced with music in a digital media application, or output in hardcopy as a poster. Programs, or application software, are what you use to get the job done. Application software is discussed in detail in the next section.

3.2 | SECTION REVIEW

CHECK YOUR UNDERSTANDING

1. What is the basic function of the operating system?
2. What is a computer platform?
3. Which type of system software assists in managing and optimizing a computer's performance?
4. What are special system software programs that provide instructions to the operating system for using a peripheral device?
5. Which type of system software is used to complete specific activities?

IC3 CERTIFICATION PRACTICE

The following question is a sample of the type of questions presented on the IC3 exam.

1. Which of the following is *not* a feature of an operating system?
   A. Communicate between the application software and the peripheral devices.
   B. Allocate memory.
   C. Save and retrieve files and data.
   D. Edit a photo.
   E. Provide utilities.

BUILD YOUR VOCABULARY

As you progress through this course, develop a personal IT glossary. This will help you build your vocabulary and prepare you for a career. Write a definition for each of the following terms and add it to your IT glossary.

accessibility options	power down
check box	power options
desktop theme	power states
device driver	radio button
drop-down menu	sleep
hibernation	system software
language packs	user account
platform	utility programs

APPLICATION SOFTWARE

michaeljung/Shutterstock.com

Application software is what you use to make the computer work for you. This may mean creating a letter or editing a photograph. You may wish to play an MP3 file or watch a movie. All of these tasks are done with application software.

Essential Question

How does application software affect your daily life?

All software must be used in a legal manner. In order to do so, the user must understand the license assigned to the software. Additionally, it is important to understand how software developers keep track of different versions of software. When installing software, a user must know the system requirements of the software version and be able to determine if his or her computer system can run the software.

LEARNING GOALS

- Explain software licenses.
- Describe application software.
- Install application software.

TERMS

application software
bugs
desktop publishing (DTP)
end user license agreement (EULA)
file format
for-purchase software
freeware
integrated development environment (IDE)
open-source software

podcasting
proprietary software
raster-based software
shareware
system requirements
template
vector-based software

Software Licenses and Versions

Writing software requires time, talent, and dedication from programmers. When a company develops software, it makes money by selling a license to use the software. In some cases, advertising may be embedded in the software to earn money for the developer. Then, the software is made available for free.

Licenses

Software programs are governed by an end user license agreement. The **end user license agreement (EULA)** is a contract outlining the set of rules that every user must agree to before using the software. Some EULAs allow the software to be installed only once on one machine. Other agreements may allow the software to be installed multiple times on the same machine to allow for reinstallation after a hard drive failure. A *site license* allows the software to be installed on any machine owned by the company that purchased the software. Large organizations, such as school systems or large companies, will purchase a site license to receive a volume discount. Single-seat licenses generally have higher per-seat fees than site licenses.

One type of software license is proprietary software or closed software. **Proprietary software** or *closed software* is owned by the creator and cannot be sold, copied, or modified by the user without permission from the creator. The actual code written by the programmers is not available to the user.

Open-source software is software that has no licensing restrictions. The base code is available for anyone to distribute, copy, and modify, as shown in Figure 3-14. However, part or all of the code of open-source

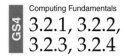

Computing Fundamentals
GS4 **3.2.1, 3.2.2, 3.2.3, 3.2.4**

GS5 Living Online
1.1.5.2

GS4 Living Online
4.2.6

FYI

If open-source software is the basis for a new application, credit should be given to the original programmers even if it is not required.

Goodheart-Willcox Publisher

Figure 3-14. SourceForge is an online community for open-source software.

software may be owned by an individual or organization. Generally, attribution must be made to the original software developers. Open-source software can be an alternative to proprietary software. Unlike proprietary software, these applications may not offer technical support. Open-source software depends on the members of the user community to assist each other and offer solutions.

Alternative-usage rights for software programs are typically covered by the GNU General Public License. The GNU General Public License (GNU GPL) guarantees all users the freedom to use, study, share, and modify the software. Open-source software usually has the GNU GPL assigned to it.

There may be shareware, freeware, and for-purchase options for software. **Shareware** is software that can be installed and used, then purchased if you decide to continue using it. Shareware usually has a notice screen, time-delayed startup, or reduced features. Purchasing the software removes these restrictions. **Freeware** is fully functional software that can be used forever without purchasing it. To be considered freeware, the software should not be a restricted version of for-purchase software. If it does, the software is considered shareware. **For-purchase software** is software you must buy to use, although you can often download a timed or limited-use demo.

The difference between a demo of for-purchase software and shareware is subtle. Typically, shareware software is not time-limited, meaning that the software remains functional forever with the restrictions in place. Shareware is based on the honor system where those who continue to use the software purchase the software. A demo of for-purchase software, however, typically stops working after a period of time. In the case of a limited-feature demo, the best features are either not functional or functional for a limited time.

Software Versions

Software developers constantly try to improve their software with new features and by eliminating bugs. **Bugs** are programming errors or oversights. Developers use a system of software versions to keep track of what has changed and when.

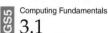

Computing Fundamentals
3.1

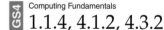

Computing Fundamentals
1.1.4, 4.1.2, 4.3.2

The first version of a software program is generally given the number 1. Later versions are given higher numbers. For example, there are several versions of Windows. The first version was Windows 1.0, which was released in late 1985. Windows 8 was released in late 2010. Windows 10 was released in July of 2015.

When small changes are made to the software, the version number is assigned a number following a decimal point. For example, Windows 8.1 is the second version of Windows 8, with the original version being Windows 8.0. Generally, these "point releases" or "dot releases" correct bugs that are discovered after the general public has had a chance to use the software.

FYI

There are many versioning systems used by software developers. Some are based on dates, numbers, or letters.

HANDS-ON EXAMPLE 3.3.1

 GS5 Computing Fundamentals 3.1

SOFTWARE VERSIONS

Programmers include notation of the software version within the software. When troubleshooting problems with the software, technical support staff will ask the user to identify which version he or she is using. In this activity, you will find the version of Windows and Microsoft Office installed on your computer.

1. In Windows 10, right-click on the **Start** menu button. In Windows 8, click the **Apps** button. In Windows 7, click the **Start** button on the taskbar.
2. Click **Control Panel** in the menu. The Control Panel window is displayed.
3. Click **System and Security** in the Control Panel window. Note: if you do not see this option, click the **View by:** link at the top of the dialog box, and click **Category** in the drop-down menu.
4. Click the **System** heading. The Control Panel window displays information about the computer system, including information about Windows.
5. Close the Control Panel window.
6. Launch Microsoft Word.
7. In Microsoft Word 2013, click **Account** on the **File** tab of the ribbon. In Microsoft Word 2010 or 2007, click the **Office** button and click **Word Options** in the menu to display the **Word Options** dialog box.
8. Locate the version of Microsoft Word, as shown.

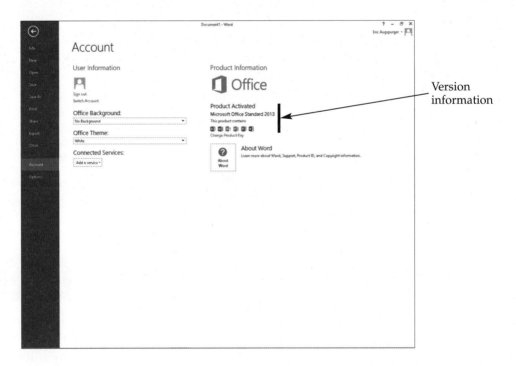

Version information

Application Software

Application software allows the user to perform specific activities, such as writing term papers, sending e-mail, paying taxes, editing photos, playing games, and taking online courses. There are four general types of application software: productivity, entertainment and educational, utility, and development.

Most application software can save information in various file formats. The **file format** indicates the manner in which the data the file contains are stored on the disk. The primary file format for given software is said to be the software's *native format*. There is usually a header portion of the file that contains information about the document. The content of the header is determined by the software that created the file. The header may contain information on what program was used to create the file; what language it is written in; and formatting settings, such as margins and fonts. Following the header is the body of the file. This contains the data the user added to the file. The purpose of the file format is to make it easy to reopen the file and arrange it on the screen. On a Windows system, the file name extension indicates the file format.

Application software does not have to be present on one's desktop, tablet, or smartphone. It can be licensed and accessed through the web. Software as a service (SaaS), introduced in Chapter 1, is a software-delivery method that provides remote access to functions as a web-based service. SaaS is a form of web application. The software is written to be compatible with desktops, tablets, or smartphones. SaaS pricing is often based on a monthly subscription fee. This allows organizations to conduct business at a lower cost by paying for the software only as long as they are using it, rather than paying for a perpetual license. It also eliminates the need to invest in installation, set-up, and maintenance as well as additional hardware.

Apps

Apps are small, self-contained programs used to enhance existing functionality, in a simple, user-friendly way. Smartphones all come with powerful web browsers. However, inputting URLs or managing bookmarks on a mobile phone is cumbersome. Many online sites and services offer a standalone app as a way to access content. This gives the user better control, thereby making everything simpler and quicker to open and use.

For example, if the user signs in to a bank's website using the phone's browser, it will be difficult for text entry and resizing the display to see the text box for entering the PIN. A banking app simplifies the process, storing the login information for next time, and making the critical data more readable on a smaller display.

Examples of functions offered by other apps include calculating tips, keeping one's day organized, calculating fuel usage, and tracking when the car needs an oil change. However, there are also apps called

Green Tech

Green Team
There are many ways to go green in the workplace. Assembling an employee green team is a good place to start. Most green teams focus on addressing employee workplace habits, such as implementing a recycling program and purchasing software as downloads instead of as boxed CDs. Companies that work toward sustainability are socially responsible and create goodwill.

Computing Fundamentals
6.5.4

Key Applications
6.1.1, 6.1.2, 6.2.1, 6.2.2, 6.2.3, 6.2.4, 6.2.5, 6.2.6, 6.3.1

Living Online
1.1.3.8

GS5

"time killers." These include video game, crossword puzzle, and video streaming apps.

Many apps are free, while some are premium apps that must be purchased. Obtaining apps is easy. For iPhones, the most popular place to get apps is in the Apple App Store. For Android phones, most people get their apps from the Google Play site. For different smartphones, conduct an Internet search with the brand of the phone followed by the word apps, such as Palm apps.

Make sure the app will run on your operating system and device before downloading it. Some apps will only run on a tablet or smartphone, some only on a desktop or laptop computer, and some on all platforms. Additionally, some apps are not downloads, but rather are browser-based and can run on all platforms and operating systems.

Users need data plans in order to download apps directly from the phone's mobile browser. Additionally, some apps, such as certain phone-tracking applications, require the user to have a data plan. Any apps that upload information collected by the application to a web-based server will require that the phone have a data plan. A data plan is a way to pay for Internet connection when the user is not able to connect to the Internet via a Wi-Fi hotspot.

Productivity Software

Productivity software is software that supports the completion of tasks. This group includes software for word processing, creating spreadsheets and presentations, editing graphics and video, and managing databases, among many other tasks. Productivity software often contains templates to help the user get started on a task or wizards to simplify complex tasks.

A *suite* is a group of programs, usually with similar interfaces, that provide complementary tasks. All of the individual programs function independently. When used together, data can be easily shared across the suite. The most common programs in an "office suite" are word processing, spreadsheet, presentation, and database management software, as shown in Figure 3-15. Microsoft Office and Corel Office are examples of suites of integrated productivity software. The software in these two suites is proprietary. Open-source alternatives for office suites are OpenOffice and LibreOffice.

Documents

GS4
Computing Fundamentals
3.3.5

When personal computers became popular, word processors were one of the first types of programs written for them. Word-processing software assists the user with composing, editing, designing, printing, and publishing documents. All modern word-processing software makes it possible to quickly enter text, complete insertions and deletions, correct mistakes, make revisions, check for spelling and grammar, combine documents, and add illustrations. Word processors are the most common type of application software.

Goodheart-Willcox Publisher

Figure 3-15. The Microsoft Office suite contains many programs. Depending on which version of Microsoft Office you have, there may be other programs not shown here or some of the programs shown here may not be included.

When a word processor is launched, it creates a blank document or offer the option to select a template. A **template** has formatting and organizational suggestions that can help the user create a professional-looking document. For example, Microsoft Word offers templates for letters, flyers, faxes, meeting agendas, budgets, and many more.

Microsoft Word is a common word processor. LibreOffice Write and AbiWord are open-source alternatives. These word-processing programs can read each other's data. When opening a file created in one of the other word processors, all text will be present, but the document may not look exactly the same. This is because the programs support different features. The native file format for Microsoft Word is the DOCx format. The native file format for LibreOffice Write is the ODT format. The native file format for AbiWord is the ABW format.

While word processors may offer some basic page-layout functions, they are not desktop publishing software. **Desktop publishing (DTP)** is the process of using a computer to typeset text and place illustrations to create, edit, and publish documents. Desktop-publishing software offers complex features for setting up text boxes and manipulating artwork. It is used to create newspapers, newsletters, brochures, advertisements, books, and many other types of documents.

Web-authoring software provides tools for designing and creating web pages. A web page is simply a text document that contains the code for how the page will appear and function. Web-authoring software, such

FYI

Open-source software alternatives are available for most common commercial application software.

Computing Fundamentals
3.3.3

as Adobe Dreamweaver, reduces or eliminates the need to write lines of code to create web pages.

Spreadsheets

Spreadsheet software is used to create, organize, and edit data in a table composed of rows and columns, as shown in Figure 3-16. The cells in the table can contain text, numbers, or mathematical equations. Each table or grid, which is the spreadsheet, is called a worksheet. Each spreadsheet document file may contain multiple worksheets.

Spreadsheet software is very popular with accountants, payroll administrators, and financial managers. It can perform complex calculations. It makes keeping a grade book, balancing a checkbook, or computing the monthly payment on a car loan easy. Spreadsheet software is also very useful in creating colorful graphs based on data entered in table format.

Microsoft Excel is an example of spreadsheet software. An open-source alternative is LibreOffice Calc. The native file format for Microsoft Excel is the XLSx format. The native file format for LibreOffice Calc is the ODS format.

Data Management

A database is information stored in tables. Database software is used for tracking large amounts of data. It is useful because it can retrieve a small part of the data that the user requests.

Businesses use databases to monitor all of the information about clients. The benefit of a database is seen when the user asks, or *queries*, the database to show a specific piece of information. For example, the user

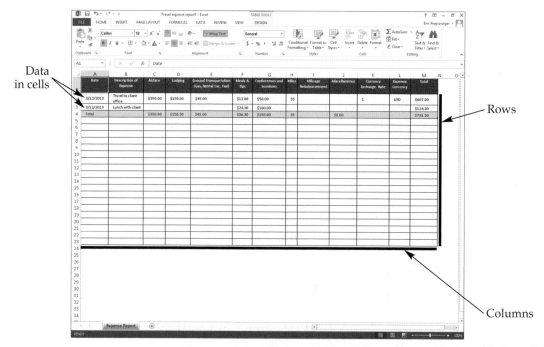

Goodheart-Willcox Publisher

Figure 3-16. A spreadsheet contains data arranged in rows and columns.

could request just the information of clients in one particular location. Most businesses also use database software to track their employees and related data, such as address, job title, salary, and certifications. Schools use database software to track information about students, including courses, grades, and attendance.

The most common database software includes Microsoft Access, SQL Server, MySQL, and Oracle. The native file format for Microsoft Access databases is the ACCDB format.

Presentations

Presentation software provides tools to combine text, photographs, clip art, video, and graphs into a series of slides for playback. A presentation allows a speaker to visually enhance the topic of the speech. Enhancing the experience of the audience can make the event more memorable. Slide shows are used extensively in classroom lectures, business presentations, company meetings, sales events, and conferences.

Computing Fundamentals
3.3.4

Presentations, or slide shows, are normally projected onto a large screen for viewing by a group of people. Sometimes presentations are intended for individual viewing on a computer screen. Often, a slide show presented to a group is later posted to the Internet for individual viewing.

Presentation software includes tools to add transitions between slides. The elements on each slide can be animated to add movement. Speaker notes can also be included to help the presenter.

Common presentation software includes Microsoft PowerPoint, Google Slides, and Zoho Show. Google Slides and Zoho Show are cloud-based solutions. LibreOffice Impress is an open-source alternative. The native file format for Microsoft PowerPoint data is the PPTx format. The native file format for LibreOffice Impress is the ODP format.

HANDS-ON EXAMPLE 3.3.2

OFFICE SUITE SOFTWARE

The programs in the Microsoft Office suite of software share a similar interface. It is common for the software in a suite to have similar functions in similar locations.

1. Close any open applications.
2. Open Microsoft Word, and start a blank document.
3. Open Microsoft Excel, and start a blank workbook.
4. Open Microsoft PowerPoint, and start a blank presentation.

HANDS-ON EXAMPLE 3.3.2 (CONTINUED)

5. Right-click on the Windows taskbar, and click **Show windows stacked** in the shortcut menu, as shown.

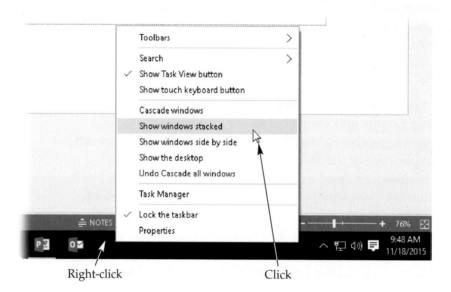

Right-click   Click

6. List the ribbon tabs that are in all three programs. For example, all three programs have a **Home** tab.
7. Click the **Home** tab in each program.
8. List the group names on the **Home** tab that are in all three programs. For example, all three programs have a **Clipboard** group on the **Home** tab.
9. Which one group on the **Home** tab contains the same tools in all three programs?

Computing Fundamentals
3.3.7

FYI

All digital photographs and scanned images are raster images.

Graphics

Graphics are pictures, drawings, photographs, and images used as decoration or to enhance or illustrate a topic. Generally, graphics can be called artwork. Graphics software is used to create, edit, print, and distribute the artwork. Professional artists use graphics software as a primary tool. However, there is graphics software designed for novice users as well. There are two types of graphics software: raster and vector.

Raster-based software creates graphics composed of dots or pixels, as shown in Figure 3-17. Each pixel is assigned a specific color and location. All of the colored pixels are mapped to form the image. Therefore, a raster image is often called a *bitmap*. As a raster image is scaled up or down, there is a loss of quality because the computer must calculate the changes in color for each pixel.

Raster-based software is used to edit digital photographs and similar graphics. Artwork created as a raster image may include commercial logos, advertisements, images for CD covers, and backgrounds for magazine and book covers. An example of basic raster-based software is Microsoft Paint, which is included in the Windows OS. Advanced

Figure 3-17. Raster images become pixelated when enlarged, but vector images can be infinitely scaled without loss of clarity.

raster-based software contains tools for adjusting color, brightness, and contrast; removing red-eye; applying filters for artistic effect; and other functions. Advanced raster-based software includes Adobe Photoshop, Corel Painter, Picasa, and GIMP. Picasa is freeware from Google. GIMP is an open-source alternative.

Vector-based software creates graphics composed of lines, curves, and fills based on mathematical formulas. Instead of storing the image definition as a map of colored pixels, each element in the image is created by its mathematical definition. Since the image is defined by a mathematical formula, it can be infinitely scaled up or down without loss of quality.

Vector-based software is used to create line drawings. Artwork created as line drawings may include diagrams, cartoons, logos, and floor plans. Vector-based software generally falls into one of two categories, creating illustrations and drafting. Examples of vector-based software used to create illustrations include Adobe Illustrator, Corel Designer, Inkscape, and LibreOffice Draw. Inkscape and LibreOffice Draw are open-source alternatives. Examples of vector-based software used for computer-aided drafting and design (CAD) include AutoCAD, LibreCAD, and SketchUp. LibreCAD is an open-source alternative.

Graphics can be saved in many different file formats. Common raster file formats include JPEG, TIFF, GIF, and PNG. Common vector file formats include EPS, AI, SVG, WMF, and DXF.

HANDS-ON EXAMPLE 3.3.3

RASTER IMAGE EDITING

Microsoft Paint is basic raster-based software. It contains basic tools for creating and editing raster images, such as digital photographs.

1. Insert your PRINC-OF-IT flash drive into the computer.
2. Create a folder on the flash drive named Chap03.
3. Navigate to the student companion website at www.g-wlearning.com, download the data files for this chapter, and save them in the Chap03 folder on your flash drive.
4. In Windows 10, click the **Start** menu button, click **All apps**, expand the **Windows Accessories** group by clicking it, and then click **Paint**. In Windows 8, click the **Apps** button, followed by **Paint** in the **Windows Accessories** category. In Windows 7, click the **Start** menu button, followed by **All Programs**>**Accessories**>**Paint**. Microsoft Paint is launched.
5. In Windows 10 and Windows 8, click the **File** tab followed by **Open**. In Windows 7, click the **Paint** button to the left of the **Home** tab, and click **Open** in the menu. A standard Windows open dialog box is displayed.
6. Navigate to your working folder where the data files for this class were downloaded.
7. Select the Moorhen.tif image file, and click the **Open** button. The photograph is opened in Paint.
8. Maximize the Paint window by clicking the **Maximize** button. This button is located in the upper-right corner of the window to the left of the **Close** button (X).
9. Click the **View** tab, and then click the **Zoom out** button. The display size of the image is reduced, but the actual size of the image is unchanged.
10. Click the **Home** tab, and then click **Rotate** button. A drop-down menu is displayed.
11. Click **Rotate right 90°** in the drop-down menu. The image is rotated 90 degrees clockwise, as shown.

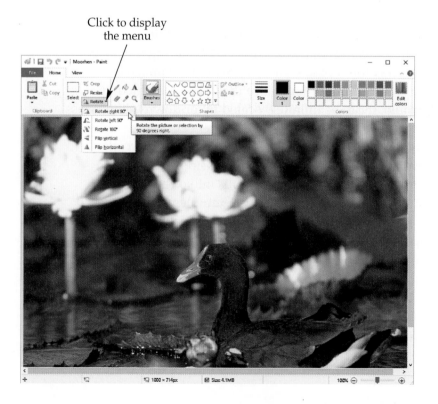

Click to display
the menu

HANDS-ON EXAMPLE 3.3.3 (CONTINUED)

12. Experiment with other features of Paint.
13. Click the **Close** button (X). When prompted to save changes, click the **Don't Save** button.

Digital Audio

Digital-audio software is used to create and edit music, narration, and other sounds in digital format. The resulting audio files can be played on computers, portable music players, or entertainment centers or added to videos or web pages. Podcasting is another use for digital audio. **Podcasting** is the distribution of audio files, such as episodes of radio or music broadcasts, over the Internet via automated or subscribed downloads.

Software for composing music includes MAGIX Music Maker, Apple GarageBand, and LMMS. LMMS is an open-source alternative. These programs have instruments built into the software. They can also edit the audio. Audio-editing software includes Sony ACID Pro, Sony Sound Forge, and Audacity. Audacity is an open-source alternative.

Two common audio file formats are waveform audio file (WAV) and MP3. The WAV format is the primary format used in Windows for uncompressed audio. The MP3 format is highly compressed. This allows the size of recordings to be reduced. For example, if a CD holds 10 uncompressed songs, it may be able to hold over 100 of those songs if they are compressed in the MP3 format.

Videos

Video software is used to create, edit, and publish digital video recordings. Using this software, titles, animation, audio, and effects can be added to video recordings. Additionally, the video itself can be trimmed and spliced to remove unwanted footage. Many video-editing programs use drag-and-drop techniques that make it possible to create professional-looking products with little training.

The equipment necessary to create digital video recordings is small, light, and portable. It uses built-in hard drives, flash drives, or DVDs to record many hours of video. Digital camcorders are available in a range of prices and features. Smartphones can also be used to record video, typically at a lower quality than a digital camcorder can create.

Several programs are available, from ones that offer full-scale special effects to more moderately priced options. Adobe After Effects, Apple Final Cut Pro, Apple iMovie, Microsoft Live Movie Maker, and Avidemux are examples of full-feature video software. Avidemux is an open-source alternative.

Entertainment and Educational Software

Some application software is designed for entertainment and educational purposes. This software is not used to create an end product, like productivity software does. Rather the software is used for the joy of using it or to learn new information.

Entertainment

GS4
Computing Fundamentals
3.3.6

Entertainment software provides amusement to the person using it. This software may be a video game, allow the user to watch movies or listen to music, or simulate a realistic environment, as shown in Figure 3-18. Video games are perhaps the most popular type of entertainment software.

Video games have evolved into many different categories, including simulations, action, puzzles, and sports, among others. Multiplayer games make it possible for two or more players to participate in the same game. Online games use the Internet to allow players to participate and communicate while they play from different locations. Video games can create virtual realities that are sophisticated, artificial environments, which in turn create realistic experiences for the players.

Entertainment software often requires a fast CPU, a high-powered video card, a significant amount of RAM, and a large hard disk. Some digital games require unique hardware that is sold with the software, such as a controller in the shape of a musical instrument. Internet-based entertainment software often requires a high-speed Internet connection.

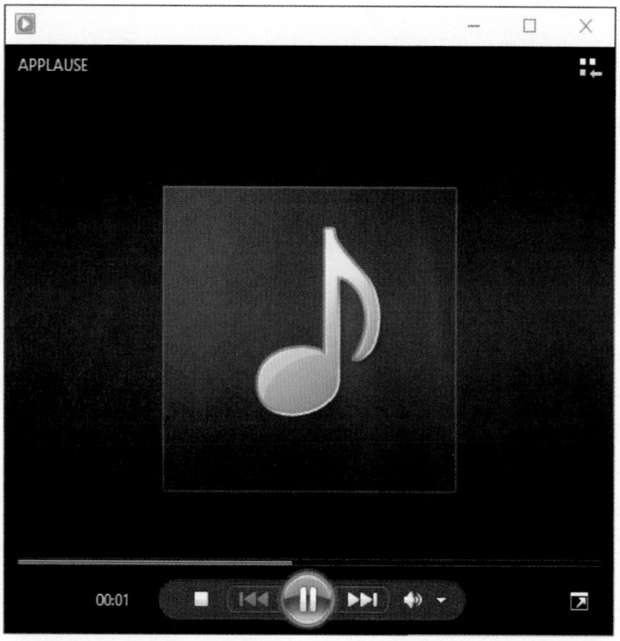

Goodheart-Willcox Publisher

Figure 3-18. Windows Media Player is an example of entertainment software. It can be used to play music, sound files, or videos.

Education

Educational software teaches the user a new skill or provides new knowledge. This software may teach users how to type, speak a foreign language, or play a musical instrument.

Personal computers and the Internet provide an opportunity for mass education. Taking classes online is becoming more popular. Online courses allow students to attend a class when it is convenient for them and eliminates having to travel to a physical site.

Simulation programs allow users to practice skills in a virtual environment instead of a real-world environment. This is a benefit since users can experience a potentially hazardous environment without suffering the consequences of a mistake. Examples include simulating landing a helicopter, piloting a ship into a narrow harbor, using surgical instruments, and performing a complex machine operation.

Simple tutorial programs can teach users how to use new software. There are also tutorial programs for preparing students for national exams, such as SAT, ACT, MCAT, LSAT, GRE, and GMAT.

Application Utility Software

A certain number of small application utilities are supplied with the Windows operating system. They include a calculator, a clock and calendar, a basic text editor, and others. The calculator and notepad are located in the Windows Accessories group in the **Start** menu in Windows 10 or the **Apps** menu in Windows 8. In Windows 7, they are located in the Accessories folder in the **Start** menu. Other programs are accessed through the system tray. The system tray, or *systray*, is located on the right-hand side of the taskbar. The clock and calendar and speaker volume control are located in the systray.

Development Software

Development software is a program used to create new software programs. Software programs are written in a high-level language and then compiled into machine language. An **integrated development environment (IDE)** provides editing capability to write and correct program codes, compilers to convert the code into machine language, and linkers to make executable files. An IDE may contain a software development kit (SDK), library of code snippets, toolkit, application programming interface (API), and overall framework.

Microsoft Visual Studio (VS) is one such IDE. VS supports programming in a variety of languages and generates executable programs for Microsoft systems. Game engines are another example of IDEs. These programs provide the tools needed to design and implement video games. Unity and Multimedia Fusion are just two examples of the dozens of game engines that are IDEs.

Installing Software

Computing Fundamentals
3.12.1, 3.12.2

Computing Fundamentals
1.1.3

When a user chooses what software to use, the software program must be placed on the system. This is called *installing* the software or *setup*. The process for installing software is created by the programmers who developed the software. Simple applications might just require copying the program files to the hard drive. More complex software generally requires an advanced procedure that modifies the operating system, as shown in Figure 3-19. Software can be installed from a CD, DVD, or a flash drive. It can also be downloaded from the Internet.

Before attempting to install software, the user should verify that the software and the computer are compatible. This means checking that the software is made for the installed operating system and that there is enough space to install the program files. Each software program should list the **system requirements**, which are specifications for the processor speed, RAM, hard drive space, and any additional hardware or software needed to run the software.

Goodheart-Willcox Publisher

Figure 3-19. Most programs have an installer that is used to properly set up the software on the computer.

GS4 Computing Fundamentals
3.1.1

New Installation

For Windows-compatible products, a standard setup procedure is dictated by Microsoft. This procedure performs several steps:
- determine if the software already exists
- look for enough space to install
- copy the program files onto the disk
- set up data files and folders
- create shortcuts to the program in the **Start** or **Apps** menu and optionally on the taskbar or desktop
- enter a file association for each file type that is created by the new program

Some installation utilities offer options for the advanced user. For example, a software program may allow a full or partial installation. A full installation would consist of all files required for the program to work plus other files such as samples or a library. A partial installation consists of only the files required for the program to work. In some cases, a partial installation will allow the user to select some of the additional files to be installed.

FYI

If you are unsure of what features to install, it is generally safe to accept the default settings.

HANDS-ON EXAMPLE 3.3.4

SYSTEM REQUIREMENTS

Memory and storage specifications are two common system requirements. In Windows, it is easy to find out how much memory and storage exist on the system.

1. In Windows 10, click **File Explorer** in the **Start** menu, and then click This PC in the tree on the left-hand side of File Explorer. In Windows 8, click the **Apps** button, and click **This PC** in the **Windows System** group. In Windows 7, click the **Start** menu button, and click **Computer** in the right-hand pane. Windows Explorer is launched with the computer selected.

2. Scroll down until the local hard drive (C:) is visible in the right-hand pane, as shown. Write down the amount of free space reported. This is the amount of space available for software installation, although never allow a hard drive to be completely full.

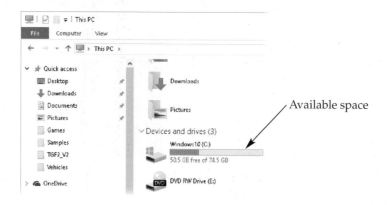

Available space

HANDS-ON EXAMPLE 3.3.4 (CONTINUED)

3. Click **System properties** in the ribbon or on the menu bar. Windows Explorer displays basic information about the computer in the right-hand pane, as shown.

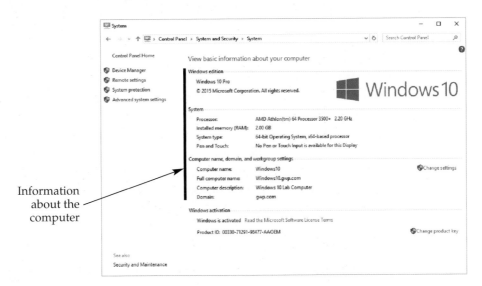

Information about the computer

4. In the **Windows** section of the information, determine the operating system. Record this information.
5. In the **System** section of the information, determine the amount of memory installed. Record this information.
6. Go to a store, either online or a physical store, that sells software. Select a program that interests you. Determine if your computer system meets the operating system, memory, and storage system requirements of the software.

Updates

Updates, sometimes called *patches* or *service packs*, are fixes to the software to correct bugs, remove security issues, or otherwise improve a version of a software program. When a software update becomes available, it is a good idea to apply it.

GS4 Computing Fundamentals
1.1.4, 3.4.2, 4.1.1

Microsoft automatically handles updates on its operating systems. Part of the shutdown process involves connecting with the Microsoft website to see if any updates need to be loaded. If an update is available, the system will automatically download and install it. Microsoft will report to the user how many updates are being applied as well as the progress of the installation. In some cases, an update requires the system to be restarted to activate the upgrade.

Some PCs are rarely turned off. In this case, Windows can be configured to automatically install updates without a shutdown. It is common in business and school settings for computers to remain on overnight so that updates can be installed without interrupting work.

Most software will have updates throughout the life of a version. If the software is registered, the developer will generally send a notification

FYI

The computer should not be turned off until the update procedure is complete.

when a new update is available. Many software programs automatically check for updates whenever the computer is connected to the Internet.

Uninstallation

GS4
Computing Fundamentals
3.1.2

A software program should be removed when it is no longer needed or seems to be causing a problem on a system. The process of removing software is called *uninstallation*. Often, this is referred to as performing an *uninstall*.

When a program is installed, many files are copied to the hard drive, often in many locations. Many installations also alter the operating system. The proper way to remove software is to use the uninstall option that came with the software. Running this option will remove all of the files that were installed, reverse any alterations to the OS, and remove shortcuts to the program. If an uninstall feature is not included with the software, use the **Add or Remove Programs** function in the Windows Control Panel to remove the program, as shown in Figure 3-20.

Reinstallation

GS4
Computing Fundamentals
3.1.3

Reinstallation is the process of reloading a software program on the computer system, usually in the same location as an existing installation of that software. Reinstallation, often called *performing a reinstall*, is

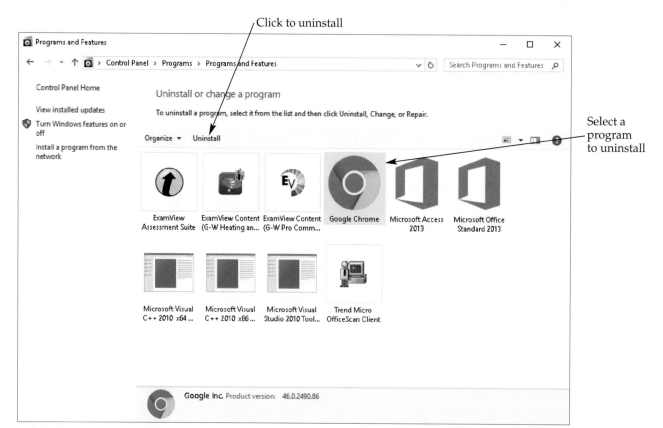

Goodheart-Willcox Publisher

Figure 3-20. Windows contains a utility that is used to remove installed programs from the computer.

usually done to reset an installed program to its defaults or to fix the program if it has become corrupted.

To reinstall software, take the same steps as installing new software. Follow the installation program wizard. Many installation programs will detect if the software is already installed and give the user the option to repair or fully reinstall the software. In some cases, the software cannot be reinstalled unless the previous version has been removed. The installation wizard should step through whatever process is needed to reinstall or repair the software.

3.3 SECTION REVIEW

 ### CHECK YOUR UNDERSTANDING

1. What is the name given to the permission to use a software program?
2. What does the file format indicate?
3. Describe the difference between raster and vector graphics.
4. What should be listed in the system requirements for software?
5. Describe the purpose of a patch or service pack.

IC3 CERTIFICATION PRACTICE

The following question is a sample of the type of questions presented on the IC3 exam.

1. Determine whether each feature is a function of the OS or the application software.

OS	App	Feature
		Restart system
		Format a document
		Communicate with the peripheral devices
		Install or Uninstall a program
		Start a program

 ### BUILD YOUR VOCABULARY

As you progress through this course, develop a personal IT glossary. This will help you build your vocabulary and prepare you for a career. Write a definition for each of the following terms and add it to your IT glossary.

application software
bugs
desktop publishing (DTP)
end user license
 agreement (EULA)
file format
for-purchase software
freeware
integrated development
 environment (IDE)

open-source software
podcasting
proprietary software
raster-based software
shareware
system requirements
template
vector-based software

Chapter Summary

Section 3.1
Language of Computers

- Communication inside a computer is conducted through a series of on-off signals. These signals are electrical in an electronic computer and represent either 1 or 0.

- There are various number systems in the world. Computers are based on the binary and hexadecimal systems.

- Code is computer-readable instructions. Programs are compiled to create computer-readable code.

Section 3.2
System Software

- The operating system performs communication with the user and the hardware. There are several different operating systems supporting several platforms.

- System utility programs assist in managing and optimizing a computer's performance. These programs may provide security, assistance, or communication, among other things.

- Device drivers provide instructions to the operating system for particular hardware. Device drivers are used to simplify the process of creating compatible hardware and software.

- Programs are what you use to get the job done. Programs may allow you to create and edit documents, play music, create images, and many other tasks.

Section 3.3
Application Software

- The software license specifies how the software may be legally used. Versions

of software are created to correct bugs or offer new features.

- Application software allows the user to perform specific activities. The software may be related to productivity, entertainment, education, or other tasks.

- Software must be installed in order for it to be used. Once installed, software may need to be updated, uninstalled, or reinstalled.

Now that you have finished this chapter, see what you know about information technology by scanning the QR code to take the chapter posttest. If you do not have a smartphone, visit www.g-wlearning.com.

Chapter 3 Test

Multiple Choice

Select the best response.

1. Programs written in a high-level language are always:
    A. interpreted at run-time.
    B. readable by the CPU.
    C. translated into machine language.
    D. linked for all computers.

2. The value 3.1415926 would belong to which data type?
    A. integer
    B. floating point
    C. string
    D. date

3. Languages are used in computer programming to:
   A. speak with a computer.
   B. write computer instructions at a human level.
   C. segment the hard drive.
   D. communicate with the hardware.

4. Small files that facilitate the operating system's communication with peripherals are _____.
   A. utilities
   B. boot procedures
   C. help files
   D. device drivers

5. Open source software is characterized by:
   A. proprietary copyright.
   B. free distribution of derivative applications.
   C. publicly available programming development files.
   D. costly software updates.

Completion

Complete the following sentences with the correct word(s).

6. Decimal, binary, and hexadecimal are examples of _____.

7. Object-oriented programming languages are known as _____-level languages.

8. The _____ performs communication with the hardware.

9. _____ software has no licensing restrictions.

10. _____ supports the completion of tasks, such as creating documents or spreadsheets.

Matching

Match the correct term with its definition.

   A. base-16 arithmetic
   B. data type
   C. operating system
   D. device driver
   E. proprietary software

11. Hexadecimal notation.

12. Manages the activities on a computer such as communicating with the hardware and running the software.

13. Cannot be sold, copied, or modified by the user without permission from the creator.

14. Description of values or information that can be accepted.

15. Used by OS to communicate with hardware.

Application and Extension of Knowledge

1. Research the history of the Hindu-Arabic numeral system. Write a one-page paper describing the origin of this system and its spread throughout the world.

2. Identify five computer programming languages. Classify each as a high- or low-level language. Prepare for a class discussion explaining why you classified each as you did.

3. Use the search function in the Windows **Start** screen or menu to search for resmon. This is the Resource Monitor utility. Launch it. Click the **Overview** tab in the Resource Monitor. Examine what information is displayed in the graphs on the right. Identify the percentage of CPU usage. Speculate how this utility can help examine the performance of the computer system.

REVIEW AND ASSESSMENT

4. Write a one-page paper that compares and contrasts the various types of software licenses. Provide examples of software available for each type of license. Speculate why a business may consider each type of license when obtaining software.

5. Identify three application software programs on your computer. Compare and contrast their functions and why you use them. Prepare for a class discussion on the importance of application software to your daily life.

Online Activities

Complete the following activities, which will help you learn, practice, and expand your knowledge and skills.

Certification Practice. Complete the certification practice test for this chapter.

Vocabulary. Practice vocabulary for this chapter using the e-flash cards, matching activity, and vocabulary game until you are able to recognize their meanings.

Communication Skills

College and Career Readiness

Speaking. Most people in the United States act as responsible and contributing citizens. How can a person demonstrate social and ethical responsibility in a digital society? Can you think of ways that are not discussed in this chapter?

Listening. Passive listening is casually listening to someone speak. Passive listening is appropriate when you do not have to interact with the speaker. Listen to a classmate as he or she is having a conversation with you. Focus attention on the message. Ask for clarification for anything that you do not understand. Provide verbal and nonverbal feedback while the person is talking.

Writing. Generate your own ideas relevant to using digital technology in the appropriate manner. Use multiple authoritative print and digital sources and document each. Write several paragraphs about your findings to demonstrate your understanding of digital citizenship.

Internet Research

Personal Information Management (PIM). Research personal information management (PIM) applications using various Internet resources. Identify a system that would work for you. Explain how you can apply a PIM system to your daily schedule.

Teamwork

Working with your team, research e-mail software. Make a chart showing at least five options, the system requirements, and the cost to purchase. One of the software options should be freeware. Write a memo to your supervisor (your teacher) listing the options and recommending an e-mail software program.

Portfolio Development

College and Career Readiness

Hard Copy Organization. As you collect material for your portfolio, you will need an effective strategy to keep the items clean, safe, and organized for assembly at the appropriate time. Structure and organization are important when working on an on-going project that includes multiple pieces. A large manila envelope works well to keep hard copies of documents, photos, awards, and other items. A three-ring binder with sleeves is another good way to store your materials.

Plan to keep similar items together and label the categories. For example, store sample documents that illustrate your writing or technology skills together. Use notes clipped to the documents to identify each item and state why it is included in the portfolio. For example, a note might say, "Newsletter that illustrates desktop publishing skills."

1. Select a method for storing hard copy items you will be collecting.

2. Create a master document to use as a tracking tool for the components of your portfolio. You may list each document alphabetically, by category, date, or other convention that helps you keep track of each document that you are including.

3. Record the name of each item and the date that you stored it.

CTSOs

Objective Test. Some competitive events for CTSOs require that entrants complete an objective component of the event. This event will typically be an objective test that includes terminology and concepts related to a selected subject area. Participants are usually allowed one hour to complete the objective test component of the event. The Global Business event may also include a team activity, case, or role play. To prepare for an objective test, complete the following activities.

1. Read the guidelines provided by your organization.

2. Visit the organization's website and look for objective tests that were used in previous years. Many organizations post these tests for students to use as practice for future competitions.

3. Look for the evaluation criteria or rubric for the event. This will help you determine what the judge will be looking for in your presentation.

4. Create flash cards for each vocabulary term with its definition on the other side. Ask a friend to use these cards to review with you.

5. Ask your instructor to give you practice tests for this chapter of the text that would prepare you for the subject area of the event. It is important that you are familiar with answering multiple choice and true/false questions. Have someone time you as you take a practice test.

4

FILE MANAGEMENT

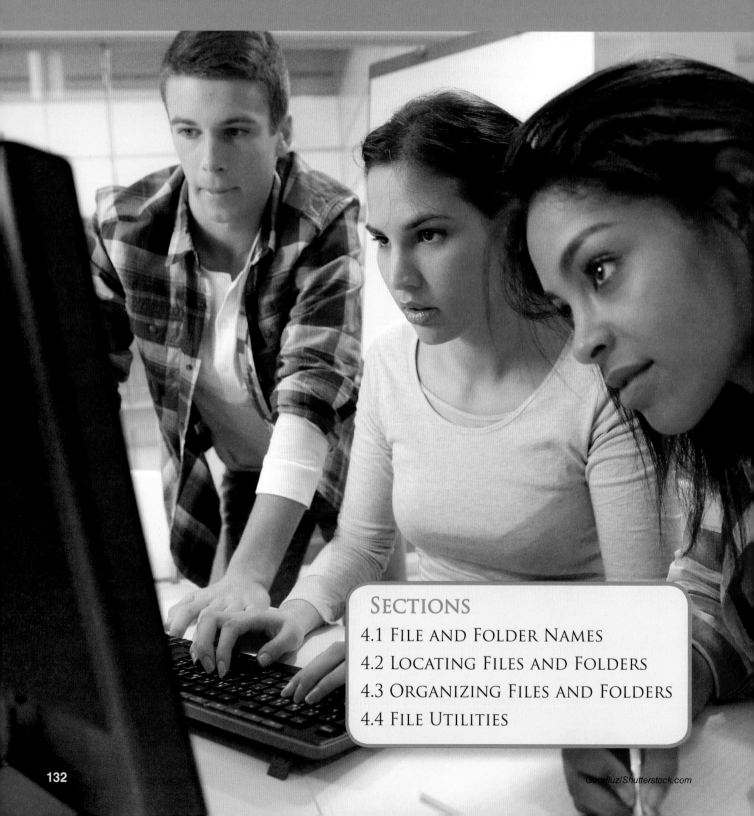

Good file management means that the user knows how to organize information on a computer. Not only do files need to be named in a meaningful way, the user must be able to locate files when necessary. A sign of poor file management is file names that do not indicate what the file contains. Not keeping track of where files are saved is also a sign of poor file management.

Files can be lost for many reasons: accidental deletion, unintentional overwriting with another file, theft, misplaced removable media, hard disk failure, or loss of the computer. Part of good file management is keeping multiple copies of a file in case of a loss. Good file management also implies that the user has created a safe location for saving the files. In a networked environment, many opportunities are present for other users to accidentally or intentionally cause file losses.

IC3 CERTIFICATION OBJECTIVES

GS5

Computing Fundamentals

Domain 3.0 Computer software architecture
　Objective 3.6 Know file structures and file/folder management
　Objective 3.7 Document management
　Objective 3.9 Searching for files
　Objective 3.10 Rights and permissions (administrative rights)

Domain 4.0 Backup and restore
　Objective 4.1 Understand backing up concepts

Domain 5.0 File sharing
　Objective 5.1 Understand file transfer options and characteristics

Key Applications

Domain 1.0 Common features
　Objective 1.8 Be able to drag and drop

Domain 2.0 Word processing
　Objective 2.10 Understand which file types are compatible or editable with word processors

Domain 3.0 Spreadsheets
　Objective 3.11 Understand compatible spreadsheet file types

Domain 5.0 Presentations
　Objective 5.1 Understand file types compatible with presentation software

GS4

Computing Fundamentals

Domain 1.0 Operating system
　Objective 1.2 Manage computer files and folders
　Objective 1.3 Manage computer configureation, Control Panel, OS drivers

Domain 3.0 Computer software and concepts
　Objective 3.4 Software tools

Domain 4.0 Troubleshooting
　Objective 4.4 Backup/restore

Key Applications

Domain 1.0 Common features and commands
　Objective 1.3 Navigating

College and Career Readiness

Reading Prep. Arrange a study session to read the chapter aloud with a classmate. Take turns reading each section. Stop at the end of each section to discuss what you think its main points are. Take notes of your study session to share with the class.

SECTION 4.1

FILE AND FOLDER NAMES

Essential Question

How is a file-naming scheme important to good computing?

A computer file is a collection of 1s and 0s that has meaning. This collection resides in computer memory or in a storage location. Software programs may create temporary files that are deleted when the software program no longer needs them. Other files contain information created by a user, and the software allows the user to save and open the file for further use. When a file is saved, it is given a file name so that the file can be located and used again. It is a good practice to assign meaningful and memorable file names so you or another person can recognize the files.

Windows uses a system of named folders to catalog and contain files. Notice that the names in Windows echo activities in an office or school setting. When students save paper files that belong together, they often use a manila folder. A Windows folder performs the same function for electronic files. Folders allow similar files or all files for a project to be organized together. This section discusses the naming of files and folders.

Goodluz/Shutterstock.com

TERMS

CamelCase
file association
file name
file name extension
file path
file tree
folder

folder name
library
naming convention
nested
reserved symbols
subfolder

LEARNING GOALS

- Explain how to create meaningful, legal file names.
- Use Windows Explorer to rename files and folders.

Windows File and Folder Names

The **file name** is a label that identifies a unique file on a computer system. There are three parts to a file name in the Windows operating system:

- the file name
- a period (or "dot")
- the file name extension

For example, consider abcde.ext as the file name. In this example, abcde is the file name and ext is the file name extension. The period separates the file name and the file name extension. Notice that Windows uses the term *file name* for both the whole name and the part of the name before the period.

A **folder** is a container in which files are stored. A **subfolder** is a folder contained within another folder. A subfolder is said to be **nested** within the parent folder. There may be several levels of nesting, as a subfolder may itself contain a subfolder that in turn contains another subfolder, as shown in Figure 4-1. A **folder name** is a label that identifies a unique folder on a computer system. In the Windows operating system, a folder name consists of only a name. There is no extension, so there is no period, either.

Legal Names

File names in Windows are limited by the number of characters in the folders and subfolders that hold the file. For example, C:\Program Files\abcde.ext indicates a file named abcde.ext that is located in

GS4 Computing Fundamentals
1.2.1, 1.2.2

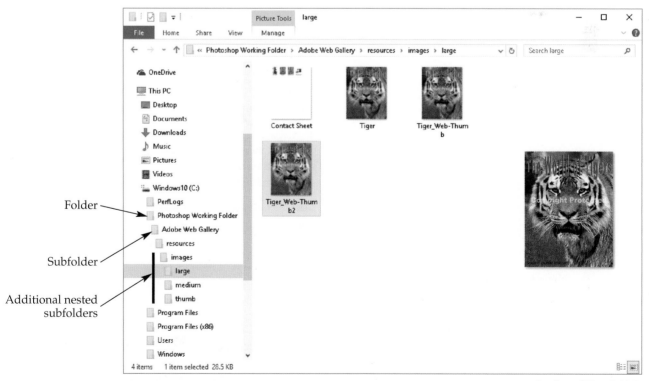

Goodheart-Willcox Publisher

Figure 4-1. A folder may contain many subfolders, each of which may contain additional subfolders.

the Program Files folder on the C: drive. This string is called the **file path**, which is the drive and folder location of a file plus its file name. The total number of characters in the file path cannot exceed 260 characters. Notice that the path includes the colon (:) for the drive letter and backslashes (\) to indicate where there is a change in folder.

The file path can be seen in the **Properties** dialog box. Right-click on a file, and click **Properties** in the shortcut menu. The file name is listed at the top of the **General** tab, and the path to the folder containing the file is shown in the **Location:** area, as shown in Figure 4-2. The full file path is the location plus the file name.

The limit of 260 characters provides ample space for writing a clear and unique name for each file and folder. Any character from the keyboard may be used in a name *except* for a few reserved symbols. **Reserved symbols** are characters that Windows uses for special meaning. The reserved symbols are shown in Figure 4-3.

Although Windows allows spaces in names, spaces cause problems in other software environments. Some software will stop reading the name at the first space. A URL or web address that contains a space will be misinterpreted. For example:

http://www.pages.com/my document.doc

will be read as:

http://www.pages.com/my

For this reason, it is best to not use spaces in file and folder names.

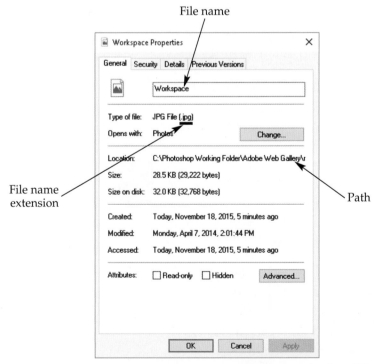

Goodheart-Willcox Publisher

Figure 4-2. The file name, file name extension, and file path are shown in the **Properties** dialog box.

Symbol	Description
<	Less than symbol or left chevron
>	Greater than symbol or right chevron
:	Colon
"	Double quote
/	Forward slash
\	Backslash
|	Vertical bar or pipe
?	Question mark
*	Asterisk

Goodheart-Willcox Publisher

Figure 4-3. Reserved symbols cannot be used in file or folder names.

All files and folders should have unique names. Although most operating systems will allow you to create many files with the same name as long as they are in different folders or drives, this is not a good idea. When looking for a specific file and several appear, the user will not know which one is correct.

Meaningful Names

The file name should clearly describe what is in the file. For example, suppose a student uses labReport to name a biology project. This may be satisfactory if there is only one lab report. However, if another lab report is created later, it would not be clear which file is for which report. Instead, more descriptive file names such as LabReportBio and LabReportDNA better describe the content of the files. A **naming convention** is a pattern that is followed whenever a file name is created.

Without spaces between words, long file names can be hard to read. For example, the name reportforlabexperiment is difficult to read. This name would be easy to read if there was an indication of the individual words. **CamelCase** is a naming convention in which the beginning of each word in the name is capitalized. This allows the file name to be read easily. For example, the name reportforlabexperiment becomes ReportForLabExperiment in CamelCase. The CamelCase naming convention got its name due to the apparent humps the capital letters make in the name, as shown in Figure 4-4.

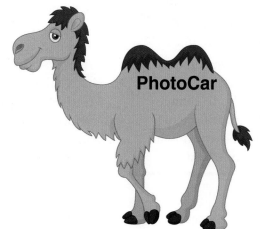

Goodheart-Willcox Publisher; Teguh Mujiono/Shutterstock.com

Figure 4-4. CamelCase is using a capital letter for the first letter in each word in a file name.

Monkey Business Images/Shutterstock.com

Computer files for schoolwork can be arranged in folders to keep everything orderly.

FYI

Changing the file name extension does not change the format of the file. To change the format of the file, it must be saved in a different format.

File Name Extensions

The second part of the file name is the period. Although the first part of the file name may contain periods as well, the last period on the right is the one Windows uses to begin the file name extension.

The third part of the file name is the file name extension, which follows the last dot. The **file name extension**, or file extension, tells the Windows operating system which software to use to open the file. The file name extension *indicates* the format of the file, but does not control the format of the file. The software saving the file controls the format.

Generally, when saving a file, the user adds the file name and Windows adds the correct file name extension. For example, if the user saves a document from Microsoft Word, the software saves the file as a Word document and adds the extension of .docx. It is good practice to let Windows choose the file name extension. Windows determines the file name extension based on the software program used to create the file. When performing a "save as" in many programs, the user can select one of many different file types in which to save the file. For example, image editing software, such as Photoshop or GIMP, may have a native file format, but also allows saving in several other formats, such as TIFF or JPEG.

When a file icon is double-clicked, Windows will locate software to open the file, launch the software, and load the file. This is made possible by a feature called file association. **File association** is a process in which Windows links a file name extension to a software program. For example, if a file has an extension of .docx, double-clicking on the file icon causes Windows to launch Microsoft Word and load the file into Word.

Figure 4-5 shows a few common file name extensions and the Windows program commonly associated with the file type. In Windows,

Extension	File Type	Associated Application
.avi	Video	Windows Media Player
.css	Cascading style sheet	Default browser
.doc, .docx	Document	Microsoft Word
.exe	Executable application	Windows operating system
.htm, .html	Hypertext markup (web page)	Default browser
.jpg, .jpeg	Compressed image	Default image editor
.m4a	Audio-only MPEG4	Windows Media Player
.mp3	Music or sound	Windows Media Player
.pdf	Portable Document Format	Adobe Reader
.pps	Slide show	Microsoft PowerPoint
.ppt	Presentation	Microsoft PowerPoint
.rtf	Rich text format document	Default document editor
.swf	Flash format	Flash Player
.tif, .tiff	Compressed image file	Windows Photo Viewer
.txt	Text	Notepad
.wpd	Document	Corel WordPerfect
.xls, .xlsx	Spreadsheet	Microsoft Excel
.zip	Compressed archive	Windows Explorer

Goodheart-Willcox Publisher

Figure 4-5. These are common file name extensions.

these associations may be changed using the **File Associations** dialog box. To access this, open the Control Panel window, click **Programs**, click **Default Programs**, and then click **Associate a file type or protocol with a program**.

Do not manually change a file name extension unless there is a very good reason to do so. Changing the extension removes the file association. Additionally, some software will not recognize or open a file using **File>Open** unless the file has the proper extension.

Naming a Group of Related Files

A project may contain several related files. Using a similar word pattern in the file names of these files reminds the user that the files are all related. For example, after completing a science experiment on determining the boiling points of different liquids, the students have been asked to record the following.

- hypothesis and methods in a text document
- data and charts in a spreadsheet
- experiment setup in a photograph
- photograph and results on a web page
- results in a presentation

A good way to organize similar files is to begin each file name with a common word. In this example, all documents relate to the boiling lab, so the word boiling can start each file name followed by the detail of each document:

- BoilingDescription.doc
- BoilingData.xls
- BoilingSetup.jpg
- BoilingResults.htm
- BoilingPresentation.ppt

Another naming convention is to include the creation date in the file name. The date a file was created or last updated is automatically recorded and can be displayed in Windows File Explorer. However, in some cases, adding a date to the file name is more useful because that will not change each time the file is saved. This is often done to maintain a date record or to help in sorting files. For example, the file name 160513LabResults.doc refers to the result of a lab test conducted in the year 2016 (16), in the month of May (05), and on the thirteenth day (13). Using this naming convention allows lab results from many different dates to be sorted by the year, then the month within a year, and finally by the day within a month regardless of when the content of the file had been updated.

Windows File Explorer

GS4
Computing Fundamentals
1.2.1

Windows File Explorer is a file-management utility with a graphical user interface that can be used to find anything in the computer's storage areas. The Windows File Explorer is part of the Windows operating system and controls parts of the GUI, including the desktop and the **Start** or **Apps** menu.

The first version of Windows contained MS-DOS Executive as the file utility. It also served as the graphical user interface instead of the **Start** or **Apps** menu and desktop found in later versions of Windows. MS-DOS Executive gave way to File Manager in Windows 3.0, at which time the program no longer served as the GUI and was strictly a file management utility. Windows File Explorer and the **Start** menu first appeared in Windows 95. At this point, the program again became part of the GUI. The **Apps** menu is used in Windows 8.

Windows File Explorer contains the address bar and ribbon or toolbar at the top of the window, as shown in Figure 4-6. Along the left-hand side of the window is the navigation pane. This pane contains a list of the available drives and folders shown in a tree format. On the right-hand side of the window is the file list. This shows the files and folders contained within what is selected in the navigation pane. Above the file list is the search box. This is used to locate files and folders, as discussed in the next section.

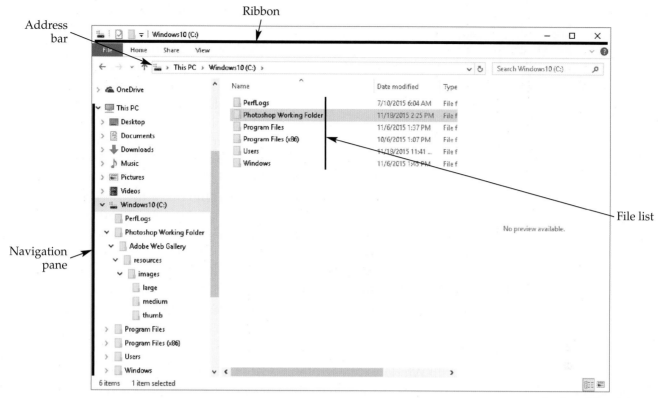

Figure 4-6. Windows File Explorer is used to locate and manage files in the Windows operating system.

The list of available drives and folders shown in the navigation pane is a tree. A **file tree** can be expanded to display subfolders and the files contained within them, as shown in Figure 4-7. Each folder in the tree is called a branch. The last item in an expanded branch is called a leaf. To expand a branch in the file tree, move the mouse over the folder name until a triangle is displayed to the left of the folder icon. Then, click the triangle. If the folder contains subfolders, they will be displayed indented below the parent folder. To collapse a branch in the file tree, click the triangle next to an expanded branch.

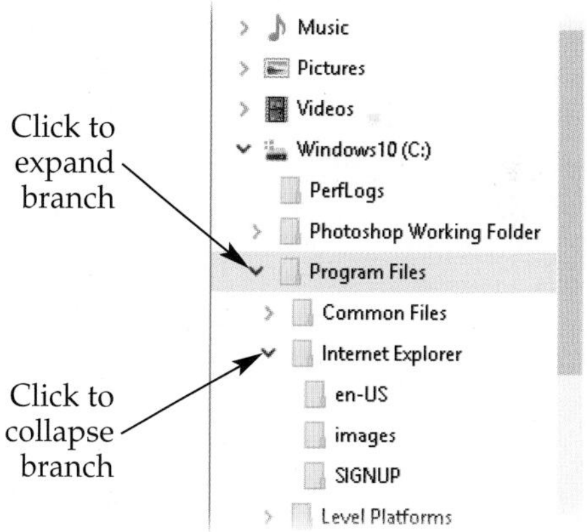

There are several folder views in which the content of a folder can be displayed. Some of these views include changing the size of the icons for files and folders, displaying the icons in a list, and displaying detailed information about the files and folders.

Figure 4-7. The navigation pane displays the folder structure using a tree metaphor.

Folders

Folders provide an organizational tool that can be used to keep similar files together. Similar files may be related to the same event, of the same file type, or for any reason meaningful to the user. A folder having

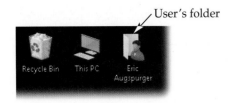

User's folder

Goodheart-Willcox Publisher

Figure 4-8. The user's Documents folder appears by default on the Windows desktop.

the current user's name appears by default on the Windows desktop, as shown in Figure 4-8. This is the user's Documents folder. Double-clicking a folder on the desktop launches Windows File Explorer, which displays the content of the folder.

A general rule of thumb is to keep only as many files in a folder as can be displayed in Windows File Explorer without scrolling. If there are more files than that, it is likely the files can be organized into subfolders. For example, suppose a user creates a folder name SchoolWork within his or her Documents folder. Items in the Documents folder that are related to schoolwork can then be moved into the SchoolWork folder. This reduces the number of files located in the Documents folder.

A folder is simply a special type of file. Therefore, follow the same naming rules used for other files. However, as stated earlier, a folder name does not have a file name extension.

Ethics

File Sharing

There are many types of computer files, from program files such as executables to document files such as songs, photographs, and e-books. However, almost all files are owned by someone. It is unethical and, in many cases, illegal to share files for which you are not the owner.

Libraries

In Windows File Explorer, a **library** is a collection of similar files and folders that are displayed together, but that may be stored in different locations. A library displays all of the common files available to all users and the current user's files in the same view. The library structure was introduced in Windows 7 to help multiple users run the same computer. Unlike a folder, there is no file or folder connected to a library. If a library is deleted, the files and folders displayed in the library are unaffected.

The idea behind a library is there may be several folders on the disk drive containing similar files that commonly need to be accessed at the same time. For example, the Pictures library, which appears in Windows File Explorer in the Libraries branch, displays the folders My Pictures and Public Pictures. These folders are not subfolders within a *folder* named Pictures, they are simply displayed in the *library* named Pictures for easy access. This is the concept of libraries.

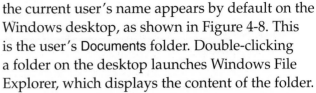

HANDS-ON EXAMPLE 4.1.1

WINDOWS FILE EXPLORER

The ability to effectively use Windows File Explorer is an essential skill for any computer user. Begin by learning the different elements of Windows File Explorer and how to navigate the folder and library structures. Note: libraries are disabled by default in Windows 8.1.

1. In Windows 10, right-click on the **Start** menu button, and click **File Explorer** in the shortcut menu. In Windows 8, launch File Explorer by clicking the **Apps** button and then clicking **File Explorer** in the **Windows System** group of the **Apps** menu. In Windows 7, right-click on the **Start** menu button, and click **Open Windows Explorer** in the shortcut menu.

HANDS-ON EXAMPLE 4.1.1 (CONTINUED)

2. In Windows 8, click the **View** tab, click the **Navigation Pane** button, and click **Show libraries** in the drop-down menu so it is checked. Leave it checked if already checked. This ensures libraries are visible.
3. Locate the elements of the Windows File Explorer window shown in Figure 4-6.
4. Single-click the Libraries branch in the navigation (left-hand) pane. The defined libraries are displayed in the file list in the right-hand pane. Note: in Windows 10, the libraries are not listed as subfolders within a Libraries branch.
5. Double-click the Pictures library in the file list. The Libraries branch is expanded in the navigation pane, the Pictures branch is highlighted, and the content of the Pictures library is displayed in the file list.
6. In Windows 7, double-click the Sample Pictures library in the file list. Note: Windows 10 and Windows 8 do not include any of the sample files and folders found in Windows 7.
7. In Windows 10 and Windows 8, click the **View** tab, and click **Medium Icons** in the **Layout** group. In Windows 7, click the **View** pull-down menu, and click **Medium Icons** in the menu.
8. Applying what you have learned, expand the tree in the navigation pane to show the folders on the local drive, the subfolders within the Windows folder, the subfolders within the Web subfolder, the subfolders within the Wallpaper subfolder, and the files within the Windows subfolder (C:\Windows\Web\Wallpaper\Windows). This nested folder should contain at least one image file.
9. Select an image file by single-clicking it. Notice the details pane updates with information about the file and the menu bar contains more options. The details pane is turned off by default in Windows 10 and Windows 8. To turn it on, click the **Details Pane** button in the **Panes** group on the **View** tab of the ribbon.

Displaying File Name Extensions

By default, the file name extensions are hidden by the operating system. This can lead to confusing situations if there are several files with the same name, but different file name extensions. Turning on the display of file name extensions can help the user tell one file from another file with the same name.

For example, it is a common practice to name image files by the content of the image. The files Jellyfish.jpg and Jellyfish.bmp are both image files. However, with the file name extensions hidden, the user will see both files as only Jellyfish when viewed in Windows File Explorer. It is only when the file name extensions are displayed that the difference between the files becomes clear, as shown in Figure 4-9.

FYI

The icon associated with a file helps indicate the file type, but many file types share the same icon or similar icons.

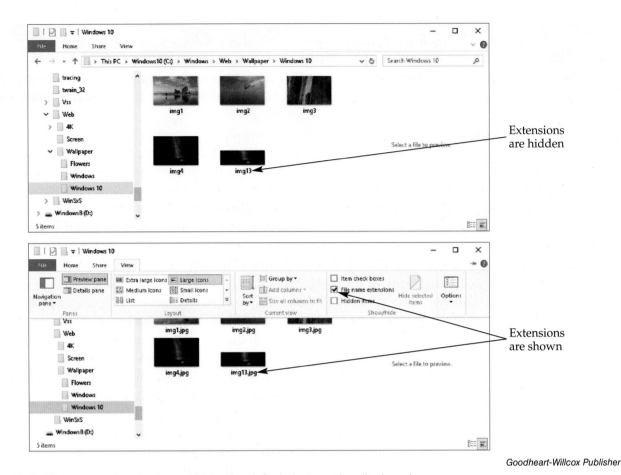

Figure 4-9. File name extensions are hidden by default, but can be displayed.

TITANS OF TECHNOLOGY

David A. Huffman, a computer scientist and inventor, was an early pioneer in the development of computers. He won many awards. However, the one he earned in 1998 from the IEEE Information Theory Society made a big impact on data compression technologies. This award recognized his invention of the Huffman minimum-length lossless data-compression code. The compression code was the topic of a term paper he wrote while a graduate student at the Massachusetts Institute of Technology in 1952. Before his method was used, file compression tended to lose some or much of the fidelity of the original file. Huffman's idea defined a compression scheme whereby none of the data were lost. Decompression restored the file to its original fidelity. This data compression method has since been used to compress image files as well as the data stream for high-definition television (HDTV) broadcasts. The technology is also used in fax machines and modems. The compression method is known as Huffman encoding. Huffman was also very interested in origami, the ancient Japanese art of paper folding. He contributed to the branch of mathematics involved in the paper folding techniques.

HANDS-ON EXAMPLE 4.1.2

DISPLAYING FILE NAME EXTENSIONS

File name extensions are hidden by default. However, many users prefer to have file name extensions visible. This is a simple setting in Windows.

1. Launch Windows File Explorer.
2. Applying what you have learned, navigate to the C:\Windows\Web\Wallpaper\Windows folder.
3. In Windows 10 and Windows 8, click the **View** tab, and click the **Options** button (not the drop-down arrow below it). In Windows 7, click the **Organize** button on the toolbar, and click **Folder and search Options** in the drop-down menu that is displayed. The **Folder Options** dialog box is displayed.
4. Click the **View** tab in the dialog box. Notice all of the settings for how files are displayed.
5. Scroll down in the **Advanced Settings** list, and uncheck the **Hide extensions for known file types** check box, as shown.

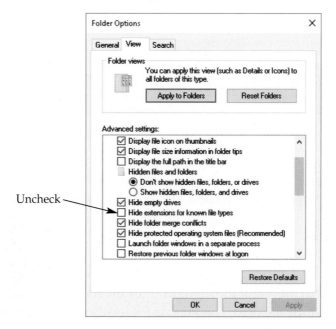

6. Click the **Apply to Folders** button at the top of the tab so file name extensions will be displayed in *all* folders.
7. Click the **OK** button to apply the change and close the dialog box. Notice the file name extension is displayed for the file in the folder. In this case, the file in the folder is in the JPG format, which is a graphics file.
8. Double-click on the file to open it in the program associated with the .jpg file extension.

Renaming Files and Folders

Often, a file or folder must be renamed. This may be done to correct spelling, make the name more descriptive, or simply to change the name to suit the user. However, only the file name should be changed, not the file name extension. If the file name extension is changed, the file association may be broken. This may make the file unrecognizable by the associated software.

There are several ways to rename a file or folder in Windows File Explorer. One way is to right-click on the file or folder and click **Rename** in the shortcut menu. Another way is to single-click twice on the file or folder in the file list. A third way is to select the file or folder in the file list, and then in Windows 10 and Windows 8, click the **Rename** button in the **Organize** group on the **Home** tab of the ribbon. In Windows 7 click **Rename** in the **File** pull-down menu. With any of these methods, the file name is replaced with an edit box, and the current file name is highlighted and ready for editing. Once the file name is highlighted, edit the name, and press the [Enter] key once to complete the process.

FYI

Two single clicks must have enough time between them so the operating system will not interpret the clicks as a double-click.

HANDS-ON EXAMPLE 4.1.3

NAMING FOLDERS

Removable media, such as flash drives, are commonly used by students to maintain schoolwork. In Chapter 2, you began setting up a flash drive for use in this class. Now you will add folders to this device for a class named Physical Science.

1. Insert the flash drive set up in Chapter 2 into the computer. If the **AutoPlay** dialog box appears, cancel it.
2. Launch Windows File Explorer.
3. In the navigation pane on the left, highlight the PRINC-OF-IT flash drive.
4. Click the arrow to the left of the drive icon for the flash drive to expand the folder tree for the drive. Currently, the drive contains no folders (unless folders have previously been added), so there is nothing to expand.
5. Make sure the flash drive is highlighted in the navigation pane. When creating a folder, it will be placed in whatever location is currently highlighted in the navigation pane.
6. In Windows 10 and Windows 8, click the **New Folder** button in the **New** group on the **Home** tab of the ribbon. In Windows 7, click the **New Folder** button on the toolbar. A new folder is added to the file list, and the default name of New Folder is highlighted for editing. The folder tree for the flash drive also is automatically expanded in the navigation pane.

HANDS-ON EXAMPLE 4.1.3 (CONTINUED)

7. Change the default name to SciencePhysical, and press the [Enter] key to finish creating the folder.
8. Highlight the SciencePhysical folder in the navigation pane.
9. Applying what you have learned, add a subfolder named BoilingLab in the SciencePhysical folder.
10. Click the arrow to the left of the SciencePhysical folder in the navigation pane to expand the folder tree. The BoilingLab folder is displayed below the SciencePhysical folder in the tree, which indicates it is a subfolder.
11. Right-click on the SciencePhysical folder in the navigation pane, and click **Rename** in the shortcut menu.
12. Change the name of the folder to PhysicalScience, and press the [Enter] key. Notice how the BoilingLab subfolder remains in the parent folder even after the parent is renamed, as shown.

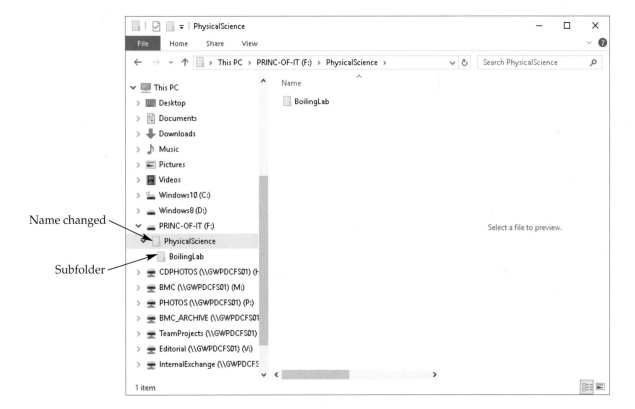

4.1 SECTION REVIEW

↗ CHECK YOUR UNDERSTANDING

1. What are the three parts of a file name?
2. What are the two parts of the file path?
3. Write this file name in CamelCase: My Picture of Venice.jpg.
4. What is a library in Windows Explorer?
5. Why would you turn on the display of file name extensions?

IC3 CERTIFICATION PRACTICE

The following question is a sample of the types of questions presented on the IC3 exam.

1. The dialog box displays the properties of a file. What is the file size?
   A. 16,045 KB
   B. Not displayed
   C. 15.6 KB
   D. 15.6 MB

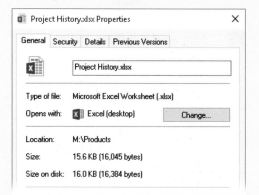

↗ BUILD YOUR VOCABULARY

As you progress through this course, develop a personal IT glossary. This will help you build your vocabulary and prepare you for a career. Write a definition for each of the following terms and add it to your IT glossary.

CamelCase	folder name
file association	library
file name	naming convention
file name extension	nested
file path	reserved symbols
file tree	subfolder
folder	

LOCATING FILES AND FOLDERS

bikeriderlondon/Shutterstock.com

It is not unusual to hear novice computer users say that they cannot find files they created. This may be explained by the fact that disk drives may have gigabytes or terabytes of storage space and contain hundreds or thousands of folders. However, being unable to locate a file often means the user did not have a plan for saving and locating files.

Windows provides an organizational plan for collecting files of a similar type in one location. This organizational scheme includes folders for My Documents, My Music, My Pictures, and My Videos. However, many users create custom folders to group files according to their own ways of working. Some choose to group files by creation dates, while others group files around a certain topic, such as vacations or school courses. Each person should choose a scheme that makes sense for him or her and that will support rapid retrieval of each file. A good guide is the English proverb, "A place for everything and everything in its place."

Essential Question

How does your ability to locate files impact your productivity?

TERMS

file management
root
sorting
wildcards

LEARNING GOALS

- Locate files and folders on a computer system.
- Sort the list of files in a folder.
- Discuss sharing files online.

Locating Files and Folders

File management is working with files on the hard disk or other storage medium. Good management involves organizing files in logical locations. Doing so makes it easier for users to recall where a file is saved.

All files are stored in a hierarchy that begins at the top folder of the drive. This top folder is called the **root**. For example, some folders that exist at the root of the primary hard drive in the Windows operating system include Program Files, Users, and Windows. The file path begins at the drive root.

Media Reader Devices

A media reader device uses digital files in standard formats to recreate the original content. The media may be video, photos, audio, or text such as an e-book. To locate the files, open the corresponding app. For example, to locate e-book files, open the e-book–reader app. To locate image files, open the photograph-viewer app.

Files may be stored on the device or in the cloud. E-book readers support a file management tool called the *library.* Users can view titles and add or delete e-book files using this tool. Music readers may use CDs, DVDs, SD cards, or direct download to access songs. Often connecting a reader device to a PC provides additional file-management capability. Songs can be swapped from the reader to the PC in order to conserve storage space on the reader device.

Image Files on Mobile Devices

Most mobile devices include a camera for taking photos and videos. These files are saved on the mobile device. Newer devices create images with high resolution, resulting in very large files. Because the files are digital, it is easy to take many shots of a subject until a satisfying image is created. It is possible to run out of storage space on mobile devices. To regain storage space, delete all photos of lesser quality or that are unneeded.

The files can be sorted into folders by date or topic. These folders are called *albums.* Create an album, and then drag photos into it. It is also possible to copy these photos to a computer. The synchronization, or syncing, process makes a copy of every photo on the device. When the mobile device is connected to the computer, it becomes a device on that computer. Navigate to the location of the photos, select the photos to copy, and copy them to the desired folder on the computer. It is important to monitor the number of photos on the device so that new photos are not missed due to insufficient storage, or time is not lost deleting photos on the fly.

Searching for Files

The search box in Windows File Explorer is used to locate files and folders. To conduct a search, first highlight the drive, folder, or subfolder to search in the navigation pane. The default text in the search box reflects what is selected. For example, if the Desktop branch is selected in the navigation pane, the default text in the search box is Search Desktop.

Next, click in the search box and enter the name of the file or folder for which to look. If the entire name is not known, a partial name can be entered. When the [Enter] key is pressed, the search begins. A green bar slides across the address bar to indicate the search progress. Every file found matching the search criteria will be displayed in the file list. Scroll through the list to locate the correct file or folder.

Sometimes the list of files found is longer than a user wants to sift through. Suppose a user was hunting for a picture file and simply entered pictures in the search box. Many unwanted files would be suggested. Narrowing the search criteria will speed up locating the file. **Wildcards** can be used in the search box to represent unknown characters. An asterisk (*) represents one or more characters in a file name. A question mark (?) represents just one character.

For example, to find all of the boiling lab files, enter boiling*. To find the boiling lab files that end in 1, enter boilinglab?1. This will return the files boilinglab01 and boilinglab11. However, the file boilinglab111 will not be returned because there is an extra character and the ? wildcard allows for one character.

It is possible to search for only files of a certain type by entering the asterisk wildcard and the file name extension. For example, to locate all JPEG images, enter *.jpg. This method can be combined with part of the file name to limit the search by file type. For example, to locate all boiling lab files that are in Excel format, enter boiling*.xlsx or boilinglab*.xlsx.

Searching Inside Files

By default, Windows File Explorer searches inside certain file types. During a search, Windows not only looks for file and folder names that meet the search criteria, but also looks at the content of these files. For example, the DOC and DOCx file types are by default set to have the content of the file searched. If a search is conducted with the phrase boiling, the results would include not only the files BoilingLab01.xlsx and BoilingLab02.xlsx, but also the file Results.docx if the word *boiling* is contained in that document.

Windows can be told to search the content of *all* file types. This may be useful, but it may also increase the amount of time it takes to conduct a search. In Windows 10 and Windows 8, click the **Options** button on the right-hand side of the **View** tab in the ribbon of File Explorer. In Windows 7, click **Folder options...** in the **Tools** pull-down menu of Windows Explorer. In the **Folder Options** dialog box that is displayed, click the **Search** tab, as shown in Figure 4-10. In Windows 10 and Windows 8, check the **Always search file names and contents** check box. In Windows 7, click the **Always search file names and contents** radio button. Click the **OK** button to apply the setting and close the dialog box.

FYI

A file search will take less time if the search is the content of a specific folder rather than an entire drive.

FYI

Instead of setting Windows to search the content of all file types, it is possible to add specific file types to the list of files whose content will be searched using the **Indexing Options** link in the Control Panel window.

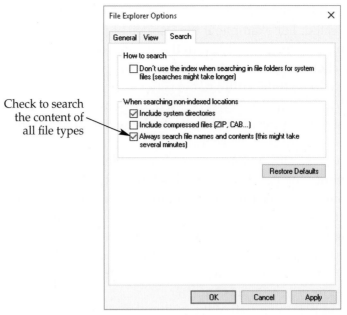

Check to search the content of all file types

Figure 4-10. By default, Windows searches the content of certain file types, but it can be set to search the content of all file types.

Hands-On Example 4.2.1

Searching for Files and Folders

The ability to search for files is critical to becoming a successful computer user. It is not uncommon for a computer user to work with hundreds if not thousands of files over the course of a year. Even the best computer users will need to search for files and folders.

1. Launch Windows File Explorer.
2. Expand the folder tree for the primary hard drive (C:) in the navigation pane on the left, and highlight the Windows folder. The search box should display Search Windows.
3. Click in the search box. The default text is replaced with a vertical bar cursor. For a few seconds, a list of recent search phrases is also displayed.
4. Enter *.jpg in the search box. When the [Enter] key is pressed, the search begins.
5. A green bar appears in the address bar to indicate the progress of the search. When the green bar reaches the right-hand side of the address bar and disappears, the search is complete. The file list displays the files found in the Windows folder, as well as all of its subfolders, that are of the JPG type.

Sorting Files

Sorting is arranging a list by a certain criterion, such as alphabetically, by date, or by size. This can help locate the file or folder. By default, Windows File Explorer shows files sorted alphabetically by name, from A to Z. Sorting files by date is also useful to show which files have been saved more recently than others. Sorting by date is especially useful if multiple versions of the same file exist in different locations.

To sort files, display the details view. In Windows 10 and Windows 8, click the **View** tab, and click **Details** in the **Layout** group. In Windows 7, click the **View** pull-down menu, and click **Details** in the menu. In the details view, headers are displayed in the file list, as shown in Figure 4-11. Clicking the Name header toggles between sorting the files alphabetically from A to Z and from Z to A. Clicking the Date header toggles between sorting the files from oldest to newest and newest to oldest. A small triangle pointing either up or down in one of the headers in the file list indicates which header is used as the sort criterion. The direction the triangle is pointing indicates if the sort is *ascending* (A to Z, for example) or *descending* (Z to A, for example).

FYI

Click the drop-down arrow in the header in the file list to show additional sorting options.

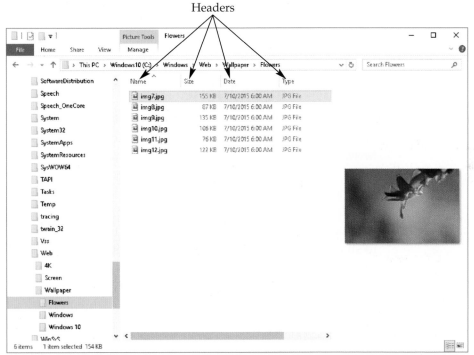

Goodheart-Willcox Publisher

Figure 4-11. The details view displays headers, which can be used to sort files.

HANDS-ON EXAMPLE 4.2.2

SORTING FILES

Sorting files is useful when a search returns a long list of files. However, sorting can be useful anytime the content of a folder is displayed.

1. Launch Windows File Explorer.
2. Highlight the Windows folder in the navigation pane on the left.
3. In Windows 10 and Windows 8, click the **View** tab, and click **Details** in the **Layout** group. In Windows 7, click the **View** pull-down menu, and click **Details** in the menu.
4. Scroll through the list of files and folders. When sorted in ascending alphabetical order, all folders are listed before the files.
5. Click the Date modified header so the triangle points down. Notice that the file list displays the files at the top in ascending order of when they were last modified. In ascending order of date, the most recent file is at the top. The folders are at the bottom of the list after the files and are also sorted in ascending order by date.
6. Click the Date modified header to toggle the sort to descending order. Now the folders appear first in the list with the oldest one at the top. The files appear after the list, also sorted in descending order.
7. Click the Name header so the triangle points up. All of the files and folders are now in ascending alphabetical order with the folders at the top of the list and the files after the folders.

Sharing Files Online

Computing Fundamentals
5.1.2, 5.1.3

New technologies provide storage not on a local computer that also support sharing files. Some of these technologies, such as Dropbox (www.dropbox.com) and Google Cloud (www.google.com/cloud), are free to use. In some cases, there is a maximum of free capacity that can be expanded by purchasing a subscription.

Each user creates an account on these file sharing sites. Personal files may be uploaded or downloaded. Only a user's e-mail address is required to share files or a link to a file or folder with another user. To share with the public, a file is selected and the option to share publicly is clicked. Options include how much access to the file is permitted. Choices are full edit capability that includes ability to delete the file, or read access that allows only being able to read the content of the file.

Caution must be taken to protect the files on these cloud technologies. A publically shared file can be seen by anyone. You may be able to restrict what can be done to the file, but if it is public, anyone can see it. A privately shared file can be seen only by those who have been given access to the file.

4.2   SECTION REVIEW

CHECK YOUR UNDERSTANDING

1. What is the top folder of the file tree called?
2. In which utility is the file search option found in Windows?
3. Which wildcard represents a single unknown character?
4. What should be entered to search for all image files with the .jpg file name extension?
5. How are files sorted by date in Windows Explorer?

IC3 CERTIFICATION PRACTICE

The following question is a sample of the types of questions presented on the IC3 exam.

1. Select the best choice for the statement. A computer icon is a(n):
   A. file containing the full image of the small one displayed.
   B. folder.
   C. small image on a Windows screen that represents a file or folder.
   D. embedded computer.

BUILD YOUR VOCABULARY

As you progress through this course, develop a personal IT glossary. This will help you build your vocabulary and prepare you for a career. Write a definition for each of the following terms and add it to your IT glossary.

file management
root
sorting
wildcards

ORGANIZING FILES AND FOLDERS

Essential Question

What is the most efficient way to copy a file from one folder to another?

Operating systems allow users to create their own folders and subfolders. Organizing personal storage locations helps the user to save and retrieve data. Using Windows File Explorer, the user can easily view and create new folders. When using an external drive, it is a good idea to create the same folder hierarchy that is used on the internal drive. Having the same organizational scheme across devices will provide a more efficient transfer of files folders from one device to another. Locating files on the external drive will be easier, too.

When files or folders are transferred from one device to another, they can be either copied or moved. There is a big difference between copying a file or folder and moving it. There is an even bigger difference when files or folders are copied or moved across devices. This section explains how to copy and move files and folders.

Ermolaev Alexander/Shutterstock.com

LEARNING GOALS

- Explain the difference between copying files and moving files.
- Delete files and folders from a computer system.

TERMS

copy
destination
drag and drop
move
recycle bin
shortcut menu
source

Copying and Moving Files and Folders

Files and folders can be easily moved around any storage drive or between devices. The **source** is the folder where the file or folder being transferred is originally located. The **destination** is the folder to where the file or folder is being transferred. The transfer can be move or copy.

There are often several methods to accomplish a task in Windows. Copying and moving files and folders are examples of where there is more than one way to do something. Particularly useful is the shortcut menu. The **shortcut menu** is a point-of-use menu displayed by right-clicking. Many software programs, including the Windows OS, have various shortcut menus. A shortcut menu is context-sensitive and anticipates common actions that a user may take. *Context-sensitive* means what is displayed in the menu is based on what was right-clicked. For example, to copy a file from one drive to another, right-click on that file and click **Copy** in the shortcut menu, as shown in Figure 4-12.

Selecting Files and Folders

To select, or highlight, a single file or folder, simply single-click it in Windows File Explorer. However, there are a couple of ways to select multiple files or folders. Once a selection is made, whether it consists of a single file or folder or multiple ones, it can be copied, moved, or deleted.

One way to select multiple files or folders is to drag a selection window around them in Windows File Explorer. Click in a blank area above the first file or folder name to select, hold down the left mouse button, and drag to the last file or folder to select. As you drag, a box

Computing Fundamentals
GS5 **3.6.1**

Computing Fundamentals
GS4 **1.2.2**

FYI

Most standard open and save dialog boxes in Windows can be used to perform some file management, such as copying, moving, renaming, and deleting files or folders.

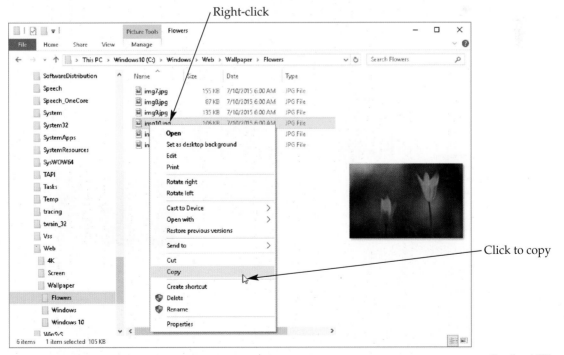

Right-click

Click to copy

Goodheart-Willcox Publisher

Figure 4-12. The shortcut menu can be used to copy or move a file.

called a selection window is drawn. Any files or folders within the selection window will be selected, as shown in Figure 4-13. When the files and folders to select are highlighted by the selection window, release the left mouse button. This method only works to select files or folders in sequence.

Another way to select files or folders in sequence is to use the [Shift] key. This is often easier than trying to drag a selection window. To use this method, click the first file or folder to select it. Then, hold down the [Shift] key, and click the last file or folder in sequence. The first and last file or folder and all files or folders between them are selected.

To select individual files or folders that are not in sequence, the [Ctrl] key must be used. Hold down the [Ctrl] key, and then click the files and folders to select. The files and folders do not need to be in sequence, but they must be in the same parent folder.

Copying Files and Folders

A **copy** of a file or folder is an exact duplicate of the original at the time the copy was made. When a file or folder is copied from one folder to another, there are two versions of the file. One version exists in the source folder and one version exists in the destination folder. To copy a file or folder using the shortcut menu:

1. Right-click on the file in the source folder. This selects the file and displays the shortcut menu.
2. Click **Copy** in the shortcut menu. A copy of the file is placed on the system clipboard.

Files to be selected   Drag a window

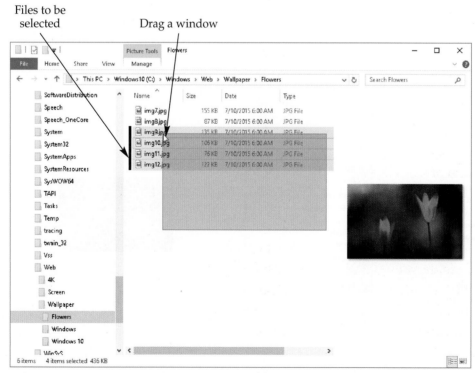

Goodheart-Willcox Publisher

Figure 4-13. Multiple files can be selected by dragging a window around them.

3. Select the destination folder in the navigation pane.

4. Right-click in a blank area of the file list, and click **Paste** in the shortcut menu. A copy of the original file is created from the content on the system clipboard and placed in the destination folder.

On occasion, a file of the same name may be in the destination folder. Windows will prompt the user to choose what to do, as shown in Figure 4-14. There are three options:

- **Copy and Replace**
- **Don't copy**
- **Copy, but keep both files**

The **Copy and Replace** option overwrites the file or folder of the same name in the destination folder. This means the original file in the destination folder will be gone. It is important to be sure that it is appropriate to overwrite the file or folder in the destination folder before choosing this option.

The **Don't copy** option cancels the action. The file or folder remains in the source folder. The file or folder of the same name in the destination folder is also unaffected. Choosing this option provides an opportunity to go to the destination folder, determine whether or not the file or folder with the same name may be deleted, and then restart the copy procedure, if appropriate.

The **Copy, but keep both files** option preserves the file in the destination folder. The copy being created is placed in the destination folder with the original name appended with a number. Choosing this method provides an opportunity to examine both files.

> **FYI**
>
> If the source and destination folders are the same, the copy is automatically renamed to end with – Copy to avoid conflicting file names.

Click to overwrite the file

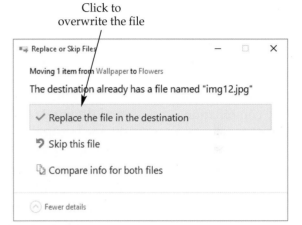

Goodheart-Willcox Publisher

Figure 4-14. If a file of the same name exists in the destination folder, you are asked what to do.

Moving Folders and Files

To **move** a file or folder means to remove it from the source folder and place it in the destination folder. When a file or folder is moved, there is only one version of it. After the action, the file or folder appears only in the destination folder. To move a file or folder using the shortcut menu:

1. Right-click on the file in the source folder. This selects the file and displays the shortcut menu.

2. Click **Cut** in the shortcut menu. The original file is removed from the source folder and placed on the system clipboard.

3. Select the destination folder in the navigation pane.

4. Right-click in a blank area of the file list, and click **Paste** in the shortcut menu. The original file is placed in the destination folder. It also remains on the system clipboard.

The only difference between the procedures for copying and moving using the shortcut menu is the file or folder is *cut* instead of *copied*. Cutting removes the original from the source folder and places it in the

GS5 Key Applications
1.8

GS4 Computing Fundamentals
1.2.2

FYI

The keyboard shortcuts for copy, cut, and paste can be used in many software programs to edit content. The [Ctrl][Z] key combination is standard for reversing an action.

destination folder. In effect, the file or folder is moved to the destination folder. If the destination folder contains a file or folder with the same name as the original, the user is prompted to choose what to do, just as with copying a file.

Other Methods to Copy and Move

There are keyboard shortcuts that can be used to copy and move files and folders. To copy a file or folder, first select the item. Then, press the [Ctrl][C] key combination. This copies the file or folder to the system clipboard. To move a file or folder, select the item, and press the [Ctrl][X] key combination to cut the item. To complete either operation, select the destination folder in the navigation pane, and press the [Ctrl][V] key combination to paste the content of the system clipboard. To undo an operation, press the [Ctrl][Z] key combination. Note that the keys [Z], [X], [C], and [V] are next to each other on the keypad, which makes it easy to complete these common tasks with the left hand.

Another alternate method to copy or move a file or folder is to drag and drop it. **Drag and drop** is a procedure in which an item is selected in one location, moved with the mouse, and placed in another location. To drag, click the item in the source location, hold down the left mouse button, and move the mouse to the destination location. To drop, release the mouse button. To cancel a drag and drop, press the [Esc] key before dropping the item. When drag and drop is used between two drives, the operation is *copy*. When drag and drop is used between locations on the same drive, the operation is *move*. It is important to remember this default behavior.

The default drag and drop behavior can be modified with the [Ctrl] and [Shift] keys. To copy a file or folder, regardless of whether the operation is between drives or on the same drive, hold down the [Ctrl] key, then drag and drop the item into the destination location. To move a file or folder, hold down the [Shift] key, then drag and drop the item into the destination location.

Another way to modify the default drag and drop behavior is to right-click instead of left-click. Right-click on the item to copy or move, hold down the right mouse button, and drop the item in the destination location. When the item is dropped, a shortcut menu is displayed that contains options to copy or move the item or cancel the operation.

HANDS-ON EXAMPLE 4.3.1

COPYING FILES

The ability to copy and move files is a critical skill for a successful computer user. Many users prefer to drag and drop files instead of using the keyboard.

1. Insert your PRINC-OF-IT flash drive into the computer.
2. Launch Windows File Explorer.

HANDS-ON EXAMPLE 4.3.1 (CONTINUED)

3. Applying what you have learned, search the Windows folder for any file with the .jpg file extension.
4. Select any one image file in the file list by left-clicking on it once.
5. Hold down the [Ctrl] key, and click any two other image files to select them. Because the [Ctrl] key is held down, the files do not need to be sequential to the first file.
6. Press the [Ctrl][C] key combination to copy the selected image files.
7. Select the PRINC-OF-IT flash drive in the navigation pane.
8. Applying what you have learned, create a folder on the flash drive named Images.
9. Select the new folder in the navigation pane.
10. Press the [Ctrl][V] key combination to paste the copied image files into the Images folder.
11. Applying what you have learned, search the Windows folder for any file with the .jpg file extension.
12. Click and hold any image file in the file list, drag the file to the Images folder on the flash drive, and drop the file. If the file tree for the flash drive is not expanded, hold the file over the flash drive icon for a couple of seconds until the tree is automatically expanded. Then, drop the file into the Images folder. Because this operation is across drives, not within the same drive, it is a copy operation, not a move operation.

Deleting Files and Folders

In order to effectively manage files, you need to be able to remove files and folders that are no longer useful. In Windows, deleting a file or folder is a simple process. Restoring a deleted file or folder is also a simple process.

Deleting

To delete a file or folder, select it and press the [Delete] key or right-click on it and click **Delete** in the shortcut menu. In Windows 10 and Windows 8, you can also click the **Delete** button in the **Organize** group on the **Home** tab of the ribbon in File Explorer. In Windows 7, you can also click the **Organize** button on the Windows Explorer toolbar and then click **Delete** in the drop-down menu. No matter which method is used, a dialog box appears asking to confirm the deletion. Click the **Yes** button to delete the selected file or folder. Click the **No** button to cancel the operation.

Restoring

When asked to confirm a deletion, the dialog box asks Are you sure you want to move this folder to the Recycle Bin? Windows uses the concept of a recycle bin as an *undelete* function for deleted files and folders. The **recycle bin** is a special folder used as a collection point for all files and folders that have been deleted. It can hold a certain volume of deleted material, and the maximum size can be changed. As long as a deleted file or folder is stored in the recycle bin, it can be restored or undeleted.

FYI

Select a group of files or folders to delete the entire group in one step.

Career Skills

Graphic Artist
Graphic artists are often called on to determine which file format to use for an online production. They must learn to balance the image quality with the file size. Their aim is to produce the finest quality image while ensuring the smallest file size for fast transmission, all without violating the integrity of the original image.

To restore a file or folder, display the content of the recycle bin. This can be done by double-clicking the **Recycle Bin** icon on the desktop or, in Windows 7, by selecting the Recycle Bin branch in the navigation pane in Windows Explorer. With the content of the recycle bin displayed, right-click on the file or folder to restore, and click **Restore** in the shortcut menu. In Windows 10 and Windows 8, you can also select the file or folder, and click the **Restore the selected items** button in the **Restore** group on the **Manage** on-demand tab in the ribbon. In Windows 7, you can also select the file or folder, and click the **Restore this item** button on the toolbar. Once restored, the item is removed from the recycle bin and placed in the location from where it was deleted.

The recycle bin is a folder, and its content takes up storage space. To free this storage space, the recycle bin can be emptied. However, doing so permanently removes the deleted files and folders, and they cannot be restored. To empty the recycle bin, display its contents. Then, in Windows 8, click the **Empty Recycle Bin** button in the **Manage** group on the **Manage** on-demand tab of the ribbon. In Windows 7, click the **Empty Recycle Bin** button on the toolbar. A message appears asking to confirm removing the items from the recycle bin. Click the **Yes** button to remove the items or the **No** button to cancel the operation.

4.3 SECTION REVIEW

CHECK YOUR UNDERSTANDING

1. The _____ is a point-of-use menu displayed by right-clicking.
2. How do you select a file or folder in Windows Explorer?
3. What is the difference between copying a file and moving it?
4. What is the key combination for cutting a file instead of copying it?
5. What is the location in Windows from where a deleted file can be restored?

IC3 CERTIFICATION PRACTICE

The following question is a sample of the types of questions presented on the IC3 exam.
1. Perform this simulation.
   Locate the file named Lighthouse.jpg in the C:\Libraries\Pictures\Sample Pictures folder, and move it to the folder C:\Libraries\Pictures\Sample Pictures\Flowers.

BUILD YOUR VOCABULARY

As you progress through this course, develop a personal IT glossary. This will help you build your vocabulary and prepare you for a career. Write a definition for each of the following terms and add it to your IT glossary.

copy
destination
drag and drop
move

recycle bin
shortcut menu
source

FILE UTILITIES

Steve Cukrov/Shutterstock.com

Windows Explorer is an example of a file utility. File utilities perform common functions such as backing up and restoring files as well as displaying and editing a file's properties. These programs are called utilities because they help the user perform useful, repetitive tasks. One of the most important file-management tasks is to back up files in the event that the original files are lost, deleted, or corrupted. Utilities also assist in determining the most recent version of a file.

Sending large files as attachments to an e-mail message or copying large files to a flash drive may be a problem. Large files take more time to copy or move through the e-mail network. A file utility that can make files smaller is an advantage here. Utility programs can be accessed through the Control Panel window and through the Accessories folder in the **Apps** or **Start** menu.

Essential Question

How would society be impacted if social media websites did not back up their data?

TERMS

backup
extracting
file attribute
file compression
file properties
help
system image

LEARNING GOALS

- Use the Windows help system.
- Explain the properties associated with a file.
- Describe the process of backing up files and folders.
- Discuss file compression methods.

Windows Help

Help is a resource to assist the user in learning how to use a feature of the program. It is a knowledge database of topics related to the software. Help is provided by almost all software programs, including the Windows operating system.

The help feature for Windows File Explorer can be launched by clicking the **Help** button (question mark) in the upper-right corner of the window. The **Windows Help and Support** dialog box is displayed. Because help was accessed from within Windows File Explorer, the initial content displayed is related to file management. However, the **Windows Help and Support** dialog box is the interface for the entire Windows help feature.

At the top of the **Windows Help and Support** dialog box is a search box. Enter a word or phrase related to the topic you wish to view, and click the **Search** button (magnifying glass). A list of related topics is displayed. The name of each topic is a hyperlink. Clicking the hyperlink displays the full article. For example, if the phrase folder management is entered in the search box, a list of topics related to managing files, folders, and other items is displayed.

Windows will try to rank topics in an order most likely to match the search phrase, but do not assume the first topic will contain the information you seek. Carefully read the name of each topic. Evaluate how closely the words in the title match the search phrase. Once you have determined which topic is most likely to contain the information you seek, click the hyperlink. Then, scan the article to see if it appears to contain the information. If not, click the **Back** button and evaluate other topics. Otherwise, read the details of the article.

FYI

The help feature for Windows can also be accessed through the **Apps** or **Start** menu. When accessed in this way, the initial topics are for Windows in general.

File Properties

The **file properties** are all information about the file, but not the data contained within the file. Properties include, among other things, the creation date, date of the last save, current permission setting, and whether or not it is hidden. The file properties are displayed in the **Properties** dialog box. To open this dialog box, right-click on a file, and then click **Properties** in the shortcut menu.

In most cases, there are three tabs in the **Properties** dialog box, as shown in Figure 4-15: **General**, **Security**, and **Details**. In Windows 7, there is usually a fourth tab named **Previous Versions**. In some cases, depending on the file type and system configuration, there may be more tabs. Under each tab are options and settings that may be displayed or edited.

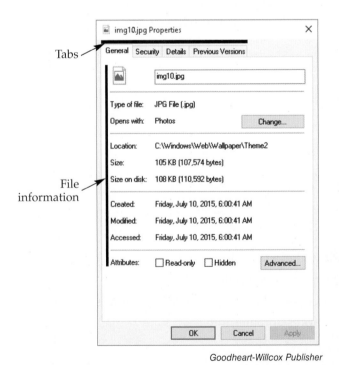

Tabs

File information

Goodheart-Willcox Publisher

Figure 4-15. The **Properties** dialog box contains information about the file.

General Tab

The **General** tab of the **Properties** dialog box lists information such as the file type, the size of the data contained and the size of the file on the disk, and the path to the folder where the file is located. The file name is displayed in a text box at the top of the tab and may be renamed there. Also listed are three dates and times.

- Created is the date and time when the file was created.
- Modified is the date and time when the file was last changed.
- Accessed is the date and time when the file was last opened, but not saved.

The software program associated with the file type is indicated in the **Opens with:** area. This is the software that will be launched when the file icon is double-clicked in Windows File Explorer. To change the associated software, click the **Change...** button. In the **Open with** dialog box that is displayed, a different software program can be selected. The association is applied to all files of the file type.

A **file attribute** is a characteristic of a file about the display, archiving, and save status of files. There are two file attributes that can be set on the **General** tab:

- read-only
- hidden

Read-only permits no editing, saving, or deleting. Check the **Read-only** check box to guard against accidental overwriting. Users may view it, but may not overwrite it. Hidden keeps the file from being listed in

bikeriderlondon/Shutterstock.com

Good file management is a key to successful computing.

Windows File Explorer. Many system files have the **Hidden** check box checked. Clicking the **Advanced** button opens a dialog box in which other settings regarding the save process for a file can be made.

Security Tab

The **Security** tab of the **Properties** dialog box permits the author to modify the permissions for sharing a file with other users on a network. Windows lets users form a workgroup when PCs are connected to a network. In addition, multiple users on a Windows PC may share files with one another. Some users only require need-to-know access to a file's contents. Permissions allow restricted access to a file. Permissions are an extension of the **Read-only** attribute available on the **General** tab.

For example, people may be working on developing a certain project as a group. Instead of carrying the common files around on a flash drive, Windows allows users in a group to see each other's files on their own computers. This means they can allow other users to modify the file or simply read it. One user may create a file and give permission to other users to view the file content, but not change it. For example, it may be a final version that has been adopted in some manner and no one should be able to change it unless authorized. These permissions are settings in the file properties.

Permissions are important to an organization for several reasons. The information of a company must be secured. Workers who need to read a document may not be authorized to make changes to it. In addition, organizations can monitor who has attempted to access files for which they have no permission via log files. This monitoring can identify a potential security threat to the information. Permissions protect a document from unauthorized modifications or scrutiny.

Details Tab

The **Details** tab of the **Properties** dialog box provides extra data about the creation of the file and information related to authorship. On this tab, the file can be assigned a title and subject, rated, tags added, and comments added. It is here that the author's name may be entered. The tab also summarizes all of the selections on the first two tabs. This tab is context-sensitive and differs by file format.

Previous Versions Tab

The **Previous Versions** tab of the **Properties** dialog box lists when the file was backed up and supports restoring an earlier version of the file. This is very helpful if changes have been made and the file saved, thereby overwriting the earlier version. If the user decides not to make those changes, an earlier version of the file can be retrieved from the backup files. This function applies only to files that have been backed up with Windows Backup and Restore, which is discussed later.

The information on this tab also helps when a program crashes, or unexpectedly stops working. When Windows crashes, it is expected to try

Computing Fundamentals
GS5 **3.6.2, 3.10**

Computing Fundamentals
GS4 **1.3.6**

STEM

Engineering
Engineering applies scientific theory to the design of materials for technological use. There are many branches of engineering, but the main branches are chemical engineering, civil engineering, electrical engineering, and mechanical engineering. Each branch has subdisciplines, which each have specialties. For example, a subdiscipline of electrical engineering is software engineering. This area specializes in creating software, from designing the functionality to writing the code.

to restore the user's work from previous saved versions. The information on this tab provides details to step through the restore operation.

HANDS-ON EXAMPLE 4.4.1

FILE ASSOCIATION

By default, in Windows the JPG file type is associated with an image viewer, such as Photos or Windows Photo Viewer. However, it may be more efficient to have the image file opened in an editor, such as Microsoft Paint.

1. Launch Windows File Explorer.
2. Applying what you have learned, search the Windows folder for any file with the .jpg file extension.
3. Right-click on any image file, and click **Properties** in the shortcut menu.
4. Click the **General** tab in the dialog box.
5. Look at the program listed in the **Opens with:** area. The default program is Windows Photo Viewer.
6. Click the **Change...** button. In Windows 10 and Windows 8, click the **More apps** or **More Options** link in the dialog box, and then the **Look for another app on this PC** link. The **Open with** dialog box is displayed, as shown.

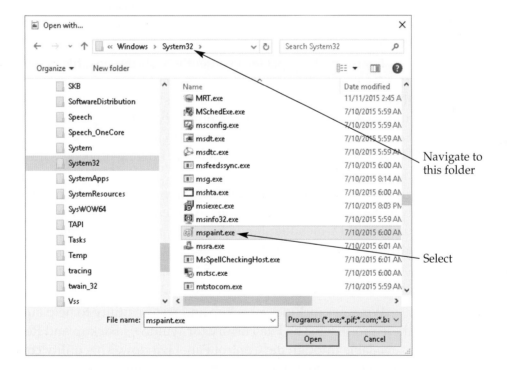

7. Navigate to the Windows\System32 folder, and select the mspaint.exe file. Click the **Open** button. The association for the JPG file type is changed to Microsoft Paint. The **Properties** dialog box is updated to reflect this.
8. Click the **OK** button to close the **Properties** dialog box.
9. Double-click on any JPG file in Windows File Explorer. Microsoft Paint is launched, and the image file is loaded into Paint.

GS5
Computing Fundamentals
4.1

File Backups

A **backup** is a copy of a file that can be safely retrieved if anything unfortunate happens to the most recent version of the file. Mishaps are common in file management. Files can be accidentally deleted, overwritten, modified, or corrupted. A file becomes corrupted when something happens to affect the storage location of the file. Users create backups to ensure that all is not lost if something happens to a file.

Saving Copies of Files

GS4
Computing Fundamentals
4.4.1, 4.4.2, 4.4.3

The simplest way to back up a file is to save it on a different storage device. If the user is saving data files on a course flash drive, the files should also be saved on another flash drive, a server, or in the cloud. An advantage of using the cloud is that the file is offsite. The cloud service being used also has backup measures to protect the file. When creating a backup on a different device, the user must remember where the copy is and to keep it current.

Saving Versions of Files

GS4
Computing Fundamentals
4.4.4

Another backup scheme is to save versions of the file. This method allows restoring one of many earlier states of a file, thus reversing changes. Most software programs offer a **Save As** function for saving a file under a different name. This function can be used to easily create versions.

For example, suppose a student is working on a file named TermPaper.docx. It is easy to save a newer version as TermPaperV1.docx, then TermPaperV2.docx, and so on. The student edits the newest version and saves it as the next version number after enough changes have been made that he or she wants to keep intact. After the final version is complete and the earlier versions are no longer needed, they may be deleted to clean up the folder.

When working on a team, it is important to establish the naming convention for creating versions. All members of the team must understand which file should be in use at any given time. The read-only attribute is useful in locking all files that should not be edited.

> ## FYI
>
> Always back up a file before a significant amount of work is to be done and after that work has been completed.

Windows Backup and Restore

Windows includes a backup and restore utility to help automate these processes. The File History (or Windows Backup and Restore) utility is available through the Control Panel window. This utility compresses all data files and saves them to another disk volume. A *disk volume* acts like a separate physical drive, but is really contained on the same drive. The utility prompts the user through restoring one of the files to the disk. This utility can also be used to create a system image, as shown in Figure 4-16.

A **system image** is a backup that is an exact duplicate of all data on the drive, including the drives required for Windows to run, your system settings, programs, and document files. A system image allows you to

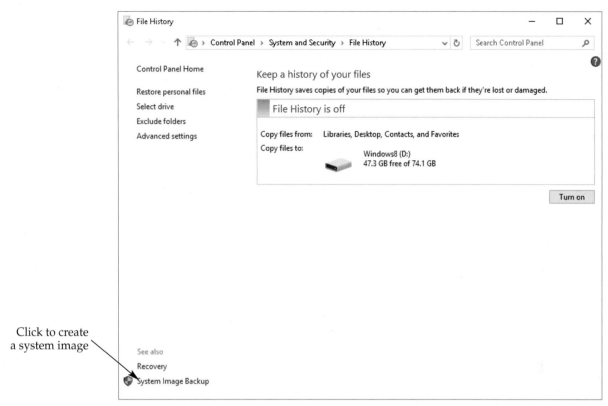

Figure 4-16. The Windows Backup and Restore utility is used to back up files and create a system image.

completely restore all data to a previous point that was working. This is usually done to correct a serious problem that causes the system to stop working.

There are many third-party backup utilities available. Some are freeware and some are for-purchase software. Most backup programs can be scheduled to automatically run at periodic intervals established by the user. It is common to set a backup utility to run overnight when there is no user activity on the system.

File Compression

The amount of space a file takes up on the disk is not as great of a concern today as it was when disk drives were very limited in size. However, when sharing files, file size is a concern. Large files take longer to move across a network than small files. Many e-mail services limit the size of a file that can be attached to a message. Large files take up more space on an external drive and may quickly fill up the device. The solution is file compression. **File compression** is a process of compacting the data in a file or group of files to reduce the overall size.

When a file is created by a software program, it is generally formatted so that reloading the file is quick and efficient. As a result, the file may be larger than it needs to be. Some file-compression technologies eliminate repeated patterns in a file to reduce the overall size. There are other steps to take to compress a file, but the result is the same. The original content of the file is preserved, but the file is smaller.

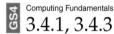
Computing Fundamentals
GS5 3.6.5, 5.1.4

Computing Fundamentals
GS4 3.4.1, 3.4.3

FYI

Some compressed file types, such as JPG, may be "lossy," which means some of the original bits may be removed during compression.

FYI

The ZIP file type is just one of many for compressing files and folders. Other common file types include 7Z, RAR, SIT, and TAR.

FYI

Some software can open a file directly from within a compressed file without the need to extract the file.

Many image file types are automatically compressed. The JPG or JPEG file type is a compressed image file. Trying to compress this file type or any of the other compressed file types will not yield much reduction in file size.

Compress Files Using Windows File Explorer

Windows File Explorer provides a utility that compresses one file or a group of files at the same time. To do this, first select the file, group of files, or a folder. Next, right-click on the selection, and click **Send to>Compressed (zipped) folder** in the shortcut menu. All of the files selected are compressed into a single file, which in Windows is considered a folder. The default name of the ZIP file is the same name as the first file or folder selected based on the current sort. The ZIP file is placed in the same location as the original selection. The original selection is unaltered.

Extract Files Using Windows File Explorer

Extracting is what Windows calls the process of taking a file out of a ZIP file. Other software may call this process *unzipping*, *unpacking*, or *unstuffing*. Because the files have been compressed, the original software for the file association no longer recognizes the file as a type it can read. The file must be uncompressed.

Double-click on a ZIP file to begin the extraction process. The content of the file is displayed in Windows File Explorer, as shown in Figure 4-17. Notice the **Extract all** button on the ribbon or toolbar. Clicking this button will copy all files and folders in the ZIP file to their uncompressed formats. The user specifies the location to where the files will be extracted. Files and folders can also be extracted using the drag-and-drop file management method.

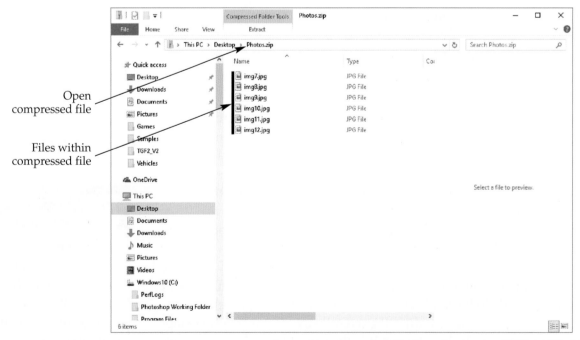

Goodheart-Willcox Publisher

Figure 4-17. Double-clicking on a ZIP file displays its contents in Windows File Explorer.

HANDS-ON EXAMPLE 4.4.2

COMPRESSING FILES

It is a common practice to compress multiple files into a single ZIP file in order to e-mail them. This not only reduces the overall size, it allows the recipient to save a single ZIP file from the e-mail instead of having to save multiple files.

1. Launch Windows File Explorer.
2. Applying what you have learned, search the Windows folder for any file with the .jpg file extension.
3. Applying what you have learned, select three or four image files.
4. Right-click on the selection, and click **Send to**>**Compressed (zipped)** folder in the shortcut menu. Because Windows cannot create a ZIP file in the search results, a message appears asking if you would like to create the ZIP file on the desktop. Click the **Yes** button.
5. Display the Windows desktop. The easiest way to do this is to use the [Alt][Tab] key combination to navigate through open windows. When the desktop is displayed, release the [Alt] key.
6. Locate the new ZIP file on the desktop. The icon for the file looks like a folder with a zipper on it. The name of the ZIP file will be the same as the first file you selected in the file list.
7. Double-click the ZIP file to display its contents in Windows File Explorer. Notice that the image files you selected are contained in the ZIP file.

4.4 | SECTION REVIEW

 CHECK YOUR UNDERSTANDING

1. How is help launched for Windows Explorer?
2. What are file properties?
3. Read-only and hidden are examples of file _____.
4. List three ways to back up your work.
5. How do you compress a group of files selected in Windows Explorer?

IC3 CERTIFICATION PRACTICE

The following question is a sample of the types of questions presented on the IC3 exam.

1. Perform this simulation.
   Select these files and compress them into a zipped folder: Paper.docx, Presentation.pptx, and Results.xlsx.

BUILD YOUR VOCABULARY

As you progress through this course, develop a personal IT glossary. This will help you build your vocabulary and prepare you for a career. Write a definition for each of the following terms and add it to your IT glossary.

backup   file properties
extracting   help
file attribute   system image
file compression

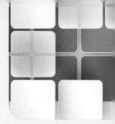

4 REVIEW AND ASSESSMENT

Chapter Summary

Section 4.1
File and Folder Names

- The file name is a label that identifies a unique file on a computer system. A folder is a container in which files are stored.
- Windows File Explorer is a file-management utility with a graphical user interface that can be used to find anything in the computer's storage areas. The list of available drives and folders shown in the navigation pane is a file tree.

Section 4.2
Locating Files and Folders

- Good file management involves organizing files in logical locations. The ability to locate files is a key skill in good computer use.
- Files and folders can be arranged by a certain criterion, such as alphabetically, by date, or by size. This can help locate a file or folder.
- Files can be shared online, either publically or privately. When shared publically, anyone can view the file. A privately shared file can be seen only by those given access to it.

Section 4.3
Organizing Files and Folders

- Files and folders can be easily copied or moved about any storage drive or between devices. The source is the original location, while the destination is the new location.
- Deleting files and folders is an important part of good file management. A deleted file or folder can be restored if needed.

Section 4.4
File Utilities

- Help is a resource to assist the user in learning how to use a feature of the program. Help is provided by almost all software programs, including the Windows operating system.
- The file properties are all information about the file, but not the data contained within the file. The file properties are displayed in the **Properties** dialog box.
- A backup is a copy of a file that can be safely retrieved if anything unfortunate happens to the most recent version of the file. A backup can be created on a different device or versions of the file can be created.
- File compression is a process of compacting the data in a file or group of files to reduce the overall size. File compression can be done to save disk space or to reduce the file size for e-mail transmission.

Now that you have finished this chapter, see what you know about information technology by scanning the QR code to take the chapter posttest. If you do not have a smartphone, visit www.g-wlearning.com.

Chapter 4 Test

Multiple Choice
Select the best response.

1. Using capital letters to show where new words start in a file name is called _____.
   A. CamelCase
   B. title case
   C. uppercase
   D. lowercase

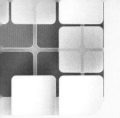
2. Which of the following is not a good file-management practice?
   A. Create descriptive names for folders and files.
   B. Store all of the data files at the top level of the drive to make them easier to find.
   C. Remove folders and files when they are no longer needed.
   D. Make enough subfolders so that the files in any one folder are readily visible.

3. What are used in the search box to represent unknown characters?
   A. digits
   B. characters
   C. blanks
   D. wildcards

4. Which key combination is used to copy a file?
   A. [Ctrl][X]
   B. [Ctrl][C]
   C. [Ctrl][V]
   D. [Ctrl][Z]

5. Where are deleted files and folders stored in Windows?
   A. In the recycle bin.
   B. In the root folder of the drive.
   C. In the original folder.
   D. They are not retained.

Completion

Complete the following sentences with the correct word(s).

6. The three parts of a file path in Windows are the _____.

7. A(n) _____ is a pattern that is followed whenever a file name is created.

8. The asterisk (*) and question mark (?) are _____ to use in names when searching for files or folders.

9. _____ is a procedure in which an item is selected in one location, moved with the mouse, and placed in another location.

10. File properties are displayed in the _____ dialog box.

Matching

Match the correct term with its definition.

A. Subfolder
B. Rename
C. Sort
D. Copy
E. Backup

11. Make copies of files in case of loss.

12. Put a file in a new location while keeping the original file in its place.

13. Nested within the parent folder.

14. Arrange files based on their properties.

15. Single-click twice on the file or folder in the file list.

Application and Extension of Knowledge

1. You and your team must create a display of these ecosystems: desert, rainforest, deciduous forest, tundra, and marine. The display will include images of the ecosystems and the animals, trees, and flowers found in them. There will also be documents for annual rainfall, manufacturing, human habitation, and traffic. Plan a folder structure so that each team member can locate the proper place to store relevant files. Create a naming convention that will make it clear what each file contains.

2. Using the naming convention created in #1, set up the folder structure. Where will the project folder be located? Will each team member have access to this folder?

3. Using Windows Explorer, search the Windows folder and all of its subfolders for any file with the .jpg file name extension. How many files are located? Sort the files by date, from newest to oldest. Copy the newest file to your flash drive.

4. Display the **Properties** dialog box for the image file copied to your flash drive in #3. What is the size of the file? When was the file created? Is the file a read-only file? Display the **Details** tab in the dialog box. Examine the information provided on this tab, and write one paragraph summarizing what is provided.

5. Write one paragraph that summarizes what a system image is, how it is created, and why it is important to create a system image.

Online Activities

Complete the following activities, which will help you learn, practice, and expand your knowledge and skills.

Certification Practice. Complete the certification practice test for this chapter.

Vocabulary. Practice vocabulary for this chapter using the e-flash cards, matching activity, and vocabulary game until you are able to recognize their meanings.

Communication Skills

College and Career Readiness

Speaking. All careers require that individuals be able to participate and contribute to one-on-one discussions. Developing intrapersonal communication skills is one way to achieve career opportunities. As your instructor lectures on this chapter, contribute thoughtful comments when participation is invited.

Listening. Hearing is a physical process. Listening combines hearing with evaluation. Effective leaders learn how to listen to their team members. Listen to your instructor as a lesson is presented. Analyze the effectiveness of the presentation. Listen carefully and take notes about the main points. Then organize the key information that you heard.

Writing. Consider entering a command using either the mouse or keyboard shortcuts, such as copying and pasting a file. Which method do you think is the most efficient? Would your answer change if you had to use the command many times in a short span? Write several paragraphs explaining which method you believe is most efficient and why.

Internet Research

IT Careers. Using various Internet resources, research the current job opportunities and general qualifications for an IT career that interests you. Use the career clusters as a starting point. Write a one-page report about job prospects that evaluates your findings. Include data from your research in the report. Use correct grammar, punctuation, spelling, and terminology to write and edit the document.

Teamwork

Work with your team to develop a list of questions that could be used to gather information about what electronics are purchased or used by young adults. Next, create a focus group for the research. Appoint a mediator who will ask the questions and a recorder who will record the answers. As a team, interpret the results of the focus group.

Portfolio Development

College and Career Readiness

Digital File Formats. A portfolio will contain documents you created electronically as well as documents that you have in hard copy format that will be scanned. It will be necessary to decide file formats to use for both types of documents. Before you begin, consider the technology that you might use for creating and scanning documents. You will need access to desktop publishing software, scanners, cameras, and other digital equipment or software.

For documents that you create, consider using the default format to save the files. For example, you could save letters and essays created in Microsoft Word in DOCx format. You could save worksheets created in Microsoft Excel in XLSx format. If your presentation will include graphics or video, confirm the file formats that are necessary for each item. Use the appropriate formats as you create the documents.

Hard copy items will need to be converted to digital format. Portable document format, or PDF, is a good choice for scanned items, such as awards and certificates.

Another option is to save all documents as PDF files. Keep in mind that the person reviewing your digital portfolio will need programs that open these formats to view your files. Having all of the files in the same format can make viewing them easier for others who need to review your portfolio.

1. Establish the types of technology that are available for you to create a digital portfolio. Will you have access to cameras or studios? Do you have the level of skill needed to create videos?

2. Decide the type of presentation you will use. Research what will be needed to create the final portfolio product.

CTSOs

Teamwork. Some competitive events for CTSOs have a teamwork component. If it is a team event, it is important that the competing team prepares to operate as a cohesive unit. To prepare for teamwork activities, complete the following activities.

1. Review the rules to confirm whether questions will be asked or if the team will need to defend a case or situation.

2. Practice performing as a team by completing the team activities at the end of each chapter in this text. This will help members learn how to interact with each other and participate effectively.

3. Locate a rubric or scoring sheet for the event on your organization's website to see how the team will be judged.

4. Confirm whether visual aids may be used in the presentation and the amount of setup time permitted.

5. Make notes on index cards about important points to remember. Team members should exchange note cards so that each evaluates the other person's notes. Use these notes to study. You may also be able to use these notes during the event.

6. Assign each team member a role for the presentation. Practice performing as a team. Each team member should introduce himself or herself, review the case, make suggestions for the case, and conclude with a summary.

7. Ask your instructor to play the role of competition judge as your team reviews the case. After the presentation is complete, ask for feedback from your instructor. You may also consider having a student audience listen and give feedback.

5

PURCHASING, MAINTAINING, AND TROUBLESHOOTING

Purchasing the correct type of computer is important in matching the computer to the goals of the technology. There are vast differences between computers. This means that the user has to assess his or her needs before purchasing a new system. Once the correct computer is purchased, it will be a wonderful tool as long as everything is working. Preventive maintenance on a computer system is just as important to keeping everything running as it is for an automobile. There are actions the user can take to minimize possible problems.

More software vendors than ever before are developing programs and more choices exist for hardware. Developers work very hard to make the installation an easy, problem-free experience. Yet, each time a new software program is installed or a new hardware device is attached, there is an opportunity for things to go awry. In addition, previously working parts may fail and cause problems. Fortunately, there are many avenues of help for resolving these problems. Developing troubleshooting skills means that each mishap can be dealt with in a direct manner. This chapter outlines steps to take when purchasing a system and when resolving technical problems.

IC3 CERTIFICATION OBJECTIVES

GS5

Computing Fundamentals

Domain 1.0 Mobile devices
  Objective 1.2 Be familiar with cellular-enabled tablets
Domain 3.0 Computer software architecture
  Objective 3.12 Know how to install, uninstall, update, repair software
  Objective 3.13 Troubleshooting
Domain 4.0 Backup and restore
  Objective 4.2 Know how to back up and restore
  Objective 4.3 Know how to complete a full system restore on a personal device

GS4

Computing Fundamentals

Domain 3.0 Computer software and concepts
  Objective 3.4 Software tools
Domain 4.0 Troubleshooting
  Objective 4.1 Software
  Objective 4.2 Hardware
  Objective 4.3 Devices and peripherals

Reading Prep. Before reading the chapter, skim the photos and their captions. As you read, determine how these concepts contribute to the ideas presented in the text.

College and Career Readiness

PURCHASING A SYSTEM

How can conducting a needs assessment save you money when purchasing a computer?

Many categories of computers are available to the individual including desktops, notebooks, tablets, and even smartphones. Many choices exist within each category, and computer technology is always changing. One of the most important tasks before making a new purchase is to research the recent additions to the market.

In addition to finding the availability of new choices, reviews by the early adopters of the new technology should be read. These reviews can show what people who are actually using the technology think about it. Topics for research include initial purchase cost; suitability of the system to a user's needs, compatibility with current systems, amount of time required to master the new devices, and follow-on costs. A user must evaluate the purpose for the purchase and compare this assessment with time and budget constraints.

dotshock/Shutterstock.com

LEARNING GOALS

After completing this section, you will be able to:
- Identify basic computer models.
- Perform a needs assessment for a computer system.
- Describe recommended standard computer configurations.

TERMS

all-in-one computer
computer model
needs assessment

Computer Models

The **computer model** is the form the computer takes. As discussed in Chapter 2, the three basic models of personal computers are desktops, laptops, and mobile devices. Within the laptop type, there are laptops, notebooks, netbooks, subnotebooks, ultrabooks, and convertibles. Mobile devices include tablets, mini tablets, phablets, and smartphones. When selecting a computer, the choices can be generalized between desktops, laptops, and tablets.

FYI

The model of computer is often the first decision made when purchasing a computer.

Desktop

Desktop computers are the most common type of computer found in office settings. In the home, desktops can be used as media centers or gaming machines in addition to typical computer uses. In general, you will get more computer for the money with a desktop model over other types of computers. The tradeoff is the larger size and lack of portability.

The monitor, keyboard, and mouse easily fit on most desks. The computer box often sits on the floor under or beside the desk. When combined with a comfortable chair and all-around ergonomic environment, desktop computers are a good choice for prolonged, stationary work.

A typical desktop computer setup may consist of:
- medium- or high-speed processor;
- high-powered video card;
- 4 GB to 6 GB of RAM;
- 500 GB to 2 TB hard drive;
- 24-inch flat-screen monitor; and
- DVD-ROM drive.

This configuration usually can be purchased for around $600 for the essentials to about $1,500 for the most powerful models. Systems designed specifically for gaming or high-end graphics work may cost between $2,000 and $3,000.

Laptop

Many laptops can run all of the software necessary to be used as a primary home or office computer. Their portability makes them very desirable, as shown in Figure 5-1. There is a wide range of laptops. All laptops resemble each other, but vary in size, power, storage, weight, and battery life.

The laptop or notebook model, which is generally the largest, may contain:
- high-speed processor;
- graphics processor separate from the CPU;
- 8 GB of RAM;
- 750 GB hard drive;

Flashon Studio/Shutterstock.com

Figure 5-1. One of the biggest advantages of laptop computers is portability. They can be used anywhere, unlike a desktop computer, which must be plugged into an electrical outlet.

- 17-inch monitor; and
- DVD drive.

This setup can run many high-end video games and video-editing software as well as standard office applications. The cost is usually around $1,000 to $2,000, but may be as much as $5,000 for a high-end gaming machine.

A smaller laptop model, such as an ultrabook, generally weighs less than four pounds and may contain:

- low-power processor;
- long-life battery;
- 4 GB of RAM;
- 13-inch screen; and
- solid-state hard drive.

It can be used to run office software and play music, but usually does not have an internal DVD drive. The cost of an ultrabook varies from around $1,000 to about $2,500.

Tablet

Computing Fundamentals
1.2.1

Tablets are mobile devices. They come in many sizes, but the most notable characteristic of a tablet is its compact size and lack of a mouse and keyboard. All data entry and pointing are performed via a touch screen. The high-powered CPU and communication capability of a tablet make it possible to watch videos, play basic games, and browse the Internet.

A 10-inch model tablet may contain:

- dual or quad core 800MHz to 2 GHz processors;
- 3 GB of RAM;
- proprietary operating systems; and
- proprietary software.

The weight of a 10-inch tablet is about 1.5 pounds. The cost generally ranges from $300 to $500.

The 7-inch model tablet is best used for reading e-books, browsing the Internet, and playing basic games. This model weighs less than one pound and costs around $200.

Needs Assessment

How the computer system is going to be used determines the requirements for the computer system. A **needs assessment** is a process of examining the current condition or state and determining how it differs from the desired condition or state. In terms of purchasing a new computer, look at how the current computer does not meet the user's needs. The needs of the user are the most important in the selection of a computer system. It may very well be that the needs result in a combination of the examples given here. Care must be taken to study the user's needs before purchase.

Green Tech

Electronic Waste
Electronics should be properly disposed of, not just placed in the trash. Before discarding electronic waste, research how the item should be properly disposed. Sometimes, charities and community groups that are in need of electronics can refurbish and use older equipment. However, if the equipment is beyond repair, it should be recycled.

Most productivity software, such as word processing, spreadsheet development, or presentation creation, has low computer requirements, as shown in Figure 5-2. These computer systems will also support Internet use and playing basic games. These devices may be a desktop or laptop model, depending on the mobility requirement of the user.

Multimedia, gaming, desktop publishing, and video-editing applications have higher requirements, as shown in Figure 5-3. Working with these software packages and files puts more demand on processing resources. Both desktop and laptop computers can be configured to

Processor Speed	All current processors are more than capable of running most productivity software. High-end quad-core processors are not required.
Monitor	One large monitor or a dual-monitor setup will aid productivity, especially for wide spreadsheets.
Memory Size	Most productivity software does not have a high RAM requirement. However, more RAM usually provides better response in loading and saving of files. If spreadsheet files have many calculations, more RAM will speed up that process.
Disk Size	The location of file storage is the consideration. If files are to be saved on the computer, a large disk drive will speed up loading, saving, and access times. If they are to be saved to the cloud or on a network computer, a large disk drive is not required.
Optical Drive	In most cases, a basic CD-ROM drive will be sufficient. However, consider if the productivity software is available on CD or DVD. A DVD-ROM drive may be required to install the software. For saving backups or to remove files for storage, a rewritable drive is a good choice. A Blu-ray player is needed to watch HD movies.
Keyboard	A physical keyboard is recommended over a virtual keyboard. The better choice for high-volume data entry is an ergonomic keyboard.
Pointing Device	A mouse is preferred over a touchpad for applications that involve frequent cursor movement or for precision placement. For applications that require frequent scrolling, such as word processing, a mouse with a wheel is recommended.
Operating System	A 32-bit system will suffice. Most productivity software applications will not make use of the advantages offered by a 64-bit system.
Software	Most productivity software is available for any of the operating systems found on desktop and laptop computers. However, the software is not cross-platform. If changing operating systems, and in many cases different versions of the same operating system, new software may need to be purchased. Also consult the system requirements of the software to ensure the computer system will run the software.
Internet	Most Internet browsers can run on any computer system. Most browsers are free, and many can carry over settings to the new system. However, if the system is to be equipped with a wireless card, consider the card's performance. Transmission speeds are due, in part, to the Internet service provider (ISP), but getting the proper router for the system is a consideration.
Printers	Depending on the amount of printing that is required, a low- to high-end printer is required. The cost of the printer is rarely a primary consideration. The primary consideration is usually how much it costs to replace the ink or toner cartridges. Print quality and speed are also considerations.

Goodheart-Willcox Publisher

Figure 5-2. For most productivity software, only a basic computer system is needed.

Processor Speed	A dual-core processor with a high speed rating is required. A quad-core processor is often recommended, especially for high-end gaming and graphics applications.
Monitor	Large dual-monitor setups are common in the graphics and video industries. A dual-monitor setup facilitates a better working environment for detail work. Many gaming applications support dual monitors, but most gaming systems have a single large, widescreen monitor with a low dot pitch.
Memory Size	It is recommended to get as much RAM as can be installed. The files used in high-end graphics and video work can be very large. The more RAM a system has, the better it will be able to handle large files and computation-intensive applications. Fortunately, RAM is relatively inexpensive.
Disk Size	In many high-end graphics and video-editing applications, the files are stored on the local hard disk drive or on a network drive while at work. If files are to be stored on the local drive, a large hard disk drive is needed. Additionally, high-end graphics and video-editing applications need a large temporary file on the local drive, called the swap file or page file. A large hard drive is needed for this.
Optical Drive	Most high-end games are provided on DVD, if not downloaded from the Internet. A DVD-ROM drive is required for installation from a disc. A DVD-ROM drive also allows the system to be used as a media center for watching movies on disc.
Keyboard	Most users of high-end graphics and video-editing software make extensive use of keyboard shortcuts. A physical keyboard is recommended. As usually only one hand is on the keyboard while the other is on the pointing device, an ergonomic keyboard is not needed, but can be used if preferred.
Pointing Device	A trackball pointing device is often the choice for many users of video-editing software. Users of high-end graphics software often prefer a stylus or a trackball over a mouse, but many use a standard mouse. Systems for gaming may require a joystick or other specialized input device.
Operating System	A 64-bit operating system is recommended. The advantage of a 64-bit system is it has improved data throughput when compared to a 32-bit system. Additionally, most high-end software has a 64-bit version written to specifically take advantage of a 64-bit operating system. In order to run a 64-bit OS, the CPU must be a 64-bit processor.
Software	Most popular multimedia development software is expensive and not cross platform. If you are changing manufacturers, you may need to purchase new development software to use on the new computer.
Internet	Transmission of large files, such as those created by high-end graphics software, across the Internet through e-mail or file transfer protocol (FTP) require higher transfer speeds than smaller files, such as created by office suite software. Additionally, online gaming requires high-speed Internet access. For these reasons the wireless card or Ethernet setup is a concern. Transmission speeds are in part due to the Internet service provider (ISP), but getting the proper router for the system is a consideration.
Printer	Depending on the specific application, a printer may not be required. Gaming and video-editing applications are rarely used to create printouts. Users of high-end graphics software will print often, but their machines are often connected to a network printer. If a printer is required for the local machine, graphics output generally dictates the printer be a high-quality color printer.

Goodheart-Willcox Publisher

Figure 5-3. A higher-end system is needed for gaming, desktop publishing and video editing.

handle these heavy loads. The requirement for mobility determines that choice. For casual e-book reading, high portability, light Internet browsing, and causal gaming, a low-end, small tablet may suffice.

Recommended Standard Configurations

Cost goes up with capability. It is always a balancing act between the cost and the capability of the system. The following are some recommendations for average use.

Desktop models with medium speed, 1 TB of storage, and a 24-inch monitor can be purchased for around $600. The advantage of this configuration is the suitability to an office or home environment. Generally, this system will be more powerful than a laptop or tablet purchased for the same amount of money.

Laptops with a 15-inch screen and 500 GB of storage can be purchased from $500 to $700. The advantage of a laptop is its portability. The "all in one" aspect of a laptop also omits the need for a standard office setup. An **all-in-one computer** is one in which all of the hardware, from input devices to processor and display, are contained in a single unit. Laptops can be used in work, school, or any other location.

Tablets with a 10-inch monitor and 64 GB of storage can be purchased for around $500. The purpose of this type of device is mostly recreational. Tablets are lighter than even the smallest laptops and have a longer battery life.

HANDS-ON EXAMPLE 5.1.1

EVALUATE COMPUTER SYSTEMS

You have decided to purchase a computer for school use. Create a table similar to the one shown to compare features of three computers from three different manufacturers. Use the Internet or visit a store to complete the table. Evaluate the results, and select a computer. Write one paragraph explaining which computer you selected and why.

Type (desktop, laptop, tablet, etc.)	Manufacturer	Processing Speed (GHz)	Hard Drive Capacity (GB)	RAM (GB)	Display Size (Inches)	Operating System	Price

5.1   SECTION REVIEW

 CHECK YOUR UNDERSTANDING

1. What are the three basic models of personal computers?
2. Which model of computer generally provides more computer for the money than other models?
3. What is a needs assessment?
4. Which needs are the most important when conducting a needs assessment?
5. What is an all-in-one computer?

IC3 CERTIFICATION PRACTICE

The following question is a sample of the types of questions presented on the IC3 exam.

1. Which of these types of computers cannot be classified as a mobile device?
   A. Phablet
   B. Desktop
   C. Smartphone
   D. Tablet

 BUILD YOUR VOCABULARY

As you progress through this course, develop a personal IT glossary. This will help you build your vocabulary and prepare you for a career. Write a definition for each of the following terms and add it to your IT glossary.

all-in-one computer
computer model
needs assessment

BASIC MAINTENANCE

Distrikt 3/Shutterstock.com

Setting up procedures to ensure the efficient operation of the hardware and software provides a good return on investment for the expense of a computer system. The life of a system can be extended and repair costs minimized by performing preventive maintenance. Keeping the hardware in the system free of dust and placing the computer in a cool, dry location go a long way toward the goals of extending the computer's life and reducing repair costs.

The least-reliable components of a computer system are those with moving parts. Printers, mice, and keyboards tend to require the most attention. However, software needs some attention as well. The program files can become corrupted and in need of repair, but also temporary files need to be deleted on a routine basis. Almost all software has a help feature that can provide insight on how to care for the software.

?Essential Question

What impact does computer maintenance have on your productivity?

TERMS

disk cleanup
hardware maintenance
repair function
sectors
software maintenance

LEARNING GOALS

After completing this section, you will be able to:
- Identify basic hardware maintenance tasks.
- Describe software maintenance tasks.

STEM

Science

Connectors are made of or contain metal to conduct signals between the cables that they connect. Pure silver, pure copper, pure gold, and aluminum make for the best conductors. Copper is commonly used in network cabling and can be found in both UTP and coaxial cabling.

FYI

Wiping the keyboard with a mild cleaning fluid is a good procedure to minimize the spread of germs among users.

Maintaining the Hardware

Hardware maintenance is the process of keeping the computer hardware in good working order. Computer systems do not operate well when the hardware is covered in dust, dirt, food crumbs, or other physical contaminants. Cleaning hardware devices helps to keep them functional. Inside the computer box, the ventilation system is the most prone to grime. Externally, keyboards are the most vulnerable.

Keyboard

The best advice for avoiding a malfunctioning keyboard is to follow the no-eating, no-drinking rule when using the computer. Contaminants, such as liquids and food particles, can interfere with the connection of the keys to the switches in the keyboard. Sticky beverages are the worst.

To clean a keyboard, first turn off the system. Next, disconnect the keyboard, turn it upside down, and gently shake it so all loose particles fall out. A small vacuum cleaner designed for cleaning computer systems can suck away smaller debris that does not shake loose. A can of compressed air can be used to force out the remaining particles from between the keys. However, use caution to avoid flying particles getting in your eyes.

The keys can be wiped with a mild cleaning fluid. Using a strong cleaning fluid may remove the printed characters from the keys. Allow the keyboard to dry before reconnecting it.

Ventilation

Keeping computers cool is necessary for optimal operation. The internal fans continuously run to help maintain a safe temperature for the system. However, the fan is very small and collects dust, dirt, and other particles, as shown in Figure 5-4. To clean the fans and vents, first disconnect power from the computer. Then, open the case, and use a small vacuum cleaner or compressed air to remove the dust and dirt.

Processors, hard drives, and graphic cards generate significant amounts of heat, and they are sensitive to temperature. An overheated system may crash or shut down. Desktop computers should be placed where air can freely circulate around them when running, not in a cabinet or a drawer. Laptops or notebooks are the most prone to overheating because of their compact size. To help avoid overheating of these computers, turn them off when not in use, work in a well-ventilated area, or place the unit on a chill mat while working.

Andrew Safonov/Shutterstock.com

Figure 5-4. The computer fan brings air into the computer box. This allows dust and dirt to collect on the internal parts.

Monitor

Cleaning procedures differ depending on the type of monitor, but the monitor should be turned off. Older CRT monitors with a glass screen can be cleaned with any glass-cleaning solution. However, because an LCD or flat-panel screen scratches easily, a special procedure is required for these monitors. A soft, dry cloth should be used, and gently wipe the screen. If fingerprints or dirt do not wipe off, a small amount of rubbing alcohol may be put onto the cloth. Do not apply rubbing alcohol directly to the screen.

Maintaining the Software

GS5 Computing Fundamentals
3.12.1, 3.12.2

GS4 Computing Fundamentals
3.4.2, 3.4.3, 4.1.1

Software maintenance is keeping the software, from the operating system to all applications, in good working order. For the most part, software is installed and just keeps running. On occasion, a program file may become corrupted. Removing the program and reinstalling it may clear up that problem. Keep the original disc and access code on hand for any proprietary software. Some software is installed with a repair function. A **repair function** allows the current installation to be corrected without completely uninstalling and reinstalling the software. Uninstallation and installation are covered in Chapter 3.

Often, a software developer makes updates to its program. These updates may include minor enhancements and bug fixes. Software often has the capability to check for updates whenever an Internet connection is sensed and to alert the user that an update is available. Generally, these updates are free to registered users.

FYI

In most cases, it is a best practice to install updates when available.

Disk Cleanup

Disk cleanup is an automated process of removing unneeded files. After performing a disk cleanup, there should be more free space on the disk and the computer may run faster. At any given time, there are a number of files on the hard drive that are not needed. These may be temporary files, system files that are no longer used, and files in the recycle bin. However, how does a user know which files are not needed and where the files are stored? The Windows Disk Cleanup utility automates the process of deleting these files, as shown in Figure 5-5. To run the Disk Cleanup utility:

1. In Windows 10, right-click on the **Start** menu button, and click **Control Panel** in the shortcut menu. In Windows 8, click the **Apps** menu button, and then click **Control Panel** in the **Windows System** group. Then, click **System and Security** followed by the **Free up disk space** link under the **Administrative Tools** heading. In Windows 7, click the **Start** menu button, and then click **All Programs>Accessories>System Tools>Disk Cleanup**.

Check which types of files to delete

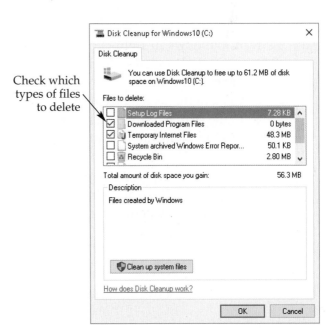

Goodheart-Willcox Publisher

Figure 5-5. The Disk Cleanup utility automates the process of removing certain files that are not needed.

2. If prompted to select the drive to clean up, choose the local hard disk, and click the **OK** button. Windows analyzes the drive, which may take a few seconds. Then the **Disk Cleanup** dialog box is displayed, as shown in Figure 5-5.
3. Check the check boxes for the locations where files will be deleted.
4. Click the **OK** button.
5. When prompted to confirm the deletions, click the **Delete Files** button.

GS4 Computing Fundamentals
3.4.3

FYI

With modern OSs and fast hard drives, disk fragmentation is not as critical of an issue as it was in the early days of personal computers.

Disk Defragmenter

Hard drives store files in locations on the hard drive called **sectors**. As a file is saved over and over, the file is broken up into clusters of data saved in sectors across the hard drive. This leads to a scattered or *fragmented* pattern. Accessing the data in a file could be sped up if the pieces of the file, or clusters, were close together. Windows 10 and Windows 8 have a utility program called Optimize Your Drives (Disk Defragmenter in Windows 7) that rearranges the clusters so they are next to each other. The utility is located in the Control Panel. Another function of the disk defragmenter is to rearrange other files to make room on the hard drive. In general, solid-state disks should not be defragmented.

HANDS-ON EXAMPLE 5.2.1

DISK DEFRAGMENTING

Fragmentation on a hard drive can sometimes cause problems, such as slow performance or software glitches. Defragmenting the hard drive is simple.
1. In Windows 10, right-click on the **Start** menu button, and click **Control Panel** in the shortcut menu. In Windows 8 and Windows 7, click the **Apps** or **Start** menu button, and click **Control Panel** in the menu.
2. Click in the search box at the top of Control Panel, and enter defrag.
3. In the search results, click **Defrag and optimize your drives** (or **Defrag your hard drive**). The disk defragmenter is launched. In Windows 8, this is called Optimize Your Drives. In Windows 7, this is called Disk Defragmenter.
4. Select the local hard drive (C:), and click the **Analyze** or **Analyze disk** button.
5. What percentage of fragmentation is reported?
6. Close the disk defragmenter.

Virus and Malware Scans

Viruses and malware are computer programs designed to damage a computer, steal data, or otherwise cause harm. These programs are usually transmitted through the Internet, e-mail, or infected shared files. Antivirus, antimalware, and antispyware software is used to avoid viruses and malware and to clean the computer when it is infected by a virus or malware. Virus and malware scans should be run on a regular basis. This topic is covered in detail in Chapter 16.

Computing Fundamentals
3.4.4, 4.1.3

5.2 | SECTION REVIEW

CHECK YOUR UNDERSTANDING

1. What is the best advice for avoiding a malfunctioning keyboard?
2. Which model of computer is the most prone to overheating?
3. What does a software repair function allow?
4. Which Windows utility automates the process of removing unneeded files?
5. What are the locations on a hard drive where file data are saved?

IC3 CERTIFICATION PRACTICE

The following question is a sample of the types of questions presented on the IC3 exam.

1. Interactive question:

    Demonstrate the procedure for running the disk defragmenter on the C: drive.

BUILD YOUR VOCABULARY

As you progress through this course, develop a personal IT glossary. This will help you build your vocabulary and prepare you for a career. Write a definition for each of the following terms and add it to your IT glossary.

disk cleanup
hardware maintenance
repair function
sectors
software maintenance

Essential Question

Why is it important for all computer users to have basic troubleshooting skills?

Computers are electronic appliances that have an expected life span. The average life span of a computer is from three to five years. Some sources estimate the average to be as low as two years. An average life span of two years does not mean the computer will break after two years. In fact, a computer may break down well before two years, while some users keep their computers functioning well beyond.

It is frustrating to sit down at the computer to get some work done and have a computer failure. The failure may be in the hardware or software, but the frustration is the same. Many users, especially novice users, become concerned that the problem may not be fixed in a timely manner or at all. However, having a clear plan for troubleshooting and resolving the problem will likely get the problem fixed and the user back to work quickly.

Rob Byron/Shutterstock.com

LEARNING GOALS

After completing this section, you will be able to:

- Explain a basic procedure for troubleshooting computer problems.
- Identify the steps for analyzing hardware problems.
- Describe common troubleshooting steps for software problems.

TERMS

device firmware upgrade (DFU) mode
factory-default settings
hard reboot
hard stop
rebooting
restore point
safe mode
soft reboot
task manager
troubleshooting

Troubleshooting

It is a worrisome situation for the user when the computer begins to show signs of trouble. The problems can come from hardware malfunctions or software issues. Sometimes the problems are created by the user. The basic maintenance discussed in the previous section goes a long way toward avoiding problems. However, when problems do occur, there are a few general actions to take in troubleshooting. **Troubleshooting** is systematically analyzing the problem to find a solution. If the user can analyze the nature of the problem, that is a good step in solving the problem.

1. Identify the symptom of the problem. If the system was working before, something has changed. Try to find what has changed.
2. If the system is not running, be sure electricity is available and there is power going to the system. A laptop or tablet may have drained its power without your noticing.
3. If the system is still running, look for messages on the display. Windows will try to alert the user to any problems and will suggest remedies.
4. Launch the Windows Help and Support feature. Search for troubleshooting.
5. Visit online forums to read what others have done or to post a question on the forum.
6. Ask a knowledgeable friend or colleague. If the device is a work or school computer, ask the IT department for help.
7. Contact technical support for the computer manufacturer, software developer, or hardware developer.

Many times, rebooting may solve the problem. **Rebooting** is restarting the system. A **soft reboot**, or *warm reboot*, is using the restart function of the operating system, as shown in Figure 5-6. A **hard reboot**, or *cold reboot*, is powering down, or shutting off, the system and then restarting it. Booting is described in detail in Chapter 2.

Getting Troubleshooting Help

There is an extensive help and support feature in Windows. In Windows 10, enter a search term directly in the search box on the taskbar. In Windows 8, the help feature is accessed through the charms menu. The easiest way to access the help feature in Windows 7 is to press the [F1] function key. Be sure the desktop or the **Start** menu is active before pressing the [F1] key, otherwise help may be displayed for the active software.

In addition to using the Windows knowledge base, forums and self-help websites can provide insight into the problems and their resolutions. A forum is a large database of conversations consisting of help topics for installing, operating, and fixing software and hardware. Assisted by search, users can ask questions and wait for answers by knowledgeable members of the forum or they can search for answers that other members have logged.

Computing Fundamentals
GS5 3.13.1, 3.13.2, 3.13.3

Career Skills

IT Technician

Although almost every field requires IT support, schools and educational institutions often have an entire team of trained IT specialists who purchase, maintain, and troubleshoot problems with a school's computers and other technology. These IT technicians manage networks, communications, hardware, and software to provide a seamless integration of technology and learning.

Computing Fundamentals
GS4 4.1.5

FYI

Most Windows applications use the [F1] key to launch help.

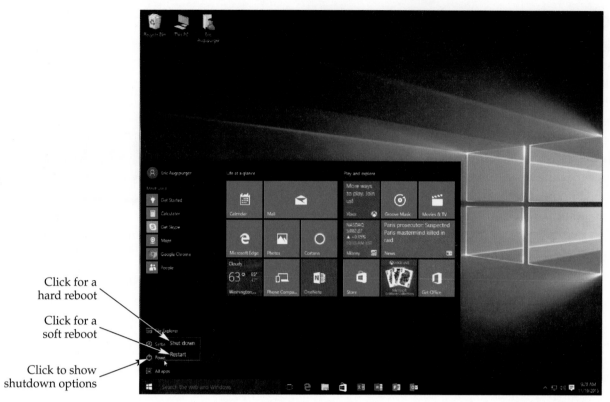

Click for a
hard reboot

Click for a
soft reboot

Click to show
shutdown options

Figure 5-6. Use the **Restart** option to perform a soft reboot of the system.

To conserve paper and to reduce shipping costs, vendors do not bundle user printed manuals with their products. A setup guide is usually included, but for help in greater detail, online user manuals are generally available. These manuals may be useful because all of the information about a particular device is gathered in one location.

When searching for a user manual on the Internet, be specific with the search phrase. A basic search phrase of user manuals will yield tens of millions of returned results, most of them not even related to IT. Suppose the task is to troubleshoot a printer with a model number of HP 6490. Perform an Internet search with the search phrase HP 6490 user manual. The first few returned results will most likely be either the user manual for this printer or troubleshooting information related to the printer.

HANDS-ON EXAMPLE 5.3.1

Computing
Fundamentals
4.1.5

ONLINE TROUBLESHOOTING HELP

Know where to look to solve a hardware problem. Because printed manuals are no longer produced, use a search engine to locate online manuals.

1. In Windows 8, move the cursor to the lower-right corner of the screen to display the charms menu, and then click **Settings** followed by **Help** in the menu. In Windows 7, click the **Start** menu button, and then click **Help and Support**. Note: in Windows 10, enter the search term directly in the search box on the taskbar.

HANDS-ON EXAMPLE 5.3.1 (CONTINUED)

2. In the **Windows Help and Support** dialog box that is displayed, verify that the **Online Help** option is selected in the lower-right or lower-left corner. If not, click the button, and click **Get Online Help** in the shortcut menu.
3. Click in the search box, and enter troubleshoot as the search term.
4. Click the **Search** button (magnifying glass). A list of specific troubleshooting topics is displayed.
5. Click the topic **Troubleshoot Problems with Installing Updates** or other topic. Make note of how the material is organized. Each help topic is called an article. Many articles contain links to either expand the current article, display a different article, or launch an application, such as a troubleshooting wizard.
6. Click the **Back** button at the top of the dialog box to return to the previous screen. Navigation within the help function is much like a web browser.

Safe Mode

Safe mode is a Windows boot setting in which the computer starts up with the minimum of functions necessary to run. It is a troubleshooting mode that allows the computer to start up in most cases after an error has occurred. Only a limited part of the operating system is loaded. Enough functionality is present to permit an experienced troubleshooter to investigate what is wrong. The keyboard, mouse, and screen will be on, but all other peripheral devices may not be functional. The screen does not display the normal GUI, rather the background is black and the letters are white or gray. In safe mode, the hardware or software that is not working can be located and uninstalled.

GS4 | Computing Fundamentals
4.1.4

Troubleshooting Checklist

It is a good idea to have a set sequence of steps to take to ensure all issues are considered. Figure 5-7 provides a two-stage checklist. The first stage is for assessing the problem. The second stage is for applying the fix. These are general checklists that provide a basic foundation for troubleshooting.

Troubleshooting Hardware Problems

The most dreaded hardware failure is the hard stop. A **hard stop** occurs when the computer completely ceases to function. In the Windows environment, it has been nicknamed the "blue screen of death" due to the blue background of the message screen displayed when a hard stop occurs. The usual GUI is not displayed on the monitor, rather the message on the blue screen indicates the system cannot recover from an error. The computer can no longer understand input. The system is not helping you analyze the cause. If the screen just displays indecipherable lines, the graphic card may be broken. At this point, a hard reboot may resolve the problem, at least temporarily. If the problem persists, the situation requires expert technical assistance.

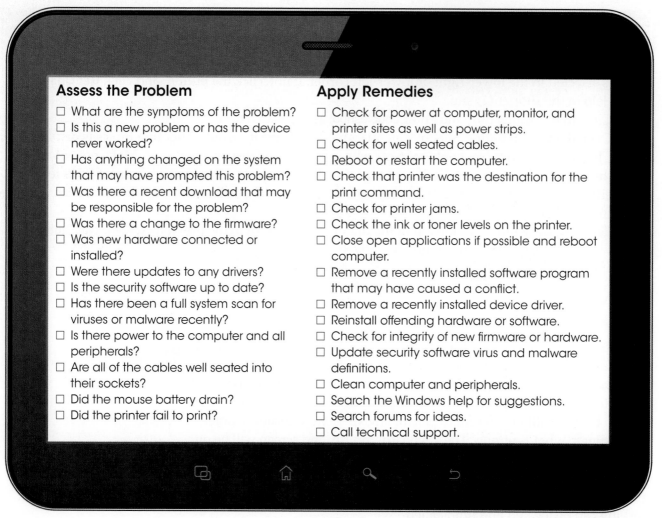

Assess the Problem

☐ What are the symptoms of the problem?
☐ Is this a new problem or has the device never worked?
☐ Has anything changed on the system that may have prompted this problem?
☐ Was there a recent download that may be responsible for the problem?
☐ Was there a change to the firmware?
☐ Was new hardware connected or installed?
☐ Were there updates to any drivers?
☐ Is the security software up to date?
☐ Has there been a full system scan for viruses or malware recently?
☐ Is there power to the computer and all peripherals?
☐ Are all of the cables well seated into their sockets?
☐ Did the mouse battery drain?
☐ Did the printer fail to print?

Apply Remedies

☐ Check for power at computer, monitor, and printer sites as well as power strips.
☐ Check for well seated cables.
☐ Reboot or restart the computer.
☐ Check that printer was the destination for the print command.
☐ Check for printer jams.
☐ Check the ink or toner levels on the printer.
☐ Close open applications if possible and reboot computer.
☐ Remove a recently installed software program that may have caused a conflict.
☐ Remove a recently installed device driver.
☐ Reinstall offending hardware or software.
☐ Check for integrity of new firmware or hardware.
☐ Update security software virus and malware definitions.
☐ Clean computer and peripherals.
☐ Search the Windows help for suggestions.
☐ Search forums for ideas.
☐ Call technical support.

Goodheart-Willcox Publisher

Figure 5-7. Use these sequences to approach troubleshooting in a methodical way.

Analysis

Other situations may occur that are not as drastic as a hard stop. If the GUI is still functioning, there are steps that can be taken to analyze the problem. Make notes of what you have tried and investigated so this can be shared with a technician if you cannot solve the problem on your own. Another good reason to keep notes is so you do not waste time repeating tests or strategies.

1. Write down any error messages that are displayed. Also note any other relevant information, such as what actions were being performed when things went awry.

2. If a hardware component has flashing LEDs or ones are on that are normally off, try to determine what this indicates. Check the installation and user manuals for the hardware device for the interpretation code.

3. Check to see that all cables are properly connected. Occasionally the vibrations or movement of the computer may wiggle the connections loose. Ensure that the cable connectors are well seated.

4. Restart the stalled device. If there is a reset button, use that. Otherwise it may be necessary to turn off the device and restart it. Finally, disconnect the device from the computer, wait a minute, and then reassemble the device.

5. Slowly pass a hand over the hardware parts. If they seem too warm, that is an indication of a problem. Shut down the system, and allow the components to cool. Investigate the item that overheated. On occasion the system will shut itself down leaving a message on the screen detailing that the system overheated.

6. Run antispyware, antimalware, and antivirus software. Malicious programs that have been introduced can cause the system to act strangely, but can also damage the system. This topic is discussed in detail in Chapter 16.

7. In Windows 10, click the **Start** menu button, click **Power** in the menu, and click **Restart** in the shortcut menu that is displayed. In Windows 8, move the cursor to the lower-right corner of the screen to display the charms menu, then click **Power** followed by **Restart**. In Windows 7, click the **Start** menu button, click the arrow next to **Shutdown**, and click **Restart**. If the menu is not functioning, press the [Ctrl][Alt][Del] key combination. On the screen that appears, click the arrow next to the **Shutdown** button, and click **Restart** in the menu, as shown in Figure 5-8.

8. If available, use the diagnosis assistance provided by Windows. This provides suggestions for ways to correct the problem.

FYI

If a computer is not operable, use another system and enter the symptoms into the diagnosis assistance provided by Windows.

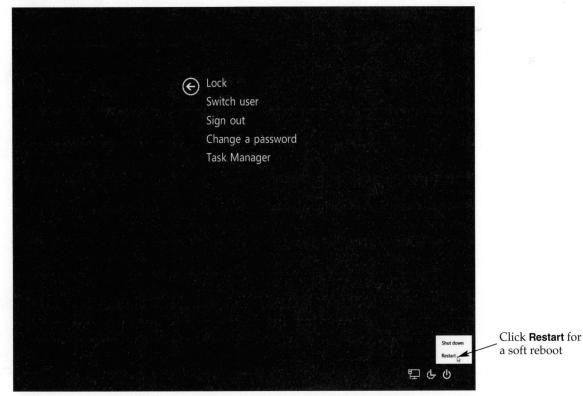

Click **Restart** for a soft reboot

Goodheart-Willcox Publisher

Figure 5-8. Performing a soft reboot.

Computing Fundamentals
4.2.1, 4.3.1

Firmware

Firmware is permanently stored software. Updates to firmware include changes to hardware-related instructions. In most cases, firmware will not be the cause of a problem. However, if a firmware update is needed, a device driver will need to be installed to perform the update.

The Apple device family is unique when it comes to firmware. The iOS devices have a **device firmware upgrade (DFU) mode** that provides the ability to upgrade or downgrade the firmware. DFU mode essentially places the device in a recovery mode. This allows any iOS device to be restored to original firmware programming.

Updating the firmware on an iOS device is not to be confused with updating an app from the Apple App Store. Apps are extra software programs installed by the user, not firmware. These more volatile apps are included in the synchronization process for backup.

Cables and Connections

Computing Fundamentals
4.2.2

In addition to verifying cable connections are secure, it is important to check that the cables are in good condition. On occasion, exposed cables can be worn due to people walking over them or by pets chewing on them. If the protective Mylar cover is damaged, the wires may be damaged as well. Also be sure the cables are proper for the application.

Inspect the connectors on the cables, as shown in Figure 5-9. Look for bent or missing pins or incorrect matching of the socket to the connector. Look for frayed wires at the junction of the connector and the cable. Look for an excessively long or joined Ethernet cable. A long length of Ethernet cable may degrade the transmitted signal.

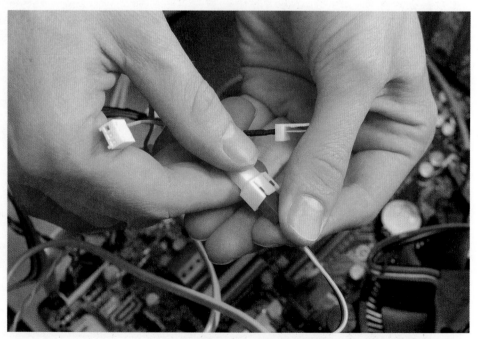

Smileus/Shutterstock.com

Figure 5-9. Troubleshooting hardware may involve inspecting connectors and cables for damage.

Troubleshooting Devices and Peripherals

Installation of a new device or peripheral frequently causes problems in the computer system. The devices may arrive with a device driver on an installation disc. Likely this information is out of date and may conflict with updates to the computer system itself. Always download and install the newest drivers. Even the installation of the device may cause a conflict in the system that must be fixed.

External Storage

Most external storage devices do not have on-and-off switches. They are supposed to be recognized and powered as soon as the device is connected to a USB port. These devices are prone to problems because they are inserted and removed so many times. If the system does not identify an external storage device when it is connected, the system needs to be rebooted with the device already connected.

Take care to properly remove external storage devices. This can help avoid the problem of an unrecognized device. To properly remove an external storage device, click the **Safely Remove Hardware and Eject Media** icon in the system tray (systray) on the taskbar, as shown in Figure 5-10. Then, click **Eject** in the menu that appears. A message will be displayed when it is safe to disconnect the device.

Printers

Printers experience issues such as an empty paper tray or low ink or toner. Common minor mechanical problems with printers are paper jams and incorrectly installed cartridges. If a printer is not printing, a message generally will be displayed on the printer's screen after the system has diagnosed the nature of the problem. In many cases, the computer operating system also displays the error message.

Another problem that may occur with printers is that the device driver has become corrupted or has otherwise developed an error. In this case, there are two solutions. The driver can be reinstalled from either the CD that came with it or a new copy can be downloaded from the manufacturer over the Internet. When searching the Internet for the driver, search by manufacturer and model number. Downloading a new

GS4 Computing Fundamentals
4.3.3

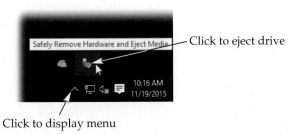

Click to eject drive

Click to display menu

Goodheart-Willcox Publisher

Figure 5-10. When disconnecting a flash drive, be sure to use the icon in the system tray.

driver may be the best option because always doing so ensures the most up-to-date version is installed.

Computing Fundamentals
4.3.2

OS Versioning

The drivers that are supplied with a device will support certain operating systems. If the operating system is upgraded to a newer version, the device driver may not be compatible and can cause problems. It is important to match device drivers to the OS version on the computer. If the OS is upgraded or changed, be sure to update all device drivers. This will ensure all devices have the most current drivers and that the drivers are compatible with the operating system.

Troubleshooting Software Problems

For the most part, software runs well and has no problems. On occasion, a program may become unresponsive or react in an unexpected way to your interaction. Software problems become apparent when a particular application stops working or does not respond to mouse or keyboard input. Other symptoms of a software problem may include a slowdown during loading of an application or a lag in responding to commands.

Each major software company, whether a developer of system or application software, provides online support for its programs. Similarly, there are websites and forums to consult in the case of mishap. A key tool in managing the software on a Windows system is the Task Manager.

Computing Fundamentals
4.1.2

Operating Systems

The operating system is composed of many different programs. If one of them develops a problem, the OS is said to be corrupted. The system may be difficult to start, freeze up, not permit data entry, or generally act unstable. The corruption within the OS can be for no apparent reason or can be introduced through malicious software from the Internet, e-mail, or a shared file.

There are a wide variety of operating systems and different versions of each. When troubleshooting a computer, it is important to identify the installed OS and version. If the computer does not have the latest version of the operating system installed, important updates to the operating system are missing. It may be that the problem at hand is due to an out-of-date OS. On Windows systems the operating system version number is located through the Control Panel, as shown in Figure 5-11.

If the OS is showing signs of a problem, first try rebooting the system. If possible, follow the proper shutdown procedure. If this is not possible, such as when the OS is frozen, press and hold the power button until the computer turns off. Next, wait five seconds, and then turn on the system.

If a reboot does not fix the issue, the Windows troubleshooting guide may help. This feature provides a wizard-like interface that will step the user through diagnosing various problems. If the troubleshooting guide does not help correct the problem, contact technical support or a computer-service company.

Ethics

Customer Data

Some company websites gather personal and confidential information from customers such as credit card numbers or phone numbers. Sharing or tampering with personal information is not only unethical, but may also be illegal. Protecting the customers' data will help protect the reputation of the business and encourage customer loyalty.

Version number

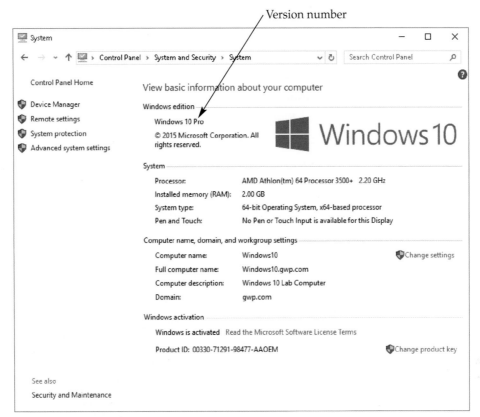

Figure 5-11. The Windows version can be displayed using the Control Panel.

Using Task Manager

The Windows Task Manager is an excellent utility for monitoring the software activity of a system. Each operating system has a task manager, but by a different name, such as Activity Monitor for the Mac iOS. The **task manager** analyzes what is going on in the system and reports the results. In addition, the task manager can be used to close, or terminate, a program or service that is not responding.

Computing Fundamentals
4.1.6

There are several ways to launch the Windows Task Manager. The traditional method is to press the [Ctrl][Alt][Del] key combination and then click **Start Task Manager** in the menu that is displayed. Another method is to right-click on an empty space in the taskbar, and click **Task Manager** or **Start Task Manager** in the shortcut menu. In Windows 10 and Windows 8, there are seven tabs in Task Manager:

- **Processes**
- **Performance**
- **App History**
- **Startup**
- **Users**
- **Details**
- **Services**

In Windows 7, there are six tabs:

- **Applications**
- **Processes**
- **Services**
- **Performance**
- **Networking**
- **Users**

FYI

Do not terminate a process without knowing exactly what function it is performing for the system. Terminating a process may make the system unstable.

The **Processes** tab lists all of the currently running processes and the percentage of CPU time each is consuming. Some processes are started by the OS, while others are started by an application. This tab can be used to see which processes are creating the greatest load on the CPU.

In Windows 10 and Windows 8, the **Processes** tab also lists currently running applications (apps) along with the status of each. In Windows 7, these are listed on the **Applications** tab, and the running applications are called tasks. Each application or task should be a program name that you recognize because these are programs you launched. If the Status column reports the program as Not Responding, the program is frozen. The choices are either to wait until the OS and the program try to resolve the issue or to forcibly terminate the program. The problem with terminating the program is that most software performs a cleanup operation during normal exiting. Terminating the program may not permit that to occur.

The **Performance** tab displays a time line of the CPU and RAM usage, as shown in Figure 5-12. This information shows the load on the system.

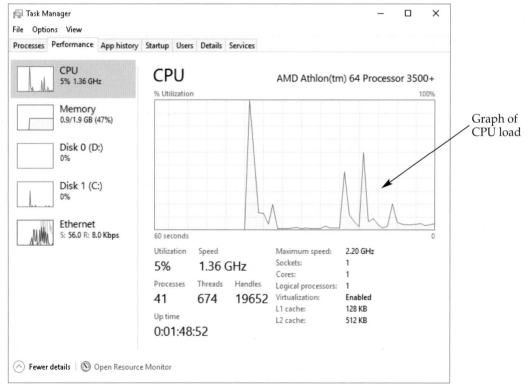

Goodheart-Willcox Publisher

Figure 5-12. The Task Manager can provide much information about the system, including the load on the CPU.

If the load is consistently heavy, this may indicate the need for a more powerful CPU or more RAM. In Windows 8, a time line of the available network connections and activity are also displayed on the **Performance** tab. In Windows 7, this is displayed on the **Networking** tab.

The **App History** tab lists how much CPU time has been used by each app in the Metro applications. It also shows how much data have been transferred via the network by the apps.

The **Startup** tab lists the programs and services that are automatically launched when Windows 10 or Windows 8 is started. During installation, many software programs add startup files to the computer configuration. These startup files create processes that consume system resources. Some are for programs that are regularly used and make the loading of larger programs go more quickly. Some of these are for programs that are seldom used, yet the startup program is loaded every time the system is booted or rebooted. If there are many of these, the system will run more slowly. Startup programs that are not frequently used should be disabled.

The **Users** tab shows the users who are currently logged into the computer. For most computers, there will be only one user. If the computer is a server, this tab will list all of the users currently using the server's services.

The **Details** tab lists the currently running processes with expanded information not displayed in the **Processes** tab. The priority of a process can be set on the **Details** tab by right-clicking on the process name, and then clicking **Set priority** in the shortcut menu. The **Details** tab only appears in the Windows 10 and Windows 8 Task Manager, but it is very similar to the **Processes** tab found in the Windows 7 Task Manager.

The **Services** tab lists the programs operating in the background. These programs support logging in users, monitoring the health of the system, scheduling processes, and making user notifications. The information on this tab is display only. It cannot be changed or edited, however a service can be started or stopped by right-clicking on it. To manage the services, click the **Open Services** link or the **Services...** button.

Stopping Applications

If a program has become unresponsive, the title bar of the application window will indicate this. Task Manager can be used to terminate an application that has become unresponsive. Launch Task Manager, and display the **Processes** tab in Windows 10 and Windows 8 or the **Applications** tab in Windows 7. Click the name of the application that is frozen, and then click the **End Task** button at the bottom of the Task Manager, as shown in Figure 5-13. The application will be terminated, and it will no longer appear in the list.

Computing Fundamentals
4.1.6

Stopping Processes

Some processes are necessary, while others are not always needed. Processes that are not currently needed slow down the system. Processes can be terminated using Task Manager. Launch Task Manager, and

Computing Fundamentals
4.1.6

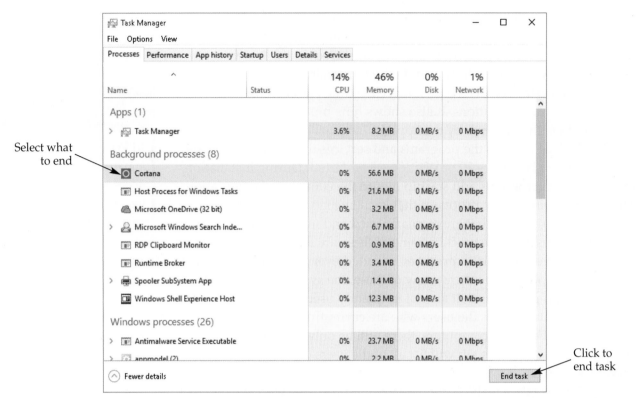

Select what to end

Click to end task

Goodheart-Willcox Publisher

Figure 5-13. Task Manager can be used to end an application that has stopped working.

display the **Processes** or **Details** tab in Windows 10 and Windows 8 or the **Processes** tab in Windows 7. Click the name of the process to terminate, and then click the **End Task** or **End Process** button at the bottom of the Task Manager. The process will be terminated, and it will no longer appear in the list.

HANDS-ON EXAMPLE 5.3.2

TERMINATING A PROGRAM

Task Manager is a utility that can be used as part of the troubleshooting process for software. It displays the current system activity. It can also be used to terminate a program.

1. Launch Notepad. This is located in the **Windows Accessories** or **Accessories** group in the **Start** or **Apps** menu.
2. Launch Task Manager.
3. In Windows 10 and Windows 8, click the **Processes** tab. In Windows 7, click the **Applications** tab. Notepad appears in the list of currently running applications. A button for Notepad appears on the Windows task bar, which indicates that it is running.
4. In Task Manager, select Notepad in the list of running applications.
5. Click the **End Task** button at the bottom of Task Manager. Notice that Notepad disappears from the list in Task Manager, and the button on the task bar is no longer displayed. Notepad has been terminated.

TITANS OF TECHNOLOGY

Peter Norton was the first person to develop utilities and sell them to the general public. In 1982, he founded Peter Norton Computing, inventing an industry for troubleshooting help for personal computers. The same year, his company introduced Norton Utilities. His most popular utility was UNERASE, which was for recovering erased files from DOS disks. Today, computer users are familiar with the Recycle Bin or Trash, but at the time UNERASE was the first readily available way to restore a deleted file. Norton sold his company to Symantec Corporation in 1990. Norton has published many books and articles on personal computer technology. His first book was published in 1983. He also wrote monthly columns in computer magazines in the 1980s. During this time, he became a recognized authority on PC technology. Norton supports many philanthropic efforts through the Peter Norton Family Foundation and other organizations. He has also accumulated a vast collection of modern art, many pieces of which are displayed in various locations around the world.

Windows 7 Startup Programs

The System Configuration utility is a troubleshooting tool used to help diagnose problems with Windows startup. It displays which processes are included in the startup configuration file. These processes can be turned on and off to isolate a problem. To run the utility, open the **Run** dialog box by pressing the [Windows Key][R] key combination. Enter msconfig in the text box in the **Run** dialog box, and click the **OK** button. The System Configuration utility is displayed, as shown in Figure 5-14.

Click the **Startup** tab in the System Configuration utility. All of the processes that are launched whenever Windows is started are displayed. To disable a process, uncheck the check box to the left of its name. Click the **OK** button to apply the change. A message appears indicating the

FYI

The System Configuration utility is available in Windows 8, however the startup configuration must be set using Task Manager.

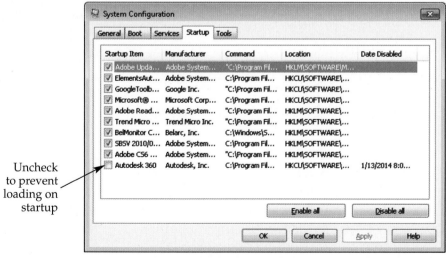

Uncheck to prevent loading on startup

Goodheart-Willcox Publisher

Figure 5-14. In Windows 7, the System Configuration utility can be used to disable processes that load on startup.

system must be restarted for the change to be activated. Either click the **Restart** button to restart the computer or click the **Exit without restart** button to restart the computer at a later time.

HANDS-ON EXAMPLE 5.3.3

STARTUP PROCESSES

Many software programs add a startup process during the installation process. Often, these processes are not needed and can cause the system to slow down.

1. In Windows 10 and Windows 8, launch Task Manager. In Windows 7, launch the System Configuration utility.
2. Click the **Startup** tab.
3. Make note of the processes that are loaded on Windows startup.
4. Use a web browser and Internet search engine to research what one of the listed programs does. In Windows 10 and Windows 8, right-click on the item, and click **Search Online** in the shortcut menu. Speculate if the process is one that should be enabled on startup.

System Restore

Computing Fundamentals
4.2, 4.3

In some cases, it may be necessary to perform a system restore to fix a problem. In Windows, System Restore is a utility that returns system files and settings to the state they were in, or **restore point**, at an earlier date or time, as shown in Figure 5-15. A restore point is a copy of the system files in their state at the earlier date or time. Windows creates a restore point weekly and also whenever a change is made to the system files. It is also possible to manually create a restore point.

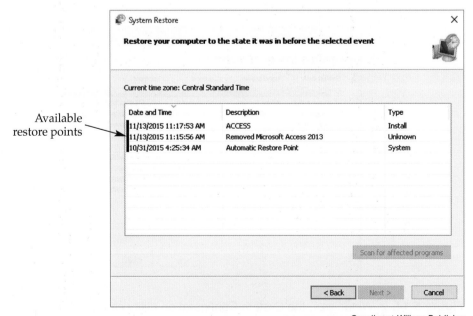

Goodheart-Willcox Publisher

Figure 5-15. System Restore can be used to reset the computer to an earlier state, which can be helpful when troubleshooting software problems.

System Restore does not affect the user's documents, such as text files, image files, or e-mails. However, for some applications, such as games, System Restore may reset the application to an earlier state. Even though System Restore does not affect user files, using it is often a last resort. It reverses security updates, driver updates, and, in some cases, antivirus software updates. After using System Restore, it is necessary to make sure all of these critical items are updated.

On mobile devices, a similar function is available. Often this is in the Settings app and the feature is called Reset. Options are available to reset all or part of the device. A reset restores the device to factory default settings. The **factory-default settings** are the original settings that the device had when it was new before the user made any changes. Because it may not be possible to fix a problem by selectively undoing specific settings, restoring the factory-default settings may be required to back out of a problem.

5.3 | SECTION REVIEW

 ## CHECK YOUR UNDERSTANDING

1. What is the difference between a soft reboot and a hard reboot?
2. What is safe mode in Windows?
3. What has been nicknamed "the blue screen of death" in the Windows environment?
4. Which utility in Windows can be used to stop a process or application that is not responding?
5. Which utility restores the hard drive to a previously saved point?

IC3 CERTIFICATION PRACTICE

The following question is a sample of the types of questions presented on the IC3 exam.

1. Interactive question:

   Use Task Manager to locate a nonresponsive program and terminate the task.

BUILD YOUR VOCABULARY

As you progress through this course, develop a personal IT glossary. This will help you build your vocabulary and prepare you for a career. Write a definition for each of the following terms and add it to your IT glossary.

device firmware upgrade (DFU) mode
factory-default settings
hard reboot
hard stop
rebooting
restore point
safe mode
soft reboot
task manager
troubleshooting

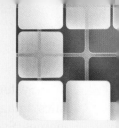

Chapter Summary

Section 5.1
Purchasing a System

- The computer model is the form the computer takes. The three basic models of personal computers are desktops, laptops, and mobile devices.

- A needs assessment is a process of examining the current condition or state and determining how it differs from the desired condition or state. Look at how the current computer does not meet the user's needs because the needs of the user are the most important.

- When purchasing a system, balance the cost with the capability of the system. A general desktop model can be purchased for around $600, a laptop for between $500 and $700, and a tablet for around $500.

Section 5.2
Basic Maintenance

- Hardware maintenance is the process of keeping the computer hardware in good working order. Inside the computer box, the ventilation system is the most prone to grime, while externally keyboards are the most vulnerable.

- Software maintenance is keeping the software, from the operating system to all applications, in good working order. Often, software programs have updates made available, which may include enhancements or bug fixes.

Section 5.3
Troubleshooting Basics

- Troubleshooting is systematically analyzing the problem to find a solution. A few general actions can be taken to help the user analyze the nature of the problem.

- The most dreaded hardware failure is the hard stop, which occurs when the computer completely ceases to function. Other situations may occur with hardware that are not as drastic as a hard stop.

- A software program may become unresponsive or react in an unexpected way to your interaction. Windows Task Manager can be used to stop programs and functions that are not responding, and the System Restore function can reset the system to a previously working point.

Now that you have finished this chapter, see what you know about information technology by scanning the QR code to take the chapter posttest. If you do not have a smartphone, visit www.g-wlearning.com.

Chapter 5 Test

Multiple Choice

Select the best response.

1. What is the most important consideration in purchasing a new computer system?
   A. clock speed
   B. user's needs
   C. amount of RAM
   D. size of the hard disk

2. Which of these environmental factors may cause a computer to shut down?
   A. overheating
   B. dust in a keyboard
   C. printer jam
   D. low lighting

3. Which Windows utility automates the process of removing unneeded files?
   A. Antivirus
   B. Task Manager
   C. Disk Cleanup
   D. Optimize Your Drive or Disk Defragmenter

4. Working systematically to uncover and repair computer problems is called:
   A. defragmenting
   B. updating
   C. uninstalling
   D. troubleshooting

5. What does the task manager do?
   A. Cleans up the hard drive by removing unneeded files.
   B. Analyzes what is going on in the system and reports the results.
   C. Moves clusters on the hard drive so they are next to each other.
   D. Configures the system.

Completion

Complete the following sentences with the correct word(s).

6. The three models of personal computer are _____.

7. When conducting a(n) _____, look at how the current computer does not meet the user's needs.

8. To help prevent overheating of a laptop, place it on a(n) _____ while working.

9. _____ is systematically analyzing the problem to find a solution.

10. _____ is a boot setting in which only the minimum of functions are supported.

Matching

Match the correct term with its definition.

A. mobile devices
B. needs assessment
C. hardware maintenance
D. sectors
E. hard reboot

11. Cleaning devices helps to keep them functional.

12. Determining how the current state differs from the desired state.

13. Shutting off the system and then restarting it.

14. Includes tablets, mini tablets, phablets, and smartphones.

15. Locations on the hard drive where data are stored.

Application and Extension of Knowledge

1. Research tablet computers. Select one unit, and make a list of its specifications. Compare that with your current computer. Determine if an upgrade to the tablet is a good idea. Be prepared to justify your answer in a class discussion.

2. Identify a device attached to your computer, such as a CD-ROM drive. Locate the manufacturer and model number. Visit the manufacturer's website and locate the most up-to-date device driver.

3. Identify three third-party software solutions that offer to help maintain your computer. Create a chart that compares cost, platforms served, features, advantages, drawbacks. Determine if you need one of these packages. Write one paragraph for each solution that describes why you would or would not select it.

4. Research troubleshooting checklists. Locate an example checklist for computer troubleshooting. Identify a step included in that checklist not discussed in this chapter. Apply critical thinking skills to determine if the step should be included.

5. Open the Windows Control Panel. Click in the search box at the top, and enter troubleshooter. In the search results, click **Troubleshooting**. On the new page that is displayed, click **Troubleshoot audio playback**. A wizard is launched. Step through the wizard, providing answers to any questions. Make note of how the troubleshooter functions. Did it find any problems?

Online Activities

Complete the following activities, which will help you learn, practice, and expand your knowledge and skills.

Certification Practice. Complete the certification practice test for this chapter.

Vocabulary. Practice vocabulary for this chapter using the e-flash cards, matching activity, and vocabulary game until you are able to recognize their meanings.

Communication Skills

College and Career Readiness

Reading. After you have read this chapter, identify the explicit details, as well as the author's main idea for the chapter. Apply appropriate reading techniques to identify the main ideas and purpose of the information that is presented. Draw conclusions about the author's purpose. Share your findings with the class.

Writing. Standard English means that word choice, sentence structure, paragraphs, and the format of communication follow standard conventions used by those who speak English. Research the topic of language use in social media as it relates to Standard English. Write an informative report, consisting of several paragraphs to describe your findings. Edit the writing for proper syntax, tense, and voice.

Speaking. The workplace requires that employees adapt to diversity of the many individuals with whom they will come in contact. The interaction can be in formal or informal situations. Make a list of potential barriers that can evolve and solutions to eliminate those barriers. Share your list with the class.

Internet Research

Annotation Techniques. Using the Internet, research different ways to annotate and take notes as you read. Which techniques are commonly used? Did you learn about any new ones? Write a brief summary of the techniques you researched. Then, create a system for annotating works, such as color coding, a symbol system, or listing topics of interest.

Teamwork

Form a team with three to four classmates. Together, you will create a digital media presentation in the form of an infomercial for your school's STEM department. The goal of the presentation is to make the audience aware of the subjects that are available to learn, the real-world applications of these subjects, and the opportunities to have experiences beyond the traditional

academic setting. As a team, work through the planning stages, determine what form the presentation will take, create or obtain all components of the presentation, create the presentation, and package and deliver the presentation.

Portfolio Development

College and Career Readiness

Digital Presentation Options. Before you begin collecting items for a digital portfolio, you will need to decide how you are going to present the final product. For example, you could create an electronic presentation with slides for each section. The slides could have links to documents, videos, graphics, or sound files. This will dictate file naming conventions and file structure.

Websites are another option for presenting a digital portfolio. You could create a personal website to host the files and have a main page with links to various sections. Each section page could have links to pages containing your documents, videos, graphics, or sound files. (Be sure you read and understand the user agreement for any site on which you place your materials.)

Another option is to place the files on a CD. The method you choose should allow the viewer to easily navigate and find items. There are many creative ways to present a digital portfolio.

1. Establish the types of technology that are available for you to create a digital portfolio. Will you have access to cameras or studios? Do you have the level of skill needed to create videos?

2. Decide the type of presentation you will use. Research what will be needed to create the final portfolio product.

CTSOs

Ethics. Many competitive CTSO events include an ethics component that covers multiple topics. The ethics component of an event may be part of an objective test. However, ethics may also be a part of the competition in which teams participate to defend a given position on an ethical dilemma or topic. To prepare for an ethics event, complete the following activities.

1. Read the guidelines provided by your organization.

2. Make notes on index cards about important points to remember. Use these notes to study.

3. To get an overview of various ethical situations that individuals encounter, read each of the Ethics features that appear throughout this text.

4. Ask someone to practice role-playing with you by asking questions or taking the other side of an argument.

5. Use the Internet to find more information about ethical issues. Find and review ethics cases that involve business situations.

UNIT 2
KEY APPLICATIONS

Goodluz/Shutterstock.com

This section provides an overview of using industry-standard software technologies: the office suite of productivity tools. A suite of office software shares a similar interface, and many features and tools are found in all of the programs in the suite. First, you will learn the common features to the office suite. Then you will apply these features as you investigate each specific program. The programs covered in this unit are word processing software, presentation software, spreadsheet software, and database management software.

With this unit, the textbook continues to provide information and activities that support the objectives for the IC3 Digital Literacy Certification. This information will help you prepare for taking this certification exam. Certification is important to demonstrate a mastery of Internet and core computing skills.

G-WLEARNING.com

While studying, look for the activity icon for:

- Pretests and posttests
- Vocabulary terms with e-flash cards and matching activities
- Formative assessment

6

COMMON OFFICE APPLICATION FEATURES

SECTIONS

6.1 STARTING WORD, EXCEL, AND POWERPOINT

6.2 SAVING, PRINTING, AND OPENING DOCUMENTS

6.3 EDITING AND FORMATTING

6.4 DOCUMENT VIEWS, OPTIONS, AND HELP

An office suite is used to create and share personal and business documents. The most common software in an office suite includes word-processing, spreadsheet, presentation, and database programs. An advantage of purchasing an office suite is that the basic functions work similarly in all of the software. For example, once a user learns how to save a file in one of the applications, or modules, he or she can do the same thing in other modules because the procedure is the same in all of the applications. Because the user has a basic set of directions common to all applications in the suite, it is easy to switch from one application to another.

The most common office suites are Microsoft Office, OpenOffice, LibreOffice, Google Docs, and Zoho Office Suite. Microsoft Office 2013 is the most popular office suite and what is demonstrated in this text. The programs included in the Microsoft Office suite are Word, Excel, PowerPoint, Access, and others.

College and Career Readiness

Reading Prep. As you read the chapter, record any questions that come to mind. Indicate where the answer to each question can be found: within the text, by asking your teacher, in another book, on the Internet, or by reflecting on your own knowledge and experiences. Pursue the answers to your questions.

IC3 CERTIFICATION OBJECTIVES

GS5

Computing Fundamentals

Domain 3.0 Computer software architecture
  Objective 3.3 Have a general understanding of operating systems and software settings
  Objective 3.4 Set software preferences
  Objective 3.8 Menu navigation

Key Applications

Domain 1.0 Common features
  Objective 1.1 Know copy, cut, and paste keyboard equivalents
  Objective 1.5 Know the find/replace feature
  Objective 1.6 Be able to select text or cells
  Objective 1.7 Be able to redo and undo
  Objective 1.9 Know the read-only view
  Objective 1.10 Understand what a protected mode means
  Objective 1.11 Be able to use the zoom feature

Domain 2.0 Word Processing
  Objective 2.4 Create and save files
  Objective 2.6 Know how to print a word processing document
  Objective 2.7 Use and configure print views
  Objective 2.10 Understand which file types are compatible or editable with word processors

Domain 3.0 Spreadsheets
  Objective 3.11 Understand compatible spreadsheet file types
  Objective 3.12 Be able to use spreadsheet templates to increase productivity

Domain 4.0 Databases
  Objective 4.4 Know what metadata is

Domain 5.0 Presentations
  Objective 5.1 Understand file types compatible with presentation software

Domain 7.0 Graphic modification
  Objective 7.1 Be able to import and insert images into documents
  Objective 7.2 Understand how to crop images

GS4

Key Applications

Domain 1.0 Common application features
  Objective 1.1 Common features and commands
  Objective 1.2 Formatting
  Objective 1.3 Navigating
  Objective 1.4 Working with multimedia files

Domain 2.0 Word-processing activities
  Objective 2.1 Organizing data

Domain 6.0 Collaboration
  Objective 6.2 Sharing files

STARTING WORD, EXCEL, AND POWERPOINT

Essential Question

Why does the common interface of the Microsoft Office suite increase productivity?

Microsoft Office is a software suite designed for home users, large and small businesses, and students. Methods of creating, retrieving, and saving files are consistent throughout the suite. Entering, editing, and formatting text have standard procedures. Steps for printing are also the same throughout the application. The help files built into the applications provide essential assistance.

Opening the application of an office suite is standard throughout the suite. Whenever the user starts one of these applications, templates for a new blank document, spreadsheet, or presentation appear. Another advantage of Microsoft Office is the ability to open more than one application at a time. Then the user can view them on the same screen. Also, the user can have more than one document (spreadsheet or presentation) visible at a time to compare or edit.

michaeljung/Shutterstock.com

TERMS

access key
active window
cell
dialog box launcher
document template
insertion point
key tip badges
maximized

minimized
on-demand tab
presentation
restoring
ribbon
spreadsheet
windowed

LEARNING GOALS

After completing this section, you will be able to:

- Launch a Microsoft Office application.
- Describe features common to Microsoft Office applications.
- Explain the process of displaying multiple windows.

Launching Applications

Like all applications in Windows, the Microsoft Office suite is accessed via the **Start** or **Apps** menu. In Windows 10, click the **Start** menu button, click **All apps**, and scroll to and expand the **Microsoft Office** group, as shown in Figure 6-1. In Windows 8, click the **Apps** menu button to display the **Apps** menu. Then, scroll to the **Microsoft Office** group. In Windows 7, click the **Start** menu button to display the **Start** menu. Then, click **All Programs** followed by the **Microsoft Office** folder.

Launching Microsoft Word

To launch Microsoft Word, click the **Word 2013** icon in the **Start** or **Apps** menu. Wait for the program to load and display the startup screen. Word 2013 begins by presenting the user with the choice to open a document, begin a new blank document, or begin a document based on a template.

A blank document contains no text and has a minimum number of standard formatting styles. A **document template** is a document preformatted for a specific use and may contain placeholder text or images the user replaces with actual content. Word contains many templates. Templates are also found in Microsoft Excel and Microsoft PowerPoint.

Microsoft Word is able to save documents in a variety of file formats. For example, a document created in Microsoft Word 2013 can be saved

Key Applications
GS5 **2.4**

Key Applications
GS4 **1.3.3**

FYI

Versions of Microsoft Word previous to Word 2013 automatically open a blank document when launched.

Key Applications
GS5 **2.10.1**

Microsoft Office group →

Goodheart-Willcox Publisher

Figure 6-1. The applications in the Microsoft Office suite are accessed in the Windows 10 **Start** menu.

in a format that can be read by earlier versions of Microsoft Word. In addition, Microsoft Word documents can be saved in other formats. A popular format is portable document format (PDF). Documents saved in PDF format have all text and graphics intact, but cannot be edited by the PDF-reader software. Files can also be saved as Extensible Markup Language (XML) documents, which are used for web pages. It is also possible to save Word files into a format that can be read by OpenOffice, an open-source word-processing program. Also, Word files can be saved as plain text with the .txt extension. This is the most portable format since any other software that can read text can read this format.

Launching Microsoft Excel

Key Applications
3.12

To launch Microsoft Excel, click the **Excel 2013** icon in the **Start** or **Apps** menu. Wait for the program to load and display the startup screen. Excel 2013 begins by presenting the user with the choice to open a spreadsheet, begin a new blank spreadsheet, or begin a spreadsheet based on a template.

A **spreadsheet** is a special type of document in which data are organized in columns and rows. The individual box where a row and column intersect is called a **cell**. When a cell is selected, its border is thicker than normal. This is called the *active cell*. Text or numbers that are entered are placed in the active cell.

Key Applications
3.11

Microsoft Excel is able to save spreadsheets in a variety of file formats. As with Microsoft Word, Microsoft Excel can save spreadsheets in a format for earlier versions of the software. Microsoft Excel can also save files in PDF, XML, and text formats. Microsoft Excel files can be saved for the OpenOffice spreadsheet function as well. Another popular format is called comma-separated values (CSV). It is the most portable format for copying spreadsheet data into other applications.

Launching Microsoft PowerPoint

To launch Microsoft PowerPoint, click the **PowerPoint 2013** icon in the **Start** or **Apps** menu. Wait for the program to load and display the startup screen. PowerPoint 2013 begins by presenting the user with the choice to open a presentation, begin a new blank presentation, or begin a presentation based on a template.

A **presentation** contains individual slides used to communicate information to an audience. Each slide may contain text, images, sounds, tables, or other information. The presentation is played back as a slide show.

Key Applications
5.1.2

Microsoft PowerPoint is able to save spreadsheets in a variety of file formats. Files can be saved in a format for earlier versions of the software. Files can also be saved as PowerPoint Show (PPS) files, which allows sharing with others who do not have Microsoft PowerPoint. Less-popular formats for presentations include PDF, XML, and text files. Files can also be saved in the OpenOffice format.

Common Features and Functions

The interface of each application in a suite is similar. This is to allow a user to learn basic commands and features once instead of individually for each program. For example, each program in the Microsoft Office suite contains the **Quick Access** toolbar. It contains the **Save**, **Undo**, and **Redo** or **Repeat** buttons in each program of the suite. The **Quick Access** toolbar is always displayed above the ribbon in the Microsoft Office suite.

Basic Option Settings

Microsoft Office applications have common basic option settings that the user can adjust. These options are found in the backstage view, which is displayed by clicking the **File** tab in the ribbon. Click **Options** on the left-hand side of the backstage view to open the **Options** dialog box.

In the **Options** dialog box, click **General** on the left-hand side. General options include choosing interface, personalization, and startup options. For example, the mini toolbar that is normally displayed when text is selected can be disabled. Also, you can enter your name and initials so tracked changes will be recorded as made by you.

Click **Proofing** on the left-hand side of the dialog box. There are several check boxes on this screen that allow you to set what is checked or ignored during a spelling and grammar check. The **AutoCorrect Options...** button opens the **AutoCorrect** dialog box for making settings on automatic spelling corrections.

Click **Save** on the left-hand side of the dialog box. The options on this screen allow you to select how often the file is automatically saved, where it is saved, and in which format. To change the default file format, click the **Save files in this format:** drop-down list. To change the location of auto recover files, enter the path in the **AutoRecover file location:** text box.

Insertion Point

The **insertion point** is the location where text or images will be placed within the document. It appears as a vertical line within the document. To avoid errors, it is important to be aware of the location of the insertion point before adding text or images. The insertion point appears the same in all Office suite applications.

Ribbon Interface

The **ribbon** is the main command interface for the Microsoft Office suite of software. It consists of tabs, each containing commands arranged in groups, as shown in Figure 6-2. The name of each ribbon indicates the type of commands it contains. The groups on each tab contain similar or related commands. To activate a command on the ribbon, click the command button using the mouse.

In Microsoft Office 2013, each application contains the **File**, **Home**, **Insert**, and **Review** tabs in the ribbon. Other tabs will be present,

GS5 Computing Fundamentals
3.4

Career Skills

Agriculture and Food Science Technician
Agricultural and food science technicians often work in laboratories assisting agriculture and food scientists. They perform duties such as measuring and analyzing food quality. They use word processing, spreadsheets, and databases to analyze and report on the research results. On occasion they prepare presentations for the scientists as well.

GS5 Computing Fundamentals
3.8.1, 3.8.2, 3.8.3, 3.8.4

Tab   Command button

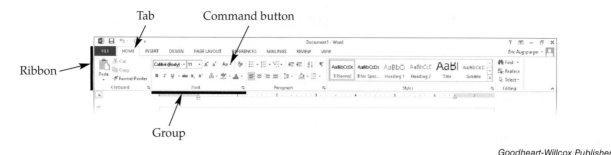

Ribbon

Group

Figure 6-2. The ribbon is the main command interface in the Microsoft Office suite of software.

depending on the application. Additionally, one or more on-demand tabs may be present. An **on-demand tab** is displayed depending on what is selected in the program document.

In the lower-right corner of most groups on the ribbon is a small arrow. This is called a **dialog box launcher**. Clicking the arrow opens a dialog box related to the commands in the group.

Keyboard Navigation

The ribbon is designed for using a mouse to select commands. However, the keyboard can also be used to navigate the ribbon and select commands. This allows the user to quickly complete tasks without removing his or her hands from the keyboard to use the mouse. Access keys are used to navigate the ribbon with the keyboard. An **access key** is the keyboard key or key combination used instead of the mouse to activate a command. These are often called *keyboard shortcuts*.

Access keys are displayed by pressing the [Alt] key on the keyboard. Little boxes called **key tip badges** appear over each command in the **Quick Access** toolbar and the ribbon tabs, as shown in Figure 6-3. To activate a command on the **Quick Access** toolbar, press the key or key combination shown in the key tip badge corresponding to the command. To access a command on the ribbon, first press the access key for the tab, even if the tab is currently visible, and then press the key or key combination shown for the command.

Key tip badges

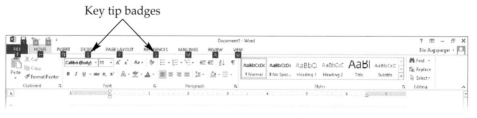

Figure 6-3. Key tip badges are displayed on the ribbon when the [Alt] key is pressed.

HANDS-ON EXAMPLE 6.1.1

KEYBOARD NAVIGATION OF THE RIBBON

Learning to navigate the ribbon and activate commands using the keyboard can improve your efficiency using the software. Once learned, a keyboard shortcut is usually a much faster way to activate a command than using the mouse.

1. Launch Microsoft Word, and click Blank Document in the startup screen to begin a new document.
2. Press and release the [Alt] key. Key tip badges are displayed on the **Quick Access** toolbar and the ribbon.
3. Press the [W] key to activate the **View** tab in the ribbon. Make note of the access keys for commands on this tab.
4. Press the [1] key (number one) to display a full-page view of the document.
5. Applying what you have learned, use the keyboard to display the key tip badges on the **View** tab.
6. Press the [I] key (letter i) to display the document at a zoom level in which the width of the document fills the width of the window.

Toggle Buttons

Many command buttons on the ribbon are toggles. If a toggle button is clicked, the command is either activated or deactivated. Clicking the button toggles the command on and off. The **Show/Hide** button in the **Paragraph** group on the **Home** tab of the ribbon in Word is an example of a toggle button. It displays nonprinting characters found on the page. For example, when this button is clicked, a paragraph symbol, called a *pilcrow*, is shown at the end of each paragraph. Clicking the button again hides the paragraph symbols along with all other nonprinting characters.

Other toggle buttons include the **Bold**, **Italic**, and **Underline** buttons located in the **Font** group on the **Home** tab of the ribbon in Word. These buttons are used to change the formatting of text, such as to emphasize it. The **Bold** button makes the lines composing the individual text characters thicker. For example, this text is bold: **bold**. The **Italic** button makes the characters slanted. For example, this text is italicized: *italic*. The **Underline** button adds a rule under the selected word or characters. For example, this text is underlined: <u>underline</u>. Clicking any of these buttons a second time toggles off the corresponding formatting for the selected word or characters.

HANDS-ON EXAMPLE 6.1.2

TOGGLE BUTTONS

Many command buttons in the Microsoft Office suite of software are toggles. The concept of toggle buttons is important to understand.

1. Launch Microsoft Word, and click Blank Document in the startup screen to begin a new document.

¶
Show/
Hide

2. Click the **Show/Hide** toggle button so it is on.
3. Add your first and last names to the document. Notice that the insertion point and paragraph symbol move to the right as characters are entered.
4. Select your first name by double-clicking it. Selected text is highlighted.

B
Bold

5. Click the **Bold** button in the **Font** group on the **Home** tab of the ribbon. The button is toggled on, and the text is bolded.
6. Applying what you have learned, select only your last name.

I
Italic

7. Click the **Italic** button in the **Font** group on the **Home** tab of the ribbon. The button is toggled on, and the text is italicized.
8. Select both names by clicking at the beginning of your first name, holding down the left mouse button, and dragging to the end of your last name. Then release the left mouse button. Both names should now be highlighted.

U
Underline

9. Click the **Underline** button in the **Font** group on the **Home** tab of the ribbon. The button is toggled on, and the text is underlined. Note: the underline may not be visible if Word thinks your names are misspelled words and places a red squiggly line under them to indicate this.
10. Applying what you have learned, select only your last name.

I
Italic

11. Click the **Italic** button in the **Font** group on the **Home** tab of the ribbon. The button is toggled off, and your last name is no longer italicized, but it remains underlined.
12. Close Word by clicking the **Close** button (X) in the upper-right corner of the window. When asked to save the file, click the **No** button.

Displaying Multiple Windows

GS5 Computing Fundamentals
3.3.2

GS4 Key Applications
1.3.4

FYI

A window that is in the windowed state may be referred to as *restored down*.

Each application in the Microsoft Office suite is opened in its own window. Additionally, by default, each document that is open in a Microsoft Office application appears in its own window. The current window, which is called the **active window**, is where any command that is entered will be applied.

When a window fills the entire screen, it is **maximized**. Other applications may be running in other windows, but those windows will not be visible except as buttons on the taskbar. To see more than one window, a maximized window must be resized smaller. A window that is visible, but does not fill the entire screen, is **windowed**. This is done by clicking the resizing button in the upper-right corner of the window. It is to the left of the **Close** button (X), and the button icon looks like two windows, one behind the other, as shown in Figure 6-4. Once the button is clicked, the window is resized smaller. The button also changes to the maximize button.

A window can be resized once it is no longer maximized. Resizing a window is easy. Move the cursor over an edge of the window until it changes to a standard resizing cursor. A resizing cursor looks like two arrows pointing in the directions the window can be resized. When the cursor is over a left or right edge, the arrows will point horizontally. When the cursor is over a top or bottom edge, the arrows will point vertically. When the cursor is over a corner, the arrows will point diagonally. Once the resizing cursor is displayed, click, hold, and drag to resize the window.

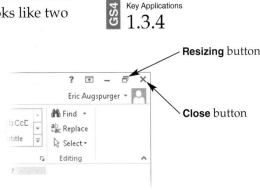

Goodheart-Willcox Publisher

Figure 6-4. The resizing button is used to window the application. The standard Windows **Close** button is used to close the application.

Moving a window is easy. Click and hold on the window's title bar, and drag the window to a new location. If the window is dragged to the top of the screen, it will be maximized. If the window is dragged to the left side of the screen, the window will be resized to fill the left half of the screen. If the window is dragged to the right side of the screen, the window will be resized to fill the right half of the screen. If the title bar of a maximized window is grabbed and dragged, the window will be placed in a windowed state.

Multiple open windows also can be automatically arranged next to each other or one above the other. To do so, right-click on a blank area of the taskbar at the bottom of the screen to display a shortcut menu, as shown in Figure 6-5. The choices to arrange window positions include **Cascade windows**, **Show windows stacked**, and **Show windows side-by-side**, as discussed in Chapter 3.

A window can be removed from the desktop area without closing the window. A window in this state is called minimized. A **minimized** window is still running, but hidden from view except for the button on the taskbar corresponding to the application. To minimize a window, click the minimize button in the upper-right corner of the window. This button is to the left of the resize button, and its icon looks like a dash or hyphen, as shown in Figure 6-4. To display a minimized window, which is called **restoring** the window, click the application's button in the taskbar. The window is restored to its previous state, either maximized or windowed.

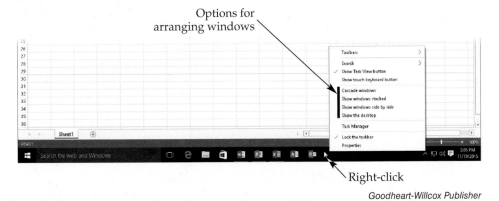

Goodheart-Willcox Publisher

Figure 6-5. Open windows can be arranged in one of several different ways.

If multiple documents are open for an application, after clicking the application button on the taskbar, click which document to restore. A window can also be restored using the [Alt][Tab] key combination to cycle through open application windows.

HANDS-ON EXAMPLE 6.1.3

MANAGING OPEN WINDOWS

It is quite common to have multiple application windows open at any given time. An essential skill for any computer user is managing open windows.

1. Launch Microsoft Word, and click Blank Document in the startup screen to begin a new document.
2. Launch Microsoft Excel, and click Blank Workbook in the startup screen to begin a new spreadsheet.
3. Launch Microsoft PowerPoint, and click Blank Presentation in the startup screen to begin a new slide show. There should be a button on the taskbar for Word, Excel, and PowerPoint because all three applications are running.
4. With PowerPoint the active window, click the standard close button (X) in the upper-right corner of the window to close the program. Since there were no entries or changes made, it will close immediately. The button on the taskbar corresponding to PowerPoint disappears.
5. If Word is not the active window, make it active by clicking the button on the taskbar corresponding to Word.
6. Add this line of text to the document: Principles of Information Technology.
7. Minimize the Word window by pressing the minimize button in the upper-right corner of the window. Although the window is no longer visible, Word is still loaded in the computer's memory. The button corresponding to Word is still displayed on the taskbar.
8. If the Excel window is not active, make it active by clicking the button on the taskbar corresponding to Excel.
9. Click cell A1, which is the upper-left cell, so that it is active (surrounded by a thick border).
10. Enter your first name in cell A1.
11. Press the [Tab] key to fix the content of cell A1 and make cell B1 the active cell.
12. Enter your last name in cell B1. Do not be concerned if part of the first name is overwritten.
13. Press the [Enter] to fix the content of cell B1 and make cell A2 active.
14. Enter this formula in cell A2: =TODAY().
15. Press the [Enter] key to fix the content. Today's date appears in cell A2.
16. Right-click on an empty space on the taskbar to display a shortcut menu.

HANDS-ON EXAMPLE 6.1.3 (CONTINUED)

17. Click **Show windows side by side** in the shortcut menu. The Word and Excel windows are resized and positioned to be side by side, as shown. To make either window active, click anywhere within that window.

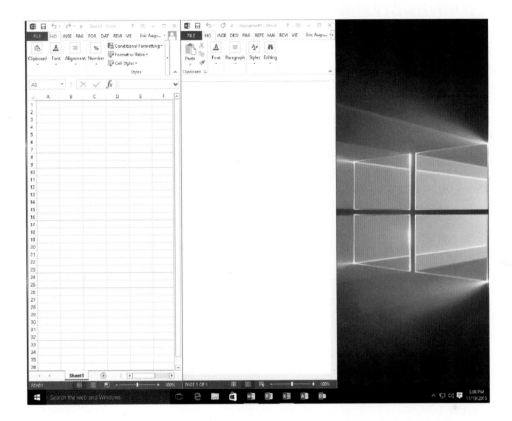

18. Applying what you have learned, use the shortcut menu to display the windows stacked and then cascading.
19. Applying what you have learned, minimize each window so the desktop is visible.

6.1 | SECTION REVIEW

 ## CHECK YOUR UNDERSTANDING

1. What is the location where text or images will be placed within the document?
2. What is the name of the command interface that appears at the top of all Microsoft Office applications?
3. Which command tabs are present in all Microsoft Office 2013 applications?
4. What happens if a toggle button is clicked?
5. What is the window called if it is running, but hidden from view except for a button on the taskbar?

IC3 CERTIFICATION PRACTICE

The following question is a sample of the types of questions presented on the IC3 exam.

1. The **Show/Hide** button that displays all non-printing characters is found on the _____ tab in the _____ group.
   A. **Home**; **Font**
   B. **Insert**; **Page Layout**
   C. **Design**; **Format**
   D. **Home**; **Paragraph**

BUILD YOUR VOCABULARY

As you progress through this course, develop a personal IT glossary. This will help you build your vocabulary and prepare you for a career. Write a definition for each of the following terms and add it to your IT glossary.

access key	minimized
active window	on-demand tab
cell	presentation
dialog box launcher	restoring
document template	ribbon
insertion point	spreadsheet
key tip badges	windowed
maximized	

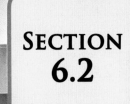

SAVING, PRINTING, AND OPENING DOCUMENTS

wavebreakmedia/Shutterstock.com

Documents, spreadsheets, and presentations are created to be viewed again or printed on hard copy. While creating a document, spreadsheet, or presentation in Word, Excel, or PowerPoint, the information is stored in the computer's RAM. RAM is temporary and will hold the information as long as the computer is on and the application is open. That information has to be moved to a permanent storage location.

Microsoft Office can save and recover files if something causes the system to crash. This protects the user from lost data. The state of the program is also remembered. For example, Microsoft Office will remember how many windows were open and what applications were being displayed.

 Essential Question

Why does software not automatically save a new file as soon as it is created?

TERMS

backstage view
closing
collate
landscape
opening
portrait
print preview
printing
virtual printer

LEARNING GOALS

After completing this section, you will be able to:
- Describe the process for saving files.
- Explain how to print files.
- Close files and applications.
- Discuss opening of files.

GS5 Key Applications
2.4

GS4 Key Applications
6.2.2, 6.2.3

FYI

If the file has not yet been saved, clicking the **Save** button on the **Quick Access** toolbar will begin the "save as" function.

Saving Files

The procedure for saving files is standard. Files can be saved on the computer's local hard disk drive, a network drive, a removable drive, or the cloud. When the user saves a file on the local hard drive or a portable flash drive, that same computer or flash drive must be used to retrieve the file. When the file is saved on a network, it is stored on a hard drive that can be reached from any computer on the network. If the user saves the file in the cloud, the file can be accessed from any location by means of an Internet connection.

Saving Files for the First Time

The first time a file is saved, it must be given a name. Click the **File** tab in the ribbon. The view that is displayed is called the **backstage view**, as shown in Figure 6-6. Click either **Save** or **Save As** in the backstage view. Since the file has not been saved, either command begins the "save as" function, which is used to name the file. To complete the save, select a location in the **Recent Folders** list or click the **Browse** button to navigate to a folder. A standard Windows **Save As** dialog box is displayed. Finally, enter a name for the file in the **File name:** text box in the **Save As** dialog box, and click the **Save** button. Be sure the correct location is current in the **Save As** dialog box before clicking the **Save** button.

Click either to save the file for the first time

Goodheart-Willcox Publisher

Figure 6-6. Clicking the **File** tab displays the backstage view. What is shown in the backstage view depends on which category is clicked on the left-hand side.

After the initial save when file is named, the **Save** command can be used to save the file quickly. The **Save** command is found in the backstage view of the **File** tab or on the **Quick Access** toolbar. If the **Save As** command is used after the file has been saved at least once, a copy of the file is created under a different name or in a different location. The original document is no longer open.

Key Applications
GS4 1.3.2

HANDS-ON EXAMPLE 6.2.1

SAVING AN OFFICE DOCUMENT

Saving a document is one of the most basic skills a computer user must have. Until a document is saved the first time, it exists only in the computer's volatile memory. If the power is shut off, the document is lost unless it has been saved.

1. Insert your PRINC-OF-IT flash drive into the computer.
2. Applying what you have learned, create a folder on the flash drive named Chap06.
3. Applying what you have learned, maximize Microsoft Word if it is open, or launch Word and begin a new blank document.
4. If not already in the document, add this line of text: Principles of Technology.
5. Click the **Save** button on the **Quick Access** toolbar. Since the document has not yet been saved, the **Save As** function is started.
6. Click the **Browse** button and navigate to the Chap06 folder on your flash drive.
7. Click in the **File name:** text box in the **Save As** dialog box, and enter your last name, as shown.

Save

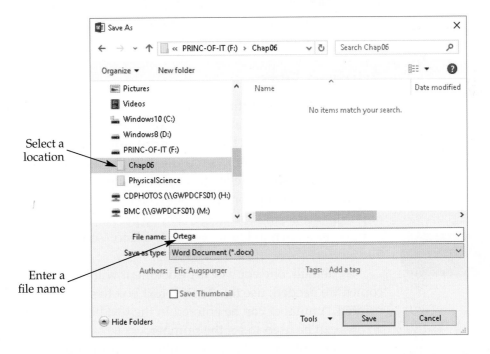

Select a location

Enter a file name

8. Click the **Save** button in the **Save As** dialog box. The document is saved to the flash drive with your last name as the file name. The .docx file name extension is automatically added to the file name. The file name becomes the name of the document, which is displayed in the title bar of the Word window.

HANDS-ON EXAMPLE 6.2.1 (CONTINUED)

9. Applying what you have learned, maximize Microsoft Excel if it is open, or launch Excel and begin a new blank document.
10. If not already in the spreadsheet, add this formula to cell A2: =TODAY().
11. Click the **Save** button on the **Quick Access** toolbar. Because the spreadsheet has not yet been saved, the **Save As** function is started.
12. Applying what you have learned, navigate to the Chap06 folder on your flash drive.
13. Click in the **File name:** text box in the **Save As** dialog box, and enter your first name.
14. Click the **Save** button in the **Save As** dialog box. The document is saved to the flash drive with your first name as the file name. The .xlsx file name extension is automatically added to the file name. The file name becomes the name of the document, which is displayed in the title bar of the Excel window.
15. Launch Windows Explorer, and display the content of the Chap06 folder on the flash drive. Verify that the DOCx and XLSx files you just saved are in the folder.

FYI

The [Ctrl][S] key combination is a shortcut to save a file that is common to most software.

Key Applications
2.6, 2.7

Key Applications
1.1.4

FYI

The [Ctrl][P] key combination is a shortcut to print a document that is common to most software.

Updating Files

Once a file has been saved, updating it is a quick process. Clicking the **Save** button on the **Quick Access** toolbar or clicking **Save** in the **File** tab immediately saves the current state of the file under the same file name. The original file is overwritten with current changes.

To create a copy of a file, first save the file to update it. Then, use the **Save As** command to save a copy under a different name or location. It is important to remember that after the **Save As** command, the active document is the copy with the new name, not the original file.

Printing Files

Printing is outputting the content of a file, usually as a hardcopy on paper. Before printing a document or spreadsheet, Microsoft Office offers the user a print preview screen. A **print preview** shows the document exactly how it will look when printed. If the document has more than one page, the user can click through the pages one by one. Most software also allows many options to be set when printing a file. Microsoft Office applications use the backstage view to preview the printing and set options, as shown in Figure 6-7. This is accessed by clicking **Print** in the **File** tab.

By default, one copy of the document will be printed. If additional copies are needed, use the **Copies:** text box to set how many will be printed. A number can be entered in the text box or the up and down arrows can be used to set the number.

A computer may have more than one printer installed. Some computers have access to printers over a network. In addition, some virtual printers may be installed, such as the Microsoft XPS Document Writer. A **virtual printer** outputs a file instead of a physical hardcopy. Select the appropriate printer using the **Printer** drop-down list.

Click
to print

Make settings
as needed

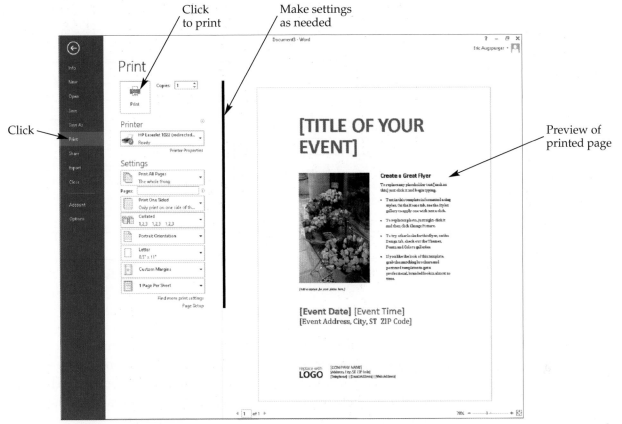

Click

Preview of
printed page

Goodheart-Willcox Publisher

Figure 6-7. The backstage view is used to preview the document before it is printed.

Options are selected under **Settings**. The specific options available may differ by application, but most Microsoft Office applications have similar options.

The first option allows the user to choose how much of the document to print. Depending on which application is printing, settings may include printing the entire document; printing specific pages, slides, or workbooks; or printing only what is selected in the document.

To **collate** is arranging multiple copies of a document so all pages are in the correct order. For example, if two copies of a five-page document are printed, collating prints pages one through five and then one through five again instead of printing two copies of page one, two copies of page two, and so on. There is an option to print collated or not collated.

The page layout is how the document will be placed on the sheet. The layout can be portrait or landscape, as shown in Figure 6-8. **Portrait** layout or orientation is when the long edge of the paper is on the sides. **Landscape** layout or orientation is when the long edge is on the top and bottom. When a layout option is selected, the preview is updated to reflect it.

Ethics

Bias-Free Language
As you go to work or school each day, you may encounter others who categorize people using biased words and comments. Using age, gender, race, disability, or ethnicity as a way to describe others is unethical and sometimes illegal. Use bias-free language in all of your communication to show respect for others.

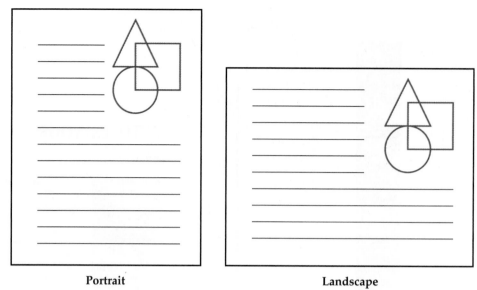

Portrait   Landscape

Goodheart-Willcox Publisher

Figure 6-8. The page layout can be either portrait or landscape.

The paper size should be set to the size of paper that is loaded in the printer. In some cases, such as with Excel, the document can be scaled down (reduced in size) to fit better on the selected paper size. The **Fit Sheet on One Page** option in Excel is handy if the spreadsheet is larger than one page.

In some applications, such as Word and PowerPoint, the number of pages printed on each sheet of paper can be set. The default is one page per sheet. Printing more than one page per sheet decreases the size of each page. How it will appear is not reflected in the preview. Printing more than one page per sheet is useful for creating handouts, but can make the individual pages hard to read.

HANDS-ON EXAMPLE 6.2.2

PRINTING AN OFFICE DOCUMENT

It is common to print a document, whether on paper or to a file via a virtual printer. It is important to understand how to make settings when printing a document.

1. Applying what you have learned, maximize Microsoft Excel if it is open, or launch Excel and begin a new blank document.
2. If not already in the spreadsheet, add this formula to cell A2: =TODAY().
3. Click the **File** tab to display the backstage view.
4. Click **Print** in the backstage view to display the print preview and the options.
5. Select the printer specified by your instructor.
6. In the **Settings** area, click the bottom drop-down list, and click **Fit Sheet on One Page**. This option forces the spreadsheet to print on a single page, although in this case the content of the spreadsheet would fit on a single page without using this option.
7. Click the **Print** button at the top of the backstage view.

Closing Files and Applications

Closing means removing a file or application from RAM. When a file is not going to be used for a period of time, it should be closed. The same is true of a software application. This is a good practice because closing files and applications frees up space in memory for other applications.

To close a file in a Microsoft Office application, click the **File** tab, and then click **Close**. If the file has no unsaved changes, it is immediately closed, and the application remains open. If there are unsaved changes, the user is prompted to save the file before closing it.

An easy way to close an application is to click the standard Windows close button (X). This method can be used to close any Microsoft Office application or any other application.

Opening Files

Just as knowing how to save a file is a basic computer skill, knowing how to open a file is a basic skill. **Opening** a file is placing its content into RAM so the content can be used. Opening a file is a simple process: activate the **Open** command, navigate to the file location, and select the file.

In Microsoft Office, click **Open** in the **File** tab. Then, click **Computer** in the backstage view, followed by the **Browse** button, as shown in Figure 6-9. A standard Windows **Open** dialog box is displayed. Navigate to the location where the file is saved, select the file, and click the **Open** button. The file contents are loaded into RAM and displayed in the application window.

Key Applications
GS4 1.3.1

The [Ctrl][O] key combination is a common shortcut for opening a file in an application.

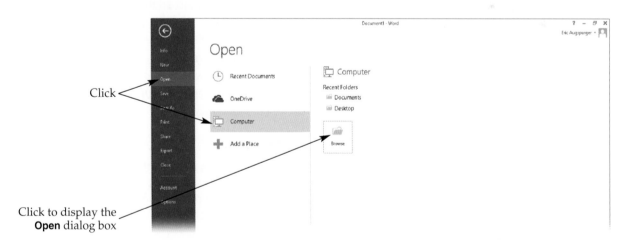

Click

Click to display the **Open** dialog box

Goodheart-Willcox Publisher

Figure 6-9. Opening a document in a Microsoft Office application.

HANDS-ON EXAMPLE 6.2.3

OPENING AN OFFICE DOCUMENT

One of the most basic skills a computer user must have is the ability to open a file. It is important to understand where documents are stored and to select the correct document for opening.

1. Insert your PRINC-OF-IT flash drive into the computer.
2. If any Microsoft Office application is open, close it by clicking the standard Windows close button (X).
3. Launch Microsoft Word, and click **Open Other Documents** in the startup screen.
4. In the **Open** dialog box, navigate to the Chap06 folder on your flash drive.
5. Select the file named with your last name. By default, only Word files are displayed in the dialog box, but the file type can be changed if needed.
6. Click the **Open** button. The file is opened and displayed in the Word application window. Notice that the file content is the same as when it was last saved.

6.2 SECTION REVIEW

 ## CHECK YOUR UNDERSTANDING

1. What does the **Save** command do if the file has not yet been saved?
2. How is the backstage view displayed in Microsoft Office?
3. What are the two options for how the printed page is arranged or laid out on a sheet of paper?
4. What are two ways to close a Microsoft Office application?
5. What is placing a file's content into RAM so the content can be used called?

IC3 CERTIFICATION PRACTICE

The following question is a sample of the types of questions presented on the IC3 exam.

1. Which of the following commands is used to save the current file under a new name?
   A. **File>Save As**
   B. **File>Save**
   C. **Home>Clipboard/Paste**
   D. **File>New**

BUILD YOUR VOCABULARY

As you progress through this course, develop a personal IT glossary. This will help you build your vocabulary and prepare you for a career. Write a definition for each of the following terms and add it to your IT glossary.

backstage view
closing
collate
landscape
opening

portrait
print preview
printing
virtual printer

EDITING AND FORMATTING

wavebreakmedia/Shutterstock.com

The applications in the Microsoft Office suite use the same techniques for editing and formatting text. To edit text means inserting, deleting, replacing, formatting, and copying and pasting text. Revising text is an important feature in all applications, not just Microsoft Word. One of the most valuable aspects of using Office is that you can quickly revise data. Editing and formatting skills form the foundation of all text-based activities throughout the suite.

The insertion point is where changes will take place. To set the insertion point, click at the location. Then the arrow keys on the keyboard can also be used to move the insertion point around the document. Keyboard navigation is often quicker than using the mouse.

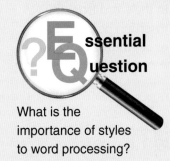

Essential Question

What is the importance of styles to word processing?

LEARNING GOALS

After completing this section, you will be able to:

- Describe basic ways in which to edit text.
- Manipulate inserted media files.
- Reverse errors in a document.
- Discuss finding and replacing text.
- Explain how to move, copy, cut, and paste text and images.
- Apply formatting to text.

TERMS

ascending order	handles
bulleted list	inserting
character style	move
copy	numbered list
crop	paragraph style
cut	paste
descending order	sorting
drag-and-drop	style
editing	system clipboard
format painter	typeface
formatting	

FYI

Holding down the [Ctrl] key before pressing the [Delete] or [Backspace] key will delete all characters in the word from the insertion point to the end or beginning of the word.

GS5 Key Applications
1.6

GS4 Key Applications
1.1.9

FYI

The [Ctrl][A] key combination is used in many software programs to select all content.

Editing Text

Editing a document is making changes to the text, format, layout, or other aspects of the content. The insertion point is where changes will take place. To set the insertion point, click at the location. The arrow keys on the keyboard can also be used to move the insertion point around the document.

Deleting Text

The [Delete] key erases one character at a time to the right of the insertion point. The [Backspace] key erases one character at a time to the left of the insertion point. If a word, sentence, or paragraph is selected, either key erases the selection. If text is added, the selection is erased and replaced with the new text.

Selecting Text

To select an entire word, double-click the word. To select an entire line of text, move the cursor to the left of the line until it changes to an arrow. Then, click once. This selects a line of text, not a sentence, as shown in Figure 6-10. To select a sentence, hold down the [Ctrl] key, and then click anywhere in the sentence. This only works if there is not currently a selection. To select a paragraph, move the cursor to the left of the paragraph until it changes to an arrow, and then double-click. To select the entire document, move the cursor to the left of any paragraph, and then either triple-click or hold down the [Ctrl] key and click once. You can also press the [Ctrl][A] key combination to select the entire document.

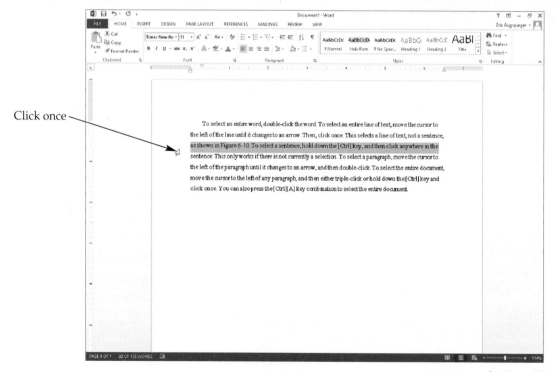

Click once

Goodheart-Willcox Publisher

Figure 6-10. When the cursor changes to an arrow, click once to select a line of text.

Selecting Nonadjacent Items

Sometimes it is necessary to select words, sentences, lines, or paragraphs that are not adjacent, or next to each other. Scrolling over the words will not work. Instead, select the first item, and then press and hold the [Ctrl] key. With the [Ctrl] key held down, additional items can be selected that are not adjacent to the first item. This selection method is useful if several nonadjacent items in a list, for example, need to be formatted the same.

Key Applications
1.1.9

Creating and Working with Lists

Lists are short lines or paragraphs of information, each typically only a few words in length, of related data. For example, a list may be the names of members in a class or the steps in the procedure for filling a car with gasoline. Lists are useful for displaying several small pieces of data in a format that is easy to read.

Key Applications
2.1.2

In a text or slide show document, there are two types of lists: bulleted and numbered. A **bulleted list**, also called an *unordered list*, consists of separate lines of text with a small graphic such as a dot in front of the line, as shown in Figure 6-11. A **numbered list**, also called an *ordered list*, consists of separate lines of text with numbers in sequential order in front of the text.

Creating a List

To create a bulleted list in Microsoft Word or Microsoft PowerPoint, select the lines that will compose the list. Then, click the **Bullets** button in the **Paragraph** group on the **Home** tab of the ribbon. The selected paragraphs are converted to an automatic bulleted list. Each item in the list is indented on the left and a bullet is added to the beginning of each paragraph. You can also click the button, and then enter text.

To create a numbered list in Microsoft Word or Microsoft PowerPoint, select the lines that will compose the list. Then, click the **Numbering** button in the **Paragraph** group on the **Home** tab of the ribbon. The selected paragraphs are converted to an automatic numbered list. Each item in the list is indented on the left and a number is added to the beginning of

> ## FYI
>
> Due to the nature of Microsoft PowerPoint, most of the slide templates are set up to create automatic bulleted lists whenever text is added.

Bulleted List

- Describe basic ways to edit text.
- Manipulate inserted media files.
- Reverse errors in a document.
- Discuss finding and replacing text.

Numbered List

1. Buckle your seatbelt.
2. Put your foot on the brake.
3. Start the car.
4. Check for traffic and pedestrians.

Goodheart-Willcox Publisher

Figure 6-11. A bulleted list is in no particular order. A numbered list presents information in a specific order.

Anytime you are working with lists, you may find the need to sort the items.

Key Applications
GS4 **1.1.9**

FYI

A spreadsheet is basically a series of lists. Each column can be thought of as a vertical list consisting of rows.

each paragraph. By default, the first number is 1, and each item in the list is sequentially numbered from there.

If the [Enter] key is pressed at the end of any paragraph in the list, the following line is automatically formatted as part of the bulleted or numbered list. To cancel the automatic bulleting or numbering on this new line, either press the [Enter] key a second time or click the button in the **Paragraph** group on the **Home** tab of the ribbon.

Sorting a List

Sometimes, it is not enough just to create a list, but the items in the list must be placed in a certain order. **Sorting** is arranging a list in either ascending or descending order. **Ascending order** is when the lowest value, such as A or 1, is at the top of the list. This is often called *A to Z order*. **Descending order** is when the highest value, such as Z or 10, is at the top of the list. This is often called *Z to A order*.

Sorting can be used on a series of single words or numbers, numbered lists, and bulleted lists. The items to be sorted must be adjacent. Sorting is particularly useful when working with tables. The first character in each cell in the table is read and the table sorted accordingly. Microsoft Word and Microsoft Excel can sort lists.

To sort a list in Microsoft Word, first select all items to be sorted. Then, click the **Sort** button in the **Paragraph** group on the **Home** tab of the ribbon. The **Sort Text** dialog box is displayed, as shown in Figure 6-12. Select whether to sort in ascending or descending order, and click the **OK** button to sort the list. Any empty lines, rows, or paragraphs will be placed either at the top or bottom of the list.

To sort a list in Microsoft Excel, first select all items to be sorted. This may be an entire column, selected adjacent cells within a column, or

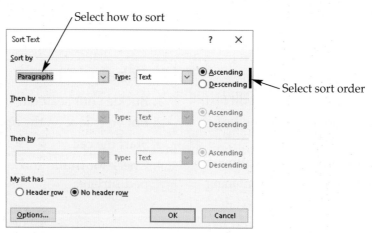

Figure 6-12. Sorting text in Microsoft Word.

multiple columns. Then, click the **Sort & Filter** button in the **Editing** group on the **Home** tab of the ribbon, as shown in Figure 6-13. In the drop-down list that is displayed, click **Sort smallest to largest** to sort in ascending order or **Sort largest to smallest** to sort in descending order.

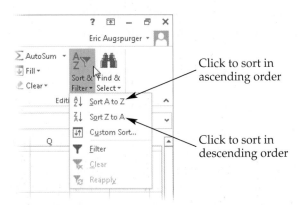

Click to sort in ascending order

Click to sort in descending order

Figure 6-13. Sorting data in Microsoft Excel. Note that ascending order is **Sort A to Z** and descending order is **Sort Z to A**.

HANDS-ON EXAMPLE 6.3.1

CREATING AND SORTING A LIST

Creating lists is a basic skill to have for creating documents. Many documents contain lists, such as sales data, addresses, names, or many other items.

1. Launch Microsoft Word, and begin a new blank document.
2. Enter the last names of five of your friends, each on a separate line (paragraph).
3. Move the cursor to the left of the first name in the list until it changes to an arrow, click and hold, and drag down to the last line in the list. When the entire list is highlighted, release the mouse button. The list is selected.

Bullets

4. Click the **Bullets** button in the **Paragraph** group on the **Home** tab of the ribbon. The list is converted to an automatic bulleted list.

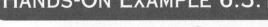

Sort

5. Click the **Sort** button in the **Paragraph** group on the **Home** tab of the ribbon. The **Sort Text** dialog box is displayed.
6. In the **Sort by** area of the dialog box, click the left-hand drop-down arrow, and click **Paragraphs** in the list. This tells Word that the breaks between items are indicated by returns (paragraphs).
7. Click the right-hand drop-down arrow, and click **Text** in the list. This tells Word to sort letters.
8. Click the **Ascending** radio button. This tells Word to sort the list in A to Z order.
9. Click the **OK** button to sort the list.
10. Double-click the first name in the list to select it.
11. Hold down the [Ctrl] key, and double-click the third name in the list.
12. Hold down the [Ctrl] key, and double-click the last name in the list. The first, third, and fifth names should be highlighted to indicate they are selected, but the second and fourth names should not be selected.

Key Applications
7.1

Inserting Media Files

It is possible to insert various media files, such as images, into documents using office suite software and then manipulate them. In Microsoft Office, the ribbon interface includes on-demand tabs. For example, when an image is selected, the **Format** on-demand tab is available in the ribbon. This tab contains commands related to working with images, such as changing the border, wrapping text around the image, adding shadow effects, aligning the image on the page, and changing the size of the image.

Key Applications
1.4.2

Inserting a Media File

Adding a media file to a document is called **inserting** or *attaching*. Depending on which Microsoft Office application is being used, images, videos, and sounds can be inserted. For example, to insert an image into Microsoft Word, Microsoft PowerPoint, or Microsoft Excel, click the **Pictures** button in the **Illustrations** group on the **Insert** tab of the ribbon. A standard open dialog box is displayed. Navigate to the location where the image file is saved, select the file, and click the **Insert** button. The image is added to the document at the current insertion point.

Key Applications
1.4.1

Image Location and Size

When an image is selected, small squares or dots, called handles, are displayed in the middle of each edge and at the corners, as shown in Figure 6-14. **Handles** are used to change the size of the image. The corner

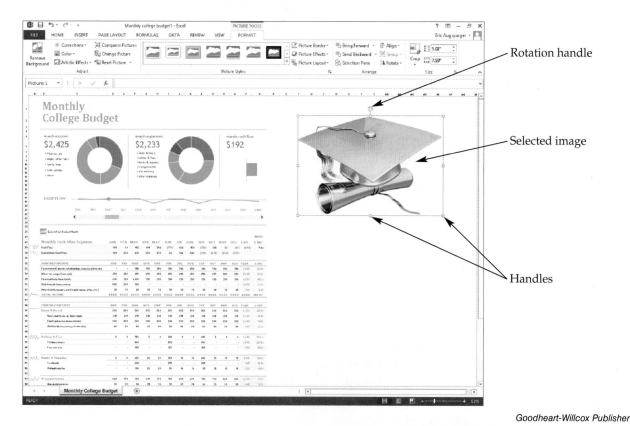

Goodheart-Willcox Publisher

Figure 6-14. When an image is selected, handles are displayed that can be used to resize the image.

handles are used to resize the image proportionally. This means the ratio of height to width remains the same. The handles on the top, bottom, and sides are used to resize the image nonproportionally. The ratio of height to width will change when these handles are used.

The location of an image can be adjusted by dragging the frame. Click on the outer edge of the selected image, not on a handle, and drag the image to a new location. Note: depending on how the image was inserted, its position may be locked.

FYI

Photographs and images should always be resized proportionally.

Cropping an Image

In some cases, only part of the image is needed. For example, a photograph may show a group of people, but only one person needs to be shown. It is possible to cut away the rest of the photograph. To **crop** an image is to trim the outer portion.

Key Applications
7.2

Key Applications
1.4.1

To crop an image in Microsoft Office, first select it. Then, click the **Crop** button in the **Size** group on the **Format** on-demand tab of the ribbon. New handles are displayed on the image. Click one of the handles and drag inward to specify the area to keep. The portion that will be cropped is grayed out. The size of the image will be reduced without changing the proportions by removing the portion of the image that is grayed out. To complete the operation, click anywhere outside of the image.

Rotating an Image

In Microsoft Office, an image can be rotated on an imaginary axis projecting out of the screen. It can be rotated in 90-degree increments either clockwise or counterclockwise or manually rotated to any angle. An image can also be flipped horizontally or vertically.

Key Applications
1.4.1

To rotate an image to any angle, first select the image to display the handles. There is a special handle displayed at the top-middle of the image that looks like a circular arrow. Click this handle and drag to rotate the image. Holding down the [Shift] key while dragging limits the rotation to 15 degree increments.

The ribbon can also be used to rotate an image. Select the image, and then click the **Rotate Objects** button in the **Arrange** group on the **Format** on-demand tab of the ribbon to display a drop-down menu, as shown in Figure 6-15. Options in this menu allow the image to be rotated 90 degrees clockwise or counterclockwise or to be flipped horizontally or vertically.

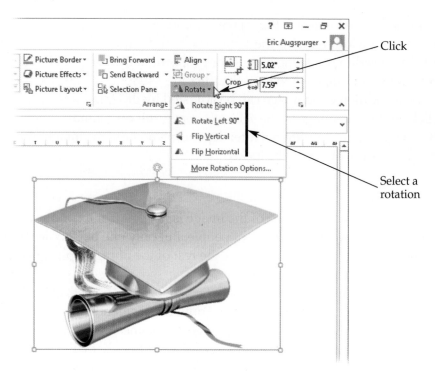

Figure 6-15. Using commands in the ribbon to rotate an image.

HANDS-ON EXAMPLE 6.3.2

GS4 Key Applications 1.4.2

MANIPULATING A MEDIA FILE

Photographs come in many different sizes. Once a photograph is inserted into a document, its size and location can be adjusted to fit the document. Additionally, the photograph itself can be manipulated, such as adding a border.

1. Insert your PRINC-OF-IT flash drive into the computer.
2. Navigate to the student companion website at www.g-wlearning.com, download the data files for this chapter, and save them in the Chap06 folder on your flash drive.
3. Applying what you have learned, open the Baltimore1 document file from the Chap06 folder on your flash drive.
4. Click at the end of the first paragraph. The insertion point is placed at that location.

Pictures

5. Click the **Pictures** button in the **Illustrations** group on the **Insert** tab of the ribbon. A standard open dialog box is displayed.
6. Navigate to the Chap06 folder on your flash drive, select the FortMcHenry.jpg image file, and click the **Insert** button. This photograph is inserted, but notice that it is very large in relation to the document.
7. If the image is not already selected, click it to select it.
8. Click the handle at the lower-right corner of the photograph, and drag it toward the middle of the image.
9. Resize the image so it is about 2″ × 3″. The size of the image is displayed in the **Height:** and **Width:** text boxes in the **Size** group on the **Format** on-demand tab in the ribbon.

Wrap Text

10. With the photo selected, click the **Wrap Text** button in the **Arrange** group on the **Format** on-demand tab in the ribbon to display a drop-down menu.

11. Click the **Square** option in the drop-down menu. The text is shifted up to fill the space to the right of the photo.

Picture Border

12. With the photo selected, click on the **Picture Border** button in the **Picture Styles** group on the **Format** on-demand tab in the ribbon to display a color palette.

13. Click a blue color swatch in the palette. A blue border appears around the photo, as shown.

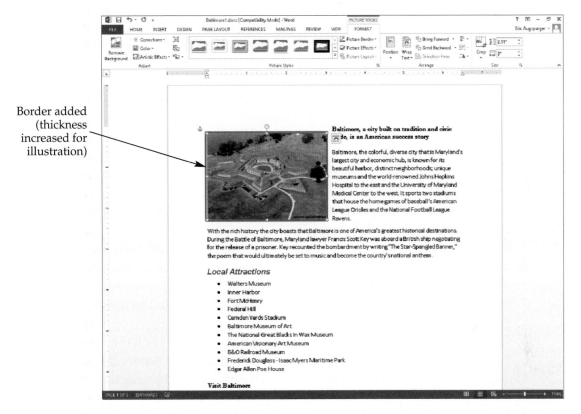

Border added (thickness increased for illustration)

14. Applying what you have learned, save the file as *LastName*Baltimore1 in the Chap06 folder on your flash drive, where *LastName* is your last name.

Reversing Errors

Most actions in software can be reversed, or undone. If an action cannot be undone, software will usually warn the user the action about to be taken is permanent. However, actions such as deleting, formatting, and moving text as well as many other actions can be quickly reversed with the **Undo** command. It is also possible to redo an action that was reversed with the **Undo** command. The **Redo** command restores the last action undone.

Key Applications
1.7

FYI

The **Repeat** command can be used to duplicate the last action.

In Microsoft Office, the **Undo** and **Redo** commands are located on the **Quick Access** toolbar. Clicking the **Undo** button reverses the last action. The [Ctrl][Z] key combination is the shortcut for undo. Clicking the drop-down arrow next to the **Undo** button displays a list of actions that can be undone. This list allows the user to select multiple actions to undo in one step, but actions must be undone in order. You cannot pick and choose which actions to undo. Clicking the **Redo** button restores the last undone action. The [Ctrl][Y] keyboard combination is the shortcut for redo. Only one action can be redone at a time.

HANDS-ON EXAMPLE 6.3.3

EDITING A DOCUMENT

The ability to edit a document is one of the most basic computer skills to have. Another basic computer skill is to be able to undo and redo changes.

1. Insert your PRINC-OF-IT flash drive into the computer.
2. Launch Microsoft Word.
3. Applying what you have learned, open the file *LastName*Baltimore1 from the Chap06 folder on your flash drive.
4. In the first line of text, click to the right of the letter g in the word bustling to place the insertion point at that location.
5. Press the [Backspace] key nine times to erase the word and one space.
6. Use the arrow keys to move the insertion point to the left of the letter q in the word quirky in the second paragraph.
7. Press the [Delete] key eight times to erase the word as well as the comma and space that follow it.
8. In the first line of the list under the paragraphs, double-click the word Area to select it. Notice that a mini toolbar is displayed when the cursor is over the selection.
9. Add the text Local. As soon as the first letter is added, the selection is replaced by the character.
10. Move the cursor to the left of the line in the list containing the text Federal Hill. When the cursor changes to an arrow, click once to select the entire line.
11. Press the [Delete] key to erase the line. In this case, the entire paragraph is deleted because the line was a single paragraph.
12. Click the **Undo** button on the **Quick Access** toolbar. The paragraph containing the text Federal Hill is restored as deleting it was the last change made to the document.
13. Applying what you have learned, move the insertion point to the end of the last line, which begins with the text Frederick Douglass.
14. Press the [Enter] key to add a new paragraph.
15. On the new line (paragraph), add the text Edgar Allen Poe House.
16. Save the file.

Undo

Searching for Text

Locating specific text within a document is very easy. This is accomplished with the **Find** and **Replace** commands. The ability to locate text is particularly valuable for long documents. If many instances of text appear in a document and must be changed, replacing the text is more efficient than editing each individual instance. Formatting and special characters can also be located and, if needed, replaced.

Key Applications
1.5

Finding Text

To locate specific text in Microsoft Office, click the **Find** button in the **Editing** group on the **Home** tab of the ribbon or press the [Ctrl][F] key combination. In Microsoft Excel, the **Find and Replace** dialog box is displayed (or the **Find** dialog box in Microsoft PowerPoint). In Microsoft Word, the **Navigation** pane is displayed on the left side of the window. To display the **Find and Replace** dialog box in Word, click the arrow next to the search box in the **Navigation** pane, and click **Advanced Find...** in the drop-down list.

To use the **Navigation** pane in Word, click in the search box, and enter the word or phrase to locate. All instances of the search word are listed in the **Navigation** pane and highlighted throughout the document, as shown in Figure 6-16. Clicking an entry in the list automatically jumps the view of the document to that location and selects the word.

Key Applications
1.1.5, 1.3.5

FYI

The [Ctrl][F] key combination is a shortcut common to most software for activating the **Find** command.

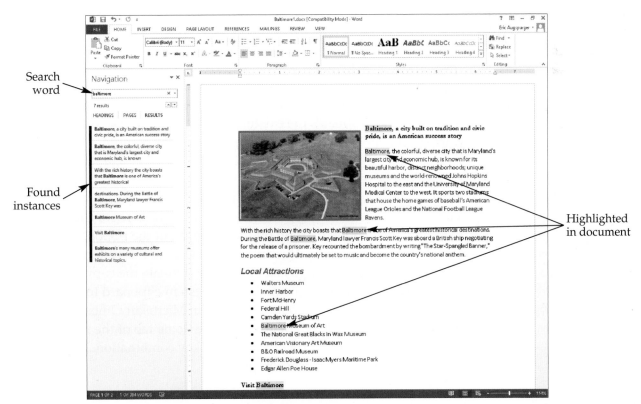

Goodheart-Willcox Publisher

Figure 6-16. Using the **Navigation** pane in Microsoft Word to locate text in the document.

To use the **Find and Replace** dialog box to locate text, click the **Find** tab in the dialog box (this is not in PowerPoint). Then, click in the **Find what:** text box, enter the word to locate, and click the **Find Next** button. The view of the document is automatically centered on the first instance of the word, and the word is selected. By default, the search is conducted from the insertion point downward. To find the next instance of the word, click the **Find Next** button again. Once the dialog box is closed after conducting a search, the [Ctrl][Page Down] and [Ctrl][Page Up] key combinations can be used to quickly find the next or previous instance of the last search word.

Replacing Text

To replace specific text in Microsoft Office, click the **Replace** button in the **Editing** group on the **Home** tab of the ribbon or press the [Ctrl][H] key combination. The **Find and Replace** dialog box is displayed (or the **Replace** dialog box in Microsoft PowerPoint). Click in the **Find what:** text box, and enter the word to locate. Next, click in the **Replace with:** text box, and enter the word to substitute. Click the **Find Next** button. The view of the document is automatically centered on the first instance of the word, and the word is selected. To replace that instance, click the **Replace** button, and the next instance is automatically located. To leave the located instance the way it is, click the **Find Next** button. To replace all instances in the document, click the **Replace All** button. The **Replace All** option should be used carefully as you will not have the opportunity to confirm each replacement.

Moving, Copying, Cutting, and Pasting Text and Images

The system clipboard is used to copy and paste content. The **system clipboard** is a virtual container for storing data. When new data are placed on the clipboard, the existing clipboard content is deleted. The current content of the clipboard remains until the computer is turned off or restarted.

A copy of text or an image is an exact duplicate of the original at the time the **copy** was made. The content exists in two locations. To copy content in Microsoft Office, first select what to copy. Then, click the **Copy** button in the **Clipboard** group on the **Home** tab of the ribbon or press the [Ctrl][C] key combination. The content is placed on the system clipboard. Then, the content can be pasted elsewhere to create the copy.

To **paste** is to add the content of the system clipboard to the document at the insertion point. To paste in Microsoft Office, click the **Paste** button in the **Clipboard** group on the **Home** tab of the ribbon, as shown in Figure 6-17, or press the [Ctrl][V] key combination. The clipboard content is added at the insertion point.

FYI

The shortcut menu can be used to copy, cut, and paste content.

GS5 Key Applications
1.1

GS4 Key Applications
1.1.1, 1.1.2

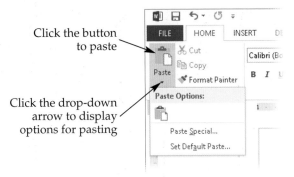

Click the button to paste

Click the drop-down arrow to display options for pasting

Figure 6-17. The ribbon can be used to paste content or the [Ctrl][V] key combination can be used.

To **cut** content means to remove it from the document and place it on the system clipboard. To cut content in Microsoft Office, first select what to cut. Then, click the **Cut** button in the **Clipboard** group on the **Home** tab of the ribbon or press the [Ctrl][X] key combination. The content is removed from the document and placed on the system clipboard. By cutting and pasting, the content is, in effect, *moved* from one location to another.

To **move** content means to remove it from the source location and place it in the destination location. Cutting and pasting moves content, but the mouse can also be used to move content. First, select what is to be moved. Then, by clicking and holding down the left mouse button, the content can be *dragged* to the new location. Releasing the mouse button causes the content to be *dropped* into the new location. Therefore, this operation is called **drag-and-drop.** The system clipboard is not involved in this procedure.

Key Applications
1.1.6

HANDS-ON EXAMPLE 6.3.4

Key Applications
1.1.6, 1.1.9

COPYING CONTENT BETWEEN DOCUMENTS

It is a common task to copy text from one document to another. An even more common task is to move text from one point in a document to another location in the same document.

1. Be sure the data files for this chapter have been downloaded to the Chap06 folder on your flash drive.
2. Launch Microsoft Word, and open the file *LastName*Baltimore1 from the Chap06 folder on your flash drive, if it is not already open.
3. Open the file Baltimore2 from the Chap06 folder on your flash drive.
4. Select all text in the Baltimore2 document by pressing the [Ctrl][A] key combination.

HANDS-ON EXAMPLE 6.3.4 (CONTINUED)

Copy

5. Click the **Copy** button in the **Clipboard** group of the **Home** tab of the ribbon, as shown. All text in the document is placed on the system clipboard.

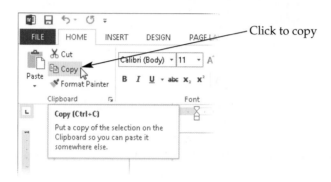
Click to copy

6. Close the Baltimore2 file without saving it.
7. In the *LastName*Baltimore1 file, place the insertion point at the end of the document.
8. Applying what you have learned, create a new line (paragraph).

Paste

9. Click the **Paste** button in the **Clipboard** group on the **Home** tab of the ribbon. The content of the system clipboard, which is the text from the other document, is placed at the insertion point.
10. Applying what you have learned, select the line at the end of the document with the text Matisse's Marguerite: Model Daughter.
11. Click on the selection, hold, and drag the text to the beginning of the line above it. As you drag, a small rectangle appears next to the cursor.
12. Release the mouse button. The selected text is moved to the new location.
13. Save the file.

FYI

The mini toolbar displayed when text is selected is intended for making formatting changes.

Key Applications
1.2.2

Formatting Text

Formatting text means changing the appearance of the characters. Bold, italic, and underline are examples of text formatting. Other examples include making the characters larger or smaller, striking a line through them, and changing their color. Formatting changes are applied to selected text or the text where the insertion point is located.

Fonts

A **typeface** is a design of characters. In common usage, the term *font* is used to mean typeface, although technically these are not the same thing. Common typefaces are Arial, Times New Roman, and Courier. Dozens of typefaces are installed with Windows and Microsoft Office. In Microsoft Office, the typeface is selected in the **Font** group on the **Home** tab of the ribbon. Click the **Font** drop-down arrow to see a list of installed fonts. The name of a font appears in a preview of the typeface. To change the typeface of the selection, click the font name in the list.

The size of the selected text can be changed using the **Font Size** text box or drop-down list in the **Font** group on the **Home** tab of the ribbon.

The size of text is measured in points. There are 72 points per inch, so an uppercase letter set in 11 point type is about 5/32″ tall, as shown in Figure 6-18.

Other text formatting options that can be set in the **Font** group on the **Home** tab of the ribbon include bold, italic, underline, strikethrough, subscript, superscript, and color. Bold, italic, and underline are discussed earlier in this chapter. Strikethrough is a horizontal line through the middle of characters. Click the **Strikethrough** button to format the selected text as strikethrough. Superscript is formatting that sets the character smaller than normal and raised, such as the 2 in X^2. Click the **Superscript** button to make the selected text superscript. Subscript is formatting that sets the character smaller than normal and lowered, such as the 1 in Y_1. Click the **Subscript** button to make the selected text subscript. To change the color of the selected text, click the drop-down arrow next to the **Font Color** button, and select a new color in the palette that is displayed.

Figure 6-18. Type is measured in points. There are 72 points per inch. Note: the measurement includes an allotment for the part of some letters that descends below the line.

Styles

A more efficient and complete method of formatting text is using styles. A **style** is a group of formatting settings that can be applied in one step. The look of text can be quickly changed by picking a new style. It immediately changes the typeface and paragraph properties of the text.

For text documents, there are two basic types of styles: paragraph and character. A **paragraph style** defines the formatting for a paragraph, including the text formatting. A **character style** defines the text formatting for individual characters. Paragraph-related formatting, such as margins and indents, are not part of a character style.

To see a list of the available styles in Microsoft Word, click the **More** button in the gallery in the **Styles** group on the **Home** tab of the ribbon, as shown in Figure 6-19. Clicking a style name in the gallery immediately applies the formatting defined in the style to the selected text.

STEM

Engineering

The steps of the engineering design process are define the problem, do research, specify requirements, brainstorm solutions, choose the best solution, do development work, build a prototype, and test and redesign. Software engineering follows these steps in general, but a piece of software goes through various prototyping stages. Features are added or refined at each stage until the final product is achieved.

Default styles

Figure 6-19. The gallery in the **Styles** group contains the default Microsoft Word styles.

Be careful when applying styles. In Microsoft Word, if a character or word is selected, the style may be applied as a character style. Many of the built-in styles can be either paragraph or character styles. However, a new style can be defined to be only a paragraph or a character style. This helps avoid accidentally applying the wrong type of style.

Microsoft Word 2013 also contains collections of styles called style sets. A style set is a group of styles that have been designed to work together visually. To see the available style sets, click the **More** button in the gallery in the **Document Formatting** group in the **Design** tab of the ribbon. Clicking a style set name in the gallery makes all of the styles within the set available for use in the document.

HANDS-ON EXAMPLE 6.3.5

FORMATTING TEXT

To create professional documents, you must be able to change color, size, font, style, and paragraph formatting. The use of styles allows consistent formatting within a document.

1. Launch Microsoft Word, and open the file *LastName*Baltimore1 from the Chap06 folder on your flash drive, if it is not already open.
2. Place the insertion point anywhere in the first line at the top of the document.
3. Click the Heading1 style in the gallery in the **Styles** group on the **Home** tab of the ribbon. Since no text is highlighted, the style is applied to the entire paragraph instead of as a character style.
4. Applying what you have learned, apply the Heading2 style as a paragraph style to the line Local Attractions, as shown.

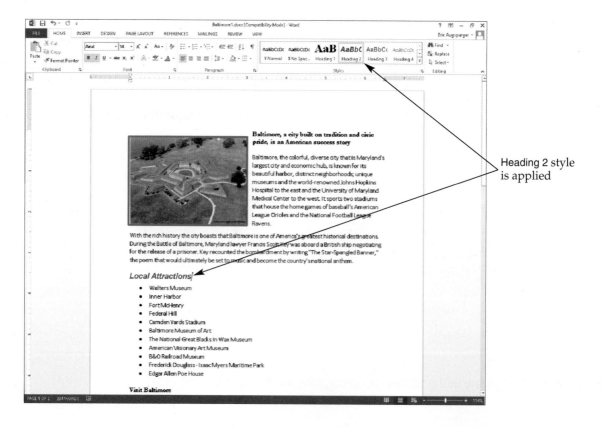

Heading 2 style is applied

HANDS-ON EXAMPLE 6.3.5 (CONTINUED)

5. Applying what you have learned, select the entire first paragraph (the one in Heading1 style).
6. Click in the **Font Size** text box in the **Font** group on the **Home** tab of the ribbon, and enter 20. This sets the point size to 20 points.
7. Select all lines of text in the list under Local Attractions, from Walters Museum to Edgar Allen Poe House.
8. Applying what you have learned, convert the lines of text to an automatic bulleted list.
9. Select the lines of text in the second list, from Divided Voices to Passages through Fire.
10. Applying what you have learned, convert the lines of text to an automatic bulleted list.
11. Save the file.

Format Painter

A useful tool for formatting text is the format painter. The **format painter** copies the formatting applied to selected text and then applies that formatting to a second text selection. To use the format painter, select the text with the formatting to copy. Then, click the **Format Painter** button in the **Clipboard** group on the **Home** tab of the ribbon. Finally, click the text to which the formatting is to be applied.

HANDS-ON EXAMPLE 6.3.6

FORMAT PAINTER

There are times when formatting must be applied many times. For example, suppose a document has important words in red and this must be changed to purple throughout. After reformatting the first instance, the format painter can be used to apply the new formatting to the other important words.

1. Launch Microsoft Word, and open the file *LastName*Baltimore1 from the Chap06 folder on your flash drive, if it is not already open.
2. Applying what you have learned, select the first paragraph (the one in Heading1 style).
3. Applying what you have learned, change the size of the text to 12 points.
4. With the text selected, click the **Font** drop-down arrow in the **Font** group on the **Home** tab of the ribbon, and click **Garamond** in the drop-down list. If Garamond is not available, select a different typeface.

Format Painter

5. With the text selected, click the **Format Painter** button in the **Clipboard** group on the **Home** tab of the ribbon. The cursor changes to a paintbrush.
6. Select the line of text that states Visit Baltimore. The text assumes all of the formatting applied to the first paragraph, including the style setting.
7. Save the file.

TITANS OF TECHNOLOGY

Jakob Nielsen, a cofounder of the Nielsen Norman Group, is a consultant on the usability of the World Wide Web and holds a PhD. in human-computer interaction. He studies user interactions and proposes quick and easy ways to implement software functions that increase user productivity. Early in his career, Dr. Nielsen worked mostly on large-scale software applications. However, while at Sun Microsystems in the 1990s, he switched to studying the usability of what was then the emerging technology of the World Wide Web. While his focus has been on the Internet, his advice to keep common actions performed in the same way is a key concept in the design of user interfaces. Dr. Nielsen has published many books and articles. His 1989 text *Coordinating User Interfaces for Consistency* is considered a standard in how to design a consistent look and feel for software. It is still in demand and frequently cited.

6.3 SECTION REVIEW

 CHECK YOUR UNDERSTANDING

1. What key combination is used to select all text in a document?
2. What is trimming the outer portion of an image called?
3. Which command or function is used to locate specific text and substitute other text for it?
4. When text is cut, where is it placed?
5. What is the difference between a paragraph style and a character style?

IC3 CERTIFICATION PRACTICE

The following question is a sample of the types of questions presented on the IC3 exam.

1. To move text or an image, which command(s) are used?
   A. **Copy**; **Paste**
   B. **Move**
   C. **Cut**; **Paste**
   D. **Cut**; **Move**

BUILD YOUR VOCABULARY

As you progress through this course, develop a personal IT glossary. This will help you build your vocabulary and prepare you for a career. Write a definition for each of the following terms and add it to your IT glossary.

ascending order
bulleted list
character style
copy
crop
cut
descending order
drag-and-drop
editing
format painter
formatting
handles
inserting
move
numbered list
paragraph style
paste
sorting
style
system clipboard
typeface

DOCUMENT VIEWS, OPTIONS, AND HELP

michaeljung/Shutterstock.com

To make software easier to learn and use, developers have included shortcuts, dialog boxes, ability to manipulate views, options, and help functions. This makes it possible to modify the program and decrease the time it takes to produce a document, spreadsheet, or presentation. Views of the file being worked on are easily adjusted for size.

The user can create many personalized settings, including general activities, saving, proofing, and customizing the ribbon. The help function of Microsoft Office is all-encompassing and always up-to-date. It replaces the printed user manuals that in the past were supplied with software. The help function is accessed in the same fashion from all Office applications.

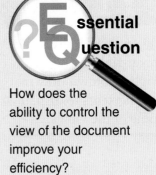

Essential Question

How does the ability to control the view of the document improve your efficiency?

TERMS

metadata
protected view
read-only
zooming

LEARNING GOALS

After completing this section, you will be able to:
- Explain how to change the view of a document.
- Discuss options that can be set in the Microsoft Office suite.
- Describe how to use the help function.

Key Applications
1.3.6

FYI

There are buttons in the lower-right corner of the application window that are shortcuts to display some of the views.

Document Views

There are many ways to view a document in Microsoft Office. The way a user views a document is largely a personal preference. For example, some users like to see a text document on a simulated page. Other users would rather not see the page, only the text. The view of the document does not affect how the document is constructed. Microsoft Word, Microsoft Excel, and Microsoft PowerPoint have various views for displaying the document. These views can be categorized as overall or protected.

Overall Views

Microsoft Word has five overall views: reading mode view, print layout view, web layout view, outline view, and draft view. Microsoft PowerPoint has eight overall views: normal view, outline view, slide sorter view, notes page view, and reading view for slides and slide master view, handout masters view, and notes master view for slide masters. Microsoft Excel has three overall views: normal view, page break view, and page layout view along with an option to create custom views. All views are set using the **View** tab of the ribbon, as shown in Figure 6-20. The five overall views in Microsoft Word are described here.

Word Overall Views

The print layout is the default view. In the print layout view, a simulated page is displayed so the margins can be seen. To display this view, click the **Print Layout** button in the **Views** group on the **View** tab of the ribbon.

The draft view is useful when the margins and the edges of the page do not need to be seen. In this view, the style area can also be displayed along the left edge, as shown in Figure 6-21. The style area is a quick reference for which styles are applied to the text. Many experienced users prefer to use the draft view. To display this view, click the **Draft View** button in the **Views** group on the **View** tab of the ribbon.

The outline view is ideal for organizing the content of a document. In this view, the levels of heads can be displayed with the body copy hidden, just as if you were creating an outline on paper. The heads can be rearranged in this view, and the associated body copy will be moved as well. To display the outline view, click the **Outline View** button in the **Views** group on the **View** tab of the ribbon.

The web layout view displays the document as it will appear as a web page. The simulated page and the vertical ruler are not displayed.

Views

Figure 6-20. The document view can be set using the **View** tab in the ribbon.

Draft view is displayed

Applied styles are listed

Figure 6-21. When the document is displayed in the draft view, the style names can be displayed along the left side of the document.

When using Word to create a web page, it is important to use this view to check for display issues. To display this view, click the **Web Layout** button in the **Views** group on the **View** tab of the ribbon.

The reading mode view displays the document similar to how an e-book reader displays content. The document is displayed in spreads. A spread is a left- and right-hand page displayed side by side. The user can easily move from spread to spread using the controls in the view. However, the ribbon is not displayed. This is the only overall view in Word in which the document cannot be edited. To display the reading mode view, click the **Read Mode** button in the **Views** group on the **View** tab of the ribbon.

Zooming

Zooming is changing the magnification of the view. There are several commands in the **Zoom** group on the **View** tab of the ribbon that can be used to change the magnification level. Clicking the **Zoom** button displays the **Zoom** dialog box in which a magnification level can be selected. Clicking the **100%** button sets the magnification level to actual size. The magnification level can also be adjusted using the slider at the lower-right corner of the application window. Depending on the Office application, there are also options for displaying one or two full pages, setting the magnification to the width of the document page, zooming to the selection, and fitting the document in the window.

Key Applications
1.11

FYI

Holding down the [Ctrl] key and using the mouse wheel is a quick way to zoom in or out.

GS5 Key Applications
1.9, 1.10

GS4 Key Applications
1.3.6

Protected Views

A **protected view** is one in which most or all of the editing functions have been locked. If a document is going to be sent to others, it can be saved as read-only. **Read-only** means the file can be opened and viewed, but cannot be changed. Making a document read-only prevents changes to the file, but does not prevent someone from saving a copy under a different name. The original file will remain intact, but the copy can be edited.

To save a Microsoft Word document as read-only, click the **Restrict Editing** button in the **Protect** group on the **Review** tab of the ribbon. The **Restrict Editing** pane is displayed on the right-hand side of the screen, as shown in Figure 6-22. In the **Editing restrictions** area of the panel, check the **Allow only this type of editing in the document:** check box, and click **No change (Read-only)** in the drop-down list. Finally, click the **Yes, Start Enforcing Protection** button in the **Start enforcement** area of the pane. A Microsoft Excel spreadsheet can be similarly set as read-only, but there are different options.

File Metadata

GS5 Key Applications
4.4

Metadata are details about a file that describe or identify it. Metadata are also known as document properties. Metadata include features such as the document author's name, subject, file size, date the file was created or updated, and any keywords set up by the user. When a file is selected in Windows File Explorer, the metadata from that file may be displayed at the bottom of the window. Metadata are also used by databases, such as a

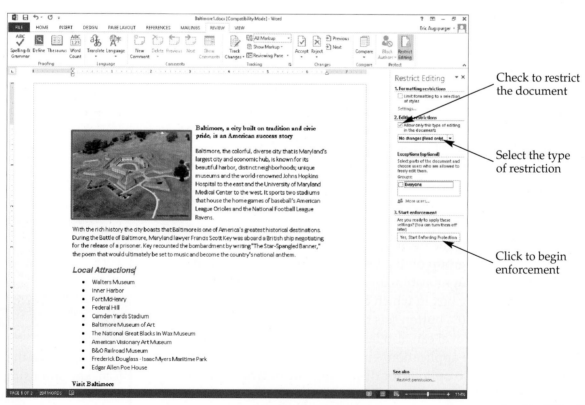

Goodheart-Willcox Publisher

Figure 6-22. A document can be restricted so no changes can be made to it.

Microsoft Access database. In this application, metadata are details about a database entry.

To view the metadata in any Microsoft Office file, click the **File** tab in the ribbon and then **Info**. The metadata will be displayed on the right-hand side of the backstage view.

Removing metadata is easy in Microsoft Office. Click the **Check for Issues** button in the **Info** backstage view, and then click **Inspect Document** in the drop-down menu. The **Document Inspector** dialog box is displayed in which you can choose which metadata to look for in the document. If any of the selected metadata are found, you are given the opportunity to remove the metadata. When the file is saved again, these properties will no longer be included in the file.

Office Options

Each Microsoft Office application has various options that can be set to match more closely how a user prefers to work. For example, the number of recent documents displayed on the opening screen can be changed. To change options, click **Options** in the **File** tab to open the **Options** dialog box. Settings made in the **Options** dialog box affect the entire Office application, not just the document that is open. The commonly changed settings are found in the **General**, **Proofing**, **Save**, and, in Microsoft Word, **Display** categories. To display the settings in a category, click the category name on the left side of the **Options** dialog box.

Key Applications
1.1.7

General

The **General** category contains choices the user can make related to the user interface, personalizing the application, and startup options. This includes the display of the mini toolbar when text is selected, showing a live preview when text is edited, permitting the display of screen tips, and entering a name for the user.

To display the mini toolbar or show a live preview, check the corresponding check box. There are three choices for how screen tips are displayed. The user name and initials can be entered in the corresponding text boxes. These are used as the document's author name and for marking changes.

Proofing

The **Proofing** category contains options for how the software helps the user correct mistakes. Clicking the **AutoCorrect Options...** button displays a dialog box for entering items to automatically change, as shown in Figure 6-23. When the user enters something that matches an item in this dialog box, the specified correction is automatically made. For example, a default entry is "teh". When the user enters this, it will be automatically changed to "the".

In addition, this category allows the user to decide how to handle certain spelling errors. The user can choose to have the application flag repeated words, ignore uppercase words, or ignore words with numbers.

Green Tech

Cleaning Products
Products used to clean buildings and workstations can impact the environment. Toxic chemicals in many traditional cleaning products can pollute water sources and other business assets. They are also hazardous for employees to use. Conversely, green cleaning products are safe to use on almost any surface and are also safer for the employee using them.

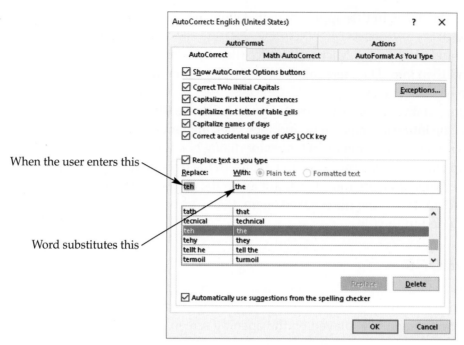

When the user enters this

Word substitutes this

Figure 6-23. The autocorrect feature can be used to automatically correct common misspellings.

Many other proofing settings are available in this category. Proofing is discussed in more detail in Chapter 7.

Save

The **Save** category contains options related to how files are saved. One of the most important options is how often the auto recover information for files is automatically saved. The user can also specify where the auto recover information will be saved. The auto recover feature is used to restore the file if the application or system crashes. Set the save time to as much work as you are willing to redo. If you are willing to redo 30 minutes of work, this can be the time interval.

This category also provides options for the default file format and the default location of files. The location of files is the folder that will be displayed when opening or saving a file for the first time when the application is launched. It is common to set this to a project folder.

Display

The **Display** category is unique to Microsoft Word. The options in this category set how the document will be shown on the screen and when printed. There are options for showing white space and how hidden characters should appear. For example, the user can decide to show hard returns (paragraph marks), tabs, and text anchors. Options for printing include printing drawings, background colors, properties, and hidden text.

Resetting Defaults

If changes are made to the default option settings, each can be reversed by simply changing the setting back to the default. This must

Key Applications
1.1.7

be done one at a time. However, if the ribbon has been customized, all changes can be reversed in one step. To help reduce the complexity of the ribbon, the user can customize it. Tabs that the user does not need can be removed. If, however, at a future time, the user wishes to have the ribbon appear with the original choices, it can be reset with one command.

To customize the ribbon, click the **Customize Ribbon** category in the **Options** dialog box. Then, add or remove buttons, groups, and tabs as needed, as shown in Figure 6-24. To return the ribbon to its default state, click the **Reset** button. Then, in the drop-down menu that is displayed, choose to reset only the selected tab or the entire ribbon.

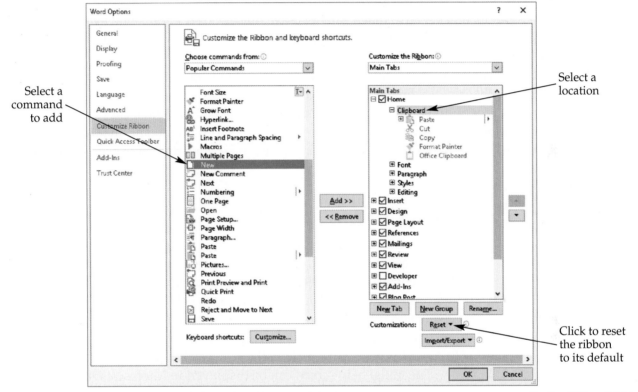

Goodheart-Willcox Publisher

Figure 6-24. The ribbon can be customized in the **Options** dialog box. It can also be reset to the default.

HANDS-ON EXAMPLE 6.4.1

OFFICE OPTIONS

The Microsoft Office applications have default settings that will be acceptable to the greatest number of users. However, many users prefer to customize option settings once they discover how they are most comfortable working with the software.

1. Launch Microsoft Word, Microsoft PowerPoint, or Microsoft Excel.
2. Click **Options** in the **File** tab. The **Options** dialog box is displayed with the **General** category active.
3. Locate the **Personalize your copy of Microsoft Office** area on the right-hand side of the dialog box.
4. Click in the **User name:** text box, and enter your first and last name. This will be assigned as the creator of any new documents you save.

HANDS-ON EXAMPLE 6.4.1 (CONTINUED)

5. Click in the **Initials:** text box, and enter your initials. These will be used to indicate which comments or tracked changes you added to the document.
6. Click the **Proofing** on the left-hand side of the dialog box to display the options in that category on the right-hand side.
7. In the **When correcting spelling in Microsoft Office programs:** area, uncheck the **Ignore words in UPPERCASE** check box. This tells the software to spell-check any words that are set in all uppercase characters.
8. Click the **Save** category on the left-hand side of the dialog box to display the options in that category on the right-hand side.
9. In the **Save** documents area, make sure the **Save AutoRecover information every** check box is checked, and then click in the corresponding text box and enter 5. This tells the software to save a backup copy of the file every five minutes.
10. Click the **Customize Ribbon** category on the left-hand side of the dialog box to display the options in that category on the right-hand side.
11. Click the **Reset** button on the right-hand side of the dialog box. Then, click **Reset all customizations** in the drop-down list that is displayed. The ribbon and the **Quick Access** toolbar are restored to their default states. All customizations that have been made are removed.

Office Help

Key Applications
1.1.8

There are many ways to get help when using an office suite. When office suites were first created, the software came with large printed manuals. Now, all instructions, tips, and troubleshooting advice are available online and easily accessible through the software's help system. One of the greatest advantages of online help over a printed manual is the ability to search based on keywords. The help database consists of many articles of varying lengths. Because the articles are online, they are easily updated by the developers.

The initial help screen can be displayed in Microsoft Office by pressing the [F1] key or by clicking the help button in the upper-right corner of the screen, as shown in Figure 6-25. The software tries to make it easy to find solutions to common problems. The most popular topics that users ask about are listed on the initial screen of the online help.

For example, suppose a user is looking for keyboard shortcuts. Press the [F1] key to launch help, enter keyboard shortcuts in the search box, and click the **Search** button. The help system returns a list with many articles that it thinks are related to keyboard shortcuts. Evaluate the title of each article to locate one that best matches the information being sought, and click the title to display the article.

Using the software's online help is the fastest way to answer questions related to the application. However, there may be other ways to get help. Additional online help is available by contacting the software vendor. If a company has many computer users, it will usually have a dedicated

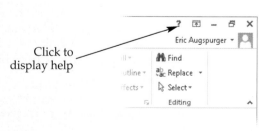

Click to display help

Goodheart-Willcox Publisher

Figure 6-25. The help function can be accessed by pressing the [F1] key or clicking the help button.

IT staff that assists employees through a help desk. It is also possible that a coworker will know the answer to a software question. For many types of software, users have formed online forums or groups where questions can be posted and answered by other users.

HANDS-ON EXAMPLE 6.4.2

OFFICE HELP

Being able to use the online help system in an application is essential to learning how to use the software. Even after becoming proficient with the software, there will be times when help must be consulted.

1. Launch Microsoft Word.
2. Add your first and last name to the document.
3. Press the [F1] key to launch the online help system.
4. Click in the search text box, enter WordArt, and click the **Search** button. WordArt is a method of applying decorative effects to text.
5. Locate an article that discusses how to insert WordArt, click the title to display the article, and read it.
6. Use the [Alt][Tab] key combination to switch to the document window.
7. Using the information in the help article, change your name into WordArt. As needed, use the [Alt][Tab] key combination to switch between the document window and the help article.
8. Applying what you have learned, save the file as *LastName*WordArt in the Chap06 folder on your PRINC-OF-IT flash drive.

6.4 SECTION REVIEW

CHECK YOUR UNDERSTANDING

1. What are the two categories of views in Microsoft Office?
2. What is zooming?
3. What can be done in a read-only file?
4. How do you undo any customizations made to the ribbon?
5. Which key is used to access the help function?

IC3 CERTIFICATION PRACTICE

The following question is a sample of the types of questions presented on the IC3 exam.

1. In which dialog box is the mini toolbar set to display?
   A. **View**
   B. **AutoCorrect**
   C. **Toolbar**
   D. **Options**

BUILD YOUR VOCABULARY

As you progress through this course, develop a personal IT glossary. This will help you build your vocabulary and prepare you for a career. Write a definition for each of the following terms and add it to your IT glossary.

metadata   read-only
protected view   zooming

6 REVIEW AND ASSESSMENT

Chapter Summary

Section 6.1
Starting Word, Excel, and PowerPoint

- The Microsoft Office suite is accessed via the **Apps** or **Start** menu.
- The ribbon is the main command interface for the Microsoft Office suite of software and consists of tabs, each containing commands arranged in groups.
- The active window is where any command that is entered will be applied.

Section 6.2
Saving, Printing, and Opening Documents

- The first time a file is saved, it must be given a name. After the initial save when the file is named, the **Save** command can be used to quickly save the file or the **Save As** command can be used to rename the file.
- Printing is outputting the content of a file. This is usually done as a hardcopy on paper, but a virtual printer may be used to print to a file.
- Closing means removing a file or application from RAM. An easy way to close an application is to click the standard Windows close button (X).
- Opening a file is placing its content into RAM so the content can be used. Activate the **Open** command, navigate to the file location, and select the file.

Section 6.3
Editing and Formatting

- Editing a document is to make changes to the text, format, layout, or other aspects of the content. Properly selecting text is important to correctly applying an edit.
- Media files, such as images, can be inserted into documents.
- Most actions in software can be reversed using the **Undo** command. The **Redo** command restores the last action undone.

- The **Find** command is used to locate specific text within a document. The **Replace** command not only locates specific text, it substitutes it for text the user enters.
- The system clipboard is a virtual container for storing data. It is used to copy or cut content and paste it elsewhere in the document.
- Formatting text means changing the appearance of the characters. A style is a group of formatting settings that can be applied in one step, which is an efficient method of formatting text.

Section 6.4
Document Views, Options, and Help

- There are many ways to view a document in Microsoft Office, such as appearing on a simulated page or only the text.
- Each Microsoft Office application has various options that can be set to more closely match how a user prefers to work.
- The help function provides information on how to use the software.

Now that you have finished this chapter, see what you know about information technology by scanning the QR code to take the chapter posttest. If you do not have a smartphone, visit www.g-wlearning.com.

Chapter 6 Test

Multiple Choice

Select the best response.

1. What is the vertical line called that shows where text will be inserted?
   A. clipboard
   B. pilcrow
   C. cell reference
   D. insertion point

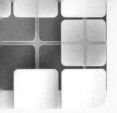

2. Which type of button turns a feature on and off?
   A. screen tip
   B. mini toolbar
   C. live view
   D. toggle

3. Which option shows exactly how the document will look when printed?
   A. virtual printer
   B. print preview
   C. **Print** tab
   D. **Options** dialog box

4. What is another name for an unordered list?
   A. numbered list
   B. free-structure list
   C. bulleted list
   D. paragraph list

5. Changes to the ribbon can be made in which dialog box?
   A. **Options**
   B. **File**
   C. **Ribbon**
   D. **Print**

Completion

Complete the following sentences with the correct word(s).

6. _____ is displaying a minimized window.

7. _____ means removing a file or application from RAM.

8. _____ is a sort in which the lowest value appears at the top of the list.

9. Formatting applied to one section of text can be copied to another section of text using the _____.

10. To access the Microsoft Office help system, press the _____ key.

Matching

Match the correct term with its definition.

A. ribbon
B. backstage view
C. typeface
D. [Ctrl] key
E. read-only

11. Displayed by clicking the **File** tab.

12. A mode in which a file is open, but changes cannot be saved.

13. A design of characters.

14. Used to select nonadjacent items.

15. The main command interface in Microsoft Office.

Application and Extension of Knowledge

1. Launch Microsoft PowerPoint. List the tabs available in the ribbon. Do the same for Microsoft Excel and Microsoft Word. Can you identify any patterns in which tabs are available and the order in which they appear? Write a one-page paper explaining the interface of Microsoft Office. Discuss similarities and differences between the applications.

2. Launch Microsoft Excel, begin a blank spreadsheet, and save it as *LastName*Invoice in the Chap06 folder on your PRINC-OF-IT flash drive. Enter the data shown below to create an invoice. Apply the formatting as shown.

Invoice number:	42111
Service	**Fee**
Professional résumé	$ 325.00
Down payment	$ (100.00)
Student discount	$ (25.00)
Total due	$ 200.00

Copyright Goodheart-Willcox Co., Inc.

Chapter 6 Common Office Application Features

3. Open the *LastName*Invoice Excel file created in #2. Display the print preview by clicking **Print** in the **File** tab. List what settings can be made in the print preview. Write one or two sentences about what each setting does.

4. Launch Microsoft Word, begin a new blank document, and save it as *LastName*Resume in the Chap06 folder on your PRINC-OF-IT flash drive. You will be creating the beginning of a résumé. Enter the following contact information on separate lines: your first and last name, your street address, your city and state, your e-mail address. Enter the text shown below as the introduction to the résumé. Change your name to bold and 20 points in the typeface of your choice. Center your contact information. Italicize the word Objective. Save the file, and then use the "save as" function to save it as a PDF file. Open the PDF and try to make changes; can you?

Objective

Challenging position in operations management where over twenty years of experience in top-level administration, financial management, budgeting, logistics, compliance, and information technology can be combined with skills in negotiation, leadership, communication, analysis, team building, problem solving, and attention to detail to maximize the success of a nonprofit organization.

---

5. Launch Microsoft PowerPoint, and begin a new blank document. Launch the help function, and search for help on adding a motion path. How many results are returned? Evaluate the returned results for relevance, and click the article that appears most relevant. Read the article, and write a one-page paper summarizing your findings.

Online Activities

Complete the following activities, which will help you learn, practice, and expand your knowledge and skills.

Certification Practice. Complete the certification practice test for this chapter.

Vocabulary. Practice vocabulary for this chapter using the e-flash cards, matching activity, and vocabulary game until you are able to recognize their meanings.

Communication Skills

College and Career Readiness

Reading. Read a magazine, newspaper, or online article about an IT company. Analyze the article and distinguish the facts from the author's point of view on the subject. Write a report in which you draw conclusions about the importance of information technology. Use visual support, such as graphs, to share specific evidence from the article with your class to support your understanding of the topic.

Speaking. Select three of your classmates to participate in a cooperative learning situation such as a discussion panel. Acting as the team leader, name each person to a specific task such as timekeeper, recorder, etc. Discuss the topic of buying an electronic store franchise or a local electronics business that is available for sale. What are the advantages and disadvantages of not starting a business from scratch? Keep the panel on task and promote democratic discussion.

Writing. Making small improvements in the way things are done can bring about great benefits. Choose three entrepreneurs in the information technology field, and explain how they used innovation to start a new company or improve an existing product.

Internet Research

Typeface Anatomy. Research typeface anatomy using various Internet resources. What does the term mean? Create a list of some of the common terms used to describe a typeface. Illustrate your examples.

Teamwork

Working with your team, make a list of good listening skills versus bad listening skills. After you have completed the list, prepare a short skit that demonstrates both types of listening skills in an IT help desk setting. Incorporate both verbal and nonverbal communication tools to show active listening, such as body language, asking questions, or note-taking. Perform your skit in front of the class. Afterward, ask the audience to give feedback on the information you provided them.

Portfolio Development

College and Career Readiness

File Structure. After you have chosen a file format for your documents, determine a strategy for storing and organizing the materials. The file structure for storing digital documents is similar to storing hard copy documents.

First, you need a place to store each item. Ask your instructor where to save your documents. This could be on the school's network or a flash drive of your own. Next, decide how to organize related files into categories. For example, Certificates might be the name of a folder with a subfolder Community Service Certificates and a subfolder that says School Certificates. Appropriate certificates would be saved in each subfolder. The names for folders and files should be descriptive but not too long.

1. Decide on the file structure for your documents.

2. Create folders and subfolders on the school's network drive or your own flash drive.

CTSOs

Extemporaneous speaking. Extemporaneous speaking is a competitive event you might enter with your CTSO. This event allows you to display your communication skills, specifically your ability to organize and deliver an oral presentation. At the competition, you will be given several topics from which to choose. You will also be given a time limit to create and deliver the speech. You will be evaluated on your verbal and nonverbal skills as well as the tone and projection of your voice. To prepare for an extemporaneous speaking event, complete the following activities.

1. Ask your instructor for several practice topics so you can practice making impromptu speeches.

2. Once you have a practice topic, jot down the ideas and points to cover. An important part of making this type of presentation is that you will have only a few minutes to prepare. Being able to write down your main ideas quickly will enable you to focus on what you will actually say in the presentation.

3. Practice the presentation. You should introduce yourself, review the topic that is being presented, defend the topic being presented, and conclude with a summary.

4. Ask your instructor to play the role of competition judge as you give the presentation. Afterward, ask for feedback from your instructor. You may also consider having a student audience listen and give feedback.

5. For the event, bring paper and pencils to record notes. Supplies may or may not be provided.

7 WORD-PROCESSING SOFTWARE

SECTIONS
7.1 CREATING A DOCUMENT
7.2 PROOFING TEXT

Word-processing software is the most popular productivity software. Microsoft Word has an estimated half billion users around the world. Word-processing software helps users with the writing of all kinds of documents, from a five-page term paper to a brochure for a home-based business or a personal résumé. It allows the user to let ideas flow. The user can enter his or her thoughts without worrying about how the text will look or where the margins are. These elements are automatically applied, but can be modified to alter the appearance of the document.

Users can improve the quality of their written product by using the word processor's many features. A full-featured word processor includes ways to check spelling and grammar, look up synonyms, write tables of contents, automatically number pages, and apply citations. The readability of the document can be quickly measured, which allows the user to make edits to improve readability. A full-featured word processor also has methods to easily incorporate graphics and photographs as well as ways to perform basic edits to these elements. This chapter discusses the process of creating a document.

IC3 CERTIFICATION OBJECTIVES

GS5

Key Applications

Domain 1.0 Common features
Objective 1.3 Know how to use spelling check
Objective 1.4 Know how to use reviewing features

Domain 2.0 Word processing
Objective 2.1 Perform basic formatting skills
Objective 2.2 Adjust margins, page sizes, and page orientation
Objective 2.3 Alter text and font styles
Objective 2.5 Know page layout concepts
Objective 2.8 Use reviewing options within a word processing document
Objective 2.9 Be able to use tables
Objective 2.10 Understand which file types are compatible or editable with word processors

GS4

Computing Fundamentals

Domain 3.0 Computer software and concepts
Objective 3.3 Software usage

Key Applications

Domain 1.0 Common application features
Objective 1.1 Spell-check, find/replace, redo/undo
Objective 1.2 Formatting

Domain 2.0 Word processing activities
Objective 2.1 Organizing data
Objective 2.2 Layout

Domain 6.0 Collaboration
Objective 6.1 Review comments

College and Career Readiness

Reading Prep. Before reading this chapter, flip through the pages and make notes of the major headings. Analyze the structure of the relationships of the headings with the concepts in the chapter.

CREATING A DOCUMENT

?**Essential Question**

How does the layout of a document affect the message trying to be communicated?

Making a document more readable is the goal of using word-processing software. Being able to control exactly how and where the words will appear on the page is beneficial. Choosing where to start a new page and adding a photo or illustration also increases interest in the document.

Word-processing software can be used to create many types of documents. The most common type of document written with word-processing software contains text only, such as a business letter or research report. Both of these documents are discussed in detail later. However, word-processing software can also be used to create documents that incorporate graphics or photographs, such as business cards, newsletters, and advertising flyers.

Goodluz/Shutterstock.com

TERMS

desktop publishing
font
justification
leading
line spacing
margins
master page
orphan
page break

page layout
serifs
style sheet
tabs
touch system
typeface
visual design
widow

LEARNING GOALS

After completing this section, you will be able to:
- Explain how to start a document in Microsoft Word.
- Identify elements of a table.
- Discuss the use of templates.
- Describe desktop publishing.

Starting a Document

As discussed in Chapter 3, word-processing software assists the user with composing, editing, designing, printing, and publishing documents. There are many terms associated with word-processing software. Some common terms and their explanations are shown in Figure 7-1.

To create a new document in Microsoft Word 2013, click **New** in the **File** tab. The backstage view displays many templates as well as the choice of starting a blank document. Click the Blank document tile. The default display is the print layout view showing a simulated sheet of paper. The **Home** tab in the ribbon is active by default because it contains the most common tools for creating a document. The groups on the **Home** tab are **Clipboard**, **Font**, **Paragraph**, **Styles**, and **Editing**.

FYI

When Microsoft Word 2013 is launched, a startup screen is displayed that allows the user to begin a new blank document.

Alignment	How text or other element is positioned on the page. Horizontally, the element may be flush left, flush right, or centered left-to-right. Vertically, the element may be flush top, flush bottom, or centered top-to-bottom.
AutoCorrect	A feature in the software that automatically replaces certain text with specified text.
Citation	A notation indicating the source of information in a document.
Endnote	A notation placed at the end of the document. May be a citation or other information.
Font	A set of characters of a typeface in one specific style and size.
Footer	Text that appears at the bottom of every page in a document or section of a document.
Footnote	A citation placed at the bottom of the page.
Format	The appearance of text or other element.
Grammar-check	A feature in the software that examines the document for proper use of grammar.
Header	Text that appears at the top of every page in a document or section of a document.
Heading	A word or phrase placed at the beginning of a passage to indicate the topic of the passage.
Indentation	The amount text is moved in from the standard margin.
Margin	The locations where text will begin and end and beyond which there is no printing.
Merge	To combine two elements into one, such as two cells in a table into a single cell.
Orientation	The direction in which the page or element is aligned; portrait or landscape.
Pagination	Adding page numbers to a document or the page numbers themselves.
Paragraph	Part of a document that typically deals with a single idea or thought and begins and ends with a hard return.
Spell-check	A feature in the software that examines the document for properly spelled words.
Thesaurus	A feature in the software that suggests alternate words with similar meanings.
Typeface	The design of characters. Maybe be serif, sans serif, or decorative.

Goodheart-Willcox Publisher

Figure 7-1. Common terms related to word processing and a brief explanation of each.

Entering Text

To be proficient in creating a document, the user must learn to enter text. The most efficient users employ the touch system or method for entering text, numbers, and other data. In the **touch system**, the user does not look at the keyboard when entering information because he or she has memorized the location of keys based on hand position. Using the touch system, a person can very quickly enter information because he or she does not need to look for the characters on the keyboard when thinking or reading what needs to be entered.

Efficient users in the accounting area employ the touch system on the number keypad. Since these users do not have to look at the number keys, they can keep their eyes on the data to be entered. This increases their efficiency while entering numerical data.

Many software programs are available to help in becoming more skillful at entering text. These targeted exercises are designed to improve the speed and accuracy of the user in entering text and data.

A word-processing document is based on paragraphs. In Microsoft Word, a paragraph is defined as any text that is followed by a hard return. Pressing the [Enter] key adds a hard return to start a new paragraph. A paragraph in Microsoft Word may consist of one word, one sentence, or several lines of text.

As text is added to a document, it is part of the paragraph where the insertion point is located. When enough text is added, the line of text will wrap to a new line, but will remain part of the same paragraph. This continues until the [Enter] key is pressed to begin a new paragraph. When enough lines of text or paragraphs have been added to the document, a new page is automatically added to make room for the text.

To move through the document one page at a time, press the [Page Up] key to move to the previous page or the [Page Down] key to move to the following page. When working with long documents, it is helpful to be able to move quickly to the end or the beginning of the document. The [Ctrl][End] shortcut key combination moves the insertion point to the end of the document. The [Ctrl][Home] shortcut key combination moves the insertion point to the beginning of the document. The arrow keys and the mouse wheel can also be used to navigate.

Career Skills

School Counselor
Educational, guidance, school, and vocational counselors work to improve the lives of their students. They evaluate a student's current needs, publish a written treatment plan, enact the plan, and follow through. Recordkeeping is constant and electronic records are essential to the effectiveness and support of these human services workers.

HANDS-ON EXAMPLE 7.1.1

ENTERING TEXT

The purpose of a word processor is to create a document. Therefore, the most basic skill when using a word processor is entering text.
1. Insert your PRINC-OF-IT flash drive into the computer.
2. Applying what you have learned, create a folder on the flash drive named Chap07.
3. Launch Microsoft Word, and begin a new blank document.

HANDS-ON EXAMPLE 7.1.1 (CONTINUED)

Show/Hide

4. Click the **Show/Hide** button in the **Paragraph** group on the **Home** tab of the ribbon to activate it. A paragraph symbol should appear at the end of the first line in the document.
5. Add your name, and press the [Enter] key to begin a new line.
6. Add your street address, and press the [Enter] key.
7. Add your city, state abbreviation, and ZIP code.
8. Applying what you have learned, save the file as MyLetterhead.docx in the Chap07 folder on your flash drive.

Formatting Text

When people used typewriters, the choice in formatting was limited to selecting uppercase or lowercase characters. In some cases, the user could choose between blue, black, or red ink. If the size, formatting, and color of the text had to be controlled, professional printers and typesetters composed the document. Word-processing software was a revolutionary development. It allowed users to control the size, formatting, and color of text as well as many other aspects of formatting a document.

As discussed in Chapter 6, the **typeface** is the design of characters. The technical definition of a **font** is a set of characters of a typeface in one specific style and size. For example, Garamond may be the typeface, and the font may be bold, 11 point. In common usage, *font* is used to mean *typeface*, but this is not technically correct. In software such as Microsoft Word, when you select the *font*, you are technically selecting the *typeface*. By applying formatting such as bold or italic and setting the size of the characters, you are technically selecting the font of the current typeface.

Typefaces are divided into three broad categories: serif, sans serif, and decorative. **Serifs** are small marks that extend from the end strokes of characters, as shown in Figure 7-2. A sans serif typeface does not have serifs. Most text should be set in either a serif or sans serif typeface. Serif typefaces tend to be used for long passages. Sans serif typefaces tend to

GS5 Key Applications
2.1, 2.3

FYI

It is a good practice to limit the number of typefaces in a document to two or three.

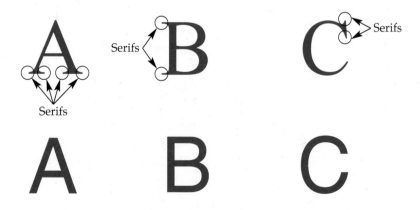

Goodheart-Willcox Publisher

Figure 7-2. A comparison of serif and sans serif typefaces.

be used for short text, such as headings. Decorative typefaces, such as script typefaces, have limited applications and should be used only for artistic presentations.

The height of the characters is called the *text size*. The text size is measured in points. Recall from Chapter 6 that there are 72 points per inch. The main body text in a document is usually between 10 and 12 points, and 11 points is very common. For younger and older readers, the text may need to be a bit larger than 12 points. Headings and titles should be larger than the body text.

Formatting that can be applied to text includes bold, italic, underlined, and color. Bold text, or boldface text, is the typeface with thicker lines. Italic is the typeface with the characters tilted or slanted. Underlined is a horizontal line underneath the characters in the typeface. If the characters are not bold, italic, or underlined, the typeface is said to be roman. Figure 7-3 shows a comparison of roman, bold, italic, and underlined type. These formats can be combined. The characters can also be set in any color. This is a common practice by accountants who use black characters to show positive amounts and red characters to show negative amounts.

To highlight text is to place a colored background behind it. This is similar to taking a highlighter marker to a printed page. Highlighting places much emphasis on the text. It should be used sparingly. Many people apply highlighting only for their own use, such as a reminder of an important sentence or paragraph.

roman

bold

italic

<u>underlined</u>

bold, italic

Goodheart-Willcox Publisher

Figure 7-3. A comparison of several fonts in the Times New Roman typeface. These examples are all 14 point type.

HANDS-ON EXAMPLE 7.1.2

FORMATTING TEXT

There are many times when the formatting of certain text within a document must be changed. This is easy to do using the commands in the ribbon in Microsoft Word.

1. Navigate to the student companion website at www.g-wlearning.com, download the data files for this chapter, and save them in the Chap07 folder on your flash drive.
2. Launch Microsoft Word, and open the Lighting1.docx file from the Chap07 folder on your flash drive.
3. Applying what you have learned, save the document as *LastName*Lighting.docx in the Chap07 folder on your flash drive
4. Applying what you have learned, select the whole document.
5. Click the **Font** drop-down arrow in the **Font** group on the **Home** tab of the ribbon, and click **Times New Roman** in the drop-down list. The typeface for the entire document is changed.
6. Click the **Font Size** drop-down arrow in the **Font** group on the **Home** tab of the ribbon, and click **11** in the drop-down list. The size of all text is changed to 11 points.

HANDS-ON EXAMPLE 7.1.2 (CONTINUED)

Bold

7. Select the title Home Lighting, and click the **Bold** button in the **Font** group on the **Home** tab of the ribbon. The font is made boldface.
8. Applying what you have learned, change the point size for the title to 14.
9. Press the [Enter] key twice to leave a blank space, and add your name.
10. Applying what you have learned, format your name as not bold in 12 points.

Font Color

11. Select your name, and click the drop-down arrow next to the **Font Color** button in the **Font** group on the **Home** tab of the ribbon. In the color palette that is displayed, click the color swatch for a dark color of your choice. The font color is changed.
12. Applying what you have learned, use the format painter to copy the formatting on the title to these headings: Interior Lighting, Exterior Lighting, Lighting for Energy Efficiency, and Summary.
13. Save the file.

Page Layout

Page layout refers to how the type is placed on the page. Formatting an entire document includes deciding on page orientation, setting up margins, and adjusting tabs. A tool that is useful when formatting a document is the ruler.

GS5 Key Applications 2.2

Ruler

The ruler displays inch divisions for the page. It shows the user where the text is on the page. It also shows where the margins are located as well as any indents. It also displays if any tabs have been set up, and the types of tabs. To display the ruler, check the **Ruler** check box in the **Show** group on the **View** tab of the ribbon. The horizontal ruler can be displayed in the draft, print layout, and web layout views. The vertical ruler can only be displayed in the print layout view.

GS5 Key Applications 2.5.5
GS4 Key Applications 2.2.1

The horizontal ruler can be used as a shortcut for changing the margins, indents, and tabs. By sliding the triangles that mark the indents and left and right margins, the user can change those values without using the ribbon. The vertical ruler can be used to slide the bottom and top margins up or down. However, it should be noted that these adjustments are style overrides. Style overrides are discussed later in this chapter.

Orientation

The orientation is how the document will be placed on the sheet. This is similar to the page layout for printing discussed in Chapter 6. The orientation can be portrait or landscape. By default, new blank documents in Microsoft Word are set up in portrait orientation on a letter-size sheet of paper. This means the paper is 8.5″ × 11″ with the long edge along the side. In landscape orientation, the long edge is along the top.

GS5 Key Applications 2.5.6
GS4 Key Applications 2.2.1

To set the orientation, click the **Change Page Orientation** button in the **Page Setup** group on the **Page Layout** tab of the ribbon. Then, click either **Landscape** or **Portrait** in the drop-down menu. The change in orientation will only be visible in the page layout view.

Page Margins

GS5 Key Applications 2.5.3

GS4 Key Applications 2.2.1

Each new blank document in Microsoft Word is formatted with preset margins. **Margins** are the points at the top, bottom, left, and right of the page beyond which text is not placed. The default value in Word for all margins is 1″, but the value for each margin can be changed.

The easiest way to change the page margins in Microsoft Word 2013 is to use the ruler. It is a good idea to be at the beginning of the document so the overall effect can be seen.

To change the left-hand margin using the ruler, hover the cursor on the left-hand side of the ruler between the upward- and downward-pointing triangles until the double-arrow cursor appears, as shown in Figure 7-4. The help text will display Left Margin. The downward-pointing triangle controls the first line indent. The upward-pointing triangle controls the hanging indent. If both of these markers are at the same location, as they are by default, it can be difficult to position the cursor for adjusting the left-hand margin.

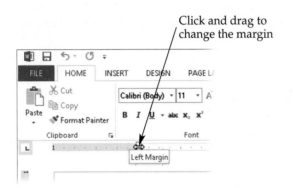

Click and drag to change the margin

Goodheart-Willcox Publisher

Figure 7-4. Using the ruler to change the left-hand margin.

Once the double-arrow cursor appears and the help text reads Left Margin, click, hold, and drag to adjust the left-hand margin.

The other margins are similarly adjusted. To adjust the right-hand margin, hover the cursor on the right-hand side of the ruler until the double-arrow cursor is displayed and the help text displays Right Margin. To adjust the top margin, hover the cursor on the top end of the ruler until the double-arrow cursor is displayed and the help text displays Top Margin. To adjust the bottom margin, hover the cursor on the bottom end of the ruler until the double-arrow cursor is displayed and the help text displays Bottom Margin. Then, click, hold, and drag to adjust the margin.

The margins can also be adjusted using the **Page Layout** tab. This allows for a precise adjustment of the top and bottom margins, where the ruler allows for only an approximation. Click the **Adjust Margins** button in the **Page Setup** group on the **Page Layout** tab to display a drop-down menu. Then, click a new margin arrangement in the drop-down menu or click **Custom Margins…** to display the **Page Setup** dialog box. This dialog box allows the user to set the margins to values not offered in the drop-down menu.

FYI

Adjusting the left- and right-hand page margins should not be confused with adjusting the indentation of a paragraph.

HANDS-ON EXAMPLE 7.1.3

ADJUSTING MARGINS

For some documents, the default margin values are fine. However, for many documents, the margin values need to be changed.

1. Launch Microsoft Word, and open the MyLetterhead.docx file from the Chap07 folder on your flash drive, if it is not already open.
2. Applying what you have learned, display the page layout view, if it is not already displayed.
3. If the rulers are not visible along the top and left sides of the document, check the **Ruler** check box in the **Show** group on the **View** tab of the ribbon.
4. Scroll to the beginning of the document.
5. Hover the cursor over the top margin indicator in the vertical ruler. The portion of the ruler that is outside the margin is darker than the portion that is inside the margin.
6. When the double-arrow cursor is displayed and the help text displays Top Margin, click, hold, and drag the margin indicator down approximately .5". Notice how the ruler shifts as you drag, so you can only approximate the new margin value.

Adjust Margins

7. Click the **Adjust Margins** button in the **Page Setup** group on the **Page Layout** tab of the ribbon, and click **Custom Margins...** in the drop-down menu.
8. On the **Margins** tab of the **Page Setup** dialog box, click in the **Top:** text box, and enter 1.5". This precisely adds .5" to the default 1" margin.
9. Click the **OK** button to update the margin setting.

Tabs

Tabs help to organize and space the text, which improves the readability of the document. For example, the beginning of each paragraph in the body of the letter can be indented with a tab. **Tabs** are preset horizontal locations across the page in a document. The term is more accurately *tab stops* because these are the locations where the insertion point will stop when the [Tab] key is pressed. The term originated with typewriters where a metal tab would be pulled out to set the stops.

There are several types of tabs, as shown in Figure 7-5. The most commonly used tab is the left tab, which left-aligns the text to the tab position. Microsoft Word has default left tabs at half-inch intervals. As the [Tab] key is pressed, the insertion point moves across the page one-half inch at a time.

Tabs can be easily added to a document in Microsoft Word. First, select the type of tab to add using the selector at the left-hand end of the ruler. Then, click on the horizontal ruler at the location where the tab should be. A tab indicator is added to the ruler. The default tabs up to that point are removed, but there will be no visible indication of this. Once a tab is added to the ruler, it can be moved left or right to adjust the location.

GS5 Key Applications
2.5.5

GS4 Key Applications
2.2.1, 2.2.3

FYI

In most cases, the tab stops should be set in the style, not manually added using the ruler.

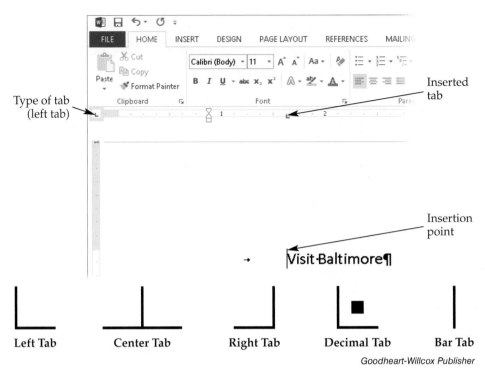

Type of tab
(left tab)

Inserted
tab

Insertion
point

Visit·Baltimore¶

| Left Tab | Center Tab | Right Tab | Decimal Tab | Bar Tab |

Figure 7-5. There are several different types of tabs that can be added.

Key Applications
2.5.4, 2.5.7

Key Applications
2.2.2

FYI

In most cases, line spacing and alignment should be set in the style, not manually set using the commands in the ribbon.

Modifying Line Spacing and Paragraph Alignment

How much space is present between lines or paragraphs can be changed. **Line spacing** is the amount of space between lines of text. The space between paragraphs is controlled by the *space before* and *space after* settings. **Leading**, pronounced *led-ing*, is the technical term for vertical spacing between lines of text and paragraphs. The term comes from early printing technology when slabs of metal were placed between lines of text. Long passages of text can be made easier to read by adding more spacing between lines. Adding space between paragraphs also makes long passages easier to read and helps define where a paragraph begins and ends.

To change the line spacing for a paragraph, place the insertion point within the paragraph. Then, click the **Line Spacing** button in the **Paragraph** group on the **Home** tab of the ribbon to display a drop-down menu. The numbered entries in the drop-down list refer to the line spacing, and the current setting is checked. Options include single spaced (**1**), double spaced (**2**), and one-and-a-half spaced (**1.5**), among others. Space before or after the paragraph can be removed or added using this drop-down menu as well.

A paragraph can be aligned to the left margin, to the right margin, centered, or fully justified (aligned left and right). **Justification** is the technical term for paragraph alignment. The easiest way to read text is to have it left-justified. Titles or headings are sometimes centered for emphasis. There are four buttons in the **Paragraph** group on the **Home** tab of the ribbon that control justification: **Align Text Left**, **Center**, **Align Text Right**, and **Justify**. The current setting for the paragraph in which the insertion point is located is indicated by which button is on (depressed).

HANDS-ON EXAMPLE 7.1.4

ADJUSTING LINE SPACING

The default line spacing in Microsoft Word 2013 is 1.08. This is okay for short lines of text, but for multiple lines and paragraphs, the line spacing may need to be increased.

1. Launch Microsoft Word, and open the MyLetterhead.docx file from the Chap07 folder on your flash drive, if it is not already open.
2. Select the three lines of text (name and address).
3. Click the **Line and Paragraph Spacing** button in the **Paragraph** group on the **Home** tab of the ribbon, and click **1.5** in the drop-down menu. This sets the line spacing to one-and-a-half times that of single-spaced text.
4. Select the first line of text, click the **Line Spacing** button again, and click **Add Space Before Paragraph** in the drop-down menu. The paragraph shifts down slightly as space is added before it.
5. Save the file.

Line and Paragraph Spacing

Paragraph Styles

As discussed in Chapter 6, a *paragraph style* defines the formatting for a paragraph. Paragraph formatting includes indentation, line spacing, text formatting, and tabs, among other things. Using styles saves time. All of the formatting can be applied to text in one step. Using styles also ensures that similar parts of a document will be consistently formatted.

Microsoft Word contains default styles. Many of these are displayed in the style gallery in the **Styles** group on the **Home** tab of the ribbon. To see additional styles, click the **More** button on the gallery. Clicking the dialog box launcher in the **Styles** group displays the **Styles** palette, as shown in Figure 7-6. To apply a style, click it in the gallery or the **Styles** palette.

Key Applications
1.2.1

> ## FYI
>
> A different style set can be selected by clicking it in the gallery in the **Document Formatting** group on the **Design** tab of the ribbon.

TITANS OF TECHNOLOGY

In 1979, Rob Barnaby of MicroPro International created WordStar for a microprocessor platform. It was the first commercially successful word-processing software produced for microcomputers. To users of a current word processor, such as Microsoft Word, WordStar would seem clunky and hard to use. For example, it had no mouse support, no function keys, and could not use arrow keys. Navigation was accomplished by a combination of the [Ctrl] key and letter keys. In addition there were no font choices or other advanced features that are taken for granted today. However, at the time, WordStar was a significant step forward as it was the first what you see is what you get (WYSIWYG) text editor. Within three years of its release, WordStar was the most popular word-processing software. Other companies began developing word-processing software to compete with WordStar. An early leader was WordPerfect, which is now part of the Corel office suite. Microsoft also developed Word.

Style gallery

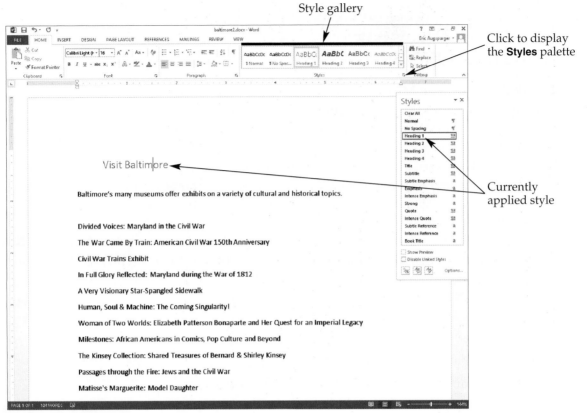

Click to display
the **Styles** palette

Currently
applied style

Goodheart-Willcox Publisher

Figure 7-6. The **Styles** palette can show all of the styles in the document, but by default will show recommended styles.

FYI

To create a new style, click the **New Style** button in the **Styles** palette or click the **More** button in the styles gallery in the **Styles** group on the **Home** tab of the ribbon and click **Create a Style** in the expanded gallery.

The settings for a default style can be changed or a new style can be created. To modify a style, right-click on it in the gallery in the **Styles** group on the **Home** tab of the ribbon or in the **Styles** palette, and click **Modify...** in the shortcut menu. The **Modify Style** dialog box is displayed, as shown in Figure 7-7. This is the same dialog box used to create a new style, except the name is different. Set the formatting for the style, and click the **OK** button to update (or create) the style. Some formatting can be changed directly in this dialog box. Clicking the **Format** button displays a menu for selecting additional formatting options to change. Each option in this menu opens a new dialog box related to the menu entry.

Applying formatting using the commands in the ribbon is called *style override*. When one of these formatting elements is changed using the commands in the ribbon, the settings of the style are overridden. The best way to make these changes is by modifying the style or by creating a new style to apply to the paragraph.

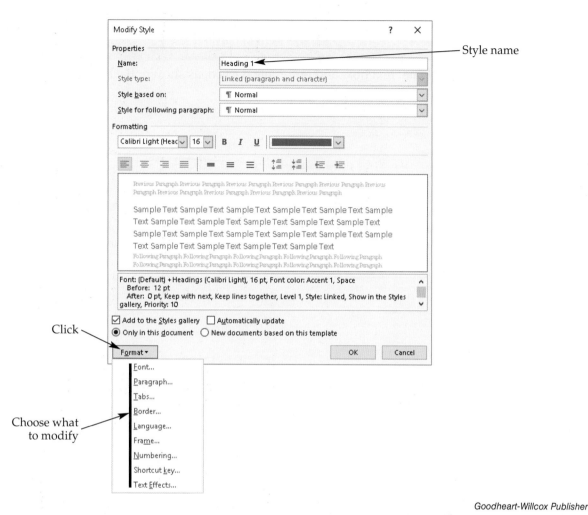

Goodheart-Willcox Publisher

Figure 7-7. This dialog box is used modify a style. The same dialog box (with a different name) is used to create a new style.

HANDS-ON EXAMPLE 7.1.5

CREATING A STYLE

Styles are an effective and efficient way to control formatting. Creating a style is easy in Microsoft Word.

1. Launch Microsoft Word, and open the MyLetterhead.docx file from the Chap07 folder on your flash drive, if it is not already open.
2. Place the insertion point at the end of the ZIP code, press the [Enter] key to start a new line, and add the text Introduction.
3. Click the dialog box launcher on the **Styles** group on the **Home** tab of the ribbon to display the **Styles** palette.
4. Click the **New Style** button in the **Styles** palette. The **Create New Style from Formatting** dialog box is displayed. The default name for the style being created is Style*x*, where *x* is a sequential number.

New
Style

HANDS-ON EXAMPLE 7.1.5 (CONTINUED)

5. Click in the **Name:** text box, and enter Introduction, as shown. Each style must have a unique name.

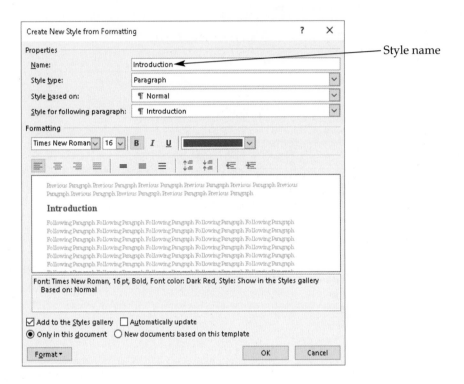

6. Using the formatting commands in the dialog box, change the typeface to Arial Black and the font size to 20 points. The changes appear in the window.
7. Click the **OK** button. The style is created and applied to the current selection.
8. Save the file.

Adding Breaks

There are several types of breaks that may appear in a document. A break is a location where there is a change, such as when the document changes from one page to the next. A break may also occur where the page layout changes, such as when the text changes from one column to two columns. This is called a section break.

Page Breaks

A **page break** is where the document changes from one page to another. Word processors automatically add page breaks when enough text is added to the document to need an additional page. Microsoft Word and most other word processors also allow the user to set where a page will end and a new page begins. This is called a manual page break and can be added at any place in the document.

To add a manual page break in Microsoft Word, place the insertion point at the location where the break should be. Then, click the **Page Break** button in the **Pages** group on the **Insert** tab of the ribbon. Or, click the **Breaks** button in the **Page Setup** group on the **Page Layout** tab of the ribbon and choose the type of page break. The shortcut key for adding a page break is [Ctrl][Enter]. In page layout view, a new simulated page is visible. In draft view, a horizontal line and the text Page Break are added if nonprinting elements are displayed (**Show/Hide** button).

Section Breaks

A section break is a point in the document where page formatting changes. One document can have several different sections. Each section can have its own header and footer, page orientation, margins, page borders, and number of columns. Using section breaks allows much more control of the document and how you want it to look.

To add a section break, place the insertion point at the location where the break should occur. Then, click the **Insert Page and Section Breaks** button in the **Page Setup** group on the **Page Layout** tab of the ribbon. The types of section breaks appear on the lower part of the drop-down menu that is displayed. Select the type of section break to add.

GS5 Key Applications
2.5.2

GS4 Key Applications
2.2.1

FYI

Some actions, such as changing the number of columns for selected text, automatically add section breaks.

HANDS-ON EXAMPLE 7.1.6

ADDING A PAGE BREAK

In many cases, the content in a document should begin on a new page even if the previous page is not full. For example, an introduction to a technical report may be less than one page, but often this type of introduction appears on a page by itself.

1. Launch Microsoft Word, and open the Library1.docx file from the Chap07 folder on your flash drive.
2. Applying what you have learned, save the file as *LastName*Library in the Chap07 folder on your flash drive.
3. Place the insertion point after the word Sincerely and the following comma.
4. Press the [Enter] key twice to add two blank lines.
5. Add your first and last names followed by a comma, a space, and the word Director.
6. With the insertion point after the word *Director*, press the [Ctrl][Enter] key combination to insert a manual page break.
7. Applying what you have learned, display the draft view.
8. Press the [Page Up] key to display the previous page.
9. Click the **Show/Hide** button in the **Paragraph** group on the **Home** tab of the ribbon so it is on (depressed). Notice code in the document for the page break.
10. Save the file.

Show/Hide

Key Applications
GS5 2.9

Tables

A table in a word-processing document is similar to a spreadsheet. Tables increase readability for complex or mathematical text. Data are organized in columns and rows, and the box where a row and column intersect is called a cell. Being able to view data in columns and rows helps the reader find information. A table can list numerical information or organize the appearance of text on page.

Creating and working with a table in Microsoft Word is simple. A table is added at the insertion point. When creating a table, you should have an idea of its dimensions. However, adding or deleting extra rows and columns is easy. The column and row widths are easy to manipulate. Colors and shading can be added to rows, columns, and cells.

Creating a Table

To create a table, click the **Add a Table** button in the **Tables** group on the **Insert** tab of the ribbon. A drop-down menu containing a grid is displayed, as shown in Figure 7-8. Move the cursor to highlight the number of columns and rows desired, and click to create the blank table. The table is ready for data to be entered.

Data in the columns can be aligned to the right or centered. Left alignment is the default. To change the width and height of the table or cells within it, move the cursor over a cell margin line. When the cursor changes to a resizing cursor, click and drag to change the size.

To convert text into a table, there should be some type of punctuation to tell the software how to separate the text into columns and rows. Commas or tabs can be used to indicate where columns will be. Hard returns indicate where rows will be. Once this is set up, select the text.

FYI

The [Tab] key, [Shift][Tab] key combination, and arrow keys can be used to navigate a table.

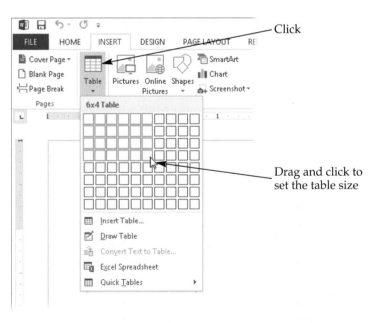

Goodheart-Willcox Publisher

Figure 7-8. Adding a table to a document by specifying the number of columns and rows.

Then, click the **Add a Table** button in the **Tables** group on the **Insert** tab of the ribbon, and click **Convert Text to Table...** in the drop-down menu. The **Convert Text to Table** dialog box is displayed, as shown in Figure 7-9. At the bottom of the dialog box, choose how the text is separated, then click the **OK** button to create the table.

Tables can be converted to text. Select the table, and click the **Convert to Text** button in the **Data** group on the **Layout** on-demand tab in the ribbon. In the **Convert Table to Text** dialog box that is displayed, choose how the text will be separated, and click the **OK** button.

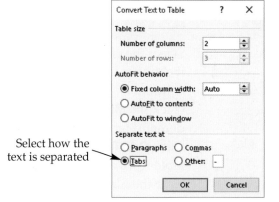

Select how the text is separated

Goodheart-Willcox Publisher

Figure 7-9. Converting text into a table.

HANDS-ON EXAMPLE 7.1.7

CREATING A TABLE

There are many times when a table can improve the presentation of information in a document. For example, a schedule may be better presented as a table than as a bulleted list.

1. Launch Microsoft Word, and open the file FitnessOpportunities.docx from the Chap07 folder on your flash drive.
2. Applying what you have learned, save the file as *LastName*FitnessOpportunities.docx in the Chap07 folder on your flash drive.
3. Place the insertion point at the end of the paragraph that begins with the text The following.
4. Press the [Enter] key to add a blank line.

Add a Table

5. Click the **Add a Table** button in the **Tables** group on the **Insert** tab of the ribbon to display a drop-down menu, as shown.
6. Move the cursor over the grid in the drop-down menu until two columns and six rows are highlighted. The top of the grid should display **2 × 5 Table**. Then, click to add the blank table.
7. Enter this text into the table:

Volleyball Area	2 hours
Soccer Fields	2 hours
Baseball Diamonds	2 hours
Basketball Courts	1 hour
Tennis Courts	1 hour

8. Select the right-hand column by moving the cursor to the top of the column until it changes to a downward pointing arrow, and then click.

Align Right

9. Click the **Align Right** button in the **Paragraph** group on the **Home** tab of the ribbon. Notice how the table is too wide. With this text alignment, the right-hand text is too far from the left-hand text.
10. Move the cursor over the right-hand border until it changes to a double arrow.
11. Click and drag the right-hand border to the left to narrow the column. When the column is about as wide as the longest entry, release the mouse button.

HANDS-ON EXAMPLE 7.1.7 (CONTINUED)

12. Select the entire table by moving the cursor to the top of the left-hand column until it changes to a downward pointing arrow, and then click and drag to the right-hand column.
13. Click the **More** button in the styles gallery in the **Table Styles** group on the **Design** on-demand tab of the ribbon to show the expanded gallery.
14. Click **Grid Table 4 – Accent 4** in the expanded gallery. The design is applied, and the table rows are shaded in color.
15. Save the file.

Key Applications
2.1.1

FYI

A shortcut to adding a row at the end of a table is to place the cursor in the bottom-right cell, and press the [Tab] key.

Key Applications
2.1.1

Adding Columns and Rows

To add a column or row to a table, click in the table, and then click the **Layout** on-demand tab. The **Rows & Columns** group on this tab contains buttons for adding a row above or below the current cell and adding a column to the right or left. Click the appropriate button.

Another way to add a row or column is to use the shortcut menu. Right-click on the cell to use as the reference point for the insertion. Then, click **Insert** in the shortcut menu to display a cascading menu, and click the appropriate command for adding a row or column.

Splitting and Merging Cells

Occasionally, one cell must be split into two or two cells must be combined into one. To split a cell, click in the cell. Then, click the **Split Cells** button in the **Merge** group on the **Layout** on-demand tab of the ribbon. In the **Split Cells** dialog box that is displayed, set the number of columns and rows to create, and click the **OK** button.

To merge cells, first select which cells will be combined. Then, click the **Merge Cells** button in the **Merge** group on the **Layout** on-demand tab of the ribbon. The cells are combined into one cell. If multiple cells contained data, the data from each cell is placed on its own line within the new single cell.

HANDS-ON EXAMPLE 7.1.8

MODIFYING A TABLE

Sometimes you will need to make changes to an existing table. For example, a table may need additional columns, descriptive column headings, and adjustments to the column widths.

1. Launch Microsoft Word, and open the file *LastName*FitnessOpportunities.docx from the Chap07 folder on your flash drive, if it is not already open.
2. Click anywhere within the first row of the table.

HANDS-ON EXAMPLE 7.1.8 (CONTINUED)

Insert
Rows
Above

Insert
Columns
to the
Left

Autofit

3. Click the **Insert Rows Above** button in the **Rows & Columns** group on the **Layout** on-demand tab of the ribbon. A new row appears at the top. Notice that the new first row assumes the dark shading set by the table style.
4. Add the text Fitness Area into the first cell in the first row. Do not press the [Enter] key because that will start a new line in the same cell.
5. Press the [Tab] key to move to the second cell in the first row.
6. Add the text Reservations.
7. With the insertion point in the right-hand cell in the first row, click the **Insert Columns to the Left** button in the **Rows & Columns** group on the **Layout** on-demand tab of the ribbon. A middle column is added to the table.
8. Add the text Description to the middle cell in the first row. Notice that the columns are not equal widths.
9. With the insertion point anywhere within the table, click the **Autofit** button in the **Cell Size** group on the **Layout** on-demand tab of the ribbon, and click **AutoFit Contents** in the drop-down menu. Each column is resized to fit the widest cell content in the column.
10. Save the file.

Templates

As discussed in Chapter 6, a document template is a document preformatted for a specific use and may contain placeholder text or images the user replaces with actual content. They are designed to aid the user in creating professional-looking documents. Templates are available for brochures, flyers, newsletters, reports, invitations, certificates, calendars, and many other types of documents. A template typically contains some basic instructions on how to use it to the best advantage.

Key Applications
2.10.2

For example, a template can be used to create an academic calendar for next month and add some personal events. The template can be easily updated for any month and year. Depending on the template used, it may include room for notes or display the previous and next months as thumbnails for at-a-glance scheduling.

Another example of using a template is to create a newsletter or flyer. These templates may have placeholders for text, images, and a logo. To replace any placeholder text with your own, click the placeholder and enter text. To replace a photo or logo, typically the procedure is to right-click on the placeholder, and then click **Change Picture** or similar command in the shortcut menu.

HANDS-ON EXAMPLE 7.1.9

CREATING A DOCUMENT FROM A TEMPLATE

Templates provide a quick way to create a professional-looking document. The user can focus on the content instead of the format.

1. Launch Microsoft Word 2013.
2. On the startup screen, click in the search text box, enter Academic Calendar, and click the **Search** button. Note: the computer must be connected to the Internet.
3. In the list of returned results, click **Academic Calendar (one month, any year, Monday start)** in the list of templates.
4. In the preview that is displayed, click the **Create** button to start a new document based on the template, as shown.

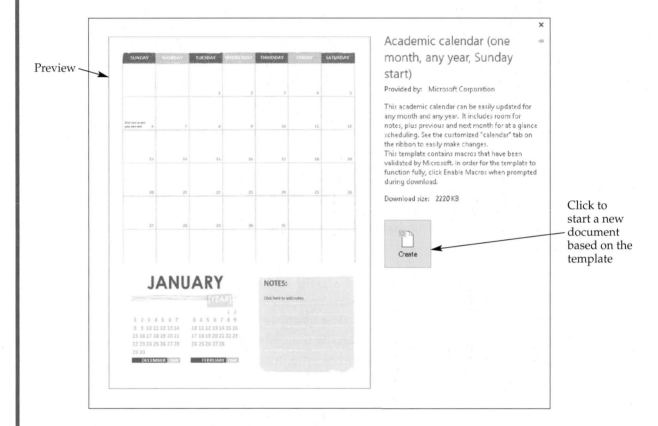

5. In the **Select Calendar Dates** dialog box that appears, choose next month and the current year in the drop-down lists, and then click the **OK** button. If a message appears, click the **OK** button to dismiss it.
6. Click the **Calendar** tab in the ribbon, if it is not already active.
7. Click the placeholder text in the Notes: area of the template. The placeholder text states Click here to add notes.
8. Add the note Study for Chapter 7 test.
9. Save the file as *LastName*MonthCalendar.docx in the Chap07 folder on your flash drive.

but only the end result is visible. To display the changes, click **All Markup** or **Simple Markup** in the drop-down list.

To start tracking changes, click the **Track Changes** button (not the drop-down arrow) in the **Tracking** group on the **Review** tab of the ribbon. This is a toggle button. To stop tracking changes, click the **Track Changes** button again. When tracked changes is off, any existing markups are kept. However, any new changes are not tracked as markups. Turning track changes on begins logging markups again. Only markups made with track changes on will be logged.

When the editing is complete, the tracked changes must be set as final. This is done by accepting or rejecting each change. Move to the beginning of the document. Then, click the **Next Change** button in the **Changes** group on the **Review** tab of the ribbon. This locates the first markup in the document. If the change is okay, click the **Accept and Move to Next** button in the **Changes** group on the **Review** tab of the ribbon. If the markup should not be made, click the **Reject and Move to Next** button in the same group. The change is either applied or not applied, and then the next markup is located. Continue doing this until there are no more markups in the document.

Checking Spelling and Grammar

Spelling and grammar mistakes distract readers. More importantly, they show a lack of quality and concern for the work. To help find spelling and grammar errors, use the spell-check feature of the word processor. However, it is important to keep in mind that a spell-check may not find all mistakes. It is a tool to help you, but it should not be a substitute for manually reviewing and proofreading the document.

Many word-processing programs, including Microsoft Word, check spelling and grammar as words are entered by default. When these words are flagged, you can right-click on the word, and alternate spellings or words will be displayed in the shortcut menu. However, a manual spell-check should always be the last thing you do to a document before declaring it completed.

To start a manual spell-check, click the **Spelling & Grammar** button in the **Proofing** group on the **Review** tab of the ribbon or press the [F7] key. If no errors are found, a message is displayed indicating this. If errors are found, the **Spelling** pane is displayed with the first error display, as shown in Figure 7-12. The error is also selected in the document. Select the correct spelling from the options displayed, and click the **Change** button. If the word is not an error, click the **Ignore** button. If this spelling will appear many times in the document, click the **Ignore All** button so the spell-checker will not stop on all of the instances. After clicking the **Change**, **Ignore**, or **Ignore All** button, Word will locate the next error. Continue making changes as needed until there are no more errors found in the document.

Key Applications
1.3

Key Applications
1.1.5

FYI

In versions of Microsoft Word before 2013, the **Spelling and Grammar** dialog box is used instead of the **Spelling** pane.

Questioned word   Suggestions

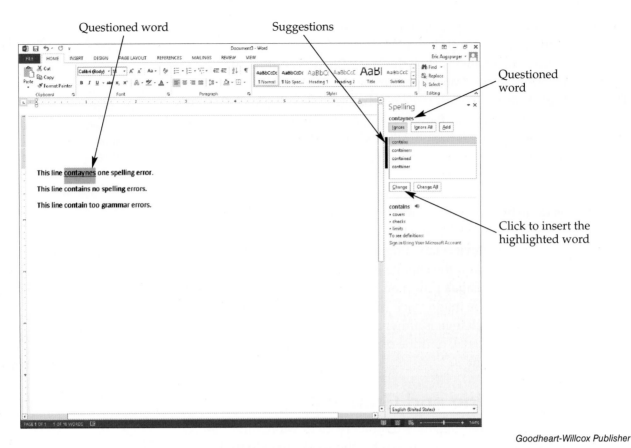

Questioned word

Click to insert the highlighted word

This line contaynes one spelling error.

This line contains no spelling errors.

This line contain too grammar errors.

Goodheart-Willcox Publisher

Figure 7-12. The spell-check feature is used to check for misspellings and can be set to check for proper grammar as well.

HANDS-ON EXAMPLE 7.2.2

CHECKING SPELLING AND GRAMMAR

It is important to use proper spelling and grammar in all documents. Misspelled words or improper usage of grammar are signs of lack of quality and professionalism.

1. Launch Microsoft Word 2013, and open the file *LastName*Library.docx from the Chap07 folder on your flash drive, if it is not already open.
2. Place the insertion point at the beginning of the document.
3. Click the **Spelling & Grammar** button in the **Proofing** group on the **Review** tab of the ribbon or press the [F7] key. Because there are spelling errors in this document, the **Spelling** pane is displayed on the right-hand side of the window, and the first questionable word is highlighted in the document. Note: earlier versions of Word will display the **Spelling and Grammar** dialog box.
4. In the list of spelling alternatives offered, select the correct spelling, and click the **Change** button. The word is changed, and the next questionable word is highlighted in the document.

Spelling & Grammar

HANDS-ON EXAMPLE 7.2.2 (CONTINUED)

5. Continue correcting the document. If the questioned word is correct, click the **Ignore** button. If the correct word does not appear in the list of spelling alternatives, click in the document and manually correct the word. When the last questionable word has been addressed, the **Spelling** pane is closed, and the **Readability Statistics** dialog box is displayed.
6. Make note of the reading level and reading ease scores, and then close the **Readability Statistics** dialog box.
7. Save the file.

Readability

Readability is a measure of how easy it is for the reader to understand and locate information within a document. It includes the visual appearance of text on the page, but also included are the length of words, sentences, and paragraphs. When proofing a document, it is important to remember that somebody will be reading the document. Therefore, readability should always be considered.

Visual Appearance

The arrangement of information in relation to the white space on the page contributes to readability. White space includes margins, space between paragraphs, and any other blank space on the page.

Kerning is the amount of space between two letters. Letters in words that have little space between them creates a crowded look. Letters in words with too much space between them can be hard to read.

As discussed earlier in this chapter, leading is the amount of space between lines of text and paragraphs. Similar to kerning, lines of text that have little space between them create a crowded look. Lines with too much space between them also can be difficult to read.

Also discussed earlier in this chapter is paragraph alignment. Alignment can effect readability. The pages may be left aligned, right aligned, or centered. Additionally, text may be *ragged*, meaning there are uneven end points for each line, or fully justified. How these aspects affect readability vary based on other factors, such as the typeface, point size, length of text, and page and text color.

Reading Level and Readability Scores

Readability and reading level scores help authors and educators adjust a document so it fits the needs of the target audience. These scores predict how difficult the material is to read. The two publications

Green Tech

Repurpose Electronics
Most electronics cannot just be thrown away. They have to be recycled due to harmful chemicals. Sometimes they can be repurposed. For example, a wireless router can be reprogrammed and repurposed to act as a signal amplifier or repeater. By repurposing electronics, a company can save hundreds of dollars on the disposal of old products and even more on the purchasing on new ones.

with the largest circulations, *TV Guide* (13 million) and *Readers Digest* (12 million), are written at the ninth-grade level. This means that anybody with education of at least ninth grade should be able to read the material without difficulty. Some of the most popular novels are written at the seventh-grade level. Two common measures of readability are Flesch Reading Ease and Flesch-Kincaid Grade Level.

The Flesch Reading Ease test produces a rating based on a 100-point scale. The higher the score, the easier it is to understand the document. For most audiences, the target score should be between 60 and 70.

The Flesch-Kincaid Grade Level test produces a rating that corresponds to a school grade level in the United States. For example, a score of 8.0 means the average eighth grader should be able to understand the material. For most audiences, the target grade should be between 7.0 and 8.0.

These tests look at the average number of syllables per word and the number of words per sentence. To improve the readability of a document, edit it to reduce the number of words used in each sentence. Also, try to use words that have no more than two syllables. Words with one or two syllables do not affect the scores.

To set up Microsoft Word to display readability statistics, click **Options** in the **File** tab. In the **Options** dialog box, select **Proofing** on the left-hand side. Under the **When correcting spelling and grammar in Word** heading, check the **Check grammar with spelling** check box. This enables the **Show readability statistics** check box. Check this check box, and then close the **Options** dialog box. The next time a document is spell-checked, the readability statistics dialog box will be displayed after the spell-check is completed, as shown in Figure 7-13.

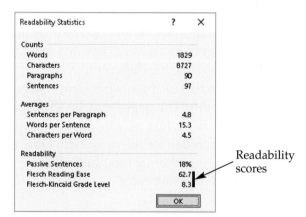

Goodheart-Willcox Publisher

Figure 7-13. Readability statistics can be displayed after a spell-check. In this example, the document has a high reading level.

FYI

Microsoft Outlook can also be set up to display readability statistics for composed e-mails.

7.2 | SECTION REVIEW

 ## CHECK YOUR UNDERSTANDING

1. What does proofing a document involve?
2. How is Microsoft Word set to check spelling as text is entered?
3. What are the two things that the track changes feature logs?
4. What are two ways to start a manual spell-check?
5. How can the reading level of a passage be reduced?

IC3 CERTIFICATION PRACTICE

The following question is a sample of the types of questions presented on the IC3 exam.

1. On which tab is the **Track Changes** button located?
   A. **Proofing**
   B. **References**
   C. **Review**
   D. **Editing**

BUILD YOUR VOCABULARY

As you progress through this course, develop a personal IT glossary. This will help you build your vocabulary and prepare you for a career. Write a definition for each of the following terms and add it to your IT glossary.

kerning
proofing
readability
track changes

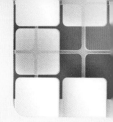

Chapter Summary

Section 7.1
Creating a Document

- Starting with a blank document, text can be entered and formatted. The page layout can be modified, and paragraph styles can be used to control the formatting of the text.

- Tables can be added to a document. A table can be created from existing text, and an existing table can be converted into text.

- A document template is a document preformatted for a specific use. It is intended to be an aid in creating professional-looking documents, such as brochures, flyers, newsletters, reports, invitations, certificates, and calendars.

- Desktop publishing is using software to lay out text and graphics for professional-looking documents, such as newspapers, books, or brochures. As important as the content in a desktop-publishing document is the visual design, which is the arrangement of the visual and artistic elements used to accomplish a goal or communicate an idea.

Section 7.2
Proofing Text

- Proofing is the process of checking the document for errors, such as misspellings, grammar mistakes, and formatting problems. The tools in word processors that help in proofing a document should be considered aids, not replacements for manually reviewing a document for accuracy.

- The track changes feature of word processors is used to log markups made to the document. When finalizing the document, review the markups and either accept or reject each one.

- Spelling and grammar mistakes not only distract readers, they show a lack of quality and concern for the work. A spell-checker can help find spelling and grammar errors along with a manual review of the document.

- Readability is a measure of how easy it is for the reader to understand and locate information within a document. The visual appearance of the document affects readability, and readability scores can be used to assign a score.

Now that you have finished this chapter, see what you know about information technology by scanning the QR code to take the chapter posttest. If you do not have a smartphone, visit www.g-wlearning.com.

Chapter 7 Test

Multiple Choice

Select the best response.

1. Which of the following key combinations moves the insertion point to the end of the document?
   A. [Page Down]
   B. [Ctrl][Page Down]
   C. [End]
   D. [Ctrl][End]

2. Which of the following is not a category of typefaces?
   A. serif
   B. bold
   C. decorative
   D. sans serif

3. Which of the following should be checked when editing a desktop publishing project?
   A. Typefaces and font styles are appropriately applied.
   B. Graphics are appropriately labeled.
   C. Headings are accurate.
   D. All of the above.

4. Which proofing feature can be used to automatically change a misspelled word to the correct spelling?
   A. spell-check
   B. AutoCorrect
   C. AutoChange
   D. SmartCorrect

5. In order for readability statistics to be displayed, what additional function must be done?
   A. Use the **Readability** command.
   B. Apply correct styles.
   C. Check grammar with spelling.
   D. None of the above.

Completion

Complete the following sentences with the correct word(s).

6. The vertical ruler can only be displayed in the _____ view.

7. A(n) _____ is a desktop publishing file that saves the attributes of every font that will be used in a project.

8. _____ is examining a document for misspellings and grammatical mistakes.

9. To start a manual spell-check, press the _____ key.

10. In the Flesch Reading Ease measurement, the _____ the score, the easier it is to understand the document.

Matching

Match the correct term with its definition.

A. typeface
B. orientation
C. tabs
D. kerning
E. Flesch-Kincaid Grade Level

11. The amount of space between two letters.

12. How the document will be placed on the sheet.

13. The design of characters.

14. A measure of readability.

15. Preset horizontal locations across the page in a document.

Application and Extension of Knowledge

1. Create a three-column table in a Microsoft Word document that outlines each hour of your day. The cells in the left-hand column should indicate the hour. The middle column should list the name of each activity. The right-hand column should include any notes, such as "study for test tomorrow" or "bring new shoes to practice." Resize each column as needed. For example, the notes column may need to be wider than the other two columns.

2. Begin a new blank document. Create four new styles: *LastName*Heading1, *Last-Name*Heading2, *LastName*Heading3, and *LastName*Body. Set the formatting of each to your preference. Do not use more than two typefaces. Vary the formatting to make each style look different. Save the file in a location where you will be able to access it in the future.

3. Begin a new blank document. Change the page orientation to landscape. Create a new style named TabStops. Set the line spacing for the style to double. In the style, add a left tab at 1", a center tab at 4.5", and a right tab at 8". Change the typeface and formatting to your preference. Save the file in a location where you will be able to access it in the future.

4. Research three local attractions that your local tourism board may highlight to encourage visitors. Write a report describing what a visitor might find at each of the three sites. Include an introduction and a separate page for each of the three attractions. Use page breaks. Include a table that summarizes the entrance fees for children and adults for weekdays and weekends. Spell-check the document, and display the readability statistics.

5. Research careers that may interest you. The career clusters (www.careertech.org) and Bureau of Labor Statistics (www.bls.gov) are good places to start. Select one career. Write a brief summary of what types of activities are involved in the career. Include a table that outlines the educational requirements, average entry-level salary, number of current jobs in the field, and expected number of jobs in the future. Create styles as needed to format the document. Spell-check the document.

Online Activities

Complete the following activities, which will help you learn, practice, and expand your knowledge and skills.

Certification Practice. Complete the certification practice test for this chapter.

Vocabulary. Practice vocabulary for this chapter using the e-flash cards, matching activity, and vocabulary game until you are able to recognize their meanings.

Communication Skills

College and Career Readiness

Writing. There will be many instances when you will be required to persuade the listener. When you persuade, you convince a person to take a proposed course of action. Prepare for a conversation with a person in the community about who should be responsible for paying for collection or pickup and then disposal of electronic waste. Ask for assistance to help you plan a focused presentation that argues your case and shows solid reasoning that will influence the listener's understanding of the topic.

Reading. Imagery is descriptive language that indicates how something looks, feels, smells, sounds, or tastes. After you have read this chapter, find an example of how the author used imagery to appeal to the five senses. Analyze the presentation of the material. Why did you think this appealed to the senses? How did this explanation create imagery? Describe how it influenced your mood.

Speaking. Word-processing software is used to create written documents. How can a written document help prepare for an oral presentation? Prepare for and participate in a discussion describing your answer to this question.

Internet Research

Famous Speakers. Research famous speakers and select one that captures your attention. The speaker can be in politics, sports, or another realm of life. For the person you selected, note characteristics such as profession, age, business, or other facts that define the person. Listen to speeches this individual has given. Using presentation software, summarize this

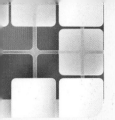

speech and explain how or why this speech was effective. What did you learn?

Teamwork

Collaborating with your team, make a list of the various types of reading materials that you regularly use to find specific information. Examples include a bus schedule, onscreen TV guide, blogs, text messages, newspapers, and magazines. For each type of medium, list the information you are reading to find and discuss strategies for finding it quickly.

Portfolio Development

College and Career Readiness

Certificates. Exhibiting certificates you have received in your portfolio reflects your accomplishments. For example, a certificate might show that you have completed a training class. Another one might show that you can key at a certain speed.

Include any certificates that show tasks completed or your skills or talents. Remember that this is an ongoing project. Plan to update when you have new certificates to add.

1. Scan the certificates that will be in your portfolio.
2. Give each document an appropriate name and save in a folder or subfolder.
3. Place the hard copy certificates in a container for future reference.
4. Record these documents on your master spreadsheet that you started earlier to record hardcopy items. You may list each document alphabetically, by category, date, or other convention that helps you keep track of each document that you are including.

CTSOs

Written Events. Many competitive events for career and technical student organizations (CTSOs) require students to write a paper and submit it either before the competition or when the student arrives at the event. Written events can be lengthy and take a lot of time to prepare, so it is important to start early. To prepare for a written event, complete the following activities.

1. Read the guidelines provided by the organization. The topic to be researched will be specified in detail. Also, all final format guidelines will be given, including how to organize and submit the paper. Make certain you ask questions about any points you do not understand.
2. Do your research early. Research may take days or weeks, and you do not want to rush the process.
3. Set a deadline for yourself so that you write at a comfortable pace.
4. After you write the first draft, ask an instructor to review it for you and give feedback.
5. Once you have the final version, go through the checklist for the event to make sure you have covered all of the details. Your score will be penalized if you do not follow instructions.
6. To practice, visit your organization's website and select a written event in which you might be interested. Research the topic and then complete an outline. Create a checklist of guidelines that you must follow for this event. After you have completed these steps, decide if this is the event or topic that interests you. If you are still interested, move forward and start the writing process.

8

FORMAL DOCUMENTS

SECTIONS

CHECK YOUR IT IQ

Before you begin this chapter, see what you already know about information technology by scanning the QR code to take the chapter pretest. If you do not have a smartphone, visit www.g-wlearning.com.

In the modern world of text messaging and other real-time communication, it is common to see invented spelling and improper grammar. For informal communication between family and friends, these behaviors are accepted. However, formal business communication should reflect a high level of written communication skill. When employers are asked what they are looking for in a new hire, most say they want workers who can show up on time, work a good day, and have excellent oral and written communication skills.

Good communications skills include use of clear, concise sentences with proper sentence structure. Good communicators use proper grammar and spelling. Words are spelled out, not abbreviated. No slang is used. Fortunately, as discussed in the previous chapter, Microsoft Word has built in features to assist with proper written communication. The format of formal communication is commonly used in business. Business letters and interoffice memos use this formal way of communicating. This chapter assists in the development of good written communication for business.

IC3 CERTIFICATION OBJECTIVES

GS5

Key Applications
Domain 2.0 Word processing
   Objective 2.1 Perform basic formatting skills
   Objective 2.5 Know page layout concepts
Living Online
Domain 1.0 Internet (navigation)
   Objective 1.1 Understand what the Internet is

GS4

Key Applications
Domain 2.0 Word processing activities
   Objective 2.2 Layout
Living Online
Domain 4.0 Digital citizenship
   Objective 4.2 Legal and responsible use of computers

College and Career Readiness

Reading Prep. Before reading this chapter, review the objectives. Based on this information, write down two or three items that you think are important to note while you are reading.

CREATING A BUSINESS LETTER

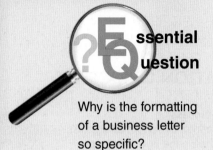

?E ssential Question

Why is the formatting of a business letter so specific?

One of the most common uses for word-processing software in the professional world is to create a letter. Readers expect professional documents to appear a certain way. By using the appropriate format, the reader can immediately tell what type of document is being received. Standard formatting is a generally accepted way to format a document so its appearance follows a convention. Writers use standard formatting so their business documents are consistent in appearance with what the reader expects.

The appearance of a document is the first impression your writing makes on the reader. That first glance at the message should be an open invitation to the receiver. The arrangement of text in relation to the white space on the page determines the visual appeal to the reader. Without properly formatted elements, the reader can easily become lost or distracted.

Rob Marmion/Shutterstock.com

TERMS

block-style letter
body
complimentary close
copy notation
enclosure notation
inside address
letterhead
mixed punctuation

modified-block-style letter
open punctuation
postscript
reference initials
salutation
signature block
subject line

LEARNING GOALS

After completing this section, you will be able to:

- Describe the standard business letter formats.
- Identify standard letter elements.
- Discuss elements beyond standard letter elements.
- Format a business letter.

Standard Business Letter Format

Letters are messages printed on stationery and should conform to workplace standards. Stationery used for business purposes is often letterhead stationery. A **letterhead** includes information about an organization, such as its name, address, contact information, and a logo. Letterhead is preprinted on high-quality paper so organizations do not have to add this information on every correspondence. In the case of a letter concerning personal business, the letterhead is replaced by the return address of the sender.

Businesses generally use one of two standardized letter formats: block or modified block. The **block-style letter** is formatted so all lines are flush with the left-hand page margin, as shown in Figure 8-1. No indentions are used. The **modified-block-style letter** places the date, complimentary close, and signature to the right of the center point of the letter. All other elements of the letter are flush with the left-hand page margin. Figure 8-2 shows a letter formatted in the modified-block style.

Standard Letter Elements

Standardized letter formats contain various elements. Block-style and modified-block-style letters include the same elements:

- date
- inside address
- salutation
- body
- complimentary close
- signature
- notations

If not using a letterhead, a return address should also be included.

TITANS OF TECHNOLOGY

Charles Simonyi and Butler Lampson were early developers of word-processing software. Many people would say that word processing began with the electric typewriter, which allowed, for the first time, someone to edit his or her work and reprint the document. However, others claim the first true word processors were the software programs for the minicomputers and microcomputers that allowed formatting of a document. Simonyi and Lampson were two researchers at Palo Alto Research Center (PARC), the research arm of Xerox Corporation, when they developed Bravo in 1974 for the Alto minicomputer. However, the earliest word processor for home microcomputers was Electric Pencil, which was developed by Michael Shrayer, a computer club enthusiast. Other early word-processing programs included WordStar, Word Perfect, Apple Writer, and Easy Writer. The word-processing programs of today are descendants of these early software applications.

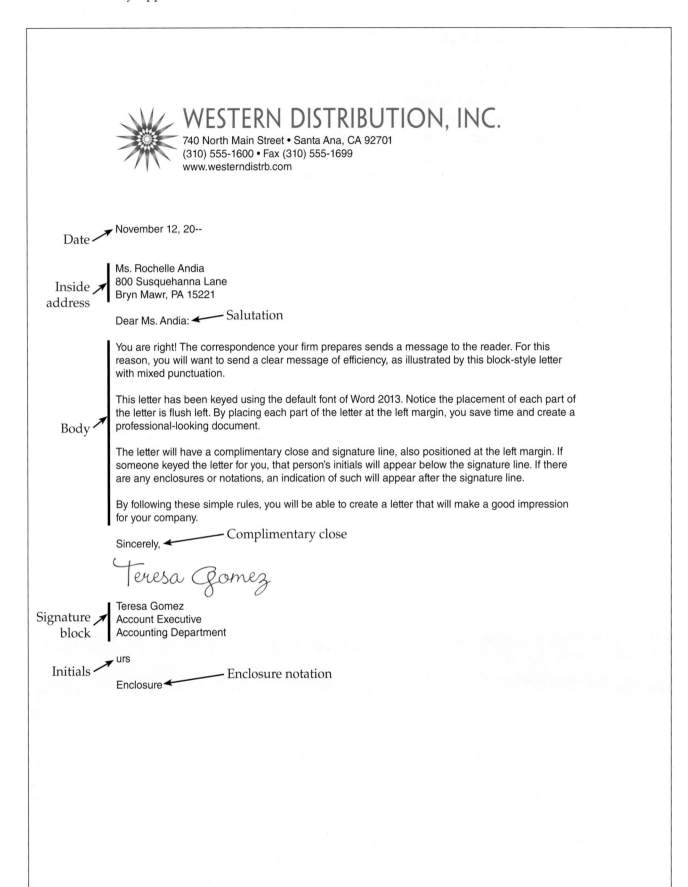

Figure 8-1. This letter is formatted in block style with mixed punctuation.

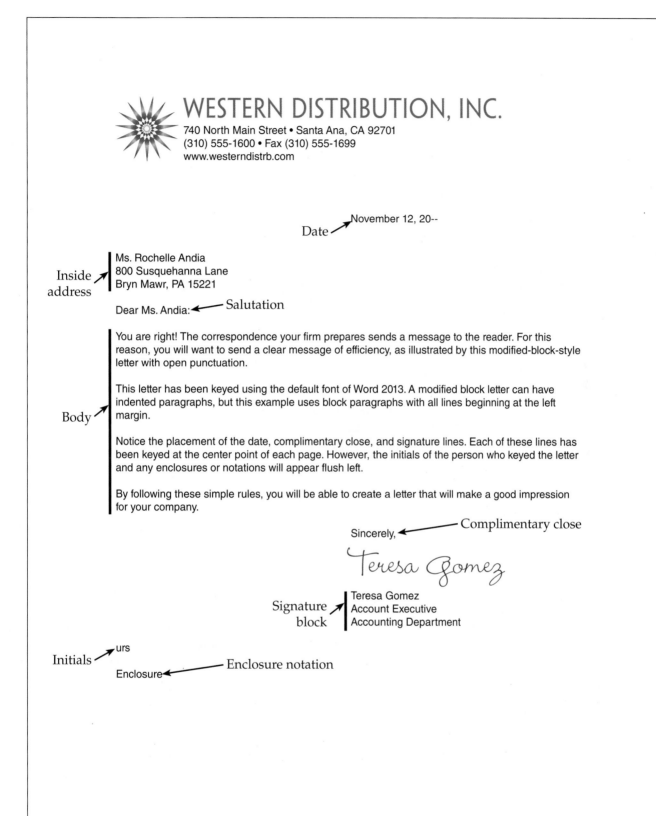

Figure 8-2. This is similar to the letter shown in Figure 8-1, but formatted in modified-block style with open punctuation.

Career Skills

Destination Marketing Manager

A destination marketing manager works for a variety of employers to attract visitors to a particular destination. They coordinate the destination activities of agencies, convention bureaus, or marketing firms who choose their particular destination. Using business communications standards and promotional materials, these marketing managers target travelers within a certain budget range.

Date

The date consists of the month, day, and year. The month is spelled in full. The day is written in figures and followed by a comma. The year is written in full and consists of numbers. For example:

> December 18, 20xx

where xx is the current year. This is the standard for the United States. International uses may require a different format for the date.

Inside Address

The **inside address** is the name, title, and address of the recipient. The two examples that follow show how to format an inside address.

> Mr. Angelo Costanzo, Manager
> Griffin Plumbing Supply Co.
> 1987 Susquehanna Avenue
> Wilkes-Barre, PA 18701

> Ms. Denise Rodriquez
> President & CEO
> Urban Development Council
> 150 Grosvenor Avenue
> Washington, DC 30005

For addresses in the United States, the last line must be the city, state, and zip code. Note that the state abbreviation is always two letters and in all capital letters.

Salutation

The **salutation** is the greeting in a letter and always begins with *Dear*. This is followed by the recipient's first name or, according to your relationship, title and last name.

There are two types of punctuation used in letters. **Mixed punctuation** is a style in which a colon is placed after the salutation and a comma after the complimentary close. **Open punctuation** is a style in which there is no punctuation after the salutation or complimentary close.

Always address a letter to a specific person unless it is being intentionally directed to an organization. It may take a phone call or Internet search to get the correct name, but it is worth the effort to personalize business messages. Also, make sure the receiver's name is correctly spelled and the appropriate title used, such as *Dr.*, *Mr.*, or *Ms.* The title *Mrs.* is rarely used in business writing. Spell out and capitalize titles such as *Professor* and *Reverend*. If you are unsure of a person's gender, use the full name.

If you need to write a letter without the name of a specific person, do not use generic greetings such as *Dear Sir* or *Gentlemen*. You may use *Ladies and Gentlemen*; however, the best course is to use words that describe the role of the person:

Dear Customer:
Dear Circulation Manager:
Dear Editor:

Body

The **body** of the letter is the message. Format the body according to the block or modified-block style. Most businesses use the block style. Single-spaced letters are standard. However, some businesses prefer the default setting of the word-processing software used. In Microsoft Word 2013, this is 1.08.

Complimentary Close

The **complimentary close** is the sign-off for the letter. Only the first word is capitalized. The style used in the complimentary close—mixed or open punctuation—must match the salutation. The complimentary close follows the body of the letter and is appropriately spaced, as shown in Figure 8-1 and Figure 8-2. The most commonly used closings are as follows.

Mixed Punctuation
Sincerely,
Sincerely yours,
Cordially,
Cordially yours,

Open Punctuation
Sincerely
Sincerely yours
Cordially
Cordially yours

Signature Block

The writer's name and title are called the **signature block** or *signature*. The writer's job title and department appear beneath the name, unless a letterhead is used that contains this information. Begin the signature block below the complimentary close. The blank lines of space are used for the handwritten signature.

Sincerely,

Margaret Shaw
Coordinator
Business Development

When the message is from the company rather than an individual, the company name may appear in all-capital letters below the complimentary close. In this situation, there is no signature.

Sincerely,

JIMENEZ-BRADFORD REALTY

Notations

Letters may include reference initials. **Reference initials** indicate the person who keyed the letter. If the writer keyed the letter, initials are not included. Reference initials are lowercase letters.

Cordially yours,

Margaret Shaw
Senior Vice President

smb

An **enclosure notation** alerts the reader to materials that are included in the mailing along with the letter. Spell out and capitalize the word *Enclosure*. If there is more than one enclosure, indicate the number of items included or list them. The word *Attachment* may be used instead of the word *Enclosure*.

Enclosures
Enclosures: 3
Enclosures: Statement
                    Check
                    Letter

A **copy notation** is needed when others are being sent a copy of the letter. The notation appears below the signature, as shown in Figure 8-1 and Figure 8-2. If there are enclosure notations or reference initials, the copy notation appears below these. Use *c* for copy or *cc* for carbon copy or courtesy copy. The copy notation is followed by a colon and a list of the full names of individuals receiving copies.

cc: Tina Ricco
        Gary Kowalski

Additional Letter Elements

The previously described elements are the most common elements of a business letter. However, there are three additional letter elements that are sometimes used in a business letter. These are the attention line, subject line, and postscript.

Attention Line

There is a wealth of resources available to the writer, such as the Internet and company databases, that make it largely unnecessary to address correspondence without an individual's name. However, if this circumstance does occur, substituting a position or department title for a specific name is a good solution. For example, you may know the marketing manager is to receive the letter, but cannot find the name of the person. In this situation, it is appropriate to include an attention line that says *Attention Marketing Manager*. This line is positioned as part of the inside address:

> Attention Marketing Manager
> Urban Development Council
> 150 Grosvenor Avenue
> Washington, DC 30005

Subject Line

A **subject line** in a letter helps the reader know the content of the message before reading. The subject line may be in all caps or initial caps and the word *subject* is optional. The subject line appears after the salutation and before the body of the letter.

> Dear Mr. Ramito:
>
> SUBJECT: MINUTES OF SUMMER MEETING
>
> Thank you for attending the summer meeting of the Green Entrepreneur that was held last month in Orlando. We appreciate your attendance and your contribution to this meeting...

Postscript

Postscript means *after writing* and is information included after the signature. In business letters, the postscript is no longer used to represent an afterthought. For example, in the past a writer may have included an omission as a postscript, such as:

> P.S. I forgot to tell you we're moving. After June 1, you can reach us at our new address.

With the advent of word-processing software, the need for postscripts disappeared. If you discover that something important was omitted from the body of a letter, simply edit the letter and include it.

Occasionally, however, a writer uses a postscript to emphasize or personalize a point. Sales letters often use postscripts for special effect.

> P.S. Remember, our sale ends this Thursday. Don't miss the wonderful savings in store for you!

Use postscripts sparingly. Frequent use of postscripts may suggest to the reader that you did not plan your message.

STEM

Technology
A word processor is an electronic device or software application that allows the composition, editing, formatting, and printing of written material. Word processors have evolved from large computerized systems to electronic typewriters to software such as Microsoft Word. Modern word processors have font selection, spelling and grammar check, and automatic text correction, among other features.

HANDS-ON EXAMPLE 8.1.1

CREATING A PERSONAL BUSINESS LETTER

There will be many times throughout your career when you will need to create a business letter. The ability to create a proper business letter is an important skill to develop.

1. Launch Microsoft Word, and begin a new blank document.
2. Save the file as *LastName*BusinessLetter.docx in the Chap08 folder on your flash drive.
3. Add the text University of New Hampshire, and press the [Enter] key.
4. Add a one-line street address, and press the [Enter] key.
5. Add a city, a state abbreviation, and a zip code, and press the [Enter] key.
6. Enter today's date. Notice that when Word recognizes you are entering a month, it suggests the current month. Accept this by pressing the [Enter] key. Then, once you press the space bar, Word suggests today's date. Accept this by pressing the [Enter] key.
7. Enter the following text on separate lines. The body should be two paragraphs.

> Dr. Kathleen Augustino
> University of Baltimore
> 1420 North Charles St
> Baltimore, MD 21201
>
> Dear Dr. Augustino,
>
> Please let me know who on your faculty is in charge of coordinating student internships for international studies for the spring and summer semesters. We have several very good candidates who are bilingual.
>
> Our candidates are fluent in French, Spanish, German, and Arabic. They are all US citizens. Several have grown up in bilingual households. Others have spent time learning the languages through total immersion. You can reach me through e-mail at languages@arc.xyz or 999-555-1234. Thank you.
>
> Sincerely,

8. Enter your name. The letter is now composed, but it needs to be properly formatted. This will be done in the next exercise.
9. Save the document.

Formatting a Business Letter

GS5 2.1 Key Applications

There is an accepted standard format for business letters. It is important to follow the accepted standard. Using nonstandard formatting makes the letter appear unprofessional. As a result, the reader may not take the letter seriously or the message of the letter may not be effectively communicated.

If you will be creating letters on a regular basis, the best approach is to create paragraph styles for each element of the letter. Also set up the page margins. Then, save the document as a template. Whenever a letter needs to be created, begin a new blank document based on this letter template. All of the paragraph styles and page formatting will be set up automatically.

Then simply write the letter and apply the proper paragraph styles to each element. However, if you do not frequently write letters, you may choose to manually format the page and paragraphs each time.

Common Formatting

The left- and right-hand page margins should be 1″. The bottom page margin should also be 1″. The top page margin should be 2″. However, if the letterhead extends more than 2″ from the top edge of the page, the date line should be placed two lines below the bottom of the letterhead. If the letter is longer than one page, the top margin on the second and remaining pages should be 1″.

The typeface used in a letter is largely a personal preference, but many people use the default typeface in the word processor. The typeface may be a serif typeface or a sans serif typeface, as discussed in Chapter 7. A common serif typeface is Times New Roman. A common sans serif typeface is Arial. Do not use decorative typefaces, such as Flemish Script, Monotype Corsiva (a calligraphy-style typeface), or Comic Sans. These typefaces are not appropriate for a business letter and their use decreases the readability of text.

Business letters should have single line spacing. However, some word-processing software has a default setting that is not single spaced. For example, the default line spacing in Microsoft Word 2013 is 1.08, as shown in Figure 8-3. Many companies use the default setting for line spacing, but single line spacing is the traditional standard. To use single line spacing, either modify the paragraph setting or style or use the [Shift] [Enter] key combination to add a soft return.

If writing a personal business letter with a return address, leave two blank lines between the return address and the date. Otherwise, the date should begin at the top margin. There should be two blank lines between the date and the inside address. After the inside address, there should be one blank line before the salutation. Leave one blank line after the salutation and begin the body. If the body is longer than one paragraph, leave one blank line between each paragraph. After the body, leave one blank line and then add the complementary close. Between the complementary close and the signature block, there should be two blank lines. This is the space where the writer will sign the letter. For additional elements, such as reference initials or an enclosure notation, leave one blank line between each element.

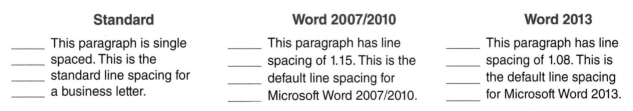

Goodheart-Willcox Publisher

Figure 8-3. The standard line spacing for business letters is single spaced, but some companies allow the Microsoft Word default setting to be used.

Block Style versus Modified-Block Style

In a block-style letter, all elements are flush to the left-hand page margin. There should be no indentation on any line. This can be set up in the paragraph styles. If manually formatting the letter, it is easiest to remove the indentation before writing the letter so each new line will not be automatically indented.

In a modified-block-style letter, the date, complimentary close, and signature are flush left with the center point of the page. The horizontal center of the page for a standard letter-size sheet is 4.25", which becomes 3.25" on the ruler when the 1" page margin is subtracted. This point can be set in the paragraph style or the left indentation can be manually shifted over by 3.25". All other elements are flush to the left-hand page margin. The first line of body paragraphs may be indented or not. If indentation is used, the indent should be .5". This can be set up in the paragraph style or, if manually formatting the letter, a tab stop can be manually added at this location.

HANDS-ON EXAMPLE 8.1.2

FORMATTING A BUSINESS LETTER

Composing the message in a letter is only an initial step. The letter must be properly formatted following accepted guidelines to be final.

1. Launch Microsoft Word, and open the *LastName*BusinessLetter.docx file in the Chap08 folder on your flash drive, if it is not already open.

Adjust
Margins

2. Click the **Adjust Margins** button in the **Page Setup** group on the **Page Layout** tab of the ribbon, and click **Custom Margins** in the drop-down menu. The **Page Setup** dialog box is displayed with the **Margins** tab selected, as shown.

Set the margins

3. Click in the **Top:** text box, and enter 2. This sets the top page margin to 2″.
4. Enter 1 in the **Bottom:**, **Left:**, and **Right:** text boxes to set the corresponding page margins to 1″.
5. Click the **OK** button to close the dialog box and set the margins. The first line should shift down slightly to match the new top margin.
6. Click at the end of the first line in the return address, press the [Shift][Enter] key combination, and press the [Delete] key. This adds a soft return and makes the first and second lines of the return address in the same paragraph. Essentially, this two-line paragraph becomes single spaced.
7. Applying what you have learned, make the third line in the return address part of the same paragraph as the first two lines.
8. Click after the ZIP code in the return address, and press the [Enter] key twice. This manually adds two blank lines between the return address and the date.
9. Click after the date, and press the [Enter] key twice to manually add two blank lines between the date and the inside address.
10. Applying what you have learned, add soft returns to single space the inside address.
11. Click after the ZIP code in the inside address, and press the [Enter] key once. This manually adds one blank line between the inside address and the salutation.
12. Click after the salutation, and press the [Enter] key once to manually add one blank line between the salutation and the body.
13. Click at the end of the first paragraph of the body, and press the [Enter] key once to manually add one blank line between the paragraphs in the body.
14. Applying what you have learned, select all of the text in the document, including blank lines.
15. Click the dialog box launcher in the **Paragraph** group on the **Home** tab of the ribbon. The **Paragraph** dialog box is displayed with the **Indents and Spacing** tab selected, as shown.

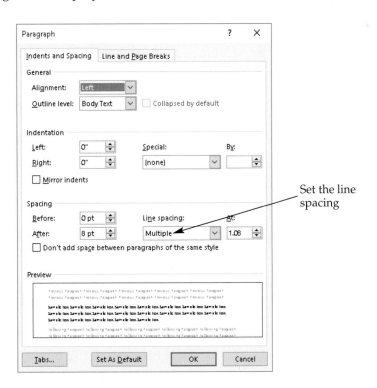

Set the line spacing

HANDS-ON EXAMPLE 8.1.2 (CONTINUED)

16. Click the **Line spacing:** drop-down arrow, and click **Single** in the drop-down list. This manually sets the line spacing for the selected text, which is the entire document, to single spaced.
17. Enter 0 in the **Before:** and **After:** text boxes. This sets the amount of space (in points) that appears before and after each paragraph.
18. Click the **OK** button to update the line spacing.
19. Click at the end of the last line in the body, and press the [Enter] key to manually add one blank line between the body and the complimentary close.
20. Click at the end of the complimentary close, and press the [Enter] key twice to add two blank lines between the complimentary close and your name. The letter is now properly formatted in block style.

8.1 SECTION REVIEW

 ### CHECK YOUR UNDERSTANDING

1. What are the two standardized letter formats used by businesses?
2. Which standard letter element contains the address of the person for whom the letter is intended?
3. What is the purpose of the subject line on a letter?
4. If you will be creating letters on a regular basis, what is the best approach to formatting the text of the letters?
5. What is the traditional line spacing used in a business letter?

IC3 CERTIFICATION PRACTICE

The following question is a sample of the types of questions presented on the IC3 exam.

1. Perform this simulation.

   Create a new paragraph style named Letter_ Body that is single spaced, has no paragraph indent, and has three points before and after the paragraph.

BUILD YOUR VOCABULARY

As you progress through this course, develop a personal IT glossary. This will help you build your vocabulary and prepare you for a career. Write a definition for each of the following terms and add it to your IT glossary.

block-style letter	modified-block-style letter
body	open punctuation
complimentary close	postscript
copy notation	reference initials
enclosure notation	salutation
inside address	signature block
letterhead	subject line
mixed punctuation	

CREATING A REPORT

Air Images/Shutterstock.com

Reports provide facts and information from which conclusions are drawn. They also discuss problems and recommend solutions. In the workplace, reports are often used to convey information that is used as the basis for making business decisions. In school, students are often required to write reports to provide information on specific topics related to coursework.

Reports may be developed for use inside an organization. They may also be sent to people outside of the organization, such as governmental agencies, stockholders, members, investors, clients, customers, and to the media. No matter who the audience is for a report, the manner in which the report is presented represents the writer. A properly formatted report will communicate professionalism. It may also set the stage for how the reader will view the validity of the information presented in the report.

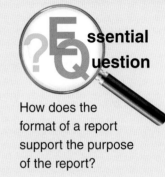

Essential Question

How does the format of a report support the purpose of the report?

LEARNING GOALS

After completing this section, you will be able to:
- Describe the process of creating a report.
- Format a report.

TERMS

analytical reports
citations
conclusions
data
endnotes
folio
footnotes
headings
informational reports

introduction
primary research
proposals
qualitative data
quantitative data
recommendations
secondary research
table of contents

Creating a Report

Reports are documents used to present information in a structured format to a specific audience for a defined purpose. There are three common types of reports:

- informational reports
- analytical reports
- proposals

Informational reports contain facts, data, or other types of information. They do not attempt to analyze the data or persuade the reader. **Analytical reports** contain both information and analysis of the data. They often provide conclusions or recommendations drawn from the analysis. **Proposals** typically contain a specific idea and attempt to persuade the reader to take a certain course of action. Extensive research and analysis often go into a proposal.

A choice must be made when planning the document in order to achieve the desired outcome. The direct or indirect approach can be applied to the content of a report. When using the direct approach, start with a general statement of purpose. Follow this with supporting details. The direct approach is desirable when the reader is expecting a straightforward message. When using the indirect approach, discuss supporting details upfront to prepare the reader for your general statement of purpose or conclusions.

Planning a Report

Planning is the most important stage of preparing a report. It involves focusing on the subject and outlining the content. Writing a report should always follow the steps of the writing process, shown in Figure 8-4. Begin planning by completing the first step in the writing process, which is prewriting. Prewriting helps you identify the purpose and audience of the report. In prewriting, answer the questions of who, what, when, where, why, and how.

- Who is the audience?
- What do you want to communicate?

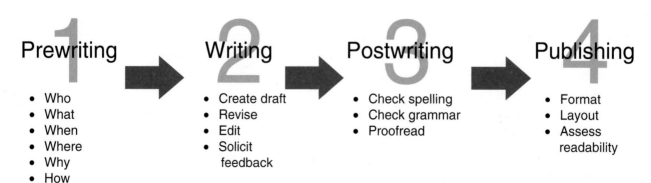

Goodheart-Willcox Publisher

Figure 8-4. There are four stages in the writing process.

- When must the report be complete?
- Where is the information?
- Why are you writing?
- How should the information be organized?

The questions can be answered in any order. After you have completed the prewriting steps, you will be able to begin the research.

Researching a Report

Collecting data is an important step in preparing to write a report. **Data** are the pieces of information gathered through research. Research techniques include studying written information on the topic and conducting surveys, focus groups, or interviews. Research might include consulting experts or convening a taskforce or committee to work on different aspects of the report.

Whatever the length or purpose of a formal report, the goal is to prepare a valid, useful, and informative document. Consider the type of information needed to make the report credible. Information usually falls into one of two categories: qualitative or quantitative data. **Qualitative data** are the information that provides insight into how people think about a particular topic. An example of qualitative data is a customer's feelings after speaking with a customer service agent. **Quantitative data** are the facts and figures from which conclusions can be drawn. An example of quantitative data is the number of customers who requested to speak with a customer service agent after using a certain product.

Primary research is first-hand research conducted by the writer in preparation for writing a report. The most common methods of primary research for a business report are interviews, surveys, and experiments.

Secondary research is data and information already assembled and recorded by someone else. This might include published materials or resources available to you on the job. In many cases, you will conduct secondary research first to find credible information to support your ideas. You will conduct primary research only when key data are not found.

Writers can reference material from other authors provided proper credit is given. This is done by summarizing the work in your own words, which is called *paraphrasing*, or by directly quoting a small part of the work. It is necessary to credit, or cite, sources when referencing or paraphrasing someone else's work. In general, the following information is needed to create citations.

- author's name
- publication title
- name and location of the publisher
- publication year
- website name, URL, and date of retrieval

Citations are discussed later in this section. Ethical use of information is discussed later in this chapter.

FYI

The root of the word *qualitative* is *quality*. The root of the word *quantitative* is *quantity*.

Green Tech

Unplug Electronics

Electronics that are plugged into an outlet use standby power, which is the minimum power usage when the item is plugged in. That means that even if it is turned off, an electronic device is still drawing power and costing money to run. To make sure that electronics will not waste power, unplug them entirely.

Writing a Report

Once the research is completed and the sources are organized, you are ready to continue the writing process and compose the report. Complete a first draft and revise the document as many times as necessary to create the final product.

Title Page

All formal reports should have a title page designed for readability and visual appeal. These elements belong on the title page:

- name of the report
- name of the person or group for whom the report was written
- name of the author of the report
- date the report is distributed

Sometimes other information, such as the location of the company, organization, or school, may also be needed. A sample title page is shown in Figure 8-5.

Table of Contents

The **table of contents**, or TOC, lists the major sections and subsections within the report with page numbers, as shown in Figure 8-6. A table of contents is necessary so the reader knows what is included in the report. This page may be referred to as *table of contents* or *contents*.

Introduction

Capture the reader's attention by giving an overview of the report's contents. A formal report usually contains an introduction. The **introduction** discusses the purpose of the report and the benefits of the ideas or recommendations you are presenting. The introduction of the report often covers the following information, but what is included in the introduction varies based on the needs of the report.

- History or background that led to the preparation of the report.
- Scope of the report, including what is covered and, if necessary, what is not covered.
- Purpose for which the report was written, including the need or justification for the report.
- Method of gathering information, facts, and figures for the report.
- Definitions of terms that may present problems for certain readers.

Refer to Figure 8-7 for an example of an introduction. Note that the order of information in an introduction may differ based on the requirements for the report you are writing.

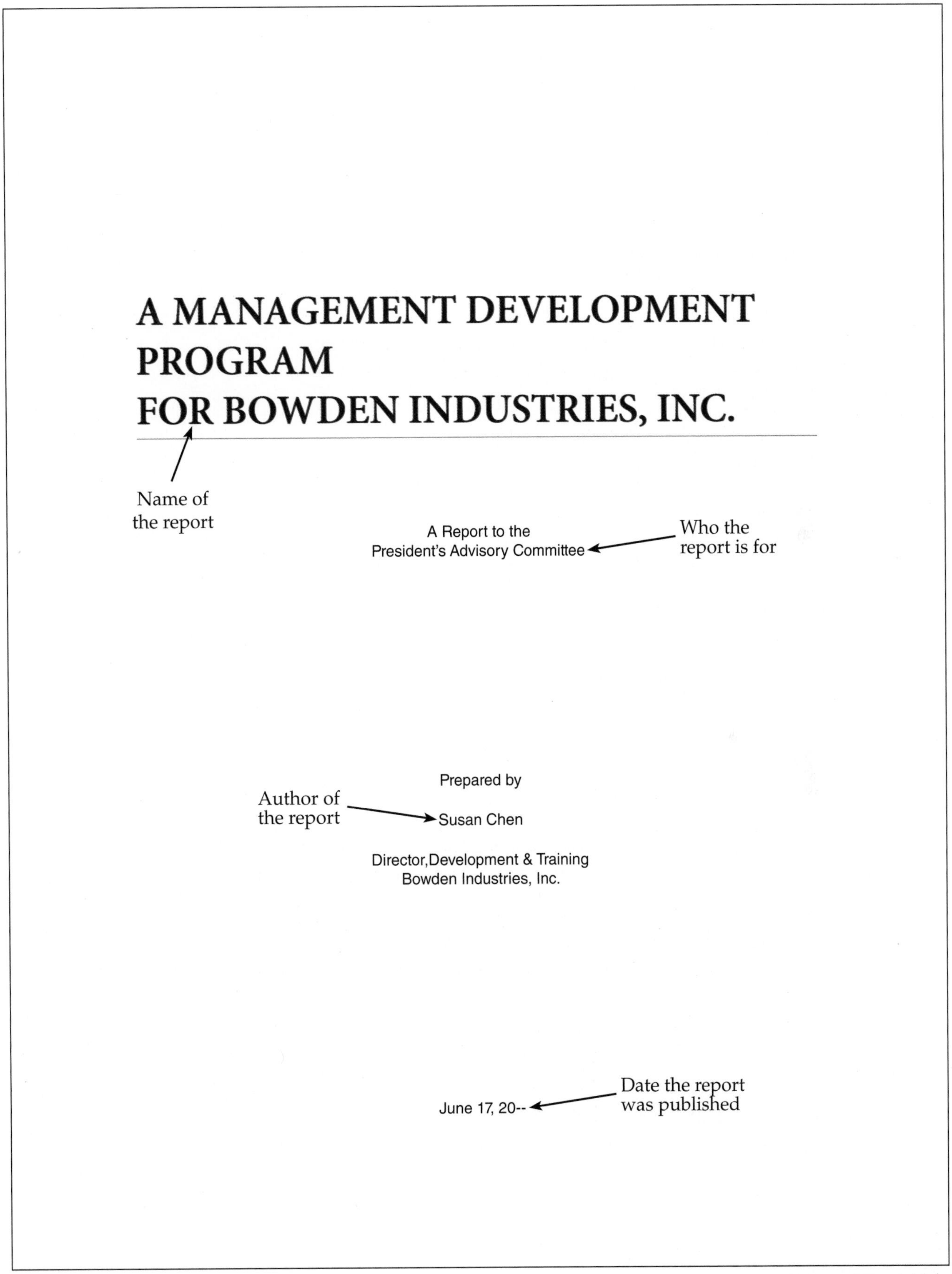

A MANAGEMENT DEVELOPMENT PROGRAM
FOR BOWDEN INDUSTRIES, INC.

A Report to the
President's Advisory Committee

Prepared by

Susan Chen

Director,Development & Training
Bowden Industries, Inc.

June 17, 20--

Name of the report
Who the report is for
Author of the report
Date the report was published

Goodheart-Willcox Publisher

Figure 8-5. This is an example of a title page.

Begin introduction
on page 1 and use
Roman numerals for
preceding pages

CONTENTS

ii

Goodheart-Willcox Publisher

Figure 8-6. This is an example of a table of contents (TOC).

INTRODUCTION

Bowden Industries, Inc., is often referred to as "a family that keeps outgrowing its home." This implies little planning, innovation, and management leadership in the company's twelve years of existence, which is simply not true. Product diversification, innovative marketing and manufacturing, and sound financial management all attest to the effective leadership with which the company has been blessed.

At the May 9 meeting of the President's Advisory Committee, the question was asked, "Where will the managerial expertise needed for future growth and expansion come from?" The purpose of this report is to provide possible answers to that vital question.

History

In the past, Bowden has depended largely on universities and executive placement agencies for sources of managerial talent—and, of course, on its own promotion-from-within policy. By and large, these have been good sources of talent and, no doubt, will continue to be used. However, training and developing those new management hires has been through hit-or-miss, largely unstructured, on-the-job supervision. The results are mixed. Some people were well trained and quickly moved up when positions became available. Others languished and, seeing no opportunity for growth, left the company.

Scope

The term "management" in this report refers to all positions from first-line supervisors (classified as Levels 13 and 14 by the Human Resources Department) right on up to the top executive positions. No attention has been given to lower-level jobs in this report, although this is obviously a subject that deserves full exploration later.

Statement of Problem

During the past year, 44 vacancies occurred in management positions. Of that number, 22 were the result of retirement because of age or health, 13 resigned to accept positions in other companies, and the remaining nine were the result of newly created positions within the company.

It is interesting to find that 27 of the 44 openings had to be filled from the outside. In other words, only 17 employees were considered ready to accept the greater responsibilities of management. Actually, few of the people recruited from the outside were actually ready either (the unknown often looks better than the known); many required a long break-in period. Besides having a negative effect on employees who were denied promotion, outside recruiting and on-the-job adjustment are very expensive.

Goodheart-Willcox Publisher

Figure 8-7. An introduction states the purpose of the report. A page number does not appear on the first page of the introduction.

Body

The body of the report contains all of the information, data, and statistics you assemble. Organize ideas in a logical manner. Provide supporting facts and figures from reliable sources for all information. Do not report your position based solely on opinion. In many formal reports, a conclusion must be drawn, but it should be based on facts presented in the report.

If the topic you are writing about is very high level, such as a detailed proposal that will cost a great deal of money, a conversational tone could take away from the objectivity that the audience might expect. You want to convince the reader you have thoroughly studied the matter and that your facts and figures are highly trustworthy. A more formal tone is more likely to achieve this goal.

If, on the other hand, you are writing a report on activities that boost morale and create a sense of team, a conversational tone would be appropriate. This tone is friendlier and will help set the stage for the theme of the report.

A report addressed to the company president is likely to be formal in tone. If you have a friendly relationship with your supervisor or instructor, a report you write for her or him may be more conversational.

Conclusion

The closing should summarize the key points. In some cases, the report will close with conclusions and recommendations based on your study or analysis. **Conclusions** are the writer's summary of what the audience should take away from the report. **Recommendations** are actions the writer believes the reader should take, as shown in Figure 8-8. Both of these should follow logically from the information presented in the body of the report. If you make a leap in logic, you risk losing credibility with the audience.

RECOMMENDATIONS

On the basis of this study, there would appear to be a definite need for a well-rounded education program at Bowden Industries, Inc. There are numerous possible methods of operating and conducting it. The following recommendations are offered.

1. Appoint a Director of Management Development, preferably a person with sound academic credentials (possibly a Ph.D.), teaching experience in management at the undergraduate and graduate levels, and broad business experience in supervision and management. The appointed person would report directly to the Executive Vice President or to the President.

2. Appoint a Management Education Committee, consisting of the top executive of each of the six divisions in the company and the Executive Vice President (ex officio). This committee would advise the Director of Management Development in planning and operating the program, using as many of the sources described in this report as feasible.

Goodheart-Willcox Publisher

Figure 8-8. Recommendations provide the writer's suggestions for a course of action.

Formatting a Report

The appearance of the document is important. Many organizations have formatting guidelines for reports, while other organizations use templates provided in Microsoft Word or other word processing software. When the topic covers more than one key point or important issue, headings should be used as a design element.

GS5 Key Applications 2.1

Headings

Headings are words and phrases that introduce sections of text. Headings are tiered, beginning with the section opener title and continuing with the main heading and subheadings. They organize blocks of information in a document and serve as guideposts to alert the reader to what is coming.

Most narrative text can be divided into main topics and subtopics usually with no more than three levels of headings. Figure 8-9 shows examples of different head levels in a document. If a given heading has subheads, it should have at least two subheads. Never have only one subhead below any heading.

Headings are formatted so the main heads have a greater visual impact than the subheads. The lowest level of subhead should have the least visual impact. For example Heading 1 is in a much larger point size than Heading 3.

The report title is usually set in the default Title style of the word processor. The default settings for this style in Microsoft Word 2013 are 28 points, Calibri Light, and font color Automatic (black).

The first level of head, usually called a *level 1 head* or a *side head*, should begin at the left-hand page margin. Capitalization should follow *title case* in which the first word and all main words in the head are

FYI

If planning to use Microsoft Word's automated table of contents feature, it is very important to use the built-in heading styles.

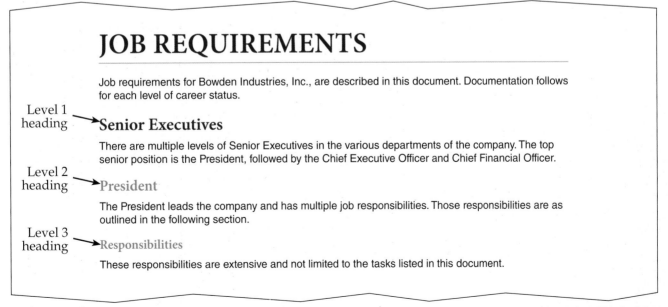

JOB REQUIREMENTS

Job requirements for Bowden Industries, Inc., are described in this document. Documentation follows for each level of career status.

Level 1 heading → **Senior Executives**

There are multiple levels of Senior Executives in the various departments of the company. The top senior position is the President, followed by the Chief Executive Officer and Chief Financial Officer.

Level 2 heading → **President**

The President leads the company and has multiple job responsibilities. Those responsibilities are as outlined in the following section.

Level 3 heading → Responsibilities

These responsibilities are extensive and not limited to the tasks listed in this document.

Goodheart-Willcox Publisher

Figure 8-9. Levels of headings within the body of a document help to organize information and guide the reader.

capitalized. The default Heading 1 style of the word processor can be used. In Microsoft Word 2013, the default settings are 16 point, Calibri Light, and font color Blue Accent 1 Darker 25%.

The second level of head, usually called a *level 2 head*, should begin at the left-hand page margin. Capitalization should follow title case. The default Heading 2 style of the word processor can be used. In Microsoft Word 2013, the default settings are 13 point, Calibri Light, and font color Blue Accent 1 Darker 25%.

The third level of head, usually called a *level 3 head*, should begin at the left-hand page margin. Capitalization may follow title case or sentence case. In *sentence case*, only the first letter on the line is capitalized. The default Heading 3 style of the word processor can be used. In Microsoft Word 2013, the default settings are 12 point, Calibri Light, and font color Blue Accent 1 Darker 50%.

In most cases, a report should not contain more than three levels of headings. However, if a level 4 head, or paragraph head, is needed, a run-in style should be used. A run-in head is the first sentence in a paragraph. The line should begin at the left-hand page margin. The typeface should be the same as the body text and in the same point size, but should be bolded and is often italicized as well. The font color is usually black, but may be a color if the formatting guidelines allow it. The first word of the run-in head is capitalized, as are any proper nouns. The run-in head should end with a period even though it is not a complete sentence.

Spacing

The left- and right-hand page margins of a report should be 1″ each. The bottom page margin should not be less than 1″. A bottom page margin greater than 1″ is acceptable for pages on which it would be impossible to have the margin be exactly 1″. For example, a heading should not be at the bottom of the page and the first line of body copy underneath it starting at the top of the next page. In this case, add a manual page break before the heading to run the page short and keep the heading with the first line of text beneath it. The top page margin on the first page should be 2″. On all other pages of the report, the top page margin should be 1″.

The report should be single spaced, but the default setting for line spacing of the word processor can be used. In Microsoft Word 2013, the default line spacing is 1.08. Leave a blank line between paragraphs in the report. This can be easily achieved with a paragraph style.

FYI

If the report is to be placed in a binder, the left-hand page margin should be increased to allow for the binding.

HANDS-ON EXAMPLE 8.2.1

FORMATTING A REPORT

The formatting of a report sets the stage for how the reader will view the information. A properly formatted report communicates professionalism to the reader.

1. Navigate to the student companion website at www.g-wlearning.com, download the data files for this chapter, and save them in the Chap08 folder on your flash drive.
2. Launch Microsoft Word, and open the LandscapeOptions.docx file from the Chap08 folder on your flash drive.
3. Place the insertion point in the first line of the document.
4. Click the Title style in the gallery in the **Styles** group on the **Home** tab of the ribbon. The style is applied to the paragraph.
5. Place the insertion point in the first heading, Landscaping as a Weather Barrier.
6. Click the dialog box launcher in the **Styles** group on the **Home** tab of the ribbon. The **Styles** pane is displayed, as shown.

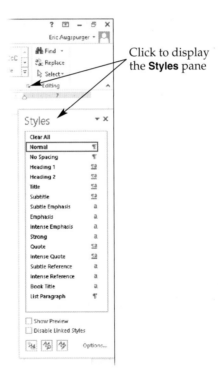

Click to display the **Styles** pane

7. Click the Heading 1 style in the **Styles** pane to apply that style.
8. Applying what you have learned, assign the style Heading 1 to the remaining two headings, Landscaping that Attracts Butterflies and Landscaping to Minimize Water Use.
9. Applying what you have learned, add a blank line between paragraphs in the report. You should add a total of four blank lines.
10. Save the file as *LastName*LandscapeOptions.docx in the Chap08 folder on your flash drive.

GS5 Key Applications
2.5.1

GS4 Key Applications
2.2.1

FYI

Page numbers are automatically updated if edits cause pages to change.

Page Numbering

The **folio**, or page number, is placed outside of the body copy. The header is at the top of the page, and the *footer* is at the bottom of the page. When content is placed in these areas, it appears on every page. The page number can be placed in the header or footer area, but the standard location is in the header on the second and subsequent pages. The page number should be flush right to the right-hand page margin. A page number is not usually included on the first page of the report. If one is required, it should be placed in the footer and center-aligned.

In addition to the page number, a user may choose to add the document name or a copyright date to the header or footer. For example, a book often displays the chapter number or title in the header along with the page number.

HANDS-ON EXAMPLE 8.2.2

ADDING PAGE NUMBERS

When creating a document for schoolwork, it may be a good idea to include your name in the header or footer. In this way, should the pages of the printout become mixed with those of other students, it will be easy to locate your work.

1. Launch Microsoft Word, and open the *LastName*LandscapeOptions.docx file from the Chap08 folder on your flash drive, if it is not already open.

Add a Header

2. Click the **Add a Header** button in the **Header & Footer** group on the **Insert** tab of the ribbon. A drop-down menu is displayed.

3. Click the Blank style in the drop-down menu. The header and footer areas are activated, as shown.

Header area is activated

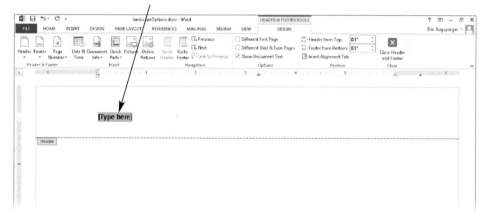

4. Applying what you have learned, replace the placeholder text with your last name, a comma, and a space.

Align Right

5. Click the **Align Right** button in the **Paragraph** group on the **Home** tab of the ribbon. The header is aligned to the right-hand margin.

HANDS-ON EXAMPLE 8.2.2 (CONTINUED)

Add Page Numbers

6. With the insertion point at the end of the header, click the **Add Page Numbers** button in the **Header & Footer** group on the **Design** on-demand tab in the ribbon. A drop-down menu is displayed.

7. Click **Current Position**>**Plain Number** in the drop-down menu that is displayed. A page number is added after your last name.

Close Header and Footer

8. Click the **Close Header and Footer** button in the **Close** group on the **Design** on-demand tab of the ribbon. The header and footer areas are deactivated, and the page layout view of the document is displayed.

9. Scroll through the document, and verify that your name and the page number appear on every page.

10. Save the file.

Title Page

The title of the report should be the first item on the title page. It should begin 2″ from the top page margin and be aligned to the left-hand page margin. The font should be 14 points and bold. The text should be set in all uppercase.

Below the title, place the target audience. This is the group or organization for whom the report was written. The text should be center-aligned, and the font should be 11 points.

Below the target audience, place the author's name. The name should begin 5″ from the top page margin and be center-aligned. The font should be 11 points, and the text should be set in title case. Using the same formatting, leave a blank line after the author's name, and place the name of the organization to which the author belongs. Below that, using the same formatting, place the date of the report. The date should begin 9″ from the top page margin.

Table of Contents

The table of contents (TOC) usually lists the level 1 and level 2 heads in the document. It is not common to list level 3 heads, but if needed these can be included as well. The page number on which the head appears is placed to the right of the head listing in the table of contents. A dotted line, called a leader, is placed between the head listing and its page number. The table of contents usually begins on a new page and ends with a page break so the report content begins on the following page.

Enter the text Table of Contents 2″ below the top page margin. Leave two blank lines, and then enter the first level 1 head of the document. Enter a tab and the page number for the heading. On the next line, enter the next head. If a level 2 head, indent the line .5″. Level 3 heads should be indented an additional .5″.

Many word processors have a feature that automates the creating of a table of contents. The automatic table of contents feature of Microsoft Word is based on the use of predefined styles. Many organizations

FYI

The leader style is set with the tab formatting.

allow the default settings to be used, but the styles can be modified to match accepted standards. When Word generates a table of contents, it will include any text that has been assigned the Heading 1, Heading 2, or Heading 3 style. The page numbers are automatically included.

HANDS-ON EXAMPLE 8.2.3

CREATING A TABLE OF CONTENTS

The table of contents is an important element for long reports. It allows the reader to quickly locate information within the report.

Table of Contents

1. Launch Microsoft Word, and open the *LastName*LandscapeOptions.docx file from the Chap08 folder on your flash drive, if it is not already open.
2. Place the insertion point at the beginning of the document. The table of contents will be added at the insertion point. Note: when the title page is added later, it should come before the table of contents.
3. Click the **Table of Contents** button in the **Table of Contents** group on the **References** tab of the ribbon. A drop-down menu is displayed.
4. Click **Automatic Table 2** in the drop-down menu. The table of contents is automatically generated. Note what is included. Also make note of the page numbers listed.
5. Applying what you have learned, add a manual page break after the table of contents and before the title text.
6. Scroll to the table of contents, and click anywhere in it. The table of contents changes into a table format, which is used to update the TOC.
7. Click the **Update Table…** button above the TOC. The **Update Table** dialog box is displayed.
8. Click the **Update entire table** radio button, and click the **OK** button. The page numbers in the TOC are updated to reflect the addition of the page break.
9. Click anywhere outside of the table of contents to deselect it.
10. Save the file.

Citations

When writing a research paper, many ideas and factual information come from other publications. The author must tell the reader exactly where the information originated. This is done through citations. **Citations** generally include the author, publication date, source document, URL, and other relevant information for material that is referenced or paraphrased within the document. It is necessary to provide citations for both print and electronic sources.

Citations usually appear as footnotes or endnotes. **Footnotes** are numbered annotations that appear once at the bottom of a page, as shown in Figure 8-10. **Endnotes** perform the same job, but appear at the end of document, and contain the same information as a bibliography. Many word processors, including Microsoft Word, have a function to automatically create a bibliography of the sources used to write a report.

WORKS CITED

Arbor, Jonathan Cole, "Training That Works." *Train the Trainer* (March 20--) pp. 23–25.

Coletta, Nicole, *The Essentials of Performance Management*. New York: Future Publishing, 2010.

Newberg, Alexis, "Formal Training Programs at Bowden Industries," Report Submitted to the Executive Board, Bowden Training Department, 2009.

Goodheart-Willcox Publisher

Figure 8-10. Always cite works that are referenced in the document.

There are many ways to format citations. In general, it is best to follow the formatting specified by a style guide. Style guides are specifications for formatting, word usage, and other aspects of creating a document. Common style guides include APA, MLA, Chicago, and AP. Microsoft Word allows the user to select between many common style guides to control how automatically generated bibliographies appear.

APA Style

The *Publication Manual of the American Psychological Association*, which is usually simply called the APA style guide, is popular in many fields, including the sciences. The writing style dictated by this guide is also known as the Harvard Style of writing.

The APA style guide calls for reports to be double-spaced on 8 1/2 × 11 inch paper set in Times New Roman typeface in 10 or 12 points. Note that this differs from the specifications outlined in this chapter. The paper should have a title page, an abstract, a main body, and references. The report title and the folio should appear in the header right-aligned.

A citation is listed in a bibliography at the end of the document. Where the citation is referenced in the body of the document, the notation is placed within the sentence so it is clear what information is being quoted or paraphrased and whose information is being cited. Many other specifications appear in the guide.

MLA Style

The *MLA Style Manual and Guide to Scholarly Publishing* is popular for English classes, graduate classes, and general papers. It is published by the Modern Language Association of America.

The MLA style calls for no title page or abstract section. The author's name, the instructor's name, the course, and the date are placed in the upper left-hand corner of the first page. The author's last name followed by a space and page number is placed in the header and right-aligned. This is similar to the header created earlier. The bibliography is called Works Cited and appears at the end of the document. Many other specifications appear in the guide.

HANDS-ON EXAMPLE 8.2.4

ADDING CITATIONS

When other information is paraphrased in a report, the source of the information must be cited. This provides validity to the information and acknowledges the owner of the material.

1. Launch Microsoft Word, and open the *LastName*LandscapeOptions.docx file from the Chap08 folder on your flash drive, if it is not already open.
2. Click the **Bibliography Style:** drop-down arrow in the **Citations & Bibliography** group on the **References** tab of the ribbon, and click **MLA** in the drop-down list. This sets the style guide to use.
3. In the numbered list in the document, place the insertion point after the final *d* in the line *Willow hybrid*.

Insert Citation

4. Click the **Insert Citation** button in the **Citations & Bibliography** group on the **References** tab of the ribbon, and click **Add New Source...** in the drop-down menu. The **Create Source** dialog box is displayed, as shown.

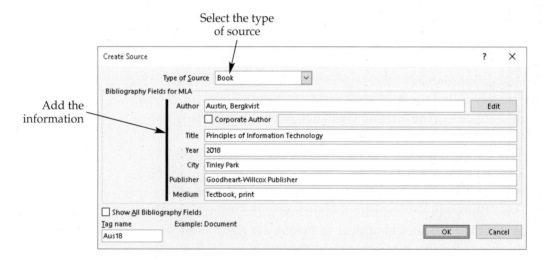

Select the type of source

Add the information

5. Click the **Type of Source** drop-down list at the top of the dialog box, and click **Book** in the list.
6. Fill in the fields in the dialog box using information for this textbook. Notice that information appears at the bottom of the dialog box related to which text box is active. Use this to help fill in the proper information.
7. Click the **OK** button to add the citation. The author's name appears in parentheses where the insertion point was.
8. Applying what you have learned, add a new page to the end of the document.

Bibliography

9. Click the **Bibliography** button in the **Citations & Bibliography** group on the **References** tab of the ribbon, and click **Works Cited** in the drop-down menu. The bibliography is automatically created and follows the MLA style for citations.
10. Save the file.

8.2 | SECTION REVIEW

 CHECK YOUR UNDERSTANDING

1. What are the three common types of reports?
2. What is the first step in the writing process, and what is its purpose?
3. What is the folio?
4. How many levels of headings are usually listed in the table of contents?
5. When is a citation needed?

IC3 CERTIFICATION PRACTICE

The following question is a sample of the types of questions presented on the IC3 exam.

1. Which of the following steps will add page numbers to the Microsoft Word document?
   A. **Page Layout>Header & Footer>Top of Page>Plain Number 1**
   B. **Insert>Page Number>Top of Page**
   C. **Insert>Header & Footer>Page Number>Current Position>Plain Number**
   D. **Home>Insert>Page Number>Current Position**

 BUILD YOUR VOCABULARY

As you progress through this course, develop a personal IT glossary. This will help you build your vocabulary and prepare you for a career. Write a definition for each of the following terms and add it to your IT glossary.

analytical reports	introduction
citations	primary research
conclusions	proposals
data	qualitative data
endnotes	quantitative data
folio	recommendations
footnotes	secondary research
headings	table of contents
informational reports	

ETHICAL PRACTICES FOR INTELLECTUAL PROPERTY

Essential Question

How does protection of intellectual property benefit society?

With so much information available on the Internet, it is possible to read about almost any topic. At one time, this information was only found in encyclopedias or reference volumes in libraries. The ease of access to information as well as the ability to copy material reinforces the importance of properly using the information. Just because information can be quickly located and accessed from home does not mean the information is free to use. Laws are in place to protect information. Improper use of information is not only unethical, in most cases it is illegal.

Ethical use of computers and information is an important part of society. Ethics are common standards of moral behavior. Computer ethics defines how people use computers in morally acceptable ways. What users do with information, how they acknowledge its source, and to whom they give it all have ethical implications.

Dragon Images/Shutterstock.com

TERMS

antipiracy technology

common knowledge

copyright

Creative Commons (CC) license

Electronic User's Bill of Rights

fair use doctrine

intellectual property

licensing agreement

open source

paraphrasing

patent

piracy

plagiarism

public domain

quotation

service mark

trademark

LEARNING GOALS

After completing this section, you will be able to:

- Explain intellectual property.
- Identify software piracy.
- Properly use information.
- Discuss the Electronic User's Bill of Rights.

Intellectual Property

The Internet provides countless sources for obtaining text, images, video, audio, and software. Even though this material is readily available, this does not make it free to use however you choose. The creators or owners of this material have certain legal rights. **Intellectual property** is something that comes from a person's mind, such as an idea, invention, or process. Intellectual property laws protect a person's or a company's inventions, artistic works, and other intellectual property. These laws apply not only to material on the Internet, but to printed materials, broadcast media, and materials in any form.

GS5 Living Online **1.1.4**
GS4 Living Online **4.2.3**

Copyright

A **copyright** acknowledges ownership of a work and specifies that only the owner has the right to sell the work, use it, or give permission for someone else to sell or use it. Any use of copyrighted material without permission is called *infringement*. Copyright laws cover all original work, whether it is in print, on the Internet, or in any other form.

GS5 Living Online **1.1.6**
GS4 Living Online **4.2.5**

Most information on the Internet is copyrighted, whether it is text, graphics, illustrations, or digital media. This means you cannot reuse it without first obtaining permission from the owner. Sometimes, the owner of the material has placed the material on the Internet for others to reuse. However, if this is not explicitly stated, assume the material is copyrighted and cannot be freely used.

Copyrighted material is indicated by the © symbol or the statement "copyright by." However, lack of the symbol or statement does not mean the material is not copyrighted. All original material is automatically copyrighted as soon as it is in tangible form. An idea cannot be copyrighted. It is the expression of an idea that is copyrighted. A copyright can be registered with the US Copyright Office, which is part of the Library of Congress. However, original material is still legally protected whether or not the copyright is registered or the symbol or statement is included.

Fair use doctrine allows individuals to use copyrighted works without permission in limited situations under very strict guidelines. Fair use doctrine allows copyrighted material to be used for the purpose of describing or reviewing the work. For example, a student writing about the material in an original report falls under fair use doctrine. Another is a product-review website providing editorial comment. Fair use doctrine does not change the copyright or ownership of the material used under the doctrine.

GS5 Living Online **1.1.9**

In some cases, individuals or organizations may wish to allow others to use their intellectual property without needing permission. Sometimes this type of use assignment is called copyleft, which is a play on the word copyright. One popular method of allowing use of intellectual property is a Creative Commons license. A **Creative Commons (CC) license** is a specialized copyright license that allows free distribution of copyrighted work. If the creator of the work wants to give the public the ability to use, share, or advance his or her original work, a Creative Commons license

GS4 Living Online **4.2.7**

provides that flexibility. The creator maintains the copyright and can specify how the copyrighted work can be used. For example, one type of Creative Commons license prohibits commercial use.

Public domain refers to material that is not owned by anybody and can be used without permission. Material can enter the public domain when a copyright expires and is not renewed. Additionally, the owner of material may choose to give up ownership and place the material in the public domain. Much of the material created by federal, state, or local governments is often in the public domain. This is because taxpayer money was used to create it. However, in some cases material from governmental sources may be copyrighted, so be sure to verify the status before using the material.

Patent

A **patent** gives a person or company the right to be the sole producer of a product for a defined period of time. Patents protect an invention that is functional or mechanical. The invention must be considered useful and nonobvious, and it must be operational. This means that an idea may not be patented. A process can be patented under certain conditions. The process must be related to a particular machine or transform a substance or item into a different state or thing.

Trademark

A **trademark** protects taglines, slogans, names, symbols, or any unique method to identify a product or company. A **service mark** is similar to a trademark, but it identifies a service rather than a product. Trademarks and service marks do not protect a work or product, they only protect the way in which the product is described. The term "trademark" is often used to refer to both trademarks and service marks. Trademarks never expire.

The symbols used to indicate a trademark or service mark are called graphic marks. Some graphic marks can be used without being formally registered, as shown in Figure 8-11.

Correct Usage of Graphic Marks	
TM	Trademark, not registered
SM	Service mark, not registered
®	Registered trademark

Goodheart-Willcox Publisher

Figure 8-11. Graphic marks are symbols that indicate legal protection of intellectual property.

Living Online
1.1.5.1, 1.1.5.2

Living Online
4.2.4

Software Piracy

Piracy is the unethical and illegal copying or downloading of software, files, or other protected material. Examples of protected material include images, movies, and music. It is illegal to copy protected material or download it from the Internet if the owner has not given permission to do so. Software installed at your school or office is licensed to that entity. It is piracy to take that software and install it at home. Piracy is a form of stealing and carries a heavy penalty, including fines and incarceration.

A software or video game developer will work for months, investing time and money, to make a program or a game. The developer not only owns the software, but also wants to earn a return on the investment of time and money. Piracy hurts the developer because it is the theft of the developer's product. To counter piracy, **antipiracy technology** has been developed that makes it very difficult for someone to use pirated software. Common antipiracy technology for software includes the activation key and the device ID. An activation key is a code the user must enter during the installation process. A device ID is a unique identifier based on the machine on which the software is installed, and the software will function only on that machine.

An organization called the BSA/The Software Alliance is an advocate for the software industry. Among its many efforts, it tracks pirated software. In its most recent report, dated 2014, it concluded that 43% of all software used in the world is pirated. It estimates 74% of the computers in one non-Western country use pirated software. Conversely, in the United States an estimated 18% of the computers use pirated software. Even though this figure is lower, it still represents that nearly one-fifth of all software in the United States is being used illegally. The commercial value of software used illegally world-wide is estimated to be nearly $63 billion, which is money lost to the software industry.

There is legislation in place in most countries to prevent software piracy. However, the laws have to be strongly enforced by the local government. The use of pirated software is most prevalent in developing countries.

Licensing Agreement

A **licensing agreement** is a contract that gives one party permission to market, produce, or use the product or service owned by another party. The agreement grants a license in return for a fee or royalty payment. When buying software, the purchaser is agreeing to follow the terms of a license, which is the legal permission to use a software program. All software has terms of use that explain how and when the software may be used. Figure 8-12 explains the characteristics of different software licensing.

Characteristics of Software Types			
Characteristics	**Software Type**		
	For-Purchase	**Freeware**	**Shareware**
Cost	• Must be purchased to use • Demo may be available	• Never have to pay for it	• Free to try • Pay to upgrade to full functionality
Features	• Full functionality	• Full functionality	• Limited functionality without upgrade

Goodheart-Willcox Publisher

Figure 8-12. Each type of software has specific licensing permissions.

Alternative-usage rights for software programs are typically covered by the GNU General Public License (GNU GPL). The GNU GPL guarantees all users the freedom to use, study, share, and modify the software. The term **open source** applies to software that has had its source code made available to the public at no charge and with no restrictions on use or modification. Open-source software can be downloaded and used for free and can also be modified and distributed by anyone. However, part or all of the code of open-source software may be owned by an individual or organization.

Ethics

Terms of Use

All software has a terms of use agreement. Social media sites also have terms of use agreements. Most websites that you have to "join" have terms of use agreements. It is unethical, and in many cases illegal, to violate the terms of use.

Living Online
1.1.8

Terms of Use

Many websites list rules called the *terms of use* that must be followed for downloaded files or for participating in the online community. The agreement may come up automatically, for example, if you are downloading a file or software application. If you want to use an image or text from a website, look for the terms of use. Unless the terms of use specifically states that you are free to copy and use the material, assume the material cannot be reused without permission.

Proper Usage of Information

Scanning or photocopying a document does not make the content yours. Similarly, copying someone's published work is unethical and illegal. It is very easy to copy and paste text from electronic resources. Therefore, it is important for users to know what constitutes proper usage of information.

Plagiarism

Plagiarism is claiming another person's material as your own, which is both unethical and illegal. If you must refer to someone else's work, follow intellectual property laws to ethically acquire the information. Use standard methods of citing sources, as discussed earlier in this chapter. However, if you *copy* the work of others without permission, even if you credit the source, you are committing plagiarism.

Computer technology has also made it fairly easy to detect plagiarism. There are services that scan for plagiarism. Educators can use these services to check the originality of a student's paper. Businesses can use the services to check the originality of submitted material. Programs such as Turnitin, Grammarly, Dustball, Dupli Checker, and Viper can check documents. There are student versions of this type of software that can be used so a student can determine if an assignment contains all required citations. Some are free. However, they must be downloaded on a personal system.

Another way of using the Internet to find the original source of published text is to enter that text directly into a search engine. Depending on the search engine's capabilities, it may locate a source for the text.

HANDS-ON EXAMPLE 8.3.1

LOCATING INFORMATION'S SOURCE

The Internet is a great resource for locating information. It can be used to find material to support your original work or to locate the source of information.

1. Launch a web browser, and navigate to a search engine.
2. Enter the following quotation into the search box *exactly* as shown, including punctuation. Be careful not to mistype or misspell anything.

   > But where do we stand today? The government's official measure of poverty shows that poverty has actually increased slightly since the Johnson administration, rising from 14.2 percent in 1967 to 15 percent in 2012.

3. Count the number of websites that contain these exact words.
4. Identify the publication in which the original work appeared.
5. Identify the authors of the original work.

Common Knowledge

Common knowledge consists of notions and factual information that can be found in a variety of places. Nobody can claim ownership of common knowledge and, therefore, it can be used by anybody. When using ideas that are common knowledge, the author does not need to let the reader know the source. A citation is not required for common knowledge.

An example of common knowledge is that a water molecule is composed of hydrogen and oxygen. Another example is Jupiter is the largest planet that revolves around the Sun. These are both examples of factual information.

Paraphrasing

Paraphrasing means expressing an idea using different words. It is summarizing the work in your own words. When using someone else's material as the basis for your own work, such as a report, do not copy the material. Instead, paraphrase portions of the work and use that to support your own original material. Note, however, that extensive paraphrasing is generally considered to be the same as copying the original material. In other words, use limited paraphrasing to *support* your original work, but do not use paraphrasing as a *replacement* for your original work.

When something has been paraphrased, the thought or research is not original. Therefore, a citation is required. This properly credits the original source of the material.

Quotation

In some cases, the best way to present another's words is exactly as they were originally written. A **quotation** is an exact repeat of a passage of another author's work. A quotation should generally be short, such as a single sentence or a brief paragraph. While there is no set rule as to the acceptable length of a quote, presenting a quote longer than this is generally considered to be a *copy* of the original material, not a quotation of it. It is important that the quotation not be used out of context or in a manner that changes its meaning or implies an intention not present in the original work. As with paraphrasing, a quotation should support your original work, not be a substitute for your original work.

The quotation must be placed within opening and closing quotation marks ("…"). Often, quotations are indented from the body text on both the left- and right-hand sides. Quotations must be properly cited to credit the original source.

Electronic User's Bill of Rights

The **Electronic User's Bill of Rights** details the rights and responsibilities of both individuals and institutions regarding the treatment of digital information. It was originally proposed in 1993 by Frank W. Connolly of American University. It is modeled after the original United States Bill of Rights, although it contains only four articles. The articles are not legally binding, but contain guidelines for appropriate use of digital information. The articles in the Electronic User's Bill of Rights are:

- Article I: Individual Rights
- Article II: Individual Responsibilities
- Article III: Rights of Educational Institutions
- Article IV: Institutional Responsibilities

Article I focuses on the rights and freedoms of the users of computers and the Internet. It states "citizens of the electronic community of learners" have the right to access computers and informational resources. They should be informed when their personal information is being collected. They have the right to review and correct the information that has been collected. Users should have freedom of speech and have rights of ownership for their intellectual property.

Article II focuses on the responsibilities that come with those rights outlined in Article I. A citizen of the electronic community is responsible for seeking information and using it effectively. It is also the individual's responsibility to honor the intellectual property of others. This includes verifying the accuracy of information obtained electronically. It also includes respecting the privacy of others, and using electronic resources wisely.

Article III states the right of educational institutions to access computers and informational resources. Like individuals, an educational institution retains ownership of its intellectual property. Each institution has the right to use its resources as it sees fit.

Article IV focuses on the responsibilities that come with the rights granted in Article III. Educational institutions are held accountable for the information they use and provide. Institutions are responsible for creating and maintaining "an environment wherein trust and intellectual freedom are the foundation for individual and institutional growth and success."

8.3 | SECTION REVIEW

CHECK YOUR UNDERSTANDING

1. What acknowledges ownership of a work and specifies that only the owner has the right to sell the work, use it, or give permission for someone else to sell or use it?
2. How does the fair use doctrine allow the use of protected material?
3. What illegal act is a person committing who creates an unauthorized copy of software?
4. If you submit somebody else's term paper as your own, what have you committed?
5. What does the Electronic User's Bill of Rights describe?

IC3 CERTIFICATION PRACTICE

The following question is a sample of the types of questions presented on the IC3 exam.

1. Which of the following tabs in Microsoft Word is used to set the style guide to use for the document?
   A. **Insert**
   B. **Review**
   C. **References**
   D. **Home**

BUILD YOUR VOCABULARY

As you progress through this course, develop a personal IT glossary. This will help you build your vocabulary and prepare you for a career. Write a definition for each of the following terms and add it to your IT glossary.

antipiracy technology	open source
common knowledge	paraphrasing
copyright	patent
Creative Commons (CC) license	piracy
	plagiarism
Electronic User's Bill of Rights	public domain
	quotation
fair use doctrine	service mark
intellectual property	trademark
licensing agreement	

8 REVIEW AND ASSESSMENT

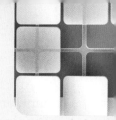

Chapter Summary

Section 8.1
Creating a Business Letter

- Letters are messages printed on stationery, often letterhead, and should conform to workplace standards. The two standard formats for a business letter are block style and modified-block style.

- Standardized letter formats contain various elements. Block-style and modified-block-style letters include: date, inside address, salutation, body, complimentary close, signature, and notations.

- Beyond the standard elements, a business letter may contain other elements. The attention line, subject line, and postscript may or may not be included.

- It is important to follow the accepted standard format for business letters. Using nonstandard formatting makes the letter appear unprofessional, and the message of the letter may not be effectively communicated.

Section 8.2
Creating a Report

- The three common types of reports are informational reports, analytical reports, and proposals. Informational reports contain facts, data, or other types of information; analytical reports contain both information and analysis of the data; and proposals typically contain a specific idea and attempt to persuade the reader.

- Many organizations have formatting guidelines for reports or a template can be used. When the topic covers more than one key point or important issue, headings should be used as a design element.

Section 8.3
Ethical Practices for Intellectual Property

- Intellectual property is something that comes from a person's mind, such as an idea, invention, or process. Intellectual property laws apply not only to material on the Internet, but to printed materials, broadcast media, and materials in any form.

- Piracy is the unethical and illegal copying or downloading of software, files, or other protected material. To counter piracy, antipiracy technology has been developed that makes it very difficult for someone to use pirated software.

- Plagiarism is claiming another person's material as your own, which is both unethical and illegal. The work can be paraphrased to support your own work, but it must be properly cited.

- The Electronic User's Bill of Rights details the rights and responsibilities of both individuals and institutions regarding the treatment of digital information. Its articles are Article I: Individual Rights, Article II: Individual Responsibilities, Article III: Rights of Educational Institutions, and Article IV: Institutional Responsibilities.

Now that you have finished this chapter, see what you know about information technology by scanning the QR code to take the chapter posttest. If you do not have a smartphone, visit www.g-wlearning.com.

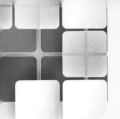

Chapter 8 Test

Multiple Choice

Select the best response.

1. Which of the following is not included in a letterhead?
   A. Company name
   B. Date
   C. Address
   D. Logo

2. What always begins a salutation?
   A. Hello
   B. Dear
   C. Hi
   D. There is no beginning to a salutation.

3. Which of the following is primary research?
   A. Reading a newspaper article.
   B. Locating an analytical report on the Internet.
   C. Interviewing several people who witnessed an event.
   D. Watching a documentary on an event.

4. Which of the following styles will be automatically included in the table of contents in a Microsoft Word document?
   A. Normal
   B. Title
   C. Footnote
   D. Heading 1

5. What is the term describing something that comes from a person's mind, such as an idea, invention, or process?
   A. Intellectual property
   B. Copyright
   C. Plagiarism
   D. Common knowledge

Completion

Complete the following sentences with the correct word(s).

6. In a(n) _____-style letter, all elements are to be flush to the left-hand page margin.

7. _____ are words and phrases that introduce sections of text in a document.

8. APA, MLA, Chicago, and AP are examples of _____, which contain specifications for formatting, word usage, and other aspects of creating a document.

9. _____ is copying information and claiming it as your own.

10. The act of copying video games without permission of the author is considered _____.

Matching

Match the correct term with its definition.

A. endnotes
B. table of contents
C. fair use doctrine
D. complimentary close
E. MLA

11. Sign-off for a letter.

12. Lists the major sections and subsections within the report with page numbers.

13. Numbered annotations that appear at the end of document.

14. A style guide for formatting, word usage, and other aspects of creating documents.

15. Allows individuals to use copyrighted works without permission in limited situations under very strict guidelines.

Application and Extension of Knowledge

1. Start a new document, and create paragraph styles for the parts of a business letter. Define each style according to the formatting described in this chapter. Write a two-paragraph letter to your instructor explaining how useful word processing is in your schoolwork.

2. Use the help feature in Microsoft Word to find out how to print an envelope for the letter you created in #1. Using what you learned, print the envelope, enclose the letter, and give it to your instructor.

3. Conduct research comparing and contrasting desktop-publishing software and word-processing software. What features and functions are shared? What features and functions are unique? Prepare a presentation illustrating the similarities and differences. Use specific software examples.

4. Identify a well-known business of your choosing. Investigate the company to see if it has any trademarks and patents. Go to the corporate website and look for a copyright statement. Based on your findings, prepare for a class discussion to describe how this company protects its intellectual property. Include the consequences of violating trademark, patent, and copyright laws.

5. Use the help feature in Microsoft Word to find out how to add a table of contents to a document. List the steps for creating a TOC. Include an explanation of how to update the TOC after changes have been made to the document.

Online Activities

Complete the following activities, which will help you learn, practice, and expand your knowledge and skills.

Certification Practice. Complete the certification practice test for this chapter.

Vocabulary. Practice vocabulary for this chapter using the e-flash cards, matching activity, and vocabulary game until you are able to recognize their meanings.

Communication Skills

College and Career Readiness

Writing. Writing style is the way in which a writer uses language to convey an idea. Select a page or pages of notes you have taken during a class. Evaluate your writing style and the relevance, quality, and depth of the information. Once you have done so, write a one-page paper that synthesizes your notes into complete sentences and thoughts. Organize your material so that it is logical to the reader. Describe what you have learned to the class.

Reading. After you have read this chapter, determine the central ideas and review the conclusions made by the author. Take notes to identify the chapter's purpose and intended audience. Demonstrate your understanding of the information by retelling or summarizing what you read.

Speaking. To become career ready, it is necessary to utilize critical-thinking skills in order to solve problems. Give an example of a problem that you needed to solve that was important to your success at work or school. How did you apply critical-thinking skills to arrive at a solution? Explain your solution to the class.

Internet Research

Skills Search. Self-assessment tools can help you decide which career opportunities might be a good fit for you. Visit the O*NET Resource Center online and select one of their assessments called Career Exploration

Tools. Create a chart listing skills you possess, careers that match those skills, and skills you will need to develop for those careers. Share your findings with the class.

Teamwork

Meet with a group of your classmates and take turns describing IT skills that you have acquired in school or elsewhere, such as volunteer or after-school work, or in your free time. Using word-processing software, list one or two skills for each team member. Working together, write a description of each skill in a way that would impress an employer hiring for an IT job. Practice using action verbs and keywords.

Portfolio Development

College and Career Readiness

Schoolwork. Academic information is important to include in a portfolio in order to show your accomplishments in school. Include items related to your schoolwork that support your portfolio objective. These items might be report cards, transcripts, or honor roll reports. Diplomas or certificates that show courses or programs you completed should also be included. Other information can be included as a list, such as relevant classes you have taken.

1. Create a Microsoft Word document that lists notable classes you have taken and activities you have completed. Use the heading "Schoolwork" on the document along with your name.

2. Scan hard-copy documents related to your schoolwork, such as report cards, to serve as samples. Place each document in an appropriate folder.

3. Place the hard-copy documents in the container for future reference.

4. Update your master document.

CTSOs

Public Speaking. Public speaking is a competitive event you might enter with your Career and Technical Student Organization (CTSO). This event allows you to showcase your communication skills of speaking, organizing, and making an oral presentation. This is usually a timed event you can prepare for before the competition. You will have time to research, prepare, and practice before going to the competition. Review the specific guidelines and rules for this event for direction as to topics and props you will be allowed to use. To prepare for a public speaking event, complete the following activities.

1. Read the guidelines provided by your organization. Review the topics from which you may choose to make a speech.

2. Locate a rubric or scoring sheet for the event on your organization's website.

3. Confirm whether visual aids may be used in the presentation and the amount of setup time permitted.

4. Review the rules to confirm if questions will be asked or if you will need to defend a case or situation.

5. Make notes on index cards about important points to remember. Use these notes to study. You may also be able to use these notes during the event.

6. Practice the presentation. You should introduce yourself, review the topic that is being presented, defend the topic being presented, and conclude with a summary.

7. After the presentation is complete, ask for feedback from your instructor. You may consider also having a student audience listen and give feedback.

9

PRESENTATION SOFTWARE

SECTIONS

9.1 CREATING A PROFESSIONAL PRESENTATION

9.2 ADDING TRANSITIONS AND ANIMATIONS

9.3 CHARTS, TABLES, AND HANDOUTS

Presentation software is used to present information in a visual medium. When given to an audience, the presentation is usually projected on a large screen or screens for the audience to see. A presentation can also be distributed for individual viewing. A presentation is commonly posted on a website so the audience can access it later or for those who could not attend. This is also a way to distribute the presentation instead of delivering it in front of an audience in a room.

Presentation software provides the ability to create, edit, and display the slides. The three major functions of the software are: a text editor, allowing words to be inserted and formatted; a technique for adding and manipulating graphic images; and a slide-show system to display the contents. Graphic and textual elements can be animated with smooth transitions between slides. Handouts can be created from a presentation to provide the audience with a copy of the presentation to take with them.

IC3 CERTIFICATION OBJECTIVES

GS5

Key Applications

Domain 5.0 Presentations

Objective 5.1 Understand file types compatible with presentation software

Objective 5.3 Be able to use presentation views and modes

Objective 5.4 Know how to add animations, effects, and slide transitions

Objective 5.5 Know how to create and organize slides

Objective 5.6 Know how to design slides

Objective 5.7 Identify presentation software options

GS4

Key Applications

Domain 4.0 Presentation activities

Objective 4.1 Inserting content

Objective 4.2 Slide management

Objective 4.3 Slide design

College and Career Readiness

Reading Prep. Examine the visuals in the chapter before you read it. Write down questions you have about them. Try and answer the questions as you read.

SECTION 9.1

CREATING A PROFESSIONAL PRESENTATION

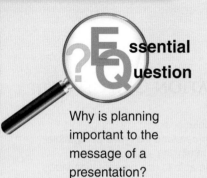

Essential Question

Why is planning important to the message of a presentation?

Presentation software is used to create presentations in a slide show format. The Microsoft Office software used to create presentations is Microsoft PowerPoint. This software contains features to present information in colorful, interesting formats. Text and graphics can be added to slides to enhance the information. Graphics can also be used to improve the visual interest and provide a mood for the presentation.

Creating a professional presentation begins with defining the purpose and planning the presentation. Everything added to the presentation should support the purpose. It is easy to add graphics, animations, and transitions, but this does not mean that the presentation should be filled with these elements. This section discusses how to create a professional presentation by modifying an existing presentation.

VGstockstudio/Shutterstock.com

LEARNING GOALS

After completing this section, you will be able to:
- Plan a formal presentation.
- Discuss how to navigate through a presentation.
- Explain how to rearrange, delete, and copy slides.

TERMS

attention grabber
clincher
external audience
graphics
internal audience
presentation
scope
slide master
theme

Purpose and Planning

A **presentation** is a speech, address, or demonstration given to a group. This type of presentation is sometimes called *public speaking.* Presentation software is used to create a slide show to accompany a presentation. The goal of creating a slide show, or visual presentation, is to educate or entertain an audience. To accomplish this requires engaging both visual and auditory learning mechanisms of the audience. A visual presentation is an excellent teaching tool because it can be used to simplify complex material. Presentation software can help create a strong impression through use of color, and it can help a speaker make efficient use of the time during a presentation. There are many terms associated with presentation software, as shown in Figure 9-1.

When designing a presentation, it is important to consider who the intended audience is and where the presentation will be viewed. A large audience in an auditorium will see and hear things differently than a small group in a classroom. The speaker can maximize readability by formatting the presentation so it can be easily viewed by everyone, regardless of the size of the room.

Planning a Formal Presentation

Formal presentations vary greatly in length, topic, and level of formality. Sometimes one speaker does all of the talking. In other presentations, two or more people share the responsibility, as in a panel discussion. Often the presentation includes a question-and-answer

Green Tech

Green Presentations
Many companies find that being good stewards of the environment can help increase sales and profits. This is because consumers often hold companies in higher regard when they have environmentally friendly policies. Green presenters post presentations to a website. Interested audience members can review information about the presentation online. This saves a number of resources.

Alignment	How text or another element is positioned on the slide. Horizontally, the element may be flush left, flush right, or centered left-to-right. Vertically, the element may be flush top, flush bottom, or centered top-to-bottom.
Bulleted list	Separate lines of text with a small graphic such as a dot in front of the line. Also called an unordered list.
Citation	A notation indicating the source of information in a document.
Font	A set of characters of a typeface in one specific style and size.
Footer	Text that appears at the bottom of every slide in a presentation.
Format	The appearance of text or other elements.
Heading	A word or phrase placed at the beginning of the slide to indicate the topic of the slide; also called a title.
Indentation	The amount text is moved in or out from the standard margin.
Margin	The points at the top, bottom, left, and right of the slide beyond which text is not placed.
Numbered list	Consists of separate lines of text with numbers in sequential order in front of the text. Also called an ordered list.
Orientation	How the slide will be placed on the sheet when printed and on screen.
Typeface	The design of characters. May be serif, sans serif, or decorative.

Goodheart-Willcox Publisher

Figure 9-1. Common terms related to presentations and a brief explanation of each.

session, allowing the audience to participate. The audience may be coworkers or customers. It may be professionals from other companies or some other group with a shared interest in the topic.

Why Are You Presenting?

When writing a formal presentation, first determine the purpose. Speeches are generally made for the purpose of informing or persuading the listener. Speaking to inform usually includes sharing descriptions or definitions about a topic. The content is structured and may sound like the speaker is telling a story. Speaking to persuade involves convincing a person to take the course of action you propose. A persuasive speech requires that the presenter be clear about what is needed from the audience. It has the goal of trying to convince the listeners to agree with the information that is being shared.

Who Is the Audience?

It is important to identify who will be attending your presentation. First, note whether the individuals are internal or external to the organization. An **internal audience** has a specific background and experience. It can be assumed the listeners have a basis for and can relate to at least some of the information that is being conveyed. An **external audience** will probably need more background information about your topic. Analyze the audience to evaluate interest in what you have to say. You can then determine the best way to gain their attention.

What Is the Topic?

Before writing a presentation, the subject must be selected. The subject is a broad idea of what the presentation will be about. Many times, the subject will be assigned to you. There may be other times when it is necessary for you to select the subject. After the subject is selected, narrow the larger idea to a specific topic.

Next, consider the scope of the content for the presentation. The **scope** of the presentation is the guideline of how much information will be included. It will be necessary to narrow the topic so that the content is manageable as well as meaningful. Will the information be detailed or general? Scope defines what should be included and what should be left out of the presentation.

Where Is the Information?

Once the topic of the presentation is set, research will be necessary to support the points made in the presentation. Researching for a presentation is similar to researching for a written report. Chapter 8 explains the research process. The same steps are applied to gathering information for a presentation.

You may need to conduct primary research, secondary research, or both. Remember the importance of crediting secondary sources. Mention

Career Skills

Management Analyst
Management analysts work with managers to improve an establishment's efficiency. They identify ways to cut costs and raise revenues. The analysis process is supported by use of all productivity tools, especially spreadsheets and databases. Analysts often communicate with managers through presentation software and documents created with word processing software.

the source during the presentation when you discuss your research findings. Source citations add to speaker credibility and the overall believability or acceptance of the presentation. Formally cite the sources in any handouts or printed reports accompanying the presentation.

When Is the Presentation?

Most often, formal presentations must be given on a certain date, at a certain place, and for a specific occasion. Time is an important element when preparing for a presentation. When you begin prewriting, identify the date of the presentation. If you are not given a date to have the presentation finished, select a date of your own.

Writing a presentation takes time, so do not underestimate the effort that will be required. Schedule your writing or preparation time just as you would schedule appointments or activities. Allow appropriate time to research, write, and practice the presentation. Rushing through the writing process could result in a presentation that appears unprofessional.

How Should the Presentation Be Organized?

As you prepare to write the presentation, select an approach that supports the message you want to convey. The approach of the document is how the information is presented. The direct approach works well when delivering an informative speech. The topic is introduced first and then followed by descriptive details. The indirect approach works well for persuasive messages. Details are given first and are then followed by the main idea. Begin with information that prepares the reader to respond in the manner you want him or her to respond.

Next, prepare an outline. The outline will serve as a guideline to identify the information to be presented and its proper sequence. One way to create an outline is to make a numbered list of the key points. These should be the main ideas about the topic. If using the direct approach, start with the main ideas followed by the details, as shown in Figure 9-2. If using the indirect approach, do the reverse. These will be considered as the headings in the outline. Start recording the main ideas in the order in which you think of them. Then, reorder the points until they reflect the order in which the information will be presented.

As you compose the outline, keep in mind how much time has been allotted for the presentation. The amount of detail in certain parts of the presentation may need to be adjusted so the presentation will fit into the available time. Facts and figures might need to be provided to the audience as handouts instead of being explained during the presentation.

Presentation Outline
I. First main point
a. Subpoint
b. Subpoint
II. Second main point
a. Subpoint
b. Subpoint
III. Third main point
a. Subpoint
b. Subpoint

Goodheart-Willcox Publisher

Figure 9-2. Developing an outline helps organize a presentation.

Preparing Content for a Presentation

When the outline is completed, it is time to begin the writing stage for the presentation. To begin drafting the presentation, follow the outline. Write sentences, words, or phrases next to each topic on the outline to act as cues for what you want to say. If you are a beginning speaker or if the topic is complex, you might opt to draft your presentation word for word. As you write, think about how spoken language differs from written language. Aim for a less formal, more conversational delivery. Be sure to identify any words that might be unfamiliar to the audience and plan to explain them.

Introduction

The introduction of the presentation serves several purposes. It should introduce the topic of the presentation and preview the main points. In other words, "tell them what you are going to tell them."

The introduction should also draw the listener into the presentation. This important function is often overlooked. Include something to arouse the interest of the audience. This is often called an **attention grabber.** Common attention grabbers include asking a question, citing a surprising statistic, reciting a relevant quote, and telling a story. If you are giving a presentation to coworkers about team-building methods, the attention grabber might be to ask, "What do you think you know about teamwork?"

Body

The body of the presentation is where the main points are made and supported. These points should be presented using the direct or indirect approach. Having too many main points can lead to a long, drawn-out presentation. This usually loses the attention of the audience. Be concise. Keep the number of main points manageable. Following each main point, briefly summarize it.

Two techniques that can enhance a presentation are the use of facts and humor. Using reliable, informative facts is an important part of any good presentation. Humor can also be a way to win over an audience, provided you use it correctly.

Conclusion

The conclusion summarizes the entire presentation. In other words, "tell them what you said." Conclude the presentation by restating the main points. Relate each point back to the purpose of the presentation. This will help the audience more easily retain the information.

The conclusion is often where the presenter will answer audience questions. Having time for questions helps engage the audience with the presentation. It also allows the audience to get clarification on any points that were not understood.

After you have adequately concluded the speech and answered any audience questions, close with a clincher. A **clincher** is a statement to finish the presentation that will make an impact on the audience. It is similar to the attention grabber in the introduction. This is the chance to leave a lasting, positive impression on the audience.

Tips

Use a simple typeface, as shown in Figure 9-3. A sans serif typeface is commonly used in presentations because in general these are easy to read. Do not use decorative typefaces, such as Comic Sans. Make sure the point size of the text is large enough to allow all of the audience, even those at the back of a large room, to read the slides.

Use the 7 × 7 rule for textual elements. This rule limits you to no more than seven items on a slide or seven words per item. That means if the slide has a title, there should not be more than six bullets below it. Split the information over two or more slides with the same title if needed. Also, do not have more than seven words in a bullet. Often articles—*the*, *a*, and *an*—are omitted from presentations. This helps reduce the number of words on the screen.

When adding text, highlight the important points. The speaker is the one with the message. If there is a large amount of text on a slide, the audience will tend to read instead of listen.

Create focus on slides with large images. This can draw attention to the presentation. The images should help the audience relate to the topic.

Just because images can be easily added using the software, this is not a reason to do so. Unnecessary graphics may distract from the

FYI

Some experts recommend the 4 × 5 rule over the 7 × 7 rule: no more than four lines and no more than five words per line.

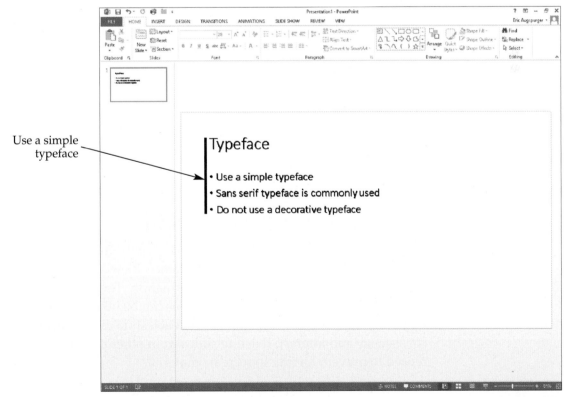

Use a simple typeface

Goodheart-Willcox Publisher

Figure 9-3. A simple, sans serif typeface is easy to quickly read, so often the choice for a presentation.

message. Only include graphics that add to or support the message. Do not clutter the slides.

Elements in a presentation can be animated. However, too much animation or too many different types of animation may distract from the message. Use animation to add interest to the presentation, but use it sparingly.

Consider the makeup of the audience when designing the presentation. A business presentation or academic presentation should be polished and professional. Do not overuse cartoons or silly photographs in these types of presentations.

HANDS-ON EXAMPLE 9.1.1

COMPARING SLIDE COMPOSITION

The design of a presentation can have an impact on how the audience receives the message. One of the best ways to develop a sense for the impact a design can have is by comparing two presentations.

1. Insert your PRINC-OF-IT flash drive into the computer.
2. Applying what you have learned, create a folder on the flash drive named Chap09.
3. Navigate to the student companion website at www.g-wlearning.com, download the data files for this chapter, and save them in the Chap09 folder on your flash drive.
4. Launch Microsoft PowerPoint by double-clicking on the Comparison.pptx file in the Chap09 folder on your flash drive. Each slide in this presentation represents the title slide of a separate presentation.
5. Examine the first slide. The goal of the presentation is to highlight features of a bicycle tour in Alaska. Notice that the title indicates to the audience the slide topic with text details. The photograph reminds the viewer of the activity. Does this image make the viewer want to try the activity?
6. Press the [Page Down] key to view the second slide. Another goal of the presentation is to make the participants want to go to Alaska for bicycling. Notice that the text is minimal. Instead, the message of the experience is conveyed with a large photograph. What details can be learned by viewing this slide?

Working with a Presentation

The features of presentation software give the author enormous possibilities to create interest for an audience. New slides can be added to the presentation to include more information. Text can be easily added to expand the content. Images and shapes can be inserted onto slides to add visual interest. Various elements of each slide can be formatted for consistency and interest. Existing slides from other presentations can be reused to prevent having to recreate material.

Navigating a Presentation File

A presentation will usually contain many slides. To navigate through the presentation file, use the scroll bar along the side of the application window. The up and down arrow keys on the keyboard can also be used to navigate through the file. Pressing the key will display either the next or previous slide in the file. The [Ctrl][Home] key combination displays the first slide in the file. The [Ctrl][End] key combination displays the last slide in the file.

In the default view of Microsoft PowerPoint, the current slide is displayed on the right-hand side of the application window. The slide takes up most of the space in the window. As the user navigates through the file, the current slide is always displayed on the right-hand side of the window. A highlight surrounds the thumbnail on the left for the current slide.

Most presentation software has a slide-sorter feature. In Microsoft PowerPoint, the slide sorter is displayed as a separate view, but it also includes thumbnails along the left-hand side of the application window, which serves as a slide sorter. The slide sorter can be used to navigate through the presentation file. To display a slide, click its thumbnail.

Adding New Slides and Text

GS5 Key Applications
5.5.1, 5.6.1, 5.7.2

GS4 Key Applications
4.1.1, 4.2.1, 4.3.1

When adding a new slide in most presentation software, there are several styles or templates to choose for the new slide. These styles or templates are usually called slide masters. A **slide master** is a predefined slide on which the position and formatting of text boxes and graphics is specified. Whatever appears on the slide master will appear on each slide in the presentation based on that master.

For example, Microsoft PowerPoint 2013 offers nine slide masters when inserting a new slide, as shown in Figure 9-4. Two of these are most commonly used. The Title Slide slide master is used for a title and subtitle for the presentation. Whenever a new blank presentation is started, the default slide in the presentation is based on the Title Slide slide master. The Title and Contents slide master is set up to allow the user to enter a title for the slide and associated bullet points. This is the slide master most people use to add content to the presentation.

Slides can be added in any location in the presentation file. In Microsoft PowerPoint, an inserted slide will be placed after the current slide. So, navigate to the slide after which the slide should be inserted, and then insert the new slide. Slides can be rearranged. If a slide is inserted in the wrong location, it is easy to move it to the correct location.

Text is added to a slide in Microsoft PowerPoint through the use of text boxes. The default slide masters all contain text boxes, with the exception of the Blank slide master. The placeholder text in a text box will be Click to add. To add text, click in the text box. The text box is activated, the placeholder text disappears, and the insertion point within the text box indicates where text will be added.

FYI

In Microsoft PowerPoint, the [Ctrl][M] key combination can be used to insert a new slide based on the same slide master as the last inserted slide.

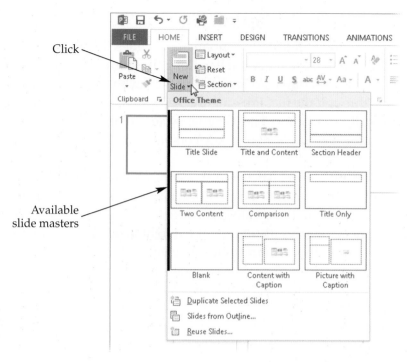

Goodheart-Willcox Publisher

Figure 9-4. When inserting a new slide, you can select a slide master on which to base the new side.

HANDS-ON EXAMPLE 9.1.2

ADDING SLIDES AND TEXT

One of the most basic skills for creating a presentation is the ability to add slides and content. Slides and content are added when creating a presentation from a blank starting point and when modifying an existing presentation.

1. Launch Microsoft PowerPoint, and open the Presentation1.pptx file in the Chap09 folder on your flash drive.
2. Save the file as *LastName*Presentation.pptx in the Chap9 folder on your flash drive.
3. Use the arrow keys, scroll bar, or [Page Up] and [Page Down] keys to navigate through the slides in the file. Notice that the first slide has a different format from the rest. The Title Slide slide master was used for this slide. The Title and Content slide master was used for the remaining slides. Each slide contains text boxes in which text is placed.
4. Navigate to the first slide.
5. Click after the *t* in the word PowerPoint to place the insertion point there. The text box is activated, and its extents are indicated by the dashed rectangle.
6. Press the [Enter] key, and add your name to the text box.
7. Press the [Enter] key, and add today's date.
8. Navigate to the last slide, which is slide 4.
9. Click the **New Slide** button in the **Slides** group on the **Home** tab of the ribbon. Do not click the drop-down arrow next to the button. A new slide is added after slide 4. Notice that the same slide master as slide 4, which is Title and Content, is used for the new slide.

New
Slide

HANDS-ON EXAMPLE 9.1.2 (CONTINUED)

10. Click the placeholder text in the title text box, and add the text What Are the Features? to the text box.

11. Click the placeholder text in the content text box, and add the following text on separate lines. The content will be automatically formatted as a bulleted list.

> Presents information in colorful, interesting format
> Creates handouts for distribution to audience
> Can be set to run continuously
> Does not require PowerPoint be installed

12. Applying what you have learned, add a new slide to the end of the presentation, enter the title How Do I Write a Presentation?, and add the following text on separate lines.

> Identify the purpose
> Identify the audience
> Determine what the audience needs to know
> Know where presentation will be given

13. Save the file.

Adding Graphics

Graphics are illustrations, photographs, and drawing shapes, as shown in Figure 9-5. Graphics add interest and provide a realistic view of the information being presented. An audience should be able to interpret the graphics and understand what is conveyed. Some viewers will look at the graphics first, so each image should be clear and well-designed. Consider the audience and the purpose of the information when choosing graphics. Select the most appropriate visual for the content being presented.

While visuals can add interest and emphasis, care must be taken to avoid overuse. Too many visuals in a presentation will become distracting, and the information will lose its effectiveness. If a presentation is cluttered, the message can be lost.

Illustrations are also called line art. Line art is an image created by drawing lines of various widths and colors. Often, colors fill in the space between the lines.

Photographs are still images created by capturing a real-life scene. Photographs are usually created with a digital camera, either a dedicated device or a device that is part of a mobile device such as a smartphone. However, continuous tone photographs (printed) may be scanned and used in digital form.

Drawing shapes are basic forms created in the software, such as rectangles and circles. Shapes are a basic type of line art created directly within the software application, not imported or inserted from another source.

GS5 Key Applications
5.5.2
GS4 Key Applications
4.1.5

FYI

Graphics can be downloaded from various online sources and inserted into a presentation. Properly credit the source.

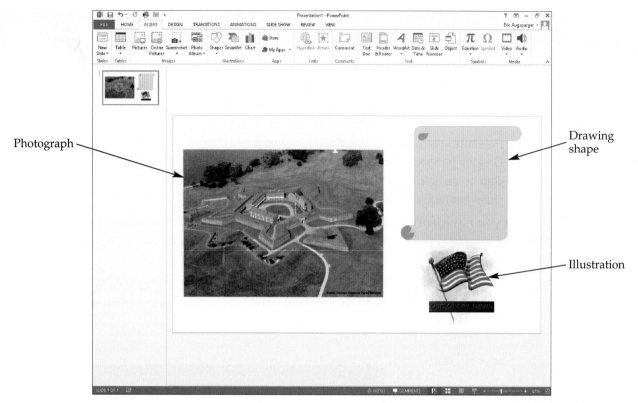

Goodheart-Willcox Publisher

Figure 9-5. Illustrations, photographs, and drawing shapes are called graphics, which can add interest to a presentation.

HANDS-ON EXAMPLE 9.1.3

ADDING GRAPHICS

When properly used, graphics can enhance the message of a presentation. Be sure not to overuse graphics to avoid cluttering the presentation.

1. Launch Microsoft PowerPoint, and open the *LastName*Presentation.pptx file in the Chap9 folder on your flash drive, if it is not already open.
2. Navigate to the What Is Presentation Software? slide, which is slide 3.

HANDS-ON EXAMPLE 9.1.3 (CONTINUED)

Shapes

3. Click the **Shapes** button in the **Illustrations** group on the **Insert** tab of the ribbon. A drop-down menu is displayed containing the various drawing shapes that can be inserted, as shown.

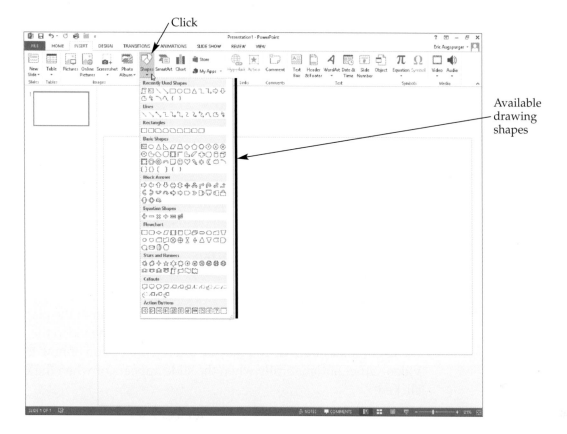

4. Click the **Right Arrow** shape in the **Block Arrows** area of the drop-down menu. The cursor changes to indicate a shape can be drawn.
5. Click to the left of the third bullet, drag to the left, and release. An arrow drawing shape is added to the slide.
6. Navigate to the What Are the Features? slide, which is slide 5.

Online
Pictures

7. Click the **Online Pictures** button in the **Pictures** group on the **Insert** tab of the ribbon. The **Insert Pictures** dialog box is displayed, which contains a search box.
8. Click in the search box, enter printers, and click the **Search** button (magnifying glass).
9. Scroll through the list of results to find a photograph of a printer producing handouts, click the image, and then click the **Insert** button. The photograph is placed on the slide. It is automatically selected with resizing handles displayed.
10. Click and drag one of the corner handles on the image to resize it. The corner handles maintain the height-to-width ratio, and the image is proportionally resized. Resize the image so it is about one-half of the height of the slide.
11. Click and hold on the image and drag it to the right of the bulleted list. The image will likely overlap the text.
12. Click anywhere in the bulleted list in the text box. Handles appear on the text box.

HANDS-ON EXAMPLE 9.1.3 (CONTINUED)

13. Drag the right-center handle to the left to resize the text box. When the right-hand edge of the text box clears the image, release the mouse button. The lines of text will wrap as the text box is resized.
14. Navigate to the last slide. Notice that the word audience is used twice on this slide. This would be a good topic of a graphic to place on this slide.
15. Applying what you have learned, search for a photograph of students in a classroom, insert the image, and resize it for the slide. Resize the text box on the slide as needed so all text is visible.
16. Save the file.

Key Applications
5.5.2

Adding Video

Video files saved on a local or network drive can be inserted into presentations. This is different from inserting a hyperlink to a video stored online. The video itself can be inserted into the presentation. Anyone opening the presentation will have access to the video even if the computer is not connected to the Internet or does not have access to the original video file.

The easiest way to insert a video is by using the content placeholder on a Title and Content slide. Click the **Insert Video** icon in the placeholder to display a standard open dialog box. Browse for the video file, and click the **OK** or **Insert** button. You may be offered the option of how to play the video, either automatically when the slide appears or when the video is clicked.

Key Applications
5.6.1, 5.7.5

Formatting a Presentation Using a Theme

A presentation can be enhanced by the use of themes. A **theme** is a set of specified colors, fonts, and effects, as shown in Figure 9-6. Themes are used to standardize these items across all slides in a presentation.

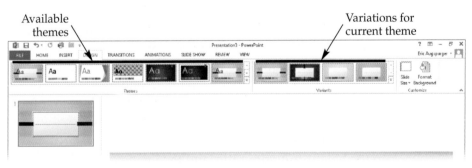

Goodheart-Willcox Publisher

Figure 9-6. A theme can be applied to standardize colors, fonts, and effects. There may be variations available for the current theme.

By having consistency throughout the presentation, the message of the presentation can be reinforced. Inconsistency leads to distraction, and the audience may not fully receive the message of the presentation. Themes add professionalism to the final product.

Themes can be added before creating the presentation or at any other time. Microsoft PowerPoint is supplied with many default themes. Additional themes can be downloaded from the Internet. Additionally, the user can create and save themes. The default themes in Microsoft PowerPoint also have variants. Variants are based on the main theme, but have some of the elements changed. For example, the background may be lighter or darker than the main theme. They offer the same design with different color schemes.

A dark blue background with light-colored lettering is the easiest on the eyes of the audience. Red should be used sparingly and only for emphasis. The eye tires from seeing too much red.

HANDS-ON EXAMPLE 9.1.4

APPLYING A THEME

The use of a theme is an easy way to maintain consistency in a presentation. It is very easy to apply a theme to a presentation at any point.

1. Launch Microsoft PowerPoint, and open the *LastName*Presentation.pptx file in the Chap9 folder on your flash drive, if it is not already open.
2. Navigate to the first slide of the presentation.

More

3. Click the **More** button in the gallery in the **Themes** group on the **Design** tab of the ribbon. Several themes are displayed in the expanded gallery. The name of each theme is displayed as help text when the cursor is hovered over the preview.
4. Scroll through the expanded gallery, and click the Damask theme. If this theme is not available, choose a different theme. The theme is applied to all slides in the presentation.
5. In the gallery in the **Variants** group on the **Design** tab of the ribbon, click the preview for the variation you prefer. The slides are updated.
6. Navigate through the presentation to see how the titles and text are formatted on the slides. Text should always begin in the same location from slide to slide. Otherwise the text will appear to jump or bounce during the presentation.
7. Move text boxes on each slide as needed so the text begins in the same location. To move a text box, click in it to display the handles and border, then click and drag the border.
8. Navigate to the How do I Write a Presentation? slide, which is slide 6.
9. Click the photograph to select it.
10. Click **Simple Frame, White** in the gallery in the **Picture Styles** group on the **Format** tab of the ribbon. A white frame is added around the photograph to emphasize the image.
11. Save the file.

Key Applications
5.5.1

Reusing Slides

Information in a presentation may need to be repeated in a different presentation. Slides in existing presentations can be reused in a new presentation. This saves the time needed to recreate what already has been created. The content can be copied and pasted. However, in Microsoft PowerPoint, there is a function that allows inserting slides from an existing presentation. The reused slides automatically take on the formatting of the new presentation.

HANDS-ON EXAMPLE 9.1.5

REUSING SLIDES

If needed information already exists on slides in another presentation, it is more efficient to reuse those slides than to recreate them. It is easy to reuse slides in Microsoft PowerPoint.

1. Launch Microsoft PowerPoint 2013, and open the *LastName*Presentation.pptx file in the Chap9 folder on your flash drive, if it is not already open.
2. Navigate to the last slide.

New Slide

3. Click the drop-down arrow next to the **New Slide** button on the **Home** tab of the ribbon, and click **Reuse Slides...** in the drop-down menu. Note: do not press the **New Slide** button. The **Reuse Slides** pane is displayed on the right-hand side of the application window, as shown.

Click to locate a file

4. Click the **Browse** button on the **Reuse Slides** pane, and then **Browse File...** in the drop-down menu that is displayed. In the standard open dialog box that is displayed, navigate the Chap09 folder on your flash drive, select the InsertPresentation.pptx file, and open it. The slides in the file are displayed in the **Reuse Slides** pane.

HANDS-ON EXAMPLE 9.1.5 (CONTINUED)

5. Click each preview in the **Reuse Slides** pane one at a time. Each slide is added to the presentation after the current slide. There should be a total of 11 slides after inserting the reused slides.
6. Close the **Reuse Slides** pane.
7. Applying what you have learned, review the inserted slides for formatting and adjust text boxes and images as needed.
8. Save the file.

Proofing and Displaying a Presentation

Before displaying the presentation, review it for any errors. It is necessary to review both the content and the layout. Review the layout and visual design to:

- ensure every item appears as intended;
- check that typefaces and font styles are appropriately applied;
- examine consistency in typefaces, spacing, and other important elements; and
- look for correct slide masters used for all slides.

Read through the final product. Run the spell-check function to locate spelling errors, but do not depend on software to "think" for you. Read for spelling and grammatical errors that the spell-checker may not find.

To run the spell-checker in Microsoft PowerPoint, click the **Spelling** button in the **Proofing** group on the **Review** tab of the ribbon. If any spelling errors are identified, they are displayed one by one in the **Spelling** pane (2013) or **Spelling** dialog box (2010 and earlier). The function of the spell-checker is similar to the same function in Microsoft Word, as discussed in Chapter 7. Note, however, grammar-checking is not part of the function.

When ready to display the presentation, Microsoft PowerPoint gives you the option to view the entire presentation from the beginning or only the portion of the presentation from the current slide forward. The option to view the presentation from the current slide is useful for testing only a portion of the presentation. For example, to test only the current slide, use this option and then press the [Esc] key after viewing the current slide. The [Esc] key always exits the playback.

To view the entire presentation, click the **Start From Beginning** button in the **Start Slide Show** group on the **Slide Show** tab of the ribbon. The presentation is displayed in full-screen mode starting with the first slide, as shown in Figure 9-7. To view the presentation starting with the current slide, click the **Start From This Slide** button in the **Start Slide Show** group on the **Slide Show** tab of the ribbon. During presentation playback, left-click, press the space bar, or press the down arrow or [Page Down] key to advance to the next slide. In some cases, depending on how the slides have been set up, the slides may automatically advance. If there is a need to return to the previous slide, press the up arrow or [Page Up] key.

FYI

The [F7] key is a shortcut for launching the spell-checker in most Microsoft Office applications.

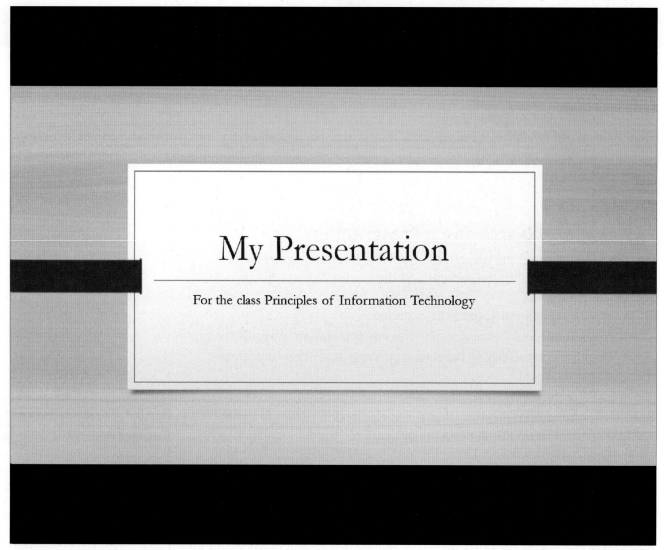

Figure 9-7. When the slide show is played, the presentation is displayed in full-screen mode.

HANDS-ON EXAMPLE 9.1.6

DISPLAYING A PRESENTATION

The end result of creating a presentation is to display the presentation. Before displaying the presentation, be sure to proof it for errors.

1. Launch Microsoft PowerPoint 2013, and open the *LastName*Presentation.pptx file in the Chap9 folder on your flash drive, if it is not already open.

HANDS-ON EXAMPLE 9.1.6 (CONTINUED)

Spelling

2. Click the **Spelling** button in the **Proofing** group on the **Review** tab of the ribbon. Because there are spelling errors in this document, the **Spelling** pane is displayed on the right-hand side of the window, and the first questionable word is highlighted in the document. Note: earlier versions of PowerPoint will display the **Spelling and Grammar** dialog box.

3. In the list of spelling alternatives offered, select the correct spelling, and click the **Change** button. The word is changed, and the next questionable word is highlighted in the document.

4. Continue correcting the document. If the questioned word is correct, click the **Ignore** button. If the correct word does not appear in the list of spelling alternatives, click in the document and manually correct the word. When the last questionable word has been addressed, the **Spelling** pane is closed.

5. Navigate to the third slide in the presentation.

6. Click the **Start From Beginning** button in the **Start Slide Show** group on the **Slide Show** tab of the ribbon or press the [F5] key. Playback of the presentation begins with the first slide.

7. Left-click, press the space bar, or press the down arrow or [Page Down] key to advance slides. Notice that some of the slides include animations. You will learn how to do this later in this chapter.

8. Press the [Esc] key to exit playback. Notice that the current slide in PowerPoint was the last slide displayed during playback.

9. Save the file.

Sharing a Presentation

After a presentation is completed, it can be saved in a PDF format for sharing with others who do not have the presentation software. A PDF can be viewed on any computer or can be used to prepare the file for commercial printing. This format does not permit the presentation to be edited. Other ways to share a presentation include saving it as a show, which can be viewed without PowerPoint, or as image files. A presentation can also be shared through e-mail, posted to the web, or saved in the cloud and shared.

The presentation can be saved to a CD using a special function in PowerPoint. This is an important option to allow viewing of the presentation, slide by slide, on most any other computer. Instead of saving the file, the presentation is exported using the **Package Presentation for CD** option. During the process, instructions are added to the file to tell other computers how to run the presentation. Exporting a presentation can also be used to create a video of the file if narration needs to be added.

GS5 Key Applications
5.1.1, 5.1.2, 5.7.1

Managing the Presentation

GS5 Key Applications
5.3

FYI

Double-clicking a slide thumbnail in the Slide Sorter view will display the Normal view with that slide current.

Microsoft PowerPoint offers several ways in which to view a presentation during development. The Normal view is the default view. This view displays the current slide in a large size as well as thumbnails of the other slides in the presentation. The Outline view also displays the current slide in a large size, but in place of the thumbnails the text content of all slides is displayed on the left. The Slide Sorter view displays only thumbnails of all slides, as shown in Figure 9-8. This view is very helpful when looking at the presentation as a whole. Most often, the Normal view along with the Slide Sorter view are used to manage the presentation, which includes inserting, rearranging, deleting, and copying slides. Inserting slides is discussed earlier in this chapter.

To change views in Microsoft PowerPoint, click the **View** tab in the ribbon. The buttons for changing views are located in the **Presentation Views** group on this tab. Buttons for displaying the Normal and Slide Sorter views are also located in the lower-right corner of the application window. These buttons are always visible no matter which tab is active in the ribbon, which makes it easy to restore one of these views at any time.

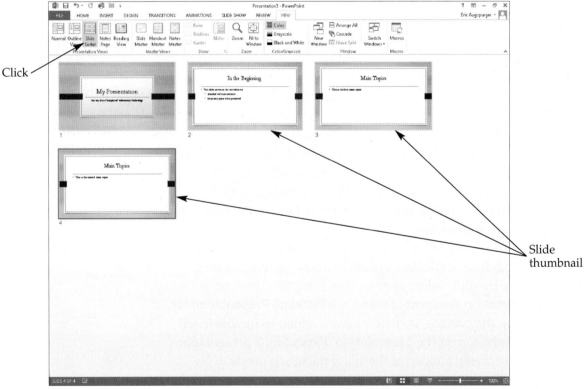

Goodheart-Willcox Publisher

Figure 9-8. The Slide Sorter view displays all of the slides in the presentation and can be used to rearrange slides.

TITANS OF TECHNOLOGY

John W. Thompson's education is in business management, but he has always worked with, and ultimately led, some of the most productive technology companies in the world. In 2014, Thompson was named Chairman of the Board of Microsoft Corporation, replacing Bill Gates in that position. Concurrently, since 2012 he has been the CEO of Virtual Instruments. His career has also included tenures at IBM, serving as Vice President and General Manager of IBM Americas, and Symantec, where he was President and CEO leading the cloud security giant. Thompson began his career working in sales at IBM and would spend the next 28 years in various positions at the company before leaving for the CEO position at Symantec.

After leaving Symantec in 2009, Thompson joined Virtual Instruments. He was named CEO in 2010. Virtual Instruments was a startup company in 2009, having been founded one year earlier. Virtual Instruments is an information technology company that helps other companies migrate to cloud computing.

Rearranging Slides

As a presentation is developed, slides often need to be rearranged in a different order. Sometimes this is because a slide is accidentally inserted in the wrong order. However, frequently the writer will decide the overall order of content needs to be changed. In Microsoft PowerPoint, slides can be rearranged in the Normal or Slide Sorter view. To move a slide to a different order, click and hold the thumbnail for the slide to move, drag it to the new location, and drop to reorder the slides.

GS5 Key Applications
5.7.4

GS4 Key Applications
4.2.3

FYI

Slides can be rearranged in the Outline view in Microsoft PowerPoint by dragging the square in front of the content.

Deleting Slides

There are times when all of the content on a slide is no longer needed. The easiest way to remove this content from the presentation is to delete the slide. Slides can be deleted in the Normal, Slide Show, or Outline view in Microsoft PowerPoint. In the Normal and Slide Show views, click the thumbnail for the slide to delete. In the Outline view, click the square next to the slide number in the outline. When a slide is selected, the thumbnail or the square will be outlined. With the correct slide selected, press the [Delete] key to remove the slide.

GS5 Key Applications
5.7.3

GS4 Key Applications
4.2.2

Copying Slides

Slides can be copied. This is useful if the slide contains a significant amount of information, but the user wants to make subtle changes to it to enhance the visual flow. Slides can be copied in the Normal, Slide Show, or Outline view in Microsoft PowerPoint. First, select the slide to copy. Then, click the **Copy** button in the **Clipboard** group on the **Home** tab of the ribbon or press the [Ctrl][C] key combination. Next, select the slide *after* which the copy should be placed. Finally, click the **Paste** button in the **Clipboard** group on the **Home** tab of the ribbon or press the [Ctrl][V] key combination.

In Microsoft PowerPoint, there is also a duplicate function. This function is used to create a copy of a slide and automatically paste it after the current slide in one step. First, select the slide to copy. Then, click the drop-down arrow next to the **Copy** button in the **Clipboard** group on the **Home** tab of the ribbon, and click **Duplicate** in the drop-down menu. The slide is automatically copied and pasted after the current slide.

HANDS-ON EXAMPLE 9.1.7

MANAGING A PRESENTATION

Managing a presentation involves many tasks, including inserting, rearranging, deleting, and copying slides. These are common tasks throughout development of a presentation.

1. Launch Microsoft PowerPoint 2013, and open the *LastName*Presentation.pptx file in the Chap9 folder on your flash drive, if it is not already open.

Slide Sorter View

2. Click the **Slide Sorter View** button in the **Presentation Styles** group on the **View** tab of the ribbon. The Slide Sorter view is displayed in which all slides are displayed as thumbnails.

3. Select the last slide in the presentation by clicking on it. The thumbnail will be outlined to indicate the slide is selected.

4. Press the [Delete] key to remove the selected slide.

5. Applying what you have learned, select the To Create an Effective Presentation slide (slide 8).

6. Click and hold on slide 8, drag to the end of the presentation, and drop the slide. The slides are automatically rearranged with the To Create an Effective Presentation slide at the end.

7. Applying what you have learned, view the slide show.

Normal View

8. Click the **Normal View** button in the **Presentation Styles** group on the **View** tab of the ribbon.

9. Save the file.

9.1 SECTION REVIEW

 ## CHECK YOUR UNDERSTANDING

1. What are the six questions that should be asked when planning a formal presentation?
2. What is the 7 × 7 rule?
3. If an object appears on a slide master, where else will it appear?
4. What happens if too many graphics are used in a presentation?
5. How are slides rearranged in a presentation?

IC3 CERTIFICATION PRACTICE

The following question is a sample of the types of questions presented on the IC3 exam.

1. Which of the following views allows the user see all slides in a presentation on the screen at one time?
   A. Zoom
   B. Slide Sorter
   C. Cascade
   D. Outline

 ## BUILD YOUR VOCABULARY

As you progress through this course, develop a personal IT glossary. This will help you build your vocabulary and prepare you for a career. Write a definition for each of the following terms and add it to your IT glossary.

attention grabber
clincher
external audience
graphics
internal audience
presentation
scope
slide master
theme

SECTION 9.2

ADDING TRANSITIONS AND ANIMATIONS

Essential Question

How do animations and transitions impact the message of a presentation?

Presentation software is not only used to create a presentation that communicates information, it is used to make the information more educational or entertaining for the audience. A presentation that is only text on the screen is not very engaging for the audience. The message of the presentation is likely to be lost. There are many ways to improve the visual aspect of the presentation.

There are also ways to provide information that is not part of or that supports the main focus. As with most types of documents, there are header and footer areas in a presentation that can be used to provide supplemental information, such as the name of the speaker. This section covers designing a presentation from scratch and including advanced features to improve a presentation.

Stephen Coburn/Shutterstock.com

LEARNING GOALS

After completing this section, you will be able to:
- Create a new presentation.
- Discuss advanced features of presentation software.

TERMS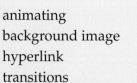

animating
background image
hyperlink
transitions

Creating a New Presentation

Creating a presentation from scratch first requires writing. Before writing the text, create an outline of the important points. As discussed earlier, answer these questions:

- Why are you presenting?
- Who is the audience?
- What is the topic?
- Where is the information?
- When is the presentation?
- How should the presentation be organized?

From the answers, formulate the introduction, body, and conclusion.

In Microsoft PowerPoint 2010 and earlier, a blank presentation is automatically started whenever the software is launched. To create a new presentation in Microsoft PowerPoint 2013, launch the software. The startup screen is displayed. A template can be selected in the startup screen if appropriate. To begin a blank presentation, click Blank Presentation on the right-hand side of the startup screen, as shown in Figure 9-9. A new blank presentation is started and displayed in the Normal view.

By default, a blank presentation in PowerPoint includes a slide based on the Title Slide slide master, as shown in Figure 9-10. If a title slide is not required, a different slide master can be applied to the default slide or the slide can be deleted. Add slides and content as needed to develop the presentation.

FYI

A theme can be applied to a blank presentation at any point to add color and visual interest.

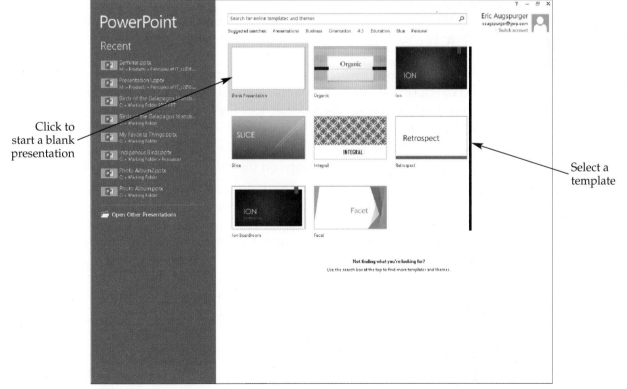

Click to start a blank presentation

Select a template

Goodheart-Willcox Publisher

Figure 9-9. Starting a new, blank presentation in Microsoft PowerPoint 2013.

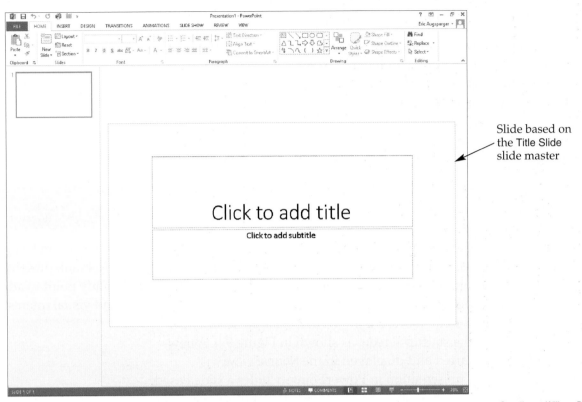

Figure 9-10. A slide based on the Title Slide master slide is automatically included in a new, blank presentation.

HANDS-ON EXAMPLE 9.2.1

CREATING A NEW PRESENTATION

There are many different goals for which a presentation may be created. For example, a presentation may need to educate an audience on the steps to take in preparing a presentation.

1. Launch Microsoft Word, and open the Seminar.docx file in the Chap09 folder on your flash drive. Leave Word and this file open.
2. Launch Microsoft PowerPoint 2013.
3. On the startup screen, click Blank Presentation on the right-hand side to begin a new presentation.
4. Display Word by using the [Alt][Tab] key combination or by clicking the button on the taskbar.
5. Applying what you have learned, select the text A Guide to Winning Business Seminar, and copy it to the system clipboard.
6. Display PowerPoint.
7. Click the placeholder text for the title, and paste the copied text.
8. Click the placeholder text for the subtitle, and enter Presented by *your name* and today's date on separate lines.
9. Applying what you have learned, add a new Title and Content slide.
10. Applying what you have learned, copy the next title from Word, and paste it into PowerPoint.

HANDS-ON EXAMPLE 9.2.1 (CONTINUED)

11. Copy the bulleted text from Word, and paste it into PowerPoint as the content.
12. Applying what you have learned, add a new Title and Content slide.
13. Applying what you have learned, copy the next title and content from Word, and paste it into PowerPoint.
14. Applying what you have learned, add a new Title and Content slide.
15. Applying what you have learned, copy the final title and content from Word, and paste it into PowerPoint.
16. Navigate to slide 2.

Pictures

17. Click the **Pictures** button in the **Images** group on the **Insert** tab of the ribbon. A standard open dialog box is displayed.
18. Navigate to the Chap09 folder on your flash drive, and open the Seminar.jpg image file.
19. Move and resize the image as needed.
20. Applying what you have learned, insert the Idea.jpg image file on slide 3.
21. Applying what you have learned, insert the Leader.jpg image file on slide 4.
22. Applying what you have learned, apply the Wisp theme and the blue variant. If this theme is not available, select one of your own choice.
23. Click **Save** in the **File** tab of the ribbon, and save the file as *LastName*Seminar.pptx in the Chap09 folder on your flash drive. Since this is the first time the file has been saved, the save as function is automatically used.

Advanced Features

Most presentation software contains many techniques to add sophisticated features. In Microsoft PowerPoint, these techniques include adding effects that appear when moving from slide to slide, including hyperlinks, and inserting a background image. Other presentation software will typically include these or similar features.

Adding Transitions

Transitions are the methods of shifting from one slide to the next. Rather than abruptly showing the next slide, the software can make the slides gradually move from one to the next, as shown in Figure 9-11. There are many types of transitions that can be applied. Slides can dramatically split, come in from the top or bottom, fly in from the left or right, or one of many other entrances.

Transitions can add visual interest to a presentation. However, do not overuse transitions. Also, limit the types of transitions used in a presentation. Generally, one or two types of transitions are fine for most applications. Some transitions may be harsh. Harsh transitions are dramatic, but they tend to focus the audience's attention away from the message. Simple transitions are best in most cases.

GS5 Key Applications
5.4

GS4 Key Applications
4.3.3

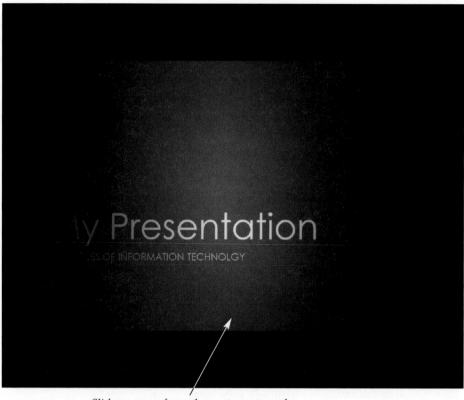

Slide appears from the center outward

Goodheart-Willcox Publisher

Figure 9-11. Transitions can be used to gradually shift from one slide to another.

HANDS-ON EXAMPLE 9.2.2

ADDING SLIDE TRANSITIONS

While transitions can add visual interest, they should not be overused. A subtle animation from one slide to the next is interesting, but not distracting.

1. Launch Microsoft PowerPoint, and open the *LastName*Seminar.pptx file in the Chap9 folder on your flash drive, if it is not already open.
2. Applying what you have learned, display the Slide Sorter view.
3. Select slide 1.
4. Click **Split** in the gallery in the **Transitions to This Slide** group on the **Transitions** tab of the ribbon. The transition is previewed and applied.
5. Applying what you have learned, apply a split transition to slide 2.
6. Applying what you have learned, apply a glitter transition to slide 3. You will need to expand the gallery to locate this transition. Glitter is a harsher transition compared to split.
7. Save the file.

Animating Objects

Text and graphics can be made to move on the screen. **Animating** is the process of adding motion to an object. An animation is the resulting scene.

A common animation used in presentations is each bullet point entering the slide one at a time. This is a good way to focus the audience on the new topic. Shapes can be animated to provide a simple demonstration. This may more effectively communicate the action than describing it with text. Combining the use of slide transitions with animated objects can add drama to the flow of the presentation.

The number of animations should be kept to a minimum. Overuse of moving objects tends to distract the audience. Also, motion should be used for a purpose, such as emphasizing a bullet point. Just because an object *can* be animated does not mean it *should* be animated. Motion without a purpose is likely to be distracting to the audience.

Key Applications
4.3.2

FYI

Be sure not to overpower the purpose of the presentation with unneeded graphics, transitions, and animations.

HANDS-ON EXAMPLE 9.2.3

ADDING ANIMATIONS

An effective use of motion in a presentation is to animate bullet points to appear one at a time. Combining a slide transition with this animation can make the presentation more dramatic.

1. Launch Microsoft PowerPoint, and open the *LastName*Seminar.pptx file in the Chap9 folder on your flash drive, if it is not already open.
2. Applying what you have learned, navigate to slide 4, and display the Normal view.
3. Click at the beginning of the first bullet, press the [Shift] key, and click at the end of the last bullet. This selects the bulleted list.
4. Click **Appear** in the gallery in the **Animation** group on the **Animations** tab of the ribbon. The animation is previewed and applied. Notice the number 1 appears next to each bullet. This indicates the order in which animations will be applied. In this case, all bullets are animated together, which is why they all have the number 1 next to them.
5. Click the **Start** down-down arrow in the **Timing** group on the **Animations** tab in the ribbon, and select **On Click** in the drop-down list. Now the bullets are numbered 1 through 6, as shown. This indicates the animation will be applied individually. In this case, one bullet will appear each time the mouse is clicked.

Animation order →

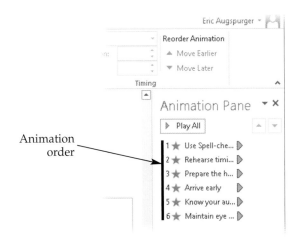

HANDS-ON EXAMPLE 9.2.3 (CONTINUED)

6. Applying what you have learned, view the presentation from the beginning. Verify that the bullets on slide 4 appear one at a time as the mouse is clicked.
7. Navigate to slide 3. This slide currently has a glitter transition applied, which is a harsh transition.
8. Applying what you have learned, apply the origami transition to slide 3.
9. Applying what you have learned, view the presentation from this slide forward.
10. Save the file.

Key Applications
4.1.3

Ethical Messages

Sometimes it is necessary to write a sales message or other type of document for your company. Embellishing a message about a product or service or intentionally misrepresenting a product or service is unethical and possibly illegal. There are truth-in-advertising laws that must be followed. Focus on the truths of the message to generate interest.

Creating a Hyperlink

Another tool for an effective presentation is the ability to add a link to additional information. A **hyperlink** is an electronic link between a marked place in a document to another place in the document or to another document, file, or web page.

For example, it may be appropriate to show the audience an informative video on the topic being discussed. Instead of embedding the video in the presentation, a hyperlink can be placed in the presentation. That link is clicked to access the video on the Internet or as a file saved on the hard drive. In another example, you may wish to show the audience how to locate information on a website. By including a hyperlink to the site, you can quickly access the site. A hyperlink can also be used to navigate to a different slide in the presentation, such as a slide containing glossary definitions.

A hyperlink is attached to a word or object in the presentation. For the presentation to be able to find the linked information, it must know the path. The path is found in the hyperlink. When the object containing the hyperlink is clicked during the slide show, the target is opened. The target may be an Internet address, a file on the local drive or a network drive, or another location in the current presentation or a different presentation.

An object that acts as the trigger must be set up and placed on a slide. In most presentation software, the procedure is to select the object, initiate the command for attaching a hyperlink, and enter the path to the target. In Microsoft PowerPoint, the command is initiated by clicking the **Add a Hyperlink** button in the **Links** group of the **Insert** tab or by pressing the [Ctrl][K] key combination.

HANDS-ON EXAMPLE 9.2.4

ADDING A HYPERLINK

Many times it is important to show more information than is appropriate to include in the presentation itself. While showing a video may enhance the presentation, embedding it in the file will increase the file size.

1. Launch Microsoft PowerPoint, and open the *LastName*Seminar.pptx file in the Chap9 folder on your flash drive, if it is not already open.
2. Applying what you have learned, add a new Title and Content slide at the end of the presentation, and display the Normal view.
3. Applying what you have learned, insert an online picture of a microphone. Place the image in the center of the slide.
4. Launch a web browser, navigate to www.YouTube.com, and locate the video entitled Four Steps to Great Speaking by Connor Neill. If you cannot locate this video, search for another professional video that discusses public speaking.
5. Watch the video to see that it is suitable. Click the **Share** link below the video player. The URL of the video appears in a text box.
6. Select the URL, and copy it to the system clipboard.
7. Close the web browser, and return to PowerPoint.
8. Select the microphone image, and click the **Add a Hyperlink** button in the **Links** group on the **Insert** tab of the ribbon. The **Insert Hyperlink** dialog box is displayed, as shown.

Add a
Hyperlink

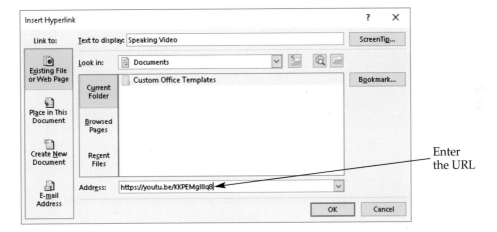

Enter
the URL

9. Click in the **Address:** text box, and paste the URL copied from the web browser. Click the **OK** button to attach the hyperlink to the image.
10. Applying what you have learned, view the presentation from the current slide.
11. Hover the cursor over the microphone image. The URL is displayed as help text.
12. Click the image to activate the hyperlink. The default web browser is launched, the YouTube page is displayed, and the video is played.
13. Close the web browser, and end the PowerPoint presentation.
14. Save the file.

GS4 Key Applications
4.1.5

Inserting a Background Image

A **background image** is an overall image that appears behind all other elements on the slide. It is usually included as a way to make the presentation attractive. A background image can enhance the feeling of a presentation. It can draw increased attention to the presentation or it can be soothing to the audience.

A background image usually should not be the main focus of the slide. It should be visible, but it should not compete with the content on the slide for the audience's attention, as shown in Figure 9-12. If a photograph is used as a background image, a level of transparency is usually assigned to it. This allows the image to recede into the background yet be visible to the audience.

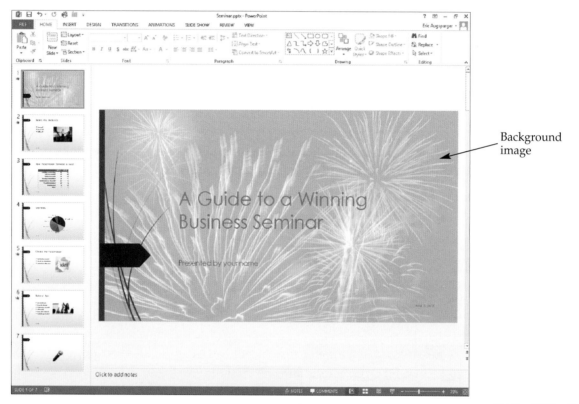

Goodheart-Willcox Publisher

Figure 9-12. A background image can be used to enhance a presentation, but it should not be the main focus.

HANDS-ON EXAMPLE 9.2.5

INSERTING A BACKGROUND IMAGE

A background image on the title slide can set the mood for a presentation. For example, a background image of fireworks will communicate excitement.

1. Launch Microsoft PowerPoint 2013, and open the *LastName*Seminar.pptx file in the Chap9 folder on your flash drive, if it is not already open.
2. Navigate to the title slide (slide 1).

HANDS-ON EXAMPLE 9.2.5 (CONTINUED)

3. Right-click on the slide or its thumbnail image, and click **Format Background** in the shortcut menu. The **Format Background** pane is displayed on the right-hand side of the application window, as shown. Note: in Microsoft PowerPoint 2010 and earlier, the **Format Background** dialog box is displayed.

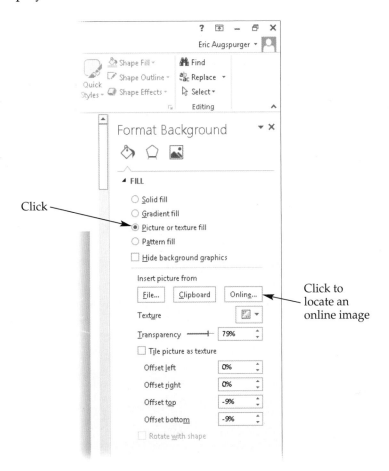

4. Click the **Picture or texture fill** radio button in the **Format Background** pane. The options in the pane change to reflect the selection.
5. Click the **Online...** button in the pane. The **Insert Pictures** dialog box is displayed.
6. Applying what you have learned, locate an image of holiday celebration fireworks and insert it. The image is added to the slide behind all other elements. Notice how the image is fully visible and the slide text is hard to read.
7. Click the **Transparency** slider, and drag to the right until the text on the slide is readable. The value in the **Transparency** text box increases as you drag, and the effect is previewed on the slide.
8. Close the **Format Background** pane.
9. Save the file.

FYI

Headers and footers are commonly omitted from presentations.

Adding Headers and Footers

The *header* is at the top of the slide, and the *footer* is at the bottom of the slide. Each is outside of the area where the main content is placed. When content is placed in the header or footer, it appears on every slide. The header and footer can be used to include slide numbers, a date, or information about the presentation file. This information may be useful if the presentation is to be distributed for individual viewing instead of displayed to an audience.

HANDS-ON EXAMPLE 9.2.6

ADDING A HEADER AND FOOTER

Sometimes information is included in the header or footer as a courtesy to those viewing the presentation. Information may also be included to state ownership of the material.

1. Launch Microsoft PowerPoint, and open the *LastName*Seminar.pptx file in the Chap9 folder on your flash drive, if it is not already open.
2. Navigate to the title slide (slide 1).
3. Delete the date from the subtitle content.

Header & Footer

4. Click the **Header & Footer** button in the **Text** group on the **Insert** tab of the ribbon. The **Header and Footer** dialog box is displayed, as shown.

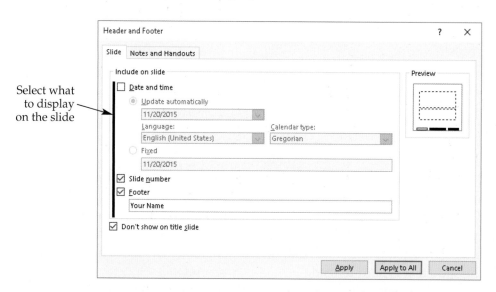

5. Check the **Slide number**, **Footer**, and **Don't show on title slide** check boxes. This specifies the footer and slide number will be placed on all the slides except the title slide.
6. Click in the **Footer** text box, and enter your name.
7. Click the **Apply to All** button.
8. Applying what you have learned, view the presentation from the beginning. Notice the slide number appears in the upper-left corner of the slide, and your name appears in the lower-left corner.
9. End the playback, and navigate to the title slide.
10. Applying what you have learned, open the **Header and Footer** dialog box.

HANDS-ON EXAMPLE 9.2.6 (CONTINUED)

11. Check the **Date and time** check box.
12. Click the **Update automatically** radio button.
13. Click the **Update automatically** drop-down arrow, and select the month, day, year format in the drop-down list.
14. Uncheck the **Don't show on title** slide check box.
15. Click the **Apply** button, *not* the **Apply to All** button. The **Apply** button applies the settings to only the current slide.
16. Applying what you have learned, view the presentation from the beginning. Notice on the title slide that there is no slide number and the date is in the footer instead of your name.
17. Save the file.

9.2 | SECTION REVIEW

 CHECK YOUR UNDERSTANDING

1. What slide is included by default in a blank Microsoft PowerPoint file?
2. What is the difference between a transition and an animation?
3. What can a hyperlink be attached to in a Microsoft PowerPoint presentation?
4. Where does a background image appear on a slide?
5. Where are the header and footer located on a slide?

IC3 CERTIFICATION PRACTICE

The following question is a sample of the types of questions presented on the IC3 exam.

1. Entrances such as wipe, fade, push, and cut are examples of:
   A. transitions
   B. slide advances
   C. preview mechanisms
   D. animations

BUILD YOUR VOCABULARY

As you progress through this course, develop a personal IT glossary. This will help you build your vocabulary and prepare you for a career. Write a definition for each of the following terms and add it to your IT glossary.

animating
background image
hyperlink
transitions

SECTION 9.3

CHARTS, TABLES, AND HANDOUTS

Essential Question

What is the importance of providing handouts to the audience of a presentation?

Properly used, assembled, and presented, statistics and other types of numerical data can be powerful devices in a presentation. A great number of data can be illustrated so that many individual items can be dealt with as one thought. Lists of numbers are not visually appealing or easy to understand in a presentation. However, presentation software makes it possible to visualize summary statistics.

Many people in the audience will want to take notes during a presentation. If the audience is provided with a hard copy of the presentation, that can be used for notes. Most presentation software is capable of printing the presentation with several slides per page to use as a handout for the audience. This section covers creating tables, charts, speaker notes, and handouts.

Alex Brylov/Shutterstock.com

LEARNING GOALS

After completing this section, you will be able to:
- Describe how to create a table.
- Explain the purpose of charts in a presentation.
- Discuss when to use speaker notes.
- Create handouts for a presentation audience.

TERMS

chart
handouts
presentation notes

Creating Tables

Tables are often used to present data, such as numerical figures or statistics. The table format makes it easy for the audience to view this type of information. A table, which looks similar to a spreadsheet, consists of columns, rows, and cells.

Tables are easy to add to a presentation. A table in a presentation is similar to a table in a word-processing document, as discussed in Chapter 7. The standard format for a table sets the first row as a header row, as shown in Figure 9-13. A header row is used to indicate what the data in each cell mean. The spacing, font, and column and row sizing for a table can all be customized.

There are a couple of ways to add a table to a presentation in Microsoft PowerPoint. The commands on the **Insert** tab of the ribbon can be used. Click the **Table** button in the **Tables** group on the **Insert** tab of the ribbon. The drop-down menu that is displayed contains a grid representing rows and columns. Highlight the number of rows and columns for the table using this grid. The table is previewed on the slide as the grid is highlighted. When the correct number of rows and columns are highlighted in the grid, click to insert the table.

Another way to add a table is by clicking **Insert Table...** in the drop-down menu. This displays the **Insert Table** dialog box. Enter the number of rows and columns for the table, and click the **OK** button to insert the table.

Also, any of the content text boxes on the default slide masters contain embedded helper icons, as shown in Figure 9-14. One of these is the **Insert Table** icon, which looks like a small table. This is a shortcut for inserting a table into the text box. Clicking the icon displays the **Insert Table** dialog box. If this icon is present, using it is the most efficient way to access the command.

Key Applications
4.1.2

> **FYI**
>
> Navigating the table is done with the arrow keys, the mouse, or the [Tab] and [Shift][Tab] key combinations.

> **FYI**
>
> The number of rows and columns in a table can be adjusted after the table is inserted.

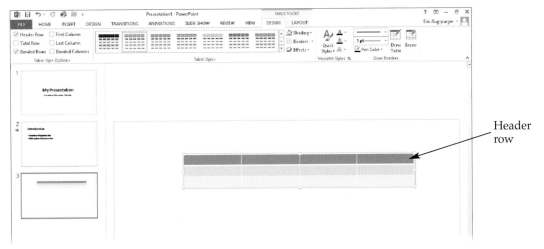

Header row

Goodheart-Willcox Publisher

Figure 9-13. A header row is the first row in a table, which indicates what the data in each column mean.

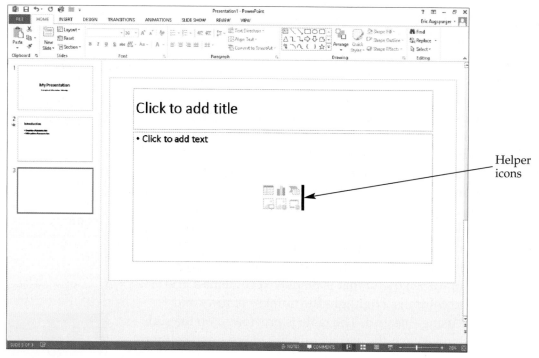

Figure 9-14. Content text boxes contain helper icons, which are shortcuts to adding content.

HANDS-ON EXAMPLE 9.3.1

ADDING A TABLE

Tables can be used in a presentation to present numerical data. However, a table can also be used to organize textual information as well.

1. Launch Microsoft PowerPoint, and open the *LastName*Seminar.pptx file in the Chap9 folder on your flash drive, if it is not already open.
2. Applying what you have learned, add a new Title and Content slide after slide 2.
3. Enter How Presentation Software Is Used as the title content.
4. Click the **Insert Table** icon in the content text box. The **Insert Table** dialog box is displayed.
5. In the **Insert Table** dialog box, enter 3 in the **Columns:** text box and 9 in the **Rows:** text box. Click the **OK** button to create the table.
6. Enter the following data into the table.

	Employees	Students
Education and teaching	72	97
Talks and meetings	70	32
Private ceremonies	32	40
Company presentations	43	11
Conferences and trade fairs	39	7
Product presentations	30	8
Entertainment	8	10
Other	1	1

HANDS-ON EXAMPLE 9.3.1 (CONTINUED)

7. Select all text in the table by clicking in the upper-left cell and dragging to the bottom-right cell.
8. Click the **Font Size** drop-down arrow in the **Font** group on the **Home** tab of the ribbon, and click **16** in the drop-down list to change the size of the text.
9. Applying what you have learned, select the numerical data in the table.
10. Click the **Align Right** button in the **Font** group on the **Home** tab of the ribbon.
11. Move the cursor to the top of the right-hand column until it changes to a downward arrow, and click to select the column.
12. Click in the **Width:** text box in the **Cell Size** group on the **Layout** on-demand tab of the ribbon, and enter 1.2″.
13. Applying what you have learned, reduce the width of the middle column to 1.4″.
14. Applying what you have learned, select the entire table.
15. Choose **Light Style 2 – Accent 3** in the gallery in the **Table Styles** group on the **Design** on-demand tab in the ribbon. The table is complete, as shown.

Align Right

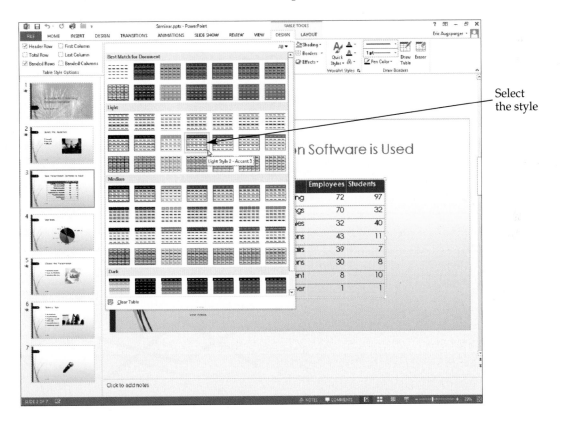

Select the style

Creating Charts

Charts are another way to present data. A **chart,** or *graph,* illustrates data in a picture-like format. Many times it is easier to understand the data if they are shown in graphical form instead of in numerical form in a table. The meaning of the data can be absorbed in one glance without

Key Applications
4.1.4

Mathematics

Graphs are used to illustrate data in a picture-like format. Often, it is easier to understand the data if they are shown in graphical form instead of numerical form. For example, a line graph can show the trend of data over time. Common types of graphs are bar graphs, line graphs, and pie charts.

reading each number. For example, a line chart can be used to show the trend of financial markets over time. Common charts include bar, line, and pie, as shown in Figure 9-15.

Most presentation software has commands to create various charts. In Microsoft PowerPoint, either click the **Insert Chart** icon in a content text box or click the **Insert Chart** button in the **Illustrations** group on the **Insert** tab of the ribbon. The **Insert Chart** dialog box is displayed, which is used to select the type of chart to create. Once the type of chart is selected, a placeholder chart is added to the slide, and a spreadsheet is displayed for entering data, as shown in Figure 9-16. As data are entered in the spreadsheet, the placeholder chart is updated to reflect the data. When all data have been entered, close the spreadsheet.

Once a chart is created, it can be formatted. In Microsoft PowerPoint, there are various options on the **Design** and **Format** on-demand tabs for changing the appearance of the chart. The basic formatting style of the chart can be changed. The colors used in the chart can be changed. Even the type of chart can be changed. The same data will be represented in the new type selected.

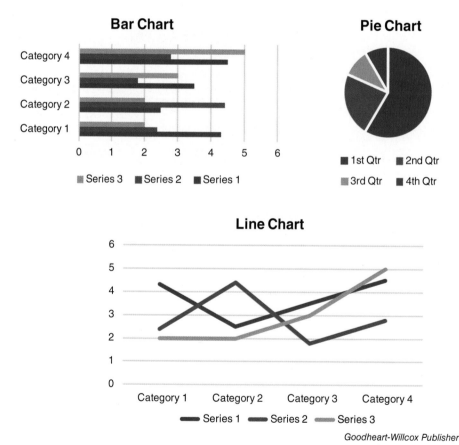

Goodheart-Willcox Publisher

Figure 9-15. The most common types of charts are bar, line, and pie.

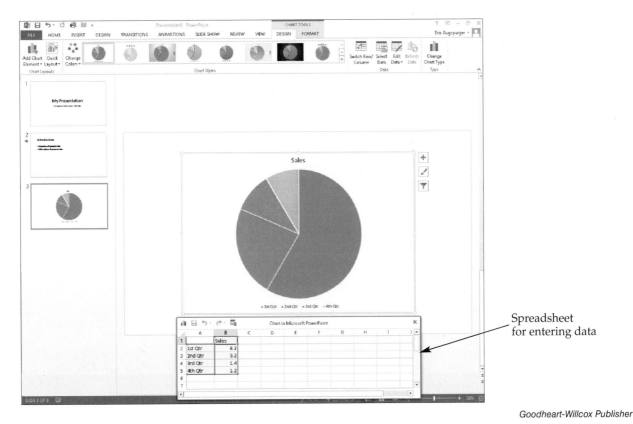

Goodheart-Willcox Publisher

Figure 9-16. When inserting a chart, an embedded spreadsheet is used to enter the data.

HANDS-ON EXAMPLE 9.3.2

ADDING A CHART

Charts can provide a way for the audience to quickly understand the meaning of data. For example, a pie chart can be used to quickly show the occurrence of various phobias among the general population.

1. Launch Microsoft PowerPoint, and open the *LastName*Seminar.pptx file in the Chap9 folder on your flash drive, if it is not already open.
2. Applying what you have learned, add a new Title and Content slide after slide 3.
3. Enter Top Fears of the General Public as the title content.
4. Click the **Insert Chart** icon in the content text box, which appears as a small bar chart, to display the **Insert Chart** dialog box.
5. Click **Pie** in the **Insert Chart** dialog box to specify the type of chart to create.
6. Click the **OK** button. A placeholder pie chart is added to the slide, and a spreadsheet containing placeholder data is displayed below the chart.

HANDS-ON EXAMPLE 9.3.2 (CONTINUED)

7. Replace the placeholder data in the spreadsheet with the following information, as shown. Do not worry if the text appears cut off as it is entered, it will appear correctly in the chart.

	Percentage
Public speaking	71
Heights	32
Insects	24
Finances	23
Deep water	22
Sickness	20
Death	19
Flying	18

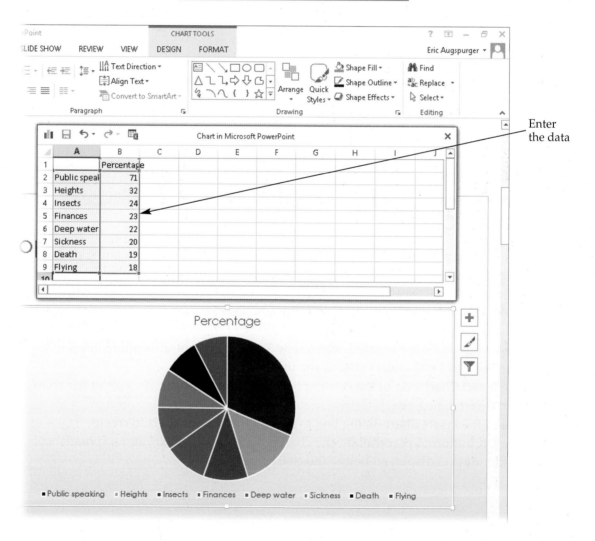

Enter the data

HANDS-ON EXAMPLE 9.3.2 (CONTINUED)

8. Close the spreadsheet by clicking the close button (X) for the spreadsheet. The spreadsheet is automatically saved when the presentation is saved.
9. With the chart selected, three buttons appear on the right-hand side of the chart. Click the **Chart Elements** button, which looks like a plus sign (+). The **Chart Elements** pane appears on the left-hand side of the chart.
10. In the **Chart Elements** pane, uncheck the **Chart Title** check box. The title Percentages is no longer displayed on the chart.
11. Click the **Chart Styles** button on the right-hand side of the chart, which looks like a paintbrush. The **Style/Color** pane is displayed on the left-hand side of the chart.
12. Click **Style 9** in the list of styles in the **Style/Color** pane. To see the name of a style, hover the cursor over the preview to display the name as help text. This style places the names of the different fears next to the corresponding slices in the pie chart.
13. Save the file.

Creating Speaker Notes

Most speakers do not memorize their speeches. Instead, they rely on notes. **Presentation notes,** or speaker notes, are notes used to keep the speaker on topic. They are used during the presentation to help you keep your place and to remind yourself of points should you forget anything.

Most presentation software offers a feature to help the speaker create presentation notes. In Microsoft PowerPoint, this feature is called speaker notes. These notes will not be visible during the presentation, but they can be printed beforehand for the speaker to use. They can also be used as notes to yourself during the development process, such as "add a photograph to this slide."

In Microsoft PowerPoint, notes can be entered below each slide. Notes can be entered for all slides or just the ones that require further explanation. The text in a presentation note should be kept to a minimum. The purpose of a note is to be a reminder, not full sentences to read to the audience.

To create a speaker note in Microsoft PowerPoint, click in the **Notes** area at the bottom of the PowerPoint window, as shown in Figure 9-17. If this area is not displayed, click the **Notes** button in the bar at the bottom of the PowerPoint window. With the insertion point in the **Notes** area, enter the text for the note. Limited formatting is available for note text. The text can be made bold, italic, underlined, or any combination of these. However, the size cannot be changed, nor can the color of the text.

FYI

Having the printed presentation with speaker notes available during the presentation can help make for a professional delivery.

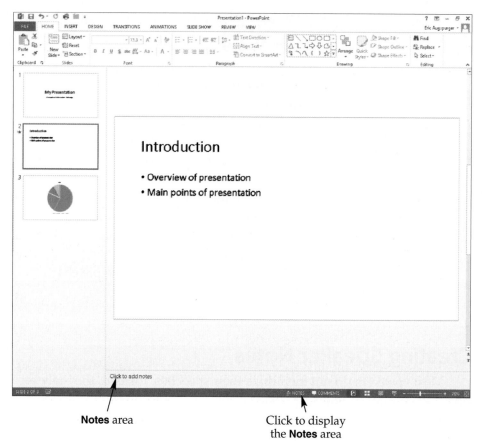

Notes area

Click to display
the Notes area

Goodheart-Willcox Publisher

Figure 9-17. The **Notes** area is displayed below the slide at the bottom of the window.

HANDS-ON EXAMPLE 9.3.3

ADDING SPEAKER NOTES

Speaker notes can be used as reminders of important points to make during a presentation. Speaker notes will not be visible during a presentation, but they can be printed beforehand.

1. Launch Microsoft PowerPoint, and open the *LastName*Seminar.pptx file in the Chap9 folder on your flash drive, if it is not already open.
2. Navigate to slide 4, and display the Normal view, if it is not already displayed. Speaker notes must be added in the Normal view.
3. If the notes area is not displayed at the bottom of the window, click the **Notes** button.
4. Click in the notes area. The placeholder text Click to Add Notes is replaced by the insertion point.
5. Enter this text:

   The word for speech anxiety, glossophobia, comes from the Greek glossa, meaning tongue, and phobos, meaning fear or dread.
6. Click **Print** on the **File** tab of the ribbon.
7. Under **Settings**, click the first drop-down arrow, and click **Print Current Slide** in the drop-down list.

HANDS-ON EXAMPLE 9.3.3 (CONTINUED)

8. Click the second drop-down arrow, and click **Notes Pages** in the drop-down menu. Notice the print preview shows slide 4 (the current slide) and the speaker notes added below the slide.
9. Click the **Print** button.
10. Save the file.

Creating Handouts

Handouts, also called *leave-behinds*, are printed materials that are distributed to the audience. Generally, handouts are used to help the listener understand the information in the presentation, provide additional information about the topic, or both. They are useful for providing an outline of key points or supplemental information that is not covered in the presentation. Figure 9-18 provides some guidelines for using handouts.

Handouts can be valuable to the audience. They serve as a review of the speaker's key points. They give the audience something to take away from the presentation. They are an important way for participants to be reminded of the key messages. Handouts are especially useful if the presentation is highly technical or complex.

However, do not overload people with a large amount of reading material. The audience should be paying attention to the key points of the presenter, not trying to read material. If listeners need the information during the presentation, distribute the materials before you begin. Place handouts on a table at the front or hand them out as people enter. If you intend to distribute the handout during the presentation, inform the listeners at the beginning of the presentation. Then they will know that they do not need to take notes. This makes it possible for them to focus their attention completely on the speaker. For distribution after the presentation, pass them out while people are still seated.

GS5 Key Applications
5.1.1

FYI

Speaker notes can be used as handouts to provide additional information.

Using Handouts
- Do not assume audience members will read your handouts.
- Keep handouts as short as possible; be concise.
- Use a format that presents the information in a way that is visually appealing and professional.
- Include your contact information and the date of the presentation.
- If the handout or presentation is available on a website, include the appropriate URL.
- Before the presentation, plan when and how you will use handouts.
- Have a plan for quickly distributing materials without distraction.
- Before referring to a handout during your presentation, be sure each person has a copy.

Goodheart-Willcox Publisher

Figure 9-18. Follow these tips when using handouts with a presentation.

Most presentation software has a function to create handouts from the slides in the presentation. This can be done to provide the audience with a copy of the presentation on which to make notes or to help those who may be in the back of the room follow the presentation. In Microsoft PowerPoint, creating handouts is part of the printing function. When selecting to print handouts, the number of slides that will appear on each printed page must be selected, from one to nine slides per page. The option for three slides per page also includes lines the audience can use to take notes. This is a good option for handouts distributed at the beginning of a presentation. The printout can be generated in color, grayscale, or pure black and white, as shown in Figure 9-19.

Option	Explanation
Color	Choose this option to output in color on a color printer. If this option is used to print on a black-and-white printer, the printout will be grayscale, but of a lower quality than when printing in grayscale.
Grayscale	Choose this option to print all objects on the page in shades of gray. This option should be used with a black-and-white printer, but it can also be used with a color printer if the output does not need to be in color.
Pure Back and White	This option prints slides in black and white. There are no shades of gray. As a result, some objects in the design theme of the slide, such as embossing and drop shadows, will not print. Text will print as black even if the text is in color.

Goodheart-Willcox Publisher

Figure 9-19. When creating a handout, decide how the color will be printed.

HANDS-ON EXAMPLE 9.3.4

PRINTING HANDOUTS

Handouts can be valuable for the audience. The handout function in Microsoft PowerPoint can be used to generate a copy of the presentation for the audience.

1. Launch Microsoft PowerPoint, and open the *LastName*Seminar.pptx file in the Chap9 folder on your flash drive, if it is not already open.
2. Click **Print** on the **File** tab of the ribbon.
3. Under **Settings**, click the first drop-down arrow, and click **Print All Slides** in the drop-down list.
4. Click the second drop-down arrow, and click **3 Slides** in the drop-down menu. Notice the print preview shows the first three slides in the presentation as well as lines next to each slide. The audience can use these lines to write notes.
5. Click the bottom drop-down arrow, and click **Grayscale** in the drop-down list. All colors in the presentation will be output as shades of gray.
6. Click the **Print** button.
7. Save the file.

9.3 | SECTION REVIEW

 CHECK YOUR UNDERSTANDING

1. What type of information is presented in a table?
2. How does a chart present data?
3. When creating a chart in Microsoft PowerPoint, how is a spreadsheet used?
4. How are speaker notes used?
5. In general, what is the purpose of a handout?

IC3 CERTIFICATION PRACTICE

The following question is a sample of the types of questions presented on the IC3 exam.

1. Which of the following are the correct steps to insert a chart into a Microsoft PowerPoint presentation?
   A. **View>Gridlines>Chart**
   B. **Insert>Illustrations>Chart**
   C. **Format>Picture Tools>Chart**
   D. **Design>Layout>Insert Chart**

 BUILD YOUR VOCABULARY

As you progress through this course, develop a personal IT glossary. This will help you build your vocabulary and prepare you for a career. Write a definition for each of the following terms and add it to your IT glossary.

chart
handouts
presentation notes

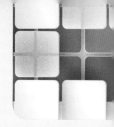

Chapter Summary

Section 9.1
Creating a Professional Presentation

- A presentation is a speech, address, or demonstration given to a group. Begin by planning the presentation, and then create the content for the presentation.

- Knowing how to navigate a presentation is important when creating and presenting. You must also be able to add slides, text, and graphics as well as be able to format the presentation.

- Managing the presentation involves rearranging, deleting, and copying slides. There are many tools available to help in managing the presentation.

Section 9.2
Adding Transitions and Animations

- A new presentation can be started from scratch or a template can be used. The new presentation will contain several slide masters that can be applied to slides in the presentation.

- Transitions are the methods of shifting from one slide to the next, while animations are objects with motion added to them. Hyperlinks can be assigned to elements in a presentation, and a background image can be added behind all other elements on a slide.

Section 9.3
Charts, Tables, and Handouts

- Tables are often used to present data, such as numerical figures or statistics. A table is similar to a spreadsheet, consisting of columns, rows, and cells.

- A chart, or graph, illustrates data in a picture-like format. This allows the meaning of data to be absorbed in one glance without reading individual numbers.

- Presentation notes help to keep the speaker on topic. They are used during the presentation to help you keep your place and to remind yourself of points should you forget anything.

- Handouts, also called leave-behinds, are printed materials that are distributed to the audience. They are useful for providing an outline of key points or supplemental information that is not covered in the presentation.

Now that you have finished this chapter, see what you know about information technology by scanning the QR code to take the chapter posttest. If you do not have a smartphone, visit www.g-wlearning.com.

Chapter 9 Test

Multiple Choice

Select the best response.

1. When identifying who will attend a presentation, what are the two types of audiences?
   A. Students and professionals.
   B. Internal and external.
   C. Experienced and novice.
   D. Top-down and bottom-up.

2. Which of the following is the key combination to navigate to the beginning of a presentation in Microsoft PowerPoint?
   A. [Ctrl][Page Up]
   B. [Home]
   C. [Ctrl][Home]
   D. [Shift][Home]

3. Overuse of moving objects tends to do what?
   A. Distract the audience.
   B. Emphasize a point.
   C. Add interest to the presentation.
   D. Create visual appeal.

4. What happens when the item containing a hyperlink is clicked during the slide show?
   A. The hyperlink is inactive during the slide show.
   B. The target defined in the hyperlink is opened.
   C. A new presentation window is opened.
   D. The presentation is closed and the target is opened.

5. Where are speaker notes entered in Microsoft PowerPoint?
   A. As a comment on the slide.
   B. In the **Notes** dialog box.
   C. Below the slide.
   D. In the Notes view.

Completion

Complete the following sentences with the correct word(s).

6. The introduction should also draw the listener into the presentation with a(n) _____.

7. _____ are used to standardize colors, fonts, and effects across all slides in a presentation.

8. Rather than abruptly showing the next slide, a(n) _____ can make the slides gradually move from one to the next.

9. A table is similar to a(n) _____, consisting of columns, rows, and cells.

10. Speaker notes are intended to be used by the _____.

Matching

Match the correct term with its definition.

A. presentation
B. theme
C. transition
D. hyperlink
E. chart

11. Technique for showing data in a picture-like format.

12. Set of specified colors, fonts, and effects.

13. Method of moving from one slide to the next.

14. Electronic link between a marked place in a document to another place in the document or to another document, file, or web page.

15. Speech, address, or demonstration given to a group.

Application and Extension of Knowledge

1. Go to the Bureau of Labor Statistics website (www.bls.gov), and investigate four careers of interest to you. Create a presentation that describes these careers. Include a title slide, a slide for each career describing the skills needed, and a summary slide that compares the median salaries of the four careers. Apply the principles outlined in this chapter, including the 7×7 rule.

2. Visit a software store, either online or a physical store, and look for presentations software. Make a list of the available software. Compare the price and available features for the software you found. Choose which software you would use and prepare for a class discussion explaining your choice.

3. Select a topic of interest to you, such as a hobby or activity. Outline the three parts of a presentation explaining the topic: introduction, body, and conclusion. Make note of what you will use as an attention grabber and a clincher. Then, create the presentation applying the principles outlined in this chapter.

4. Think of a short scene that can be animated, such as a dog chasing a ball. Create a presentation, and insert images, clipart, and drawing shapes to create the scene. Then, animate the objects as needed. Use the help function as needed to investigate animation features and functions. Think of ways to use transitions between slides to help with animating the scene. When completed, prepare to present the slide show to the class and explain how you animated the scene.

5. Select one of the presentations you created. Generate handouts to distribute when you give the presentation. Determine when you will distribute the handouts and how, and follow through with this when you give your presentation.

Online Activities

Complete the following activities, which will help you learn, practice, and expand your knowledge and skills.

Certification Practice. Complete the certification practice test for this chapter.

Vocabulary. Practice vocabulary for this chapter using the e-flash cards, matching activity, and vocabulary game until you are able to recognize their meanings.

Communication Skills

College and Career Readiness

Reading. Most people use technology on a daily basis. Using technology in the workplace can help employees be more productive. In other instances, technology can be a distraction. Read about types of technology and how people can use each to be more productive in the workplace. What did you learn?

Listening. Practice active-listening skills while listening to your teacher present this chapter. Focus on the message and monitor it for understanding. Were there any barriers to effective listening? How did you use prior knowledge to help you understand what was being said? Share your ideas in the group discussion.

Speaking. Successful employees model integrity. What role do you think ethics and integrity have in deciding which graphics to use in a presentation? What process did you use to make the decision? In retrospect, do you think you made the correct decision? Make an informal presentation to your class to share your thoughts.

Internet Research

Netiquette. Research the term *netiquette* using various Internet resources. Write several paragraphs to describe what the term means, where it came from, and how it has evolved this century.

Teamwork

With your team, conduct research on the phrase *Silicon Valley*. Create a presentation

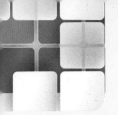

that explains what Silicon Valley is, how it got its name, and the significance of it to information technology. Each team member should conduct research and deliver a separate portion of the presentation.

Portfolio Development

College and Career Readiness

Skills and Talents. Include samples of your work that show your skills or talents. Look at past school or work assignments you have completed. Include a research paper, letter, electronic slide show, or other items that illustrate your business communication skills. Select a book report, essay, poem, or other work that demonstrates your writing talents. Look for projects that show your skills related to critical thinking and problem solving. Have you completed a long or complicated project? What career area interests you most? Select completed work from classes that will help prepare you for jobs or internships in that area.

1. Create a Microsoft Word document that lists your skills and talents. Use the heading "Skills and Talents" along with your name. Next to each skill or talent listed, write a description of an assignment and explain how your skill or talent was involved in completing it.

2. Scan hard-copy documents related to your skills and talents to serve as samples. Save the documents in an appropriate folder.

3. Place the hard copies in the container for future reference.

CTSOs

Case Study. A case study presentation may be part of a Career and Technical Student Organization (CTSO) competitive event. The activity may be a decision-making scenario for which your team will provide a solution. The presentation will be interactive with the judges. To prepare for a case study event, complete the following activities.

1. Conduct an Internet search for case studies. Your team should select a case that seems appropriate to use as a practice activity. Look for a case that is no more than a page long. Read the case and discuss it with your team members. What are the important points of the case?

2. Make notes on index cards about important points to remember. Team members should exchange note cards so that each evaluates the other person's notes. Use these notes to study. You may also be able to use these notes during the event.

3. Assign each team member a role for the presentation. Ask your instructor to play the role of competition judge as your team reviews the case.

4. Each team member should introduce him- or herself, review the case, make suggestions for the case, and conclude with a summary.

5. After the presentation is complete, ask for feedback from your instructor. You may also consider having a student audience to listen and give feedback.

10

SPREADSHEET SOFTWARE

SECTIONS

10.1 INTRODUCTION TO SPREADSHEETS

10.2 MANAGING DATA IN SPREADSHEETS

CHECK YOUR IT IQ

Before you begin this chapter, see what you already know about information technology by scanning the QR code to take the chapter pretest. If you do not have a smartphone, visit www.g-wlearning.com.

Microsoft Excel is the most popular software for creating computerized spreadsheets, but spreadsheets have a long history, originating hundreds of years before computers. Spreadsheets are used to organize, calculate, and communicate information. An individual cell in a computerized spreadsheet where a row and a column intersect can contain a variety of data, including text, numbers, or formulas to perform calculations. After data are entered, it is easy to update or edit the spreadsheet.

The data in a computerized spreadsheet can be formatted in many ways. The color of cells and the text and numbers they contain can be changed. Numbers can be formatted as percentages, currency, and many other formats. The size of individual cells can be changed, and cells can be merged. The size of rows and columns can be changed, and rows and columns can be inserted or deleted. Data in a computerized spreadsheet can be sorted and filtered as needed to display only needed information.

IC3 CERTIFICATION OBJECTIVES

GS5

Key Applications

Domain 1.0 Common features
    Objective 1.6 Be able to select text or cells

Domain 3.0 Spreadsheets
    Objective 3.1 Understand common spreadsheet terms
    Objective 3.2 Be able to insert/delete rows and columns
    Objective 3.3 Be able to modify cell sizes
    Objective 3.4 Be able to filter and sort data
    Objective 3.5 Understand functions, formulas, and operators
    Objective 3.6 Be able to enter data in a spreadsheet
    Objective 3.9 Manipulate data within a spreadsheet
    Objective 3.10 Format data within spreadsheets
    Objective 3.12 Be able to use spreadsheet templates to increase productivity
    Objective 3.13 Understand how a spreadsheet can be used as a simple database

GS4

Computing Fundamentals

Domain 3.0 Computer software and concepts
    Objective 3.3 Software usage

Key Applications

Domain 3.0 Spreadsheet activities
    Objective 3.1 Spreadsheet layout
    Objective 3.2 Data management

College and Career Readiness

Reading Prep. Skim the chapter by reading the first sentence of each paragraph. Use this information to create an outline for the chapter before you read it.

INTRODUCTION TO SPREADSHEETS

Essential **Q**uestion

How have electronic spreadsheets improved society?

Spreadsheets have long been used to record financial data. They display data in columns and rows for easy viewing and analysis. Computerized spreadsheets are basically the same as manual spreadsheets, with data arranged in rows and columns. However, computerized spreadsheets offer significant advantages.

Data can be quickly added to a computerized spreadsheet, and the spreadsheet can be easily navigated using the keyboard or mouse. One of the greatest advantages of a computerized spreadsheet is the ability to include formulas that automatically perform calculations. Another great advantage lies in the ease of editing data, either correcting errors or updating figures.

Syda Productions/Shutterstock.com

LEARNING GOALS

After completing this section, you will be able to:
- Discuss the origin of spreadsheets.
- Describe a spreadsheet.
- Enter data into a spreadsheet.
- Explain how to create a formula in a spreadsheet.
- Edit data to correct errors and update information.

TERMS

active cell
cell
columns
formulas
killer app
numbers
range

rows
spreadsheet
text
what-if analysis
workbook
worksheet

Origin of Spreadsheets

A **spreadsheet** is a collection of data arranged in rows and columns. Spreadsheets originated with bookkeepers, who recorded financial data in a ledger in rows and columns that spanned two facing pages or a single oversized page. Data were manually entered, with columns representing categories of expenditures, rows representing invoices, and cells containing the money amount. If any changes needed to be made or mistakes corrected, bookkeepers had to erase several entries and rerecord data.

Manual spreadsheets continued to be used after the advent of computerized spreadsheet software in the 1960s. Early spreadsheet software was for large mainframe computers, not personal computers. In 1978, Dan Bricklin was watching his professor at Harvard Business School solve a complex math problem on a blackboard. When the professor found an error or wanted to change a value, he had to erase several numbers and recalculate the result. Bricklin realized he could make a computer do that for him.

Bricklin and Bob Frankston invented spreadsheet software named VisiCalc for the Apple II personal computer in just two months. It became the first killer app. A **killer app** is a software application so compelling that people buy a computer just to be able to use it. VisiCalc helped change the Apple II computer from a hobbyist's device to a useful business tool. It also helped launch the widespread transition from manual spreadsheets to computerized spreadsheets.

FYI

The word *spreadsheet* comes from the publishing term *spread*, which means two facing pages of a publication, such as a book, magazine, or newspaper.

Using Spreadsheets

A spreadsheet is very helpful whenever a job requires a great deal of calculation, a graph or chart to visually display relationships, or numerical data that change from time to time. Businesses collect lots of data. Some numerical data that has to be totaled, multiplied, or otherwise analyzed include amounts of money, quantities of inventory, and numbers of hours. Spreadsheet software contains the features which make this possible. The most valuable advantage is its ability to automatically recalculate formulas and reprocess data.

GS5 Key Applications
3.13

Spreadsheet Overview

A sample computerized spreadsheet containing data and a chart is shown in Figure 10-1. The arrangement of the spreadsheet is similar to a manual spreadsheet based on a bookkeeper's ledger. The grid is the arrangement of vertical and horizontal lines. This is where the work is done. In Microsoft Excel, this grid, which is the spreadsheet, is called a **worksheet**. A **workbook**, which is the Excel file, may contain one or several worksheets.

Columns are the spaces between the vertical grid lines. In Microsoft Excel, these are named alphabetically from left to right. **Rows** are the spaces between the horizontal grid lines. In Microsoft Excel, these are sequentially numbered from top to bottom. Where a column and row

GS5 Key Applications
3.1.1, 3.1.2, 3.1.3, 3.1.5, 3.1.6

GS4 Computing Fundamentals
3.3.2
Key Applications
3.1.4

Funds Tracking

Name	January	February	March	Total	Percentage
Jimmy	$ 25.50	$ 36.25	$ 18.75	$ 80.50	37%
Carlos	$ 15.50	$ 22.00	$ 36.75	$ 74.25	34%
Stevie	$ 20.75	$ 12.75	$ 28.50	$ 62.00	29%
Monthly Total	$ 61.75	$ 71.00	$ 84.00	$ 216.75	

Goodheart-Willcox Publisher

Figure 10-1. A spreadsheet consists of columns and rows, and where they intersect is a cell.

intersect is a **cell**. Each cell has an address named for the column and row. For example, cell B2 is located in the second row (row 2) of the second column (column B), as shown in Figure 10-2. The **active cell** is the currently selected cell, which is indicated by an outline around the cell.

Navigating a Spreadsheet

A spreadsheet may be very small, consisting of just a few columns and rows, or very large, consisting of thousands of columns and rows. When a blank spreadsheet is started, only the upper-left corner of it can be seen. A few rows and columns are visible, but many more are available for use.

The mouse can be used to navigate a spreadsheet. To select a different cell, click the cell. Double-click the cell to activate its contents for editing.

GS5 Key Applications
1.6, 3.1.7

FYI

Microsoft Excel 2010 and later versions are able to accommodate 16,384 columns and over one million rows of data.

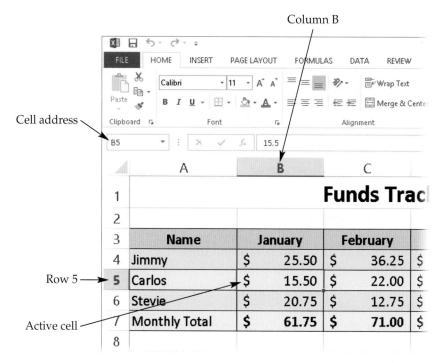

Goodheart-Willcox Publisher

Figure 10-2. A cell's address is based on the column and row where it is located.

To see rows or columns not visible in the current view, use the scroll bars to pan the view. The mouse wheel can also be used to scroll downward.

However, the most efficient users primarily navigate a spreadsheet with the keyboard. Figure 10-3 shows ways in which to use a keyboard to navigate a spreadsheet.

Saving a Spreadsheet

A spreadsheet is saved in Microsoft Excel in the same manner as a document in any Microsoft Office application. Click **Save** in the **File** tab in the ribbon, and then click **Computer** followed by the **Browse** button in the backstage view. If the file has not yet been saved, the save as function is started. Navigate to the folder where you wish to save the spreadsheet, enter a file name, and save the file. Microsoft Excel automatically adds the .xlsx extension. If the file has previously been saved, clicking **Save** will automatically save the file under the same name. To save the file under a different name, click **Save As** in the **File** tab of the ribbon.

Entering Data

As discussed in Chapter 3, there are several common data types used in computer programming:

- Integers are the positive and negative counting numbers and zero.
- Floating point numbers are decimal numbers.
- Boolean types only hold values for true or false.
- Characters are single letters, digits, or other symbols.
- Strings hold alphabetic and numeric text, along with special symbols.
- Date types hold time and date information.

Data types are also important in a computerized spreadsheet. The data type, or *format*, for a cell determines what the data entered in the cell mean. Microsoft Excel sets the default data type for the cell by the characters entered in the cell.

In general, data entered into a spreadsheet are either text, numbers, or formulas. **Text** is a string data type. It may consist of any letters, digits,

FYI

Spreadsheets usually represent many hours of work, so save your work often!

GS5 Key Applications
3.6

FYI

It is possible to format numbers and formulas as text, so if a formula is not working, be sure this is not the case.

[Enter]	Move down one row
[Tab]	Move one column to the right
[Shift][Tab]	Move one column to the left
Arrow keys	Move one cell in the direction of the arrow
[Ctrl][Home]	Move to cell A1
[Ctrl][End]	Move to the last cell that contains data (highest row number and highest column letter)
[F2] (PC), [Ctrl][U] (Mac)	Activate the current cell's content for editing

Goodheart-Willcox Publisher

Figure 10-3. The most efficient way to navigate a spreadsheet is using the keyboard.

Formula bar

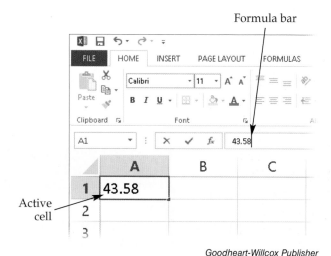

Active cell

Goodheart-Willcox Publisher

Figure 10-4. The formula bar can be used to enter or edit data or a formula. When done, press the [Enter] key or click the check mark button.

Key Applications

GS5 3.5.1, 3.5.2, 3.5.3

Key Applications

GS4 3.2.2

STEM

Mathematics

Place value is a basic element of a number system. A digit's position, or place, in a number determines the value of the digit. Each place represents ten times the place to its right. This is a *base ten system*, with the digit at the far-right of a number in the *ones* position.

or other keyboard characters. Text is used for titles, labels, and explanations. **Numbers** are a floating point number data type. Numbers can be used as data in calculations. **Formulas** are equations. The formula defines the calculation, and the result of the calculation is displayed as the value for the cell.

To enter data, first select the cell where the data are to be added. Next, use the keyboard to enter the data. Once another cell is selected, the content is set. In Microsoft Excel, data for the cell can also be entered in the formula bar, as shown in Figure 10-4, or by double-clicking to activate the cell for editing.

When text is entered, it is automatically left justified in the cell. When a number is entered, it is automatically right justified in the cell. When entering data, it may appear to extend beyond the edge of the cell. The data are contained within the cell, it just *appears* as if the data extend beyond the cell. The width of columns and height of rows can be adjusted and cells can be set to wrap text, which are discussed later in this chapter.

Using Formulas

Formulas often look like the expressions seen in math class. When a formula is entered into a cell, the software automatically executes the calculation and displays the result as the cell value. The formula can be viewed in the formula bar by selecting the cell. Double-clicking the cell to activate it for editing displays the formula in the cell.

The most basic formulas are for simple algebra: addition, subtraction, multiplication, and division. Addition is represented in a formula with the plus sign (+). Subtraction is represented with the dash or minus sign (–). Multiplication is represented with the asterisk (*). Division is represented with the forward slash (/). These characters can be entered using the standard keyboard keys or the number pad keys. All formulas in Microsoft Excel begin with an equals sign (=).

For example, assume cell A1 contains the number 5 and cell A2 contains the number 4. To create a formula that finds the sum of cells A1 and A2, select a different cell in which to add the formula, such as cell A3. Next, use the keyboard to enter this formula:

=A1+A2

As soon as the [Enter] key is pressed, the calculation is performed, and the answer displayed as the value of cell A3, as shown in Figure 10-5. Also, cell B3 is made the current cell. A different navigation key, such as an arrow key or the [Tab] key, could be used instead of the [Enter] key to set the formula and initiate the calculation.

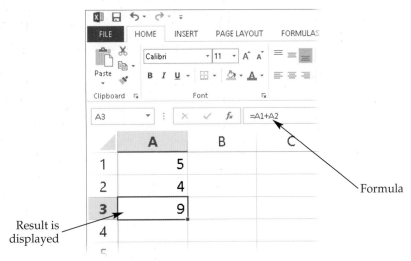

Figure 10-5. When a formula is entered into a cell, the cell displays the result of evaluating the formula.

When the data entered represent dollar amounts, do not include the dollar sign ($). The dollar sign means something special in an Excel spreadsheet. Also, for decimal numbers that end in zero, such as 34.900, the trailing zeros to the right of the decimal point are not displayed unless the cell is formatted to display them. Formatting cells is discussed later in this chapter.

FYI

Although all numbers in a spreadsheet are floating point, they can be formatted to look like integers.

HANDS-ON EXAMPLE 10.1.1

CREATING A SPREADSHEET

Microsoft Excel can be used to calculate many things. For example, a student with a part-time job can keep track of how much money has been made.

1. Insert your PRINC-OF-IT flash drive into the computer.
2. Applying what you have learned, create a folder on the flash drive named Chap10.
3. Launch Microsoft Excel, and click Blank Spreadsheet on the startup screen. Note: Excel 2010 and earlier versions automatically open a blank spreadsheet when launched.
4. Click **Save** in the **File** tab of the ribbon, and click **Computer** and then the **Browse** button in the backstage view. The **Save As** dialog box is displayed.
5. Save the file as Earnings.xlsx in the Chap10 folder on your flash drive.
6. Cell A1 should be automatically selected, as indicated by the outline surrounding the cell. Cell A1 is located where column A and row 1 intersect, which is the upper-left cell in the spreadsheet. If cell A1 is not the current cell, click it to select it.
7. Add the text Earnings History using the keyboard, and press the [Enter] key.
8. Applying what you have learned, add the text Week to cell A3 and the text Amount of Take-Home Pay to cell B3.
9. In cells A4 through A8, add the text First, Second, Third, Fourth, and Total Earnings.
10. In cells B4 through B7, add the numbers 52.83, 34.90, 23.89, and 44.32.

HANDS-ON EXAMPLE 10.1.1 (CONTINUED)

11. In cell B8, enter this formula: =B4+B5+B6+B7. The weekly earnings are in cells B4 through B7, so this formula finds the sum of all earnings. As soon as the [Enter] key is pressed to set the formula, the cell will display the total of 155.94.

12. Select cell B8. The cell displays the result of the calculation, but the formula is displayed in the formula bar, as shown.

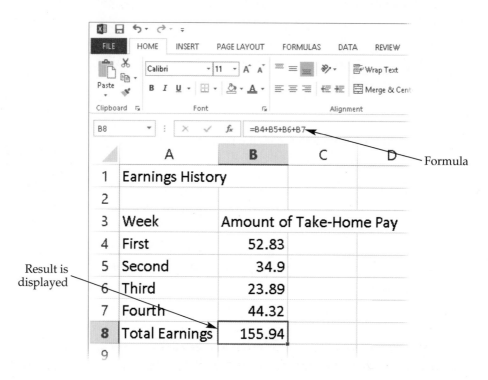

13. Save the file.

GS5 Key Applications
3.6

Editing Data

One of the biggest advantages of a computerized spreadsheet is the ability to correct errors quickly when creating the spreadsheet. However, creating the spreadsheet is usually only the first step. The real power of a computerized spreadsheet lies in the ability to change repeatedly or update data.

Correcting Errors

It is not uncommon to make an error when entering data into a spreadsheet. Fortunately, correcting errors is easy. First, locate the cell with the error and make it the active cell. Next, press the [F2] key or double-click to activate the cell for editing. Use the arrow keys or click with the mouse to position the insertion point where the edit is to be made. Then, use the [Delete] or [Backspace] key to remove the unwanted data. Finally, enter the correct data. To set the change, press the [Enter] key.

The formula bar can also be used to edit the content of a cell, as shown in Figure 10-6. First, select the cell to edit. Then, click in the formula bar and edit the data. Press the [Enter] key or click the **Enter** button (check mark) to the left of the formula bar.

The content in a cell can be erased with one keystroke. Select the cell, and press the [Delete] key. Similarly, the content in several cells can be deleted. Select the cells by clicking and dragging. To select cells that are not next to each other, click the first cell, hold down the [Ctrl] key, and click the other cells. When more than one cell is selected, the selection is called a **range** of cells. Finally, press the [Delete] key to erase the content in all selected cells. You can also right-click on the selected cells, and then click **Clear Contents** in the shortcut menu.

Updating Data

One of the best features of a computerized spreadsheet is the automatic update that occurs when changing one of the values. This allows a what-if analysis. A **what-if analysis** is changing a parameter in a data model to see how the outcome will be altered. When data are changed in a Microsoft Excel spreadsheet, Excel not only recalculates all formulas that reference those data, but also redraws any charts using those data.

Using a what-if analysis is a very valuable tool for predicting costs and other monetary scenarios. For example, if a homebuilder wants to keep track of the cost of materials to construct a particular house, each item would be listed in the spreadsheet, how many of each item is needed, and how much each item costs. A formula would be entered into the spreadsheet to multiply the quantity of each item by the cost of each item. Another formula would be entered to add the cost of all materials to yield the total cost of the house. If the price of a sheet of plywood

GS5   Key Applications
3.1.4

Green Tech

Carbon Footprints
A *carbon footprint* is a measurement of how much the everyday behaviors of an individual, company, or community impact the environment. This includes the amount of carbon dioxide put into the air from the consumption of energy and fuel used in homes, for travel, and for business.

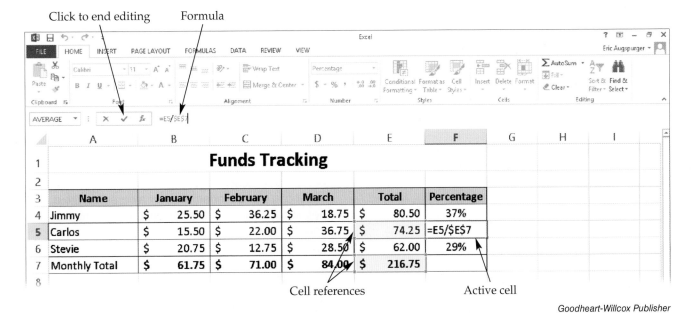

Goodheart-Willcox Publisher

Figure 10-6. Editing a formula using the formula bar. Notice the color-coding used to indicate the cells referenced in the formula.

increases, for example, the cell containing the per-item cost of that item can be quickly updated. With only this one change, the entire cost of the house would be instantly and accurately updated.

HANDS-ON EXAMPLE 10.1.2

EDITING DATA

Correcting errors is easy in Microsoft Excel. It is also easy to change or update data to create a what-if analysis.

1. Launch Microsoft Excel, and open the Earnings.xlsx file in the Chap10 folder on your flash drive, if it is not already open.
2. Select cell B3, and press the [F2] key to activate the cell for editing.
3. Press the left arrow key until the insertion point is to the left of the T in the word *Take*. You can also click at that point with the mouse.
4. Press the [Backspace] key to erase the text *Amount of* from the cell.
5. Press the [Enter] key to set the change.
6. Click cell B6 to select it.
7. Enter 32.58 to change the data in the cell. Notice how the total earnings value in cell B8 automatically changes as soon as the [Enter] key is pressed.
8. Save the file.

10.1 SECTION REVIEW

 ### CHECK YOUR UNDERSTANDING

1. Which software is considered the first killer app?
2. In Microsoft Excel, what is the difference between a worksheet and a workbook?
3. Which data type can be used in calculations in a spreadsheet?
4. In Microsoft Excel, how would the formula be written to subtract the value of cell D3 from the value of cell A5?
5. How do you select cells that are not next to each other?

IC3 CERTIFICATION PRACTICE

The following question is a sample of the types of questions presented on the IC3 exam.

1. Perform this simulation.
   Select cells A10, C5, D8, and G4.

 ### BUILD YOUR VOCABULARY

As you progress through this course, develop a personal IT glossary. This will help you build your vocabulary and prepare you for a career. Write a definition for each of the following terms and add it to your IT glossary.

active cell	rows
cell	spreadsheet
columns	text
formulas	what-if analysis
killer app	workbook
numbers	worksheet
range	

MANAGING DATA IN SPREADSHEETS

wavebreakmedia/Shutterstock.com

The data in a spreadsheet can be formatted in many ways. Microsoft Excel is part of the Microsoft Office suite of tools, so it supports many of the same formatting options found in other applications in the suite. The color of text and numbers can be changed, as can the color of cells. Numbers can be formatted as numbers, dates, percentages, and other formats. The size of rows and columns can be changed. Cells can be merged, copied, and moved. Rows and columns can be inserted and deleted.

A computerized spreadsheet can be a powerful analysis tool. It is easy to find data in the spreadsheet. Additionally, data can be sorted and filtered to focus on the needed information. A spreadsheet can be printed when a hardcopy is needed.

Essential Question

What is the importance of formatting to the purpose of a spreadsheet?

TERMS

absolute cell address
ascending order
descending order
filtering
fraction
merge
percentage
relative cell address
sorting
wrap text

LEARNING GOALS

After completing this section, you will be able to:
- Discuss ways to customize the appearance of a spreadsheet.
- Change data locations by copying and moving cells.
- Explain how to rearrange data.
- Describe ways to locate and organize data.
- Identify options for printing a spreadsheet.

Key Applications
3.10.1

Customizing the Appearance

Once data have been entered into the spreadsheet, in most cases it will be necessary to format the spreadsheet to make the data understandable. This may be as simple as adjusting the column and row sizes to ensure all data are visible. However, column and row headings can be emphasized by changing styles, size, or color. Cells can be formatted to clarify the meaning of the data they contain. Additionally, rows and columns can be added to the spreadsheet to promote readability.

Key Applications
3.2.4

Formatting Text

It is not necessary to use the default text formatting. The alignment, orientation, wrapping, and background color can be changed. The color, style, and size of the typeface can be changed as can the typeface itself. To format text, first select the cell or cells to which the formatting will be applied.

In Microsoft Excel, to change the typeface or the color, background color, size, style, or alignment of the text or the typeface, use the commands in the **Font** and **Alignment** groups on the **Home** tab of the ribbon, as shown in Figure 10-7. These commands function the same way as in Microsoft Word or Microsoft PowerPoint.

FYI

Many of the formatting choices are available in the mini toolbar displayed for a selection, which may be more efficient than using the ribbon.

One way to correct text that extends beyond the edges of a cell is to wrap it. When a cell is set to **wrap text**, a new line within the cell will be automatically started when the length of the text exceeds the width of the cell. To turn on text wrapping for the selected cell, click the **Wrap Text** button in the **Alignment** group on the **Home** tab of the ribbon.

By default, text is automatically left-aligned and numbers are automatically right-aligned. Additionally, all cells are by default bottom-aligned, which means the data will be placed at the bottom of the cell. To change the horizontal alignment of the selected cell, click the **Align Text Left**, **Center**, or **Align Text Right** button in the **Alignment** group on the **Home** tab of the ribbon. Despite the names of these commands, they work for any cell content. To change the vertical alignment of the selected cell, click the **Top Align**, **Middle Align**, or **Bottom Align** button in the **Alignment** group on the **Home** tab of the ribbon.

Key Applications
3.1.3

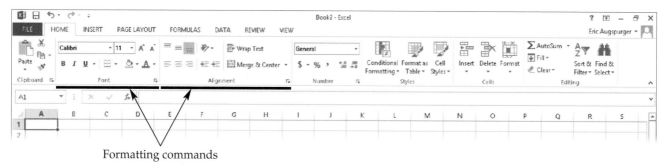

Formatting commands

Goodheart-Willcox Publisher

Figure 10-7. There are many options for formatting text in a spreadsheet.

HANDS-ON EXAMPLE 10.2.1

FORMATTING TEXT

In some cases, the default text formatting is sufficient for a spreadsheet. However, in most cases, some or all of the default formatting needs to be changed to improve the appearance of the spreadsheet.

1. Launch Microsoft Excel, and open the Earnings.xlsx file in the Chap10 folder on your flash drive, if it is not already open.
2. Right-click on cell A1. In the mini toolbar, click the **Font** drop-down list, and click **Arial Black** in the list. The typeface of the text in the cell is changed.
3. Click the **Font Size** drop-down list, and click **14** in the list. The size of the text in the cell is changed.
4. Click cell A3, hold, and drag to cell B3. This selects the range A3:B3 (A3 to B3).
5. Applying what you have learned, change the font to 12 point italic.
6. Applying what you have learned, select the range A4:A8, and change the font to 12 point.
7. With range A4:A8 selected, click the drop-down arrow next to the **Fill Color** button in the **Font** group on the **Home** tab of the ribbon, and click a light-orange color tile in the palette that appears. The spreadsheet is now formatted for better readability, as shown. Expand column A to see all of the text in cell A8.

Fill
Color

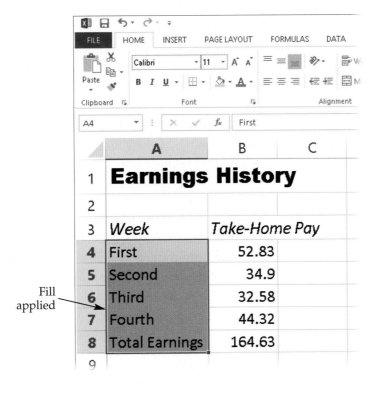

Fill
applied

8. Save the file.

Formatting Numbers

When entering numerical data, there are many choices for formatting them. Common formatting for numbers includes currency, dates, percentages, and fractions. Other formatting is also often available,

Number	12.576
Currency	$12.58
Accounting	$ 12.58
Date	6/6/1934
Time	01:49:26 PM
Percentage	1257.60%
Fraction	12 4/7
Scientific	1.26E+1

Goodheart-Willcox Publisher

Figure 10-8. There are several options for formatting a number. Here, the number 12.576 is entered in each cell, and the formatting indicated has been applied.

FYI

The dollar sign signifies a special meaning in certain situations, so the currency symbol should be added through formatting.

Ethics

Integrity

Integrity is defined as the honesty of a person's actions. Integrity and ethics go hand-in-hand in both personal and professional lives. Employees and employers both help establish the reputation of a business in the community. Company employees who display integrity help create a positive culture for the business, customers, and community.

depending on the spreadsheet software. Options for formatting are depicted in Figure 10-8.

In Microsoft Excel, the commands for applying numerical formatting to a cell are located in the **Number** group on the **Home** tab of the ribbon. The full range of cell formatting is available in the **Format Cells** dialog box, which is displayed by clicking the dialog box launcher in the **Number** group or by right-clicking on a cell and then clicking **Format Cells...** in the shortcut menu.

If the numerical data represent currency, the displayed value can be made to look as such by adding a currency symbol. In Microsoft Excel, if the currency symbol is directly entered with the data, the cell will be formatted as currency with the symbol. The symbol is automatically removed from the entered data, but the displayed value will contain the symbol. It may be easier, however, to format the cell to automatically add the currency symbol before entering the data.

Currency is most often expressed with either two decimal places or no decimal places. Choices for formatting values allow decimal places to be added or removed. In Microsoft Excel, numbers, including currency, can be formatted to contain up to 30 decimal places. To increase the number of decimal places shown in a cell, click the **Increase Decimal** button in the **Number** group on the **Home** tab of the ribbon. To decrease the number of decimal places, click the **Decrease Decimal** button in the **Number** group on the **Home** tab of the ribbon.

Numbers over 1,000 are usually rendered with commas separating each thousands place. Separating large numbers in this manner makes them more readable. In Microsoft Excel, if the commas are directly entered with the data, the cell will be formatted as a number with commas. The comma is automatically removed from the entered data, but the displayed value will contain the comma. It may be easier, however, to format the cell to automatically add the commas before entering the data.

The most common way to enter a date into a spreadsheet is as numbers separated by hyphens (dashes) or forward slashes. However, there are many ways in which the displayed value can be formatted, as shown in Figure 10-9. In Microsoft Excel, if a date is entered as mm/dd/yy, mm/dd/yyyy, mm-dd-yy, or mm-dd-yyyy, where *mm* is the numerical month, *dd* is the numerical day, and *yy* or *yyyy* is the numerical year, the cell will be automatically formatted as a date with forward slashes separating the month, day, and year with the year in a four-digit format. A cell can be formatted before or after entering the date so the displayed value will be in a different format.

A **fraction** is the number of parts of a whole. For example, the fraction 3/4 represents three parts of the whole number four. The number

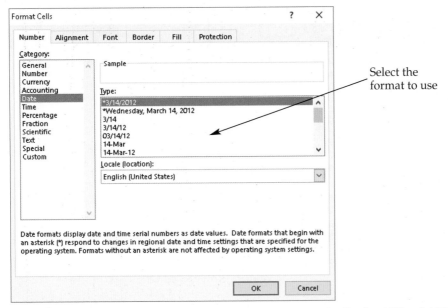

Goodheart-Willcox Publisher

Figure 10-9. When formatting a cell as a date, there are many different formats from which to choose.

on the top is the numerator, or number of parts. The number on the bottom is the denominator, or the whole. In Microsoft Excel, the fraction formatting must be applied to the cell. Usually, the formatting is applied before entering data. In this way, a fraction such as 3/4 will be accepted as a fraction, not the date March 4 of the current year.

A **percentage** is a fraction of 100. For example, 20 percent is the same as 20/100. This may also be written as .2, which is the decimal fractional equivalent. In Microsoft Excel, if the percentage is entered with the symbol, such as 20%, the cell will be automatically formatted for a percentage. The symbol is retained as part of the data. If percentage formatting is applied after the data are entered, the symbol is automatically added to the data. A data entry of .1, for example, will be converted to 10%, *not* 0.1%.

FYI

A decimal fraction is the result of dividing the numerator by the denominator, such as .75 for the fraction 3/4.

HANDS-ON EXAMPLE 10.2.2

FORMATTING NUMBERS

Numbers can represent many different things. Proper cell formatting can help give meaning to the numerical data displayed in a cell.

1. Launch Microsoft Excel, and open the Earnings.xlsx file in the Chap10 folder on your flash drive, if it is not already open.
2. Applying what you have learned, select the range B4:B8.
3. Right-click on the selection, and click **Format Cells...** in the shortcut menu. The **Format Cells** dialog box is displayed.

HANDS-ON EXAMPLE 10.2.2 (CONTINUED)

4. On the **Number** tab of the dialog box, click **Currency** in the **Category:** list, as shown. This specifies the number formatting for the selected cells.

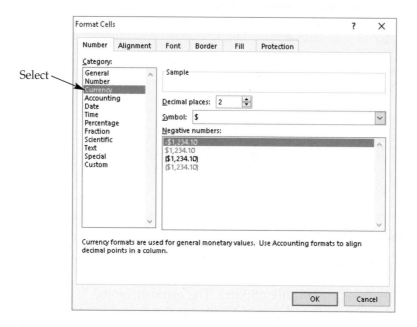

5. Click the **Symbol:** drop-down arrow, and click **$** in the drop-down list. This specifies the currency symbol to be used.
6. Click in the **Decimal places:** text box, and enter 2. Dollar values are usually represented with two decimal places.
7. Click the **OK** button to apply the formatting. Dollar signs appear in front of the value displayed in each cell. Also notice that the displayed value in cell B5 includes the trailing zero where before this was hidden.
8. Save the file.

 Key Applications
3.3

 Key Applications
3.1.2

FYI

In Microsoft Excel, double-clicking between rows or columns in the header area will automatically reduce the size of the row or column to the minimum size.

Formatting Cell Size

If part of the cell content is cut off on the right-hand side of the cell or if several pound signs (#######) appear in the cell, the cell is not wide enough. The cell width is controlled by the column width. The column must be wide enough to allow all of the characters to be visible. If part of the cell content is cut off on the bottom, the cell is not tall enough. The cell height is controlled by the row height. In Microsoft Excel, column width and row height are similarly adjusted in one of three ways.

The first method involves dragging the row or column to resize it. Move the cursor to the header area of the column or row and place it on the edge to move, as shown in Figure 10-10. When the double-arrow resizing cursor appears, click, hold, and drag to resize the column or row.

The second method allows for more precise adjustment of column width or row height. Right-click on the column or row in the header area. This selects the column or row and displays a shortcut menu. Click

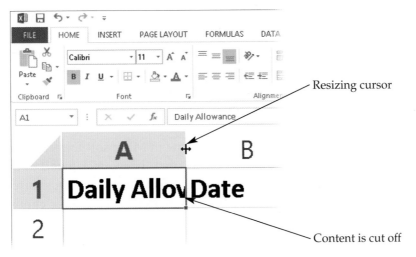

Resizing cursor

Content is cut off

Goodheart-Willcox Publisher

Figure 10-10. A row or column can be dragged to manually resize it.

Column Width… or **Row Height…** in the shortcut menu. In the **Column Width** or **Row Height** dialog box that is displayed, enter the numerical value for the height or width, and click the **OK** button.

The column width and row height can also be changed using commands in the ribbon. Click the **Format** button in the **Cells** group on the **Home** tab of the ribbon. Then, click either **Row height…** or **Column width…** in the drop-down menu. Finally, enter the new height or width in the dialog box that appears.

HANDS-ON EXAMPLE 10.2.3

ADJUSTING COLUMN WIDTH

Adjusting the column width or row height is often needed to improve the readability of the spreadsheet. In some cases, this is done to display hidden content, while in other cases doing so helps the reader locate data.

1. Launch Microsoft Excel, and open the Earnings.xlsx file in the Chap10 folder on your flash drive, if it is not already open.
2. Move the cursor to the line between columns A and B in the header row. The double-arrow cursor is displayed.
3. Click and drag the edge of column A to the right until all of the text in cell A8 is visible. Release the mouse button to set the new width of the column.
4. Save the file.

Adding Columns and Rows

After the spreadsheet is initially created, rows or columns may need to be added to allow for more data or to improve readability of the spreadsheet. To add a column in Microsoft Excel, select the column to the right of where the new column should be added. Then, click the drop-down arrow next to the **Insert Cells** button in the **Cells** group on the **Home**

Key Applications
3.2

Key Applications
3.1.1

FYI

Clicking the **Insert Cells** button instead of the drop-down arrow automatically inserts a column or row, depending on which is selected.

GS5 Key Applications
3.9.1

GS4 Key Applications
3.1.5

tab of the ribbon, and click **Insert Sheet Columns** in the drop-down menu. The new column is added to the *left* of the selected column.

To add a row in Microsoft Excel, select the row below where the new row should be added. Then, click the drop-down arrow next to the **Insert Cells** button in the **Cells** group on the **Home** tab of the ribbon, and click **Insert Sheet Rows** in the drop-down menu. The new row is added above the selected row.

Another way to insert a column or row in Microsoft Excel is to right-click on the column or row in the header area. Then, click **Insert** in the shortcut menu. If right-clicking on a cell, select **Insert...** in the shortcut menu to display the **Insert** dialog box. Then, in the dialog box, choose to insert an entire row or column.

Merging Cells

To **merge** cells is to combine them into a single cell. Cells can be merged horizontally, vertically, or both, as shown in Figure 10-11. Merging cells is usually done to improve the readability of the spreadsheet or to group columns or rows under a title. For example, the title Income may be placed across three rows that represent sources of income.

In Microsoft Excel, the content is automatically horizontally center-aligned when cells are merged. If more than one cell contains data, only the content in the upper-left selected cell is retained. If only one cell contains data, that content is retained regardless of the cell's position in the selection. The **Merge & Center** command is located in the **Alignment** group on the **Home** tab of the ribbon.

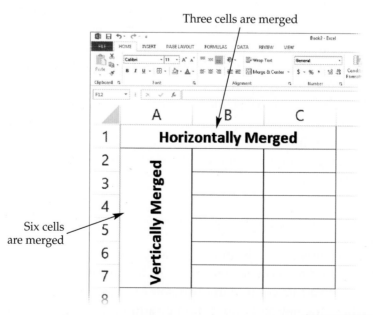

Goodheart-Willcox Publisher

Figure 10-11. Cells can be merged to improve the readability of the spreadsheet.

HANDS-ON EXAMPLE 10.2.4

ADDING COLUMNS

Frequently, a column or row must be added between existing columns or rows in a spreadsheet. Also, it is common to merge cells to improve readability of the spreadsheet.

1. Launch Microsoft Excel, and open the Earnings.xlsx file in the Chap10 folder on your flash drive, if it is not already open.
2. Click the column B header to select the column.

Insert Cells

3. Click the **Insert Cells** button in the **Cells** group on the **Home** tab of the ribbon. A column is added to the left of the selected column. Notice that the new column is column B. All columns are automatically renamed. Also notice the formatting of column A, which was the column to the left, is automatically applied to the new column.
4. Right-click the row 3 header to select the row and display the shortcut menu.
5. Click **Insert** in the shortcut menu. A new row is added above the selected row. Notice the new row is row 3 and the formatting of row 2 is automatically applied.
6. Applying what you have learned, add the text April to cell A2.
7. Applying what you have learned, add a new row at the top of the spreadsheet.
8. Applying what you have learned, add the text Budget to the first empty cell (A1).
9. Select the range A1:D1.

Merge & Center

10. Click the **Merge & Center** button in the **Alignment** group on the **Home** tab of the ribbon. The cells are merged, and the content is centered.
11. Save the file.

Deleting Columns and Rows

Just as there are times a column or row must be added to a spreadsheet, there are times when one must be deleted. Deleting a column or row also deletes all data within the cells. In Microsoft Excel, columns and rows are deleted in a similar manner. Right-click on the header for the column or row to delete, and click **Delete** in the shortcut menu. A selected column or row can also be deleted by clicking the **Delete Cells** button in the **Cells** group on the **Home** tab of the ribbon.

Changing Data Locations

Data that are already present in the spreadsheet can be copied. This is often more efficient, especially for complex data, than reentering the data. Data can also be moved from one location to a different location. Any cell content can be copied or moved. The new data will look exactly the same as the original. When moving content, any formulas that reference the content are automatically updated to the new content location.

Copying Cells

When a cell is copied, a duplicate appears in the new location. However, the original cell is unaffected, and there is no reference between the original and copied data. Any formula referencing the original cell will continue to reference the original cell.

> # FYI
>
> Pressing the [Delete] key when a column or row is selected will clear the contents, but will not remove the column or row.

Key Applications
GS5 3.9.2

To copy a cell in Microsoft Excel, select the source cell. Next, press the [Ctrl][C] key combination, click the **Copy** button in the **Clipboard** group on the **Home** tab of the ribbon, or right-click on the cell and click **Copy** in the shortcut menu. A marquee appears around the original cell to indicate this is what will be pasted, as shown in Figure 10-12. Next, select the destination cell. Finally, press the [Ctrl][V] key combination, click the **Paste** button in the **Clipboard** group on the **Home** tab of the ribbon, or right-click on the destination cell and click **Paste** in the shortcut menu. As long as the marquee appears on the source cell, the contents can be pasted into several locations. To end the operation, press the [Esc] key.

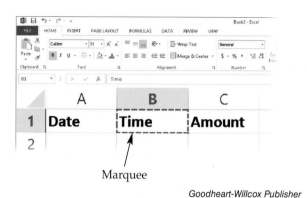

Goodheart-Willcox Publisher

Figure 10-12. The marquee indicates the cell has been copied and is ready to be pasted.

When copying a formula in Excel, any cell references in the formula will be altered based on the new location. For example, if the formula in cell A3 is =A1+A2 and is copied to cell B3, the new formula will be =B1+B2. This is because the destination cell is one column to the right of the source (from column A to column B). If the formula is copied to cell B2, a reference error will be displayed. Because the destination cell is one column to the right (from column A to B) and one row above (from row 3 to 2) the source, the formula would in essence become =B0+B1. There is no cell B0, so Excel displays the reference error. This is an important concept to remember in Excel.

Moving Cells

When a cell is moved, a duplicate appears in the new location and content in original cell is erased. Any formula referencing the original cell will be automatically updated to reference the cell in the new location. However, unlike when a cell is copied, if the moved cell contains a formula, cell references within the formula are *not* altered based on the new location.

To move a cell in Microsoft Excel, the cut function is used. First, select the source cell. Next, press the [Ctrl][X] key combination, click the **Cut** button in the **Clipboard** group on the **Home** tab of the ribbon, or right-click on the cell and click **Cut** in the shortcut menu. A flashing marquee appears around the cut cell. Next, select the destination cell. Finally, press the [Ctrl][V] key combination, click the **Paste** button in the **Clipboard** group on the **Home** tab of the ribbon, or right-click on the destination cell and click **Paste** in the shortcut menu. The operation is immediately ended. A cut cell cannot be repeatedly pasted in multiple locations.

FYI

A cell can be moved in Microsoft Excel by selecting it, clicking and dragging the outline around the cell, and dropping it in the new location.

HANDS-ON EXAMPLE 10.2.5

COPYING CELLS

Cells are often copied once a section of a spreadsheet is complete. For example, the income for one month is set up in rows and columns, these cells can be quickly copied as a starting point for the next month.

1. Launch Microsoft Excel, and open the Earnings.xlsx file in the Chap10 folder on your flash drive, if it is not already open.
2. Add the text May to cell A13.
3. Applying what you have learned, remove the background color from cell A13.
4. Select the range A4:A10.
5. Press the [Ctrl][C] key combination. A marquee appears around the range to indicate the selection is copied.
6. Select cell A14.
7. Press the [Ctrl][V] key combination. The selected range is pasted with cell A14 as the upper-left corner of the range, as shown. In this case, there is only one column in the range, so A14 is the upper cell in the pasted range.
8. Press the [Esc] key to end the operation.
9. Save the file.

Rearranging Data

On occasion, it is advantageous to copy a particular formula from one place to another in a spreadsheet. For example, when keeping a running tab of checkbook activity, each row is similar. The pattern is to add a credit or subtract a debit from the checkbook total.

What if a cell reference is used in the formula? As discussed earlier, the software will automatically update the cell reference, but what if the reference should *not* be updated? In this case, it is necessary to tell the software not to change the cell reference. In Microsoft Excel, the dollar sign ($) is used in a formula to tell Excel which references can be updated and which ones must not be changed. This character does not change the calculation, but instead acts like glue to keep the formula stuck to the original reference. The two types of cell references are relative cell addresses and absolute cell addresses.

Relative Cell Addresses

A **relative cell address** is specified as the number of rows and columns that the second cell is from the first cell. For example, if the formula stored in cell B1 is =D5–F8, D5 refers to the content of cell D5. Cell D5 is located two columns to the right and four rows below cell B1. Another way to state this is cell D5 is plus two columns and plus four rows *relative* to cell B1. Refer to Figure 10-13A.

Career Skills

Purchasing Manager
Purchasing managers, purchasing agents, and buyers acquire materials for agencies to use. They assess suppliers, evaluate product quality, and negotiate product acquisition contracts. They use technology to manage budgets, search for products, track purchases, and maintain supplier relationships. Often the program of choice is spreadsheet software because of its ability to rapidly update totals and keep track of spending.

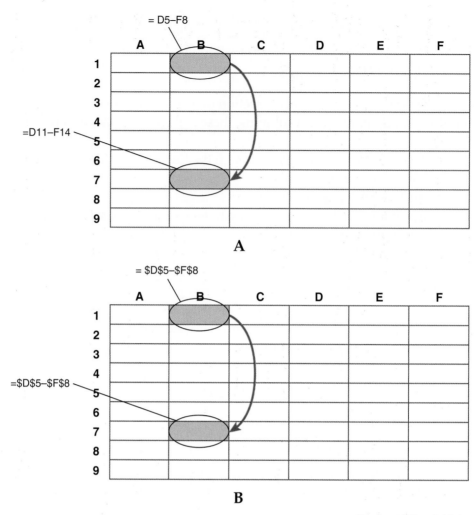

Goodheart-Willcox Publisher

Figure 10-13. A—If relative cell addresses are used, the references are automatically updated if the formula is copied. B—If absolute cell addresses are used, the references are not changed if the formula is copied.

FYI

To see which cells are referenced in a formula, double-click the cell containing the formula. The referenced cells will be outlined in the spreadsheet.

If the formula in cell B1 is copied to cell B7, the cell references in the formula will maintain this relative addressing. Therefore, the formula references cells D11 and F14. Cell D11 is two columns to the right of and four rows below cell B7. Cell F14 is four columns to the right of and seven rows below cell B7, which is the same relative address used in the original formula.

Absolute Cell Addresses

If a formula must always use the content of a specific cell, an absolute cell address must be entered. An **absolute cell address** indicates the formula will refer to the specified cell no matter where the formula is moved or copied. In Microsoft Excel, the dollar sign ($) specifies an absolute cell address. Enter dollar signs before the column letter and row number, as shown in Figure 10-13B.

For example, if the formula in cell B1 is =$D$5–$F$8, $D$5 refers to the content of the cell located in column D and row 5. If the formula in cell B1 is copied to cell B7, the cell references in the formula remain cells D5 and F8. The dollar signs tell Excel not to update the cell addresses.

A formula in a cell may contain a combination of relative and absolute cell addressing, such as =MAX(A2:A12)/$B$1. This formula tells Excel to locate the largest value of the cells in the range A2:A12 and that value is divided by the content in cell B1. If this formula is moved from cell D4 to cell D5, the formula is updated to =MAX(A3:A13)/$B$1. Notice that the relative cell address of the range is updated, but the absolute cell address of cell B1 is not updated.

HANDS-ON EXAMPLE 10.2.6

RELATIVE AND ABSOLUTE CELL ADDRESSES

Copying existing formulas is an efficient way to develop a spreadsheet. When doing so, it is important to understand how relative and absolute cell addresses are used by the software.

1. Launch Microsoft Excel, and begin a new blank spreadsheet.
2. Save the spreadsheet as Fundraising.xlsx in the Chap10 folder on your flash drive.
3. Add the text Funds Tracking to cell A1.
4. Add the text Name to cell A3.
5. Add the text January, February, and March to cells B3 through D3.
6. Add the text Total to cell E3.
7. Add your first name and the first names of two classmates to cells A4 through A6.
8. Add the text Monthly Total to cell A7.
9. Applying what you have learned, adjust the columns as needed to be as wide as the widest text entry.
10. Add dollar amounts of your own choosing to the cells in the range B4:D6. Format the cells as appropriate.
11. Enter the formula =B4+C4+D4 in cell E4. This formula totals the three values.
12. Applying what you have learned, copy cell E4 and paste it into cells E5 and E6.
13. Activate cell E6 for editing. Notice the relative cell addresses in the formula were automatically updated, as shown.

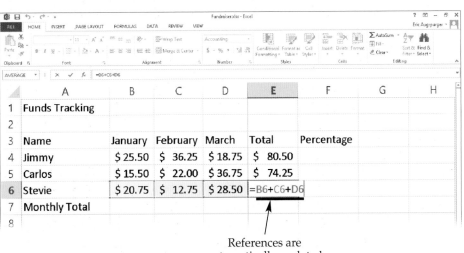

References are automatically updated

HANDS-ON EXAMPLE 10.2.6 (CONTINUED)

14. Applying what you have learned, add formulas to cells B7 through E7 to total each month and calculate the grand total. Use copy and paste as appropriate to improve your efficiency.

15. Add the text Percentage to cell F3. This column will be used to calculate what part of the total each student submitted.

16. Applying what you have learned, format the range F4:F6 for percentages.

17. Enter the formula =E4/E7 to cell F4. This formula calculates percentage of the whole by dividing the individual's total by the grand total.

18. Copy the formula in cell F4 to cells F5 and F6. Cells F5 and F6 will display a divide by zero error of #DIV/0!.

19. Select cell F5, and examine the formula in the formula bar. When the formula was copied from cell F4, both cell references were updated, however the cell containing the grand total has not moved and remains cell E7. The solution is to use an absolute cell address in the formula for cell E7.

20. Applying what you have learned, edit the formula in cell F4 so there is a $ before the column and row reference to cell E7: =E4/$E$7.

21. Copy the updated formula in cell F4 to cells F5 and F6. Notice calculated values are now displayed instead of the error message.

22. Select cell F6, and examine the formula in the formula bar. Notice the relative cell address is updated to cell E6, which is the student's total, but the absolute cell address is not updated and remains cell E7, which is the grand total.

23. Save the file.

Locating and Organizing Data

GS5 Key Applications
3.4

GS4 Key Applications
3.2.1

A large spreadsheet may contain hundreds or thousands of data. In order to use the spreadsheet, the data must be located. Instead of scrolling through the spreadsheet, the search or find function of the software can be used to locate data.

Often data are entered into a spreadsheet in the order received. This may not be the best order for evaluating the data. For example, if compiling an inventory, each item is entered when it is tallied. However, after all of the items are entered, it may make sense to view the data with similar items grouped together.

In some cases, only part of the data needs to be viewed. By excluding, or filtering, those data that do not need to be seen, the spreadsheet can be more manageable.

Finding Data

Most software that deals with text and numbers has some sort of search or find function. Spreadsheet software is no different. The basic process for locating data in a spreadsheet is the same as locating a word in a word-processing document. For example, to find all rows that include a particular name, the search or find function can be used with the name as the search phrase to locate the rows containing the name.

To find data in Microsoft Excel, click the **Find & Select** button in the **Editing** group on the **Home** tab of the ribbon, and click **Find...** in the shortcut menu. The **Find and Replace** dialog box is displayed, as shown in Figure 10-14. Click in the **Find what:** text box, and enter the data to locate. Finally, click the **Find Next** button to locate the next instance of the data from the current cell forward in the spreadsheet.

Sorting Data

Sorting is arranging data in a spreadsheet by criteria. For example, suppose the spreadsheet contains a list of movies, the date each was released, and the starring actors for each. These data can be sorted to place the list in alphabetic order by title.

To use the sort feature in Microsoft Excel, click the **Sort & Filter** button in the **Editing** group on the **Home** tab of the ribbon to display a drop-down menu, as shown in Figure 10-15. Select the appropriate command in the drop-down menu. The **Sort Smallest to Largest** command arranges the data in **ascending order**, such as A to Z or 1 to 10. The **Sort Largest to Smallest** command arranges the data in **descending order**, such as Z to A or 10 to 1. The **Custom Sort** command provides options for sorting multiple columns and rows rather than columns.

FYI

The [Ctrl][F] key combination is a shortcut to the search or find function in most software.

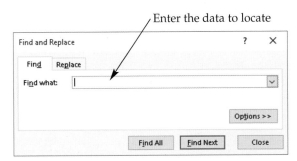

Goodheart-Willcox Publisher

Figure 10-14. The find function can be used to locate specific data.

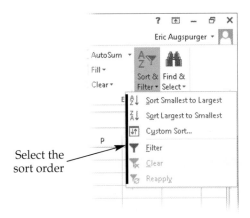

Goodheart-Willcox Publisher

Figure 10-15. Data can be sorted in ascending or descending order.

Key Applications
GS4
3.2.1

FYI

In Microsoft Excel, a sort can also be performed using the filter drop-down menu.

Filtering Data

In many cases, not all of the data need to be viewed at the same time. **Filtering** allows some data to be hidden from view. To use the filter feature in Microsoft Excel, first select a single cell within a range of data. Then, click the **Sort & Filter** button in the **Editing** group on the **Home** tab of the ribbon, and click **Filter** in the drop-down menu. Excel displays drop-down arrows in the cells it believes to be headings, as shown in Figure 10-16. To filter the data, click the drop-down arrow to display a drop-down menu, and uncheck the items to hide.

Drop-down arrows

Click to display a drop-down menu

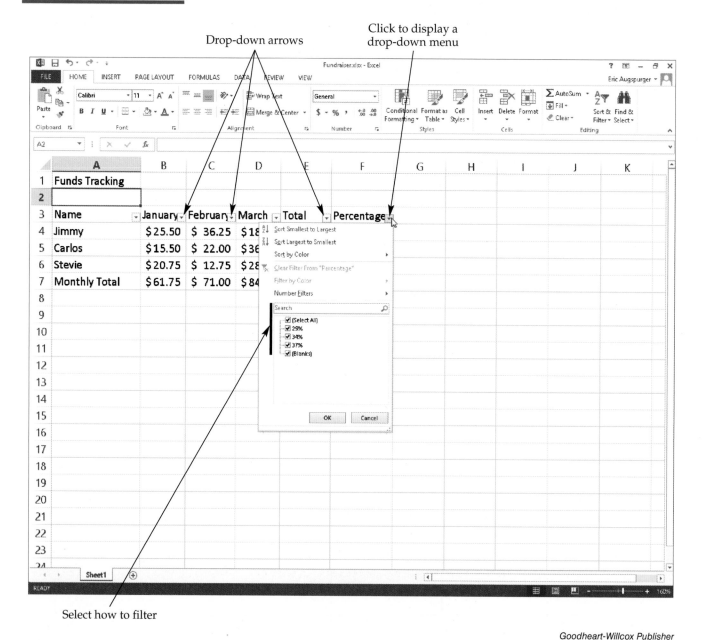

Select how to filter

Figure 10-16. To filter data, click the drop-down arrow, and then select how to filter in the drop-down menu.

HANDS-ON EXAMPLE 10.2.7

GS5 | Key Applications 3.12

SORTING DATA

One of the benefits of a computerized spreadsheet is the ability to sort data. For example, in a sales report spreadsheet, it is possible to organize data by products and isolate a certain product from all others.

1. Launch Microsoft Excel 2013.
2. On the startup screen, click in the search text box, enter sales report, and click the **Search** button (magnifying glass).
3. In the list of returned results, locate the Sales report template, and click it. Click the **Create** button in the preview that is displayed to start a new spreadsheet based on this template.
4. Examine the spreadsheet. The first row contains headings for the product, customer, and four fiscal quarters. It is currently sorted on the Product column.
5. Select any cell in the Customer column.

Sort & Filter

6. Click the **Sort & Filter** button in the **Editing** group on the **Home** tab of the ribbon, and click **Sort A to Z** in the drop-down menu. Notice how the rows of data are rearranged in alphabetical order based on the customer name, as shown.

Sorted by name

	A	B	C	D	E	F	G
1	Product	Customer	Qtr 1	Qtr 2	Qtr 3	Qtr 4	
2	Aniseed Syrup	ALFKI	$ -	$ -	$ -	$ 60.00	
3	Veggie-spread	ALFKI	$ -	$ -	$ -	$ 878.00	
4	Camembert Pierrot	ANATR	$ -	$ -	$ 340.00	$ -	
5	Alice Mutton	ANTON	$ -	$ 702.00	$ -	$ -	
6	Boston Crab Meat	ANTON	$ -	$ 165.60	$ -	$ -	
7	Ipoh Coffee	ANTON	$ -	$ 586.50	$ -	$ -	
8	Louisiana Hot Spiced Okra	ANTON	$ -	$ -	$ 68.00	$ -	
9	Ravioli Angelo	ANTON	$ -	$ 87.75	$ -	$ -	
10	Sasquatch Ale	ANTON	$ -	$ 560.00	$ -	$ -	
11	Camembert Pierrot	AROUT	$ -	$ -	$ -	$ 510.00	
12	Filo Mix	AROUT	$ -	$ 210.00	$ -	$ 56.00	

7. Applying what you have learned, sort the Qtr 1 column from largest to smallest.
8. Click the **Sort & Filter** button in the **Editing** group on the **Home** tab of the ribbon, and click **Custom Sort...** in the drop-down menu.
9. In the **Sort** dialog box that is displayed, click the **Sort by** drop-down arrow, and click **Customer** in the drop-down list.
10. Click the **Order** drop-down arrow, and click **A to Z** in the drop-down list.
11. Click the **Add Level** button to add a second sort criterion.
12. Applying what you have learned, set the second criterion to sort by product in ascending order.
13. Click the **OK** button to apply the custom sort. Notice how the data are arranged first alphabetically by customer and then alphabetically by product name for each customer.

Find & Select

14. Click the **Find & Select** button in the **Editing** group on the **Home** tab of the ribbon, and click **Find...** in the drop-down menu. The **Find and Replace** dialog box is displayed.

HANDS-ON EXAMPLE 10.2.7 (CONTINUED)

15. Click in the **Find what:** text box, and enter quick.
16. Click the **Find All** button. The locations of all instances of the text *quick* are displayed at the bottom of the **Find and Replace** dialog box.
17. Close the **Find and Replace** dialog box.
18. Select cell A1, which is the Product column heading.

Sort & Filter

19. Click the **Sort & Filter** button in the **Editing** group on the **Home** tab of the ribbon, and click **Filter** in the drop-down menu. A drop-down arrow appears in all of the heading cells in the first row.
20. Click the drop-down arrow in cell A1, and uncheck the **(Select All)** check box in the list in the drop-down menu.
21. Check the Boston Crab Meat check box in the list in the drop-down menu, and then click the **OK** button. Only the rows containing the product Boston Crab Meat are displayed in the spreadsheet. Two visual hints that the data have been filtered are the row numbers are not consecutive and a filter icon appears in drop-down arrow at the top of the Product column.
22. Click the drop-down arrow at the top of the Product column, and click **Clear Filter From "Product"** in the drop-down menu. The data are no longer filtered.
23. Close the file without saving it.

Printing a Spreadsheet

Often, a spreadsheet is used only in electronic form. However, there may be times when a hard copy of the spreadsheet is needed. To improve the readability of the printed spreadsheet, cells can be outlined or the grid set to print. Without this, there will be no visible definition of the cells on the printout other than the cell content. Additionally, before printing a spreadsheet, it should be previewed.

The steps to print in Microsoft Excel are similar to those used to print in Microsoft Word. Click **Print** in the **File** tab of the ribbon. In the backstage view, set the printing options such as which pages to print, which printer to use, and the paper orientation. A preview of the printed spreadsheet also appears in the backstage view.

Outlining Cells

A border can be drawn around cells. This can be done for emphasis or to improve readability, either on-screen or when the spreadsheet is printed. See Figure 10-17.

To add a border to cells in Microsoft Excel, first select the cell or range to which the border will be applied. Next, click the drop-down arrow next to the **Bottom Border** button in the **Font** group on the **Home** tab of the ribbon. Note: the name of this button will change based on the last selection made in the drop-down menu. In the drop-down menu, click the type of border to apply. There are many choices for borders.

FYI

The [Ctrl][P] key combination is a shortcut for the printing function in most software.

If a range of cells is selected, it is considered as one cell for applying a border. For example, if three cells are selected and the **Outside Borders** option is selected, a border is placed around the group, not each individual cell.

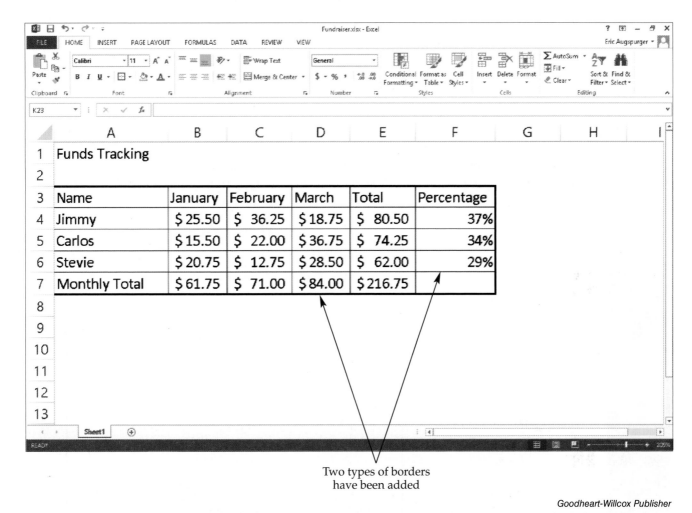

Two types of borders
have been added

Figure 10-17. Borders can be used to emphasize parts of the spreadsheet or make it easier to read.

TITANS OF TECHNOLOGY

Edward Rolf Tufte (pronounced *TOUGH-tee*) is an American statistician, political scientist, and professor. He earned his bachelor and master degrees in statistics from Stanford University and his doctorate in political science from Yale. While teaching political economy and data analysis at Princeton University in the 1970s, Tufte was asked to teach a statistics course to a group of journalists who needed to learn economics. He developed lectures on statistical graphics, which became his first book on information design, *The Visual Display of Quantitative Information*. The book quickly became a success, and he became known as an information expert as well as a political scientist. Tufte coined the term *chatjunk*, which refers to elements in graphs and charts that are useless, do not inform, or confuse the data. In 2010, President Obama appointed Tufte to the American Recovery and Reinvestment Act Independent Advisory Panel "to provide transparency in the use" of the funds.

Printing the Grid

By default, the grid is displayed in Microsoft Excel, but will not be printed. However, the grid can be set to print. This can be an alternative to applying borders to cells.

To set the grid to print, check the **Gridlines Print** check box in the **Sheet Options** group on the **Page Layout** tab of the ribbon. When this is checked, the grid will be printed in an area from the first upper-left cell containing data to the last lower-right cell containing data, as shown in Figure 10-18.

Header and Footer

A header or footer can be added to the printed spreadsheet. Just as with a word-processing document, the header and footer appear on every page. The header and footer can be used to provide information about the

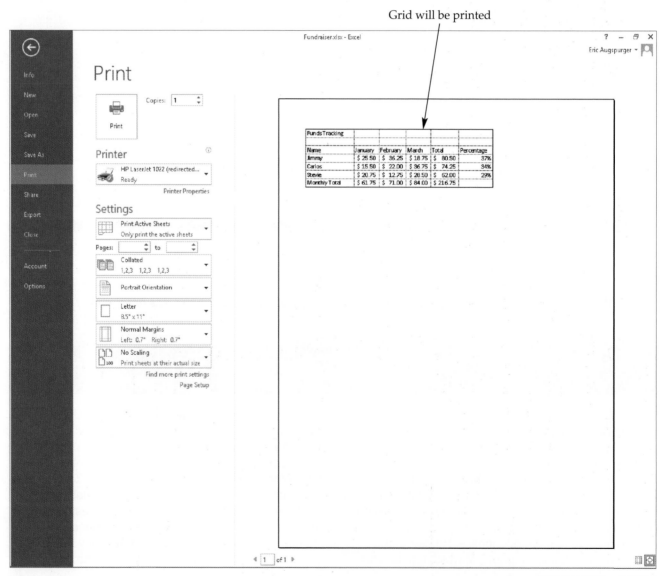

Goodheart-Willcox Publisher

Figure 10-18. The grid can be set to print. This is done in the **Page Layout** tab of the ribbon.

spreadsheet, such as the author, the date the spreadsheet was printed, or the file name of the spreadsheet file.

To add a header or footer to a spreadsheet in Microsoft Excel, click the **Header & Footer** button in the **Text** group on the **Insert** tab of the ribbon. Note: depending on your screen configuration, this group may be collapsed to a single button. The print layout view is displayed, and the center header text box is active. Enter text in this text box or click in the left- or right-hand header text box and enter text. To add text to the footer, click the **Go to Footer** button in the **Navigation** group on the **Design** on-demand tab of the ribbon. The footer similarly has left-hand, center, and right-hand text boxes.

To insert a page number in any of the header or footer text boxes, click the **Page Number** button in the **Header & Footer Elements** group on the **Design** on-demand tab of the ribbon. Other options located in the same group include **Number of Pages**, **Current Date**, **Current Time**, **File Path**, **File Name**, and **Sheet Name**.

FYI

To exit the page layout view, click outside the header or footer text box, and then click the **Normal View** button in the **Workbook Views** group on the **View** tab of the ribbon.

10.2 | SECTION REVIEW

 ### CHECK YOUR UNDERSTANDING

1. What three properties of a typeface can be changed to format the text?
2. Which key combinations are used to move the content of a cell?
3. Which type of cell address allows a formula to be automatically updated if the formula is moved?
4. What is the difference between sorting and filtering?
5. What is the purpose of adding a border around cells?

IC3 CERTIFICATION PRACTICE

The following question is a sample of the types of questions presented on the IC3 exam.

1. Write a formula that adds the value of cell A5 to B6 using an absolute address for A5.

BUILD YOUR VOCABULARY

As you progress through this course, develop a personal IT glossary. This will help you build your vocabulary and prepare you for a career. Write a definition for each of the following terms and add it to your IT glossary.

absolute cell address
ascending order
descending order
filtering
fraction
merge
percentage
relative cell address
sorting
wrap text

Chapter Summary

Section 10.1
Introduction to Spreadsheets

- A spreadsheet is a collection of data arranged in rows and columns. Manual spreadsheets continued to be used after the advent of computerized spreadsheet software until VisiCalc was created for the Apple II personal computer in the late 1970s.

- Columns are the spaces between the vertical grid lines, rows are the spaces between the horizontal grid lines, and a cell is where a column and row intersect. The mouse can be used to navigate a spreadsheet, but most efficient users primarily navigate with the keyboard.

- The data type for a cell determines what the data entered in the cell mean. There are several common data types used in computer programming.

- The most basic formulas in a spreadsheet are simple algebra. When a formula is entered into a cell, the software automatically executes the calculation and displays the result as the cell value.

- A powerful feature of a computerized spreadsheet is the ease of correcting errors. However, the real power lies in the ability to change or update data repeatedly, which allows a what-if analysis.

Section 10.2
Managing Data in Spreadsheets

- Formatting the spreadsheet may be necessary to make the data understandable. This may involve changing the column and row sizes or changing the styles, size, or color of the values displayed in cells.

- Data can be copied or moved to change their location in a spreadsheet. Any formulas that reference the content are automatically updated to the new content location.

- Data can be rearranged without cell references being automatically updated. An absolute cell address indicates the formula will refer to the specified cell no matter where the formula is moved or copied.

- There are several tools to help in locating data. The search or find function can locate specific data, the sort function displays data in ascending or descending order, and the filter function displays only data that meet certain criteria.

- In many cases, a spreadsheet is only used in electronic form, but a spreadsheet can be printed. Cells can be outlined before printing to improve readability, and headers and footers can be included on the page.

Now that you have finished this chapter, see what you know about information technology by scanning the QR code to take the chapter posttest. If you do not have a smartphone, visit www.g-wlearning.com.

Chapter 10 Test

Multiple Choice

Select the best response.

1. What is used to name each cell?
    A. worksheet name and row
    B. column and row
    C. numbers
    D. letters

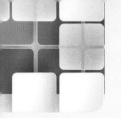

2. What determines the meaning of data entered in a cell?
   A. value
   B. format
   C. filter
   D. data type

3. Which of the following is not a common formatting for numbers in a spreadsheet?
   A. currency
   B. dates
   C. absolute
   D. fractions

4. Which of the following is the proper way to write a relative cell address?
   A. C4
   B. $C4
   C. C$4
   D. $C$4

5. What is a way in which to limit the data displayed?
   A. Filtering
   B. Searching
   C. Finding
   D. Sorting

Completion

Complete the following sentences with the correct word(s).

6. _____ is the cocreator of the first computerized spreadsheet software for personal computers.

7. By default, numbers in a cell are aligned to the _____.

8. When more than one cell is selected, the selection is called a(n) _____ of cells.

9. If _____ appear(s) in a cell, the value is wider than the cell.

10. The _____ function is used to locate specific data in a spreadsheet.

Matching

Match the correct term with its definition.

   A. active cell
   B. what-if scenario
   C. wrap text
   D. absolute cell address
   E. descending order

11. Used to lock the cell reference in a formula.

12. A new line within the cell will be automatically started when the length of the text exceeds the width of the cell.

13. Arranging data from largest to smallest.

14. Currently selected cell.

15. Used to see what happens if cell data are changed.

Application and Extension of Knowledge

1. Create a spreadsheet to keep a running balance of a debit card. Enter the data shown below. Format the cells under the Credit, Debit, and Balance headings as the accounting number format. In the Balance column, enter a formula in each cell that adds the previous balance to any credit in the row or subtracts any debit in the row. What is the formula entered in cell E4? How much money is in the account on April 10?

Item	Date	Credit	Debit	Balance
Beginning balance	April 5	$ 42.56		
Paycheck	April 6	$ 345.10		
Groceries	April 10		$ 68.97	

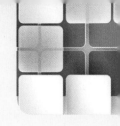

2. The value of cell A1 is 32, B1 is 42, and C1 is 2. Using a spreadsheet, find the value of each of the following formulas if entered in cell D1.
   A. =(A1+B1)*C1
   B. =A1+B1*C1
   C. =(B1–A1)/C1
   D. =B1–A1/C1

3. Create a spreadsheet to track the amount of time you spent doing certain activities or tasks throughout the day yesterday. This may include classes, homework, sports, leisure time, work, or anything else you did. Record the time as the number of minutes, such as 5, 30, or 75. Create a formula to calculate the average amount of time spent on each activity. If necessary, research how to calculate an average. What is the average amount of time you spent on each activity?

4. A checkbook register is used to manually keep track of money going into and out of a checking account. Locate an example of a blank checkbook register. Then, set up a spreadsheet to perform this function. Create formulas as needed to automate your electronic spreadsheet register.

5. The formula for calculating simple interest on a loan is A = P(1+rt), where P is the amount borrowed, r is the annual interest rate as a decimal fraction (such as .05 for 5 percent), and t is the term (time) of the loan. Select something you would like to borrow money to purchase, such as a car. Use a spreadsheet to create a what-if scenario for the simple interest on the loan. See how changing the amount borrowed, interest rate, and length of the loan affect the total amount of money you have to pay the bank.

Online Activities

Complete the following activities, which will help you learn, practice, and expand your knowledge and skills.

Certification Practice. Complete the certification practice test for this chapter.

Vocabulary. Practice vocabulary for this chapter using the e-flash cards, matching activity, and vocabulary game until you are able to recognize their meanings.

Communication Skills

College and Career Readiness

Reading. Read the Ethics features throughout this text. What role do you think ethics and integrity have in the field of information technology? Think about a time when you used your ideals and principles to make a decision related to information technology, such as software use or a digital download. What process did you use to make the decision? Looking back, did you make the correct decision?

Writing. Generate ideas for writing a paper that describes the concept of information technology as you understand it. Gather information to support your thoughts and ideas. Keep careful and accurate records of any sources you use as references. Create the notes that you could use to write a paper.

Speaking. To become career ready, it is important to learn how to communicate clearly and effectively by using reason. Create an outline that includes information about using a spreadsheet to track customer data. Consider who will be your audience as you prepare the information. Using the outline, make a presentation to your class.

Internet Research

History of the Internet. Research the history of the Internet using various resources. Why was the Internet first developed? When did the Internet become standardized? Write several paragraphs describing what you learned. Use correct punctuation as you write and edit your document.

Teamwork

By joining a CTSO, students can learn leadership qualities and how to prepare for school and career opportunities. Working with your team, make a list of the CTSOs that are available at your school. Do any of them relate specifically to information technology? What activities are provided for students in each of these organizations? What kinds of professional development activities are available? How can your school CTSO help you prepare for life after graduation? Share your findings with the class.

Portfolio Development

Technical Skills. Your portfolio should showcase your technical skills. Are you exceptionally good working with computers? Do you have a talent for creating videos? Technical skills are important for succeeding in school or at work.

College and Career Readiness

1. Create a Microsoft Word document that describes the technical skills you have acquired. Use the heading "Technical Skills" and your name. Describe the skill, your level of competence, and any other information that will showcase your skill level. Save the document file.

2. Create a master spreadsheet to track your documents.

CTSOs

Communications Skills. Competitive events may also judge communications skills. Presenters must be able to exchange information with the judges in a clear, concise manner. This requirement is in keeping with the mission of CTSOs: to prepare students for professional careers in business. Communication skills will be judged for both the written and oral presentation. The evaluation will include all aspects of effective writing, speaking, and listening skills. To prepare for the business communications portion of an event, complete the following activities.

1. Visit the organization's website and look for specific communication skills that will be judged as a part of a competitive event.

2. Spend time to review the essential principles of business communication.

3. If you are making a written presentation, ask an instructor to evaluate your writing. Review and apply the feedback so that your writing sample appears professional and correct.

4. If you are making an oral presentation, ask an instructor to review and listen for errors in grammar or sentence structure. After you have received comments, adjust and practice the presentation several times until you are comfortable.

5. Review the Communication Skills activities that appear at the end of each chapter of this text as a way to practice your reading, writing, listening, and speaking skills.

6. To practice listening skills, ask your instructor to give you a set of directions. Then, without assistance, repeat those directions to your instructor. Did you listen closely enough to be able to do what was instructed?

11
ADVANCED SPREADSHEET USES

CHECK YOUR IT IQ

Before you begin this chapter, see what you already know about information technology by scanning the QR code to take the chapter pretest. If you do not have a smartphone, visit www.g-wlearning.com.

Spreadsheet software makes it possible to complete projects that require repetitive calculations, such as budgeting, processing a payroll, maintaining a grade book, balancing a checkbook, or calculating loan payments. When financial decisions need to be made, spreadsheet software can be used to calculate how much must be paid in taxes or how much a monthly payment would be for a car loan. A what-if analysis can be devised to compare which arrangements are more advantageous before making a monetary commitment.

Spreadsheet software can also create colorful charts. Long columns of numbers can be hard to analyze. The meaning of the data may not be apparent. By displaying the data in a chart, it may be easier to decipher what the data mean. Charts created in spreadsheet software can also be used in word-processing documents. This allows data in a spreadsheet to be represented in graphic form in a report.

IC3 CERTIFICATION OBJECTIVES

GS5

Key Applications

Domain 3.0 Spreadsheets
    Objective 3.5 Understand functions, formulas, and operators
    Objective 3.7 Use and create spreadsheet charts
    Objective 3.8 Create spreadsheet tables

GS4

Key Applications

Domain 3.0 Spreadsheet activities
    Objective 3.2 Data management

Reading Prep. Skim the Chapter Test questions at the end of the chapter first. Use them to help you focus on the most important concepts as you read the chapter.

College and Career Readiness

CALCULATING WITH FUNCTIONS

Essential Question

How can advanced functions of spreadsheet software impact your life?

One method of adding the values in a column or row of numbers is to write a formula that specifies the individual cell addresses, such as =A3+A4+A5+A6. What if the sum of the content of 100 cells is needed? The address of each of the 100 cells would be in this formula. That would make for a very long formula. To enter this long formula requires some time, and the process would be tedious. The opportunities for errors in writing the formula are great.

Functions, or calculation shortcuts, built into the spreadsheet software simplify the work of creating complex formulas. These shortcuts range from commonly used formulas to complex mathematical and financial calculations. Whenever possible, functions should be used to improve efficiency and accuracy in creating formulas in a spreadsheet.

wavebreakmedia/Shutterstock.com

LEARNING GOALS

After completing this section, you will be able to:
- Describe the use of functions in a spreadsheet.
- Discuss creating complex financial formulas in a spreadsheet.
- Use logical functions in spreadsheet formulas.

TERMS

arguments
function
logical functions
principal
term

Using Functions

Most spreadsheet software contains many formulas that have already been programmed. A preprogrammed formula in spreadsheet software is called a **function**. Functions are usually divided into categories, including financial, statistical, mathematical, date and time, and logical. All of these are available through the function library.

To see a list of all available functions, click the **Insert Function** button in the **Function Library** group on the **Formulas** tab of the ribbon. The **Insert Function** dialog box appears, as shown in Figure 11-1. Click the drop-down arrow in the dialog box, and click **All** in the drop-down list. All available functions are listed in the dialog box.

Functions in Microsoft Excel are written in a specific pattern. They begin with an equals sign, just like all formulas, followed by the function name. Next are the parameters or **arguments**, which are values the function needs for the calculation, enclosed in parentheses. Sometimes the arguments can be a range of cells or a cell address that contains critical values. If multiple cell addresses are used as the arguments, they must be separated by commas.

Common Functions

Commonly used functions include **SUM**, **AVERAGE**, **TODAY**, **MIN**, **MAX**, and **IF**. These functions cover calculations for which spreadsheets are often used.

The **SUM** function finds the sum of a list of numbers or the content of a range of cells. For example, to find the sum of the content in cells C4 to C10, or the range C4:C10, the function is written as = SUM(C4:C10).

The **AVERAGE** function finds the average value of the arguments. For example, to find the average of the content in cells B12 to B25, the function is written as =AVERAGE(B12:B25).

GS5 Key Applications
3.5.1, 3.5.2, 3.5.3

GS4 Key Applications
3.2.2

FYI

A shortcut to the **SUM** function in Excel is to click the **AutoSum** button in the **Editing** group on the **Home** tab of the ribbon.

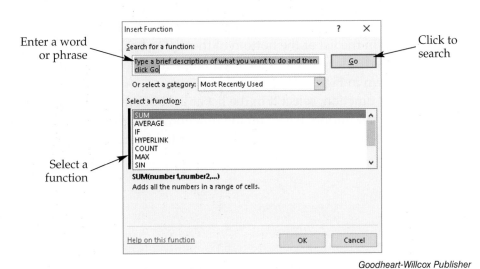

Goodheart-Willcox Publisher

Figure 11-1. The **Insert Function** dialog box can be used to help locate and insert functions.

The **TODAY** function returns the current date. This function does not require an argument, but it must still have open and closed parentheses. This function is written as =TODAY().

The **MIN** function returns the lowest value of the range specified in the argument. For example, to find the lowest value in the range A1:D5, the function is written as =MIN(A1:D5). **MIN** is short for *minimum*.

The **MAX** function returns the highest value of the range specified in the argument. For example, to find the highest value in the range C10:G25, the function is written as =MAX(C10:G25). **MAX** is short for *maximum*.

The **IF** function is a logical function, which is used to make a decision. Logical functions are discussed later in this section.

Entering Functions

GS5 Key Applications
3.5.3

GS4 Key Applications
3.2.2

To add a function to the spreadsheet in Microsoft Excel, select the cell to which the formula will be added. Then, enter the function. If you know the correct syntax of the function and arguments, the function can be directly entered using the keyboard. For example, the correct syntax to find the minimum value is =MIN(*arguments*), not =MINIMUM(*arguments*).

If you are unsure of the syntax or do not know the name of the function, use the **Insert Function** dialog box. To display this dialog box, click the **Insert Function** button in the **Function Library** group on the **Formulas** tab of the ribbon.

The drop-down list in the middle of the dialog box can be used to filter the list at the bottom of the dialog box. Click the drop-down arrow, and select the category of functions to show.

If the name of the function is not known, click in the **Search for function:** text box at the top of the box, and enter keywords for what you want to do. Then, click the **Go** button. Excel will display the functions it believes are related to the action you entered in the list at the bottom of the dialog box.

For example, if you want to find the number of cells in a range that are blank, enter blank cells in the **Search for function:** text box, and click the **Go** button. In the list at the bottom of the dialog box, select a function. The function is displayed below the list along with a description of what it does, as shown in Figure 11-2.

To insert a function, select it in the list at the bottom of the dialog box. Then, click the **OK** button. Based on the function, an additional dialog box appears for entering the arguments needed for the function.

FYI

Double-clicking the name of a function in the list in the **Insert Function** dialog box inserts the function.

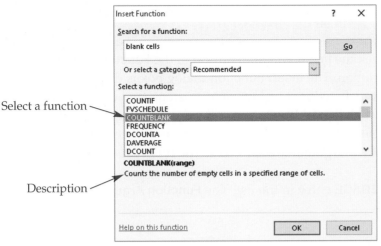

Select a function

Description

Figure 11-2. A description of the selected function appears at the bottom of the dialog box.

HANDS-ON EXAMPLE 11.1.1

INSERTING FUNCTIONS

Two commonly used functions are the **SUM** and **AVERAGE** functions. For example, these functions can be used to create a spreadsheet that tracks expenses and displays the total and average expense.

1. Insert your PRINC-OF-IT flash drive into the computer.
2. Applying what you have learned, create a folder on the flash drive named Chap11.
3. Launch Microsoft Excel, and begin a new blank spreadsheet.
4. Save the file as Expenses.xlsx in the Chap11 folder on your flash drive.
5. Applying what you have learned, format cells B3 through B8 as currency.
6. Add the following content.

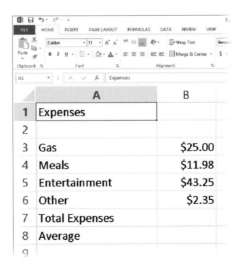

7. Select cell B7. A function will be added to this cell that totals the expenses.
8. Enter the function =SUM(B3:B6) using the keyboard. As soon as the [Enter] key is pressed, the function calculates the total of the range, and the value is displayed in the cell.

HANDS-ON EXAMPLE 11.1.1 (CONTINUED)

Insert
Function

9. Select cell B8, and click the **Insert Function** button in the **Function Library** group on the **Formulas** tab of the ribbon. The **Insert Function** dialog box is displayed.
10. Click in the **Search for a function:** text box, enter average, and click the **Go** button.
11. In the list of results, click the **AVERAGE** entry. Read the description at the bottom of the dialog box to be sure the function is appropriate. In this case, the function should return the average of the arguments supplied to the function, which the **AVERAGE** function does.
12. Double-click the **AVERAGE** entry in the list. The **Function Arguments** dialog box is displayed, as shown.

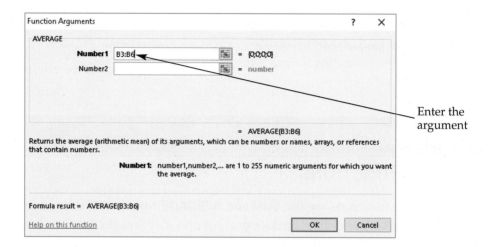

Enter the argument

13. Click in the **Number1** text box, and enter the range B3:B6. Be sure the range ends with cell B6, not cell B7. The range B3:B6 is the argument for the function.
14. Click the **OK** button to finish inserting the function. The value displayed in cell B8 is the average expense. Notice how the function appears in the formula bar: =AVERAGE(B3:B6). This could have been manually entered into the cell like the **SUM** function above to achieve the same result.
15. Save the file.

FYI

When data are entered in a date format, such as 03-14-17, Microsoft Excel will automatically format the cell as a date.

Date and Time

It is possible to insert current, past, and future dates into a spreadsheet through the use of functions. Because the computer has an internal clock, the system always knows the date and time. The computer keeps track of dates by the number of days since January 1, 1900. Time is tracked as a fraction of a day. When a date is entered into a spreadsheet, the software automatically converts it to the number of days since January 1, 1900. When the cell is formatted as a date, this number is displayed as a date. To see the number of days since January 1, 1900, format the cell as a number, as shown in Figure 11-3.

Because dates are stored as numbers, they can be easily used in calculations, such as addition and subtraction. For example, a formula can be created to calculate an age from a person's birthday by subtracting the number for the birthday from the number for today.

In Microsoft Excel, there are several functions related to date and time. These can be accessed through the **Insert Function** dialog box, but there are shortcuts in the ribbon. Click the **Date & Time** button in the **Function Library** group on the **Formulas** tab in the ribbon, as shown in Figure 11-4. Then, select the function to use in the drop-down menu that is displayed. The function is inserted into the current cell, and the **Function Arguments** dialog box is displayed for entering the arguments.

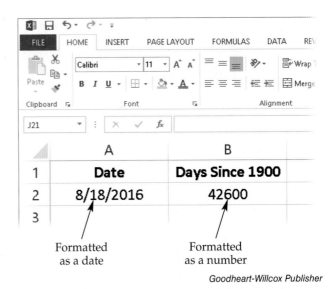

Formatted as a date

Formatted as a number

Goodheart-Willcox Publisher

Figure 11-3. To see the number of days since January 1, 1900, enter the date and then format the cell as a number.

Click

Select a function

Goodheart-Willcox Publisher

Figure 11-4. The ribbon contains shortcuts for entering date-related functions.

HANDS-ON EXAMPLE 11.1.2

USING DATE-RELATED FUNCTIONS

There are many functions in Microsoft Excel related to date and time, and these can be used in many different ways. For example, using a function it is easy to see the number of days it has been since January 1, 1900 or to calculate your age in years.

1. Launch Microsoft Excel, and begin a new blank spreadsheet.
2. Save the file as Dates.xlsx in the Chap11 folder on your flash drive.
3. Add the text Date: to cell A1.
4. Enter the function =TODAY() in cell B1. Today's date is displayed in the cell. Every time this spreadsheet is opened, Excel will check for the current date and display it here.
5. Applying what you have learned, format cell B1 as a number. The value displayed in the cell is the number of days since January 1, 1900.
6. Applying what you have learned, format cell B1 as mm/dd/yyyy. The value displayed in the cell is today's date.
7. Enter the function =TODAY() in cell D1.
8. Enter your birthday in cell D2 in the format mm/dd/yy.
9. Enter the formula =D1–D2 in cell D3. This will calculate the number of days between today's date and your birthday. This is how many days you have been alive.
10. Applying what you have learned, edit the formula in D3 to be =(D1–D2)/365, as shown. Be sure the parentheses are correctly placed so the subtraction is carried out before the division. Since ages are not usually expressed in days, dividing by 365 will approximate the number of years you have been alive, including a decimal fraction.

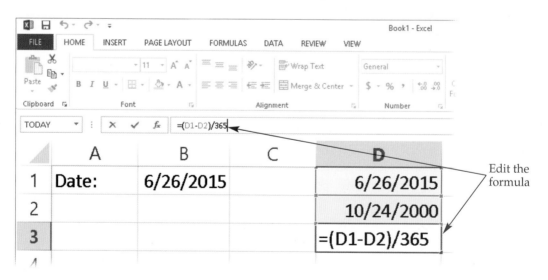

Edit the formula

11. Applying what you have learned, select cell D4, and open the **Insert Function** dialog.
12. Applying what you have learned, search for the phrase round off. In the list of results, select the **INT** function, and read the description. This function converts a decimal to an integer by dropping the decimal places.
13. Double-click the **INT** function and, in the **Function Arguments** dialog box, enter D3 as the argument and click the **OK** button to complete the function. The value displayed in cell D4 is your age as whole number of years.
14. Save the file.

Complex Financial Formulas

One of the benefits of using a computerized spreadsheet is the ability to change the data in cells to create a what-if scenario. It is possible to modify the arguments for a formula to see what the effect will be. This feature of spreadsheets provides the opportunity to analyze a variety of possibilities. It is often helpful to create a what-if scenario when making financial decisions.

An important financial decision is to purchase a car. Cars are very expensive, so many people borrow part of the money to purchase the car. Banks and other organizations that lend money make a profit by charging interest on the money borrowed. For simple interest, they calculate how much interest is owed by multiplying the loan amount by the monthly interest rate and the number of months for the loan. That amount is then added to the loan amount and divided by the number of months for the loan. However, in most cases, interest on a loan is actually calculated on a daily or continual basis, which makes the calculation complex.

Most spreadsheet software contains many preprogrammed functions that can be used to calculate payments. These functions provide an opportunity to look at scenarios to help make a decision. To have the spreadsheet do the math, three values need to be known:

- amount of the loan, also called the **principal**
- interest rate per period
- how many periods it will take to repay the loan, also called the **term**

Interest rates are generally expressed as annual rates. If the spreadsheet function requires the monthly rate, divide the annual rate by 12. The term of a loan is generally stated in years. If the spreadsheet function requires the term to be in months, multiply the number of years by 12 to find the total number of periods.

A function in Microsoft Excel that can be used to calculate payments is **PMT**. The syntax of this function is =PMT(*monthly rate, number of months, principal*). The order of the arguments is very important. Also, notice that the rate and term reference months, not years. Be sure to convert annual rates and terms to monthly rates. Otherwise, the function will return results that are not correct.

Green Tech

Automatic Lighting
Every building must be well-lighted in order for employees and customers to work and visit safely. Simple changes can make an impact in the cost of lighting. Motion sensors can be a simple solution. If the sensor detects low activity over a period of time, the lights will automatically turn off, saving money and energy.

FYI

Term is also abbreviated as *nper*, for number of periods, in the function list in Microsoft Excel.

HANDS-ON EXAMPLE 11.1.3

CALCULATING A PAYMENT

A what-if scenario can be created to help make decisions when buying a car. You can see what effect changing the principal, interest rate, or term has on the payment.

1. Launch Microsoft Excel, and begin a new blank spreadsheet.
2. Save the file as Payment.xlsx in the Chap11 folder on your flash drive.

HANDS-ON EXAMPLE 11.1.3 (CONTINUED)

3. Enter the following content.

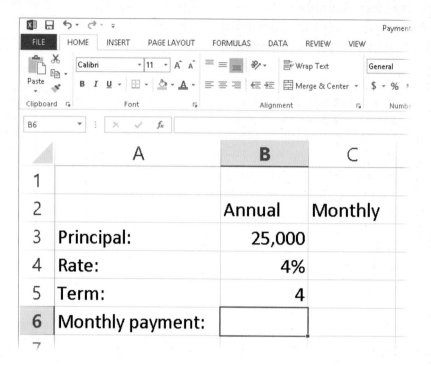

4. Enter the formula =B4/12 in cell C4. This calculates the monthly rate. The result is a decimal fraction.

5. Enter the formula =B5*12 in cell C5. This calculates the number of months for the term.

6. Select cell C6.

7. Applying what you have learned, use the **Insert Function** dialog box to enter the **PMT** function. The arguments are, in order, C4, C5, and B3. After the function is inserted, the correct value that should be displayed in cell C6 is –564.48. The value may be enclosed in parentheses without the minus sign, as (564.48), to indicate a negative value.

8. Applying what you have learned, edit the formula to include a minus sign before the function name: =PMT(C4,C5,B3). This reverses the sign of the result, so the displayed value appears as a positive number instead of a negative number.

9. To perform a what-if scenario, change the loan, rate, and term one at a time. See how each change affects the monthly payment.

10. Save the file.

Logical Functions

In addition to mathematical calculations, a spreadsheet can also determine if certain statements are true or false. Functions that test for true or false are **logical functions**. These functions can be used to add an element of decision making to the spreadsheet.

IF Logical Function

A commonly used logical function is the **IF** function. In Microsoft Excel, this function has three arguments separated by commas. The first argument is the condition to test. The second argument is the action to perform if the condition is true. The final argument is the action to perform if the condition is false. Any valid logical expression may be used in the first argument of the **IF** statement, as shown in Figure 11-5.

For example, consider the condition where a monthly payment is above or below a certain number. If the payment is less than $325 per month, then the payment is affordable. If the payment is greater than this amount, it is not affordable. The statement is:

> **IF** p<$325, then it is **TRUE** the payment is affordable, or else it is **FALSE** the payment is affordable.

where p represents the payment.

Suppose the monthly payment is in cell C6. In Microsoft Excel, the function for the above statement would be written =IF(C6 <325,"Yes","No"). If the value in cell C6 is less than $325, then the cell containing the function will display the text Yes. If the value is $325 or higher, the cell will display No.

Operator	Meaning
=	Equal to
>	Greater than
<	Less than
< >	Not equal to
>=	Greater than or equal to
<=	Less than or equal to

Goodheart-Willcox Publisher

Figure 11-5. Various operators can be used in a logical expression.

Other Logical Functions

There are several additional logical functions in Microsoft Excel. The **AND** function tests the value of two expressions. If both are true, the function returns the value **TRUE**. If both are false, the function returns the value **FALSE**. The **OR** function also tests the value of two expressions. However, if either expression is true, the function returns the value **TRUE**. If both expressions are false, the function returns the value **FALSE**.

The **NOT** function reverses the value of an expression. If the expression evaluates to **TRUE**, the **NOT** function reverses the value to **FALSE**. If the expression evaluates to **FALSE**, the **NOT** function reverses the value to **TRUE**.

The **IFERROR** function returns a specified value if the expression evaluates to an error. For example, if the expression returns a divide by zero error (#DIV/0), the text Enter a nonzero number could be displayed as the value. If the expression does not return an error, the value of the expression is displayed. In this example, the function could be written as =IFERROR(A1/A2,"Enter a nonzero number"). Notice that the string is contained in quotation marks. If the value of cell A2 is 0, then the text is displayed. If the value of cell A2 is a nonzero number, such as 5, the result of the division is displayed.

The **TRUE** function returns the value **TRUE**. The **FALSE** function returns the value **FALSE**. These functions are provided in Microsoft Excel for compatibility with spreadsheets created in other software.

Career Skills

Budget Analyst
Budget analysts help private and public institutions manage their finances. Their jobs are both reactive and proactive by studying past spending and making budget projections for management. They use spreadsheets and databases to prepare budget reports and oversee organizational spending. Often their background is a bachelor's degree in accounting and finance.

HANDS-ON EXAMPLE 11.1.4

USING A LOGICAL FUNCTION

A logical function can be used to determine if a monthly payment is within your budget. Based on the payment, the **IF** function can be used to display either Yes or No in a cell.

1. Launch Microsoft Excel, and open the Payment.xlsx file in the Chap11 folder on your flash drive, if it is not already open.
2. Add the text Affordable? to cell B7.
3. Enter the function =IF(C6<325,"Yes","No") in cell C8. Be sure to include the text in quotation marks. The value displayed in cell C8 should be either Yes or No, depending on whether or not the payment is less than $325.
4. Perform a what-if scenario by changing the principal, rate, and term amounts. Try to find a combination that results in an affordable payment.
5. Save the file.

11.1 SECTION REVIEW

CHECK YOUR UNDERSTANDING

1. What does each function in Microsoft Excel begin with?
2. Which dialog box is used to add a function to a spreadsheet in Microsoft Excel?
3. What three values are needed to calculate loan payments using the **PMT** function in Excel?
4. What does a logical function test for?
5. Which logical function is used to test the values of two expressions?

IC3 CERTIFICATION PRACTICE

The following question is a sample of the types of questions presented on the IC3 exam.

1. The formula =SUM(G7:G25) calculates the sum of the range G7:G25. Modify this formula to instead find the largest value in the same range.

BUILD YOUR VOCABULARY

As you progress through this course, develop a personal IT glossary. This will help you build your vocabulary and prepare you for a career. Write a definition for each of the following terms and add it to your IT glossary.

arguments
function
logical functions
principal
term

VISUAL ENHANCEMENTS OF DATA

racorn/Shutterstock.com

Most people are visual creatures. Highlighting certain data makes results more visible. It is easy to manually change the color of displayed values or the background color of cells in a spreadsheet. However, some spreadsheet software has the ability to automatically format cells. In Microsoft Excel, this is done through conditional formatting.

Charts graphically represent data. When the data in a spreadsheet are updated, the associated charts are automatically updated. There are several types of charts available in Microsoft Excel, such as column, line, pie, and bar. Each type has a variety of options to make it easy to create and update. The type of chart selected should be appropriate for the data that were entered into the spreadsheet. Excel helps to determine the proper type of chart by displaying tool tips for each type.

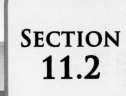

Essential Question

Does visually enhancing data improve the effectiveness of a spreadsheet?

TERMS

bar chart
chart
comma-separated values (CSV) file
conditional formatting
embedding
line chart
linking
pie chart

LEARNING GOALS

After completing this section, you will be able to:
- Apply conditional formatting to cells in a spreadsheet.
- Describe how to create a chart from spreadsheet data.
- Explain how to insert a spreadsheet chart into a text document.
- Describe how to create a basic table in a spreadsheet.
- Discuss the use of comma separated value files.

Key Applications
3.2.4

Conditional Formatting

Conditional formatting changes the appearance of a cell's value based on parameters set by the user. Conditional formatting allows the user to set up a formula that changes the color of a cell based on the value displayed in the cell. It is often used with the result of the **IF** logical function or another logical function. The result of the logical function is calculated by the software, and the color of the cell's background and content are based on that result, as shown in Figure 11-6.

For example, when looking at a list of names and numbers, conditional formatting makes it is possible to have the important cells instantly highlighted. A teacher could create a spreadsheet listing student grades and instantly see who needs extra help. Or, an inventory specialist could create a spreadsheet to track the quantities of products the company has on hand and observe which inventories are low. Conditional formatting makes this possible.

In Microsoft Excel, there are several types of conditional formatting that can be applied. To apply conditional formatting to a cell, select the cell, and click the **Conditional Formatting** button in the **Styles** group on the **Home** tab of the ribbon, as shown in Figure 11-7. Select the type of conditional formatting to apply, and then select the specific formatting in the cascading menu.

Conditional formatting can also be applied using the **New Formatting Rule** dialog box. To display this dialog box, click **New Rule...** in the drop-down menu displayed by clicking the **Conditional Formatting** button in the **Styles** group on the **Home** tab of the ribbon. To create a rule from scratch, click **Use a formula to determine cells to format** in the dialog box. Then, define the formula. For example, the formula =A1<5 tests to see if the value in cell A1 is less than 5. Finally, click the **Format...** button and define the formatting to apply if the condition is true.

FYI

Many experienced users prefer to create conditional formatting from scratch using the **New Formatting Rule** dialog box because doing so offers more control.

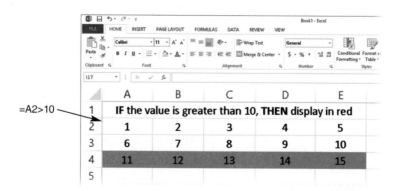

=A2>10

Goodheart-Willcox Publisher

Figure 11-6. Conditional formatting can be used to change the color of a cell's background if a certain condition is met.

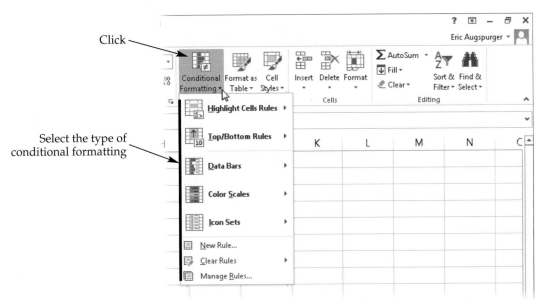

Goodheart-Willcox Publisher

Figure 11-7. There are several ways in which conditional formatting can be applied and used.

HANDS-ON EXAMPLE 11.2.1

APPLYING CONDITIONAL FORMATTING

Conditional formatting can be used to highlight values automatically if they are below a certain point. For example, grades tracked in a spreadsheet can be set up so any grade below 70% will be shown in red.

1. Launch Microsoft Excel, and begin a new blank spreadsheet.
2. Save the file as Formatting.xlsx in the Chap11 folder on your flash drive.
3. Enter the following data.

	A	B	C	D	E
1	Name	Test 1	Test 2	Test 3	Average
2	Bradley	56	34	65	
3	Kim	89	95	99	
4	Tyrese	90	94	93	
5	Sophia	87	87	89	

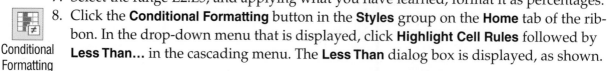

HANDS-ON EXAMPLE 11.2.1 (CONTINUED)

4. Applying what you have learned insert a function in cell E2 to find the average of the range B2:D2. Use the **Insert Function** dialog box to locate an appropriate function.

5. Applying what you have learned, format cell E2 as a number and decrease the decimal places until only a whole number is displayed.

6. Applying what you have learned, copy the function in cell E2 to cells E3, E4, and E5.

7. Select the range E2:E5, and applying what you have learned, format it as percentages.

Conditional Formatting

8. Click the **Conditional Formatting** button in the **Styles** group on the **Home** tab of the ribbon. In the drop-down menu that is displayed, click **Highlight Cell Rules** followed by **Less Than...** in the cascading menu. The **Less Than** dialog box is displayed, as shown.

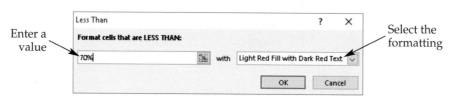

Enter a value

Select the formatting

9. Click in the **Format cells that are less than:** text box, and enter 70%.

10. Click the **with** drop-down arrow, and click **Light Red Fill with Dark Red Text** in the drop-down list.

11. Click the **OK** button to apply the conditional formatting. Any value in the Average column that is less than 70 is highlighted. All other values remain in the default formatting. In this example, only one student is below 70.

12. Change the value in cell C2 to 90. This student's average is now 70. Notice how the formatting in the Average column changed.

13. Change the value in cell D5 to 34. This student's average is now below 70. Notice how the formatting in the Average column changed.

14. Change the value in cell D5 to 50. This student's average is now above 70. Notice how the formatting in the Average column has returned to the default formatting.

15. Save the file.

Charts

Key Applications
GS5
3.7.1, 3.7.2, 3.7.3
Key Applications
GS4
3.2.5

Charts are pictures that display numerical data in a graphical format. A chart shows relationships between lists of numbers that may not be easy to see in a table format. The best charts give the viewer the quickest grasp of ideas in the shortest time. They can communicate complex ideas with clarity, precision, and efficiency. For example, financial workers often use charts of the data rather than reading columns and rows of numbers. Charts can enhance information, add visual appeal, and make it easy to analyze data. Creating a chart in spreadsheet software is straightforward:

1. Identify the purpose of the chart.

2. Select the range of cells to chart.

3. Insert the chart on the spreadsheet.

4. Select the chart type.

5. Choose chart elements to clarify data.

6. Change the chart location and size.

Most spreadsheet software can draw many types of charts. The most common types are bar, line, and pie charts, as shown in Figure 11-8. It is important to choose the type of chart that will best represent the selected data and communicate your message.

Bar charts are the best chart type for comparing individual values across categories. The bars can be arranged vertically or horizontally. A bar chart can be used, for example, to show a comparison of total sales of five companies over one year. In Microsoft Excel, a bar chart with vertical bars is called a *column chart*.

Pie charts display the relative size of each fractional part of a whole. Use a pie chart when values represent the division of a category into its parts, such as market share. A pie chart is also useful when displaying only one data series of positive values.

Line charts are used to display trends over time. For example, a line chart can be used to show the annual profit of a company over ten years. Line charts are also used to represent continuous processes rather than individual values. Data points are connected by line segments to show continuous change.

> **FYI**
>
> When creating a chart, it is very important to make sure the correct range of cells is selected; otherwise, the software may attempt to include unwanted data.

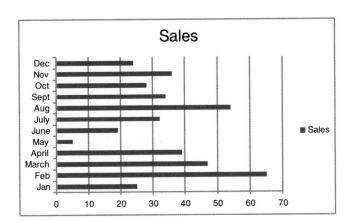

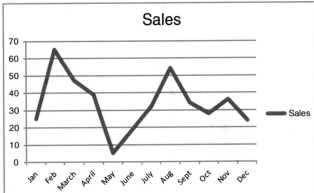

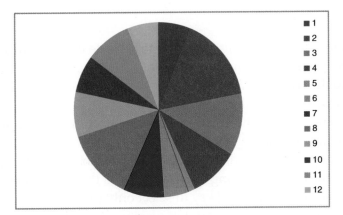

Figure 11-8. The three most common types of chart are, from top to bottom, bar, line, and pie.

HANDS-ON EXAMPLE 11.2.2

CREATING CHARTS

The Dizzy World Park wants to track the relative popularity of its theme parks among visitors from three regions of the United States and to compare total attendance between parks. A vertical bar chart will be used to track popularity by region, while a pie chart will compare total attendance.

1. Navigate to the student companion website at www.g-wlearning.com, download the data files for this chapter, and save them in the Chap11 folder on your flash drive.
2. Launch Microsoft Excel, and open the ThemePark.xlsx file in the Chap11 folder on your flash drive.
3. Select the range A3:E6. This range includes the attendance at the theme parks as well as the headings. Take care not to select the Total row or Total column.

Insert
Column
Chart

4. Click the **Insert Column Chart** button in the **Charts** group on the **Insert** tab of the ribbon, and then click **Clustered Column** in the **2D Column** area of the drop-down menu. This creates a vertical bar chart with the bars grouped in a cluster, as shown. Notice how Excel has selected three ranges within the original selection.

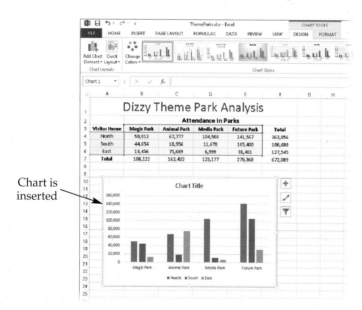

Chart is inserted

5. Double-click the default chart title to activate it for editing, and change the title to Dizzy Theme Park Attendance Analysis.
6. Move the cursor to a corner of the chart until it changes to a resizing cursor, and drag the corner to make the chart smaller.
7. Click and hold on the outside bounding box of the chart, and drag the chart to a position below the data.
8. Click anywhere outside of the chart to deselect the chart.
9. Select the cells containing the headings (B3 through E3) and the totals (B7 through E7). Hold down the [Ctrl] key to select only these cells. These cells will provide headings and data for a pie chart that displays the attendance in percentages of each theme park compared to the whole.

HANDS-ON EXAMPLE 11.2.2 (CONTINUED)

Insert Pie or Doughnut Chart

10. Click the **Insert Pie or Doughnut Chart** button in the **Charts** group on the **Insert** tab of the ribbon, and click **Pie** in the **2D Pie** area of the drop-down menu.
11. Applying what you have learned, change the default chart title to Attendance by Park.
12. Applying what you have learned, resize the chart to be the same size as the bar chart and move the pie chart below the bar chart.
13. Click the pie in the pie chart. Handles are displayed on all slices of the pie.
14. Click the slice representing Animal Park. Handles are displayed only on that slice.
15. Click and hold on the Animal Park slice, and drag the slice outside of the pie. This is called exploding the chart, and it emphasizes the Animal Park slice.
16. Deselect the chart, and then click the pie to select that element.

Add Chart Element

17. Click the **Add Chart Element** button in the **Chart Layouts** group on the **Design** on-demand tab in the ribbon, and click **Data Labels** followed by **More Data Label Options…** in the drop-down menu. The **Format Data Labels** pane is displayed on the right-hand side of the Excel window.
18. Uncheck the **Value** check box in the **Format Data Labels** pane. The total values are removed from the chart.
19. Check the **Percentage** check box in the **Format Data Labels** pane. Each slice displays a percentage of the whole.
20. Save the file.

Spreadsheet Charts in Text Documents

The data in a spreadsheet are often used to support a report. The data may support conclusions presented in the report, or the report may explain the data. Spreadsheet software is not suited to create written reports. Therefore, other software must be used to create the report and the data from the spreadsheet must be inserted into the report.

The various applications within an office suite can communicate with each other. This makes it possible to insert objects from one application into documents created by another application. For example, a chart created in Microsoft Excel can be inserted into a Microsoft Word document. There are two ways to achieve this: embedding and linking.

Embedding is a form of copying and pasting. The source object, such as a chart, is copied to the destination document. Once the object is embedded, there is no connection between it and the original from which it was created. If the original is changed, the embedded object will not reflect the changes.

Linking is similar to embedding, but a connection is maintained between the copy and the original source, as shown in Figure 11-9. If the original is changed, the linked copy is updated. For example, if the data in Microsoft Excel are updated, a chart based on those data will be updated in Excel, and a linked copy of this chart in a Microsoft Word document will also be updated. Linking is a good option to keep data synchronized. However, if either of the two files is moved or the source file is renamed, the link is broken, so good file management is necessary.

Ethics

Ethical Communication
Distorting information for a company's gain is an unethical practice. Honesty, accuracy, and truthfulness should guide all communications. Ethically, communication must be presented in an unbiased manner. Facts should be given without distortion. If the information is an opinion, it should be labeled as such.

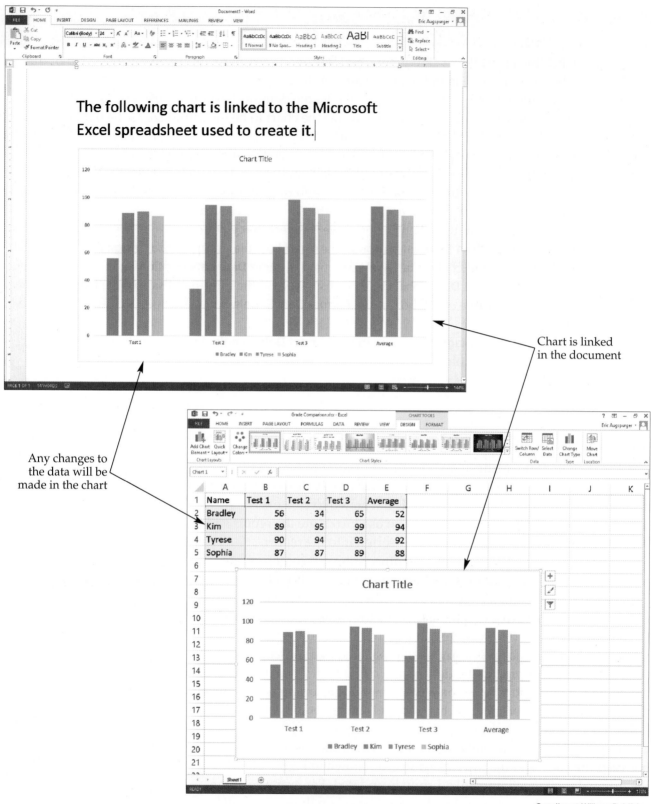

Figure 11-9. A linked object, such as a chart, maintains a connection to the original source. Any changes to the source will be reflected in the linked object.

HANDS-ON EXAMPLE 11.2.3

USING A CHART IN A DOCUMENT

Charts created in a spreadsheet can be inserted into a text document. The chart may be embedded or linked.

1. Launch Microsoft Word, and open the ParkReview.docx file from the Chap11 folder on your flash drive. A pie chart created in Microsoft Excel will be displayed below the text.
2. Launch Microsoft Excel, and open the ThemePark.xlsx file in the Chap11 folder on your flash drive.
3. Click the pie chart to select it.
4. Applying what you have learned, copy the chart to the system clipboard.
5. Return to Microsoft Word.
6. Place the insertion point at the end of the paragraph, and press the [Enter] key to start a new paragraph.
7. Click the drop-down arrow next to the **Paste** button in the **Clipboard** group on the **Home** tab of the ribbon to display a drop-down menu, as shown.

Paste

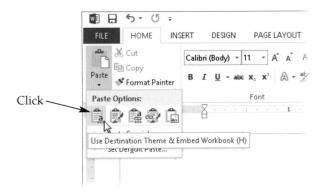

8. Click the **Use Destination Theme & Embed Workbook** button in the drop-down menu. The pie chart is inserted into the document. It is embedded, so there is no connection between it and the original pie chart.
9. Start a new paragraph below the pie chart.
10. Return to Microsoft Excel.
11. Applying what you have learned, copy the bar chart to the system clipboard.
12. Return to Microsoft Word.
13. Click the drop-down arrow next to the **Paste** button in the **Clipboard** group on the **Home** tab of the ribbon, and click the **Use Destination theme & Link Data** button. The bar chart is inserted into the document. It is linked, so it remains connected to the original bar chart.
14. Return to Microsoft Excel.
15. Change the data in cell B4 to 450,000.
16. Return to Microsoft Word. Notice that the pie chart has not changed, but the bar chart has been updated to reflect the change made in the spreadsheet.
17. Save both files.

Paste

TITANS OF TECHNOLOGY

Mitch Kapor launched Lotus 1-2-3 spreadsheet software in early 1983. It was similar in functionality to VisiCalc, but added the capability to generate charts. This software is considered the first killer app for the PC. People were buying PCs only to run Lotus 1-2-3. It soon became clear that PCs were the next big market and Microsoft took notice. Douglas Klunder headed the small team that developed Excel for Microsoft Corporation to take advantage of the PC spreadsheet market. Excel was released in late 1985. The most important elements of a good spreadsheet for advanced developers are speed of recalculations and the availability of many features. Klunder designed a recalculation algorithm that did not recalculate every cell, but only those cells affected by the changes made. This greatly increased the speed of recalculations. When it comes to spreadsheet software, Mitch Kapor and Douglas Klunder are titans of technology.

Key Applications
3.8.1, 3.8.2, 3.8.3

STEM

Mathematics

Mathematical equations can involve simple algebra, but often they are arithmetic. A powerful capability of computerized spreadsheets is not the ability to solve complex mathematical equations, but to serve as a conceptual bridge between algebra and arithmetic. In creating and entering mathematical functions in a spreadsheet, patterns must be identified, concepts generalized, and arithmetic expressions developed.

Tables

A table allows a group of related data to be analyzed. Tables have built-in filtering and sorting functions as well as row shading. To create a table in a spreadsheet, it is easiest to enter the data first. Then, select the range of cells, including the header row, to be in the table. In Microsoft Excel, click the **Table** button in the **Tables** group on the **Insert** tab of the ribbon or use the [Ctrl][T] key combination.

Once the table is created, row shading can be applied. This can be done manually by setting the fill color for each row, but styles can also be used to control the coloring. There are various other settings that can be changed to alter the appearance of the table. In Microsoft Excel, these are found on the **Design** on-demand tab in the ribbon. The basic style colors are located in the gallery in the **Table Styles** group.

In Microsoft Excel, each cell in the header row of a table contains a drop-down arrow. Clicking the arrow displays a menu that allows the data in the table to be sorted based on the value in the column. Excel recognizes that the cells in each row must remain together. Rows can also be hidden or displayed using this menu.

The **Quick Analysis** feature in Microsoft Excel offers a way to quickly apply conditional formatting to the table. First select the table to display the **Quick Analysis** button next to the table. Then, click the button and select the type of conditional formatting to apply to the table.

Comma-Separated Values Files

A **comma-separated values (CSV) file** contains data with commas to denote the beginning and end of each datum in a row. Each row is a paragraph in the CSV. A CSV file is used to share data from one application with other software. This type of file is also known as a *comma delimited file*. Other characters may be used instead of a comma, such as tabs or spaces. Figure 11-10 shows how spreadsheet data can be saved to a CSV file.

In addition, a CSV file is used to share spreadsheet data with other software that cannot read the native file format of the spreadsheet software. For example, you may have a word processor that cannot read Microsoft Excel files (XLSx). However, you may need to include the spreadsheet data in a table in the text document. By saving the data from the spreadsheet as a CSV file, the word processor can import the data and create a table.

To create a CSV file in most spreadsheet software, use either the save as or export function. A CSV file has a .csv file name extension. Select the CSV file type, navigate to the folder where the file should be saved, and name the file. In Microsoft Excel, a warning will be displayed indicating that some features of Excel will be lost. Since the CSV file type contains only data, formatting, data types, formulas, and other features are stripped out before the file is saved.

Quarter 1	$ 250
Quarter 2	$ 325
Quarter 3	$ 275
Quarter 4	$ 300

Quarter 1, $250
Quarter 2, $325
Quarter 3, $275
Quarter 4, $300

Datum separator

Goodheart-Willcox Publisher

Figure 11-10. A comma-separated values file contains only the data from a spreadsheet. Commas separate cells in a row, and each row is a separate paragraph.

11.2 SECTION REVIEW

 ### CHECK YOUR UNDERSTANDING

1. What is used to change the appearance of a cell's value based on parameters set by the user?
2. Name the three most common types of charts.
3. Which type of chart would be best to show trends over time?
4. What is the difference between embedding and linking a chart in a text document?
5. How is each datum in a spreadsheet row separated in a CSV file?

IC3 CERTIFICATION PRACTICE

The following question is a sample of the types of questions presented on the IC3 exam.

1. To add a column chart to a Microsoft Excel spreadsheet, which of the following is the command sequence?
   A. **Page Layout>Charts>Insert Column Chart**
   B. **Home>Insert Chart**
   C. **Insert>Charts>Insert Column Chart**
   D. **Data>Insert Column Chart**

 ### BUILD YOUR VOCABULARY

As you progress through this course, develop a personal IT glossary. This will help you build your vocabulary and prepare you for a career. Write a definition for each of the following terms and add it to your IT glossary.

bar chart
chart
comma-separated
   values (CSV) file
conditional formatting

embedding
line chart
linking
pie chart

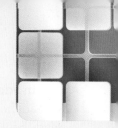

Chapter Summary

Section 11.1
Calculating with Functions

- A function is a preprogrammed formula in spreadsheet software. Arguments are values the function needs for the calculation.

- Most spreadsheet software contains many preprogrammed functions that can be used to calculate payments. It is possible to modify the arguments for the formula to create a what-if scenario to see what the effect will be on payments.

- Logical functions test for true or false. These functions can be used to add an element of decision making to the spreadsheet.

Section 11.2
Visual Enhancements of Data

- Conditional formatting changes the appearance of a cell's value based on parameters set by the user. A formula can be created to change the color of a cell based on the value displayed in the cell.

- A chart shows relationships between lists of numbers that may not be easy to see in a table format. The best charts give the viewer the quickest grasp of ideas in the shortest time.

- A chart can be created in spreadsheet software and used in other software. The chart can be embedded, which is a copy, or linked, which maintains a connection to the original chart.

- A table can be inserted into a spreadsheet based on a range of cells. Once inserted, the table can be stylized, including adding shading to rows. Conditional formatting can also be applied to the table.

- A comma-separated values file contains only the data from a spreadsheet. This file type is used to share data with other software that cannot read the spreadsheet software file format.

Now that you have finished this chapter, see what you know about information technology by scanning the QR code to take the chapter posttest. If you do not have a smartphone, visit www.g-wlearning.com.

Chapter 11 Test

Multiple Choice

Select the best response.

1. What are the values the function needs for the calculation called?
   A. pieces
   B. arguments
   C. addresses
   D. logicals

2. Which of the following is *not* a logical function?
   A. **NOT**
   B. **IF**
   C. **MIN**
   D. **AND**

3. How is the **Insert Function** dialog box displayed?
   A. **Formulas>Function Library>Insert Function**
   B. **Insert>Formulas>Functions**
   C. **Formulas>Functions>Insert**
   D. **Insert>Functions**

4. Which type of charts shows the relative size of each fractional part of a whole?
   A. graph
   B. line
   C. bar
   D. pie

5. What is the purpose of a CSV file?
   A. To share data with other software.
   B. To retain formatting and formulas.
   C. To improve readability.
   D. To use logical functions.

Completion

Complete the following sentences with the correct word(s).

6. A(n) _____ is a preprogrammed formula in spreadsheet software.

7. The _____ function returns the lowest value of the arguments.

8. The _____ logical function tests if the value of either of two expressions is true.

9. To create a conditional formatting from scratch, use the _____ dialog box.

10. A _____ is a picture that displays numerical data in a graphical format.

Matching

Match the correct term with its definition.

   A. function
   B. **MAX** function
   C. logical function
   D. bar chart
   E. linking

11. Tests for true or false.

12. A preprogrammed formula.

13. Best for comparing individual values across categories.

14. Returns the highest value of the arguments.

15. A connection is maintained between the copy and the original source.

Application and Extension of Knowledge

1. Monitor the outside temperature for your area for one 24-hour period. Use weather reports in the newspaper, on television, or on the web to fill in temperatures you cannot take yourself. Create a spreadsheet, and enter the data for each hour. Create a line chart in the spreadsheet to illustrate the changes in temperature for the day.

2. Modify the spreadsheet created in #1. Add functions to display the highest and lowest temperatures for the day. Be sure to add text to label what each value indicates so anybody viewing the spreadsheet will know. Save the spreadsheet under a new file name.

3. Modify the spreadsheet created in #2. Apply conditional formatting to the cells containing the hourly information. Change the background color of the cells so all data during the day has a light-yellow background and all data during the night has a dark-blue background. Save the spreadsheet under a new file name.

4. Create a spreadsheet to track the amount of time you spend doing certain activities or tasks throughout one week. This may include classes, homework, sports, leisure time, work, or anything else you did. Be sure to account for all of your time, include sleeping, eating, and getting to and from school. There are 168 hours in a week. Record the time as the number of hours, such as .25, .5, or 1.25. Use these data to create a pie chart illustrating what part of the whole each activity was for the week.

5. Open the file created in #4. Create CSV file from the spreadsheet. Open the CSV file in Notepad or other text editor. Write a one-paragraph paper describing what happens to the data in the spreadsheet when the CSV file was created.

Online Activities

Complete the following activities, which will help you learn, practice, and expand your knowledge and skills.

Certification Practice. Complete the certification practice test for this chapter.

Vocabulary. Practice vocabulary for this chapter using the e-flash cards, matching activity, and vocabulary game until you are able to recognize their meanings.

Communication Skills

College and Career Readiness

Speaking. Participate actively and effectively in a one-on-one oral communication with a classmate about the importance of the technology use for a business. Prepare for the conversation by creating notes that outline your opinions.

Writing. Create a Venn diagram to show the relationships between mobile and desktop computer technology. Where do the circles overlap? What do you think this overlap signifies?

Reading. There are many new vocabulary terms in this chapter that relate to information technology. Make a list of the terms and the words that are italicized. Use reference guides to confirm the meanings of new words or concepts.

Internet Research

Entering Data into a Spreadsheet. Navigate to Google Trends by keying www.google.com/trends into your web browser. Conduct a search for the term information technology. The numbers along the time line demonstrate the interest in the searched term relative to the highest point on the chart. Using spreadsheet software, build a spreadsheet consisting of the month and search interest indicator for the last 12 months. Then, turn your data into a line graph and compare it

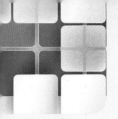

to the line graph on the website. Does yours look similar to the one on the website?

Teamwork

Knowing how to give and accept constructive criticism is a requirement in the workplace. Working with your team, use spreadsheet software to create a list of rules that should be followed when giving criticism to a peer. Next, create a list of rules that should be followed when receiving criticism. Share your findings with the class.

Portfolio Development

College and Career Readiness

Clubs and Organizations. Being involved in academic clubs or professional organizations will help you make a good impression. You can also learn a lot that will help you with your studies or your career. While in school, you may belong to clubs, such as National Honor Society and Future Business Leaders of America. When you are employed, you may belong to professional organizations related to your career area, such as American Nurses Association.

1. Identify clubs or organizations to which you belong. Create a Microsoft Word document to list the name of each organization. Use the heading "Clubs and Organizations" and your name. Briefly describe the organization, your level of involvement, and how long you have been a member. Save the document.

2. Update your master spreadsheet.

CTSOs

Client Service. Client service is a competitive event you might enter with your career and technical student organization (CTSO). This event may include an interactive simulation. The simulation will often be a case study dealing with internal and external clients. If you decide to participate in this event, you will need to review steps in resolving client issues such as inquiries, troubleshooting, and other assistance to prepare for the test. To prepare for a client services event, complete the following activities.

1. Read the guidelines provided by your organization. Make certain that you ask any questions about points you do not understand. It is important you follow each specific item that is outlined in the competition rules.

2. Review the vocabulary terms at the beginning of each chapter.

3. Review the Checkpoint activities at the end of each section of the text.

4. Ask your instructor to give you practice tests for each chapter of this text. It is important that you are familiar with answering multiple choice and true/false questions. Have someone time you as you take a practice test.

12 DATABASE SOFTWARE

Imagine trying to operate a school without knowing who the students are, who the faculty is, what courses are offered, when the students attended class, or what grades the students earned. All schools have to keep track of this type of data and much more. Schools must have these data available for parents and state officials when they ask for it. Business people also need to keep track of who their customers are, what products they sell, who their employees are, and who owes them money.

Information drives many aspects of society, which is one of the reasons this time in history is called the Information Age. Information systems help schools, businesses, and other organizations arrange information. The data are stored in a database. While similar to a spreadsheet, a database offers many advantages over a spreadsheet. A database allows information to be organized and rapidly retrieved when needed.

IC3 CERTIFICATION OBJECTIVES

GS5

Computing Fundamentals
Domain 6.0 Cloud computing
   Objective 6.5 Understand web app types
Key Applications
Domain 4.0 Databases
   Objective 4.1 Understand what data is
   Objective 4.3 Know basic concepts of a relational database

GS4

Computing Fundamentals
Domain 3.0 Computer software concepts
   Objective 3.3 Software usage
Key Applications
Domain 5.0 Basic database interactions
   Objective 5.1 Record managements

College and Career Readiness

Reading Prep. Write all of the key terms for this chapter on a sheet of paper. Highlight the words that you do not know. Before you begin reading, look up the highlighted words in the glossary and write the definitions.

INTRODUCTION TO DATABASES

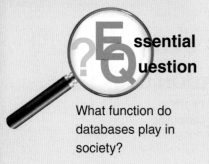

What function do databases play in society?

Databases have many uses, from simple to complex. A simple database may contain information related to recipes and ingredients. A complex database may contain information about the various configurations of a particular model of car and the tens of thousands of parts needed to manufacture each.

A database organizes data in one or more tables. Each table consists of rows and columns, like a spreadsheet. However, database software offers more powerful tools for working with the data than the tools offered by spreadsheet software. The process of creating a database is not difficult, but it may be time-consuming if the database is large.

Ammentorp Photography/Shutterstock.com

LEARNING GOALS

After completing this section, you will be able to:
- Describe the structure of a database.
- Explain how to add, edit, and delete data in a database.
- Create a database structure.

TERMS

database
database management system (DBMS)
design view
field
primary key
record
table

Overview of Databases

A **database** is a structured collection of related information organized for easily locating and retrieving the data. A database can be very large. For example, a database may contain information of sports card collections as well as all details of the related major league sports teams. Before computers became widely used, most organizations kept data on paper. Schools and businesses had to find many places to store the paper. It was also difficult to find specific pieces of information.

An electronic or computerized database is a big improvement over paper-based databases. It not only organizes the data, but offers tools to search and output the data. When people search the computerized card catalog at the library, they are using an electronic database to show, or output, the results. The World Wide Web uses databases to look up website locations. When someone places a food order by phone, a database may be used to check the customer's name, address, and ordering history.

There are many advantages to using an electronic system over a paper system. An electronic database offers faster input with fewer errors. The data are easier to maintain. All calculations are done correctly by the computer, eliminating errors that may occur with manual calculations. When a company's data are kept in an electronic form, the data can be protected by backups. Passwords can be required to provide security for the data. Electronic databases make it easy to search, find specific answers, and create reports.

The software that manipulates the data is called a database management system. A **database management system (DBMS)** handles the collection, storage, sorting, reporting, and organization of data. In a society of "knowledge workers," an understanding of databases and database management systems is critical. This chapter introduces the basic concepts of database management. Some common terms associated with a DBMS and their explanations are shown in Figure 12-1.

Customer relationship management (CRM) software is a type of database designed to manage and analyze customer data and interactions with customers. CRM programs can improve business relationships by compiling information on customers across different points of contact. These points of contact may include the company's website, telephone,

GS5 Computing Fundamentals
6.5.3

Field	Contains information about specific characteristics of the entry described in a record.
Form	Database object used to collect or display data one record at a time.
Query	Includes searching, finding, and organizing the related details of records that meet certain search conditions.
Record	A row in a database table.
Report	Output of the database of specific information requested by the user.
Sort	Arranging data in a table based on one or more field.
Table	Contains information arranged in horizontal rows and vertical columns.

Figure 12-1. Common terms related to databases and a brief explanation of each.

web-based live chat, direct mail, marketing materials, and social media. CRM systems can also give the staff detailed information on customers' personal information, purchase history, buying preferences, and concerns. With cloud-based CRM software, data are stored on an external, remote network that employees can access anytime and anywhere there is an Internet connection. Four popular vendors of CRM systems are Salesforce.com, Microsoft, SAP, and Oracle.

Tables

The foundation of a database is a table. A **table** contains information arranged in horizontal rows and vertical columns, as shown in Figure 12-2. A database table appears similar to a spreadsheet. Most databases contain more than one table. The tables are organized by topic.

Records

Rows in a database table are called records. A **record** contains information related to the entry in the first column of the record. This column is called ID by default, and the data in this column cannot be edited by the user. In most database programs, the software automatically generates the ID number. The column can be modified to make its name more meaningful, such as EMPLOYEE ID or INVENTORY NUM.

For example, if the table contains information about people who work at a particular company, each record would contain information about one person. This may include the employee's first and last names, date of hire, and Social Security number. There would be one record for each employee.

If the table contains all of the products available at a hardware store, each record would contain only data about one piece of inventory. For example, each record might contain the type of product, the name of the supplier, and the product's cost. Each product would have a separate record in the table.

Key Applications
GS5 4.3.2

Career Skills

Material-Moving Machine Operator

Material-moving machine operators work with robotic systems to load and unload high numbers of containers between large ocean-going vessels and transport vehicles in the port. Driven by a vast database and robotic movements, these systems move goods at a rapid rate. Some operators manage the systems via remote interface for a port far from their stations.

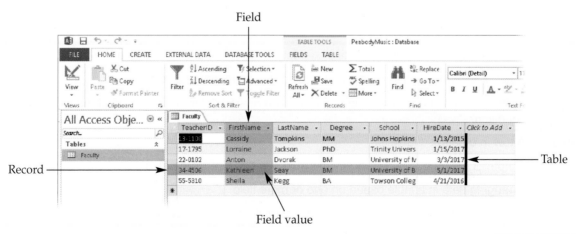

Field

Record

Table

Field value

Goodheart-Willcox Publisher

Figure 12-2. A table consists of records (rows) and fields (columns).

Fields

Columns in a database table are called fields. **Fields** contain information about specific characteristics of the entry described in a record. The names of the columns appear along the top of the table. For a table containing employee information, fields may be included for first name, last name, date of hire, and Social Security number. These labels will appear along the top of the table.

Key Applications
4.3.1

Microsoft Access

Microsoft Access is the database management software included in the Microsoft Office suite. Its best applications are for personal use or for small business management. All examples and discussions in this chapter are based on Microsoft Access. The parts of the Microsoft Access screen are identified in Figure 12-3.

Microsoft Access saves databases with the **.accdb** file extension. When a database file is saved, there will not be separate files in the folder for all of the tables, reports, forms, and queries created in the project. These items are all stored within the single database file.

As with all software, there are **Save** and **Save as** options in Microsoft Access. The **Save as** option allows the database to be saved under a different file name. The **Save** option saves the database under the current file name. However, if the file has not yet been saved, the **Save as** option will be activated.

FYI

Microsoft Access is not included in all levels of the Microsoft Office suite, but can be purchased separately.

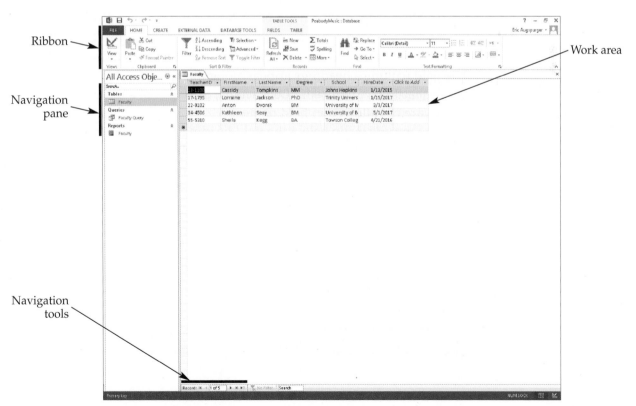

Goodheart-Willcox Publisher

Figure 12-3. The various parts of the Microsoft Access screen are identified here.

Microsoft Access is closed in the same manner as any Microsoft Office application. Click the standard close button (X) in the upper-right corner of the application window. You can also click **Close** in the **File** tab on the ribbon. Whenever Microsoft Access is closed, the database file is automatically saved.

Examining a Database

Ethics

Customer Information

A database may contain personal information about customers or employees. This information should be treated as confidential. It is unethical to share personal information about someone without his or her permission. Many people also consider the practice of selling customer data to other companies unethical. Companies often promote the fact that they do not sell customer data as a way to promote goodwill with customers.

The best way to learn about databases and a DBMS is to look at examples. First, you will examine an existing database. After that, you will look at how to create a database from scratch.

Consider the database created by the company Rizzo Landscapes. The owner is Troy Rizzo, who is a landscape architect, and his company provides a wide range of services, from site analyses and feasibility studies to drafting and administering construction documents for projects of various scales. He has set up three tables to track his data:

- customer information
- contract details
- invoices

This is the information that Troy tracks:

- contract number, which is a unique number assigned to each contract
- customer ID, which is a unique number assigned to each customer
- contract amount, which is the dollar amount for the full contract
- signing date, which is the date the customer signed the contract
- contract type, which is a brief description of the contract

Look at the Microsoft Access database shown in Figure 12-4. The title of the table is listed on the tab at the top of the table just below the ribbon. The field (column) headings appear along the top of the table. The fields are ContractNum, CustomerID, ContractAmt, SigningDate, and ContractType. Spaces are not allowed in field names.

The records begin below the field headings. In this example, there are three records. Each datum in a record is related to the entry in the first field, or left-hand column. For example, the fields in the record highlighted in blue in Figure 12-4 are all related to the same contract.

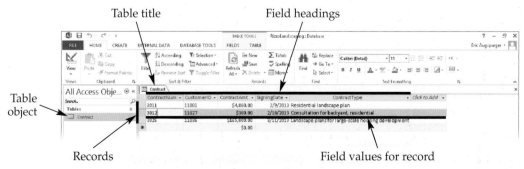

Goodheart-Willcox Publisher

Figure 12-4. Tables are the foundation of a database. The parts of a table are identified here.

HANDS-ON EXAMPLE 12.1.1

EXAMINING A DATABASE

A database consists of at least one table composed of rows and columns. The best way to learn about a database is to begin by looking at an existing database.

1. Insert your PRINC-OF-IT flash drive into the computer.
2. Applying what you have learned, create a folder on the flash drive named Chap12.
3. Navigate to the student companion website at www.g-wlearning.com, download the data files for this chapter, and save them in the Chap12 folder on your flash drive.
4. Launch Microsoft Access 2013.
5. On the startup screen, click **Open other files**, followed by **Computer** and then the **Browse** button.
6. Navigate to the Chap12 folder on your flash drive, and open the RizzoLandscaping.accdb database file.
7. If a security warning appears below the ribbon, click the **Enable Content** button.
8. Locate the navigation pane on the left, and make note of the objects that are part of the database. In this case, the database contains one object, which is a table named Contract.
9. Double-click the Contract table in the navigation pane to open the table.
10. Locate the table in the center of the screen. Notice the field labels along the top. The name of each record is determined by what appears in the first column, which in this case is the ContractNum field.
11. Right-click on the tab above the table that contains the table name, and click **Close** in the shortcut menu.
12. Click **Save As** in the **File** tab of the ribbon, and then click **Save Database As** followed by the **Save As** button.
13. In the standard save as dialog box that is displayed, save the file as *LastName*RizzoLandscaping.accdb in the Chap12 folder on your flash drive.

Adding Data

As with spreadsheets, information will be added to a database after it is created. It is easy to add a new record to a table in a Microsoft Access database. Click in the first column for the new record, and enter the necessary data. Then, use the [Tab] key to move from left to right, entering data into each field as you go. Do not enter symbols such as commas or dollar signs. The software will take care of that just as spreadsheet software does. Press the [Enter] or [Tab] key at the end of the record. Do not click the Click to Add column heading or a new field will be added to the table.

GS4 Key Applications
5.1.3

HANDS-ON EXAMPLE 12.1.2

ADDING DATA

1. Launch Microsoft Access, and open the *LastName*RizzoLandscaping.accdb file in the Chap12 folder on your flash drive, if it is not already open.
2. If a security warning appears below the ribbon, click the **Enable Content** button.
3. Double-click the Contract table in the navigation pane to open the table.

HANDS-ON EXAMPLE 12.1.2 (CONTINUED)

4. Click in the ContractNum field for the next available record. The next available record has an asterisk (*) to the left.
5. Enter 3015, and press the [Tab] key.
6. Continue adding the following data. Do not add the dollar signs or commas. Press the [Tab] key to advance through the database.

ContractNum	CustomerID	ContractAmt	SigningDate	ContractType
3015	11005	$1,500	3/1/2017	Schematic plan for backyard, residential
3022	11043	$22,000	4/14/2017	Landscape design for two entrances
3023	11071	$39,000	3/22/2017	Renovation of large multifamily housing open space

Editing Data

Key Applications
GS4 5.1.3

Data that have already been entered into a database can be easily changed. Editing data in a database table is similar to editing data in a spreadsheet. Display the table that contains the record with the information to be edited. Then, click the cell to edit, and change the entry. Unlike a spreadsheet in Microsoft Excel, clicking the cell automatically activates it for editing, placing the insertion point within the cell. So, to completely replace the existing data requires erasing what is there and then entering the new data.

Deleting Data

Key Applications
GS4 5.1.3

Incorrect data can be deleted. To delete data in a cell, click the cell in the table to activate it for editing. Then, use the [Delete] or [Backspace] key to remove the data.

Often, an entire record or field will need to be removed. This is a drastic move and should be well planned. In Microsoft Access, a deleted record or field cannot be restored using the **Undo** function. In the other Microsoft Office applications, the **Undo** function reverses the last changed. In Microsoft Access, the **Undo** function can reverse some, but not all, changes. Deleting a record or field is one of the changes that cannot be undone in Access.

To delete a record, move the cursor to the left of the record until it changes to a right-pointing arrow. Click to select the entire record or row. To select a field, move the cursor above the field until it changes to a downward-pointing arrow. With the record or field selected, press the [Delete] key. A warning appears asking to confirm the deletion and warning that the change cannot be undone, as shown in Figure 12-5. Click the **Yes** button to delete the record or field.

Goodheart-Willcox Publisher

Figure 12-5. When a record is deleted, the action cannot be undone.

HANDS-ON EXAMPLE 12.1.3

EDITING DATA

The data in a database will usually change. The ability to edit the data to update records is an important skill to master when working with databases.

1. Launch Microsoft Access, and open the *LastName*RizzoLandscaping.accdb file in the Chap12 folder on your flash drive, if it is not already open.
2. If a security warning appears below the ribbon, click the **Enable Content** button.
3. Double-click the Contract table in the navigation pane to open the table.
4. Click the cell in the 3015 record for the ContractAmt field. The cell is activated for editing, and the insertion point is within the cell.
5. Change the amount to 1750.
6. Move the cursor to the left of the record 3022 record until it changes to a right-pointing arrow, and click. The entire record is selected.
7. Press the [Delete] key.
8. Click the **Yes** button in the warning that appears. The record is permanently removed from the database.

Creating a Database Structure

Users can enjoy many benefits from a correctly designed database. In an educational or business setting, many people may want to use the data. If the organization is using a DBMS, it can improve its ability to share data. The organization can minimize inconsistencies among the different parts. As a result, the users will be able to make better decisions and be more productive.

Before a database is created, the purpose of the database must be determined. Then, how the information is to be organized into tables must be planned. First, decide exactly which information to track. These items will become the fields. Related fields will be in the same table. If necessary, additional tables can be created to group other related fields.

Data Types

Databases are particular about what type of data goes in each field. When the data types are correctly set up, the information is easier to retrieve. It also ensures that whoever is using the database is entering data in the proper manner. Deciding what type of data is going to go in a field also allows the system to establish how much room it needs to set aside. There are several different types of data that can be stored in the fields of a database, such as:

- text;
- numbers;
- currency;
- dates; and
- Boolean (yes/no).

Numbers are considered text if they are not going to be used for calculation.

Fields can be sized to control the data entry. For example, a text field may need room for 50 characters for an address. A yes-no field only needs space for one character, a Y or an N, as shown in Figure 12-6.

In the Rizzo Landscaping example in the previous section, four data types were used. The contract number and the customer ID were numeric fields. The contract amount was a currency field. The signing date was a date field. The contract type was a text field.

Creating a Table

The best way to learn how to create a database from scratch is to look at an example. In this example, a database will be created to help manage a music school. The director, Cassidy Tompkins, founded the Peabody Music School because of his popularity as a music teacher specializing in brass instruments. During the past two years, other qualified teachers have joined him to offer instruction in voice, piano, violin, cello, guitar, percussion, and other instruments. As the school continues to grow, he wants to keep track of information about students, teachers, and contracts. Mr. Tompkins wants to track this information about instructors:

- teacher ID
- first name
- last name
- degree
- school
- hire date

The database will contain fields to track this information. Once the database is set up, Mr. Tompkins will enter the data into these fields.

Defining Fields

When starting a database from scratch, begin by creating a table. When a blank database is started in Microsoft Access, a blank table is automatically created and displayed in the datasheet view. However, fields are defined in Microsoft Access in the design view. The **design view** is for developers of the database to set up fields, as shown in Figure 12-7.

Database Energy Use

Many databases are in constant use, especially those driving websites. This means the database resides on a server that is always on and consuming power. One way to make these databases more green is to choose green energy suppliers for the servers running the databases. Green energy is generated from renewable sources, whereas traditional brown energy is generated from carbon-based sources, such as coal-fired plants.

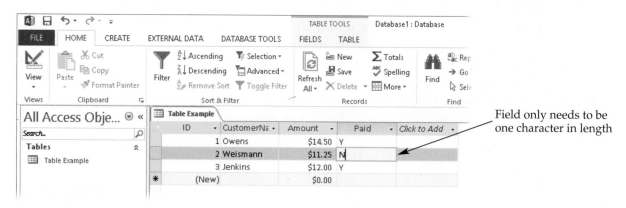

Goodheart-Willcox Publisher

Figure 12-6. The length of a text field can be set to limit entry. In this case, the length is one character to allow only an entry of Y or N.

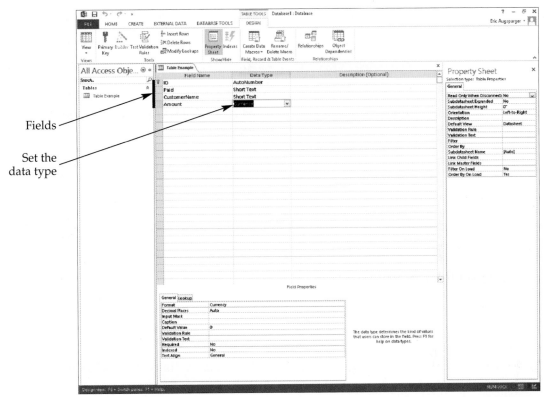

Fields

Set the data type

Figure 12-7. The design view is where fields are set up. Ordinary users of the database will not see this view.

Ordinary users of the database will not see the design view. This prevents them from changing the fields or the data type.

To display the design view in Microsoft Access, click the **View** button in the **Views** group on the **Home** tab of the ribbon. This button is a toggle between the datasheet view and the design view. The drop-down arrow below the button can also be clicked to display a drop-down menu. In some cases, there may be more views that can be displayed with this menu. When displaying a new table in the design view, it must first be named and saved.

The first field entered into a table is, by default, the primary key. The **primary key** is the field that will be used by the DBMS to keep track of records. In the design view of Microsoft Access, the row header for the primary key contains an icon of a key. There can be only one primary key in a table.

Each record must have a different value for the primary key. For example, when tracking people with a database, such as students or employees, the last name cannot be a primary key because there could be duplicates. Instead, a unique identification number should be used. Microsoft Access suggests the first field, which is the default primary key, be named ID. It also suggests the data type should be an automatic number. These can be accepted or changed as needed.

Enter the name to use in the **Field Name** column or press the [Enter] or [Tab] key to accept the default value. To set the data type, click the drop-down arrow in the **Data Type** column, and then click the data type for the

FYI

Right-clicking on the tab name of the table displays a shortcut menu that can be used to switch views.

field. For example, if the field will be a date, click **Date/Time** in the drop-down list.

Entering New Records

Once the table is set up in Microsoft Access, data are entered into the database using the datasheet view. Display the datasheet view by clicking the **View** button in the **Views** group on the **Home** tab of the ribbon. Once the datasheet view is displayed, new records are created and data entered the same as previously discussed for an existing database.

HANDS-ON EXAMPLE 12.1.4

CREATING A DATABASE

When working with databases, sometimes you will have an existing database. However, many times you will need to create a database from scratch.

1. Launch Microsoft Access 2013.
2. On the startup screen, click **Blank desktop database**. A dialog box is displayed for naming the database and specifying its location.
3. Click in the **File Name** text box, and enter PeabodyMusic.
4. Click the **Browse** button, and navigate to the Chap12 folder on your flash drive.
5. Click the **Create** button. The database is created, and an empty table appears in the datasheet view.
6. Click the **View** button in the **Views** group on the **Home** tab of the ribbon to display the design view. The **Save As** dialog box appears for naming the table.
7. Click in the **Table Name:** text box, enter Faculty, and click the **OK** button. The default for the first field, which is the primary key, is ID, and this value is active for editing.
8. Replace ID with TeacherID. Do not use spaces. This will be the field name for the primary key.
9. Press the [Tab] key to move to the Data Type column or click the cell in that column.
10. Click the drop-down arrow in the cell to view the different types. There are two types of text fields, short and long. This field will have only seven characters, which is considered short text.
11. Click **Short Text** in the drop-down list.
12. Press the [Tab] key to move to the Description column or click the cell in that column.
13. Enter Primary key in the cell, as shown. This is an optional field, but whatever is entered here will be displayed in the status bar in a form to help the user know what to enter.

Field name   Data type   Optional comment

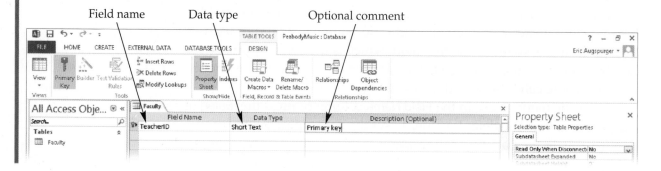

HANDS-ON EXAMPLE 12.1.4 (CONTINUED)

14. Press the [Tab] or [Enter] key to move to the next row.
15. Applying what you have learned, create the remaining fields shown below. If you need to make a change due to a typo or reconsideration, click the cell and correct the information.

Field Name	Data Type	Description
FirstName	Short Text	First name of teacher
LastName	Short Text	Last name of teacher
Degree	Short Text	Educational degree
School	Short Text	College or university attended
HireDate	Date/Time	Date hired

16. Right-click on the table name in the tab above the table, and click **Save** in the shortcut menu.

View

17. Click the **View** button in the **Views** group on the **Home** tab of the ribbon to display the datasheet view. If the table has unsaved changes, a message appears indicating the table must be saved before changing views.
18. Applying what you have learned, enter the records shown below to complete the table. In some cases, the data may extend beyond the width of the cell, which will not affect the data.

TeacherID	FirstName	LastName	Degree	School	HireDate
13-1100	Cassidy	Tompkins	MM	Johns Hopkins University	1/13/2015
17-1795	Lorraine	Jackson	PhD	Trinity University	1/15/2017
55-5310	Sheila	Kegg	BA	Towson College	4/21/2016
22-0102	Anton	Dvorak	BM	University of Maryland	3/3/2017
34-4506	Kathleen	Seay	BM	University of Baltimore	5/1/2017

Save

19. Click the **Save** button on the **Quick Access** toolbar to save the table.
20. Click the standard **Close** button (X) to close Microsoft Access.

TITANS OF TECHNOLOGY

Sergey Grin and Larry Page created Google while pursuing their PhDs at Stanford University. Google makes use of massive databases and has the most sophisticated search algorithms of any programs written. Its mission is "to organize the world's information and make it universally accessible and useful." Google runs more than one million servers in data centers around the world and processes over one billion search requests per day. Each data center is composed of high-performance computers that run all the time. Google maintains an index of websites, which is a large database. A Google search is a basic query on the index (database). According to Google, this database exceeds 95 petabytes in size, or nearly 100 million gigabytes. Google also can reach other databases of information that are not links, but can be accessed via queries.

12.1 SECTION REVIEW

 CHECK YOUR UNDERSTANDING

1. What are the columns in a database table called?
2. Which part of a database is a row?
3. How do you undo the deletion of a record in Microsoft Access?
4. In which view are fields set up in Microsoft Access?
5. What is true about the value for each record in the field set as the primary key?

IC3 CERTIFICATION PRACTICE

The following question is a sample of the types of questions presented on the IC3 exam.

1. Which of the following data types should be used to create fields that contain numerals that will not be used for calculation?
   A. number
   B. currency
   C. text
   D. date/time

 BUILD YOUR VOCABULARY

As you progress through this course, develop a personal IT glossary. This will help you build your vocabulary and prepare you for a career. Write a definition for each of the following terms and add it to your IT glossary.

database	field
database management system (DBMS)	primary key
	record
design view	table

IMPORTING AND VIEWING DATA

auremar/Shutterstock.com

There are many ways to view the data once they have been entered. Users can see all of the data in the table view as they are entered. These data can be sorted and filtered to make specific records more obvious.

Tables containing many records can present a problem for the person entering or updating the data. It can be distracting to verify that data have been entered on the correct line. This difficulty can be overcome by showing only one record at a time in a form. Another way to view the data is through a report. This can be printed and formatted so the reader does not need to know how to use the DBMS to understand it.

Essential Question

How does use of a form improve the effectiveness of information in a database?

TERMS

datasheet view
foreign key
form
one-to-many relationship
relational database
report

LEARNING GOALS

After completing this section, you will be able to:
- Explain how to import records into a database.
- Describe different ways in which to view data in a database.
- Explain the process of joining tables in a database.

Importing Records into a Database

A database can be created from scratch. New fields and records can be added to a table. If needed, new tables can be created to group related data. Data can be entered directly into the database. However, sometimes the data already exist in some other form, such as in a spreadsheet.

If the data are located in a spreadsheet, instead of manually reentering the data into the database, the spreadsheet can be imported into the database. Importing existing data is much more efficient than reentering it, especially if the quantity of data is large. Data can be imported into a blank database or a database that already contains data.

In Microsoft Access, a wizard is used to import data from a spreadsheet, as shown in Figure 12-8. The columns in the spreadsheet should match the order of the fields in the database and the data types. Both the spreadsheet and the table in Access into which the data are being imported must be closed before starting the process. During the importing process, the user is given the opportunity to check the data before importing them.

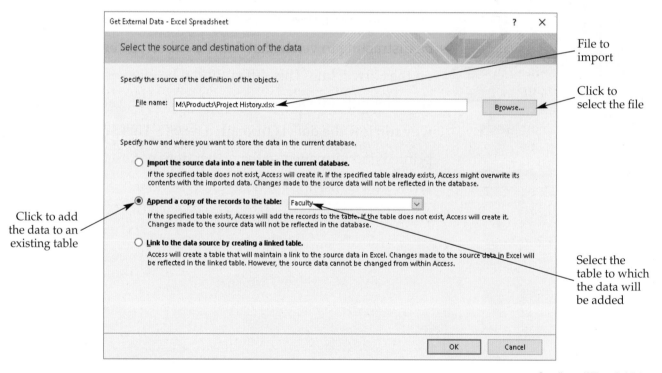

Goodheart-Willcox Publisher

Figure 12-8. Importing data from a spreadsheet into an existing table.

HANDS-ON EXAMPLE 12.2.1

IMPORTING DATA

If data exist in a spreadsheet, they should be imported into the database instead of manually reentering them. This is done through use of a wizard.

1. Launch Microsoft Access, and open the *LastName*RizzoLandscaping.accdb file in the Chap12 folder on your flash drive, if it is not already open.
2. If a security warning appears below the ribbon, click the **Enable Content** button.
3. Double-click the Contract table in the navigation pane to open the table.
4. Applying what you have learned, display the design view. Make note of the field names.
5. Launch Microsoft Excel, and open the Troy1.xlsx file in the Chap12 folder on your flash drive. Note the first row contains the same field names used in the Rizzo Landscaping database and they are in the same order.
6. Close Excel, and return to Access.
7. Right-click on the tab above the table that contains the table name, and click **Close** in the shortcut menu.

Import Excel Spreadsheet

8. Click the **Import Excel Spreadsheet** button in the **Import & Link** group on the **External Data** tab of the ribbon. A wizard is launched to guide you through the process of importing data.
9. Click the **Browse...** button on the first page of the wizard, navigate to the Chap12 folder on your flash drive, and open the Troy1.xlsx file.
10. Click the **Append a copy of the records to the table:** radio button, as shown. This tells Access to add the data to an existing table. There is only one table in this database, so it is automatically listed in the corresponding drop-down list. If there were more than one table, the drop-down list is used to select to which table the data will be added.

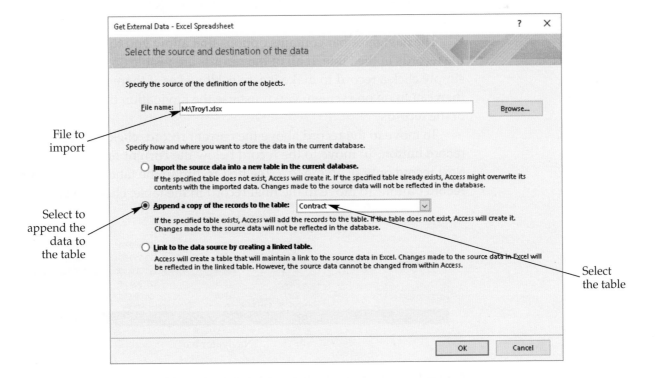

HANDS-ON EXAMPLE 12.2.1 (CONTINUED)

11. Click the **OK** button to display the next page of the wizard. This page shows the column headings in the spreadsheet as the field names for the database. The data will be imported as shown. If data are not correctly set up, click the **Cancel** button, fix the data in the spreadsheet, and start again.
12. Click the **Finish** button. The final page of the wizard is displayed, which offers the option to save the steps for importing the data.
13. Leave the **Save import steps** check box unchecked, and click the **Close** button.
14. Open the Contract table, and verify that the new data were imported.
15. Close the table.
16. Applying what you have learned, import the Troy2.xlsx spreadsheet file into the Contract table. Be sure to examine the spreadsheet file to verify the column names versus the field names in the database.

Viewing Data

The data in a database can be viewed in different ways. The basic way to view data is in table form. This is the datasheet view you have used so far. Another way to view data is in a form. Data can also be sorted, just as in a spreadsheet.

Datasheet View

In Microsoft Access, the **datasheet view** displays data in table form. When a table is open, the navigation bar appears at the bottom of the Access window, as shown in Figure 12-9. The text box indicates which record is currently selected and the total number of records.

The navigator bar contains options that allow you to move through the records in the table. If all of the records are visible on-screen, you can simply click a record to make it active. However, if there are more records than can fit on one screen, you must use the navigation options to see all of the records.

To move to the record above the current record, click the **Previous record** button. To move to the record below the current record, click the **Next record** button. To move to the first record in the table, click the **First record** button. To move to the final record in the table, click the **Last**

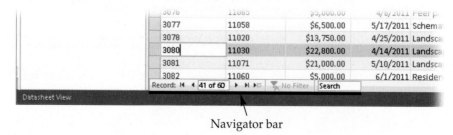

Goodheart-Willcox Publisher

Figure 12-9. The navigator bar is located at the bottom of the datasheet view and contains tools for navigating the table.

record button. If the number of the record is known, the number can be entered directly in the text box.

Clicking the **New (blank) record** button in the navigation bar adds an empty record to the bottom of the table. You can then enter the data for the record.

Sorting and Filtering Data

Each record in a database contains related field data. The database can be sorted on one field and have all related information sorted with it. This is similar to sorting data in a spreadsheet. In Microsoft Access, the data are sorted by default on the first field entered in the table.

To sort the data by a field, click the drop-down arrow in the field header, as shown in Figure 12-10. This selects the entire field and displays a drop-down menu. Notice this drop-down menu is similar to the one used to sort data in Microsoft Excel. To sort the data in ascending order based on the selected field, click **Sort A to Z** or **Sort Smallest to Largest** in the drop-down menu. To sort the data in descending order, click **Sort Z to A** or **Sort Largest to Smallest** in the drop-down menu. These options are also available as the **Ascending** and **Descending** buttons in the **Sort & Filter** group on the **Home** tab of the ribbon.

To filter the data, click the drop-down arrow in the field header or select the field and click the **Filter** button in the **Sort & Filter** group on the **Home** tab of the ribbon. The same drop-down menu is displayed as when sorting data. Uncheck the **(Select All)** check box, and then check the check boxes for the values to include in the filtered data. Finally, click the **OK** button to filter the data.

Engineering

The fields of engineering rely on data of all types, from reference articles to the empirical results of research. Databases are especially suited to store and drive access to these data. The querying, sorting, and filtering capabilities of a database can make locating specific data easy.

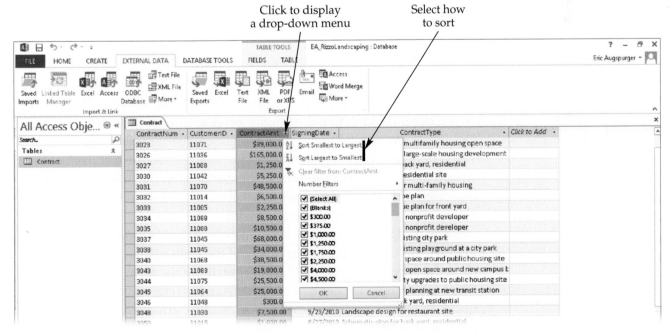

Goodheart-Willcox Publisher

Figure 12-10. To sort a table by a field, click the drop-down arrow in the field heading, and then select how to sort.

HANDS-ON EXAMPLE 12.2.2

SORTING DATA

Data in a database can be sorted by fields. This allows the data to be viewed in the order most appropriate for the information that needs to be obtained.

1. Launch Microsoft Access, and open the *LastName*RizzoLandscaping.accdb file in the Chap12 folder on your flash drive, if it is not already open.
2. If a security warning appears below the ribbon, click the **Enable Content** button.
3. Applying what you have learned, open the Contract table.
4. Applying what you have learned, select the ContractAmt field.
5. Click the **Descending** button in the **Sort & Filter** group on the **Home** tab of the ribbon. The data are sorted with the first record being contract number 3103 having a contract amount of $252,000.

Descending

6. Applying what you have learned, sort the SigningDate field in ascending order. After the sort, the first record should be contract number 3027 with a date of 4/7/2015.

Form

Key Applications
GS5
4.3.5

Looking at the data in the table view can be difficult because the records are in narrow bands across the screen. It is easier for users and those entering data to see only one record at a time. Microsoft Access contains another object in addition to a table that makes this task simpler. A **form** is a database object used to display only certain data, one record at a time.

To create a form in Microsoft Access, click the **Form Wizard** button in the **Forms** group on the **Create** tab of the ribbon. On the first page of the wizard, select which fields to include, as shown in Figure 12-11. To include a field, select it in the left-hand box, and click the single right-pointing chevron button (>). To include all fields, click the double right-pointing chevron button (>>). The fields listed in the right-hand box will be included in the form. To remove one of these fields, select it in the right-hand box, and click the single left-pointing chevron button (<). To remove all fields, click the double left-pointing chevron button (<<). On the second page of the wizard, select how the form will be arranged. The columnar layout is often the design selected. On the last page of the wizard, name the form and select whether to open the form or to modify its design. Once the form is created, it appears in the navigation pane along with the table on which it is based.

The navigation bar at the bottom of the Access window can be used to move through the form. Each page of the form displays one record. To close the form, right-click on the tab containing the form name, and click **Close** in the shortcut menu or click the standard close button (X) in the upper-right corner of the form. To open a form, double-click on it in the navigation pane.

FYI

It is a good idea to include the name of the table with which a form is associated in the name of the form.

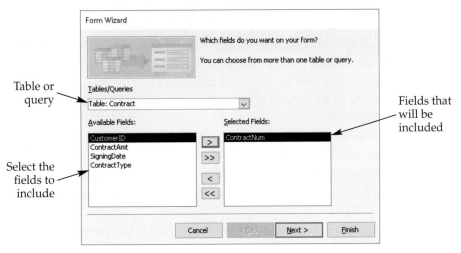

Table or query

Fields that will be included

Select the fields to include

Goodheart-Willcox Publisher

Figure 12-11. A wizard is used in Microsoft Access to create a form.

HANDS-ON EXAMPLE 12.2.3

CREATING A FORM

A form can be created to display only certain data from records. This is an easy way to limit the data to only what needs to be seen.

1. Launch Microsoft Access, and open the *LastName*RizzoLandscaping.accdb file in the Chap12 folder on your flash drive, if it is not already open.
2. If a security warning appears below the ribbon, click the **Enable Content** button.
3. Click the **Form Wizard** button in the **Forms** group on the **Create** tab of the ribbon.
4. On the first page of the wizard, click the ContractNum field in the left-hand box to select it, as shown.

Form Wizard

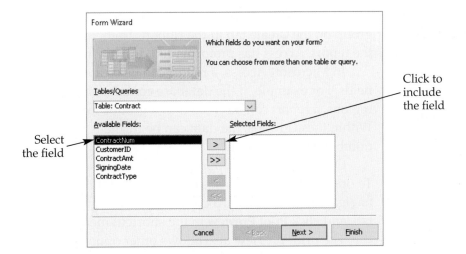

Select the field

Click to include the field

5. Click the single right-pointing chevron to move the field to the right-hand box.
6. Applying what you have learned, add the ContractAmt and SigningDate fields to the right-hand box.

HANDS-ON EXAMPLE 12.2.3 (CONTINUED)

7. Click the **Next** button to display the second page of the wizard.
8. Click the **Columnar** radio button to select that layout, and click the **Next** button.
9. On the next page of the wizard, click in the text box at the top of the page, and enter Contract Form. This is the name of the form.
10. Click the **Open the form to view or enter data** radio button. This will open the form as soon as it is created.
11. Click the **Finish** button. The form is created and opened. The first record of the database is displayed on the first page of the form. Notice that only data from the selected fields are displayed in the form.
12. Applying what you have learned, use the commands in the navigation bar to move to a new record.
13. Add the following information into the new record. Do not enter the dollar sign or comma. Press the [Enter] key after entering the last datum to save the new record.

ContractNum	3111
ContractAmt	$32,789
SigningDate	today's date

14. Applying what you have learned, open the Contract table and navigate to the record for contract number 3111. You may need to close and reopen the table to see the new record. Notice that several fields are empty. This is because they were not available in the form, so data could not be entered in these fields using the form.

Preparing a Report

Tables and forms deal with input. Another object in Microsoft Access contains output instead of input. A **report** is an output of the database of specific information requested by the user, as shown in Figure 12-12. A report is created in Microsoft Access in much the same way as a form is created. To create a report, click the **Report Wizard** button in the **Reports** group on the **Create** tab in the ribbon. Then, follow the wizard to create the report. Access has preformatted designs for creating reports.

In Microsoft Access, a report can be created that groups data by fields. For example, if the database contains sales data from four different regions, a report can be created that groups information by each region. Within these groups, the data can be further grouped by customer number or sales amount.

Once created, the report object is displayed in the navigation pane. To open a report after it has been closed, double-click on the report in the navigation pane. If a hard copy is needed, right-click on the report name tab, and click **Print Preview** in the shortcut menu.

The print preview also allows other options. The report can be sent to a printer, e-mailed, exported as an Excel spreadsheet, or converted to a PDF file. The view of the report can be zoomed and reoriented if needed.

FYI

If the report does not appear in the navigation pane, try changing the view in the pane. Right-click on the pane, and click **Category>Tables and Related Views** in the shortcut menu. Then, right-click and click **Category>Object Type** to return to the previous view.

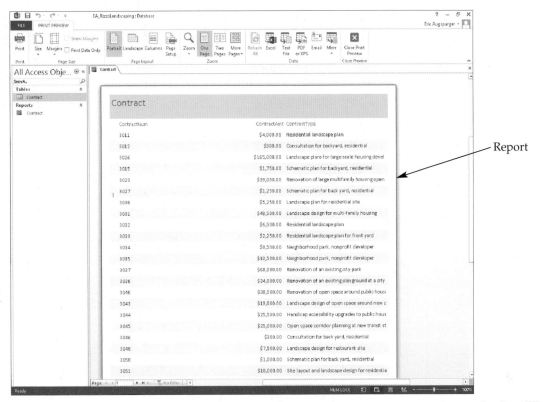

Report

Figure 12-12. A report is an output of data requested by the user.

HANDS-ON EXAMPLE 12.2.4

CREATING A REPORT

One way of outputting data from a database is to create a report. A report is created in Microsoft Access in much the same way a form is created.

1. Launch Microsoft Access, and open the *LastName*RizzoLandscaping.accdb file in the Chap12 folder on your flash drive, if it is not already open.
2. If a security warning appears below the ribbon, click the **Enable Content** button.
3. Click the **Report Wizard** button in the **Reports** group on the **Create** tab of the ribbon.

Report Wizard

4. Applying what you have learned, move the CustomerID, ContractAmt, and SigningDate fields into the right-hand box, and then click the **Next** button.
5. The next page of the wizard asks for grouping levels. Click the **Next** button to continue without creating any groups.
6. The next page of the wizard allows sorting of the data. Click the first drop-down arrow, and click **CustomerID** in the drop-down list. Click the button to the right of the drop-down arrow until it displays **Ascending**. This will sort the data by customer ID in ascending order. Click the **Next** button.
7. On the next page of the wizard, click the **Tabular** and **Portrait** radio buttons, and then click the **Next** button. This sets the layout of the report.
8. On the final page of the wizard, click in the text box, and enter Customer Signing Dates as the name of the report. This will be the title that appears on the report, so use spaces between words.

HANDS-ON EXAMPLE 12.2.4 (CONTINUED)

9. Click the **Preview the report** radio button, and click the **Finish** button. The report is generated and displayed, as shown. The **Print Preview** on-demand tab is displayed in the ribbon. Review the available commands.

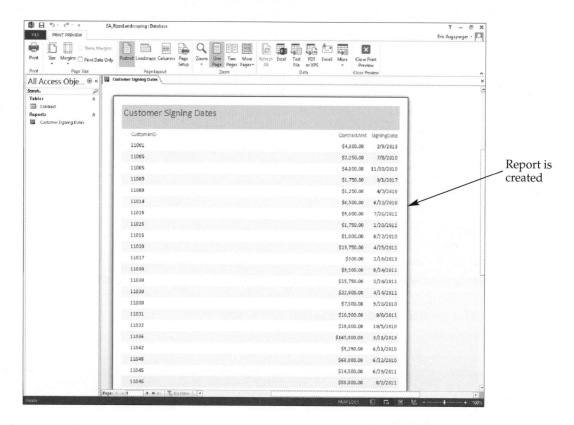

Report is created

10. Right-click on the report name tab, and click **Close** in the shortcut menu.
11. Applying what you have learned, create a new report that includes the ContractNum and ContractType fields sorted in descending order by contract number. Name the report Contract Descriptions.

Joining Tables

Most databases contain more than one table. For example, the Rizzo Landscaping database includes a table of contract descriptions. However, it would more than likely include additional tables for the contact information of customers and payment of invoices.

However, it is not a good practice to put all data in one big table. As the amount of data increases, it would take a long time to load all of the data. This would slow down the retrieval process. To solve this problem, data are organized into separate categories that become individual tables. These tables can then be joined.

With a DBMS, data can be retrieved by joining tables that have a common field. Microsoft Access is a relational DBMS. A **relational database** is a collection of tables that have been joined. These relationships make it possible to see parts of the database instead of displaying entire tables.

To demonstrate how tables are joined, continue considering the Peabody Music School example from earlier in this chapter. Mr. Tompkins, the owner of the Peabody Music School, has been keeping track of student data in a text file, as shown in Figure 12-13. This text file is difficult to read. Each piece of data in the field contains a different amount of characters. Importing the table into a database will allow better use and readability of the data.

To build a table to track the student information, analyze what is present in this file. Each of the fields is separated by commas. The text fields are enclosed within quotation marks. Numerical and date/time fields are not enclosed within quotation marks. Notice the date/time field includes the time as all zeroes for each record. These will be ignored when the data are imported into Microsoft Access. Also notice that there are no field names given in the file. The field names have to be determined by the person importing the table into the database.

Careful analysis of the text file shows that there are ten fields in this table. The first field contains data for the primary key. Other fields are included for first name, last name, street address, city, state, ZIP code, phone number, date of birth, and student gender.

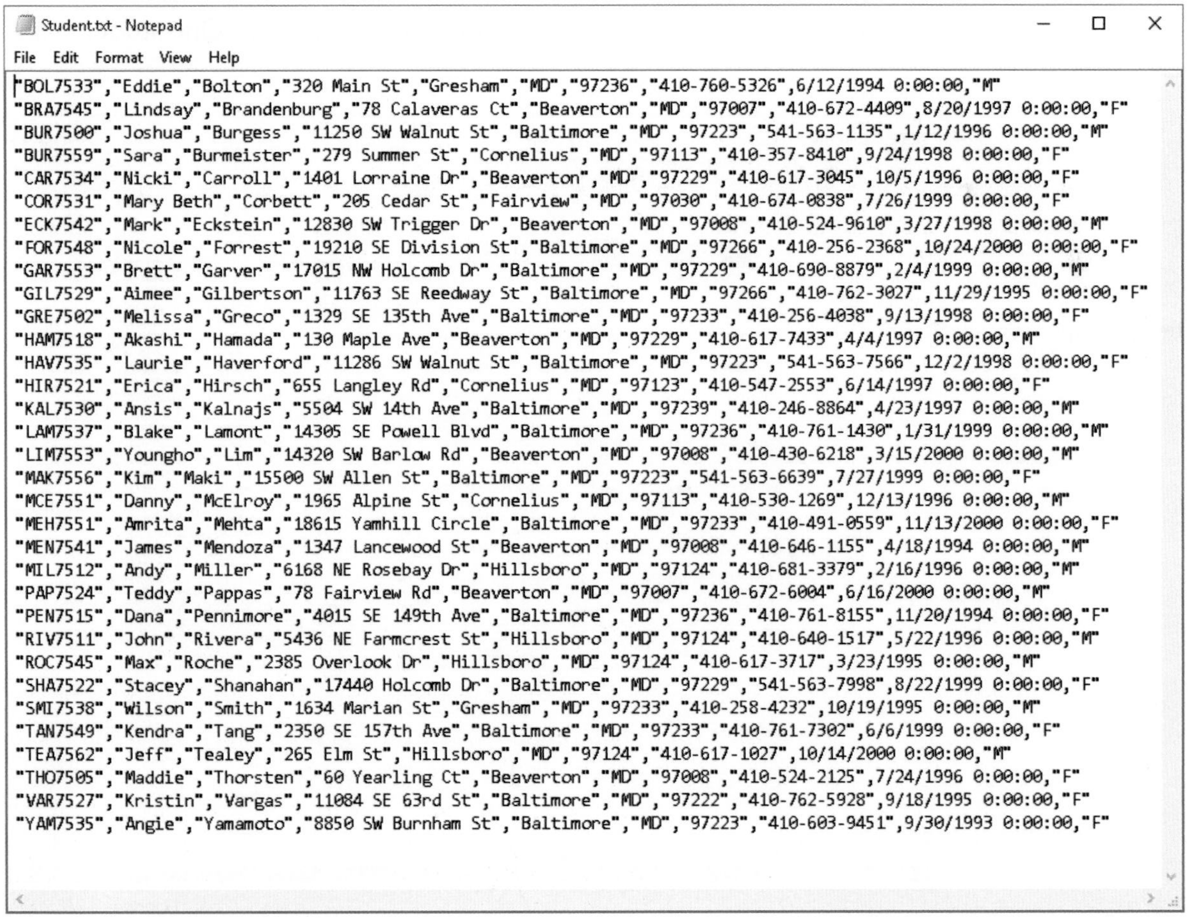
Student.txt - Notepad
File Edit Format View Help

```
"BOL7533","Eddie","Bolton","320 Main St","Gresham","MD","97236","410-760-5326",6/12/1994 0:00:00,"M"
"BRA7545","Lindsay","Brandenburg","78 Calaveras Ct","Beaverton","MD","97007","410-672-4409",8/20/1997 0:00:00,"F"
"BUR7500","Joshua","Burgess","11250 SW Walnut St","Baltimore","MD","97223","541-563-1135",1/12/1996 0:00:00,"M"
"BUR7559","Sara","Burmeister","279 Summer St","Cornelius","MD","97113","410-357-8410",9/24/1998 0:00:00,"F"
"CAR7534","Nicki","Carroll","1401 Lorraine Dr","Beaverton","MD","97229","410-617-3045",10/5/1996 0:00:00,"F"
"COR7531","Mary Beth","Corbett","205 Cedar St","Fairview","MD","97030","410-674-0838",7/26/1999 0:00:00,"F"
"ECK7542","Mark","Eckstein","12830 SW Trigger Dr","Beaverton","MD","97008","410-524-9610",3/27/1998 0:00:00,"M"
"FOR7548","Nicole","Forrest","19210 SE Division St","Baltimore","MD","97266","410-256-2368",10/24/2000 0:00:00,"F"
"GAR7553","Brett","Garver","17015 NW Holcomb Dr","Baltimore","MD","97229","410-690-8879",2/4/1999 0:00:00,"M"
"GIL7529","Aimee","Gilbertson","11763 SE Reedway St","Baltimore","MD","97266","410-762-3027",11/29/1995 0:00:00,"F"
"GRE7502","Melissa","Greco","1329 SE 135th Ave","Baltimore","MD","97233","410-256-4038",9/13/1998 0:00:00,"F"
"HAM7518","Akashi","Hamada","130 Maple Ave","Beaverton","MD","97229","410-617-7433",4/4/1997 0:00:00,"M"
"HAV7535","Laurie","Haverford","11286 SW Walnut St","Baltimore","MD","97223","541-563-7566",12/2/1998 0:00:00,"F"
"HIR7521","Erica","Hirsch","655 Langley Rd","Cornelius","MD","97123","410-547-2553",6/14/1997 0:00:00,"F"
"KAL7530","Ansis","Kalnajs","5504 SW 14th Ave","Baltimore","MD","97239","410-246-8864",4/23/1997 0:00:00,"M"
"LAM7537","Blake","Lamont","14305 SE Powell Blvd","Baltimore","MD","97236","410-761-1430",1/31/1999 0:00:00,"M"
"LIM7553","Youngho","Lim","14320 SW Barlow Rd","Beaverton","MD","97008","410-430-6218",3/15/2000 0:00:00,"M"
"MAK7556","Kim","Maki","15500 SW Allen St","Baltimore","MD","97223","541-563-6639",7/27/1999 0:00:00,"F"
"MCE7551","Danny","McElroy","1965 Alpine St","Cornelius","MD","97113","410-530-1269",12/13/1996 0:00:00,"M"
"MEH7551","Amrita","Mehta","18615 Yamhill Circle","Baltimore","MD","97233","410-491-0559",11/13/2000 0:00:00,"F"
"MEN7541","James","Mendoza","1347 Lancewood St","Beaverton","MD","97008","410-646-1155",4/18/1994 0:00:00,"M"
"MIL7512","Andy","Miller","6168 NE Rosebay Dr","Hillsboro","MD","97124","410-681-3379",2/16/1996 0:00:00,"M"
"PAP7524","Teddy","Pappas","78 Fairview Rd","Beaverton","MD","97007","410-672-6004",6/16/2000 0:00:00,"M"
"PEN7515","Dana","Pennimore","4015 SE 149th Ave","Baltimore","MD","97236","410-761-8155",11/20/1994 0:00:00,"F"
"RIV7511","John","Rivera","5436 NE Farmcrest St","Hillsboro","MD","97124","410-640-1517",5/22/1996 0:00:00,"M"
"ROC7545","Max","Roche","2385 Overlook Dr","Hillsboro","MD","97124","410-617-3717",3/23/1995 0:00:00,"M"
"SHA7522","Stacey","Shanahan","17440 Holcomb Dr","Baltimore","MD","97229","541-563-7998",8/22/1999 0:00:00,"F"
"SMI7538","Wilson","Smith","1634 Marian St","Gresham","MD","97233","410-258-4232",10/19/1995 0:00:00,"M"
"TAN7549","Kendra","Tang","2350 SE 157th Ave","Baltimore","MD","97233","410-761-7302",6/6/1999 0:00:00,"F"
"TEA7562","Jeff","Tealey","265 Elm St","Hillsboro","MD","97124","410-617-1027",10/14/2000 0:00:00,"M"
"THO7505","Maddie","Thorsten","60 Yearling Ct","Beaverton","MD","97008","410-524-2125",7/24/1996 0:00:00,"F"
"VAR7527","Kristin","Vargas","11084 SE 63rd St","Baltimore","MD","97222","410-762-5928",9/18/1995 0:00:00,"F"
"YAM7535","Angie","Yamamoto","8850 SW Burnham St","Baltimore","MD","97223","410-603-9451",9/30/1993 0:00:00,"F"
```

Goodheart-Willcox Publisher

Figure 12-13. The data in a comma-delimited text file are hard to read, but can be imported into a database.

This text file has been imported into the Peabody Music School database as a table. The database is named PeabodyMusic2 in the Chap12 folder on your flash drive. There are three tables in the database. The original table is Faculty, and the two tables that have been added are Contract and Student. Notice how the text data in the Student table are arranged in the fields, as shown in Figure 12-14. The quotation marks present in the text file were not imported when the data were imported. Also notice that the time does not appear in the BirthDate field.

Table Relationships

For a DBMS to work when a database contains multiple tables, each table must be connected to at least one other table. This is necessary so that reports can be written using information from more than one table. For example, the school administrator may want to find the names of the students taking piano lessons. These data are found in separate tables. Or, the administrator may want to know the names of the students associated with a particular teacher, which are found in different tables.

To connect the tables, the relationships among the tables need to be understood. The best kind of relationship between two tables is one-to-many. A **one-to-many relationship** occurs when a single piece of data is related to several other pieces of data. Think of the Faculty, Student, and Contract tables. One teacher can have many contracts because he or she instructs many students in a variety of instruments. One student can

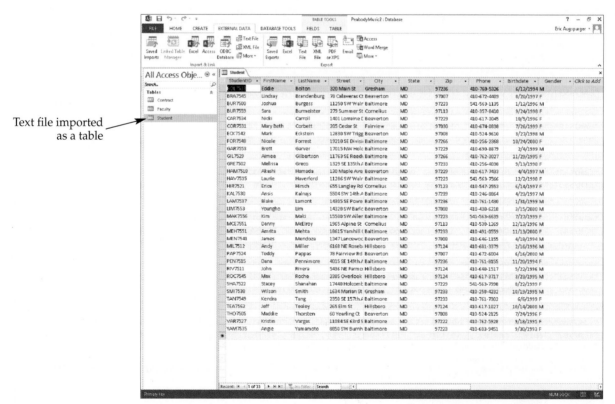

Goodheart-Willcox Publisher

Figure 12-14. When the comma-delimited text file is imported as a table, the data are automatically arranged in fields and records.

have many contracts because he or she may be taking lessons on several instruments. These are one-to-many relationships. The fields in each table need to reflect these relationships. If two tables are to be related, the table on the "many" side of the relationship must have a copy of the "one" table's primary key in its list of fields.

The Contract table is used to track the contracts made between the students and the teachers. It contains information relevant to the individual music lessons. In the design view, you can see how the table was built, as shown in Figure 12-15. Notice that it contains fields to hold the data from the primary keys of the other two tables. When tables are joined, the primary keys from other tables are called **foreign keys**. In the Contract table, the foreign keys are the StudentID and TeacherID fields, as indicated in the Description column for these fields.

Building Relationships

It is not enough to simply build tables with the extra fields in the "many" table. The DBMS does not know the tables are related until it is told so. The DBMS must also be told the exact relationships between tables. Once the relationships are set, it is possible to write reports and ask the database to find specific data from more than one table.

In Microsoft Access, relationships are easily created using a visual representation of the tables, as shown in Figure 12-16. To create a relationship, click the **Relationships** button in the **Relationships** group on the **Database Tools** tab in the ribbon. The tables are displayed in individual windows, which can be enlarged or moved using the mouse. Then, simply draw a line from the "one" table to the "many" table. Finally, specify the specific relationships.

FYI

Fields with different names can be connected, but whenever possible it is good practice to name the fields the same.

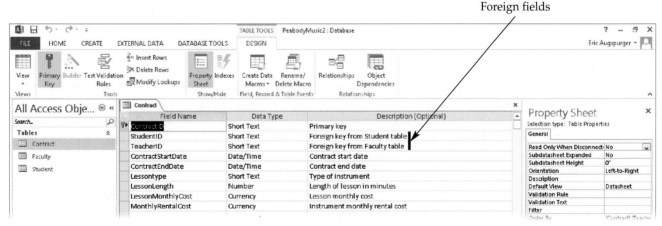

Goodheart-Willcox Publisher

Figure 12-15. The Contract table contains fields for foreign keys from the Student and Faculty tables. This is important when joining tables.

Relationships
have been created

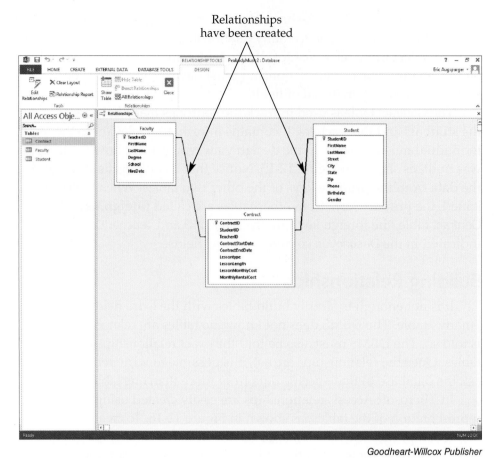

Goodheart-Willcox Publisher

Figure 12-16. Tables are joined by connecting visual representations of the tables with lines.

HANDS-ON EXAMPLE 12.2.5

JOINING TABLES

Most databases contain more than one table. To join the tables, they must be connected and the specific relationship between fields must be set.

1. Launch Microsoft Access, and open the PeabodyMusic2.accdb file in the Chap12 folder on your flash drive.
2. If a security warning appears below the ribbon, click the **Enable Content** button.

Relationships

3. Click the **Relationships** button in the **Relationships** group on the **Database Tools** tab of the ribbon. The three tables in the database are displayed as small windows within the view. Note: if a dialog box appears asking which of the three tables in the database should be included, one at a time select each table and click the **Add** button, then close the dialog box.
4. Drag the Contract table to the middle of the view.

HANDS-ON EXAMPLE 12.2.5 (CONTINUED)

5. Click the TeacherID field in the Faculty table, drag it to the TeacherID field in the Contract table, and drop it. A dialog box appears asking the developer to create a relationship between the two, as shown.

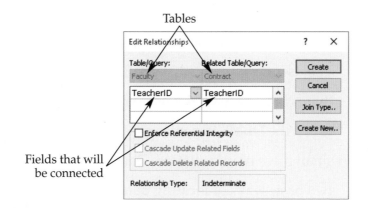

Tables

Fields that will be connected

6. Verify the TeacherID fields in the Faculty and Contract tables will be connected, and then click the **Create** button. A relationship is established between the fields. A line is drawn between the field in one table to the connected field in the other table.

7. Applying what you have learned, connect the StudentID field in the Student table to the StudentID field in the Contract table.

12.2 SECTION REVIEW

CHECK YOUR UNDERSTANDING

1. What is used in Microsoft Access to step the user through importing data from a spreadsheet?
2. Which database object displays only one record at a time?
3. What is the basic difference between a form or table and a report?
4. When two tables within a database are joined, what does the database become?
5. What is the best kind of relationship between tables?

IC3 CERTIFICATION PRACTICE

The following question is a sample of the types of questions presented on the IC3 exam.

1. Which of the following is the correct sequence to join two tables in Microsoft Access?
   A. **Database Tools>Relationships>Relationships**
   B. **Database Tools>Join>Tables**
   C. **Database Tools>Relationships>View Relationships**
   D. **Database Tools>View>Tables**

BUILD YOUR VOCABULARY

As you progress through this course, develop a personal IT glossary. This will help you build your vocabulary and prepare you for a career. Write a definition for each of the following terms and add it to your IT glossary.

datasheet view
foreign key
form

one-to-many relationship
relational database
report

QUERIES

Essential Question

What is the importance of a query to the effectiveness of a database?

Databases can be very large. The user never wants to see all data that is in it. Instead, the user wants to ask the DBMS to come up with a small piece of information. There are two basic ways of locating data in a database: searching and querying.

A database can be a powerful tool when a DBMS is used to manage the database. A DBMS can analyze all of the data in a database and generate results. Calculated fields can be included in the database to perform calculations on data. Statistical fields can be included to provide summary information on the data in a database.

Volt Collection/Shutterstock.com

LEARNING GOALS

After completing this section, you will be able to:
- Describe ways in which data can be located in a database.
- Create a calculated field in a database.
- Explain the use of statistical fields in a database.

TERMS

calculated field
criteria
query
searching
statistical field

Locating Data

Searching is defined as a method to find a particular value among a set of values. Another method used in finding information in a database is the query. A **query** includes not only searching, but also finding and organizing the related details of records that meet certain search conditions. A DBMS is very effective in quickly finding particular portions of information. When a user asks a DBMS to retrieve related pieces of information from a database, this is known as *querying* the database.

Queries are objects in a database, just as tables, reports, and forms are objects. Once a query is created, it becomes part of the database. In a Microsoft Access database, saved queries will be listed in the navigation pane.

Creating a Basic Query

The easiest way to create a basic query in Microsoft Access is to use the query wizard. It creates a query based on a single table or existing query. Click the **Query Wizard** button in the **Queries** group on the **Create** tab of the ribbon. There is a choice of four basic queries that can be created with the wizard, as shown in Figure 12-17. A description of the selected query is displayed in the lower-left area of the dialog box. The simple query is the most basic query. Once the type of query is selected, the remaining pages of the wizard are similar to those found in the form or report wizards. The table on which to base the query must be specified, fields to include must be selected, and the query must be named.

When the **Finish** button is clicked in the wizard, the query is run and displayed (if you chose to display it). The query also appears as an object in the navigation pane. To close the query, right-click on the query name tab, and click **Close** in the shortcut menu. To run the query again, double-click on the query in the navigation pane.

GS5 Key Applications
4.3.4

GS4 Key Applications
5.1.2

FYI

If the query does not appear in the navigation pane, try changing the view in the pane. Right-click on the pane, and click **Category>Tables and Related Views** in the shortcut menu. Then, right-click and click **Category>Object Type** to return to the previous view.

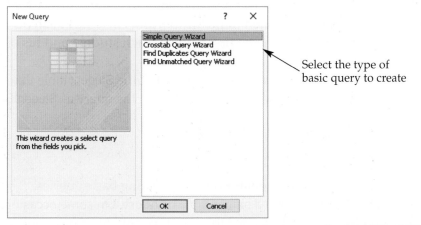

Select the type of basic query to create

Goodheart-Willcox Publisher

Figure 12-17. There are four types of basic query that can be created using the query wizard.

HANDS-ON EXAMPLE 12.3.1

CREATING A SIMPLE QUERY

A query searches for and returns data that meet criteria specified by the user. For example, in the Peabody Music School database, a query can be used to list the first names and birth dates of students.

1. Launch Microsoft Access, and open the PeabodyMusic3.accdb file in the Chap12 folder on your flash drive.
2. If a security warning appears below the ribbon, click the **Enable Content** button.

Query Wizard

3. Click the **Query Wizard** button in the **Queries** group on the **Create** tab of the ribbon. The query wizard is opened.
4. On the first page of the wizard, click **Simple Query Wizard** in the list, and click the **OK** button.
5. On the second page of the wizard, click the **Tables/Query** drop-down arrow, and click **Table: Student** in the drop-down list, as shown. This specifies the query will be based on the Student table.

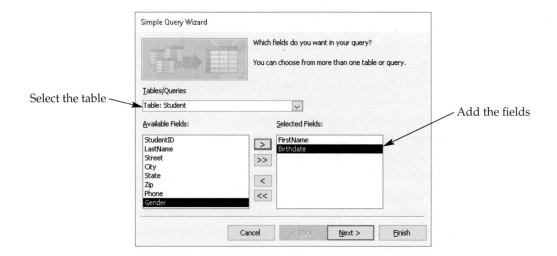

6. Applying what you have learned, move the FirstName and BirthDate fields to the right-hand box, and then click the **Next** button.
7. On the last page of the wizard, click in the text box, and enter the name StudentBirthDate.
8. Click the **Open the query to view information** radio button, and click the **Finish** button. The query is created and displayed. Only the first name of each student and his or her birth date appear in the query.
9. Applying what you have learned, create a simple query using the Student table that returns the first name, last name, and city for each student. Save the query as StudentCity.

Creating an Advanced Query

The query wizard is a tool for quickly creating basic queries. However, it can only search a single table or query. On some occasions, information from more than one table must be used to create a query. In these cases, an advanced query must be created using the query design view, as shown in Figure 12-18. To display the query design view, click the **Query Design** button in the **Queries** group on the **Create** tab of the ribbon.

For example, consider the Peabody Music School database. The user wants to see first names of the students and the instrument that each student plays. In this case, the Student table contains the first names in the FirstName field and the Contract table contains the instruments in the LessonType field. An advanced query must be created.

When the query design view is first displayed, you must select which tables and queries to show. See Figure 12-19. In the **Show Table** dialog box, click the **Table** tab, click a table to include, and click the **Add** button.

FYI

Once a query is created and saved, the design view can be displayed in the same way it is for a table.

Tables containing the fields for the query

Query is constructed

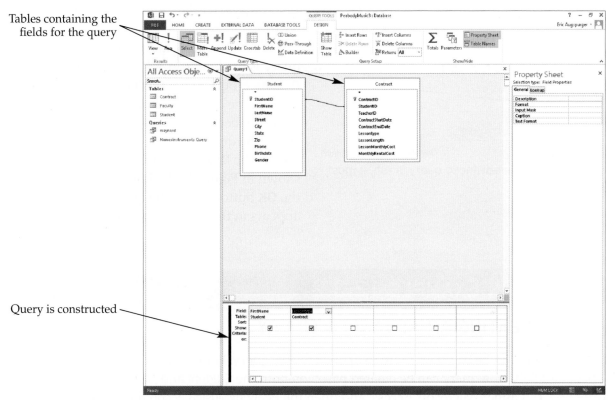

Goodheart-Willcox Publisher

Figure 12-18. An advanced query is created in the query design view. An advanced query allows fields from different tables to be included in the query.

Select the tables on which to base the advanced query

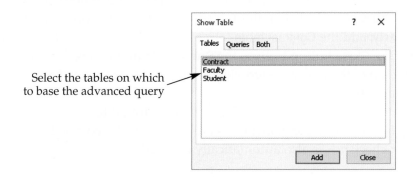

Goodheart-Willcox Publisher

Figure 12-19. When creating an advanced query, you must first select which tables contain the fields that will be included in the query. Existing queries can also be used as the basis for the advanced query.

Queries are listed in the **Queries** tab. Once all of the tables and queries are shown in the view, click the **Close** button to close the dialog box. Any relationships between the tables will be shown by lines, just as they are when joining tables.

At the bottom of the query design view is a grid for creating the query. After the tables or queries on which to base the new query are displayed in the view, fields must be added to this grid. In the grid, click the **Field:** drop-down arrow in the first column, and select the field in the drop-down list. Notice that each field name begins with the name of the table in which it is located. Once a field is selected, the entry in the **Table:** row is automatically filled in. The first column in the grid defines one criterion for the query. Additional criteria can be added using the remaining columns in the grid.

After all criteria are set for the query, the query is ready to run. Click the **Run** button in the **Results** group on the **Design** on-demand tab in the ribbon. The query is displayed, but at this point it has not been saved. Right-click on the name tab above the query, and click **Save** in the shortcut menu. The **Save As:** dialog box is displayed, as shown in Figure 12-20. Enter a name, and click the **OK** button. Once the query has been saved, it appears in the navigation pane.

Enter a name for the query

Goodheart-Willcox Publisher

Figure 12-20. After an advanced query is run, it must be saved.

HANDS-ON EXAMPLE 12.3.2

CREATING AN ADVANCED QUERY

A query can be based on more than one table or query. For example, using the Peabody Music School database, a query can be created based on both the Student and Contract tables.

1. Launch Microsoft Access, and open the PeabodyMusic3.accdb file in the Chap12 folder on your flash drive, if it is not already open.
2. If a security warning appears below the ribbon, click the **Enable Content** button.
3. Click the **Query Design** button in the **Queries** group of the **Create** tab of the ribbon. The query design view is displayed, and the **Show Table** dialog box appears.
4. Click **Student** in the list on the **Tables** tab of the dialog box, and click the **Add** button. Similarly, add the Contract table.
5. Click the **Close** button to close the **Show Table** dialog box. The two tables are displayed at the top of the query design view, and a grid for creating the query is displayed at the bottom of the view.
6. Click the FirstName field in the Student table, drag it to the first column in the grid, and drop it. The **Field:** and **Table:** rows are automatically completed in the first column. The **Show:** check box is also automatically checked.

Query Design

HANDS-ON EXAMPLE 12.3.2 (CONTINUED)

7. Click the **Field:** drop-down arrow in the second column, and click **Contract:LessonType** in the drop-down list. The **Field:** and **Table:** rows are automatically completed in the second column, and the **Show:** check box is checked. Now the design is established, and the query is ready to run, as shown.

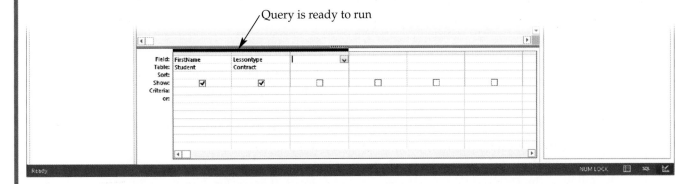

8. Click the **Run** button in the **Results** group on the **Design** on-demand tab of the ribbon. The query is created and displayed. Some student names appear more than once in the query. This means that the student has more than one contract for lessons.

Run

9. Right-click on the query name tab, and click **Save** in the shortcut menu.
10. In the **Save As:** dialog box, enter NamesInstruments as the name, and click the **OK** button. The query is named and appears in the navigation pane.

Entering Criteria

Sometimes, only certain records for a field need to be seen. Specific records can be requested by qualifying the query. The qualifiers on a query are called **criteria** in Microsoft Access. Criteria place limits or constraints on a query to fine-tune the requested information, as shown in Figure 12-21.

For example, using the Peabody Music School database, it is possible to query only the names of students who are taking flute lessons. The LessonType field contains the instruments, but a query that simply returns

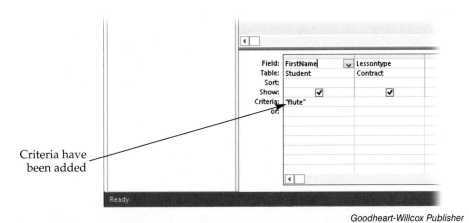

Goodheart-Willcox Publisher

Figure 12-21. Criteria can be used to limit the information from a field.

this field will list all instruments, not just flute. By entering criteria, the query can be qualified to return only those records that contain Flute in the LessonType field.

HANDS-ON EXAMPLE 12.3.3

QUALIFYING A QUERY

A query can be qualified with criteria to limit the returned results. For example, a query can be created to return the monthly cost of students for one teacher, instead of for all teachers.

1. Launch Microsoft Access, and open the PeabodyMusic3.accdb file in the Chap12 folder on your flash drive, if it is not already open.
2. If a security warning appears below the ribbon, click the **Enable Content** button.
3. Double-click on the NamesInstruments query to open it.
4. Applying what you have learned, display the design view.
5. Click in the **Criteria:** text box in the second column (LessonType) in the grid at the bottom of the design view, and enter flute. If you move to a different cell in the grid, Access will automatically add quotation marks around the term.
6. Applying what you have learned, run the query. Only the students who have taken flute lessons are returned by this query.
7. Appling what you have learned, create a query that includes the LastName field from the Faculty table and LessonMonthlyCost from the Contract table with the criteria Maynard for the LastName field. Run the query, and save it as MaynardCost.

Creating Calculated Fields

Sometimes a value needs to be known that is not found in the database, but can be calculated from the existing data. A **calculated field** is a field that performs a calculation based on data within the same table, as shown in Figure 12-22. This special field is also known as a "field on the fly."

Calculated field

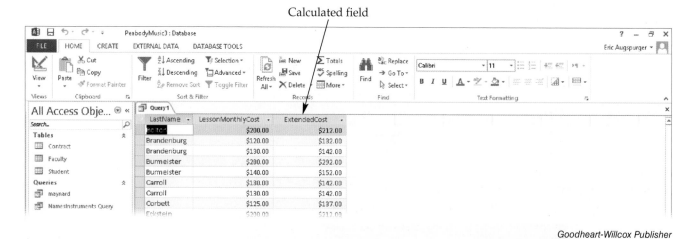

Goodheart-Willcox Publisher

Figure 12-22. A calculated field can be used to generate a value based on data in the database. Here, $12 has been added to the monthly cost of each lesson with a calculated field.

For example, the Peabody Music School may want to know how much each lesson would cost if a certain amount is added to the existing monthly fee. This information is not in the database, but a calculated field can be built to show the new amount.

HANDS-ON EXAMPLE 12.3.4

CREATING A CALCULATED FIELD

A calculated field can provide information not found in the database by performing a calculation on existing data. For example, a query can be created to display the result of adding $12 to the monthly fee for a faculty member.

1. Launch Microsoft Access, and open the PeabodyMusic3.accdb file in the Chap12 folder on your flash drive, if it is not already open.
2. If a security warning appears below the ribbon, click the **Enable Content** button.
3. Applying what you have learned, begin a new query based on the LastName field from the Faculty table and the LessonMonthlyCost field from the Contract table with the criteria "Kegg" for the LastName field. These two fields should be in the first two columns of the grid in the design view.
4. In the **Field:** row for the third column, add the following information: ExtendedCost: [LessonMonthlyCost] + 12. If necessary, you can widen the column by dragging the right-hand margin of the column.
5. Applying what you have learned, run the query. Extended Cost will appear in the query as the name of the calculated field. The values displayed in the ExtendedCost field are the values from the LessonMonthlyCost field with 12 added.
6. Applying what you have learned, save the query as ExtendedCost.

Creating Statistical Fields

A **statistical field** provides summary information related to other data within a table. It is a type of calculated field. Several built-in statistical calculations can be performed on a group of records. Some of the mathematical functions include **SUM**, **AVG** (average), **MAX** (maximum), and **MIN** (minimum). There are dozens of other built-in functions in Microsoft Access. Depending on what fields are included in the query, the statistical functions can give overall totals or totals divided by groups.

If the syntax of the function is known, the expression can be directly entered into the **Field:** row in the query design view. The expression builder in Microsoft Access can also be used to create an expression. To display the expression builder, click the **Builder** button in the **Query Setup** group on the **Design** on-demand tab of the ribbon. The **Expression Builder** dialog box is displayed, as shown in Figure 12-23. The expression is constructed in the top box. The lower-left box contains the library of functions in a tree format. When an element is selected in the lower-left box, the items it contains are displayed in the lower-middle box. When an element is selected in the lower-middle box, the functions it contains are displayed in the lower-right box. Double-click a function in the lower-right box to add it to the expression being created in the top box.

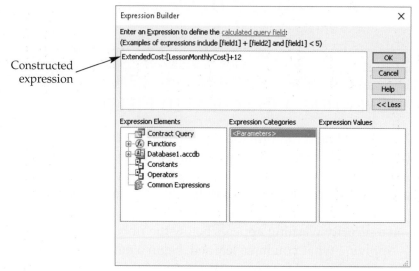

Constructed expression

Goodheart-Willcox Publisher

Figure 12-23. The expression builder can be used to help construct a calculated field or a statistical field.

HANDS-ON EXAMPLE 12.3.5

CREATING A STATISTICAL FIELD

The **SUM** function can be used to add amounts, such as the monthly cost of music lessons. Microsoft Access has an automatic totals feature that can help in applying this function.

1. Launch Microsoft Access, and open the PeabodyMusic3.accdb file in the Chap12 folder on your flash drive, if it is not already open.
2. If a security warning appears below the ribbon, click the **Enable Content** button.
3. Applying what you have learned, begin a new query based on the LessonMonthlyCost field from the Contract table and the LastName field from the Faculty table.
4. Click the **Show/Hide Column Totals in Query Results** button in the **Show/Hide** group on the **Design** on-demand tab of the ribbon. A new row called **Total:** appears in the grid.

Σ

Show/Hide
Column
Totals in
Query Results

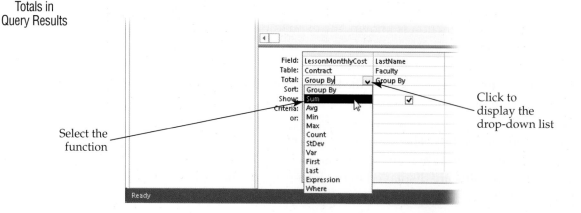

Select the function

Click to display the drop-down list

HANDS-ON EXAMPLE 12.3.5 (CONTINUED)

5. Click the cell in the first column (LessonMontlyCost) of the **Total:** row, click the drop-down arrow that appears, and click **Sum** in the drop-down list, as shown.
6. Applying what you have learned, run the query. The result displays one field that contains the total dollar amount of all lessons.
7. Applying what you have learned, save the query as LessonTotal.
8. Save the database file.

12.3 SECTION REVIEW

CHECK YOUR UNDERSTANDING

1. How does a query differ from a search?
2. What are the limits or constraints on a query?
3. How many tables or queries can a basic query in Microsoft Access search?
4. What is the type of field that can generate a value not present in the database?
5. What is the purpose of a statistical field?

IC3 CERTIFICATION PRACTICE

The following question is a sample of the types of questions presented on the IC3 exam.

1. Which of the following is the proper sequence for creating a query that can search more than one table?
   A. **Create>Queries>Query Wizard**
   B. **Insert>Queries>Query**
   C. **Create>Queries>Query Design**
   D. **Insert>Design>Query**

BUILD YOUR VOCABULARY

As you progress through this course, develop a personal IT glossary. This will help you build your vocabulary and prepare you for a career. Write a definition for each of the following terms and add it to your IT glossary.

calculated field
criteria
query
searching
statistical field

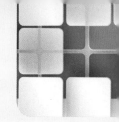

Chapter Summary

Section 12.1
Introduction to Databases

- A database is a structured collection of related information organized for easily locating and retrieving the data. It consists of data arranged in tables, records, and fields.
- Data in a database can be added, edited, and deleted. The [Tab] key can be used to navigate through fields in a record.
- When creating a database structure, decide what information will be tracked. This information will become fields in a database table.

Section 12.2
Importing and Viewing Data

- Data from a spreadsheet can be imported into a database. The data can be appended to an existing database or added to a blank database.
- The datasheet view displays data in table form. Data can be searched and sorted in the table, and reports can be created to display data.
- A database may contain more than one table, which can be joined. Joining tables creates a relational database.

Section 12.3
Queries

- A query includes not only searching, but also finding and organizing the related details of records that meet certain search conditions. Queries can be created that are very simple or advanced with qualifiers called criteria.
- A calculated field is a field that performs a calculation based on data within the same table. It reports a value that is not found in the database, but can be created from data within the database.

- A statistical field is a type of calculated field that provides summary information related to other data within a table. Microsoft Access has several built-in statistical-calculation functions.

Now that you have finished this chapter, see what you know about information technology by scanning the QR code to take the chapter posttest. If you do not have a smartphone, visit www.g-wlearning.com.

Chapter 12 Test

Multiple Choice

Select the best response.

1. Which of the following contains information about specific characteristics of the entry described in a record?
   A. table
   B. row
   C. report
   D. field

2. Which data type is used to store numbers that will be used for financial calculations?
   A. currency
   B. number
   C. general
   D. text

3. After a table has been created, which of the following options is used to add data from a spreadsheet to the table?
   A. addition
   B. navigation
   C. finish
   D. append

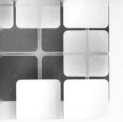

4. What feature or function includes searching, finding, and organizing the related details of records that meet certain search conditions?

   A. search
   B. find
   C. query
   D. locate

5. Which view is used to add new fields to a query?

   A. design
   B. datasheet
   C. text box
   D. navigation pane

Completion

Complete the following sentences with the correct word(s).

6. The foundation of a database is a(n) _____.

7. A row in a database contains related data and is called a(n) _____.

8. A column in a database, which contains the categories of data, is called a(n) _____.

9. A(n) _____ is a database object that illustrates only certain data one record at a time.

10. A(n) _____ performs a calculation based on data within a table.

Matching

Match the correct term with its definition.

A. DBMS
B. record
C. primary key
D. foreign key
E. statistical field

11. Type of calculated field that provides summary information related to other data within a table.

12. Handles the collection, storage, sorting, reporting, and organization of data.

13. Contains information related to the entry in the first column of the record.

14. Field in a related table with the same data as another table.

15. Unique identifier for a table.

Application and Extension of Knowledge

1. Before beginning these activities, navigate to the student companion website at www.g-wlearning.com, download the data files for this chapter, and save them in the Chap12 folder on your flash drive. You will create a database containing two tables that tracks the enrollment in a non-credit art school. Begin a new database titled Baltimore Art School, and save it in the Chap12 folder on your flash drive. Create a table, and save it as Sections. Change the name of the ID field to StudentID. Add the following fields, and save the table.

Name	Data Type
SectionID	Short text
StartingDate	Date/time
ClassName	Short text
Fee	Currency
CategoryID	Short text
Enrolled	Number

2. Open the Baltimore Art School database created in #1, if it is not already open. Import the Microsoft Excel file Sections.xlsx from the Chap12 folder on your flash drive. Append the spreadsheet data to the Sections table. Open the

Sections table. How many records were imported? Write one paragraph describing the procedure you used to import the spreadsheet data.

3. Open the Baltimore Art School database created in #2, if it is not already open. Create a second table titled Category. Add the fields shown below to the table. Then, import the Microsoft Excel file Category.xlsx from the Chap12 folder on your flash drive. Append the data to the Category table. Create a relationship between the tables using the CategoryID fields. Consider the process for creating a relationship. Write one paragraph describing the procedure you used to create the relationship.

Name	Data Type
CategoryID	Short text
CategoryName	Short text
Description	Short text
Length	Short text

4. Open the Baltimore Art School database created in #3, if it is not already open. Create a query that lists the CategoryName, StartingDate and Enrolled fields. Save it as EnrollmentByCategory. Create a second query that lists the ClassName, Fee, and Enrolled for the Beginning Watercolors class. Save it as WaterColorEnrollment. How did the process of creating these two queries differ? Write one paragraph describing the differences.

5. Open the Baltimore Art School database created in #4, if it is not already open. Copy the WaterColorEnrollment query as a basis, and name the copy WaterColorRevenue. Create a new calculated field that computes the revenue from each section. The revenue is found by multiplying the fee by the number of students enrolled in the section. Name

the calculated field Revenue. What is the formula you entered to create the calculated field? What is the revenue for each of the sections in the Beginning Watercolors class? Write one paragraph describing the formula you used and the process for creating the calculated field.

Online Activities

Complete the following activities, which will help you learn, practice, and expand your knowledge and skills.

Certification Practice. Complete the certification practice test for this chapter.

Vocabulary. Practice vocabulary for this chapter using the e-flash cards, matching activity, and vocabulary game until you are able to recognize their meanings.

Communication Skills

College and Career Readiness

Listening. Engage in a conversation with someone you have not spoken with before. Ask the person how he or she uses technology in personal circumstances and more formal circumstances such as at school or a job. Actively listen to what that person is sharing. Next, summarize and retell what the person conveyed in conversation to you. Did you really hear what was being said?

Reading. Figurative language is used to describe something by comparing it with something else. Locate an advertisement for mobile devices. Scan the information for figurative language about the product. Compare this with a description using literal language. Did the use of literal or figurative language influence your opinion of the services? Did the advertisement help you understand the service or company?

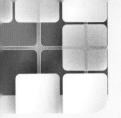

Writing. Everyone has a stake in protecting the environment. Taking steps as an individual to become more environmentally conscious is a behavior of responsible citizens. From a business standpoint, it may also help a company be more profitable. Make a list of actions a business can take to minimize risk to the environment from the technology it uses.

Internet Research

Finding Credible Sources. Research the history of databases using various Internet resources. Apply your secondary research skills to find the information in a variety of formats such as reports, graphs, or articles. Describe each stage of database development. What methods did you use to extract information from the resources? Write a short informal report on your findings. Cite each source that you use.

Teamwork

Working with a partner, navigate to your school's website and find the faculty and staff directory. Using spreadsheet software, create a worksheet that lists each faculty or staff member's name, position, and other information such as phone extension or room number. List as much information as you can.

Portfolio Development

College and Career Readiness

References. An important part of any portfolio is a list of references. A reference is a person who knows your skills, talents, or personal traits and is willing to recommend you. References will probably be someone from your network. These individuals can be someone for whom you worked or with whom you

provided community service. Someone you know from your personal life, such as a youth group leader, can also be a reference. However, you should not list relatives as references. Consider which references can best recommend you for the position for which you are applying. Always get permission from the person before using his or her name as a reference.

1. Ask several people from your network if they are willing to serve as a reference for you.
2. Create a Microsoft Access database with the names and contact information for your references. Use the file name "References" and your name.
3. Update your master spreadsheet.

CTSOs

Help Desk. Help desk is a competitive event you might enter with your Career and Technical Student Organization (CTSO). This is an individual event in which participants take an objective test. High-scoring participants also compete in a performance-based test. The ability to provide technical assistance to computer hardware and software users is the focus of the event. To prepare for a help desk event, complete the following activities.

1. Visit the organization's website well in advance of the date of the event.
2. Download any posted practice tests.
3. Conduct research on the Internet regarding the common IT assistance questions and solutions for those questions. Print out the information you find to use as study material.
4. Visit the organization's website often to make sure information regarding the event has not changed.

UNIT 3
LIVING ONLINE

Monkey Business Images/Shutterstock.com

This unit provides a background in subjects needed for using Internet-based tools, including web browsers, communication tools, search engines, and multimedia. You will be able to apply new knowledge to using communication networks and the World Wide Web. Also presented are advantages and perils of using online technologies, which will help you be aware of benefits and risks of using online resources. You will be able to apply this newly acquired knowledge in new circumstances.

Information gathered in this unit will support you in providing a foundation for further learning in the field of information technology. The material in this textbook, from provided information to acquired skills and activities, supports the objectives for the IC3 Digital Literacy Certification. Learning and studying this material will help to prepare for taking this certification exam.

While studying, look for the activity icon for:

- Pretests and posttests
- Vocabulary terms with e-flash cards and matching activities
- Formative assessment

13 INTERNET AND THE WORLD WIDE WEB

It is not uncommon to find people who think that the Internet and the World Wide Web (WWW) are the same thing. The Internet is an interconnected network of networks, while the web is a collection of documents connected by universal resource locator (URL) codes and hypertext protocol. The Internet also includes e-mail, file transfers, and instant messaging. Although many web-based services have reached out to support these protocols, these protocols were well in place before the web was created.

The Internet had its beginning in 1969 with an Advanced Research Projects Agency (ARPA) grant to create communication between remote computers. The first communications network, ARPANET, included computers at University of California at Los Angeles, University of California at Santa Barbara, University of Utah, and Stanford University. The final step that created what is known today as the Internet was the definition of the transmission control protocol/Internet protocol (TCP/IP) standards in 1982. The Internetworking Group was responsible for defining how a network of networks would communicate. The formal name of Internet came from that group's name.

College and Career Readiness

Reading Prep. As you read this chapter, stop at the Section Reviews and take time to answer the questions. Were you able to answer these questions without referring to the chapter content?

IC3 CERTIFICATION OBJECTIVES

Computing Fundamentals

Domain 2.0 Hardware devices
> **Objective 2.11** Understand concepts regarding connecting to the Internet

Domain 3.0 Computer software architecture
> **Objective 3.9** Searching for files
> **Objective 3.11** Define an IP address
> **Objective 3.13** Troubleshooting

Domain 7.0 Security
> **Objective 7.4** Connecting to secured vs. unsecured network (wired and wireless)

Key Applications

Domain 1.0 Common features
> **Objective 1.2** Understand the difference between plain text and HTML (text with markup)

Domain 4.0 Databases
> **Objective 4.2** Understand how websites utilize databases

Living Online

Domain 1.0 Internet (navigation)
> **Objective 1.1** Understand what the Internet is

Domain 2.0 Common functionality
> **Objective 2.1** Understand how to use common website navigation conventions

Domain 9.0 Digital principles/ethics/skills/citizenship
> **Objective 9.2** Understand digital wellness basics

GS5

Living Online

Domain 1.0 Browsers
> **Objective 1.1** Internet vs. browsers vs. WWW
> **Objective 1.2** Navigation

Domain 2.0 Networking concepts
> **Objective 2.2** Network types and features, capabilities
> **Objective 2.3** Network troubleshooting

Domain 4.0 Digital citizenship
> **Objective 4.2** Legal and responsible use of computers

Domain 5.0 Safe computing
> **Objective 5.2** Ergonomics

Domain 6.0 Research fluency
> **Objective 6.1** Using search engines
> **Objective 6.2** Evaluate search results
> **Objective 6.3** Using advanced features of search engines

GS4

SECTION 13.1

INTERNET AND THE WORLD WIDE WEB

Essential Question

Why is ethical use of Internet resources important to maintaining a functioning society?

The Internet is an interconnected network of networks used for communication. File transfers, electronic mail, messaging, news feeds, and the web are all made possible by the Internet. There are several parts to the Internet. These parts include computers, communication hardware, software, and standards. The Internet was designed to be redundant and fault tolerant. This means that there are many duplications to ensure the communication takes place.

The World Wide Web is a collection of programs, called web servers, running on Internet networks all over the world. On these servers are over 50 billion hypertext pages. Each page has its own uniform resource locator (URL) or web address. Searching through all of this information is supported by software called a search engine. Learning to perform good searches is important for a user and for the search engine.

Monkey Business Images/Shutterstock.com

TERMS

Boolean operators
browser
digital wellness
download
ergonomics
human-computer
  interaction (HCI)
hypertext markup
  language (HTML)
Internet service provider
  (ISP)

modem
packet
plug-in
protocol
public switched network
search engine
uniform resource locator
  (URL)
upload

LEARNING GOALS

After completing this section, you will be able to:
- Describe the operation of the Internet.
- Discuss the aspects of maintaining digital wellness.
- Use a search engine to locate information.
- Explain how to use the Internet in an ethical manner.

510

Internet

The *Internet* is a worldwide communication network that connects individual computer networks. Messages are exchanged between these networks, and then the destination network must deliver the message to the correct computer in its network. It sounds complicated, but the process is very simple to understand.

The routing mechanism is based on small file fragments called **packets**. The transmission control protocol (TCP) identifies a file to be sent and breaks it into packets, each of which is given a header. The packet *header* contains the:

- file's source computer's Internet protocol (IP) address;
- destination computer's IP address;
- packet number; and
- total number of packets in the entire file.

These packets are sent though the network of networked computers, possibly not on the same path, as shown in Figure 13-1. If a server along the way is too busy or not working, a packet sent to that server is rerouted to another network. When the packets arrive at the destination network, they are reassembled into the original file. If any packets are missing or corrupted in the transmission, messages are sent to the source computer and the lost packets are resent.

The process of creating packets and transmitting them over a network is called *packet-switching.* It happens at the speed of light. Electricity and light travel a little less than one foot in one nanosecond, or about one billion feet in one second. That is why transmissions are so quick on the Internet. A **public switched network** makes use of packet switching to transfer information and is available to the general public. Examples are the Internet and the telephone network. A private switched network is protected from the general public by security measures. An

GS5 Living Online
1.1.1.1

GS4 Living Online
1.1.1, 1.1.2, 1.1.3

GS4 Living Online
2.2.1

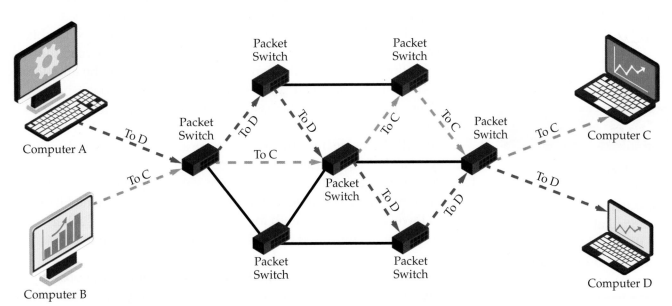

Figure 13-1. The TCP breaks a file into packets, which are then sent through the network.

example of a privately switched network is the ATM network, which requires a high degree of security.

Internet Service Provider

In order to connect to the Internet, an ISP must be used. An **Internet service provider (ISP)** is a company or organization that provides access to the Internet. The Internet is a network of networks, and each ISP owns one of those networks. Examples of ISPs are Verizon, Comcast, AOL, and many others. There is usually a fee charged by ISPs to access the Internet.

The device used to connect to the ISP is called a modem. These connections are either hardwired or wireless. A wireless connection may be cellular based or Wi-Fi. Wi-Fi is the name given to wireless networks, and the ISP owns the Wi-Fi network. Wi-Fi connections may be fee-based or offered free of charge in many public locations, such as airports, hotels, and libraries.

The task of a **modem** is to deliver the data channel for Internet transmissions. Its original use was via telephone landlines. Digital signals were modulated into analog transmissions, sent along telephone lines, and then demodulated back into digital signals for the computer. Hence the term *modem*, from *mo*dulate and *dem*odulate.

Modems come in a variety of configurations. At home or in businesses, ISPs provide modems that are wired to cable service, digital subscriber lines, or satellite dish service. Traditional landline modems are still in use, especially in remote areas where cable or satellite transmissions are not available. Cellular modems are used in mobile devices. In this case, the cellular carrier is the ISP.

Internet Protocol

A **protocol** is a system of agreed-on rules. Each network on the Internet has a unique Internet protocol address. The *Internet protocol (IP) address* is the number the networks on the Internet use to identify a particular network location. The host of the network is identified by this number. Each device on a network has a subnet address relative to the host. This allows each computer connected to the Internet to be uniquely identified. For example, the IP address 4.31.38.9 is for the Google home page. There are two schemes for assigning an address to a network: IPv4 and IPv6.

In the IPv4 scheme, four bytes of data are assigned to the address. Each byte can hold 256 numbers, from 0 to 255. That provides 4,294,967,296 unique addresses ($256 \times 256 \times 256 \times 256$). When the TCP/IP transmission scheme was invented, four billion addresses seemed like plenty. However, it is not enough for today's technology needs when there are so many embedded devices that require connection to the Internet.

The IPv6 scheme was developed to increase the number of possible IP addresses. In the IPv6 scheme, 16 bytes are assigned to each IP address. This provides 2^{128} or more than 8×10^{28} addresses. Each IPv6 address

GS5 Computing Fundamentals 2.11.1

GS5 Computing Fundamentals 3.11

Living Online 1.1.1.2, 1.1.1.3

GS4 Living Online 2.2.3, 2.3.3

FYI

The IP address of a web page or other Internet resource may be changed at some point, so the IP address you have or find may not be current.

is represented by eight groups of four hexadecimal digits separated by colons, such as 2001:0:5ef5:79fd:85c:18f2:b84c:a02a.

Conversion to the IPv6 scheme is necessary because available addresses based on the IPv4 scheme are being exhausted. However, the two schemes are not compatible, and that is slowing the adoption of IPv6.

Whichever scheme is used, such an address is too difficult for people to easily use it. The domain name system (DNS) was invented to make IP addresses easier to use. The *domain name system (DNS)* uses name servers to map the numbers and letters in an IP address to a human-readable string of characters. For example, the IPv4 address of a web server may be 216.167.196.196, but its DNS address may be www.g-w.com.

Each network belongs to a domain depending on its ownership, as shown in Figure 13-2. Figure 13-3 lists several Internet top-level domains. In addition to these top-level domains, each country has its own top-level domain, such as .us for the United States, .ca for Canada, .au for Australia, and .uk for the United Kingdom. There are many sources on the Internet that provide a comprehensive list of domains for countries.

GS4 Living Online 2.2.2

GS4 Living Online 1.2.1

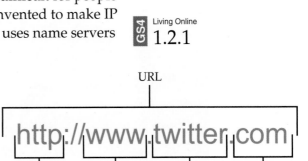

Goodheart-Willcox Publisher

Figure 13-2. A URL consists of several subparts. The second-level domain is what most people think of when talking about a website.

Top-Level Domain	Members	Example
com	Commercial entities	g-w.com
gov	US governmental agencies	whitehouse.gov
edu	US colleges and universities	stanford.edu
org	Organizations	internetsociety.org
net	Open domain, anyone can register	sourceforge.net

Goodheart-Willcox Publisher

Figure 13-3. Common top-level domains and examples of who may use them.

HANDS-ON EXAMPLE 13.1.1

GS5 Computing Fundamentals 3.13.4

FINDING AN IP ADDRESS

All computers connected to the Internet have an IP address. It is easy to find the IP address for a computer using a utility that comes with Windows.

1. In Windows 10 and Windows 7, click the **Start** button on the taskbar. In Windows 8, click the **Apps** button.
2. Click **Command Prompt** in the **Windows System** folder or area or the **Accessories** folder of the menu. The **Command Prompt** window is displayed.

HANDS-ON EXAMPLE 13.1.1 (CONTINUED)

3. Enter ipconfig.exe at the command prompt. A listing of the IP configuration for the computer is displayed, as shown.

```
Command Prompt                                                    —    □    ✕

Microsoft Windows [Version 10.0.10240]
(c) 2015 Microsoft Corporation. All rights reserved.

C:\>ipconfig

Windows IP Configuration

Ethernet adapter Wireless Network Connection:

        Connection-specific DNS Suffix  . :
        IP Address. . . . . . . . . . . . : 192.168.1.2
        Subnet Mask . . . . . . . . . . . : 255.255.255.0
        Default Gateway . . . . . . . . . : 192.168.1.1

Ethernet adapter Local Area Connection:

        Media State . . . . . . . . . . . : Media disconnected

C:\>
```

4. Identify the IPv4 address. In this example it is 192.168.1.2.
5. Identify the subnet mask. In this example it is 255.255.255.0.
6. Enter exit to close the **Command Prompt** window.

Other Protocols

The Internet protocol works together with other protocols within the Internet protocol suite. The *Internet protocol suite* is the group of network models and communication protocols used by the Internet and similar networks. The Internet protocol suite is more commonly known as *TCP/IP* for the transmission control protocol and Internet protocol standards contained within the suite. These are a few examples of protocols in the Internet protocol suite:

- transmission control protocol (TCP)
- Internet protocol (IP)
- hypertext transfer protocol (HTTP)
- post office protocol (POP3)
- Internet message access protocol (IMAP)
- simple mail transfer protocol (SMTP)
- file transfer protocol (FTP)

The transmission control protocol (TCP) provides the safe delivery of packets of information between computers on the Internet. The hypertext transfer protocol (HTTP) provides the hypermedia information system otherwise known as the World Wide Web. The post office protocol (POP3) provides retrieval of e-mail messages from a remote server over a TCP/IP connection. The Internet message access protocol (IMAP) works with POP3 to provide access to storage and retrieval of e-mail messages. The simple mail transfer protocol (SMTP) provides the sending of e-mail messages. The file transfer protocol (FTP) provides transmittal of files between hosts on a TCP network.

Upload and Download

The basic function of the Internet is to move digital files from one computer to another. These files can be text, video, image, or audio files; office documents; or any other type of digital file. There are two functions to transmitting files:

- **Upload** is a user at one computer sending a document to a server.
- **Download** is a user retrieving a document from the server to the computer.

The speeds of early Internet transmissions were too low to make the uploading and downloading of anything other than text files efficient. E-mail and basic text-only documents were transferred between computers. These transmissions each represented only a few kilobytes of data. As transmission speeds increased, larger files could be efficiently uploaded and downloaded. Now it is common to send streaming video from one machine to another, which represents the transmission of gigabytes of data.

In general, it is considered more important to provide faster download speeds than upload speeds because a user is waiting for the document. Upload on the other hand, could be handled in a slower fashion because it is simply storing the documents and no person is actually waiting for it. Because of limited resources, Internet servers ration transmission times and routinely assign faster speeds to the download function.

However, this balance between upload and download has changed with the advent of Internet-based services such as video conferencing. In these applications, it is important to provide real-time interaction. The transmission speed for both upload and download must be as fast as possible for these real-time applications.

World Wide Web

The *World Wide Web (WWW)* is a subset of the Internet that consists of a collection of documents connected by universal resource locator (URL) codes and hypertext protocol. Invented by Sir Timothy Berners-Lee in the early 1990s, the web made it easy for people who were not experts in computers to access documents stored on the Internet. Today, there are client programs that provide functionality supported by the above Internet protocols.

Servers connected to the Internet have a WWW folder at the root of the computer. Within this folder and its subfolders are all of the accessible documents for the web for the server. Figure 13-4 illustrates how the web works. These are the basic steps:

1. The user either enters a location in the navigation bar of a web browser or clicks a link on a web page, which issues the URL for a document to the browser.

GS4 Living Online
1.2.10

GS5 Living Online
1.1.3.11

GS4 Living Online
1.1.1, 1.1.2, 1.1.3

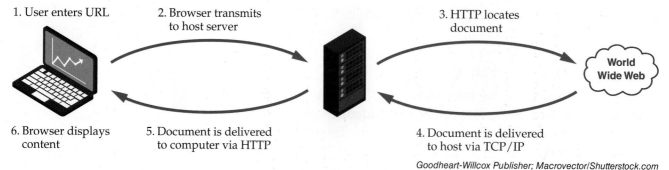

1. User enters URL

2. Browser transmits to host server

3. HTTP locates document

World Wide Web

6. Browser displays content

5. Document is delivered to computer via HTTP

4. Document is delivered to host via TCP/IP

Goodheart-Willcox Publisher; Macrovector/Shutterstock.com

Figure 13-4. The operation of the web is really just a series of simple steps.

2. The web browser transmits that to its WWW program on the host server.

3. The HTTP protocol locates the document specified by the URL and requests its delivery to the host.

4. If necessary, the document is delivered via TCP/IP packets to the host.

5. The host delivers the document to the requesting computer using HTTP.

6. The web browser determines how the document should be formatted and displays it.

The web *uses* the Internet, but it is not the Internet. The Internet is an interconnected network of networks. The Internet includes many functions that are not core to the web, such as e-mail, file transfers, and instant messaging, although these functions may be offered through web-based services. The key notions of the web are hyperlinks and uniform resource locators (URLs).

Hyperlinks

A *hyperlink* is the data needed to navigate to another resource, often a URL for a website, attached to text or an image in a document, as shown in Figure 13-5. The text or image to which the hyperlink is attached is called *hypertext*. Clicking the hypertext activates the hyperlink and retrieves the resource specified in the hyperlink. In common usage, the term hyperlink is used to mean hypertext, so one might say "click the hyperlink," or link, instead of saying "click the hypertext." However, be aware there is a technical distinction between the two terms.

Hyperlinks are one of the foundations of the World Wide Web. Web pages contain hyperlinks to other web pages or Internet resources. However, hyperlinks can also be used within documents. For example, the table of contents in a report may contain hyperlinks to the pages in the document indicated by the page numbers.

Uniform Resource Locator

A **uniform resource locator (URL)** is an address that points to a specific document or other resource on a computer network. Many people call this a *web address*, but while all web addresses are URLs, a URL is

GS4 Living Online
1.2.2

FYI

The theoretical foundation of hypertext was developed in the 1960s by Ted Nelson and Andries van Dam at Brown University based on earlier work by others.

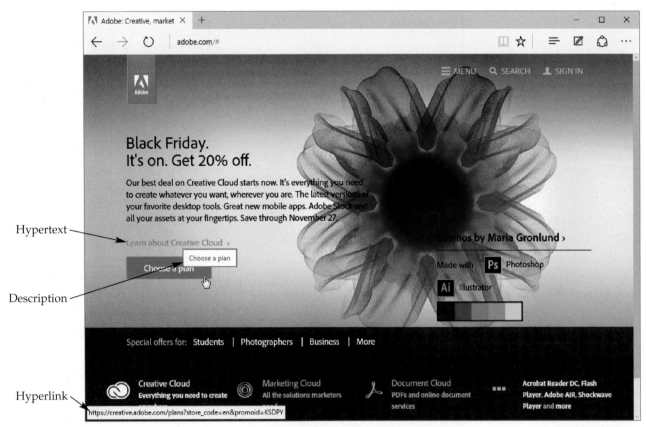

Figure 13-5. Hypertext contains a hyperlink, which is the data needed to navigate to another resource.

not necessarily a web address. Each web page on the World Wide Web has a URL, and the use of URLs is another foundation of the web. It was Berners-Lee's group that defined the URL and made each document in a WWW folder on any server discoverable.

There are several parts to a URL. Consider this URL:

http://www.internetsociety.org/deploy360/wp-content/
uploads/2014/10/IPv6-Fact-Sheet-English-v1.pdf

Beginning with the protocol, a URL provides the path to the domain, through the servers' folders, to the location of a specific document. Figure 13-6 explains the elements of this URL.

The addresses in a URL may be absolute or relative. An *absolute address* contains all of the information to locate the resource no matter from where the search begins. Think about a house address, such as:

123 Main Street
Anytown, MD 20010

The mailing address contains not only the street address, but the city, state, and ZIP code. This allows a document to be mailed to a specific address from anywhere. This is considered the absolute address of the house. An absolute URL begins at the domain of the website that contains the document.

Element	Meaning
http	The protocol, which in this case is hypertext transfer protocol
www	Third-level domain, which in this case is the World Wide Web
internetsociety	Second-level domain, which is the site name
org	Top-level domain
/deploy360/wp-content/uploads/2014/10/	Folder names, which provide a path to the intended document on the server
IPv6-Fact-Sheet-English-v1.pdf	The document name and file extension; if a document is not named, a default document is retrieved, such as index.html

Note: the colon terminates the protocol, the two forward slashes introduce the site identifier, the periods (dots) separate the domains, and single forward slashes separate folders on the server.

Goodheart-Willcox Publisher

Figure 13-6. A breakdown of the URL given in the text.

A *relative address* provides the information needed to find the resource from a known location. For example, to give somebody instructions to a house from where you are standing:

Go two streets over and down a block to 123 Main Street.

Web designers often use relative addresses when programming websites. Relative addresses are used for locations on the same domain, where absolute addresses are used for locations on other domains. Consider the previous URL. A hyperlink on a web page stored in the top folder may be:

./deploy360/wp-content/uploads/2014/10/IPv6-Fact-Sheet-English-v1.pdf

The period or dot (.) represents the current folder on the website. Therefore, this URL tells the browser to start at the current folder and then use the remaining information to locate the PDF. If a web page on another domain, such as code.org, contains a hyperlink pointing to this document, the absolute address must be used:

http://www.internetsociety.org/deploy360/wp-content/uploads/2014/10/IPv6-Fact-Sheet-English-v1.pdf

Browsers

Browsers are the user's interface to the World Wide Web. A **browser** is a computer program that retrieves hypertext documents via the HTTP protocol and displays them on the computer monitor. The name is derived from the activity of browsing, or surfing, the web to locate files. While these programs are also known as *web browsers,* browsers now offer many abilities beyond surfing the World Wide Web.

GS5 Living Online
1.1.3.10,
1.1.3.12, 2.1.4
GS4 Living Online
1.2.9

Most browsers support tabs. Tabs provide the ability to open multiple web pages at the same time, one in each tab, without opening new application windows. Without tabs, or *tab browsing*, moving to a new page overwrites the previous page. Tabs usually appear along the top of the browser window, similar to paper file folder tabs, but each browser implements the idea of tabs in its own unique way.

Examples of browsers are Chrome, Internet Explorer, Microsoft Edge, Safari, and Firefox, among others. Figure 13-7 illustrates the main features of the Microsoft Edge browser.

There are common features that every browser supports. The specific function of a feature may vary from one browser to another or by software version. Some of the common features are discussed below.

Home Page. When the browser is launched, it loads a page designated as the home page. This provides a uniform starting place for browsing. In Microsoft Edge, the option for setting the home page is found by clicking the **More Actions** button and then clicking **Settings**, as shown in Figure 13-8A. In Google Chrome, this option is found in the **Customize and Control Google Chrome** menu, as shown in Figure 13-8B. The option is similarly located in other browsers.

FYI

If you need help learning the functions of a new browser or version, hover the cursor over each icon to view the tooltip. If more information is required, use the help feature to search for the content of the tooltip.

GS4 Living Online
1.2.3

Current tab: tab navigation allows multiple tabs to be open

New tab: opens a new, blank tab

Navigator bar: shows or accepts a URL

Hub button: displays favorites, reading list, history, and downloads

Web Note button

Share button

Back button: displays the previous page

Forward button: displays the next page

More Actions

Scroll bar moves the page up and down

Goodheart-Willcox Publisher

Figure 13-7. The basic layout of the Microsoft Edge screen.

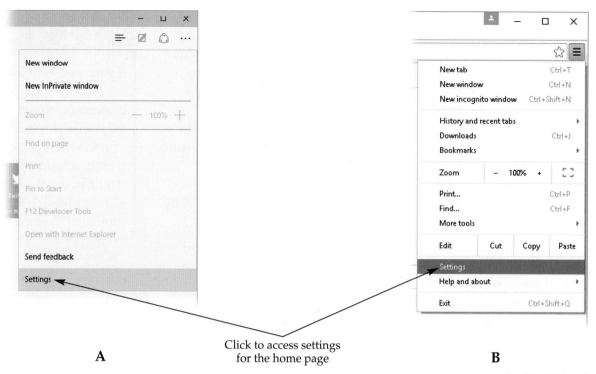

A

Click to access settings
for the home page

B

Goodheart-Willcox Publisher

Figure 13-8. The home page can be set in all popular browsers.

Some schools, businesses, or companies use an intranet. An *intranet* is an internal network similar in function to the Internet. If an intranet is used, often the home page for the browser is set to the home page of the intranet. Other users may prefer to set the home page to a search engine or even to a blank screen.

Living Online
1.1.3.11

Scroll Bars

Usually a web page is too large to fit on the display. Scroll bars are provided for the user to see the extra content that does not fit on the display. Web designers often place the attention-grabbing content on the top of the display to encourage users to scroll to see the rest. Click and drag the scroll bar up and down or use the up and down arrow buttons to move the extra content into the display. The mouse wheel can also be used to scroll the page.

Living Online
1.1.3.4

Breadcrumbs

A common type of website navigation is breadcrumbs. Breadcrumbs, or a breadcrumb trail, are hyperlinks back to each page the user has navigated to on the website. The breadcrumbs typically appear along the top of the website. A separator, usually a chevron (>), is used between each breadcrumb. These elements are called breadcrumbs because they show a trail back to the home page of the website, just as Hansel and Gretel left breadcrumbs to find their way out of the forest in the fairytale of the same name.

Mouse Actions

Moving the cursor over a hyperlink on a webpage, known as a mouse-over or roll-over, causes the cursor to change to indicate the presence of a hyperlink. The browser will display the URL of the hyperlink, typically in the status bar at the bottom of the browser window. In general, a single click selects an item on a webpage, while a double click activates an item. The exception is a hyperlink, which is activated with a single click, not a double click. A right-click displays a shortcut menu of actions including navigation and page-management tools. Generally, this shortcut menu provides browser-based actions, but it is possible for a web designer to program a shortcut menu for page-based actions.

GS5 Living Online
2.1.1, 2.1.2

Downloads

Files and applications may be downloaded to the user's computer. Browsers use file transfer protocol to bring image, text, PDF, or other files to the local computer. The process is known as *downloading*. Each browser has a default location where downloaded files are saved. For example, Microsoft Edge (Internet Explorer) in a Windows 10 environment has a default location as This PC>Download, which is the C:\Users\(*user name*)\Downloads folder. One of the settings that can be made in the browser is whether or not to prompt for a download location. A good file-management technique is to make the browser prompt for the storage location each time a download is requested. Then, save the file in your project's folder. If this setting is not to prompt, the browser automatically stores the downloaded file in the default location.

GS5 Computing Fundamentals
3.9

History. The history feature keeps track of the locations visited using the browser. This feature makes it easy to return to one of the listed pages. Figure 13-9 shows the history feature in Internet Explorer.

GS5 Computing Fundamentals
7.4.3.1
GS4 Living Online
1.2.7

TITANS OF TECHNOLOGY

Although the Internet is the result of many talented people, one person stands out as the individual who made the Internet accessible to the masses. Sir Timothy Berners-Lee conceived and built the World Wide Web. While working as a computer programmer at CERN in Bern, Switzerland, Berners-Lee noticed how very difficult it was to find and read documents of research results that were stored on the Internet. He devised the notion of the uniform resource locator (URL)

as an address for every document on the Internet. Then he used the existing technology of hypertext to describe markup rules for developing browsers to view the documents. His final step was to create the hypertext transfer protocol (HTTP) for locating and delivering the documents to the requesting computer. That was in 1989. At this time, Berners-Lee is working at the World Wide Web Consortium. He directs the World Wide Web foundation.

History

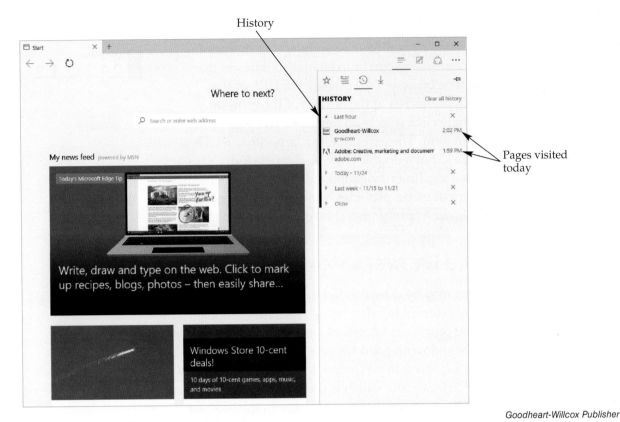

Pages visited today

Figure 13-9. The history feature keeps track of visited pages. This is the history feature for Microsoft Edge.

GS4 Living Online
1.2.4

Back, Forward, and Refresh. The back and forward functions allow you to move backward and forward through the pages you have visited. This is easier than reentering the URL of a previously visited page. The refresh function is used to reinitialize the current page. This is sometimes needed if the page has frozen or is used to update dynamic information on the page, such as the display of the amount of time left in an online auction.

GS5 Living Online
1.1.3.13

GS4 Living Online
1.2.5

Favorites or Bookmarks. Often while searching for information, several sites may prove to be helpful. Rather than writing down the URLs and reentering them later to return to the sites, it is possible to flag the sites as a favorite or bookmark. The browser stores the title and URL of the page. Opening the list of favorites or bookmarks and clicking the link retrieves that page.

Most browsers allow a specific list of bookmarks to be made that can be shared with other users. This is a useful feature when researching a group project. All of the relevant bookmarks can be kept together and shared with everybody in the group.

GS5 Living Online
1.1.3.5, 1.1.3.7

GS4 Living Online
1.2.6

Plug-ins. A **plug-in**, or add-on, is a helper file that extends the capability of a software application, in this case, a browser. For example, Adobe Flash Player is a browser plug-in. The benefit of a plug-in is that patches can be sent from the developer to update only that part of the browser. It is not necessary to install a new browser each time an update needs to be made.

Most plug-ins will be suggested when a user tries to use a feature that is not native to a browser. Suppose you click a link to play a video. If the browser is not able to play the video, it needs a plug-in that supports the format of the video being played. As a security measure, the browser makes the user choose whether or not to install a plug-in.

Once a plug-in is installed, it can be deleted or its configuration can be changed. In Chrome, enter chrome://plugins in the address bar. Then, click the **Disable** link for the plug-ins you wish to disable. In its initial release, Microsoft Edge does not support add-ons.

HANDS-ON EXAMPLE 13.1.2

SETTING THE BROWSER HOME PAGE

When launched, a browser displays what has been set as the home page. Changing the home page is easy in most browsers.

1. Launch Microsoft Edge.
2. Click the **More Actions** button, and click **Settings** in the drop-down menu. The **Settings** menu is displayed, as shown.

Home page setting

3. Click the **A specific page or pages** radio button.
4. Click the drop-down list below the radio button, and click **Custom** in the list.
5. If any pages are listed, such as about:start, click the X next to the page to remove it.
6. Click in the text box that states Enter a web address, and enter www.google.com or the address of your school's intranet.
7. Click the **More Actions** button to close the menu.

Living Online
1.1.3.1

HTML and Web 2.0

Part of the problem of using documents stored on various computers around the world was solved by the URL and web servers. Once the document could be obtained, there remained the problem of how to open it and read its contents. HTML solved this problem. As the web has advanced, new capabilities have been introduced, giving rise to Web 2.0.

HTML

Key Applications
1.2

Hypertext markup language (HTML) is a language used to create documents that tell browsers how to assemble text, images, and other content to display as a web page. It allows a universal practice of marking up the documents for browsers. The basis of HTML is tags, which are codes that let the browser know how to display a document. Figure 13-10 shows a basic web page and the HTML used to create it.

HTML provides for basic formatting for a document. A cascading style sheet provides advanced formatting and has become the standard for how to control the appearance of a website. A *cascading style sheet (CSS)* provides definitions that control the formatting of HTML documents and other markup documents.

> ## FYI
>
> JavaScript and the Java programming language are not related.

Interactive or dynamic pages require additional programming tools. JavaScript is browser-dependent, but provides interactions such as buttons and rollover image swapping. For form handling, pages that change content based on interactions, or even more advanced interactions, tools such as PHP, active server pages (ASP), and structured query language (SQL) are required. Some web pages are even programmed to allow the user to drag and drop content. Drag and drop may also be used as a navigation method for the website. In this case, the user may need to drag the image on the page to move the focus to a different area.

Living Online
2.1.3

There are software applications for building web pages, such as Adobe Dreamweaver and CoffeeCup. These are known as WYSIWYG

Web Page

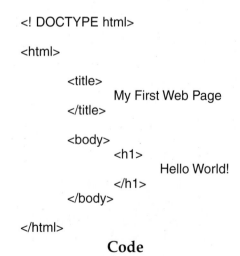

Code

Figure 13-10. Very little code is needed to create a simple web page.

editors, which stands for "what you see is what you get," because you are able to design a web page in an environment that shows how the web page will look. The software also inserts the HTML tags for you.

To learn more about programming web pages, visit the W3 Schools website (www.W3Schools.com). This is a free web-development resource. There are tutorials with many examples, language reference documents, and certification tests.

Web 2.0

Web 2.0 is a movement that promotes increased use of multimedia and social networking on the web. *Web 2.0* describes websites that provide more opportunity for people to collaborate rather than simply read static pages, as originally found on the web. The term is used to describe how the web has evolved since it was created. Twitter is an example of Web 2.0, as shown in Figure 13-11.

A major advancement of web design that led to Web 2.0 was the ease of incorporating multimedia. *Multimedia,* or many media, is a combination of text, video, graphics, animations, audio, and user interaction. There are some basic concepts that every web designer needs to understand:

- new media
- interactivity
- interaction design
- human-computer interaction

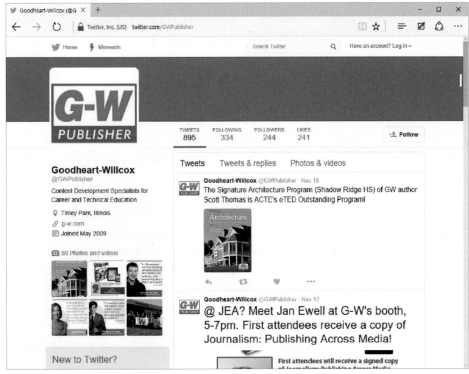

Goodheart-Willcox Publisher

Figure 13-11. Web 2.0 promotes the use of multimedia and social networking, such as Twitter.

New Media. The term *new media* refers to the Internet-based content that can be accessed on-demand on any digital device and involves user control and dialogue. The definition of new media continually changes as new interactions and models for communication are developed.

Interactivity. The magic of computers is the ability to put the user in control of the speed, order, and use of information. *Interactivity* refers to items the user can control, such as hyperlinks, text-entry boxes, selection buttons, scroll bars, video controls, and audio controls. Interactivity allows the user to be in control of gathering and providing information on each page.

Interaction Design. Online communication is facilitated by understanding what is to be communicated and presenting it in the clearest and easiest way. *Interaction design* refers to creating interactivity. All elements of the page must work together to communicate the message. The selection of typeface is an important consideration. The typefaces easiest to read on a computer monitor are sans serif fonts. Images should promote the message and not be meaningless graphics. Video should be incorporated when a series of intricate steps must be followed to perform a task. Color should be used to highlight important ideas and should not be used simply to decorate the page.

Human-Computer Interaction. The **human-computer interaction (HCI)** describes how computer users communicate with the computer. The HCI part of web design is often referred to as *usability*. Readability, ease of interaction, and intuitive use of the page are all considerations for web design. Considerations must also be included for accessibility by users with disabilities as well as others. In addition, consider how the web page design will be presented if the content is viewed on a mobile device.

Digital Wellness

With new digital technology comes new health concerns. Users can become addicted to the technologies or injure themselves as a result of use. **Digital wellness** is the area of study to discuss and remedy excessive use of screen time, online addictions, and smartphone addictions. Caution must be taken to be aware of how much time and energy is devoted to use of games or social media. Excessive use of digital technology may be considered an addiction. Smartphone use is very common across all age groups. There is a distinct difference between idle use of these technologies and smartphone use to the exclusion of other social activities. A recent Pew Research Center study found that 46 percent of smartphone owners said they "could not live without" their smartphones. Section 15.3 provides more information on good communication practices related to online and cell phone communication.

Ergonomics is the science concerned with designing and arranging things people use so that they can interact with them both efficiently and safely. In the workplace, it can include designing workstations to fit the unique needs of the worker and the equipment used. Applying

GS5 Living Online
9.2.1, 9.2.2

GS4 Living Online
5.2.1, 5.2.2,
5.2.3, 5.2.4,
5.2.5

ergonomic principles results in a comfortable, efficient, and safe working environment. Ergonomics can help make reading on a screen more comfortable. There are many types of ergonomic accessories that may improve the comfort of reading on a screen, including wrist rests; specially designed chairs, keyboards, and mice; and back supports. In addition, Figure 13-12 identifies actions that can be taken to create a comfortable environment for reading on a screen and help prevent injury or strain to the worker's body.

Using Search Engines

A **search engine** is a software program that looks through massive databases of links and information to try to identify the best matches for the search request. Web-based search engines are powerful tools for locating information on the Internet and World Wide Web. Most modern search engines have natural language processing that makes searching very easy. For example, a question such as what is the boiling point of water can be entered as the search "term."

However, the more specific the search phrase, the better the results. For example, a search using the phrase, or string, sports information may return two billion results in about a half second. To optimize the search, be as specific as possible. The search for top 2016 fielding percentage narrows the results to around three hundred thousand. This is still too many pages to read. Fortunately, the links are ordered by relevance to the search string. The links near the top are more likely to contain the information than links near the bottom. Figure 13-13 shows a page at espn.go.com that allows the user to select a season and player position to show the fielding percentage. This was one of the first links in the search results.

GS5 | Key Applications
4.2

Living Online
1.1.2.1.1

GS4 | Living Online
1.2.8, 6.1.1

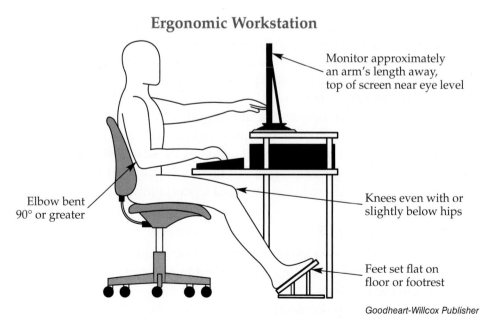

Ergonomic Workstation

Monitor approximately an arm's length away, top of screen near eye level

Elbow bent 90° or greater

Knees even with or slightly below hips

Feet set flat on floor or footrest

Goodheart-Willcox Publisher

Figure 13-12. The application of ergonomics helps prevent muscle pain, eyestrain, and headaches caused by improper placement of monitors, desks, and chairs.

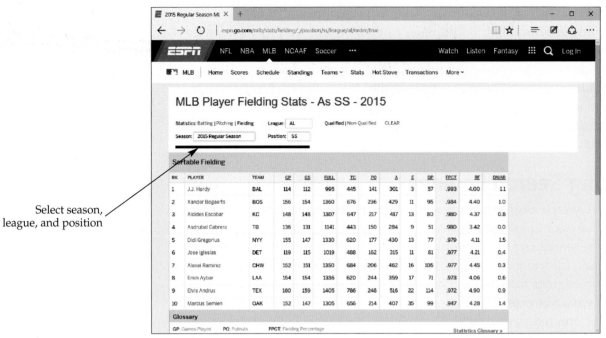

Figure 13-13. Using a specific search phrase narrowed the results to pages more likely to match, such as this espn.go.com page.

Living Online
4.2.2, 6.3.1

Search engines provide filters to help to narrow your search. For example, Google and Bing have filters for images, videos, news, and other categories. There are also sites dedicated to a particular type of media. Flickr is a website for posting and storing images. When searching for an image, using Flickr automatically limits the results to images. When searching for video, using a site for posting videos, such as YouTube, limits the results to videos. For music, search a music site such as iTunes.

A technology named Boolean logic can be used to construct very precise search strings. English mathematician George Boole invented a logical algebra, or Boolean algebra, in the 19th century. It is still relevant to computing today. **Boolean operators**, or logical operators, define the relationship between words in the search string. The Boolean operators AND, OR, and NOT can be used to create precise search strings. Also available are proximity operators such as NEAR or FOLLOWED BY. Figure 13-14 shows how the Boolean operators can be applied to a search string.

For example, to use Boolean operators to find information about space launches to Pluto near the word "stellar," enter the search string: space launches AND Pluto NEAR stellar. Without the Boolean operators, the search will return any result that includes the word space, launches, Pluto, or stellar.

Evaluating Results

Living Online
6.1.2

There are two reasons to use a search engine: acquire knowledge and solve problems. Problem solving is enhanced by use of a search engine. Problem solving involves:

- statement of the problem;
- gathering of information;

Boolean Operator	Example	Effect
AND	space launches AND Pluto	Locate information in both phrases on the same page
OR	space launches OR Pluto	Locate information on either phrase
NOT	space launches NOT Pluto	Locate information on the first phrase, exclude information on the second phrase
NEAR	space launches NEAR Pluto	Locate information where both phrases are used in close proximity on the same page
FOLLOWED BY	space launches FOLLOWED BY Pluto	The first phrase comes before the second phrase on the page

Goodheart-Willcox Publisher

Figure 13-14. Boolean operators and proximity operators can be used to improve searches.

- formulation of a solution; and
- action to resolve the problem.

Finding accurate, relevant, and valid information is critical to the problem-solving process.

Locating information on the web is relatively simple. However, it is important to evaluate the results. The criteria for evaluating results include accuracy, relevance, and validity.

Accuracy

Accuracy refers to the correctness of the information. Are the dates, places, and other factual information correct? For example, the freezing point of water is 32 degrees Fahrenheit. If the site gives the freezing point of water as some other temperature, the accuracy of all information on the site should be questioned. Does the page contain misspellings? Misspellings and grammar errors can be a sign that the information on the site is inaccurate. At the very least, it is a sign of sloppiness on the creator's part.

Relevance

Relevance refers to how the results relate to the search phrases. Do the results include all words in the search string or just one? Most browsers support the [Ctrl][F] key combination to launch a search function. After clicking a link in the search results, use this function to locate the search string on the page. If it cannot be found, the page is likely not relevant to the search string.

Validity

Validity refers to how appropriate the results are to the search question. Do the results answer the question of the searcher? It is important to verify the validity of the information that you retrieve. A method for ensuring the correctness of the information is called *triangulation*. If the same information can be located in at least three different sources, it is likely to be valid information. Another method

FYI

Anyone can create a web page. Just because information appears on a web page does not make the information true, correct, or accurate.

GS5 Living Online
1.1.2.1.1, 1.1.2.2.1

GS4 Living Online
6.2.5

used to judge validity is to examine the source of the information. Information that is part of an official site, such as a university or a news agency, is more likely to be valid. Sources that are less likely to contain valid information are blog entries, a student research paper, or a social media site where opinions rather than facts may be included.

Types of Returned Results

Living Online
1.1.2.1.1

The list of returned results for a search will likely contain links to many types of websites or sources. In evaluating the validity of the results, it is important to be aware that some types of sources will be less reliable than others. Some typical types of sources include forums, ads, sponsored links, knowledge bases, and articles.

Forums

Living Online
6.2.1

Forums are Internet sites that support conversations or posts on certain topics. These can be useful for people interested in the same subject. Forums are good for finding suggestions or solutions to common problems or having a discussion about a topic. Good forum users try to post accurate and helpful information on the topic. However, that does not make them experts on the topic. Forums are not good sources to cite for accurate and valid information.

Ads

Living Online
6.2.2

Take care to see if a page is providing accurate and valid information or if it is an advertisement for a product or service. If the page is really an ad, it is likely promoting something other than accurate, research-based information. An advertisement is not a good source of reliable information.

Sponsored Links

Living Online
6.2.3

Most popular search engines are owned by for-profit companies. Since the search engine is free to use, the search engine displays sponsored links related to the search results in addition to the results, as shown in Figure 13-15. These sponsored links are really advertisements placed by companies that pay for them, often on a per-click basis. Sponsored links may be useful if you are shopping for something specific. However, sponsored links are paid ads and not a reliable source of information.

Knowledge Bases

Living Online
6.2.4

A knowledge base is a collection of data about a certain topic, often from a manufacturer of an item or product. Help and support information is posted to these sites. When looking at the page, check the URL to see if it is the manufacturer that has posted the information about its products. If the URL is not for the manufacturer's website, the site may be fake or an advertisement posing as a knowledge base. Information posted by the manufacturer is generally accurate and valid.

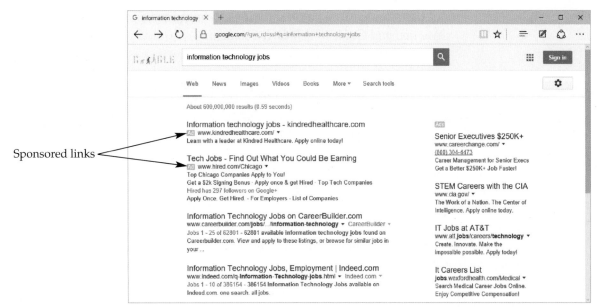

Figure 13-15. Sponsored links usually appear at the top or along the side of the search results.

Articles

Articles can contain both fact and fiction. The source of the article is important in determining the validity of the information. Professional journals, governmental sites, and educational institutions generally control their sites to maintain the value of the information. If an article is open to review, such as the Wikipedia site, the accuracy and validity of the information is more likely to be good. Personal websites, advertising websites, blogs, and forums may contain articles, but the accuracy and validity of these articles can be questionable.

Living Online
6.2.6

Ethical Use of the Internet

Similar to the concerns for plagiarism when creating word processing documents, there are ethical concerns for use of information on the Internet. The topics included in ethical use are Internet safety and intellectual property. More information on these topics is found in Chapters 8 and 16 of this textbook.

Many schools and companies provide an acceptable use policy to guide students and employees on expectations for ethical use of the Internet. An *acceptable use policy (AUP)* is a set of rules that explains what is and is not acceptable use of school- or company-owned equipment and networks. This document should describe policies on copyrights, fair use, file sharing, online privacy, cyber predators, and cyberbullying.

Every document placed on the Internet has an author, and the content is the intellectual property of that author. Intellectual property is protected by laws. Some information on the Internet is available for free use, but it must be labeled as such. If the material is not specifically labeled as free use, assume it is copyrighted. When basing your own work on material found on the Internet, proper attribution or citation of the source must be made. Most style guides, including the *MLA Style Manual and Guide to Scholarly Publishing*, provide guidelines for how to cite Internet-based work.

HANDS-ON EXAMPLE 13.1.3

CITING ONLINE SOURCES

The Internet is a great resource for information. The *MLA Style Manual and Guide to Scholarly Publishing* provides guidelines for properly citing Internet-based information.
1. Launch a browser.
2. Navigate to a search engine, such as Google or Bing.
3. Enter the search string MLA citation format for websites.
4. Evaluate the results for relevance and validity.
5. Select an appropriate link in the results.
6. Evaluate the site for accuracy.
7. Use the information on the website to determine the proper method for citing a web document.

13.1 SECTION REVIEW

CHECK YOUR UNDERSTANDING

1. Distinguish between upload and download.
2. How does the World Wide Web relate to the Internet?
3. List four programming tools used to create interactive or dynamic web pages.
4. List the three Boolean operators that can be used in a search string.
5. If basing your own work on material found on the Internet, what must you do to document that?

IC3 CERTIFICATION PRACTICE

The following question is a sample of the types of questions presented on the IC3 exam.
1. In the domain name system, which top-level domain would be used by a university?
   A. .gov
   B. .com
   C. .org
   D. .edu

BUILD YOUR VOCABULARY

As you progress through this course, develop a personal IT glossary. This will help you build your vocabulary and prepare you for a career. Write a definition for each of the following terms and add it to your IT glossary.

Boolean operators	modem
browser	packet
digital wellness	plug-in
download	protocol
ergonomics	public switched network
human-computer	search engine
interaction (HCI)	uniform resource locator
hypertext markup	(URL)
language (HTML)	upload
Internet service provider	
(ISP)	

CREATING FOR THE WEB

Paul Matthew Photography/Shutterstock.com

The primary principle for web designers is the usability of their pages. Users must be able to perform tasks with a minimum of effort. This requires a great deal of design. Once the design is in place, the pages can be created. Web pages are developed on a rising scale of complexity. For each level, more sophisticated tools are used.

The tools for creating documents for the web include HTML for simple markup of existing documents or creating of static web pages, CSS for formatting web pages, and programming and scripting languages to make dynamic pages. This section explores how to use these tools to create web pages.

Essential Question

How does the efficiency of web programming impact the usability of a web page?

TERMS

alignment
cascading style sheet (CSS)
contrast
external style
inline style
internal style
JavaScript
PHP hypertext preprocessor
proximity
repetition
semantic tag
tag
validation

LEARNING GOALS

After completing this section, you will be able to:

- Identify graphic design principles that should be applied when creating a web page.
- Explain how to create a basic web page using HTML.
- Discuss programming languages used to create web pages.

Designing for the Web

There are many commonly accepted principles of web design. At the root of these principles is the need to present information in a format that is easy to understand and visually pleasing. The first step is to determine the audience for the page and what information will be presented.

Each page on a website should be easy to understand. A web designer must consider what the user will want and present it in a clear and intuitive interface. It is important to organize the information so that it is easy to find. Help to focus the readers' attention by using typefaces that are easy to read, changing text size for emphasis, and using colors for grabbing attention.

Navigation of the site should be obvious. Make use of common conventions. For example, users expect to follow links. Make them clear. Use standard icons to help users find links to common services, such as Facebook or Twitter. When designing a website, use a storyboard to plan the navigation. Create a sketch of each page in the website. Then, arrange the sketches on a whiteboard and draw lines between the pages to illustrate the navigation. Using storyboards can also be used for time management, which is discussed in Chapter 17.

Basic graphic design principles apply to the visual design of a website. Principles such as contrast, repetition, alignment, and proximity should be followed.

kosmos111/Shutterstock.com

Figure 13-16. The colors of these umbrellas have high contrast, which makes it easy to see all of them.

Contrast

A key principle in graphic design is contrast. **Contrast** is the degree of difference between elements in a design, as shown in Figure 13-16. Mixing elements of different qualities provides interest, draws focus, and helps the user to understand the information on the page.

Contrast can be achieved by using large items with small items; a serif typeface for some elements and a sans serif typeface for other elements; bright colors with subtle colors; or by grouping some elements and separating other elements. These methods provide the opportunity to indicate importance of an item because of the contrast to other, lesser important items on the page.

Repetition

Repetition, or pattern, is when an element occurs more than once. Repeating design elements such as color choices or image treatment provides a uniform look to the pages of a website. This promotes a feeling that all of the pages belong together. It provides a sense that there is an organization to the website.

Alignment

All items on the page should look as if they are specifically placed. Nothing looks accidental. **Alignment** is placing elements in relation to key points in other elements. Proper alignment of elements gives a professional look to a page.

For example, alignment can be around a specific element or left justified to the edge of the display. Text referring to an image should be aligned with the image. Aligning elements by edge or on centers is common, as shown in Figure 13-17. The designer chooses the type of alignment to enhance the message being communicated.

Proximity

Proximity means how closely elements are placed to each other. For example, the caption for an image should be placed next to the image it describes. In this case, the caption is said to be in proximity to the image, meaning it is close to the image. People will tend to think of elements as a group if they are laid out in proximity to each other.

Science
Asymmetry is commonly used in photography and videography to create visual interest. Asymmetry is common in nature and biology. For example, the fiddler crab has one small claw and one large claw. The small claw is used for feeding, where the large claw is used for defense or courtship.

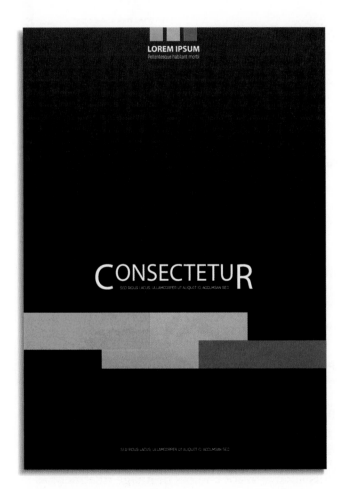 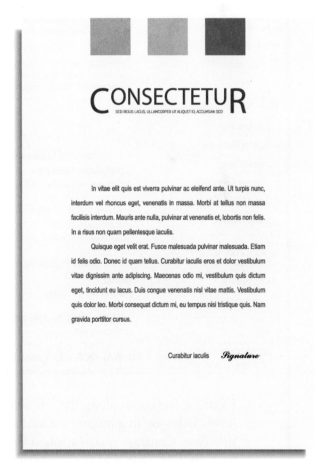

Kun Kunko/Shutterstock.com

Figure 13-17. Notice how the designer has chosen to align not only the text, but the other elements in this layout.

HANDS-ON EXERCISE 13.2.1

IDENTIFYING DESIGN PRINCIPLES

The design of a website should follow basic design principles. It should be easy to identify whether or not design principles have been followed.

1. Launch a browser.
2. Navigate to the World Wide Web Consortium website at www.w3.org, as shown. Note: the content of this page may have changed because the web is dynamic, but the basic design should appear similar.

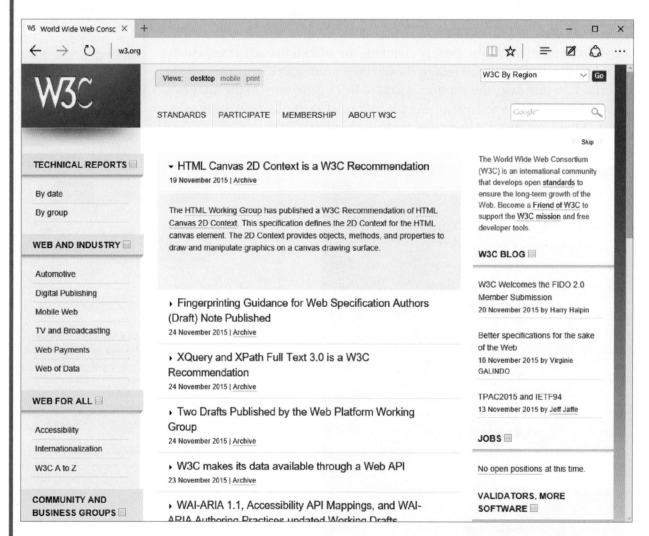

3. Examine the menu along the left side of the page. Notice the contrast used to indicate level. Titles are in a larger font and set in all caps. Subtitles are in a smaller font and set in title case. Contrast is also applied by shading the large blocks in which the titles appear of background color, and the entire menu is a different color from the main background.

HANDS-ON EXAMPLE 13.2.1 (CONTINUED)

4. Click each entry in the menu. Notice how the menu is repeated on each page. While the specific entries in the menu vary from page to page, the formatting of the menu is consistent. This repetition is useful for rapid recall.

5. Return to the website's home page. Notice the material is arranged in the three columns on the page. The text in each of the columns is left-justified. Images are also left-justified. This is the alignment.

6. Scroll to the bottom of the home page, and examine the proximity of elements. The calendar graphics are in close proximity to the related events and talks.

7. Identify one more example of each of these four design principles: contrast, repetition, alignment, and proximity.

HTML

It is very easy to make a simple web page. Only a few rules must be followed to make an HTML-based web page.

GS5 **Key Applications**
1.2

- The files must be text only.
- The file name ends in .html or .htm.
- The page must be stored in a folder or subfolder of a web server connected to the Internet.
- Tags are embedded in the file to instruct the browser how to display the page elements.

A **tag** is a code enclosed in chevrons (angle brackets) that tells the browser how to format or display the content. In general, a tag definition consists of a pair of starting and ending tags, such as <p> and </p>. Ending tags start with a slash. A few tag definitions do not have an ending tag. Figure 13-18 shows some basic tags. A comprehensive list of HTML tags is available on the W3 Schools website (www.w3schools.com) and other online resources.

The best way to see how HTML defines a web page is to create a basic page. This will show the foundation for all web page development. From there, you can develop your skills in creating web pages. The best way to learn web-page development is to make web pages and learn as you go.

FYI

The first line in an HTML file should declare the document type.

1. Launch Notepad or other plain-text editor. Do not use a word-processing program, such as Microsoft Word, because there is hidden formatting in the documents these programs create.

2. Enter the tags and text shown in Figure 13-19. Notice the spacing and indention used to separate sections of the code. This has no effect on the functionality, but it makes it easier for a person to read and understand the code.

Start Tag	End Tag	Purpose
<html>	</html>	Identifies a document as a hypertext document and contains all other HTML code.
<head>	</head>	Identifies the portion of the document that contains information about the page.
<title>	</title>	Contains the text that appears in the title bar of the browser window.
<body>	</body>	Identifies the portion of the document that is displayed in the browser window; the content of the page.
<strong>	</strong>	Contains text (content) that is important; often displayed in bold, but how it is displayed is controlled by the CSS.
<em>	</em>	Contains text (content) that is emphasized; often displayed in italic, but how it is displayed is controlled by the CSS.
<a>	</a>	Defines the anchor for a hyperlink.
<p>	</p>	Identifies a paragraph of text; text will wrap if the browser window is resized.
 	none	Defines a single line break; content after the tag is displayed on the next line.
<img>	none	Identifies an image to be displayed in the browser window; height and width of the image can also be specified.
<h1> to <h6>	</h1> to </h6>	Heading tags determine font sizes where h1 is the largest and h6 is the smallest.

Note: there is a <font> tag with more options, such as typeface, italics, etc., but this tag is not supported in HTML5.

Figure 13-18. These are basic HTML tags used in creating a web page.

```
<! DOCTYPE html>

<html>

        <title>
                My First Web Page
        </title>

        <body>
                <h1>
                        Hello World!
                </h1>
        </body>

</html>
```

Figure 13-19. The HTML code for creating a basic web page.

3. Save the file as First.html. Be sure to change the file type from .txt to .html, otherwise the browser will not be able to find the file.

4. Launch the system file explorer, navigate to where the First.html file is saved, and double-click the file. The default web browser is launched, and the page is loaded. Note: in Windows 10, you may need to right-click on the file and select **Open with** followed by either Google Chrome, Internet Explorer, or another browser other than Microsoft Edge.

5. Examine the browser window, as shown in Figure 13-20. The title bar or tab displays My First Web Page, which is defined by the <title> tag. The content in the window is Hello World!, which is defined by the <h1> tag, making it the highest level head in the body.

6. Using the browser, navigate to the NASA website (www.nasa.gov), and use the menu or search function to locate a photograph you like.

7. Right-click on the image, and click **Save picture as...** in the shortcut menu. Save the image as NASA_Image in the same folder as the First.html file. Make note of the image file type. You will need to know the file extension.

8. Switch to Notepad. Add the code shown in color in Figure 13-21. Be sure to use the correct file extension for the image file. Match the spacing and indentation shown to make the code easier to read.

9. Save the file. Note: if you receive a message that the file cannot be saved because it is being used, your file explorer may be previewing the file, in which case close the file explorer and then save the file.

Collusion

It is unethical for a business to participate in acts of collusion. *Collusion* occurs when competing businesses work together to eliminate competition by misleading customers, fixing prices, or participating in other fraudulent practices. Unethical businesses sometimes collude with others so they can dominate the marketplace. Collusion is not only unethical—it is illegal.

Goodheart-Willcox Publisher

Figure 13-20. The basic web page created with the code shown in Figure 13-19.

```
<! DOCTYPE html>

<html>

        <title>
                My First Web Page
        </title>

        <body>

                <h1>
                        Hello World!
                </h1>

                <img src="NASA_Image.jpg" alt="NASA Image">

                <h1>
                        NASA Image
                </h1>

        </body>

</html>
```

Goodheart-Willcox Publisher

Figure 13-21. Update the HTML file with the code shown here in color.

10. Switch to the web browser, and press the **Refresh** or **Reload** button for the My First Web Page tab. Notice how the edits you made to the HTML file are reflected on the web page.

Congratulations, you have created a basic web page! Use this HTML file to experiment. Try changing the number in the <h1> tags to see what happens. Be sure to change the number in both the start and end tags. Try removing the <h1> tags altogether. Change the title text to see the effect that has. By making changes to this HTML file and seeing how the changes affect the web page, you can learn how to build larger and more complex web pages.

HANDS-ON EXAMPLE 13.2.2

CREATING A BASIC WEB PAGE

It is easy to create a basic web page using a plain-text editor. For example, with a small amount of code, you can create a web page about yourself that includes a photograph.

1. Insert your PRINC-OF-IT flash drive into the computer.
2. Applying what you have learned, create a folder on the flash drive named Chap13.

HANDS-ON EXAMPLE 13.2.2 (CONTINUED)

3. Using Notepad or other plain-text editor, enter the HTML code shown.

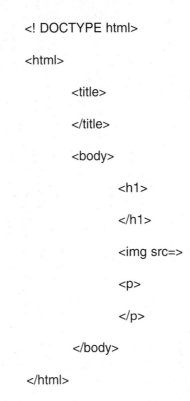

```
<! DOCTYPE html>

<html>

        <title>

        </title>

        <body>

                <h1>

                </h1>

                <img src=>

                <p>

                </p>

        </body>

</html>
```

4. Save the file as AboutMe.html in the Chap13 folder on your flash drive.
5. Using a digital camera, smartphone, or other device, take a photograph of yourself and save it in the Chap13 folder on your flash drive.
6. Applying what you have learned, edit the HTML file so the title of the web page is About Me, the heading is your name, and the image is the photograph of yourself. Refer to the example in the text if needed.
7. On the line between the paragraph tags, which are <p> and </p>, add one or two sentences describing yourself.
8. Save the HTML file, and load it into a web browser.
9. Debug the HTML file if needed. Refer to the example in the text as needed.

HTML5

There have been five revisions to the HTML standard. Each revision has added clarity and uniformity for how a browser developer should present the marked-up text. In addition, the W3C has approved additional tags for new features. The new elements for HTML5 can be presented in four groups: semantic, form control, graphics, and multimedia.

Cascading style sheets allow for much flexibility when designing website pages.

A **semantic tag** is one in which the purpose of the tag is clear from the tag name. Some of the new semantic tags are <header>, <footer>, <article>, and <section>. These help to provide contextual information for a reader of a web page.

Graphics and multimedia support have been expanded in HTML5. Now scalable vector graphic (SVG) files are supported so that changing the size of a vector graphic preserves fidelity to the original graphic. The canvas is a new feature that allows developers to draw images on the web page. The <audio> and <video> tags allow playing of sound and video files without a plug-in. Eliminating the need for plug-ins saves time for both developers and users.

CSS

A **cascading style sheet (CSS)** provides formatting information for a web page. While a CSS can be contained within an HTML file, in practice it is usually a separate file with a .css extension that is referenced by the HTML file. Separating the content of the HTML file from the formatting makes it easier to maintain an entire website. Each page can reference one CSS file. Any needed formatting changes can be made only once in the CSS file instead of in each HTML file.

The current standard for formatting web pages is maintained by the World Wide Web Consortium (W3C). There are three levels of formatting that a CSS provides:

- inline styles
- internal styles
- external styles

FYI

The website www.csszengarden.com is an interesting site that shows how changing the style sheet can change the entire design of a website without modifying the content.

Inline styles are embedded into the HTML file within the element being formatted. They are the first priority of formatting, which means they override all other styles. For example, to modify the paragraph style:

```
<p style="margin-left: 30px;">This paragraph is indented 30
pixels.</p>
```

This style is in-line with the paragraph tag <p>. The margin-left property, which sets the left-hand margin of the element, is specified as 30 pixels. Pixel is abbreviated as px. The text in the paragraph is: This paragraph is indented 30 pixels.

Internal styles are defined in the head section of the HTML file. They are the second priority of formatting, which means they override all other styles except for inline styles. To set the left-hand margin as an internal style:

```
<head>
        <style>
                p{margin-left: 30px;}
        </style>
</head>
```

This sets the left-hand margin to 30 pixels, just as the previous inline style does. However, the difference is the inline style applies only to the one paragraph where the style is defined. The internal style applies to *all* paragraphs in the web page. Any text with the <p> tag will be indented by 30 pixels.

External styles are similar to internal styles, but they are contained in a separate CSS file. They are the final priority of formatting, which means they can be overridden by internal and inline styles. To set the left-hand margin as an external style sheet, this would be included in a CSS file:

```
p{
        margin-left: 30px;
}
```

These are the most powerful because the style sheet is linked to many pages. When a style is updated in the external style sheet, every occurrence of the style in the entire website is updated. The best practice is to create external styles whenever possible.

A good question to ask is, if the external styles are the most powerful and preferred option, why are they the lowest in the cascade of formatting priorities? The answer is simple: there may be formatting needed only one time on one page. An inline or internal style can meet this need. Changing the CSS file will not affect that formatting.

An example of an external CSS is shown in Figure 13-22. It specifies that the background image of the body of the web page will be an image named watermark.png, which is stored in the same web folder as the CSS file. If it is located in a different folder, the path must be specified. The CSS also specifies that any text defined with the <h1> tag will be displayed in the dark blue color with right-hand justification (alignment). Finally, each paragraph, which is defined by the <p> tag, will be indented 30 pixels from the left-hand page margin. To use this style sheet to control

Green Tech

Digital Coupons
Many companies offer convenient digital coupons that are sent directly to customers through e-mail, text messages, or QR codes. Digital coupons eliminate the costs and resources involved in printing and physically distributing coupons. Digital coupons are a convenient and green solution that benefits both customers and businesses.

FYI

On some web servers, references to URLs are case sensitive, so always exactly match the capitalization in path and file names.

```
body {
        background-image: url("watermark.png");
}

h1 {
        color: darkblue;
        text-align: right;
}

p {
        margin-left: 30px;
}
```

Goodheart-Willcox Publisher

Figure 13-22. This is a cascading style sheet that is saved in a separate file, which is called an external style sheet.

the formatting of a web page, a link must be specified in the <head> portion of the HTML file:

```
<head>
        <link rel="stylesheet" type="text/css" href="formal.css">
</head>
```

This code specifies the relationship (rel) as a style sheet, the media type as a text or CSS file, and the URL of the file named formal.css. The href attribute specifies a URL and is found in many HTML tags. In this case, the CSS file is in the same folder as the HTML file, so only the file name and extension need to be provided. If the file is in a different folder from the HTML file, the entire path or a relative path must be specified.

FYI

The W3 Schools website (www.w3schools.com) provides comprehensive information about how to create and use a CSS.

GS5
Living Online
1.1.3.6

Web Widgets

A *widget*, or gadget, is a small limited functionality application that can be easily inserted into a web page. Examples are body mass index (BMI) calculators, holiday countdown widgets, weather apps, and others. Many widgets are free, while some must be purchased. Conduct a search for free web widgets to see the various widgets that are available.

Widgets are written in JavaScript, PHP, or other web-page programming language. Widgets generally come with instructions on how to add it to a web page. Often, you can customize a widget after which you are provided with HTML code that is to be inserted into your web page HTML definition.

HANDS-ON EXAMPLE 13.2.3

CREATING A BASIC EXTERNAL STYLE SHEET

The best practice for formatting a web page is the use of an external CSS. For example, a CSS file can be easily created to control the formatting of the AboutMe.html web page created earlier.

1. Launch a web browser, and load the AboutMe.html file in the Chap13 folder on your flash drive.
2. Launch Notepad or other plain-text editor, and save the file as Style.css in the Chap13 folder on your flash drive.
3. Enter this code into the CSS file.

```
body{
        background-color: black;
}

h1{
        color: orange;
        text-align: center;
}

p{
        font-family: Verdana, Geneva, sans-serif;
        font-size: 18 px;
        color: white;
}
```

4. Save the CSS file. Be sure it is saved as Style.css.
5. Switch to the web browser, and reload the page. What happens? Nothing changes because the CSS file has not been linked to the HTML file.
6. Using Notepad, open the AboutMe.html file. Note: you will need to open the file from within Notepad; double-clicking the file will not open it for editing.
7. After the <html> tag, press the [Enter] key to begin a new line, and add the following code.

```
<head>
        <link rel="stylesheet" type="text/css" href="Style.css">
</head>
```

8. Save the HTML file.
9. Switch to the web browser, and reload the page. The formatting of the page changes to match what is specified in the CSS file.
10. Applying what you have learned, modify the CSS to change the font size of the <h1> tag to 75 pixels. Verify the change by reloading the page in the browser.
11. Applying what you have learned, modify the CSS to change the text alignment of the <p> tag to right-hand justified, and verify the change.

Validation

HTML is a very forgiving language. Errors are not reported nor do they cause a web page not to load. If an error exists in the code, the browser ignores it and tries its best to display the remainder of the page. To keep the quality of web pages high and to confirm that a page is built according to the standards, a validation should be performed on a web page. **Validation** is a process of checking the code to ensure it contains no errors of syntax or usage.

The W3C validation site (validator.w3.org) can be used to check for valid code. Visit this site and submit a web address or a file or directly enter code to check for errors. Just for fun, examine the W3 Schools site for conformance to standards, as shown in Figure 13-23. The site passes, but two warnings are issued.

FYI

Together HTML, CSS, and validation promote sites that adhere to W3C standards.

Programming Languages

In order to add interactivity to a web page, more than HTML is required. There are several technologies used in web page development to produce interactivity. These include JavaScript, PHP, and other preprocessors.

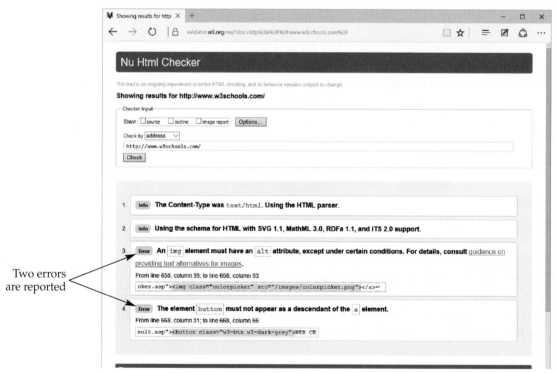

Goodheart-Willcox Publisher

Figure 13-23. The W3C validation site can be used to check for valid code. The evaluation shown here reports two errors.

JavaScript

JavaScript is an object-oriented programming language most often used in web development. When used as a browser enhancement, it allows web developers to create buttons, process forms, and vary the experience of the user based on selections made. The scripts are embedded in the HTML file itself. Because the rendering of the JavaScript to HTML is performed by the browser on the client's (user's) machine, it is called a *client-side technology*.

A simple pop-up box is produced by the **alert** command in this JavaScript statement added to an HTML file:

```
<script>
        alert("A Pop-up!");
</script>
```

The result is shown in Figure 13-24. Notice the text between the quotation marks is the text displayed in the alert. When the alert is displayed, the browser halts loading the page until the user clicks the **OK** button. When the user clicks the **OK** button, the remainder of the page is loaded.

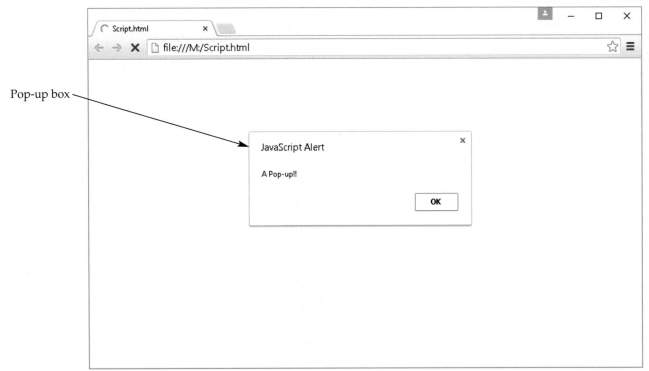

Goodheart-Willcox Publisher

Figure 13-24. This pop-up box is created with JavaScript.

HANDS-ON EXAMPLE 13.2.4

ADDING JAVASCRIPT TO A WEB PAGE

It is relatively easy to incorporate some basic JavaScript code into a web page. For example, an alert can be added to the AboutMe.html web page created earlier.

1. Applying what you have learned, open the AboutMe.html file for editing.
2. Below the <h1> end tag, enter the following code.

```
<script>
       alert ("My first Web page! Woo Hoo!");
</script>
```

3. Save the file, and load it into a web browser to see the alert.
4. Applying what you have learned, edit the script so the alert displays A short biography of *your name.*
5. Verify the change in the browser.

PHP and Other Preprocessors

A preprocessor language is required to provide database support to a web page. **PHP hypertext preprocessor** enhances interactions and supplies database support using structured query language (SQL). Early applications of PHP were address books and forum development. This functionality is not handled by the hypertext protocol. An additional program must be running on the server to handle these files. The filename extension is .php. Because the rendering of the PHP code to HTML is performed at the host, not by the user's computer, it is called a *server-side technology.*

Preprocessing functions as follows, as shown in Figure 13-25. Notice an additional step is added to the process shown in Figure 13-4 at the beginning of this chapter.

1. The user either enters a location in the navigation bar of a web browser or clicks a link on a web page, which issues the URL for a document to the browser.

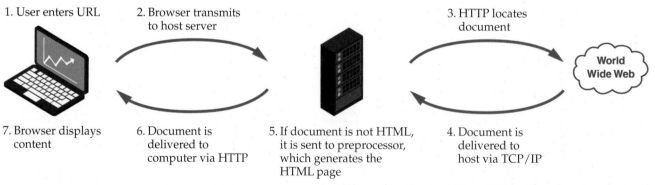

1. User enters URL
2. Browser transmits to host server
3. HTTP locates document
World Wide Web
7. Browser displays content
6. Document is delivered to computer via HTTP
5. If document is not HTML, it is sent to preprocessor, which generates the HTML page
4. Document is delivered to host via TCP/IP

Goodheart-Willcox Publisher; Macrovector/Shutterstock.com

Figure 13-25. Preprocessing involves one more step than normal web processing.

2. The web browser transmits that to its WWW program on the host server.

3. The HTTP protocol locates the document specified by the URL and requests its delivery to the host.

4. If necessary, the document is delivered via TCP/IP packets to the host.

5. If the file name extension is not .html, additional processing must take place at the host, and the file is sent to the appropriate preprocessor for translation into an HTML file.

6. The host delivers the HTML document to the requesting computer using HTTP.

7. The web browser determines how the document should be formatted and displays it.

13.2   SECTION REVIEW

 ### CHECK YOUR UNDERSTANDING

1. What are four basic design principles that should be applied to the design of a website?
2. In HTML, what are used to tell browsers how to format or display a web page?
3. What is the order of the cascade for CSS?
4. What does validation do for a web page?
5. What is required to add database support to a web page?

IC3 CERTIFICATION PRACTICE

The following question is a sample of the types of questions presented on the IC3 exam.

1. A server is a:
   A. specialized computer.
   B. conductive wireframe.
   C. set of ports to the Internet.
   D. client machine.

 ### BUILD YOUR VOCABULARY

As you progress through this course, develop a personal IT glossary. This will help you build your vocabulary and prepare you for a career. Write a definition for each of the following terms and add it to your IT glossary.

alignment
cascading style sheet
  (CSS)
contrast
external style
inline style
internal style
JavaScript

PHP hypertext
  preprocessor
proximity
repetition
semantic tag
tag
validation

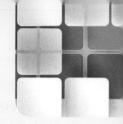
Chapter Summary

Section 13.1
Internet and the World Wide Web

- Information on the Internet and World Wide Web is transmitted in packets. The Internet protocol address uniquely identifies each computer on the network and is used to correctly route packets.

- Digital wellness is the area of study to discuss and remedy excessive use of screen time, online addictions, and smartphone addictions. Ergonomics is the science concerned with designing and arranging things people use so they can interact with them both efficiently and safely.

- A search engine examines massive databases trying to identify the best matches to the search phrases. Boolean operators can be used to fine-tune searches, and search results should be evaluated for accuracy, relevance, and validity.

- It is important to use the Internet in an ethical manner. Many schools, organizations, and companies have an acceptable use policy that outlines ethical uses of online resources.

Section 13.2
Creating for the Web

- Basic design principles such as contrast, repetition, alignment, and proximity should be followed when designing for the web. Information on a web page should be presented in a format that is easy to understand and visually pleasing.

- Hypertext markup language is a basic language used to create web pages based on tags that tell the browser how to format or display the content. A cascading style sheet is used to control formatting of web pages.

- Interactivity on a web page requires a programming language beyond HTML.

Languages often used to program interactivity include JavaScript and PHP.

Now that you have finished this chapter, see what you know about information technology by scanning the QR code to take the chapter posttest. If you do not have a smartphone, visit www.g-wlearning.com.

Chapter 13 Test

Multiple Choice

Select the best response.

1. What is the client software program that retrieves web documents and displays them to the user?
   A. preprocessor
   B. server
   C. host
   D. browser

2. What does Web 2.0 promote?
   A. WYSIWYG editors
   B. use of multimedia and social networking
   C. use of uniform resource locators
   D. relative addresses

3. Any information you retrieve from a search engine:
   A. is guaranteed accurate
   B. is correct, factual, and truthful
   C. is not to be questioned
   D. should be evaluated for accuracy, relevance, and validity

4. Which of the following is the correct pair of starting and ending tags for defining a hyperlink in a web page?
   A. <a>...</a>
   B. <h>...</h>
   C. <p>...</p>
   D. <html>...</html>

5. Which of the following can be used to add interactivity to a web page?
   A. DNS
   B. URL
   C. JavaScript
   D. HTML

Completion

Complete the following sentences with the correct word(s).

6. A(n) _____ is an address that points to a specific document or other resource on a computer network.

7. _____ involves statement of the problem, gathering of information, formulation of a solution, and action to resolve the problem.

8. A method for ensuring the correctness in which the same information can be located in at least three different sources is _____.

9. In practice, a(n) _____ is usually a separate file referenced by each page in a website to control formatting.

10. The _____ JavaScript command displays a pop-up box containing a message.

Matching

Match the correct term with its definition.

A. domain name system
B. upload
C. download
D. MLA
E. HTML

11. Source for how to properly cite information.

12. Maps the numbers and letters in an IP address to a human-readable string of characters.

13. Transmission from the host to the client.

14. Transmission from the client to the host.

15. Defines a web page.

Application and Extension of Knowledge

1. Go to the World Wide Web Consortium (W3C) website (www.w3.org). Use the site's search function, and search for a little history of the world wide web. In the search results, look for the article of the same name. Read the W3C article, and write a one-page summary of the key game-changing events. Be sure to cite the information source.

2. Go to the Wikipedia website (www.wikipedia.org). Use the site's search function, and search for programming languages used in most popular websites. If the site does not transport you directly to the article, click the link in the search results that matches the search string. Examine the information in the article. Prepare for a class discussion on the accuracy, relevance, and validity of the information on this web page.

3. Go to the NASA website (www.nasa.gov). Use the site's search function to locate an image file of a planet in our solar system, such as Venus. Make note of the URL of the image or the page on which it is displayed, and download or save the image. Using Notepad or other plain-text editor, create an HTML file to display the image. Save it in the same folder as the image file. Identify the purpose of the page in <title> and <h1> tags. Include the image file using the code <img src="*image*"> where *image* is the name of the image file. Use the <p> tag to include a proper citation of the image source. Use the <a> tag to include a hyperlink to the image URL. Make sure all tags are properly closed, then save the HTML file, and display the web page in a browser.

4. Edit the HTML file created in #3. Add this code to the <head> section,

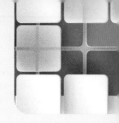

and then save and close the file: <link rel="stylesheet" type="text/css" href="mystyle.css">. Using Notepad or other plain-text editor, create the following style sheet, and save it as mystyle.css in the same folder as the HTML and image files. Display the web page in a browser, and note the color of the hyperlink before clicking it, while the cursor is over it, and after clicking it. Experiment with editing the CSS to create different colors. Use hex-code colors (search the Internet for color codes).

```
a:link{
        color: red;
}

a:visited{
        color: orange;
}

a:hover{
        color: blue;
}
```

5. Go to the W3 Schools website (www.w3schools.com). Use the site's search function, and search for my first javascript example. Evaluate the search results, and select the link for JavaScript Tutorial. The tutorial contains an example that matches the search string. Click the button in the example to display the date and time. Next, click the **Try it Yourself** button to view the HTML and JavaScript code. Notice that the button tag actually draws a button for you. Identify the part of the code that matches what is displayed on the web page button. Edit the code to change what is displayed on the button, and then click the **See Result** button at the top of the page to update the HTML code. Consider how adding a button to a website can improve the navigation. Prepare for a class discussion on that topic.

Online Activities

Complete the following activities, which will help you learn, practice, and expand your knowledge and skills.

Certification Practice. Complete the certification practice test for this chapter.

Vocabulary. Practice vocabulary for this chapter using the e-flash cards, matching activity, and vocabulary game until you are able to recognize their meanings.

Communication Skills

College and Career Readiness

Writing. Rhetoric is the study of writing or speaking as a way of communicating information or persuading someone. Identify rhetoric that could be used to persuade a customer to purchase a Mac over a PC. Write a script in a step-by-step format for presenting the item to an adult customer.

Speaking. It is important to be prepared when you are speaking to an individual or to an audience. Style and content influences how the listener understands your message. Using the script you developed in the last activity, convince a classmate to buy a Mac. Make use of visuals or demonstrations to enhance the presentation. Adjust your presentation length to fit the attention span of the audience.

Listening. Active listening is fully participating as you process what others are saying. Salespersons must practice active listening in order to fully understand a customer's need. Make a list of listening strategies that could be used to enhance listening comprehension. Examples might include monitoring the message for what is being said or focus on the message.

Discarded.

Internet Research

Boolean Searches. Using various search engines, conduct an Internet search for the term mammals. Take note of how many results you get. Next, using combinations of the Boolean search operators AND, OR, and NOT, conduct a search using the terms mammals, marine, herbivore, and monotreme. Record results for each search you conduct. Which Boolean operator yields the most results? Make a chart showing your search parameters and number of results, and share your findings with the class.

Teamwork

Working with your team, select an IT company that you think needs a new website. Or, consider proposing a site revision to your school's Career and Technical Student Organization website. First, analyze the selected website. Create a list of structural elements that need to be addressed. Identify what components work and what needs improvement. Make a list of tasks that must be considered to improve the website's structure. Outline each step that would be necessary if your team is awarded the opportunity to update and revise the website.

Portfolio Development

College and Career Readiness

Soft Skills. Employers and colleges review various qualities of candidates. For example, the ability to communicate effectively, get along with customers or coworkers, and solve problems are important skills for many jobs. These types of skills are often called soft skills. Make an effort to learn about and develop the soft skills needed for your chosen career field.

1. Conduct research about soft skills and their value in helping people succeed.

2. Create a Microsoft Word document and list the soft skills that are important for a job or career that you currently possess. Use the heading "Soft Skills" and your name. For each soft skill, write a paragraph that describes your abilities. Give examples to illustrate your skills. Save the document.

3. Update your master spreadsheet.

CTSOs

Community Service Project. Many competitive events for CTSOs include a community service project. This project is usually carried out by the entire CTSO chapter and will take several months to complete. This project will probably span the school year. There will be two parts of the event, written and oral. The chapter will designate several members to represent the team at the competitive event. To prepare for a community service project, complete the following activities.

1. Read the guidelines provided by your organization.

2. Contact the association immediately at the end of the state conference to prepare for next year's event.

3. As a team, select a theme for your chapter's community service project.

4. Decide which roles are needed for the team. There may be one person who is the captain, one person who is the secretary, and any other roles that will be necessary to create the plan.

5. Identify your target audience, which may include business, school, and community groups.

6. Brainstorm with members of your chapter. List the benefits and opportunities of supporting a community service project.

14

COMMUNICATION NETWORKS

SECTIONS

14.1 NETWORK FUNDAMENTALS

14.2 NETWORK TOPOLOGIES

14.3 NETWORK SECURITY

Communication in terms of computers refers to the transmission of signals that are ultimately interpreted as data. Networks are the systems used to connect the devices that transmit the signals. These networks are a combination of hardware and software. Most people use a variety of networks without noticing. The Internet interconnects local area networks over cables. The land-based telephone network transmits voice and data across the Integrated Digital Services Network, and the cellular telephone networks operate on microwave networks. Connection to a network can be via wires and cables or wirelessly. Today, the distinction blurs among network technologies because in many cases a network uses a variety of the available technologies.

Along with the benefits of being connected, people are subject to hazards that can compromise transmission and data. In addition, criminals commit fraud and hack into networks to access data and disrupt service. Also to be considered are the equipment breakdowns and how to troubleshoot specific network failures.

IC3 CERTIFICATION OBJECTIVES

GS5

Computing Fundamentals

Domain 2.0 Hardware devices
Objective 2.4 Understand the use of Ethernet ports
Objective 2.5 Connect a device to a wireless network (Wi-Fi)
Objective 2.7 Understand driver concepts as well as their device compatibility
Objective 2.10 Know the difference between cellular, Wi-Fi, and wired networks
Objective 2.11 Understand concepts regarding connecting to the Internet

Domain 3.0 Computer software architecture
Objective 3.13 Troubleshooting

Domain 7.0 Security
Objective 7.4 Understand connecting to secured vs. unsecured network (wired and wireless)
Objective 7.6 Know the use of firewalls and basic settings
Objective 7.8 Understand what virtual private networks (VPNs) are

Living Online

Domain 1.0 Internet (navigation)
Objective 1.1 Understand what the Internet is

GS4

Living Online

Domain 2.0 Networking concepts
Objective 2.1 Internet connection
Objective 2.2 Network types and features, capabilities
Objective 2.3 Network troubleshooting

College and Career Readiness

Reading Prep. Before reading this chapter, read the opening pages and section titles for this chapter. These can help prepare you for the topics that will be presented. What does this tell you about what you will be learning?

Although there are many types of networks, there are basic understandings common to all of them. The discussion of analog versus digital representations of the data is key to determining the transmission of the data. The hardware to connect devices in a network is specific to each type of network. The methods of connecting the user to the network services depend on the network architecture and topology.

Between each two communication devices is a channel. The channel capacity determines how much data can be transmitted and how quickly. Channel capacity is also referred to as bandwidth and is measured in bits transferred per second (bps). The transmission media used also affects the channel capacity. This section explores the basics of network structure and devices.

Zurijeta/Shutterstock.com

TERMS

analog
bandwidth
Bluetooth
client
digital
Ethernet
host
hotspot
hub

network adapter
Open Systems Interconnection (OSI) model
ports
router
sampling
switch
transmission rate
Wi-Fi

LEARNING GOALS

After completing this section, you will be able to:

- Explain the difference between digital and analog signals.
- Discuss network connection technologies.

Digital Versus Analog

Analog is a continuous signal that can vary over an infinite range. **Digital** is a signal composed of discrete or segmented chunks of data. The human voice or an audio speaker generates a waveform of air disturbance. To transmit an analog signal, the actual waveform is reproduced. The signaler continuously varies the amplitude of the waveform to replicate the vibrations caused by the original data. To transmit the waveform as digital data, a series of measurements of the amplitude of the waveform is taken and each measurement is a discrete signal.

The process of taking measurements along the analog signal to convert it into a digital signal is called **sampling** and is illustrated in Figure 14-1.The *amplitude* is the height of a waveform at any given location. The digital data are not the stepped wave shown in the Figure 14-1, but a series of numbers that each is the value of the amplitude of the analog wave at a sampling location. As you can see, there is a certain loss of information from the original wave.

The difference in quality between analog and digital signals is minimized by increasing the number of samples. This is known as sampling at a higher frequency. For example, to sample live music for CD-quality audio, measurements are taken at a rate of 192 kHz. This means 192,000 samples are taken per second. Video contains much more information than music. If sampled at this rate, digital video files would be enormous. Generally digital video files are created at a sampling rate of 48 kHz. Then, the files are compressed to make them smaller so they will transmit more quickly, as discussed in Chapter 4.

Speed is a big factor in data transmission. A **transmission rate** is the number of bits per second that can be sent from one device to another. Current transmission speeds may reach trillions of bits per second, depending on the technology.

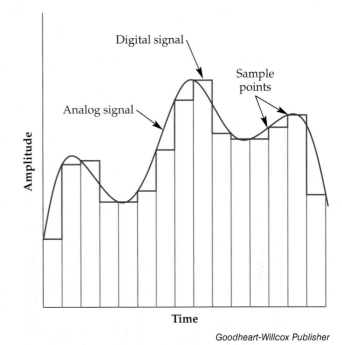

Digital signal

Sample points

Analog signal

Amplitude

Time

Figure 14-1. An analog signal must be sampled to turn it into a digital signal.

- Fiber optic cable supports a transmission rate of nearly the speed of light, 73.7 trillion bits per second (Tbit/s).
- Bluetooth has an optimal transmission rate of 24 million bits per second (Mbit/s).
- Coaxial cable has a maximum transmission rate of 10 billion bits per second (Gbit/s).
- Wi-Fi has a theoretical maximum transmission rate of 54 million bits per second (Mbit/s).

Clearly, the technologies are vastly different in supporting transmission speeds. **Bandwidth** is the rate of data transfer. The higher the bandwidth, the more bits are transmitted per second.

GS4 Living Online
2.1.1

FYI

Plain text is the easiest digital data to transmit because it is generally in smaller files and already is mapped to Unicode digital data.

GS5 Living Online
1.1.1.4

Fidelity is also a big factor in data transmissions. *Fidelity* is the degree to which a copy matches the original. Depending on the technology, data sustain a small amount of corruption and must be checked on arrival for fidelity, or compared to the original information sent. Data correction will, of course, take time to perform and reduce the theoretical transmission time.

GS5   Computing Fundamentals
2.4.1, 2.4.2, 2.5, 2.10, 2.11.4, 2.11.5

GS4   Living Online
2.1.2, 2.1.3

Network Connection Technologies

The transmission of information on the Internet is accomplished by either wired or wireless technologies, as shown in Figure 14-2. **Ethernet** is a data transmission technology that creates a wired connection between modems or routers and computers. This is referred to as being "wired." An Ethernet cable has a specific connector that plugs into the modem, router, or computer. Because of this physical connection to the network, wired devices are immobile. Once physically removed from the cable, these devices no longer have access to the network.

A newer and more flexible technology is wireless, or Wi-Fi. In **Wi-Fi**, a wireless router is placed between the modem and the computer and transmissions are sent though the air to the computers with a Wi-Fi receiver. This provides the ability to easily move computers from room to room without worrying about the Ethernet cable. However, this flexibility comes at a cost. Ethernet transmissions are faster and more secure than wireless transmissions.

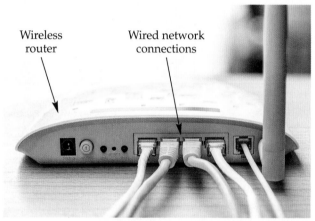

Wireless router

Wired network connections

Goodheart-Willcox Publisher; fotoslaz/Shutterstock.com

Figure 14-2. An Internet connection may be wired or wireless. Shown here is a wireless router, which is itself connected to a network by wired connections.

Networking Hardware

A network is composed of a variety of computers and peripheral devices that support input and output, save and serve data, and manage communication protocols. Devices include the host, client, cable, router, network adapter, hub, switch, and network printer or scanner.

Host

On the network, the **host** is one computer dedicated to managing the communication tasks, as shown in Figure 14-3. In the case of the local area network, the host is the hub of the network. In the case of the Internet, it may also be a network that connects to the Internet. In this case, the host is often referred to as the server, and it may do double-duty as a file server.

Client

A computer connected to and served by the host is called the **client**. There are many clients on

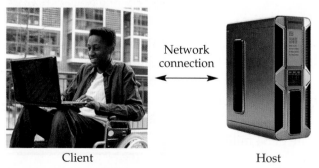

Client

Network connection

Host

Goodheart-Willcox Publisher; Michaelpuche, Sashkin/Shutterstock.com

Figure 14-3. The host manages the communication tasks, while the client is any computer connected to and served by the host.

a network. The communication between the host and the client is called the *client-server relationship.*

Cable

A cable is used to connect network devices. A network may have many cables connecting the many devices on the network. There are several types of cables used in networking.

Ethernet cable is composed of coaxial cable, twisted pair, or optical fiber, as shown in Figure 14-4. *Coaxial cable* has an inner conductor (wire) surrounded by a layer of insulation, a layer of conducting mesh shield, and an outside layer of insulation. *Twisted pair cable* contains several pairs of wires, each of which are twisted together to help cancel electromagnetic interference and represent one circuit. *Optical fiber cable* contains multiple optical fibers each of which transmit data via light. These three types of cables support a variety of transmission speeds, from 1 Mb/s to 100 Gb/s.

Since 2008, a standard has existed for high-speed communication over power lines, such as the ones providing your house with electricity. This communication scheme, known as *power-line communication (PLC),* is based on the simultaneous use of electric power transmission for data transfer and electrical supply. PLC can support home automation and broadband data communication.

Router

A **router** sends data packets between computer networks and is generally used for Internet applications. It is the job of the router to accept data packets and deliver them to the target computer on the network. A router is also used to connect multiple devices to a network.

It is important to acquire a router that can support the number of Internet-ready devices in your home or office. Transmission speeds are dependent on the bandwidth of the router and the connection to the router.

When considering a wireless router, check the router's wireless standard. There are two notable wireless standards: G and N. The N standard is the latest. Devices supporting this standard can generate speed up to 600 Mbits/sec. The AC standard is the newest standard and has been approved.

GS5 Computing Fundamentals
2.11.4

FYI

The massive amount of cabling creating core data routes on the Internet is called the *backbone*. There are many backbones in the Internet, and they are capable of very-high-speed transmissions.

GS5 Computing Fundamentals
2.11.3

FYI

The router is the descendant of the Internet Message Processor (IMP) of the ARPANET.

Coaxial Cable

Optical Fiber Cable

Twisted Pair Cable

Figure 14-4. Ethernet cable may be coaxial cable, twisted pair cable, or optical fiber cable.

Hub

A **hub** is a common connection point for devices in a network. A hub contains multiple points of connection to the network. When data arrive at the hub, they are available to all connection points.

Switch

A **switch** is a network transmission device that checks and forwards packets between parts of the network. When data arrive at the switch, the switch can determine which connection point should receive the data.

Network Adapter

For a network to function, there must be a way to transmit the data between the computers. A **network adapter** provides the interface between the computer and the network. It is either an internal card or a USB plug-in adapter.

Some computers are connected via Ethernet adapters or network-interface cards using network cabling. These connections have the highest bandwidth. Other computers are connected using a wireless adapter. Speeds of wireless connections are lower than wired connections.

Network Printer and Scanner

Printers and scanners are often connected to a network. In order to be connected to the network, the device must contain a network adapter. Network-ready printers and scanners are either connected to a specific computer with a cable and shared across the network or are wirelessly connected to the router.

A network administrator may password-protect a networked printer or scanner to limit the number of users. This is usually done to avoid congestion at the device.

Most wireless printers or scanners will automatically detect and connect to the network. However, in some cases, you may need to manually connect to the wireless network using the "add printer" feature of the OS. In Windows, use the **Add a printer** feature located in the Control Panel. You may be given the option to choose between a local printer and a network, wireless, or Bluetooth printer. Choose to add a network, wireless, or Bluetooth printer. The OS will search for all available printers. Select the correct wireless printer from the returned list. Then, follow the prompts to complete the connection. This includes installing the correct printer driver for the printer.

Network Architecture

Suppose a programmer had to consider all facets of computing to write a single application. In the one program would be all of the communication software plus all of the operating system software. There are many functions that need to be carried out to ensure a high-fidelity,

FYI

A "consumer router" unit may contain the router device, hubs, and switches.

error-free transmission of data. It would be a nightmare to support all operating systems and networks.

As with the operating system, much of the communication software is the same for most applications. It is not necessary to write it new each time an application is developed. So, the static or common elements of communication are abstracted and handled by the communication software of the operating system.

OSI Model

There is always a need for standardization in computing so that systems can be interoperable. This is the case for moving bits of data within and between networks. To accomplish this, software and hardware work together according to established protocols or rules for communicating between computers. The **Open Systems Interconnection (OSI) model** separates the functions of networking into layers that keep the same functions together for all networks. It is a product of the International Organization for Standardization (ISO).

The idea behind the OSI model is simplifying the communication software and hardware by separating the functions into smaller sections. This keeps each application programmer from having to worry about such things as whether the connection is live or what type of protocol is being used to transmit the data. All of the common features are separated into their own layer and into smaller, manageable software and hardware units.

OSI Layers

The concept of layers in the OSI model is illustrated in Figure 14-5. The easiest way to understand the layers concept is to think about questions that would be answered by a given layer. Descriptions of the seven layers help to illustrate the genius of the OSI model.

Layer 1: Physical Layer. The physical layer manages all of the hardware concerns. Is there a connection between these two computers? What is

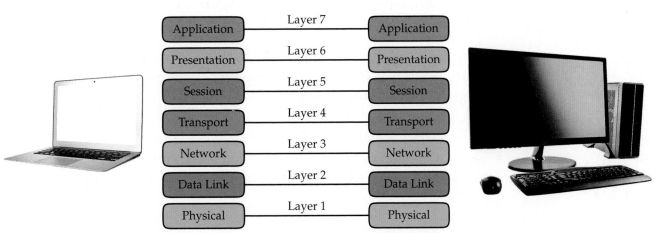

Figure 14-5. The Open Systems Interconnection model separates the network functions into layers.

the electrical connection? Is the connection Bluetooth or Ethernet? Is it wireless? Is there a network adapter?

Layer 2: Data Link Layer. The data link layer maintains the link between two connected nodes. Did an error occur in the physical layer? Are the data flowing correctly?

Layer 3: Network Layer. The network layer manages the transfer of datagrams among all of the nodes on a specific network. *Datagrams* are variable-length data sequences. How does a message get to the correct node of the network? Should this message be broken into packets for the transport layer?

Layer 4: Transport Layer. The transport layer provides reliability. Its job is to move the packets set up by the network layer between nodes on the network. Did all of the packets arrive at the destination node? Did the entire message arrive intact? Should a specific datagram be resent?

Layer 5: Session Layer. The session layer controls the connections between computers. Is there still a connection between two computers? Did the transport layer request another copy of a packet? Did it arrive error-free? Should the connection be terminated?

Layer 6: Presentation Layer. The presentation layer prepares data for the application layer. Is the arriving data packet encrypted? If it is, this layer takes care of decoding the packet. Are the data in the format that the application is expecting? Should the data being sent from the application be encrypted?

Layer 7: Application Layer. The application layer provides the interface to the user. It synchronizes network communication for applications that require it. Is there a communication need from this application? Are there resources available to support data communication? Is the communication open?

Server Operating System

The server runs a specialized operating system that includes communication software. The server operating system is what makes a computer a server. The server operating system allows files to be transferred from a computer on the network, to the server, and out to other computers on the network. The server operating system also maintains files available to all computers on the network. Password protection to limit access to files can be provided by server software.

Connection Technologies

Connections to the Internet rely on ports. **Ports** are application- or process-specific software communication endpoints in a computer's

Career Skills

Computer Systems Design
Computer systems designers evaluate an agency's current computer networks, processes, and efficiency. Based on their findings, they suggest improvements in connectivity and support for the information systems. They work with the state-of-the-art of computing and balance the capability and needs of the organization to help people work more proficiently and effectively. This career offers challenges and the ability to propose new solutions as the needs of the organizations and the power of computing change.

GS5 Computing Fundamentals 2.10

operating system. The purpose of a port is to uniquely identify different applications or processes running on a single computer. This enables sharing of a single physical connection to a packet-switched network, such as the Internet. Ports are associated with an IP address of the host as well as with the type of protocol used for communication. There are about 250 well-known ports that are reserved by convention to identify specific types of services on a host.

Every connection to the Internet "listens" on a particular port. For example, the World Wide Web service listens on port 80. A computer connects to the ISP's mail server through port 25 (the SMTP port). Depending on preferences set by the network administrator, individual ports may be opened (unblocked) or closed (blocked). These port settings affect WAN and LAN connections.

Bluetooth Technology

Bluetooth is a radio wave–based wireless connection technology that provides communication between devices within a short range of each other, generally up to about 30 feet. Its notable feature is that it carries both voice and data at the same time. The technology is named after 10th century Danish King Harald Bluetooth. He united tribes into a single group that developed into the present day countries of Norway, Sweden, and Denmark. Using the name Bluetooth for the technology hints that the technology also unites, pairing devices to work together in near proximity.

Computing Fundamentals
2.7.2

Typically it is used to connect a hands-free device to a cell phone. Many automobiles are Bluetooth enabled for this purpose. Other Bluetooth-enabled devices include PC peripherals, headphones, ear pieces, and gaming handsets. Look for the Bluetooth logo on devices indicating they are Bluetooth enabled.

To use the technology, two Bluetooth-enabled devices must be *paired*. To pair a cell phone with the car's audio system, refer to the vehicle's manual to find the steps that must be taken. Usually, this involves setting the Bluetooth "on" feature on the cell phone and then allowing the vehicle's computer to detect the device. Once paired, a user can use the cell phone hands-free while driving.

Hotspots

Any LAN that is accessible to connection by roaming users, such as airport travelers, is called a **hotspot**. Often, restaurants or other businesses offer free connection to their Internet network to bring in customers. A hotspot consists of a LAN for everyone and a virtual private network (VPN) for each user. Public hotspots are unsecured. Keep this in mind when using one.

Computing Fundamentals
7.4.3

HANDS-ON EXAMPLE 14.1.1

CONNECTING TO A NETWORK

To use a network, it is not enough just to have a network adapter installed. The computer must be connected to the network.

1. In Windows 10, click the **Start** button, and click **Settings** in the menu. Note: in Windows 8 and Windows 7, the Control Panel is used to connect to a network.
2. In the **Settings** window that is displayed, click **Network & Internet**.
3. In the **Network & Internet** window that is displayed, click the type of network you are trying to connect to, as shown.

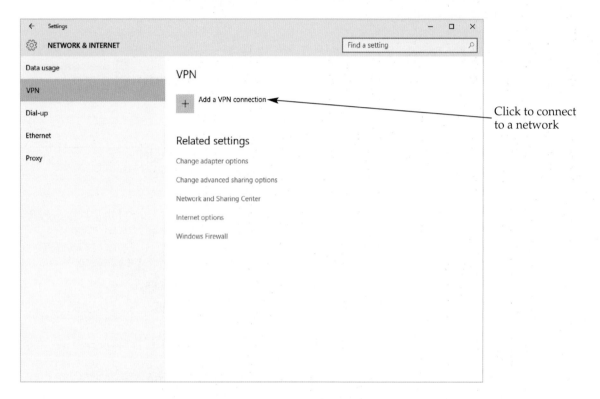

Click to connect to a network

4. Select the option to add a network connection.
5. Follow the prompts and provide the information requested to connect to the network.

14.1 SECTION REVIEW

CHECK YOUR UNDERSTANDING

1. What is the difference between transmission rate and bandwidth?
2. Which technology is capable of the highest transmission rate?
3. What are the two computers that communicate with each other on a network?
4. Which OSI layer contains the hardware?
5. What makes a computer a server?

IC3 CERTIFICATION PRACTICE

The following question is a sample of the types of questions presented on the IC3 exam.

1. Interactive question.

   Drag the labels to arrange the OSI layers with layer 1 at the bottom to layer 7 at the top.

	Transport
	Data link
	Physical
	Application
	Presentation
	Session
	Network

BUILD YOUR VOCABULARY

As you progress through this course, develop a personal IT glossary. This will help you build your vocabulary and prepare you for a career. Write a definition for each of the following terms and add it to your IT glossary.

analog
bandwidth
Bluetooth
client
digital
Ethernet
host
hotspot
hub
network adapter

Open Systems
   Interconnection (OSI)
   model
ports
router
sampling
switch
transmission rate
Wi-Fi

NETWORK TOPOLOGIES

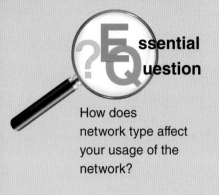

Essential Question

How does network type affect your usage of the network?

Networks are arranged in a variety of ways to create the best platform for data communication. There are several types of network, such as LAN, WAN, and VPN. The decisions for network design rely heavily on the purpose for the network, the number of people who will use it, and how far the computers are separated.

There are several choices for the arrangement, or topology, of the components in a network. The arrangement of components in a network is considered on a physical level as well as a logical level. This section discusses the types of networks and the topology of components in a network.

leo_photo/Shutterstock.com

TERMS

bus topology
daisy chain topology
extranet
Internet area network (IAN)
intranet
local area network (LAN)
mesh topology
metropolitan area network (MAN)

network topology
peer-to-peer (P2P) topology
point-to-point topology
ring topology
star topology
tree topology
virtual private network (VPN)
wide area network (WAN)

LEARNING GOALS

After completing this section, you will be able to:

- Identify network types.
- Describe network topologies.

Network Types

The Internet is a network of networks. It spans the globe. Smaller-scale networks of networks are used in smaller geographical areas. An **intranet** is a locally confined network of networks, usually within a single business or school. Intranets are closed networks available only to the specific set of users within the defined area. The open Internet allows access by all. This is generally read-only access without the ability to change things. The ability to make changes is called read-write access. When remote devices or networks are connected, the term **extranet** is used to describe the network of networks.

Labels are assigned to groups of networked devices depending on the span, location, and number of nodes in a network. Common types of networks include LAN, MAN, WAN, IAN, VPN, and ATM.

GS5 Living Online
1.1.1.1

GS4 Living Online
2.2.4

FYI

Several other lesser-used network types are self-explanatory by their names, including home area network (HAN) and near-me area network (NAN).

LAN

A **local area network (LAN)** consists of a group of computers and their devices that are locally assembled in a limited area, as shown in Figure 14-6. Generally a school's computer lab is an example of a LAN. These devices share peripheral devices such as a file server, printers, and scanners. A network within a home is also an example of a LAN.

MAN

A **metropolitan area network (MAN)** consists of a group of computers that are not in the same room or building, but in the same city or small geographical area. An example of a MAN might be the student services network for a university. Another example of a MAN is providing the Internet connection for a group of LANs.

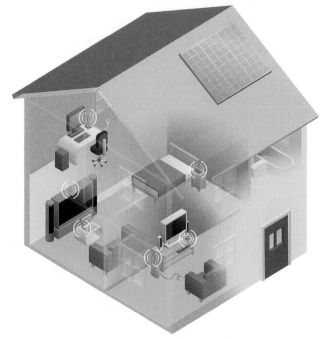

WAN

A **wide area network (WAN)** consists of a group of computers within a large geographical area. The area covered by a WAN is larger than that covered by a MAN. Businesses with offices across the country may use a WAN. The Internet is an example of a WAN. WANs are used to connect LANs and other types of networks.

Christos Georghiou/Shutterstock.com

Figure 14-6. The network within your home is a local area network (LAN).

IAN

An **Internet area network (IAN)** builds on the concept of the computing cloud to connect computers. Data are transmitted using the Internet protocol. Instead of using a LAN or WAN, computers using the IAN concept connect directly to the Internet through an Internet service provider (ISP).

GS5 Computing Fundamentals
7.8

GS4 Living Online
2.2.5

Green Tech

Computer Technology
Advances in computer technology have improved hardware capabilities and performance. Often, terminals can be set up at several workstations and connected to a single server where the applications actually run. Sharing the computing power of a single server reduces the need for multiple computers, which reduces the amount of power used by a business.

VPN

A **virtual private network (VPN)** uses the Internet as an extension of a LAN or other smaller network. As the name implies, a VPN is private. Connections to the VPN devices are hidden from casual Internet users. A VPN allows external access to a private network from a remote location. For example, a traveling sales representative may use a VPN to connect to the LAN in the home office.

ATM

Automated teller machines (ATMs) are telecommunication devices that allow certain financial transactions to be completed. These devices are connected on interbank networks, not the Internet. Classically, interbank networks are direct connections of the host to the ATM via telephone lines.

Network Topologies

Network topology is the arrangement of the components of the network. There are two general categories of network topologies: physical and logical. *Physical topology* describes the shape of the connections to the computers and devices. *Logical topology* refers to the way the signals are transmitted and tracked around the network. Several network topologies are shown in Figure 14-7.

A good question to ask is, why are there so many different network topologies? The answer is quite simple. No one topology has all of the advantages of all topologies. Each topology also has its own disadvantages.

Topologies can be mixed. A physical connection scheme can support other logical schemes. For example, Ethernet can be installed as a physical bus, but can logically act like a ring.

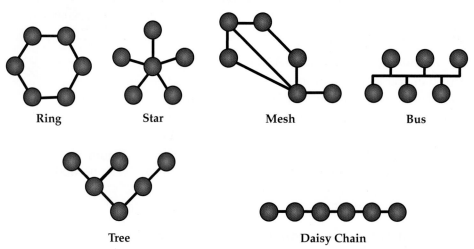

Ring   Star   Mesh   Bus

Tree   Daisy Chain

Goodheart-Willcox Publisher

Figure 14-7. There are several network topologies. These may be physical or logical.

Ring Topology

In a **ring topology**, computers and devices are connected one to another so that a circle can be drawn. A message travels around the ring until it arrives at its destination. A disadvantage of this topology is that if one computer on the network goes down, the entire network goes down.

In a *token ring topology,* a token is circulated among the computers. Only the computer holding the token can transmit to the network. This is a logical ring topology. Physically, the network has a star topology.

Star Topology

In a **star topology**, the main node is in the center. All other nodes, or computers, are connected to the main node. Messages are sent directly from the main node to the destination mode without passing through other computers. This overcomes the disadvantage of a ring topology because any computer on the network other than the main node can go down and the network will still function. The star topology is common.

Mesh Topology

In a **mesh topology**, each node in the network carries a signal to all other nodes until the message is received at its destination. A mesh may be a fully or partially connected. A fully connected mesh topology is one in which each node is connected to every other node. A partially connected mesh topology is one in which each node is connected to multiple other nodes, but not necessarily all other nodes.

Bus Topology

In a **bus topology**, each node on the network is connected to a single main transmission cable. The signal travels the main transmission cable to the end of the line looking for the address of the device for the message being carried. The bus topology requires less cable than a star topology, but if there is a problem with the single transmission cable, the network goes down.

Tree Topology

A **tree topology** connects smaller star topology networks via a bus topology. It creates a hierarchy of nodes. A tree topology is used when some nodes must have a higher priority than others. If the bus breaks down, the individual star topology networks will continue to function within themselves, but will not be able to communicate with each other.

Daisy Chain Topology

In a **daisy chain topology**, devices are added to the network at the end of the line, like the links in a chain. A message is passed through each device or computer on the chain until the destination address is reached. In this way, it acts like a bus. If the last node in the line is connected to the first node, a ring topology is formed.

Ethics

Online Merchandise
When merchandising online, IT companies should display all the information the customer needs. Details such as content, compatibility, and shipping dates should all be easily accessible and visible. Withholding any information will leave the customer uninformed and untrusting of your company. This may be considered unethical if the customer has not been properly informed.

Point-to-Point Topology

A **point-to-point topology** consists of a permanent connection between two nodes. Point-to-point topology is the basis of landline telephone connections. An example of a point-to-point topology is a dedicated service line.

Peer-to-Peer Topology

In a **peer-to-peer (P2P) topology**, all devices act like both servers and clients. Files can be shared among all of the devices without going through a main host. Resources are shared among all devices. Any given device must contribute part of its resources to the functioning of the network.

HANDS-ON EXAMPLE 14.2.1

EXAMINING NETWORK TOPOLOGY

There are many topologies that may be used in the design of a network. Each topology has advantages and disadvantages.

1. Launch a browser.
2. Navigate to the Wikipedia page en.wikipedia.org/wiki/Network_topology.
3. Visit each of the topology subtopics, and note one advantage and one disadvantage of each.
4. Using a word processor, create a chart similar to the one shown to record your findings.

Topology	Advantage	Disadvantage
Ring		
Mesh		
Star		
Bus		
Tree		
Daisy chain		
Point-to-point		

14.2 | SECTION REVIEW

 CHECK YOUR UNDERSTANDING

1. What is a WAN?
2. What is a VPN?
3. How does an ATM connect to the host?
4. In terms of network topologies, how is Ethernet employed as physical and logical topologies?
5. Which of the network topologies are basically bus topologies?

IC3 CERTIFICATION PRACTICE

The following question is a sample of the types of questions presented on the IC3 exam.

1. Which of the following is an example of a WAN?
   A. The Internet.
   B. An intranet.
   C. A physical ring.
   D. A campus network.

 BUILD YOUR VOCABULARY

As you progress through this course, develop a personal IT glossary. This will help you build your vocabulary and prepare you for a career. Write a definition for each of the following terms and add it to your IT glossary.

bus topology	network topology
daisy chain topology	peer-to-peer (P2P)
extranet	topology
Internet area network	point-to-point topology
(IAN)	ring topology
intranet	star topology
local area network (LAN)	tree topology
mesh topology	virtual private network
metropolitan area	(VPN)
network (MAN)	wide area network (WAN)

NETWORK SECURITY

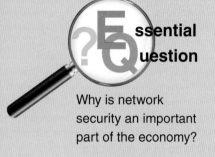

Essential Question

Why is network security an important part of the economy?

Much is written in the media about cybercriminals breaking into computer networks. Once in, they cause havoc with the transmissions and data. Care must be taken to protect the information that flows freely within a computer network from those unauthorized persons. There are particular safety topics that relate to specific network needs. There are safeguards at the key OSI layers of network, transport, and session because these three layers deal with moving the data from node to node.

In addition to security, there are issues with networks related to upkeep. Troubleshooting a network is important if the network experiences problems. This section explores methods to improve safe network use and to troubleshoot problems when they occur.

PathDoc/Shutterstock.com

LEARNING GOALS

After completing this section, you will be able to:
• Describe basic network security.
• Identify wireless network security types.
• Discuss vulnerabilities of a network.
• List network troubleshooting steps.

TERMS

authentication
encryption
firewall
password
Wi-Fi Protected Access (WPA)
Wired Equivalent Privacy (WEP)

Basic Network Security

Computers and devices are interconnected. This presents the opportunity for unauthorized users to get into the network to steal data or cause problems. A secured network requires a username and password to connect to it. Unsecured networks, such as those offered by retail shops and at transportation hubs, permit anyone who accepts the user agreement to join. Wired networks tend to be more secure than wireless networks. Using a free Wi-Fi connection in a public place where data is transmitted through the air makes all of your data vulnerable to anyone who wants to capture it. There are a few methods for preventing this activity, including password protection, firewalls, levels of access, and encryption.

Password Protection

A **password** is a code that must be entered to allow access to something. The most basic way to protect a network is to require a user name and password to unlock any computer or device on the network. However, limiting access to a network in this manner is only as secure as the complexity of the passwords.

Most people are careless and use easily guessed passwords: names of family members, pets, birthdates, and other easily obtainable information. There are guidelines for creating good passwords. At minimum, the best passwords:

- contain eight or more characters;
- use both uppercase and lowercase letters;
- contain letters, numbers, and special characters;
- are different for each account a user has;
- are not shared with others;
- are not written down in plain view of the computer;
- do not contain personal references; and
- are not English words.

However, even good passwords are not foolproof security. Hackers may develop a program to automatically generate and enter all possible passwords. A good password-protection program restricts the number of times a user can attempt to log in. This helps reduce the chance that an automatic password generator will be able to crack into the system.

Firewall

A **firewall** is a technology that creates a barrier between computers, as shown in Figure 14-8. It uses a set of defined rules to resist unwanted or unauthorized messages from passing over network channels. This security measure helps preserve network integrity.

The term firewall is borrowed from the notion of building a barrier to prevent fire from spreading from one compartment of a structure to another. The analogy is close, but not precise. In computing, a firewall

GS5 Computing Fundamentals 2.5

FYI

Key-holder programs make it easy for a person to keep all of the various passwords secure and accessible only to him or her.

GS5 Computing Fundamentals 7.6

GS4 Living Online 2.1.4

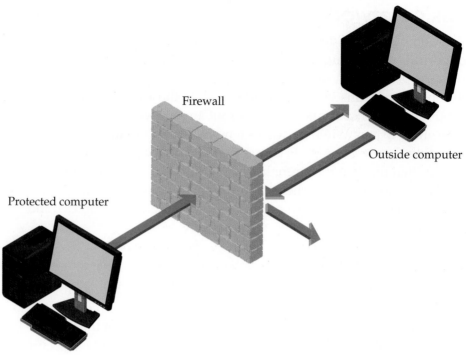

Firewall

Outside computer

Protected computer

Figure 14-8. A firewall allows or denies messages based on a set of rules.

regulates network traffic by permitting allowed messages to pass freely, but blocking unauthorized messages.

Authentication

Part of network administration is the definition and regulation of each user's access to the network. To protect the most secure parts of the network, only users who need the information to perform their work should be granted access. **Authentication** refers to providing varying levels of access to information. Some users have full read-write access, allowing them to open, create, save, and delete files. Other users will be given read-only access, which allows them only to open files. Yet other users may be denied any type of access to certain files or folders. More general information on this topic is discussed in Chapter 16.

Encryption

An easy way for the user to protect data is to encrypt all files. **Encryption** is a software process that encodes the file to make it unreadable unless the correct key is entered, as shown in Figure 14-9. An *encryption key* is like a password. The key is required to decrypt, or decode, the file. After decryption, the original file is restored intact.

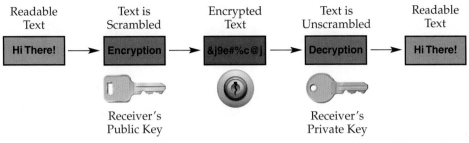

Readable Text — Text is Scrambled — Encrypted Text — Text is Unscrambled — Readable Text

Hi There! → Encryption → &j9e#%c@j → Decryption → Hi There!

Receiver's Public Key   Receiver's Private Key

Figure 14-9. Encryption makes a file unreadable to any computer that does not have the proper key.

Wireless Network Security Types

Wireless transmission is accomplished by the use of radio waves. Any capable device can receive these signals. This makes it possible for data to be stolen during wireless transmission. Therefore, wireless networks are naturally unsecure. However, in an attempt to make wireless networking more secure, protocols have been established related to encrypting data sent via radio waves. In 1999, the Institute of Electrical and Electronic Engineers (IEEE) introduced a standard named 802.11 to describe wireless networks. Included in this standard was WEP.

WEP

Wired Equivalent Privacy (WEP) is a security algorithm for wireless networks designed to protect data. Unfortunately, it is deeply flawed. It does not live up to the goal of matching the security of wired networks. The major flaw is the inability of the algorithm to keep the encryption keys protected.

WPA and WPA2

WEP has been replaced in most wireless networks by the **Wi-Fi Protected Access (WPA)** algorithm. A group known as the Wi-Fi Alliance developed this and its successor, WPA2, in an attempt to make wireless networks more secure. Unfortunately, there are weaknesses in these algorithms as well and security can be bypassed.

Unsecured

The WEP, WPA, and WPA2 algorithms provide some network security, despite their flaws. When none these algorithms is implemented, there is no encryption-based security at all. The network is said to be *unsecured*. Network security is limited to the proper use of passwords.

GS5 Computing Fundamentals
2.5

GS4 Living Online
2.1.3

FYI

Some wireless networks, primarily free Wi-Fi hotspots, continue to use the WEP algorithm.

HANDS-ON EXAMPLE 14.3.1

GS5 Computing Fundamentals 2.5

DETERMINING WIRELESS NETWORK SECURITY

Whenever a user connects wirelessly to a network, a profile for that connection is saved by the operating system. In Windows, the Control Panel can be used to check the security level of a wireless network.

Windows 10

1. Click the **Start** button, and click **Settings** in the menu.
2. In the **Settings** window, click **Network & Internet**.
3. In the **Network & Internet** window, click **Wi-Fi** on the left. A list of wireless connections is displayed. Note: if the computer is not Wi-Fi enabled, this option does not appear.
4. Click **Advanced Options** at the bottom of the window on the right. The details are listed in the **Properties** area of the new page, including the security type.

Windows 8

1. In Windows 8, swipe to view the charms bar.
2. Click the **Settings** icon.
3. Click **Change PC Settings**.
4. Click **Network**.
5. Click **Connections**.
6. If there are networks listed, click one of the network names.
7. Look for the entry **Security type**. Identify if the network is unsecured, uses WEP, uses WPA, or uses WPA2.
8. Repeat for each network listed.

Windows 7

1. In Windows 7, click the **Start** button on the taskbar.
2. Click **Control Panel** in the **Windows System** area or on the right-hand side of the menu. The Control Panel window is displayed.
3. Click the **View by:** drop-down arrow at the upper-right of the window, and click **Category** in the drop-down list.
4. Click **Network and Internet**.
5. Click **Network and Sharing Center**.
6. Click **Manage wireless networks** on the left.
7. Click **Networks you can view, modify, and reorder**. If the computer has never connected to a wireless network, this list is blank.
8. If there are networks listed, identify if each is unsecured, uses WEP, uses WPA, or uses WPA2.

Vulnerability of a Network

While security is important to most people, some people make mistakes in judgment. Sharing passwords compromises the security of the computer or network. Allowing someone with a lower access level than you to use your computer can allow problems to occur. Opening an e-mail attachment without fully understanding what the attachment is supposed to do can spread a virus or malware. In fact, opening an unknown e-mail attachment is a common way viruses and related problems enter a local computer. Figure 14-10 illustrates ten common vulnerabilities to a computer or network.

GS5   Computing Fundamentals
7.4.1, 7.4.2

The best way to keep a network secure is to implement all of the available safety precautions. For example, disabling the autorun feature can help prevent malware from running when media, such as a flash drive, is inserted into the computer. Proper training of users should include making them sensitive to threats. Give users the tools to recognize and thwart the threats. More detailed examples of how to do this are included in Chapter 16.

USB flash drive	If the computer automatically runs the flash drive on insertion, malicious code such as worms and viruses can be executed.
Laptop computer	Attaching a laptop to a network allows a new connection that can spread malicious code from the laptop to the network.
Wireless access points	Wireless access points provide easy access for intruders. Whether or not encryption is used, these access points are inherently less secure or unsecure.
USB connections	Any connection such as digital cameras, scanners, and printers can spread malicious code.
Access borrowing	A user accessing the computer of another user with a higher access level, either with or without permission, can see restricted data and parts of the network. Even well-meaning employees wanting to help out a colleague can potentially open the network to harm by doing this.
Outside service personnel	A person posing as legitimate service personnel, even unrelated to IT, may be allowed access to network hardware and software, which opens a threat of introducing malicious code or stealing data.
Optical media	Allowing users to bring in their own optical media provides a way to steal information or introduce malware to the system.
Password entry	Allowing others to watch the keystrokes of password entry compromises the password. A password obtained in this manner can be used to access the computer or network for malicious reasons.
Smartphones and other digital devices	These devices pose the same threats as laptops and flash drives.
E-mail	E-mail is not secure. Confidential information can be easily forwarded. Data thieves often send an official-looking e-mail requesting sensitive information, such as passwords or account information, in phishing scams.

Goodheart-Willcox Publisher

Figure 14-10. These are several common vulnerabilities to a computer or network along with brief explanations.

HANDS-ON EXAMPLE 14.3.2

DISABLING AUTORUN

Disabling the autorun feature will improve the network security. Even though this may make it less convenient to use USB devices, it is an important security measure.

1. In Windows 10, right-click on the **Start** button. In Windows 8, click the **Apps** button. In Windows 7, click the **Start** button on the taskbar.
2. Click **Control Panel** in the menu. The Control Panel window is displayed.
3. Click the **View by:** drop-down arrow at the upper-right of the window, and click **Small icons** in the drop-down list.
4. Click **AutoPlay**. Autorun and autoplay are controlled by the same policy in Windows, as shown.

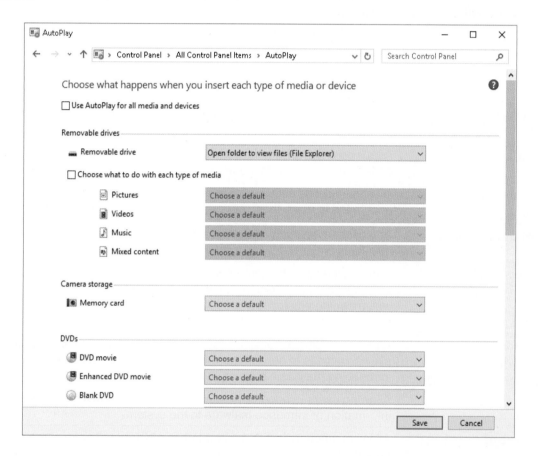

5. Uncheck the **Use AutoPlay for all media and devices** check box. The autorun and autoplay features are disabled.

TITANS OF TECHNOLOGY

Sandra Lerner teamed with Leonard Bosack to invent the router. While working as computer support personnel at Stanford University, Lerner and Bosack used university resources to wire the disconnected networks using their router. This involved physically going through underground tunnels to lay the cable. Their networking hardware and software became so successful that they left Stanford in 1984 to form Cisco Systems, which has grown into a multinational computer networking company. Stanford claimed ownership for the router and its software because it was developed there and subsequently licensed it to Cisco Systems. In 2000, Lerner was dismissed from Cisco Systems, reportedly over disputes concerning the direction of the company. Bosack resigned in protest. Together, they had made $170 million dollars with Cisco Systems. Lerner and Bosack took that money and put 70% of it into a foundation, and Lerner went on to found a line of animal-friendly cosmetics.

Network Troubleshooting

It is not unusual to read an error message that says:

Unable to connect to the network. Please try later.

In the case of a remote network, there may be nothing that can be done to solve the problem. If the problem is local, there are some quick steps to troubleshoot the disruption. Basic troubleshooting is discussed in Chapter 5. However, there are particular problems specific to network setup, transmission, and security that require special treatment.

The best way to solve a problem is to determine the exact nature of the mishap and then search for solutions. Some reoccurring problems have ready solutions. Microsoft has identified several common issues:

- a wireless network adapter switch that is not enabled
- WEP, WPA, or WPA2 security key or passphrase issues
- cables that are not properly connected
- corrupted or incompatible drivers
- missing updates
- incorrect network connection setting
- hardware or software problems

Microsoft provides a tutorial to assist in determining and repairing network problems.

GS4 Living Online
2.3.1, 2.3.2

 STEM

Science
Ohm's Law is a scientific law that states that the current moving through an electrical conductor between two points is directly proportional to the voltage across those same two points. A computer cable can be tested for the voltage drop from end to end and its resistance, and Ohm's law can be used to calculate the current running through the cable.

GS5
Computing Fundamentals
3.13.5

Often users express concern that the response time in a browser is too slow. This generally refers to the connection speed. While ISPs advertise high-speed connections for the network, the individual user may not experience those rates of transmission. Several factors affect connection speed.

- amount of RAM on the local computer
- amount of other traffic on the network
- whether the activity is upload or download
- clock speed of the local computer

There are many third-party tools that will determine the actual connection speed. Conduct an Internet search using the string how to determine connection speed to see some of the ways to find your actual connection speed.

Often the simplest repair for network issues is to disconnect the modem or router, wait a few minutes, and then reconnect it. When that does not fix the problem, a more sophisticated approach is required. Generally a step-by-step process is followed. The Microsoft Windows help feature provides an interactive troubleshooter. This may help, but often does not zero-in on the specific problem at hand.

HANDS-ON EXAMPLE 14.3.3

NETWORK TROUBLESHOOTING

Taking a Microsoft tutorial on general network troubleshooting is useful. It will be tailored to specific issues for the network at hand.

1. Launch a browser, and navigate to a search engine.
2. Enter the search string Wired and wireless network problems.
3. Click the link in the list of results that is on a windows.microsoft.com page. This link will likely be the first one listed.
4. Once the Microsoft web page is displayed, use the menu to select the version of Windows you are running. The site will likely automatically detect the version of Windows.
5. Read the introduction to the tutorial. This covers the troubleshooting interaction, explaining each step involved.
6. Use the menu to step through the tutorial.

14.3 SECTION REVIEW

CHECK YOUR UNDERSTANDING

1. How does a firewall provide network security?
2. How does encryption provide network security?
3. Which type of network is naturally unsecure?
4. What step can be taken to help protect against malware running on inserted media?
5. Where is the interactive troubleshooter located in Windows?

IC3 CERTIFICATION PRACTICE

The following question is a sample of the types of questions presented on the IC3 exam.

1. Complete this simulation.

   Perform the procedure for determining the security level of a wireless network.

BUILD YOUR VOCABULARY

As you progress through this course, develop a personal IT glossary. This will help you build your vocabulary and prepare you for a career. Write a definition for each of the following terms and add it to your IT glossary.

authentication
encryption
firewall
password
Wi-Fi Protected Access (WPA)
Wired Equivalent Privacy (WEP)

Chapter Summary

Section 14.1
Network Fundamentals

• Analog is a continuous signal that can vary over an infinite range, while digital is a signal composed of discrete chunks of data. An analog signal is sampled to create a digital signal.

• The transmission of information on the Internet is accomplished by either wired or wireless technologies. A network is composed of a variety of computers and peripheral devices that support input and output, save and serve data, and manage communication protocols.

Section 14.2
Network Topologies

• An intranet is a locally confined network of networks, while an extranet is connected remote devices or networks. Common types of networks include LAN, MAN, WAN, IAN, VPN, and ATM.

• Network topology is the arrangement of the components of the network, which may be physical or logical. There are several types of topology, including ring, star, mesh, bus, tree, daisy chain, point-to-point, and peer-to-peer.

Section 14.3
Network Security

• There are several ways to provide basic network security. These include password protection, firewalls, levels of access, and encryption.

• Since any capable device can receive wireless transmissions, the opportunity is present for data to be stolen. Protocols have been established related to encrypting wireless transmission, but there are flaws.

• There are common vulnerabilities to most computers or networks. The best way to keep a network secure is to implement all of the available safety precautions.

• The best way to solve a network problem is to determine the exact nature of the mishap and then search for solutions. The Microsoft Windows help feature provides an interactive troubleshooter that may help in the troubleshooting process.

Now that you have finished this chapter, see what you know about information technology by scanning the QR code to take the chapter posttest. If you do not have a smartphone, visit www.g-wlearning.com.

Chapter 14 Test

Multiple Choice

Select the best response.

1. Which of the following is the device that connects computers to a network?
   A. server
   B. router
   C. cloud
   D. scanner

2. What makes a computer a server?
   A. Internet connection
   B. network hardware
   C. server hardware
   D. server operating system

3. Which network topology connects each client to the host?
   A. star
   B. ring
   C. line
   D. bus

4. What is the name of the algorithm that provides absolute security for wireless networks?
   A. WEP
   B. WPA
   C. WPA2
   D. None of the above.

5. What is the best approach to troubleshoot a network problem?
   A. Reinstall the server software.
   B. Defragment the local hard drive.
   C. Determine the exact nature of the mishap and then search for solutions.
   D. Ignore the problem because it will probably fix itself.

Completion

Complete the following sentences with the correct word(s).

6. A(n) _____ provides the interface between the computer and the network.

7. The purpose of a(n) _____ is to uniquely identify different applications or processes running on a single computer.

8. The Internet is an example of a(n) _____ network.

9. In a(n) _____ topology, the main node is in the center.

10. The most basic way to protect a network is to require a(n) _____ and password to unlock any computer or device on the network.

Matching

Match the correct term with its definition.
   A. hub
   B. switch
   C. MAN
   D. mesh
   E. authentication

11. Each node in the network carries a signal to all other nodes until the message is received at its destination.

12. Network transmission device that checks and forwards packets between parts of the network.

13. Common connection point for devices in a network.

14. Providing varying levels of access to information.

15. Group of computers that are not in the same room or building, but in the same city.

Application and Extension of Knowledge

1. Some people find it difficult to memorize the seven layers of the OSI model. There are several mnemonic, or memory, devices that have been created to assist in the recall of the layer names. For example, All People Seem to Need Data Processing, where the first letter of each word stands for the layers. Create two original mnemonic devices that will help you recall the OSI layers in order. Create one for top-to-bottom order (layer 7 to layer 1) and one for bottom-to-top order (layer 1 to layer 7).

2. Interview a network administrator, such as the one at your school, to determine the topology of the computer network. Try to find out why that topology is used. Create a slide presentation that explains how the network is used and the topology. Present to the class.

3. Research symmetric key and public key data encryption methods. Determine the functions of these encryption methods and how each affects the message verification process. Write a one-page paper describing your findings.

4. Refer to the list of computer and network vulnerabilities given in Figure 14-10. Create a checklist that can be used to evaluate the threat level for a computer or network. Develop a rating system, such as 1 to 5, that will grade each threat. Use the checklist to rate the threat to a personal computer in your house and a computer in the school's computer lab. Present your findings to the class.

5. Using the Windows help feature or other information source, create a list of problems that network failures cause. Identify basic troubleshooting steps to take for each problem. Format your list in a document.

Online Activities

Complete the following activities, which will help you learn, practice, and expand your knowledge and skills.

Certification Practice. Complete the certification practice test for this chapter.

Vocabulary. Practice vocabulary for this chapter using the e-flash cards, matching activity, and vocabulary game until you are able to recognize their meanings.

Communication Skills

College and Career Readiness

Writing. Generate your own ideas relevant to using communication networks in an appropriate manner. Use multiple authoritative print and digital sources and document each. Write several paragraphs about your findings to demonstrate your understanding about the topic.

Reading. Review the vocabulary list at the beginning of this chapter. Sight words are those words that you recognize automatically. Identify the sight words with which you are familiar. For those words that are unfamiliar, write context clues that will help you decide the meaning of those words.

Listening. There are many competing companies that offer cellular service. Listen to the advertisements from at least three of these companies. How does each company try to convince you its service is better than others? Are there any differences in terms of technology, such as the cellular network? As you listen to each advertisement, make a list of key points.

Internet Research

Networking. Using various Internet resources, research the term network topology. Create a presentation that discusses the various topologies you encounter in your search, as well as the differences among them. Propose a real-world application of each topology, or provide an example of a real-world application. Share your presentation with the class.

Teamwork

Working with your team, continue the Teamwork website revision project started

in Chapter 13. Review the website analysis and the list of tasks necessary to update and revise the website. Make a list of the goals and objectives for the revised website. Choose the appropriate website products and services, and begin building web pages. Include a simple form to post on the site, such as a product survey, user poll, or other activity, that can be used to collect visitor information for market research. Create complex web pages that include frames, JavaScript applications, hyperlinks, and tables. Review keywords in the meta tags on the existing website. Revise and reorganize the keywords to optimize the page's search engine ranking.

Portfolio Development

College and Career Readiness

Hard Skills. Employers review candidates for various positions and colleges are always looking for qualified applicants. When listing your qualifications, you may discuss software programs you know or machines you can operate. These abilities are often called *hard skills.* Make an effort to learn about and develop the hard skills you will need for your chosen career.

1. Conduct research about hard skills and their value in helping people succeed.

2. Create a Microsoft Word document and list the hard skills that are important for a job or career that currently you possess. Use the heading "Hard Skills" and your name. For each soft skill, write a paragraph that describes your abilities. Give examples to illustrate your skills. Save the document.

3. Update your master spreadsheet.

CTSOs

Network Design. Network design is a team event. Teams consist of two to three members. There are two parts to this event: an objective test and an oral presentation of the design. The presentation part of the event is based on a case study of a small organization and its environment and network needs. Participants will analyze the situation and suggest a network design that meets the organization's needs. To prepare for writing a financial plan, complete the following activities.

1. Read the guidelines provided by your organization.

2. Study common networking objectives, including installation, troubleshooting, administration, Internet protocols, disaster recovery, configuration, and security.

3. Work with your team to design networks for multiple organizations of different sizes.

4. Practice presenting your network designs for a teacher or CTSO advisor. Have your audience provide feedback. If you present to your network instructor, ask for content-based feedback to make sure your terminology and logistics are accurate.

5. Review the exam requirements to make sure you will be prepared. Only the top-scoring teams advance to the presentation round, but be prepared to present regardless.

6. Visit the organization's website for other resources and to make sure information regarding the event has not changed.

15

ELECTRONIC COMMUNICATION AND COLLABORATION

SECTIONS

15.1 ELECTRONIC MAIL

15.2 REAL-TIME COMMUNICATION

15.3 GOOD COMMUNICATION PRACTICES

CHECK YOUR IT IQ

Before you begin this chapter, see what you already know about information technology by scanning the QR code to take the chapter pretest. If you do not have a smartphone, visit www.g-wlearning.com.

The Pew Internet Project recently studied mobile technology and released these facts about American adults: 90 percent have a cell phone, 58 percent have a smartphone, 32 percent own an e-book reader, and 42 percent own a tablet computer. Today's telephones are small computers with more computing power than many desktop computers of just a few years ago. Messages are shared using smartphones, other mobile devices, and traditional computers via e-mail and social media. In addition to sharing messages, people use online collaboration tools to videoconference and share files in real time. This allows projects to be staffed by people around the world.

With the increased speed of conversations occurring via e-mail and social media, taking shortcuts in writing is more common. However, this can lead to a poor image of the sender. Additionally, without the inflection and tone of voice found in face-to-face encounters, communication can be misinterpreted. Video connections tend to minimize those troubles. This chapter explores facets of online communication and collaboration.

College and Career Readiness

Reading Prep. Arrange a study session to read the chapter aloud with a classmate. At the end of each section, discuss any words you do not know. Take notes of words you would like to discuss in class.

IC3 CERTIFICATION OBJECTIVES

Computing Fundamentals

Domain 1.0 Mobile devices
  Objective 1.1 Understand cellular phone concepts
  Objective 1.4 Understand the use of hard-wired phones
  Objective 1.5 Use of instant messaging
  Objective 1.6 Know how to configure notifications

Domain 2.0 Hardware devices
  Objective 2.10 Know the difference between cellular, Wi-Fi, and wired networks

Domain 5.0 File sharing
  Objective 5.1 Understand file transfer options and characteristics

Domain 6.0 Cloud computing
  Objective 6.4 Web apps vs. local apps

Living Online

Domain 3.0 E-mail clients
  Objective 3.1 Identify e-mail applications

Domain 4.0 Calendaring
  Objective 4.1 Know how to create events and appointments
  Objective 4.2 Know how to share calendars
  Objective 4.3 Know how to view multiple calendars
  Objective 4.4 Understand how to subscribe to calendars

Domain 5.0 Social media
  Objective 5.1 Understand what a digital identity is (identity on social media)
  Objective 5.2 Recognize the difference of internal (school/business) vs. open media sites
  Objective 5.3 Know what blogs, wikis, and forums are and how they are used
  Objective 5.4 Know what cyberbullying is

Domain 6.0 Communication
  Objective 6.1 Know the best tool for the various situations and scenarios
  Objective 6.2 Know how to use SMS texting
  Objective 6.3 Know how to use chat platforms
  Objective 6.4 Understand options for and how to use distant/remote/individual learning technologies

Domain 7.0 Online conferencing
  Objective 7.1 Understand and identify online conference offerings

Domain 8.0 Streaming
  Objective 8.1 Understand what streaming is and how it works with devices

Domain 9.0 Digital principles/ethics/skills/citizenship
  Objective 9.1 Understand the necessity of coping with change in technology
  Objective 9.3 Understand an online identity management
  Objective 9.4 Know the difference between personal vs. professional identity

GS5

Key Applications

Domain 6.0 Collaboration
  Objective 6.1 Comments
  Objective 6.2 Sharing files

Living Online

Domain 3.0 Digital communication
  Objective 3.1 E-mail communication
  Objective 3.2 Real-time communication

Domain 4.0 Digital citizenship
  Objective 4.1 Communication standards

GS4

ELECTRONIC MAIL

Essential Question

What would society look like without e-mail?

Electronic mail is the process of trading digital messages from one person to one or more receivers. Early e-mail programs required both sender and receiver to be logged into the e-mail program at the same time. In function, this was more like text messaging than what today is thought of as e-mail. Now, e-mail messages are saved on a server and downloaded when a user opens the local e-mail program.

Electronic communication is supported by many devices and many software programs. Today, electronic communication is outpacing telephony, which was once the most popular method for communication between people at a distance. There are two parts to the process of sending and receiving e-mail: a client e-mail program and a server-side e-mail program. This section explores the technology of e-mail, its applications, and its features.

Rob Marmion/Shutterstock.com

TERMS

address book
archiving
auto-respond option
contact group
credential
digital citizenship
e-mail client
e-mail server
Internet message access protocol (IMAP)

junk e-mail
message header
netiquette
out-of-office message
post office protocol (POP)
simple mail transfer protocol (SMTP)
spam
username

LEARNING GOALS

After completing this section, you will be able to:

- Discuss various e-mail technologies.
- Describe typical e-mail account settings.
- Explain appropriate e-mail use.
- Manage e-mail communication.

E-mail Technologies

In the early days of the Internet, while using the FTP to send files between networks, Ray Tomlinson thought it would be nice to send a text message describing what was being transferred. To do this, he created the first electronic mail program. Electronic mail, today known as *e-mail*, is communication sent to a computer address where the message is stored to be read at a later time by the recipient.

GS5 Living Online **6.1.1**

The **e-mail client** is the program used to create and send the message. When the message is sent from an e-mail client program, it ends up on the e-mail host or server, as shown in Figure 15-1. The **e-mail server** handles the storing and delivery of the message. The message is stored there and a copy is forwarded to the recipient when that user opens his or her e-mail client. The message is stored on the client device until the user deletes it. The copy on the server is not deleted.

E-mail Message

An e-mail message has three components:
- message body
- message header
- message envelope

The *message body* contains the text of the message itself. The **message header** contains a variety of information necessary to ensure the proper delivery of the message. Items such as the sender's e-mail address, the receiver's e-mail address, the e-mail subject line, and the date and time sent are included. The *message envelope* is the encrypted bundle of the header and the body that is sent as a unit according to e-mail protocols. There are several protocols associated with e-mail, including IMAP, POP, and SMTP.

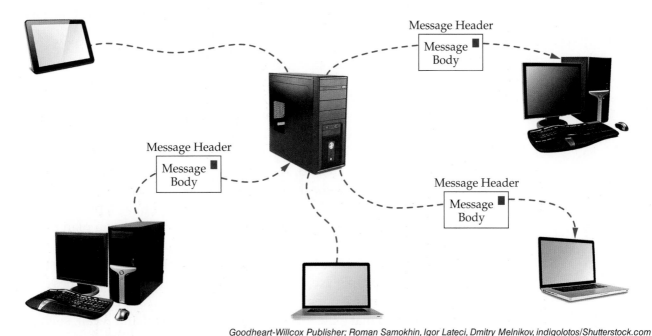

Goodheart-Willcox Publisher; Roman Samokhin, Igor Lateci, Dmitry Melnikov, indigolotos/Shutterstock.com

Figure 15-1. The e-mail server is at the center of sending and receiving e-mail messages.

IMAP

The **Internet message access protocol (IMAP)** describes how to store and retrieve e-mail messages. It is an application-layer protocol that provides an e-mail client's access to a mail server. An e-mail box is set up on the server for each user. Messages are stored in the e-mail box and delivered to the user either on demand or automatically. One of several different e-mail clients can be used to interact with the e-mail server. An e-mail application program such as Microsoft Outlook, web-based mail service, and smartphone mail programs can be used to access the e-mail server.

POP

The **post office protocol (POP)** is also an application-layer protocol that describes how to store and retrieve e-mail messages. The main difference between IMAP and POP is that in POP each e-mail client must independently download the messages from the server. POP predates IMAP, and both protocols are supported by most e-mail systems.

SMTP

The **simple mail transfer protocol (SMTP)** is used to transfer mail from one e-mail system to another over the Internet. It was the first standard that emerged from the ARPANET. SMTP is how the message gets to the e-mail server, and then IMAP or POP delivers it to the e-mail client.

E-mail Account Settings

Living Online
3.1.1

Access to an e-mail account is restricted. Each user of an e-mail system must have a unique account username. The general format for an e-mail address is the username followed by the at sign (@) and the DNS name of the e-mail server, such as JaneDoe@easymail.xyz.

Username

The **username** is the online identity of the account holder. The username must be unique for that e-mail provider to ensure the e-mail address does not conflict with other e-mail functions. Username requirements vary by e-mail system. These restrictions will be noted as an account is being created. A common example of a restriction is not permitting the use of special characters, such as /, @, and %.

If the account will be used only for personal e-mail, a playful username is acceptable, such as FunnyCat. However, if you plan to conduct business using the e-mail address, including conducting job searches, a proper username is better, such as your first and last names. Many people use variations of their own name for business e-mail usernames. Underscores, hyphens (dashes), or periods (dots) can be used to make the e-mail address easy to read and recall, such as Mateo_Vasquez@mail.xyz.

Password

Guidelines for creating a safe password are discussed in Chapter 16. Different e-mail providers may enforce stricter password rules. All rules for creating a password will be outlined as the account is created.

Some e-mail clients offer to remember your password. From a security standpoint, do not allow this. The password is meant to protect you and your messages. The time it takes to enter a password is far less than the amount of time it would take to repair damage done by unauthorized access. If you are the only user of the computer and a password is required to start the computer, you may consider allowing the e-mail client to save your password, but it is still better not to do so.

Credentials

In terms of information technology, a **credential** is a record that saves the authentication criteria required to connect to a service, such as e-mail or other database-supported resource. A credential can be as simple as a username and password. It may additionally contain security questions, require a phone number, or require a valid e-mail address. A credential is most often used to verify a user's identity. In the case of retrieving a forgotten password, the user may be required to provide information in the credential to verify he or she is the actual user, not somebody trying to hack into the system.

Microsoft Outlook

Microsoft Outlook is an e-mail client in the Microsoft Office suite. The user interface is shown in Figure 15-2. Take some time to learn the interface and investigate the features supported. Notice the common elements used by all Microsoft Office applications.

Outlook is not an e-mail *service*, it is an e-mail *client*. That is, Outlook can combine all of the e-mail accounts you have with e-mail providers, but it does not allow you to create a new e-mail service. For example, Outlook supports adding an existing Gmail account. To add an account to Outlook, use the **Add Account** command found on the **File** tab of the ribbon. A wizard guides you through adding an existing e-mail account to Outlook.

Web-based E-mail

Many e-mail clients run as a specific program on a local computer, such as Microsoft Outlook, and access to e-mail is from that client alone. This is popular with many businesses and organizations because of the control and security it offers. More flexible access to e-mail can be had with a web-based e-mail client. Examples of web-based e-mail are Gmail, Yahoo! Mail, and Outlook.com (formerly Hotmail).

The benefit of this type of e-mail client is that a user has access to it anywhere there is an Internet connection. A web browser is used to access the e-mail client via the Internet. Navigate to the log-in web page for the client, and enter your username and password. Once logged in, you will have access to the messages as well as the features of the client.

STEM

Technology
The technology used for mass communication has evolved drastically. One of the earliest known forms dates to 3000 BC, when the Egyptians perfected hieroglyphics. Just in the last 400 years, humans have gone from the first newspaper to the telegraph to video conferencing in real time on smartphones.

Living Online
3.1.1

Living Online
3.1.1.1

Web-based e-mail clients tend to be used for personal accounts. Many are free, but the user may be exposed to advertising on the website. Additionally, since these domains are widely known, they are often the targets of spam. Another downside to web-based e-mail clients is that these sites experience frequent attacks by cyber criminals.

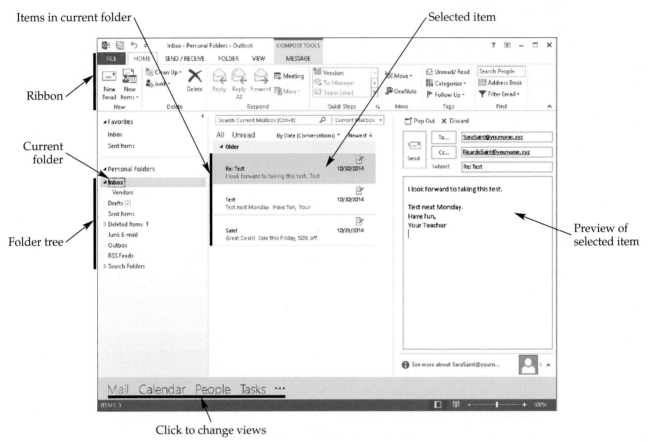

Goodheart-Willcox Publisher

Figure 15-2. Microsoft Outlook is the e-mail client for the Microsoft Office suite.

HANDS-ON EXAMPLE 15.1.1

ADDING AN ACCOUNT TO OUTLOOK

Microsoft Outlook is a personal communication tool that can be used to manage a single e-mail account or multiple accounts. A wizard is used to add an account to Outlook.

1. Launch Microsoft Outlook 2013.
2. Click the **File** tab in the ribbon to display the backstage view.
3. Click **Info** on the left of the backstage view, and then click the **Add Account** button on the right. The **Add Account** wizard is launched.

HANDS-ON EXAMPLE 15.1.1 (CONTINUED)

4. Complete the first page of the wizard by entering your name, the e-mail address you wish to add, and the password for that account, as shown.

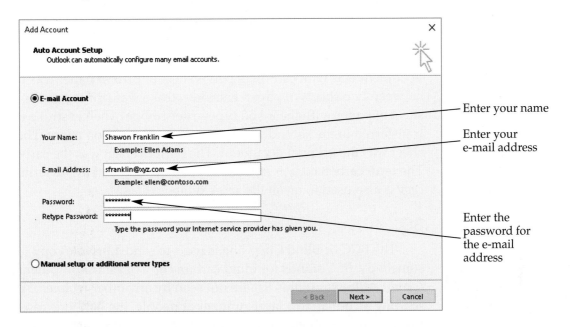

Enter your name

Enter your e-mail address

Enter the password for the e-mail address

5. Click the **Next** button. Outlook attempts to automatically configure your account.
6. When Outlook has configured the account, click the **Finish** button. Outlook displays the e-mail messages on the e-mail server waiting to be delivered to this account.

Appropriate E-mail Use

Digital citizenship is the standard of appropriate behavior when using technology to communicate. Good digital citizenship focuses on using technology in a positive way rather than using it for negative or illegal purposes. E-mail has grown beyond personal uses. In many cases, e-mail has taken the place of traditional printed business correspondence. In addition, many social engagements are set up using e-mail. It is important to use Standard English to conduct these types of communication. Complete sentences, correct spelling and proper grammar are required. For casual e-mail conversations with family and friends, less importance can be placed on this.

Living Online
3.1.2, 4.1.1

FYI

Always strive for proper spelling and grammar use, even in casual messages; it reflects on you.

Header

The header contains the e-mail addresses of all who will receive the e-mail and a subject line. The main recipients of the e-mail are listed in the To line. Enter the e-mail address of each person who is required to act on the message in this line.

In addition to the main recipients, copies of the message can be sent to other people. This is similar to other people in a room who are listening to your conversation with another person.

Living Online
3.1.2.4

GS5 Living Online
3.1.2.2

CC

The CC or Copy line is used for e-mail addresses of people who will receive the e-mail, but who are not the main recipient. Somebody who is copied on an e-mail is provided the message for informational purposes only. He or she usually is not required to act on the message. These e-mail addresses are visible to the recipients.

CC stands for carbon copy. In the past, when typewriters were used to compose letters and papers, the only way to make a copy of the document was with carbon paper. A sheet of carbon paper was placed between two sheets of paper. Each keystroke was printed on the top sheet of paper with the inked typewriter ribbon. The keystroke was also transferred to the second sheet of paper by the carbon paper. The top sheet was the original document. The bottom sheet was the carbon copy. The term carbon copy is still used for e-mail copies, but the term *computer copy* is also used to mean the same thing.

BCC

The BCC or Blind Copy line is used to send a private copy to somebody. *BCC* stands for blind carbon copy or blind computer copy. E-mail addresses in this list are not seen by any other recipient. When sending an e-mail to a large number of people, the BCC line can be used for all of the recipients. The sender enters only his or her e-mail address in the To line. This keeps all e-mail addresses confidential. Only the sender's e-mail address is visible to the recipients.

GS5 Living Online
3.1.2.2

FYI

A blind computer copy is often used to send a targeted mass e-mail, such as a product announcement, so the e-mail addresses of all recipients remain private.

Subject Line

The *subject line* should clearly and concisely state the topic of the e-mail. A clear subject line provides information to the recipient and helps to determine the priority for reading the message and where to store it. By focusing the subject line on the topic of the e-mail, readers can more easily keep track of replies.

The subject line is also important because it is the information displayed by the IMAP protocol, as shown in Figure 15-3. The sender's username or e-mail address, the subject line, and the delivery time to the server are listed along with a few words of the message body. The full message is not downloaded to the e-mail client until the message is clicked.

GS4 Living Online
4.1.3

Body

The body of the message contains all of the communication from the sender to the recipient. Until the reader replies, this is one-way communication. Therefore, take care to provide all of the information the reader needs to respond fully.

Some e-mail clients offer a choice of formatting the message as plain text, rich text, or HTML. Plain text is text only without any formatting. The rich text and HTML options support simple text formatting and including images. However, be aware that some e-mail clients do not support incoming mail in rich text and HTML formats. Recipients with

Subject line

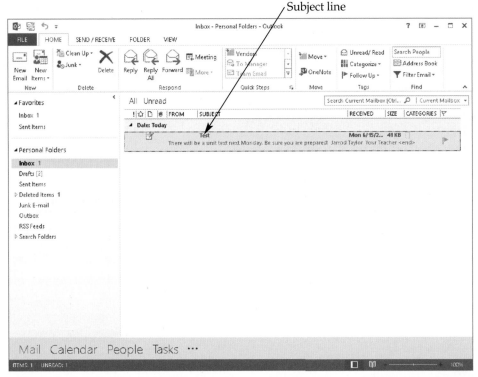

Figure 15-3. The subject line is displayed in the user's inbox when an e-mail message is received.

these clients will either receive a plain-text version of the e-mail or the e-mail will be bounced back to the sender.

When sending a formal e-mail, it should include a salutation, the message, and a complimentary close and signature. Casual e-mail to family and friends does not need to be as formal.

Salutation

The *salutation* is the greeting in the message. The general rule is to use traditional salutations, but e-mail tends to be more informal than letters. You may use the salutation "Dear" as in a letter, depending on whether you are writing a formal or informal e-mail. People often address each other by their first names in e-mails. Use your judgment based on your relationship with the recipient. If you address the recipient by first name in person, it is usually correct to do the same in written communication.

Message

Format the e-mail message the same as a letter or a memo. Use appropriate spacing, as shown in Figure 15-4. Always follow netiquette when writing both personal and business e-mails. **Netiquette**, or Internet etiquette, is a set of guidelines for appropriate behavior on the Internet, including e-mail. When you are sending e-mail as a representative of an organization or business, use Standard English and the spell-check feature before sending. Remember, your e-mail could be forwarded to others who might make judgments about what you have written.

FYI

As with all Microsoft Office applications, by default Outlook automatically displays spelling and grammar errors.

Click to add an attachment to the e-mail message

Header

Salutation

Message

Complimentary close

Signature

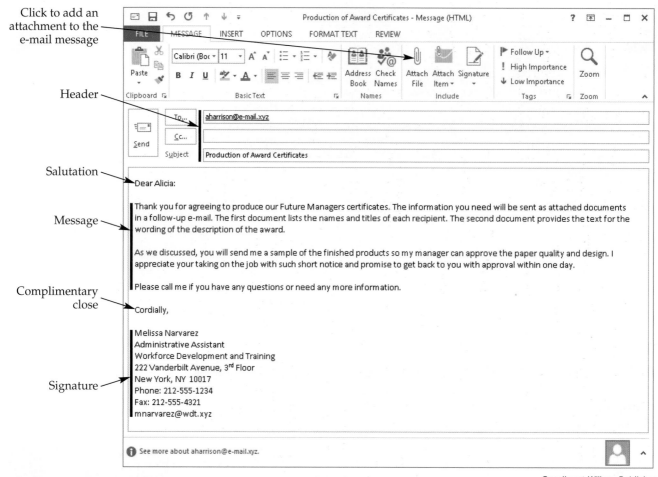

Figure 15-4. This e-mail is properly formatted.

Complimentary Close and Signature

E-mail often takes the place of routine phone calls and face-to-face conversations. Writers often forego including a closing and formal signature in these kinds of messages. However, a courteous thank-you at the end of the message is usually appropriate.

For an e-mail that is used in place of a formal letter, it is important to include a complimentary close just as in a printed letter. Include your full name and contact information at the bottom of the e-mail for the convenience of the reader. A handwritten signature can be included as a graphic, but this is not common. Most e-mail programs allow the user to set up a signature to be automatically inserted, which is discussed later in this chapter.

Replying and Forwarding Messages

If you receive an e-mail message, it may require a response. There are three basic ways to respond to an e-mail message:

- reply
- reply all
- forward

The *reply* option sends your comments to the sender. Depending on the settings of your e-mail client, the original message may or may not be included. The default is usually to include the original message. The *reply all* option sends the return message to everyone who received the original e-mail, except blind copy recipients. The *forward* option sends the reply to a new recipient. A new e-mail address must be entered in the To line.

Stay with the original topic in your reply. If you want to bring up a new topic, send a new e-mail and note the topic in the subject line. Creating a new e-mail with a new subject line makes it easier to keep the information flow understandable. Additionally, it allows both the sender and recipient of the e-mail to electronically file and organize the e-mail.

Attachments

Most e-mail clients allow files to be sent along with the text part of the e-mail message. Any type of file can be sent. It is common to share work with others by sending attachments. Reports, spreadsheets, presentations, databases, or just about any other type of work in digital form can be shared as an attachment to e-mail. Most e-mail clients use the image of a paper clip to indicate the command for attaching a file, as shown in Figure 15-4.

However, because of the danger posed by malicious attachments, some e-mail clients or servers will not accept them. One of the file types most often rejected is compressed files, such as a ZIP file. This is because compressed files can hide executable files within that may bring malware to the client computer. It may be a good idea to send an e-mail to alert the recipient you will be sending another e-mail with an attachment.

This danger is real. Any attachments that arrive on e-mail messages must be carefully handled. In general, do not open an attachment without a subject line, if you do not know the recipient, or if it is not fully explained in the body of the message.

Ensure both the e-mail client and the recipient can handle the size and type of the file. Many e-mail servers have limits on the size of files that can be received. Limits are placed on attachment size for most mobile e-mail clients as well. In general, files that are smaller than 1 MB can be accepted by most e-mail servers. If a file is larger than that, you may need to first send an e-mail to ask if the person will be able to receive a large file. For very large files, a better option may be to set up an FTP or cloud site that can be used to transfer the files.

Address Book

Remembering a variety of e-mail addresses is difficult. To accommodate this, most e-mail clients provide an electronic address book. An **address book** contains the e-mail addresses of contacts and may contain other information for each, such as a phone number and notes about the person, as shown in Figure 15-5. Most e-mail clients will suggest contacts from the address book as the To line is filled in. This makes it easy to select a recipient without having to enter the entire e-mail address.

GS5 Computing Fundamentals
5.1.1

Living Online
3.1.4

GS4 Key Applications
6.2.1

Green Tech

Paperless Society
Even though much written communication today is in the form of e-mail, paper still helps people communicate. Paper is still used in business to take notes, write reports, and perform other tasks. IT companies can take measures to reduce the consumption of paper by adopting eco-friendly practices.

GS5 Living Online
3.1.5.1

Whenever a group of people is sent the same types of messages, a contact group can be created in the address book. A **contact group** is a named collection of e-mail addresses from the address book. One name is applied to the entire list. When this name is entered in the To line of an e-mail message, the e-mail will be sent to all contacts within the group. Alternate names for contact group are distribution list, contact list, and group.

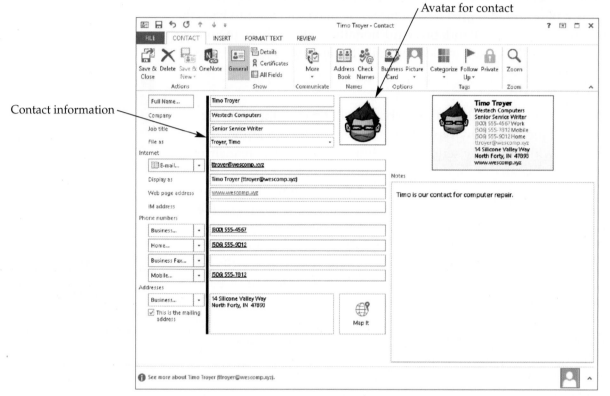

Figure 15-5. This is the information for an entry in the user's address book.

HANDS-ON EXAMPLE 15.1.2

CREATING A NEW CONTACT GROUP

Contact groups make it easy to send an e-mail to a large number of addresses at the same time. It is easy to set up a contact group in Microsoft Office.

1. Launch Microsoft Outlook 2013.

HANDS-ON EXAMPLE 15.1.2 (CONTINUED)

New
Items

2. Click the **New Items** button in the **New** group on the **Home** tab of the ribbon, and click **More Items>Contact Group** in the drop-down menu. The **Contact Group** dialog box is displayed, as shown.

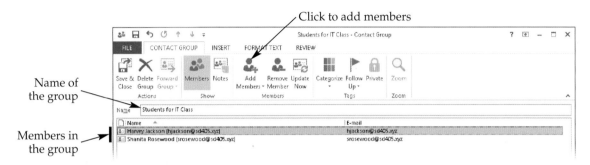

Click to add members

Name of
the group

Members in
the group

Add
Members

3. Click the **Add Members** button in the **Members** group on the **Contact Group** tab of the ribbon in the dialog box, and click **New E-mail Contact** in the drop-down menu. The **Add New Member** dialog box is displayed.
4. Click in the **Display name:** text box, and enter your first name.
5. Click in the **E-mail address:** text box, and enter your e-mail address.
6. Click the **OK** button to create the contact and add it to the contact group being created.
7. Applying what you have learned, add two more contacts using the information for two of your friends.
8. Click in the **Name** text box at the top of the **Contact Group** dialog box, and enter Me and My Friends. This is the name of the contact group. Notice the title bar of the dialog box reflects the name once the [Enter] key is pressed.

Save &
Close

9. Click the **Save & Close** button in the **Actions** group on the **Contact Group** tab of the ribbon in the dialog box.
10. Click the **New Item** button (new e-mail) in the **New** group on the **Home** tab of the ribbon. A new e-mail message is opened.

New Item

11. Click the **To...** button. The **Select Names** dialog box is displayed, which lists all of the contacts and contact groups saved in the address book.

To...

12. Select the Me and My Friends group in the list, and click the **To->** button at the bottom of the dialog box.
13. Click the **OK** button. Notice the name of the contact group appears in the **To** text box in the message. When the message is sent, it will go to all contacts in this contact group.

Managing E-mail Communication

Most e-mail clients have several features to help manage communication. Automated features can be set to send a reply or forward a message. Personal folders can be created to organize messages. Filters can be set to manage unwanted e-mail. E-mail messages can be deleted or archived.

GS4 Living Online 3.1.3

Automated Features

In today's world of instantaneous news feeds, messaging, and social media communication, often e-mail is expected to function like a text or instant message. Sometimes, it can function like that, with a reply being received seconds after the original message was sent. However, in most cases, it will take minutes, hours, or even days for somebody to reply to your e-mail. When you find yourself in a situation where you will not be able to reply to a message in a timely manner, there are automated features that can help.

Auto Respond

The **auto-respond option** sends a set reply to every e-mail message received. A message such as:

> Thank you for your e-mail. We will respond as soon as possible.

allows the sender to know you received his or her e-mail. This provides feedback even if you cannot send a direct reply. If the sender does not hear from you for a few hours or even a few days, he or she can be assured you received the e-mail. This does not, however, let him or her know whether or not you actually opened the e-mail.

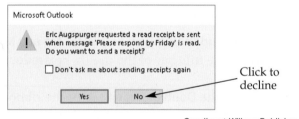

Click to decline

Goodheart-Willcox Publisher

Figure 15-6. The recipient usually can decline to send a read receipt, depending on the e-mail client.

FYI

Read receipts can be distracting to the recipient, and some people consider them rude. Use them only when there is a critical need to do so.

Read Receipt

There are times where you, as the sender, need to know if somebody read the e-mail. If the recipient has set up an auto-respond message, then you will know if he or she *received* it, but not if the message was opened. A *read receipt* is a return message sent when the original message has been opened. Not all e-mail clients support read receipts. Also, the person receiving the original message usually has the option to decline sending the read receipt, as shown in Figure 15-6. Therefore, this is not a foolproof method of knowing if somebody has read a message.

Out of Office

The **out-of-office message** is an auto-response message generated once for each user who sends e-mail to the address. When you will be unavailable for a long period of time, use the out-of-office feature to send a message stating when you will return. This is a courtesy. It allows the sender to know you are unavailable instead of not responding to his or her message.

Auto Forwarding

The auto-forwarding feature automatically sends a copy of any received e-mail to a different e-mail account. This is useful for a POP account when you will be away from the client computer for some time.

For example, you may wish to forward the e-mail to an account that can be accessed from your smartphone or other mobile device.

Signatures

A *signature,* or signature block, is content, usually text, that is automatically entered each time you start a new e-mail message. In the signature block, include your name, job title, department, and contact information. It is customary to include the e-mail address in the signature, since many e-mail clients display the sender's full name instead of the e-mail address.

It is also common to include graphics and hyperlinks in the signature. For example, many businesses and organizations will include a logo. Icons are also often included for social media, such as Twitter and Facebook. Each graphic is typically hyperlinked to the corresponding web destination.

Personal Folders

Received messages appear in the Inbox folder. Sent messages are automatically placed in the Outbox until sent by the e-mail client. Once sent, they are automatically moved to the Sent or Sent Items folder. There are typically other default folders as well, depending on the e-mail client.

GS5 Living Online
3.1.3.4

Subfolders can be created in the Inbox folder. These can be used to sort and hold your old mail messages. Create folders by project, sender, or whatever scheme you desire, as shown in Figure 15-7. The fewer files in your inbox, the faster your e-mail client will load.

Junk Mail

Unsolicited e-mail messages are known as junk or **junk e-mail**. Junk e-mails are often unsolicited marketing notices. Many junk e-mails are the result of checking or failing to uncheck a "subscribe to receive updates" check box on an order form. Once you provide an e-mail address to one company, it may be sold to other companies. The company you gave your e-mail address to in the first place may also send junk e-mails.

GS5 Living Online
3.1.2.6, 3.1.3.1

Most e-mail servers have junk e-mail filters. There are several *e-mail blacklists* the IT industry uses to help protect clients from junk e-mail. If a server IP address appears on one of these blacklists, most e-mail servers will block any e-mail from that address. Some e-mail servers are stronger in enforcing the blacklists than are other servers.

Most e-mail clients also have some form of junk e-mail filter. If an e-mail is detected as junk, it is automatically moved to the Junk or Junk E-mail folder. Unfortunately, sometimes e-mails that are not junk can be flagged and moved to the Junk folder. Therefore, it is a good idea to check the Junk folder every once in a while to see if any of the messages are not really junk. Adding the address of the misdirected e-mail message to your address book may prevent this mishap in the future.

In some e-mail clients, manually moving a message to the Junk folder will set a rule so similar e-mail messages are automatically flagged as junk.

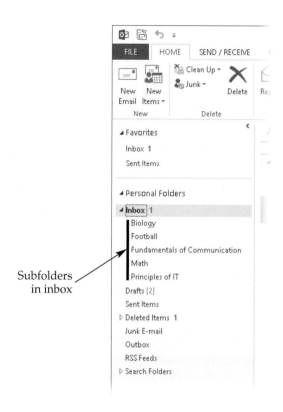

Goodheart-Willcox Publisher

Figure 15-7. Folders can be created to arrange messages by topic, such as by class or activity.

Subfolders in inbox

Living Online
3.1.2.5, 3.1.3.1

Living Online
4.1.4

FYI

The term *spam* originated as a reference to a Monty Python skit about the canned-meat product Spam. During the skit, the name Spam is repeated over 100 times.

Living Online
3.1.3.2

Spam

Spam is a type of junk mail. **Spam** is one unwanted e-mail message sent to a large number of users or multiple identical unwanted messages sent to a single e-mail address. Spamming is unethical. It is usually part of a scam or done to overload an e-mail server.

Cleaning Up E-mail Folders

When messages are kept in an e-mail Inbox folder, Sent folder, or other subfolders, disk space is consumed. Also, these messages are loaded each time an e-mail client starts up. This takes extra time. In order to free space and speed up loading, messages may be archived or deleted.

Archiving E-mail Messages

If an e-mail message is not needed at the moment, but important enough to keep, it can be archived. **Archiving** consists of storing e-mail messages in a place where they will not load every time the e-mail client is launched, but can be accessed if needed. Many e-mail clients archive e-mail messages in a compressed file that is saved on the hard drive. This file can be opened to access the messages it contains, as shown in Figure 15-8. Once the archive file is closed, the messages are no longer available until the file is again opened.

Some e-mail clients will prompt you to archive old messages. Messages can also be manually archived. This is useful to store all e-mail

Active folders

Archived folders

Goodheart-Willcox Publisher

Figure 15-8. Archived messages are not loaded each time the client is launched, but can be accessed if needed.

messages related to a project with the other project files. If personal folders are created by project, it is a simple step to archive the project e-mails.

Deleting E-mail Messages

To delete an e-mail, simply highlight it and press the [Delete] key or click the **Delete** button in the e-mail client. However, this does not remove the e-mail. Most e-mail clients move deleted e-mails to the Deleted folder. The messages remain there until the folder is emptied. Some e-mail clients are set up to automatically empty the Deleted folder when the client is closed. In other cases, the folder must be manually emptied.

What you say in an e-mail likely will always be accessible by somebody. Even when the Deleted folder is emptied, the e-mail is not permanently removed. E-mail servers generally do not delete e-mail messages for legal reasons. E-mail providers may be subpoenaed by law-enforcement agents when investigating crimes.

GS5
Living Online
3.1.3.3

15.1 | SECTION REVIEW

 CHECK YOUR UNDERSTANDING

1. What stores and delivers e-mail messages?
2. Which protocol is used to transfer e-mail from one system to another?
3. What is the simplest credential for an e-mail account?
4. Why are compressed files, such as ZIP files, sent as attachments often rejected by e-mail clients or servers?
5. How does a junk e-mail filter work?

IC3 CERTIFICATION PRACTICE

The following question is a sample of the types of questions presented on the IC3 exam.

1. Interactive question.

    Demonstrate how to set up an out-of-office reply using a Microsoft Exchange server.

 BUILD YOUR VOCABULARY

As you progress through this course, develop a personal IT glossary. This will help you build your vocabulary and prepare you for a career. Write a definition for each of the following terms and add it to your IT glossary.

address book
archiving
auto-respond option
contact group
credential
digital citizenship
e-mail client
e-mail server
Internet message access
   protocol (IMAP)

junk e-mail
message header
netiquette
out-of-office message
post office protocol (POP)
simple mail transfer
   protocol (SMTP)
spam
username

REAL-TIME COMMUNICATION

iko/Shutterstock.com

One of the most noteworthy innovations in the recent past is the development of mobile technologies. Beginning over 70 years ago with the invention of cellular technology, the evolution of the mobile industry has been fascinating. The first handheld mobile phone weighed 2.5 pounds and had a range of only five miles. Now they are pocket-sized and virtual full-fledged computers. In addition to phones, laptops and tablets provide computing on the go.

There are many technologies that support real-time communication. Technologies such as SMS and IM support text messages. MMS supports multimedia messages, while VoIP supports voice. Videoconferencing and streaming video support transfer of video. This section explores the technologies that form the foundation of mobile communication.

Essential Question

How has social media changed the way in which news is reported?

LEARNING GOALS

After completing this section, you will be able to:
- Discuss telephone technologies.
- Explain various communication tools.

TERMS

blog
carrier
cell
cellular technology
flaming
forum
instant messaging (IM)
multimedia messaging service (MMS)
really simple syndication (RSS)
short messaging service (SMS)
streaming
videoconferencing
Voice over Internet Protocol (VoIP)

Telephone Communication

The telephone is a primary means of communication for most people. A telephone is a device that converts sounds into electrical signals, transmits the signals, and converts the signals back into the same sounds. The telephone was invented in the late 19th century. Until the late 20th century, telephones were connected by wires and the electrical signals were analog. Now, telephones may be connected by wires, or may use radio waves to transmit signals. The signals may be digital or analog, although the number of analog networks is in decline.

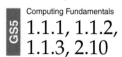

Computing Fundamentals
1.4.1, 1.4.2, 1.4.3, 1.4.4
Living Online
6.1.5

Land-line Technology

A hard-wired phone is physically connected to the telephone network by wires and optical fibers. This technology is called a *land line.* It dates to the origins of the telephone. Because land lines are fixed in place, a phone is continually connected to the telephone system. However, a land-line telephone is not mobile. It cannot be taken to school or to a friend's house. This is also a limitation in business, especially for those who must travel outside of the office.

Despite the immobility, there are advantages to a land line. The 911 system will immediately identify the location of an emergency call on a land line. To identify the location of an emergency call from a cell phone, a process known as triangulation must be done. This may take from a few seconds to a few minutes and is not always successful. Cell phones with a GPS function can be traced using that, but the location may not be precise and this process is not always successful. Additionally, if the power goes out, a land-line phone is still operational. A cell phone is only operational as long as the battery is charged and the cell towers in the area are powered. Finally, the audial quality of communication on a land line is much better than on a cell phone.

Businesses still tend to use land lines for primary communication. A business telephone system may be built on the concept of a main telephone number to reach the system and multiple telephone locations, or *extensions,* within the system. To place a call from one phone on the system to another phone on the system, a short code is entered instead of a full telephone number. To place a call to a number outside the system, typically the number 9 must be entered to reach an outside line before the telephone number is entered. From outside the system, usually the main telephone number is called, and then the extension number is entered. Calls can be transferred from extension to extension throughout the system. Most telephone systems used by businesses also support conference calling.

Cellular Technology

Computing Fundamentals
1.1.1, 1.1.2, 1.1.3, 2.10

Today, many people primarily use a cell phone instead of a land line, and some people do not even have a land line. In reality, a cellular phone (cell phone) is just a computer-controlled radio. It is a very powerful radio, but still a radio. It relies on microwave radio transmissions sent from towers in strategic locations.

Cellular technology is based on the principle of wireless transmissions distributed over groups of geographic areas. A **cell** is the area where the signal from a single tower is carried. Figure 15-9 shows how cells form a cellular network. Typically, each cell is 10 square miles around a tower. Where there are no towers, there is no cell service. It is important to understand that cellular technology is not the Internet. Some apps on mobile devices may *access* the Internet, but the connection to the mobile device is via the cellular network, as discussed later in this section.

Each cell phone–service provider, or **carrier**, has a band of frequencies on which it can transmit and receive signals. These are low-power signals so the frequencies can be reused in other cells. The cell phone contains a low-power transmitter to send data to the tower.

Using a cell phone while moving may cause the device to exit one cell and enter another. When this happens, the carrier switches the call from cell to cell. Minor disruptions in the signal may be noticed during switches. The hardware and software of cellular technology manage to keep each call connected no matter where the device is or how it moves about.

Cellular Contracts

Most carriers provide cellular service to users under a service agreement contract. These contracts offer a variety of plans. A plan defines the amount of data, text, or minutes of call time per month for the fee. Going over the limits results in *overage charges*. Some plans allow unused minutes or data to be carried over to the next month.

The service agreement contract commits the user to a specific time period. Contracts are usually for two years, but the cost of the device is greatly discounted. Many of the long-term contracts offer upgrades of the phone within the service period. There are also no-contract options. These allow you to change carriers at any time, but you have to pay the full cost of the device. Prepaid cell phones are also a no-contract option.

There are a wide variety of contracts and plans. Even for a given carrier plans can vary. Thoroughly investigate the details of service agreement and understand the specifics of each plan. Choose the carrier and plan that best suits your needs.

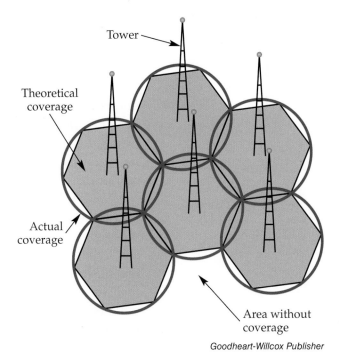

Goodheart-Willcox Publisher

Figure 15-9. Cells are considered to be hexagonal in shape, but in practice each cell is circular.

FYI

Many carriers offer service outside of the United States. Be sure to check for additional charges that may apply.

GS5 Computing Fundamentals 1.1.4

Computing Fundamentals
GS5 1.1.3

Cellular Technology and the Internet

There are two key functions of smartphones: carrying voice messages and transmitting data to and from the Internet. A *tier 1* carrier has its own network capabilities to manage both voice and data. Essentially, this type of carrier is the ISP for smartphone users. Tier 1 carriers include AT&T, Sprint, T-Mobile, and Verizon. A *tier 2* carrier purchases Internet services from the tier 1 companies. A *tier 3* carrier does not have its own networks. It purchases network access from tier 1 and tier 2 carriers. Tier 2 and tier 3 carriers are considered smaller carriers and may be regional.

Voice transmissions dropped sharply with the advent of short messaging service (SMS) texting. Even more so, SMS has gone the way of messaging apps. Additionally, users can connect to a wireless network and bypass the data service on their phones. This takes a toll on the revenue of the tier 1 companies, which depend on voice and data for their income. As smartphone use and Internet traffic increase, carriers will need to depend more on income from data transmission than voice transmission.

Cell Phone Generations

The evolution of cell phone technology is marked by generations. The generations are known as 1G, 2G, and so on. A new generation appears about every 10 years. The newest generation in development is 5G, but the current generation is 4G.

The first generation of cell phone technology was 1G. These systems were capable of transmitting analog voice signals. This was the same technology as land-based telephones, except with wireless transmissions.

In the 1990s, digital voice transmission was introduced. This marked the beginning of the second generation of cell phone technology, known as 2G. Later, Internet access and e-mail were supported. Since this was an adaptation of 2G technology, this was known as 2.5G.

In 2000, faster access to the Internet was introduced. Download rates up to 1 Mbps could be achieved. This marked the third generation, known as 3G. Worldwide roaming was introduced with the generic access network (GAN) standard. The technology in this generation also tried to address the problem of getting cell phone signals inside large buildings.

The fourth generation, known as 4G, had three versions. High-speed packet access (HSPA+) increased transmission speeds. This offered more channels and different modulation and coding techniques. Worldwide interoperability for microwave access (WiMAx) from Sprint increased transmission speeds and created a wide area network. It also added a feature for Internet service providers to boost signals using a small, indoor base station. This improved the reception in large buildings that previously blocked signals. Long term evolution (LTE) supported the highest speeds available without using Wi-Fi connections. The iPhone 5 incorporated LTE technology.

The fifth generation, known as 5G, is not yet a standard. It is a working project in keeping with expectations for the decade. Predictions

Career Skills

Public Safety Telecommunicator
Fire, police, and ambulance dispatchers work in emergency communication centers to answer emergency and nonemergency calls. They advise emergency responders of the caller's situation and location. Workers at the common public safety answering point work in a high-pressure, technology-supported role. The Automatic Location Identification technology is a database function that automatically identifies the caller's location. It is maintained by the local telephone company.

are that speeds will increase. However, the technology may have reached a physical limitation on bandwidth. A breakthrough in frequency distribution technologies may be needed to define this generation.

Communication Tools

In addition to voice, cellular channels provide for transmission of text, video, and audio. In the case of high-bandwidth requirements, transmission speeds rely on a Wi-Fi connection. Connection to the Internet via Wi-Fi or data link supports the use of many of the desktop-based tools.

When rapid wireless communication is required, it is important to understand the communication capabilities and preferences of the message receiver. Some will want a voice call for an important time-sensitive matter. Some prefer text messages. In this case, it is important to know whether SMS or IM is the better technology for reaching the receiver in the shortest time. If considering videoconferencing, ask if the participant has a webcam. Be sensitive to the throughput capability before suggesting "bandwidth hogs" such as screen sharing or streaming video.

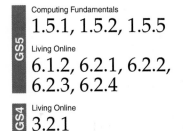

GS5 Living Online
9.1.1

Computing Fundamentals
1.5.1, 1.5.2, 1.5.5
GS5 Living Online
6.1.2, 6.2.1, 6.2.2,
6.2.3, 6.2.4
GS4 Living Online
3.2.1

SMS

Short messaging service (SMS) is a protocol for exchanging messages on a wireless network. This is the technology used for text messaging. The maximum number of characters is 160 per message. This limitation promotes very rapid transmission. It may seem like a simple application, but there is a lot that goes on to get a text message where it needs to go.

1. The phone creates the message with transmission data embedded, such as sender's phone ID, the short message center (SMC) address where the message will be sent, and the recipient's address.
2. The phone sends the message to the SMC.
3. The SMC stores the message.
4. The SMC forwards the message to the destination device using the home location register (HLR). This is a massive database of all network subscribers.
5. The message switching center (MSC) takes over and changes the connection to the destination mobile network.
6. Using the visitor location register (VLR) in the SMC, the exact cell where the destination device is currently connected is found.
7. The message is sent to the base station system (BSS), which ultimately delivers the message to the correct device.
8. If the device is not active, the SMC keeps trying to send the message until the device is online.

It is easy to detect if your texting mate is using SMS. Longer messages are broken into 160-character bursts. Some smartphone messaging apps reconstruct the message to keep the conversation continuous.

It seems likely that SMS took hold because it can be performed silently compared to a telephone call. The notion of texting is not long-term communication. Simply short bursts of key information are intended, hence the 160-character limitation. Key brief business communication can be made using SMS. It has sped up reaching people who are away from the office.

There is a basic etiquette associated with mobile communication, including text messaging. For example, it is not proper to text while speaking with another person. In an emergency, as with a phone call, explain that you must deal with the text messages and excuse yourself to a private location. In most formal social situations, a request is often made to silence cell phones. Even if the request is not made, it is still courteous to silence your phone. It is rude to text where the display light is visible and, therefore, disruptive to all around you, such as in a movie theater. Keep in mind that some communication is not proper using text. Truly sensitive conversations should be held in person, face to face.

Because of the amount of distraction created by texting, it is illegal to text while driving in almost all states. Some states ban any use of a handheld device while driving. Most states also ban younger drivers from using any mobile device while driving, even with a hands-free adaptor. There may be further restrictions on the use of devices while driving at the local level.

IM

Instant messaging (IM) is a texting technology that uses the Internet, not the phone system, to transfer messages. There is no standard for this because each IM provider maintains its own proprietary protocol. Examples of IM services are Gmail Chat, Windows Live Messenger, ICQ, and AOL Instant Messenger (AIM).

FYI

Instant messages are the precursor to today's text messages.

Computing Fundamentals
GS5 **1.5.4**
Living Online
6.1.3
GS4 Living Online
3.2.1

HANDS-ON EXAMPLE 15.2.1

Computing Fundamentals
GS5 **1.5.4**
Living Online
6.3, 7.1.2

INSTANT MESSAGING

This exercise will connect the user with another Gmail user in a video conference. Additional Gmail users may be added to the conversation. Google Chat is a web-based service, and the specifics of how to use it may change over time.

Hangouts conversations

Find people to chat with

1. Launch Gmail or Google Hangouts.
2. In Gmail, click the **Hangouts conversations** button or, in Hangouts, click the **Message** link.
3. Click the **Find people to chat with** button (magnifying glass).
4. Enter the name of a Gmail user, and select the name from the search results. The hangouts conversation window opens. This is a chat window for sending instant messages.
5. Enter the text message to send in the box at the bottom of the chat window, and press the [Enter] key. If the contact is logged in, he or she will immediately receive the message. If not logged in, the message will be received as soon as he or she logs in.

HANDS-ON EXAMPLE 15.2.1 (CONTINUED)

6. Messages from the contact to you will appear in the chat window as they are sent.
7. To end the conversation, close the chat window. The conversation is logged and appears on the sidebar in Gmail whenever the **Hangouts conversations** button is selected.

Multimedia Messaging Service (MMS)

Multimedia messaging service (MMS) is a standard for sending messages that include multimedia between mobile devices. The message content may be text, images, audio, or video. MMS technology is an extension of the functionality provided by SMS.

GS5 Computing Fundamentals
1.5.1

GS4 Living Online
3.2.2

VoIP

Voice over Internet Protocol (VoIP) is a set of technologies that supports voice and multimedia transmission over the Internet. For voice use, special VoIP telephones are required. Analog telephone adapters can be used to connect a regular phone to the service.

GS5 Living Online
6.1.4, 7.1.1

GS4 Living Online
3.2.2

Conference Communication

There may be times when you need to communicate with more than one person who is not in the same location as you. This is common in many businesses. Fortunately, technology makes it easy to communicate with multiple people in multiple locations. Ways to conduct this communication include videoconferencing, conference calls, and web-based conferencing.

GS5 Computing Fundamentals
1.5.3

Living Online
6.3, 7.1.2

GS4 Living Online
3.2.2

Videoconferencing

Videoconferencing is conducting a meeting with both audial and visual interaction between people in different locations, as shown in Figure 15-10. Before videoconferencing, to bring employees from around the country or world to a meeting, a company had to spend a lot of money on airfare and hotel rooms. In the 1990s, videoconferencing became practical. However, it was expensive. Special equipment and software along with a network that could support the transmissions were required.

Today, videoconferencing is a great deal less complex, more reliable, and supports more features. As a result, videoconferencing has become more common. Each member or group of employees logs into a software program that runs over the Internet. Examples of these programs are GoToMeeting and Unify. Features generally supported are voice, video, screen sharing, file

Andrey_Popov/Shutterstock.com

Figure 15-10. Today's technology makes it very easy to conduct videoconferences.

transfer, and chat. Skype is another technology that supports voice, video, chat, and file exchange in one application.

FaceTime is an app that provides one-on-one videoconferencing with another FaceTime user. It was originally for use by Apple iOS products, such as iPhones and iPads. Then it was expanded for Mac OS and use on PC via apps that provide support using an iOS emulator. All of this videoconferencing requires Internet access via Wi-Fi.

Conference Calls

GS5 Living Online
6.1.7, 7.1.3

A *conference call* is when three or more telephones are connected at the same time and the users can all communicate with each other. Conference calls often take the place of face-to-face meetings when people are in multiple locations. Each person on a conference call may have a single phone or several people may be in a room using a speaker phone with other callers. Conference calls are used to conduct meetings or social interaction among people at a distance. Voice over Internet Protocol (VoIP) technology allows conference calling to be conducted using the Internet instead of traditional telephone networks.

Three-way calling is an older technology that allows three telephones to be connected at the same time. This provides a limited form of conference calling. Additionally, using speaker phones, a conference call can be conducted between two telephones with multiple people in each location.

Web-Based Conferencing

GS5 Living Online
6.1.6, 7.1.4

In the interest of interaction speed and reduced travel expense, web-based conferencing was invented. Web-based conferencing may involve videoconferencing or may be voice only. Using web resources, callers may share computer screens or send files to one another. Applications of this technology are WebEx, GoToMeeting, and other apps that blend all of the features of a face-to-face meeting into an online meeting.

HANDS-ON EXAMPLE 15.2.2

GS5 Computing Fundamentals
1.5.3
Living Online
6.3, 7.1.1, 7.1.2

VIDEOCONFERENCING

Skype is a popular and free videoconferencing application. Skype is a web-based service, and the specifics of how to use it may change over time. Visit www.skype.com to download and install the application.

1. Launch Skype, and log into your account. If needed, sign up for an account.
2. Click in the **Search** text box, enter the name of the person you want to contact, and click the **Search Skype** button. Skype will display a list of all members who meet the search criteria.
3. Select the correct person in the list, and then click the **Video call** button.
4. Wait for the person to answer the call. Once the person answers, the videoconference will begin. Both video and audio are on by default.

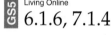
Video
call

HANDS-ON EXAMPLE 15.2.2 (CONTINUED)

5. To share the computer screen, click **Share Screens...** in the **Call** pull-down menu. The contact will see the caller's computer screen.

6. To stop sharing the computer screen, click **Call>Stop Sharing Screen**.
7. Click the **End call** button to end the videoconference.

End call   8. Click **Skype>Sign Out** to log out of Skype.

Note: closing the window does not log you out, nor does it close Skype. Skype runs in the background until you end the program. To do so, right-click on the Skype button on the taskbar, and then click **Quit Skype** in the shortcut menu.

Streaming Media

In the beginning days of the Internet, any content had to be completely downloaded before the user could start viewing it. Media files are generally very large. Waiting for a full download could take a long time, especially on mobile devices. **Streaming** is a technology that allows a multimedia file to begin playing before it is fully downloaded. The total download time is calculated and the content starts to be delivered at a point where the download will be able keep pace with the display. In an ideal situation, the final packet will be delivered exactly when the viewer needs it. However, often there are pauses in the stream as the computer *buffers*, or downloads more of the file.

Some multimedia transmissions are not prerecorded, but rather are sent via live streaming. Live audio is unrecorded sound. Live audio streaming is a technology that sends audio over the Internet in real time. The audio is not saved to a file before transmission. Of course, these streaming events can be saved to a file at the same time as the transmission for later download and playback. These archived events are often referred to as *podcasts*.

Streaming technology has made it possible to view full-length films and television shows in near-real-time on the computer and on mobile devices. Streaming technologies are used by vendors such as Netflix, Hulu, and Amazon Prime.

Computing Fundamentals
2.10
Living Online
8.1.1, 8.1.2, 8.1.3

Some Internet connections may not have enough bandwidth to support streaming video without experiencing buffering.

Blogs

Some people create a website where they can express their opinions on topics that interest them. This type of website is called a **blog**. The word is derived from the word pair *web log*. Collectively, all blogs are known as the *blogosphere*. There are several ways to get information from a blog:

- visit the website that hosts the blog
- subscribe to a mailing list for notifications from the blog
- follow the blogger on Twitter or other social media

Some blogs allow a place to make comments and respond to what is being said. If you post a comment, make it polite constructive criticism or a positive response. Posting in a negative or ill-mannered way is known as **flaming**. It is most inappropriate and may harm your reputation.

 Living Online **5.3**

 Living Online **3.2.3**

 Living Online **4.1.4**

Forums

A **forum** is a platform for holding discussions and for asking and responding to questions. Forums tend to be slightly more organized than blogs. Forums are usually focused on a very narrow topic, such as a particular video game. In general, forums are informative in intent. Peer pressure from forum members is used to keep discussions on topic.

A web-based search engine dedicated to locating forums is boardreader.com, as shown in Figure 15-11. The name references the origin of forums: bulletin boards. Bulletin boards were popular in the early days of the Internet as a way to post information for others to see. Like forums, they tended to be focused on a particular topic.

RSS

Really simple syndication (RSS) is a method of subscribing to automatic delivery of web content. Suppose you have favorite news sites or follow particular blogs. You need to go to those sites and "pull" the new posts to your computer. This is called a *pull technology*. RSS automatically delivers all new posts to your favorite sites. This is called a *push technology* because the posts are sent directly to you, or "pushed" to you. They show up in your RSS reader in near-real-time. Microsoft Outlook provides an RSS reader embedded as a feature. If a website has an RSS feed, a hyperlinked icon should appear on the page to indicate this, as shown in Figure 15-12.

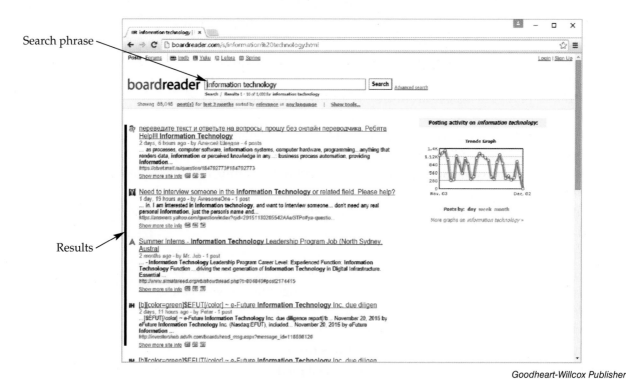

Search phrase

Results

Goodheart-Willcox Publisher

Figure 15-11. The website boardreader.com is a search engine that can be used to locate Internet forums.

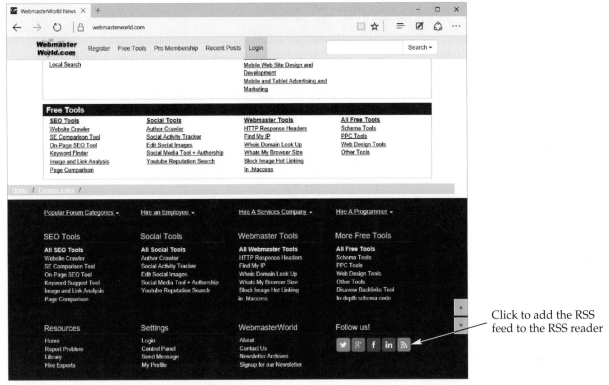

Click to add the RSS feed to the RSS reader

Figure 15-12. The RSS icon on a website means you can subscribe to the RSS feed.

HANDS-ON EXAMPLE 15.2.3

SUBSCRIBING TO AN RSS FEED

An RSS feed is a convenient way to subscribe to a blog. Microsoft Outlook can be set up to receive RSS feeds.

1. Launch Microsoft Outlook 2013.
2. Click **Options** on the **File** tab of the ribbon. The **Outlook Options** dialog box is displayed.
3. Click **Advanced** on the left-hand side of the dialog box, and scroll down to **RSS Feeds** on the right-hand side.
4. Check the **Synchronize RSS Feeds to the Common Feed List (CFL) in Windows** check box, and then click the **OK** button to apply the setting.

HANDS-ON EXAMPLE 15.2.3 (CONTINUED)

5. Right-click on RSS Feeds branch in the navigation pane, and click **Add a New RSS Feed...** in the shortcut menu, as shown.

Click to add a new RSS feed

Right-click

6. In the **New RSS Feed** dialog box, enter http://www.webmasterworld.com/feeds/forum45.rss. This is the address of a news feed from the Webmaster World forum for smartphone, wireless, and mobile technologies.
7. Click the **Add** button, and then in the message that appears click the **Yes** button to confirm the new feed. The RSS name is displayed under the RSS Feeds branch, and messages begin appearing in the inbox.

Online Calendars

Computing Fundamentals
1.6.1, 1.6.2

Living Online
4.1.1, 4.1.2,
4.2.1, 4.3, 4.4

GS5

An online calendar is a web-based application that can be used by one or more persons to record the dates and times for events, meetings, and appointments as well as add notes and reminders. Each online calendar uses a slightly different method for adding an appointment, but the most common features are the name of the appointment, the location, the time, and the day or days. It is possible to create a recurring appointment or block out the entire day for an appointment. A recurring appointment is one that happens over and over at the same time and on the same day, such as every Monday at 1:00 pm.

Most online calendars can be shared with others. Choices offered may be to share with everyone or only with specific people. Sharing only with specific people is the most secure option. This is usually done by sending an invite to the person with whom you want to share the calendar. Smartphones can display data from several shared calendars. To add a feed from a shared public calendar, visit the calendar and look for the option to add feed to your calendar. You can subscribe to multiple calendars. Each one will appear in a different color to help you keep track.

Notifications are brief messages sent to the display of a mobile device. Apps such as the calendar may send a notification of an upcoming appointment. The e-mail app may send a notification that a new message has arrived in the inbox. These messages can be configured to activate the vibrate feature or be displayed even while the screen is locked.

15.2 SECTION REVIEW

 ## CHECK YOUR UNDERSTANDING

1. What is the basic principle underlying cellular technology?
2. What was the first generation of cell phone technology?
3. How many characters can be included in an SMS message?
4. What is used to transfer an IM?
5. How does streaming function?

IC3 CERTIFICATION PRACTICE

The following question is a sample of the types of questions presented on the IC3 exam.

1. To send an IM, you must be:
   A. over 18 years old.
   B. a member of AOL.
   C. connected to the Internet.
   D. All of the above.

 ## BUILD YOUR VOCABULARY

As you progress through this course, develop a personal IT glossary. This will help you build your vocabulary and prepare you for a career. Write a definition for each of the following terms and add it to your IT glossary.

blog
carrier
cell
cellular technology
flaming
forum
instant messaging (IM)
multimedia messaging
   service (MMS)

really simple syndication
   (RSS)
short messaging service
   (SMS)
streaming
videoconferencing
Voice over Internet
   Protocol (VoIP)

SECTION 15.3

GOOD COMMUNICATION PRACTICES

Essential Question

Why are good communication practices important to the impact of social media on society?

One of the most significant changes in how people communicate was the rise of social media. Once used mainly by teens and college students, texting, tweeting, posting, and messaging are now mainstream communication methods. Television news shows respond to what is trending on Twitter. Facebook, Flickr, and Instagram are just a few of the social media websites that are part of everyday society.

Elena Elisseeva/Shutterstock.com

Etiquette has been a rule for personal social interactions for centuries. These rules govern what is deemed to be polite. While the principles of etiquette apply to online communication, there is an added concern. Online text-based communication does not provide the vocal inflections or facial expressions of the sender. Lacking these, it is easy to misinterpret intent.

LEARNING GOALS

After completing this section, you will be able to:
- Discuss the use of social media.
- Identify techniques for proper online communication.
- Demonstrate proper cell phone use.
- Describe how to collaborate with others through software.
- Explain the function of learning management systems.

TERMS

collaboration	libel
comment	online presence
cyberbullying	online status
digital footprint	slander
emoticon	social media
learning management system (LMS)	standard capitalization
	telepresence

Social Media

Social media is the tools of online communication that support creating, sharing, or exchanging information through websites and applications that promote interaction among people. A key characteristic of social media is "audience participation." The sites are constructed by the company that owns the site, but the content is delivered and managed by the users. Communication can be directed at one person or many.

Many people consider participating in social media a leisure activity. However, it has also become a serious business tool. For example, the news media very closely follow social media trends. Social media is the topic of many university research studies. Businesses and organizations use social media to promote products and services. Social media is also a way for businesses to gather customer feedback.

Living Online
5.1.1, 5.1.2, 9.3.1

Online Presence

Your online presence is how you represent yourself through social media, websites, blogs, and other Internet-based media, as shown in Figure 15-13. Any information about you that can be located with an online search is part of your online presence. Always be aware of what you make available on the Internet. There is a difference between personal online presence and professional online presence. Personal presence can be casual and fun. Professional presence speaks to your capability and can be used by clients and superiors to pre-judge your

Living Online
9.3.1, 9.4

FYI

Many employers will check an applicant's online presence as part of the hiring process.

Goodheart-Willcox Publisher

Figure 15-13. Many companies spend much time and money to create an online presence. Social media, such as Facebook and Twitter, is a common way to do this.

performance. It is poor practice to mix these in the same account. However, be aware that even your personal online presence may affect your professional online presence.

Many people are connected to social media sites all day. Many social media sites allow you to set your online status. Your **online status** is how other users will see your availability for immediate interaction. Options for online status usually are: online or offline, away, do not disturb, and invisible or visible. When the status is set to invisible, you are connected to your social media sites, but other users cannot see that you are connected.

Telepresence refers to the use of technology to help a person feel as if he or she is present with other people in a meeting or gathering at a different location. Videoconferencing and telecommuting are two activities supported by telepresence. In each case, a person is connected to a computer in one location and interacts in real time using video and voice with people or computer programs at remote locations.

Classification of Social Media Sites

Many social media sites have similar purposes, even if they may seem very different. However, there are some ways to categorize sites. In general, most social media sites will fall into one of these groups:

- social networking
- media sharing
- wikis
- social news

However, there are many other ways to classify social media sites as well.

Social Networking

The focus of social networking sites is interacting with friends; sharing personal news; and posting images, videos, and other web addresses of interest. For most of these sites, the service is free to the user, and the site is supported by advertising. Facebook, Myspace, and Twitter are examples of social networking sites.

A professional social networking site is LinkedIn. This is a tool used by professionals to share accomplishments, contact information, skill sets, and other information related to themselves or their companies. Job hunters as well as potential employers use this site for hiring people and for having professional conversations.

Some schools support local social media sites for their students. The site is monitored by administrators to prevent improper use of the site, and only students and teachers can access the site. This is an example of a *closed social media site.* An *open social media site,* such as Facebook or Myspace, can be accessed by everyone. A business can use the open-source, closed social media site Yammer to communicate and collaborate within its organization.

GS4 Living Online
3.2.2

GS5 Living Online
5.2.1

Media Sharing

On media-sharing sites, users may upload media, gain followers, and engage in discussions. The service is free to the casual user and supported by advertising. Flickr and YouTube are examples. Flickr offers 1 terabyte of storage for free and charges for using more space. Instagram is a social media site for sharing photos and video. Instagram is a blend of Facebook, where each user has a profile, and Twitter, where each user has followers and can follow other users. Instagram has been a part of Facebook since 2012.

Living Online
5.1.2

Wikis

On a wiki site, users contribute content and offer constructive criticism and modify other users' content. Examples of wikis are Wikipedia and The Vault, as shown in Figure 15-14. The Wikipedia site is an encyclopedia funded by venture capital and user donations. The Vault is a gaming wiki about the video game Fallout. It is supported by fans and advertising.

Living Online
5.3

Social News

A social news site contains user-uploaded stories. Examples of social news sites are Slashdot and Reddit. Slashdot is editor managed and supported by advertising. Reddit stories are ranked by reader reviews and scored. Users comment on each other's stories.

Ethics

Using Social Networking Media

Social networking media is used by organizations to reach existing customers and find new ones. Because it is readily available and easy to use, those who are writing communication for the organization must be ethical when using websites such as Facebook or Twitter for business purposes. Use good judgment and represent the company in a professional manner.

Goodheart-Willcox Publisher

Figure 15-14. Wikipedia is one of the best-known wikis. It is continuously edited.

GS5 Living Online
9.3.1

GS4 Living Online
4.1.5

Disadvantages of Social Media

Social media is very popular. It has caused a revolution in how people communicate. Many people engage in social media daily. Some people will check or contribute to social media every few minutes. However, there are some serious disadvantages to social media.

A disadvantage of social media is related to the ownership of the material you post. Most social media sites claim the right to use your content forever. Even if content is deleted, the backups and external storage of these sites maintain copies of it. Although the sites do not claim exclusive ownership, they have the right to use your material forever.

One aspect of social media is the ability to post and share comments. If anyone makes an untrue claim about another, a crime has been committed. **Slander** is speaking a false statement about someone that causes others to have a bad opinion of him or her. **Libel** is publishing (printing) a false statement about someone that causes others to have a bad opinion of him or her. Slander and libel can be considered crimes of defamation. It is important to choose words carefully when making comments about others, whether online or face-to-face.

Care must be taken to understand the rules for each social media site. What you post on the Internet never really goes away. For example, Facebook supports uploading and deleting of images. However, its terms of service give it the right to keep an archive copy of all images forever. A **digital footprint** is a data record of all of an individual's online activities. Even if you delete something you have posted on the Internet, it stays in your digital footprint. Always think before posting to social media sites or sending an e-mail. What you post online today could risk your future college and job opportunities. Postings of fun events may figure negatively when applying for jobs.

> ## FYI
>
> Discretion is always the better path when determining what to post, whether it is content or a comment.

HANDS-ON EXAMPLE 15.3.1

TERMS OF USE

Twitter is used by nearly 300 million people each month. Like all social media sites, Twitter has terms of service that outline its rights and the rights of users.

1. Launch a browser, and navigate to www.twitter.com.
2. If you are a user and currently logged in, log out.
3. At the bottom of the home page, click the **Terms** link. The Terms of Service page is displayed.
4. Read the first paragraph of section 5, Your Rights. Although the user maintains ownership of what is tweeted, it is not exclusive. Twitter assumes perpetual rights to use what you write.
5. Read the first paragraph of section 8, Restrictions on Content and Use of Services. Note what Twitter can do with your content.
6. Read the second paragraph of section 12C, Entire Agreement. Note how you can be bound by new terms of service.

Managing Profiles

A social media site provides each user with a profile when he or she signs up for the service. You can customize your profile on the site to suit your personality and needs. Each social media site you are a member of can have a different profile. Recall, it is important to present a profile that is appropriate for the site. A profile on a gaming site may be casual, but sites that represent you as a person should be clean and professional.

A username and password are required to log into social media sites. These are assigned when you sign up. It is important to use a different password for each site. That way, if one site is hacked, your other profiles are not affected. Also, be sure to log out of each social media site when you are done using it.

Facebook and Twitter accounts can be linked. By doing so, a post on one site automatically becomes a post on the other site. Many other social media sites can be similarly linked. This is common even for gaming sites.

Many video games have online play capability. To play online, you must create a profile like any other social media site. Some games support their own user profiles, such as Halo or Call of Duty. In other cases, the game uses a platform such as Steam to manage online activities. Steam is an online platform for distributing games and managing their digital rights. It also has a social media component where gamers can interact, including in-game chatting and voice communication, provided the game supports these features.

GS5 Living Online
9.3.2.1, 9.3.2.2, 9.3.2.3, 9.3.2.4

GS5 Computing Fundamentals
7.4.3.3

Online Communication

There is a distinct difference between oral and written communication. In most cases, except for formal speeches, oral communication is more relaxed. There also is the benefit of being able to hear inflections in the speaker's voice. In many cases, you can also see the person who is talking and pick up on nonverbal cues. No one can see the punctuation or the spelling of any of the words in a spoken conversation. However, proper grammar should be used. Written communication is expected to be correct in terms of spelling, punctuation, and grammar.

══ TITANS OF TECHNOLOGY ══

Mark Zuckerberg was writing computer programs in his early teens. He created a program that allowed communication between his family's computers. It functioned similar to an instant messaging system before AOL came out with Instant Messenger. In high school, he created a music player that learned what the user listened to. In college, Zuckerberg, together with his college roommates and fellow Harvard University students Eduardo Saverin, Andrew McCollum, Dustin Moskovitz, and Chris Hughes, launched Facebook from Harvard's dormitory rooms in 2004. Initially, it was only available to Harvard students. It was first expanded to other universities in the Boston area and then to other schools. In 2006, Facebook became available to anyone. The number of Facebook users worldwide reached a total of one billion in 2012. This number is rapidly growing.

GS4 Living Online
4.1.1, 4.1.3

FYI

Always proofread all written communication before sending it.

GS4 Living Online
4.1.2, 4.1.3

FYI

In a casual message, such as to a friend, it is okay to show emphasis by using all uppercase characters for a word.

Spelling, Punctuation, and Grammar

Most text applications have a dictionary and grammar rule base. This supports proper spelling, punctuation, and grammar. Items misspelled or misused are visually indicated by a red line or other eye-catching device, as shown in Figure 15-15. The user can then correct the errors.

Some applications have an autocorrect feature. The software determines from context what word is intended and automatically inserts it. However, the result is not always correct. This is especially true when sending text messages with a mobile device app. There often is no indication the autocorrect has taken place. This makes it very easy to send a written message that does not make sense.

Inflection and Tone

In the early days of electronic communication, it was not uncommon for a person to use all uppercase letters in the message. However, using all caps is considered rude. It is like shouting at the recipient. **Standard capitalization** involves using uppercase only for the first letter of the first word in a sentence, the first letter of all proper nouns, and acronyms. Remember, using all uppercase letters is considered shouting and is rude.

Humor is often verified by watching the speaker's facial expression or listening to the inflection in his or her voice. However, in written messages, there is no way to pick up on these cues. In order to ward off unintentional insults, emoticons were developed. An **emoticon** is a combination of keyboard characters used to represent a facial expression,

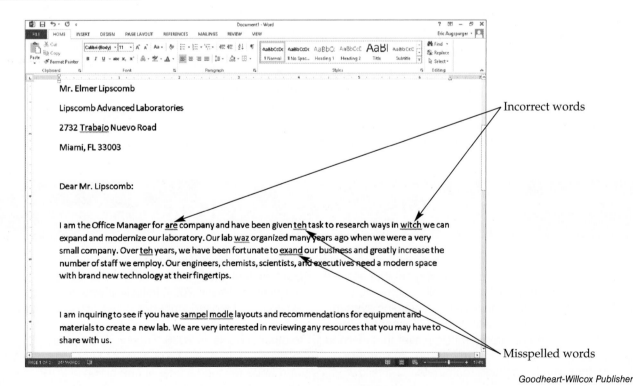

Goodheart-Willcox Publisher

Figure 15-15. Most text applications have a way to indicate misspelled words and words that are correctly spelled, but incorrectly used.

as shown in Figure 15-16. The classic emoticon is the smiley face, which is created with a colon and a closing parenthesis. Emoticons help to convey intent. Today, it is possible to incorporate actual emoticon graphics, sometimes called emoji, into a message.

Emoticon	:)	:(	;)	:-D
Meaning	happy	sad	wink	laughing
Emoji				

Goodheart-Willcox Publisher; CoolKengzz/Shutterstock.com

Figure 15-16. Emotion can be communicated in written messages with emoticons and emoji.

Keypad Shortcuts

The first cell phones that could be used for texting did not contain an alphabetic keypad. They also did not have voice-to-text capability. On these phones, text was entered by pressing the number keys multiple times. For example, the number 4 key can be used to enter the letters G, H, and I, as shown in Figure 15-17. Pressing the key one time enters the number 4 as text. Pressing the key two times enters the letter G. Pressing the key three times enters the letter H. Pressing the key four times enters the letter I.

Cyberbullying

It is important to understand the far-reaching impact of your online actions. You may post something that is hurtful to someone else. However, once a message or image is posted, it can be difficult to remove it.

Cyberbullying is harassment that takes place using electronic technology. It includes using social media, text messages, or e-mails to harass or scare a person with hurtful words or pictures. Examples of cyberbullying include mean text messages or e-mails; rumors sent by e-mail or posted on social networking sites; and posting embarrassing pictures, videos, websites, or fake profiles. A victim of cyberbullying cannot be physically seen or touched by the bully. However, this does not mean the person cannot be harmed by the actions. Cyberbullying is unethical and the offender can be prosecuted. Several states have passed antibullying laws.

GS5 Living Online
5.4.1, 5.4.2

GS4 Living Online
4.1.4

FYI

Cyberbullying is not a joking matter. If you suspect that someone is being cyberbullied, report it.

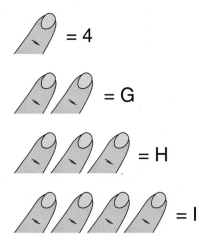

1	2 ABC	3 DEF
4 GHI	5 JKL	6 MNO
7 PQRS	8 TUV	9 WXYZ
*	0	#

= 4
= G
= H
= I

Goodheart-Willcox Publisher

Figure 15-17. Pressing the number 4 enters different data depending on how many times the button is pressed.

Cyberbullying is especially dangerous because of its relentlessness. Those who are cyberbullied are often also physically bullied. However, cyberbullying goes on twenty-four hours a day, seven days a week. It can reach those being bullied when they are alone and without support.

The federal government created the www.StopBullying.gov website to educate people about this problem. According to this website, six percent of students in grades 6–12 experienced cyberbullying during the school year studied. The report is Student Victimization in US Schools published by the US Department of Education. Additionally, 16 percent of high school students (grades 9–12) were electronically bullied in the past year according to the report Youth Risk Behavior Surveillance Survey from the Centers for Disease Control and Prevention.

HANDS-ON EXAMPLE 15.3.2

CYBERBULLYING

It is important to understand what cyberbullying is and the negative impact it can have. Protect yourself from cyberbullying, and help to protect others.

1. Launch a browser, and navigate to the www.StopBullying.gov website.
2. Using the website menu, click **Cyberbullying** and then **What is cyberbullying**, or use the search function to search for what is cyberbullying.
3. Watch the video on the web page.
4. Click the **Technology and Youth-Protecting Your Child from Electronic Aggression** link. The Centers for Disease Control and Prevention website is displayed.
5. Click the **Technology and Youth: Protecting Your Child from Electronic Aggression** link, or use the search function to locate this PDF.
6. Read the two-page report.
7. Identify the five examples of electronic aggression provided in the report. If you have experienced any of these actions, show this report to your parents so they may take action.

Cell Phone Use

A recent survey found that many people carry their cell phones at all times during the day and put them down only to sleep. Another survey conducted by a marketing firm found that the average person with a smartphone will use it 1500 times a week. That is over 200 times a day. With this constant access to communication, it is difficult to remember that a phone call is, by its very nature, an interruption to what you are doing.

Social Use

People in social situations find it offensive for a phone to ring in the middle of a movie or during a conversation. The proper etiquette is to keep the phone on silent when in a group of people. Let calls go to voice mail when you are engaged in another conversation. Additionally, some people will conduct personal conversations in public on a cell phone without regard to those around them. Talking about personal issues can be annoying to nearby listeners. Also, talking loudly into a cell phone is disruptive to social situations. At the very least, it is rude.

Emergencies are a special case, but they still must be handled with proper etiquette. If you are expecting an emergency call, politely ask permission to check the sender of the call. If it is the emergency call, excuse yourself from the conversation and leave the room to take the call.

Business Use

Computing Fundamentals
1.4.6, 1.4.7

In many cases, it is important to immediately answer a business call. However, excuse yourself from the situation you are in, whether it is a meeting or a social situation, to take the call. If it is okay to allow the call to go to voice mail, do so.

Be certain the outgoing message you have recorded for your voice mail is professional and brief. The message should identify yourself and your business. Ask for the caller's name and a return-call phone number. You may also include a brief message, such as directing the caller to another person for immediate assistance. If a personal phone is also used as the business phone, record a professional outgoing message over a friendly, casual message.

Voice Mail Messages

Computing Fundamentals
1.4.5, 1.4.7, 1.4.8

When leaving a voice mail message, be brief and clear. State your name, a return-call phone number, and a clear message. Include why the person needs to act and what is expected of him or her. Speak slowly and

StockLite/Shutterstock.com

It is important to follow proper cell phone etiquette at all times, but especially in business situations. When on the job, you represent your employer. Any positive or negative impression you make reflects on your employer.

clearly when providing the number. Pause between the three parts of the number. Most people cannot write down a phone number as quickly as other people can say it. Many people choose to repeat the phone number to give the person a second chance to hear all of the numbers without having to replay the voice mail message.

Collaboration

Collaboration is working together on a project with at least one other person. Working together at a distance has never been easier. Basic computer hardware is able to support many collaboration tools: voice, text, cloud-based file sharing, video, audio, whiteboards, screen sharing, conferencing software, and version control software. Most of these programs are easy to use. In many cases, there are free alternatives to for-purchase software. Add cloud printing and 3D printing, and the whole package is there.

Each of these technologies has been available for some time. However, current hardware and transmission speeds can make it seem as if the collaborators are in the same room. The online collaboration effort has spawned a number of startup companies and new divisions of established software companies.

Common cloud-storage technologies are examples of this development. Google Drive, SharePoint, and Dropbox each offers a common location to share files. Each is password protected and provides options for sharing files with others.

Another technology developed to support collaboration is videoconferencing, discussed earlier. Many videoconferencing sites offer the ability to edit a document simultaneously on the web with all persons in the conference.

Online collaboration presents some challenges. With so many people working in the same documents, data can be lost. Documents may be deleted or overwritten. If multiple versions of the same document exist, which version to use may not be clear. Tight control over permissions and access as well as routinely backing up files is important to reduce problems.

Features of Collaboration Software

There are common features of collaboration software, as shown in Figure 15-18. Most try to recreate an interactive experience, similar to Twitter. Not all packages support the same features. Free versions are often available with a premium paid for extra features.

Choosing Collaboration Software

The most important consideration in selecting collaboration software is how it will be used. Not all projects will require all of the features listed in Figure 15-18. Questions to ask include the following.
- How many people will be involved?
- If a large number of people are on the team, are you able to make subgroups?

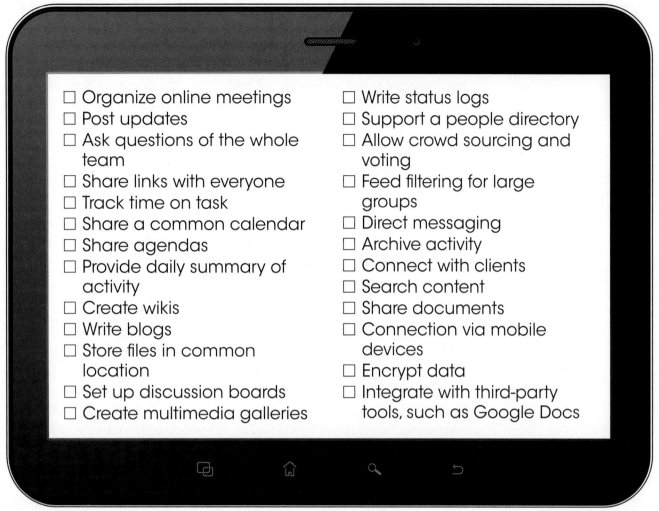

Figure 15-18. Common features of collaboration software.

- How are file versions maintained?
- Will many people be working on the same file?
- Will documents need to be shared?
- Are workers in different offices or different locations?
- Will there be a time zone conflict?
- Will real-time delivery of images be needed during a videoconference?

Collaborating Using Microsoft Office

GS4 Key Applications
6.1.1, 6.1.2, 6.1.3

Working on the same document can be confusing if users do not know what the last person did to update the file. What if the changes need to be reversed? Does the collaboration feature allow users to reinstate deleted material? As discussed in Chapter 7, Microsoft Office has a tracked changes feature to monitor the alterations each user makes. After all changes are suggested, the person in charge of the document accepts or rejects the changes.

A **comment** is a note inserted into the document, much like a sticky note. It is a communication tool among collaborators. One person may make a comment to the other collaborators, but the note is not incorporated into the main text of the document. Other collaborators may respond to the comment and make other comments of their own. Comments can be printed or the document can be printed without the comments.

GS5

Computing Fundamentals
6.4.2

Living Online
6.4.1

Learning Management Systems

Online learning is an alternative to face-to-face learning, but is also used to extend classroom learning as a blended class. Learning management systems were developed to help create an online learning environment. A **learning management system (LMS)** is a platform for managing digital content, students, and records as well as providing collaboration features. Examples are Blackboard, Moodle, and Desire2Learn.

An entire course or a portion of it, called a module, can be offered using LMS technology. Lessons are presented in text, video, and hyperlinks to external websites as well as other multimedia formats. Discussions are a key to learning in the physical classroom. Discussion boards or forums provide this key learning component on an LMS. Students can receive assistance through e-mail and chat contact with the instructor. This is important if the class is online only, not a blended class.

Students follow the curriculum outlined in the LMS, complete the work, submit documents for assignments, and answer online forms for quizzes and tests. Submitted documents are physically graded by the instructor. If online quizzes and tests are programmed to be automatically graded, the scores are automatically generated and can be auto-tracked by the student. Grades are entered in the LMS gradebook, which allows the instructor to easily track student progress. Each student can review his or her own progress at any time. Instructors also can modify content, adjust the organization of material, and run statistical reports on the class.

15.3 | SECTION REVIEW

CHECK YOUR UNDERSTANDING

1. What is the difference between libel and slander?
2. Why should all caps not be used in a message?
3. What is cyberbullying?
4. If you are speaking with another person and you receive a cell phone call, what should you do?
5. If a note is inserted into the document, much like a sticky note, what is it called?

IC3 CERTIFICATION PRACTICE

The following question is a sample of the types of questions presented on the IC3 exam.

1. Using all uppercase letters in an e-mail or text is considered what?
   A. formal
   B. exact
   C. shouting
   D. humorous

BUILD YOUR VOCABULARY

As you progress through this course, develop a personal IT glossary. This will help you build your vocabulary and prepare you for a career. Write a definition for each of the following terms and add it to your IT glossary.

collaboration	libel
comment	online presence
cyberbullying	online status
digital footprint	slander
emoticon	social media
learning management system (LMS)	standard capitalization
	telepresence

15 REVIEW AND ASSESSMENT

Chapter Summary

Section 15.1
Electronic Mail

- The e-mail client is the program used to create and send the message, while the e-mail server handles the storing and delivery of the message. There are several protocols associated with e-mail, including IMAP, POP, and SMTP.

- Each user of an e-mail system must have a unique account username, and access is restricted. A credential is a record that saves the authentication criteria required to connect to a service, such as e-mail or other database-supported resource.

- Complete sentences, correct spelling, and proper grammar are required in e-mail communication. Use Standard English in all communication.

- Most e-mail clients have several features to help manage communication. Automated features, personal folders, and filters can be used to manage communication.

Section 15.2
Real-Time Communication

- A land-line telephone is hard wired to the network via wires and optical fibers. A cell phone is not hard wired to the network. It is simply a computer-controlled radio. Cellular technology is based on wireless transmissions distributed over groups of geographic areas called cells. There have been several generations of cell phone technology.

- Cellular channels provide for transmission of voice, text, video, and audio. There are many protocols and

technologies that allow this, including SMS, IM, and MMS.

Section 15.3
Good Communication Practices

- Social media involves creating, sharing, or exchanging information through websites and applications that promote interaction among people. Your online presence is how you represent yourself through social media, websites, blogs, and other Internet-based media.

- Written communication is expected to be correct in terms of spelling, punctuation, and grammar. Standard capitalization should be used in communication.

- The proper etiquette for cell phone use in public is to have the phone on silent. Let calls go to voice mail if you are engaged in a conversation with someone else.

- Collaboration is working together on a project with at least one other person. Basic computer hardware is able to support many collaboration tools, making working together at a distance easy.

- A learning management system (LMS) is a platform for managing digital content, students, and records as well as providing collaboration features. It is used to create an online learning environment, either online only or a blended classroom.

Now that you have finished this chapter, see what you know about information technology by scanning the QR code to take the chapter posttest. If you do not have a smartphone, visit www.g-wlearning.com.

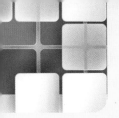

Chapter 15 Test

Multiple Choice

Select the best response.

1. Which part of an e-mail message contains information necessary to ensure the proper delivery of the message?
   A. message body
   B. message header
   C. message envelope
   D. message address

2. Which automated e-mail feature sends a reply to *every* e-mail message received?
   A. read receipt
   B. out-of-office message
   C. auto respond
   D. auto forwarding

3. How many generations of cell phone technology have been in use?
   A. one
   B. two
   C. three
   D. four

4. What is a key characteristic of social media?
   A. audience participation
   B. multimedia
   C. flaming
   D. cell phone use

5. Which of the following should *not* be used in electronic messages?
   A. all uppercase letters
   B. standard capitalization
   C. emoticons
   D. All of the above.

Completion

Complete the following sentences with the correct word(s).

6. The part of an e-mail message that most frequently contains malware is a(n) _____.

7. _____ is one unwanted e-mail message sent to a large number of users or multiple identical unwanted messages sent to a single e-mail address.

8. One cell tower typically serves an area of _____ in size.

9. A(n) _____ is a data record of all of an individual's online activities.

10. A(n) _____ is a feature that provides the ability to leave a note on a document for another collaborator.

Matching

Match the correct term with its definition.

A. username
B. netiquette
C. SMS and IM
D. VoIP
E. social media

11. Technologies that allow text messages.

12. Online platforms that encourage interaction and sharing.

13. Online identity of the account holder.

14. Guidelines for appropriate behavior on the Internet.

15. Internet-based telephone.

Application and Extension of Knowledge

1. Research the differences and similarities between the IMAP and POP e-mail protocols. Decide if you feel one appears to be better than the other. Develop a slide presentation that explains the differences, similarities, and your position on which one is better.

2. Investigate the features and functions of online chat rooms. Are chat rooms social media? Prepare to defend your position in a class discussion.

3. Visit the Wikipedia page that provides a list of emoticons. List five that have been introduced as graphics. Identify one that is new to you. Write a one-page paper describing the difference between Western, Eastern, and Unicode emoticons.

4. Research free collaboration tools. Select four of them, and identify the features of each. Make a comparison chart of features. Which ones are online and which ones can be installed on your computer? Which one would you choose? Write one paragraph to go along with the chart describing why you would make your choice.

5. Review the information on netiquette in this chapter. Conduct additional research on netiquette and cell phone manners. Can you identify any items that were not discussed in this chapter? How important do you think these are? Create a list of guidelines for proper netiquette and cell phone use. Develop a plan for enforcing these guidelines, and write one page describing the plan.

Online Activities

Complete the following activities, which will help you learn, practice, and expand your knowledge and skills.

Certification Practice. Complete the certification practice test for this chapter.

Vocabulary. Practice vocabulary for this chapter using the e-flash cards, matching activity, and vocabulary game until you are able to recognize their meanings.

Communication Skills

College and Career Readiness

Reading. After reading this chapter, what insights did you gain about social media that could be applied in a future career? Write several paragraphs describing what you learned.

Listening. Active listeners know when to comment and when to remain silent. Practice your listening skills while your instructor presents this chapter. Participate when appropriate and build on his or her ideas. Respond appropriately to the presentation.

Writing. It is important for an employee to apply both technical and academic skills in the workplace. Understanding social media is a workplace skill that may be applied each day in personal and work life. Write a paragraph describing why understanding social media is considered a workplace skill. How do you think that understanding social media will help you in your professional career?

Internet Research

E-mail. Research the advantages and disadvantages of using e-mail for business purposes using various Internet resources. Did your research result in information that was new to you? Share your lists with your classmates.

Teamwork

Working with a partner, list different social media sites. Next to each site, write a short description of how it can be used in a

professional way by an IT company or its employees, citing real-world examples for each description. Share your results with the class.

Portfolio Development

College and Career Readiness

Introduction. As you assemble your final portfolio, compose an introduction that gives an overall snapshot of who you are. This will be the first page of the portfolio that sets the stage for your presentation, so you want to make a good impression. Tell the reader who you are, your goals, and any biographical information that is relevant. You may want to highlight information by making references to sections or page numbers. There may be a website or URL to direct the reader to examples or documents of importance. In addition to the items you have already collected, there are some additional ones that you might include.

- *Résumé.* An updated résumé may be appropriate for the situation. If you have already submitted a résumé separately, it is not necessary to include.

- *Letters of recommendation.* If you have letters from instructors, employers, or others who have praised your performance, include these in this introductory section.

- *Photo.* Photos are not required. However, a photo will help the interviewer remember who you are after the interview when evaluating potential candidates.

- *Table of contents.* A table of contents will give a professional appearance to your documents. Consider title pages for each section to add clarity.

CTSOs

Proper Attire. Some Career and Technical Student Organizations (CTSOs) require appropriate business attire from all entrants and those attending the competition. This requirement is in keeping with the mission of CTSOs: to prepare students for professional careers in business. To be sure that the attire you have chosen to wear at the competition is in accordance with event requirements, complete the following activities.

1. Visit the organization's website and look for the most current dress code.

2. The dress code requirements are very detailed and gender specific. Some CTSOs may require a chapter blazer to be worn during the competition.

3. Do a dress rehearsal when practicing for your event. Are you comfortable in the clothes you have chosen? Do you present a professional appearance?

4. In addition to the kinds of clothes you can wear, be sure the clothes are clean and pressed. You do not want to undermine your appearance or event performance with wrinkled clothes that may distract judges.

5. Make sure your hair is neat and worn in a conservative style. If you are a male, you should be clean-shaven. Again, you do not want anything about your appearance detracting from your performance.

6. As far in advance of the event as possible, share your clothing choice with your organization's advisor to make sure you are dressed appropriately.

16

SECURITY, PRIVACY, AND SAFETY

SECTIONS

16.1 PREVENTING COMPUTER THREATS

16.2 IDENTITY PROTECTION AND ETHICAL BEHAVIOR

16.3 RESTRICTING ACCESS TO PERSONAL INFORMATION

CHECK YOUR IT IQ

Before you begin this chapter, see what you already know about information technology by scanning the QR code to take the chapter pretest. If you do not have a smartphone, visit www.g-wlearning.com.

The President of the United States has declared that the "cyber threat is one of the most serious economic and national security challenges we face as a nation." Because of the threat, people who have advanced computer skills are in high demand to fill thousands of cybersecurity jobs. Recent estimates suggest that the demand for cybersecurity experts is growing at a rate twelve times that of the overall job market and more than three times the overall pace of IT jobs. Master and doctorate cybersecurity degrees are now being offered in programs known as "information assurance."

However, the job of improving computer security is ultimately the responsibility of each and every computer user, and especially those users who connect to a network or to the Internet. There will always be a struggle between those who try to crack into computer systems and files and those who need to protect those systems. Everybody should know how to use computers with confidence and relative safety. This chapter discusses how to prevent computer threats, how to protect personal data, and how to promote general safe practices for computer users.

College and Career Readiness

Reading Prep. Arrange a study session to read the chapter with a classmate. After you read each section independently, stop and tell each other what you think the main points are in the section. Continue with each section until you finish the chapter.

IC3 CERTIFICATION OBJECTIVES

GS5

Computing Fundamentals

Domain 7.0 Security
   Objective 7.1 Know credential management best practices
   Objective 7.2 Know the basic threats to security of computers, data, and identity
   Objective 7.3 Understand the implications of monitoring software (surveillance)
   Objective 7.4 Understand connecting to secured vs. unsecured network (wired and wireless)
   Objective 7.5 Know the use of and importance of antivirus software
   Objective 7.6 Know the use of firewalls and basic settings
   Objective 7.7 Know e-commerce interactions and best practices

Living Online

Domain 1.0 Internet (navigation)
   Objective 1.1 Understand what the Internet is

GS4

Computing Fundamentals

Domain 3.0 Computer software and concepts
   Objective 3.4 Software tools
Domain 4.0 Troubleshooting
   Objective 4.1 Software

Living Online

Domain 2.0 Networking concepts
   Objective 2.1 Internet connection
Domain 4.0 Digital citizenship
   Objective 4.2 Legal and responsible use of computers
Domain 5.0 Safe computing
   Objective 5.1 Secure online communication or activity

SECTION 16.1

PREVENTING COMPUTER THREATS

Essential Question

What impact do computer threats have on our economy?

Protection of digital data will continue to require a combination of technologically advanced hardware, frequently updated software programs, and safe practices and procedures. Not only do you need to have the equipment, applications, and cyber-protection programs, you need to know how to properly use these items. Ultimately, it is the individual computer user who is responsible for cybersecurity.

Users also need to ensure their cyber behavior helps, rather than hurts, their own cybersecurity. Regardless of the equipment and software, the actions of computer users are largely responsible for failures to protect computer data. When devices are recycled, care must be taken to remove all data. This section discusses how to prevent computer threats and how to protect stored data.

nmedia/Shutterstock.com

TERMS 📤

adware

antivirus software

bot

cache

censorship

completely automated public Turing test to tell computers and humans apart (CAPTCHA)

computer virus

computer worm

cookies

data vandalism

hacking

malware

phishing

pop-up

ransomware

scareware

social engineering

spyware

Trojan horse

LEARNING GOALS

After completing this section, you will be able to:

- Identify types of computer threats.
- Discuss Internet security protocols.
- Explain how to protect stored data.

Computer Threats

There are many types of threats to computer systems and computer users. Malware most frequently finds its way into a computer as executable code hidden in another program. Often the computer user does not find out about the infection until long after a successful attack. Other threats come from phishing, data vandalism, cookies, and computer hacking.

Malware

Malware is software that intentionally performs actions to disrupt the operation of a computer system, collect private information, or otherwise harm the computer or user. The word *malware* comes from "malicious software," meaning software that intends to harm. Malware is a broad category of harmful software. Some threats falling under malware are:

- computer viruses;
- computer worms;
- Trojan horses;
- spyware;
- adware;
- scareware; and
- ransomware.

A **computer virus** consists of computer code carried in another program that can replicate itself in order to corrupt or otherwise harm either data files or the software used to process these files. A **computer worm** is similar to a virus. However, a worm is a standalone computer program that replicates itself in order to spread to other computers. A **Trojan horse** is a program that invites the user to run it while concealing malicious code that will be executed.

Spyware is software that secretly collects a user's data and behavior. Spyware may activate a webcam, log keystrokes, collect login passwords, collect bank and credit card information, monitor Internet habits, or create tailored pop-up ads. To avoid spyware, follow the security practices outlined in Figure 16-1. Spyware is most commonly used for advertising. When used in this manner, it is usually called adware.

Adware is software that creates advertisements designed to drive the user to another website. The other site may be useful, misleading, harmful, or just distracting. Adware is famous for using cookies to track user activity.

Scareware is software designed to cause enough anxiety so the computer user leaps at the chance to opt for a poor choice. An example is a message that warns the user of a virus infection and offers a free antivirus computer scan. However, the "scan" actually installs malicious software. Ransomware is similar to scareware. However, **ransomware** encrypts files or blocks the user's access to programs until the user pays to unlock them.

GS5 Computing Fundamentals
7.2.1, 7.2.2, 7.2.3, 7.3

GS4 Computing Fundamentals
4.1.3

FYI

A malware attack may occur when the user downloads seemingly harmless data from the Internet or transfers files from a shared flash drive.

GS4 Living Online
5.1.2

Activity	Action and Reason
Pop-up dialog boxes	Do not click links within pop-up dialog boxes. Just clicking within the dialog box or a "close" button within the window may result in spyware being installed. Instead, close the pop-up dialog box by clicking on the standard close button (X) in the upper-right corner of the title bar.
Pop-up windows on websites	These are windows created using HTML or other website-formatting language. They can be recognized because they do not look like standard dialog boxes generated by the operating system. Often, all parts of a pop-up window, including what appears to be a standard close button (X), will activate spyware. Try pressing the [Esc] key to close the window or close the browser window.
Unexpected dialog boxes	Be suspicious of unexpected dialog boxes that ask whether you want to run a particular program or perform another type of task. Close the dialog box by clicking the standard close button (X) in the title bar.
Links offering antispyware software	These links may actually install the spyware it claims to be eliminating. Only install antispyware from the developer's website, not from a third-party site.

Goodheart-Willcox Publisher

Figure 16-1. Good practices for safe use of the Internet and the World Wide Web.

Social Engineering

Computing Fundamentals
7.2.4

Distributors of malware often rely on social engineering. **Social engineering** involves manipulative techniques designed to lure unwary computer users into launching an infected file or opening a link to an infected website. Social engineering comes in many forms, such as:

- invitation to open an attached love letter or a notice of a traffic ticket;
- e-mail that imitates technical messages issued by the user's e-mail server, perhaps suggesting that storage has been exceeded and must be reduced immediately;
- message that claims to have been sent from Microsoft, perhaps saying that the attachment contains a patch that will remove Windows vulnerabilities;
- offer to reveal scandalous information on a famous person or to expand on an exciting news story;
- bank notice asking the customer to confirm account numbers or access codes; and
- attractively named files that entice the user to download them.

Attractively named files may include names such as PasswordHacker.exe, MicrosoftCDKeyGenerator.exe, JobsPayingMillions.exe, PlayStationEmulator.exe, or FreeInternetAccess.exe. Since the offer is often for something unethical or illegal, victims may not report the incident to their company or organization or to a law enforcement agency. In such cases, the cybercriminal has used a form of social engineering to deter the victim from reporting the abuse.

Cookies

Cookies are small text files that websites put on the computer hard disk drive when a user visits the websites. These are used to identify users. Cookies are often used to prepare customized web pages for the user. On many e-commerce sites, cookies are required to keep track of items in the shopping cart. Many password-protected websites also require cookies to keep the user logged in.

Cookies are also used to target the user with advertisements. For example, a user may search the Internet for "green fudge recipes". The search engine places a cookie on the user's computer containing this information. Then, the user goes to a website for the daily news, and ads for green fudge show up in a sidebar. The news site has used the cookie from the search engine to target the ad to the user. By selling cookies, the search engine generates revenue. While this use of cookies is not a threat to the computer system, it does represent collecting information about the user.

Computing Fundamentals
GS5 7.4.3.2
Living Online
1.1.3.2
GS4 Living Online
5.1.2

Cache

Speed of downloading material from the Internet is improved when frequently repeated material is temporarily stored on the computer's hard drive. The location of these files is called the **cache** (pronounced *cash*). For example, a company's logo may appear on each page of the website. Instead of having to download that image file each time a new page is displayed, the browser can retrieve it from the cache. Most browsers have controls that allow users to dictate how long a cached file is retained before it is deleted or downloaded again, called refreshing, from the website.

Computing Fundamentals
GS5 7.4.3.2
Living Online
1.1.3.3

Cookies are also cached on the hard drive. As cookies may contain personally identifiable information, routinely clear (empty) the cache, especially when using a public computer. Even when not using a public computer, it is wise to clear the cache (browser history) and clear cookies on a regular basis, especially if other people also have access to the same machine. Clearing the cache can also fix pages that freeze or do not finish loading, pages containing old content, or online applications (like games) that do not respond. Since clearing the cache deletes cookies, this can fix sign-in problems and eliminate error messages about setting user cookies.

The process for clearing a cache or cookies varies greatly depending on which browser is being used. As an example of clearing the cache, here is how to do so for Microsoft Edge:

1. Launch Microsoft Edge, and click the **More actions** button.
2. Click **Settings** in the menu.
3. In the menu that appears, under **Clear browsing data**, click the **Choose what to clear** button.
4. In the menu that appears, check the **Cookies and saved data** and **Cached data and files** check boxes. There are other categories that can be cleared as well.

5. Click the **Clear** button in the menu. Wait until the message **All clear!** appears at the top of the menu.

6. Click the **More actions** button to close the menu.

The downside of clearing the cache is that saved user names and passwords will be deleted and must then be reentered. However, the upside is that browser will work more efficiently and privacy will be improved.

Pop-ups

In terms of web browsing, a **pop-up** is a message or window that appears on top of or under the page you are viewing. Pop-ups that appear under the page are usually called *pop-unders*. Many pop-ups are considered spam and may be designed to transmit malware. There are third-party pop-up blockers, but all modern Internet browsers contain this feature already built in. The method for controlling the pop-up blocker is different in each browser, and each browser offers different options concerning the degree of pop-up protection. Here is how pop-ups can be controlled in Microsoft Edge:

1. Launch Microsoft Edge, and click the **More actions** button.

2. Click **Settings** in the menu.

3. In the menu that appears, click the **View advanced settings** button.

4. In the menu that appears, click the **Block pop-ups** button so it is on.

5. Click the **More actions** button to close the menu.

Phishing

Phishing is an attempt to get sensitive information by appearing as a harmless request. For example, a user may be told he or she has won a special prize or qualified for a no-cost introductory offer. The offer states all that is necessary is to fill out a survey. However, the survey requests sensitive information. Some information about a person that phishing scams commonly try to get includes:

- full name;
- employer's name;
- address;
- phone number;
- year of birth;
- credit card number; and
- Social Security number.

Once this information is in the hands of the phishers, it may be used to steal the person's identity or otherwise commit fraud.

Phishing also frequently comes in the form of phone fraud. This may begin with an unexpected phone call from a stranger who has a friendly voice and an appealing story. The same claims are made as in electronic phishing scams. Phone-based phishing scams often claim to be collecting for a natural disaster that is currently in the news. The sales pitch usually calls for an immediate decision. Never give out credit card details, your Social Security number, or banking information over the phone if you did

Health and Safety Engineer

Health and safety engineers design systems and create procedures to keep people from injury or illness as a result of a manufacturing problem. They are also concerned with preventing property damage. Their concerns are potential damage from substances, machines, software, equipment, and other consumer products. They rely on IT for new research, report generation, and communications.

not make the call. Be cautious even if only asked for a mailing address or e-mail address. Doing so gives the scammer another way to target you.

Data Vandalism

Data vandalism is the manipulation or destruction of data found in cyberspace. It is unethical and can be illegal, as shown in Figure 16-2. For example, a hacker may break into the school computer database and alter grades. Commercial competitors may engage in data vandalism, such as hacking a competing website to change the URLs for hyperlinks. Then, a customer who clicks a link for sports jackets, for example, instead may be sent to a page for sports shoes. That customer would quickly become frustrated and simply choose to shop at another online retailer. All of these examples demonstrate unethical uses of online resources.

Computer Hacking

Hacking is an activity by computer programmers to break into the e-mails, websites, computer systems, and files of other computer users. Hacking is often an unethical and illegal activity. However, there are legitimate hackers as well. Many companies hire hackers to find faults in their own computer systems. In this way, the faults can be fixed before they are exploited.

There are numerous ways hackers can discover a computer fault to exploit. For example, in many organizations, usernames and e-mail

FYI

Visit the consumer information section of the US Federal Trade Commission website (www.consumer.ftc.gov), and search for "phone scams" to find more information.

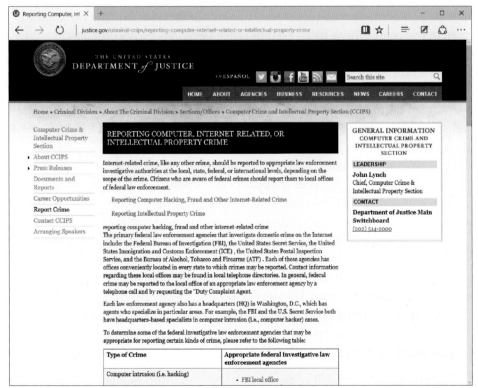

Goodheart-Willcox Publisher

Figure 16-2. The Department of Justice maintains a website for reporting computer crimes, including hacking and data vandalism.

addresses are based on the name of the user. A hacker can try to find the person by searching social media. Once a person's name and place of work are known, the e-mail address can be guessed and verified with an online service. Then, other means can be used to crack the password to gain access to the system.

HANDS-ON EXAMPLE 16.1.1

CYBERSECURITY THREATS

The federal government and the White House have undertaken many cybersecurity policy initiatives. The White House website contains information about cybersecurity threats.
1. Launch a browser, and navigate to www.whitehouse.gov.
2. Using the website's search function, search for foreign policy cybersecurity.
3. Locate an article on foreign policy related to cybersecurity. Alternatively, directly navigate to the page www.whitehouse.gov/issues/foreign-policy/cybersecurity.
4. Read the article, and summarize the government's objectives.

Censorship

GS5 Living Online
1.1.7

GS4 Living Online
4.2.1

Many schools, companies, and organizations restrict the information that their members can access. While this is usually done to prevent computer threats by blocking certain websites and other electronic access, some people consider it censorship. **Censorship** is the act of limiting access to information or removing information to prevent the information from being seen. There must be a balance between providing a safe computing environment and allowing free access to information.

Some forms of censorship can be justified. For example, it is reasonable and legal for a school or company to prevent its computer users from using the organization's time and equipment to access certain websites. For example, online blogs, such as political chat rooms and genealogical web pages; social media sites, such as YouTube, Facebook, LinkedIn, Pinterest, and Twitter; shopping sites, such as Amazon and ebay; and sites with illegal or inappropriate images may all be blocked by a school or company. It is important for the organization to establish rules related to accessing online content to protect its reputation as well as the safety of its employees and equipment. Many organizations use software to filter content and automatically prevent access to specific sites or sites matching keywords. In addition, self-censorship is appropriate while using a computer that may be seen by others. Be aware that others may view content as offensive or politically incorrect even if you do not.

Internet Security Protocols

Internet protocols tell computers, modems, routers, and networks how to communicate with each other. Protocols also provide instructions on how to verify and handle information being received and transmitted. Internet security protocols are especially important because they reduce or eliminate malicious uses of the Internet. There are several Internet protocols related to security.

However, no system, protocol, or technique can overcome lax behavior by computer users. For example, in 2014 a Russian website alerted the world to the fact that many people never bother to change the default password on video-surveillance cameras. To prove the point, the website streamed feeds from over 4,500 webcams around the world. Feeds for everything from baby bedroom monitors to hospital wards and business security systems were shown. This was possible simply because the users never changed the default passwords.

TCP/IP

The transmission control protocol (TCP) and the Internet protocol (IP) were the first networking protocols, as discussed in Chapter 13. TCP/IP provided end-to-end connectivity by specifying how data should be put into data packets, addressed, transmitted, routed, and received.

When TCP/IP was introduced during the 1980s, network or Internet security was not a serious issue. Thus, TCP/IP lacks basic mechanisms for security, such as source authentication and data encryption. Unfortunately, during the last 30 years, malicious individuals have developed techniques for misleading (spoofing) a computer concerning the real source of information. In general, this involves pretending that data are being sent from an IP address different from the actual address.

Security precautions and protocols must thus be added to TCP/IP to combat sniffing and denial of service attacks. *Sniffing* is eavesdropping that traps packets of information. A *denial of service attack* floods a service with so much traffic that the server slows down or shuts down. Most such vulnerabilities can be combated by installing the newest updates to security software and by properly configuring network applications and router settings.

SSH

A particularly important Internet security protocol is the SSH. The secure shell (SSH) is a network protocol that secures data communication and remote command execution. It is used to authenticate the client and server machines and to establish a secure channel between them. Within the SSH are three protocols: TLP, UAP, and CP.

The transport layer protocol (TLP) authenticates the server to the client and establishes a channel that the client deems secure. The user authentication protocol (UAP) authenticates the client to the server. It does this by verifying user names and passwords are matched and valid. The connection protocol (CP) distributes the secure channel into several logical channels. The CP is not really a security protocol, but is necessary.

Green Tech

Recycle and Save
Many socially responsible companies work with the community to encourage participation in recycling efforts. Several companies have in-store recycling bins for customers to deposit used electronics and ink cartridges, compact fluorescent lightbulbs (CFLs), and plastic shopping bags. Some companies also offer incentives, such as gift cards, for recycling items in the store.

HTTPS

Another very important Internet security protocol is the secure hypertext transfer protocol. The secure hypertext transfer protocol (HTTPS) secures communication over computer networks. It is widely used on the Internet to provide secure connections. HTTPS provides the user with authentication of a website and web server. In effect, the user's data can only be read by the website. HTTPS is actually the layering of other protocols to prevent various forms of wiretapping. Wiretapping is called *man-in-the-middle attacks*.

Other Protocols

There are also protocols for routers, fiber-optic channels, Bluetooth communication, and Yahoo Messenger:
- file transfer protocol (FTP)
- secure file transfer protocol (SFTP)
- simple mail transfer protocol (SMTP)
- hypertext transfer protocol (HTTP)
- secure socket layer protocol (SSL)
- Internet message access protocol (IMAP)
- bitcoin protocol

Over the past 25 years, experts have created many Internet protocols. Almost all of these play a role denying unauthorized access to computers and the data they contain. These protocols have greatly reduced hacking of computer systems and databases, virus transmission, and online identity theft. However, these protocols have not eliminated all threats.

Security Measures

Unethical Internet users may create computer programs to make massive robot-like attacks on poorly protected systems. Sometimes these attacks are done to create free e-mail accounts and send spam advertisements. Other times these attacks are for massive downloading from multimedia websites. These cyber attacks typically use web robots. A web robot, called a **bot**, is a software application that automatically performs Internet-based activities.

One common defense against bot attacks is called CAPTCHA. A **completely automated public Turing test to tell computers and humans apart (CAPTCHA)** is a brief online test to determine whether the request for access comes from a computer or a human. A common form of CAPTCHA requires the user to enter the letters and numbers shown in a distorted screen image. The image is often composed of swirled letters or blurred photos, as shown in Figure 16-3. This test is effective because humans can recognize the variety in the forms of letters and numbers, but computers cannot. This is also true for differing colors and shades. Humans can also see logical groups or segments of letters and numbers, regardless of vertical or horizontal spacing.

FYI

The Turing test, named after pioneering computer scientist Alan Turing, measures how closely a computer can imitate the intelligence of a human.

Goodheart-Willcox Publisher

Figure 16-3. A common CAPTCHA is a phrase composed of swirled letters. Most people can read the phrase shown here as Dog Tail, but it would be very hard for a computer program to decipher this.

Protecting Stored Data

The easiest way to protect information from corruption is by backing up those files in other locations. The cost of large-capacity external drives has plummeted in recent years. A reliable 2 TB portable hard drive costs less than $100. This is enough capacity to store all important, irreplaceable files from several laptop and desktop computers. Even a movie buff can store a collection of 150 or more Blu-ray movies on an external 4 TB drive. This size of drive costs only around $150.

Many computer users choose cloud-based options for backups. Services such as iCloud, Egnyte, and Dropbox are all file-storage solutions. They allow easy access via a web browser. Using a cloud-based service removes possible losses due to computer thefts, virus infections, fires, floods, and similar problems. Users can feel secure knowing that massive off-site computers with their own backup systems will retain the files.

Removing Data from Discarded Devices

The needs of a computer user will eventually exceed the capability of his or her machine. Old electronic equipment should be recycled. In many states, it is required by law. To find recycling programs, use a search engine and use a search phrase such as "computer recycling."

Data should be cleared from any computer equipment before it is recycled. Storage devices should be "wiped" to ensure all personal files are completely erased. This will protect the data from identity thieves. Using the operating system's procedures, file access can be denied. However, the file content may still be accessible to a hacker.

A very safe approach to removing data is to repeatedly overwrite the drive. Repartition the hard drive, and then overwrite all space on the drive at least three times. Alternatively, free disk-wipe software, also called data-sanitization software, can be downloaded from the Internet. The same approach can be used with a portable flash drive.

 Living Online
5.1.2

Huguette Roe/Shutterstock.com

Figure 16-4. This machine is crushing and shredding a hard drive, which will completely destroy the data on the drive.

Computing Fundamentals
7.5.1, 7.5.2

For the most sensitive data, mechanical destruction of the drive is the best solution. There are several ways to mechanically destroy a drive. One method is to shred or chop it into small pieces, as shown in Figure 16-4. Other methods include punching holes in the drive or burning it at an extremely high temperature.

Defending Against Cyber Attacks

In the rapidly changing world of cyber attacks, it is a very good idea to run cyber-defense software. Cyber-defense software, usually called **antivirus software**, detects and removes malicious software from a computer. Most also actively prevent infections. Many companies offer cyber-defense software. Some are for-purchase and some are offered as freeware or open-source software.

Some antivirus software always monitors for viruses, which is known as *real-time protection*. With some software, however, a scan must be manually started. If the antivirus software detects a virus, it should be removed as quickly as possible. Most antivirus software will remove the virus as soon as it is detected. In some cases, however, the user must manually tell the software to remove any virus that is found. This added step has the advantage of being able to tell the software that a particular file or program is safe, but this should be done only if you are certain the file is not infected. A file that antivirus software thinks is infected when, in fact, it is not is called a *false positive.*

If for any reason a virus cannot be removed, it will be quarantined. This means the virus is isolated from the rest of the files on a computer. Once in quarantine, the virus cannot infect anything else. This is especially helpful if a critical file, such as a registry file, is infected.

Cyber threats rapidly evolve. Therefore, the software must be regularly updated. In most cases, the software will check for updates at a set interval, such as once a day or once a week. In this way, the software can quickly respond to new threats.

HANDS-ON EXAMPLE: 16.1.2

COMPUTER VIRUSES

Computer viruses have been around for decades. Some viruses target a specific operating system, while others seek to exploit a fault in a general protocol.

1. Launch a browser, and navigate to Wikipedia.
2. Using the search function, enter the search phrase antivirus software.

HANDS-ON EXAMPLE 16.1.2 (CONTINUED)

3. Read the section of the article entitled Identification Methods.
4. What are the five basic methods of identifying viruses?
5. Read the section of the article entitled Issues of Concern.
6. Summarize the issues of concern.
7. Search Wikipedia for the phrase computer virus, and open the article of the same name.
8. Read the section of the article entitled "Recovery Strategies and Methods."
9. Summarize the various basic processes that can be used to remove a virus.

16.1 | SECTION REVIEW

CHECK YOUR UNDERSTANDING

1. How is a computer worm different from a computer virus?
2. When is hacking legitimate?
3. What does the HTTPS protocol do?
4. What is the purpose of a CAPTCHA?
5. List three ways to mechanically destroy a discarded hard drive.

IC3 CERTIFICATION PRACTICE

The following question is a sample of the types of questions presented on the IC3 exam.

1. Which of the following is software that secretly collects a user's data and behavior?
   A. computer virus
   B. spyware
   C. scareware
   D. hacking

BUILD YOUR VOCABULARY

As you progress through this course, develop a personal IT glossary. This will help you build your vocabulary and prepare you for a career. Write a definition for each of the following terms and add it to your IT glossary.

adware
antivirus software
bot
cache
censorship
completely automated
  public Turing test
  to tell computers
  and humans apart
  (CAPTCHA)
computer virus
computer worm

cookies
data vandalism
hacking
malware
phishing
pop-up
ransomware
scareware
social engineering
spyware
Trojan horse

IDENTITY PROTECTION AND ETHICAL BEHAVIOR

Essential Question

How does your ethical behavior online affect others in society?

Millions of people fall victim to fraud each year. In fact, the Federal Trade Commission (FTC) estimates that as many as nine million Americans have their identities stolen each year. The impact can be financially and emotionally devastating. Victims have to spend countless hours and dollars trying to correct the damage.

Computer users should protect their identities when visiting websites. Know what information is being collected, by whom, and how it will be used. Websites track visitors as they navigate through cyberspace. Most legitimate websites include a privacy statement, typically found at the bottom of the home page. This statement should detail the type of information the site collects about its visitors and how users can control the information that is being gathered.

Goodluz/Shutterstock.com

LEARNING GOALS

After completing this section, you will be able to:
- List precautions for protecting your identity on the Internet.
- Explain ways to protect your identity in e-mail communication.
- Describe ethical behavior in cyberspace.

TERMS

e-mail filters
ethics
identity theft
online piracy
pharming

Identity Protection on the Internet

Identity theft is an illegal act that involves stealing someone's personal information and using that information to commit theft or fraud. Identity theft is rampant on the Internet. This results in millions of lost dollars each day. Most credit card companies will compensate victims of online fraud. However, the victim still pays a huge price in time and aggravation. Here are steps each Internet user should take:

- Never click any links in unsolicited e-mail.
- Do not set social media profiles to public.
- Immediately delete messages from suspicious senders.
- Fill in only required fields in online forms and consider using an alternate spelling of your name.
- Carefully inspect the terms of service for websites.
- Be sure to understand the purpose of any check box relating to sharing your information.
- Ensure that the lock symbol is shown in your browser's status bar and look to see that the URL begins with https, indicating that a secure connection is being used.
- Use software that color-codes websites as to their security risk, known as secure-search software.

Living Online
5.1.1

LAN, WAN, and VPN Security

The primary goals of network security are availability, confidentiality, and integrity. But how much security can a user expect from a LAN, WAN, or VPN? All are generally secure. Security for LANs and WANs is generally very strong. However, much of the security depends on the network administrator, plus the hardware and software security resources. The network administrator must maintain server firewalls and access-control lists to prevent unauthorized access. He or she must also require appropriate credentials to access network resources. He or she must ensure all sensitive network traffic is encrypted. This makes it extremely difficult for a hacker to decipher any captured network traffic.

The best security system for portable or remote use is a VPN card. VPN software encrypts the data, inserts it into an IP packet for Internet compatibility, and sends it through a special tunnel. The packet is then decrypted at the other end of the tunnel. Several tunneling protocols are available: IP security (IPsec), point-to-point tunneling protocol (PPTP), and layer 2 tunneling protocol (L2TP). This increased security allows remote users to very securely transmit e-mail.

Wireless Network Protection

Wireless networks are not as secure as the traditional wired networks. However, the risk on a wireless network can be minimized by enabling encryption, changing the default password, changing the service set identifier (SSID) name of the network, turning off SSID broadcasting, and using the MAC filtering feature. The MAC filtering feature allows you

Living Online
2.1.3

Ethics

Bypassing Security
Computer users and network administrators take steps to ensure the security of their computers. Trying to bypass security measures is unethical and, in many cases, illegal. Breaking into a computer or network should be viewed as no different from breaking into a house or business.

to designate and restrict which computers can connect to the wireless network. Be aware that devices using wireless networks are just as vulnerable to viruses and hackers as wired devices. Only download applications from trusted sources.

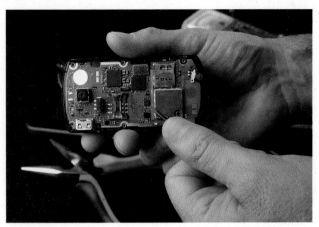

mickyso/Shutterstock.com

Figure 16-5. At its heart, a smartphone is just a computer.

Security Risks with Audio and Video Applications

All smartphones are computers, as shown in Figure 16-5. They are increasingly targets of cyber attacks. Hackers seek ways to exploit weaknesses related to text messaging via SMS. Denial of service is a common attack. Hackers can also attach virus-infected image files or ring tones that are transmitted via MMS. When these files are opened, they infect the smartphone. The virus is also forwarded to everyone in the address book.

Videoconferencing and VoIP transmissions can also be hacked. Most often, these hacks have been denial of service attacks. Hackers have also developed viruses that stop the stream of video packets and freeze the screen image. Even real-time videos being transmitted from cell phones to other computers can carry viruses. Programs have been developed to detect virus infections in near-real-time audio and video streams. These antivirus programs can detect viruses in any streaming files, such as MP3 audio files. The development of the real-time streaming protocol (RTSP) made the transmission of video and audio data more efficient and secure.

HANDS-ON EXAMPLE 16.2.1

IDENTITY THEFT

Identity theft is a real online problem. However, identity theft is not limited to online activities. The Federal Trade Commission (FTC) provides information on how to protect yourself from identity theft and what to do if you are a victim.

1. Launch a browser, and navigate to www.consumer.ftc.gov, which is the Federal Trade Commission consumer website.
2. Using the search function, enter the search phrase identify theft.
3. Locate the link for the featured information title Identity Theft. Alternately, directly navigate to www.consumer.ftc.gov/features/feature-0014-identity-theft.
4. Read the information.
5. What are the three steps to take if you have been the victim of identity theft?
6. Click the link for How to Keep Your Information Secure.
7. Read about how to keep your online information and your devices secure.

E-commerce Security

E-commerce is buying and selling products or services over electronic systems such as the Internet. E-commerce involves electronic funds transfers, online transaction processing, Internet-based marketing, electronic-data interchanges, inventory-management systems, and automated data-collection systems. Online retail sales in the United States now account for hundreds of billions of dollars each year. Recent figures estimate that over 70 percent of Americans have made online purchases. This explosion of e-commerce has led to a new generation of associated cybersecurity threats.

Privacy and data security are major concerns for both consumers and e-commerce businesses. Due to cybercriminals, millions of stolen credit- and debit-card numbers have been posted on the Internet. A major study by LexisNexis found that the value of merchant losses each year due to fraud exceeds the value of consumer losses from fraud by more than 20 times. However, consumers in the United States engaging in e-commerce are victims of fraud for billions of dollars each year.

Companies assess the risk of e-commerce transactions, often on each individual purchase. Checks include seeing whether the telephone number provided by the purchaser matches the ZIP code where the item is to be shipped and whether the IP address of the computer used to place the order is in that same region. Such instant risk analyses will also check whether the order is for a large number of high-value items, which could be fraud. The analysis will also look at the shipping address of the order. An order shipped to an unusual or foreign address also could be a possible sign of fraud. All of these checks are done through software.

Today, every e-commerce system must address the following key issues:

- privacy
- integrity
- authentication
- nonrepudiation
- protection from denial of service (DoS) attacks

Information exchanged during a transaction must be kept private at all times. Even after the transaction is complete, the information must be kept from unauthorized parties. The integrity of the information must be guaranteed by making sure no information has been altered. The information must be authenticated. This is done by forcing both parties to prove their identities. Nonrepudiation is proving that exchanged information has indeed been received. By preventing DoS attacks, the information will be available to the intended users.

Merchants assume the bulk of the risk of e-commerce. However, customers also have a responsibility to help out. Start by always providing accurate information on the online order form. When creating an account, provide the answer to the security question that would be difficult to predict. Remember, social media sites can be used to gather personal information about you, such as your pet's name. Reduce your

Internet profile. If you do so, it will be harder for cybercriminals to find information about you.

Frequently check your bank and credit card statements for fraudulent charges. If you find any fraudulent charges, *immediately* contact your bank and cancel your credit card. Never use a debit card for an online purchase. A credit card offers protection, but a cybercriminal with your debit card information can drain your bank account. Once the money is gone, it is very hard to get it back.

An alternative to using a credit card is to use a merchant service. PayPal is an example, but there are others. With a merchant service, you provide your financial information once to the service, then the service conducts the transactions. Your bank account and credit card information is never exposed to the merchant. Credit card companies also offer a similar service through single-use credit card numbers. The number is linked to your credit card, but it is good for only one purchase. In some cases, you can even specify which merchant the number is good for and for how much.

Maintain a healthy skepticism about the authenticity of e-commerce websites. Do not just click a link that says it will go to a legitimate site. Manually enter the actual URL address into the browser's address bar. If suspicious about a link to a company, look up the company directly using a search engine. Finally, just because the site shows an "official" or "verified" logo does not mean it is a legitimate site.

Be extra suspicious of foreign sites. If the IP address is in Russia or Nigeria, for example, investigate the site further before providing any information. Also look for the top-level domain. Websites based in many countries must use that country's top-level domain, such as .ru for Russia or .cy for Cypress.

Avoid sites that consist of very few web pages and offer only general descriptions of products and service. Sites that appear to have been quickly created may not be legitimate. Also be wary of websites that seem to have bugs. Programming issues may be a sign of an amateur who is unable to properly protect data.

Be suspicious of websites containing offers that are just too good to be true. For example, if major retail sites offer a sleeping bag for $75, a site offering the same sleeping bag for $15, including shipping, should raise a warning. Major retailer sites are generally trustworthy, but for smaller independent e-commerce sites, be sure to do your research before placing an order.

Always look for the HTTPS protocol in the browser's address bar before entering personal data. This indicates the site is secure. Also, most browsers will provide a visual indication, such as a lock icon, that the site is secured.

Identity Protection in E-mail

Users can take precautions to protect their personal e-mail accounts. One method is to create a "junk mail" account that you use whenever you need to enter an e-mail address in a form. This can often be done

GS5 Computing Fundamentals
7.1.1

as part of the e-mail provider's service. If not, use one of the many free e-mail services. This reserves the primary e-mail address for personal or professional e-mail. Junk mail, including spam and phishing scams, is more likely to stay out of the primary e-mail. Additionally, any mail received in the junk account can simply be deleted. Because the mail is never read, security is enhanced.

Consider creating a username that is misleading or does not reveal personal information. The name GolfSmith6503 may be good if the person does *not* play golf, is *not* named Smith, and does *not* have the number 6503 as a street address or partial phone or Social Security number. For a person named Smith who plays golf and was born June 5, 2003, this is a poor choice for a username.

Periodically check the filter and forwarding functions for each e-mail account. Hackers can enter an account and establish a rule to forward e-mail messages to an address. If you see forwarded mail that you did not forward, the e-mail account has probably been hacked. If you find your e-mail has been hacked, immediately change your password, and then perform a scan with your antivirus software.

If provided, take advantage of the option to create a specific security key. A security key is often a question that must be answered to gain access, as shown in Figure 16-6. For example, the question may ask for your pet's name or the name of your favorite grade school teacher. Some providers allow users to create their own security questions. Some providers also allow selection of a sign-in seal or a favorite color as the security key. Questions that ask for a mother's maiden name or your birthplace are poor security keys. Do not use the same questions and answers for different accounts.

FYI

Avoid setting up auto replies on your personal accounts as this will confirm the e-mail account is valid and active.

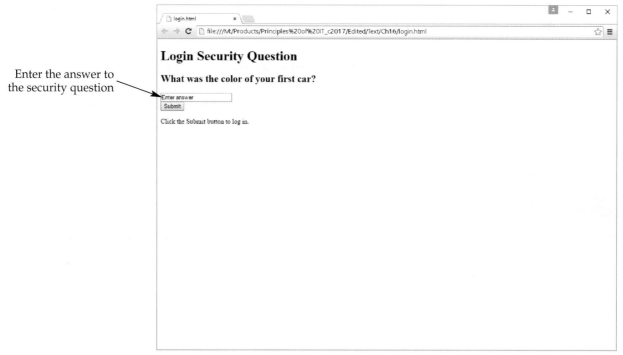

Enter the answer to the security question

Goodheart-Willcox Publisher

Figure 16-6. A common security key is a question that you have to answer.

Pharming is another way your identity can be stolen. In **pharming**, a virus or other malware infects the computer and takes control of your web browser. Then, when you enter the URL of a legitimate website, you are taken to a fake website that looks like the real website. Any information that you think you are entering on a legitimate website is instead stolen.

E-mail Awareness

Avoid downloading programs and files from unknown sources or from sources that appear to be suspicious. What makes a source suspicious? There are precautions you can take to help recognize suspicious e-mail.

Check Questionable Messages

E-mail addresses that appear to have been computer-generated should be questioned. For example, an e-mail from 67ghvv786@gmall.com is suspicious for two reasons. First, the information before the at sign (@) is just letters and numbers. This could be computer-generated. Second, the domain name after the at sign appears at a glance to be from Gmail. However, looking closely, the domain is gmall.com, *not* gmail.com. Using a domain that is very close to a well-known domain is a common way scammers try to fool people.

Be Wary of Attachments from Unknown Sources

Always be suspicious of attachments from sources you do not recognize. Never open an attached file unless you know and trust the source. Opening an attachment may launch malware. Do not rely on your antivirus software to stop the malware. Rather, be safe and do not open the attachment.

Do Not Click Links in E-mail

Offering links in an e-mail for online shopping is one of the oldest ways hackers use to carry out scams. Messages that offer sales are suspicious. If the offer appears to be from a legitimate source, open a browser and manually navigate to the site claiming to offer the sale. Then, manually search for the sale. Shop only at sites that are known and trusted. When entering payment details, make sure the URL for the page is secure. A secure URL begins with https instead of http. Also, most Internet browsers display a lock or other icon somewhere in the browser window to indicate a secure connection. After completing the order, sign out of the site or close the browser.

Every few months hundreds of people succumb to an e-mail hoax related to Microsoft patches. The phony e-mail includes a fake or stolen Microsoft logo, fake return address, and phony links. Microsoft *never* sends out patches or updates by e-mail. There are no exceptions. Similar scams involve messages designed to look like a bank trying to update its customers or a firm trying to contact lottery winners. Never follow the

FYI

Never use a debit card for online purchases because it does not offer as much protection against fraud as a credit card.

links in these e-mails. If you think your bank may be trying to contact you, manually contact the bank yourself. Mention the e-mail so the bank can alert other customers to the scam.

Stay Alert for Phishing Attempts

Ignore unsolicited e-mail that asks for personal information. These are likely phishing scams. Phishing is an attempt to get you to provide information that can be used to break into accounts and steal your identity. Phishing scams usually ask for personal information such as your address, SSN, and phone number. This information can be used to gain access to financial accounts and your online presence.

Never reply to an e-mail asking you to "verify your information" or to "confirm your user ID and password." The most common form of phishing is e-mail pretending to be from a bank, governmental agency, or legitimate retailer or organization. For example, a cyber criminal sends an e-mail that appears to be from Facebook. The e-mail states there has been unusual activity on your account and asks you to verify your username and password. However, when you enter the information, it is stolen. Your Facebook account is then hacked, and the criminal uses information found there to locate even more information about you elsewhere.

GS4 Living Online
5.1.1

FYI

Visit the website www.fraud.org run by the National Consumers League for more information on identity theft.

E-mail Filters

E-mail filters, also called rules, are used to automatically route incoming e-mail to a specified inbox folder, as shown in Figure 16-7. A filter is especially useful to send e-mail from an address known to be spam to the Trash or Junk Mail folder. However, filters can also be used to automatically send e-mail to folders based on project names, friend names, or hobbies. Most e-mail clients allow many filters or rules to be created.

One drawback to e-mail filters is that a filter may incorrectly identify incoming mail. A legitimate message may be sent directly to the Trash or Junk Mail folder without being seen by the user. Another drawback is that the user may overlook the information if it is automatically routed to another folder. However, most e-mail clients indicate how many unread messages are in each folder.

GS4 Living Online
4.2.2

E-mail Account Piracy and Protection

Some hackers focus on taking control of e-mail accounts. Once an account is hacked, it is used to send spam to the entire e-mail directory. If anybody replies to the spam, the hacker can then take control over that account, sending spam from it. How can a user prevent an e-mail account from being pirated? There are several precautions to take.

Before replying to an e-mail, verify the address. Look at the properties of the sender's name. This is usually done by hovering the cursor over the sender's name or right-clicking on the name and selecting **Properties** or **Message Options** in the shortcut menu. Make sure the e-mail address is correct. A common trick is to make an e-mail look like it came from a legitimate source, but the address is actually a scammer.

FYI

There is much information on the Internet concerning e-mail authentication.

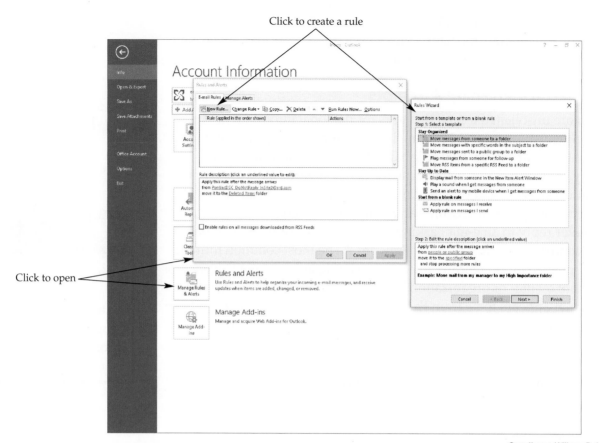

Click to create a rule

Click to open

Figure 16-7. In Microsoft Outlook, rules can be set up to automatically route incoming mail to a specific folder.

Check whether the e-mail was authenticated by the sending domain. This is usually done by right-clicking on the e-mail message and selecting **Properties** or **Message Options** in the shortcut menu. Check that the domain in the properties matches the domain shown as the e-mail address. The reply will be sent to the domain given in the properties, regardless of what is actually displayed as the e-mail address.

If using web-based mail, make sure the URL on the sign-in page is correct, as shown in Figure 16-8. For example, when logging into Gmail, does the URL actually end with google.com? Does the Yahoo Mail URL actually end with yahoo.com? If the URL is not correct, do not log in.

If anything is suspicious, contact the organization from which the message appears to have been sent. Do not reply to the message or use any links within it. Instead, visit the official website of the company in question, and find the correct contact address.

Take action quickly if you mistakenly entered personal information in a fake e-mail message. Copy the message header and the entire text of the message, and e-mail it to the Federal Trade Commission at spam@uce.gov. If you entered credit card or bank account numbers, immediately call the financial institution. If you think you are the victim of identity theft, contact local law enforcement.

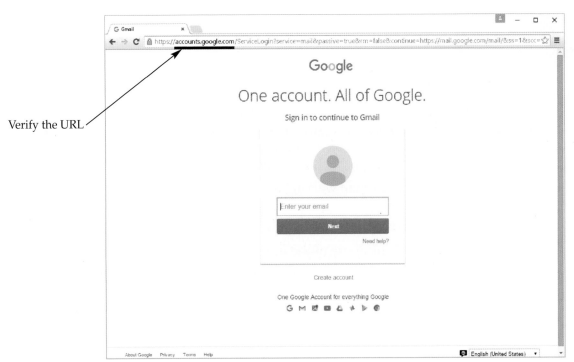

Verify the URL

Figure 16-8. If using web-based e-mail, make sure the URL on the sign-in page is correct. Here, the URL is for Google, which is correct.

Ethical Behavior in Cyberspace

Ethics are the principles of what is right and wrong that help people make decisions. Ethical actions are those actions in which the user applies ethics and moral behavior. Acting ethically means doing what most individuals and social groups believe to be morally correct and good for society. This is more than following specific rules and laws. It means doing the right thing, even when nobody is watching. Cyberbullying, which is discussed in Chapter 15, is an example of unethical behavior in cyberspace. There are legal and ethical responsibilities for everything you do online.

Legal Responsibilities

As described in Chapter 8, intellectual property is something that comes from a person's mind, such as an idea, invention, or process. The World Intellectual Property Organization (www.wipo.org) defines intellectual property as "creations of the mind, such as inventions; literary and artistic works; designs; and symbols, names, and images used in commerce." Laws protect individuals from unauthorized and unethical use of intellectual property. As discussed in Chapter 8, copyrights, patents, and trademarks protect intellectual property. These are most often enforced by national courts. The United Nations Commission on International Trade Law provides international support.

All software comes with a licensing agreement or terms of use, as described in Chapter 8. Websites that you must join, such as Facebook and Twitter, also have terms of use, sometimes called *terms of service.* This

FYI

If you check the box that says you agree to the terms, you are legally bound by them, even if you never read the document. Always read and understand the terms before agreeing to them.

legal document explains acceptable uses of the software, if the software can be copied or installed on multiple devices, and if the code or part of it can be reused. In the case of a website, the document will also explain what can be posted or shared. It is illegal to violate this agreement. Punishment may include a fine, imprisonment, or both.

Be careful on sites that share files of music, movies, games, and software. The material on these sites may be protected by copyrights. Downloading copyrighted material without permission of the copyright holder is illegal. It is theft and called **online piracy**. Online piracy is no different than walking into a store and stealing a DVD or CD.

Ethical Responsibilities

Ethical use of the Internet involves not breaking the law. It also involves respecting the intellectual property of others. As discussed in Chapter 8, plagiarism is claiming another person's material as your own, which is both unethical and illegal. If you *copy* the work of others without permission, even if you credit the source, you are committing plagiarism. However, it is entirely ethical to use the Internet while creating an original mixture of ideas. While doing this, be sure to cite known sources for all major and unusual ideas.

Copying whole sentences and paragraphs and using them as your own without attribution is unethical. However, consulting articles can be an effective first step while researching a subject. Articles can provide a general introduction to the topic. The See Also and References sections at the end of the article can also provide other sources of information.

Just as the Internet has made it easy to find information, it has made discovering plagiarism easy. There are many resources that can be used to check for plagiarism. Some of these are free, while others must be purchased. These resources make it easy for teachers and others to quickly find out if written material has been plagiarized.

Be Social Media Savvy

Make sure your social networking profiles are set to private. Sites such as Facebook and Twitter should not be allowed to display any information that can be used to identify you. Check the security settings for each account. Be careful what information you post online. Do not over-share information. There are unethical cyber surfers who troll the Internet looking for personal data to steal and sell to others. Even if a photo appears innocent, it may contain, for example, the name of your school. If you use this as part of your password, you have given hackers a hint.

Configure all of your social media accounts to control your status, who can gain access to what information, who can post, and who can share account information with others. The methods for making these security settings differ by site. Use a search engine or the site's search function to find out how to change security settings.

GS4 Living Online
5.1.1

HANDS-ON EXAMPLE 16.2.2

SOCIAL MEDIA SECURITY

Before signing up for a social media account, be sure to investigate its privacy policy. It should be easy to find this information even without logging in.

1. Launch a browser, and navigate to Facebook.
2. Click the **Privacy** link at the bottom of the page.
3. Read the information on the page. It explains Facebook's policies on how information is received, posted, and shared; how cookies are used; and what information is seen by web surfers.
4. What steps are necessary to delete information about yourself?
5. Navigate to LinkedIn.
6. Click the **Privacy Policy** link at the bottom of the page.
7. Read the information on the page. It explains LinkedIn's policies on how information is collected and saved; how information may be posted, shared, and restricted; and how account holders may access, correct, and delete information.
8. What steps are necessary to delete information?

16.2 | SECTION REVIEW

CHECK YOUR UNDERSTANDING

1. What are two indications in a browser that a secure connection is being used?
2. List four precautions you can implement to provide safety for e-mail.
3. What does an e-mail filter or rule do?
4. Which type of legal document explains acceptable uses of the software?
5. What unethical behavior is shown by copying someone else's work and claiming it as your own?

IC3 CERTIFICATION PRACTICE

The following question is a sample of the types of questions presented on the IC3 exam.

1. Which of the following is a safe practice when using web-based mail?
   A. Use only a public Internet provider.
   B. Allow the browser to save your password.
   C. Make sure the URL on the sign-in page is correct.
   D. Look for the secure icon on the web page.

BUILD YOUR VOCABULARY

As you progress through this course, develop a personal IT glossary. This will help you build your vocabulary and prepare you for a career. Write a definition for each of the following terms and add it to your IT glossary.

e-mail filters
ethics
identity theft
online piracy
pharming

SECTION 16.3

RESTRICTING ACCESS TO PERSONAL INFORMATION

Essential Question

What is the importance of restricting access to your personal information to your financial success?

Personal information should be protected as if it is as important as money. Social Security, credit card, and bank and utility account numbers can be used by cyber criminals to steal money, open new accounts, or open fraudulent credit lines. This information should not be handed out to anyone.

Each time you are asked for personal information, decide whether the requester is valid. Remember that scammers will often do anything they can to gain trust. Requests for personal information may come from web forms, e-mails, text messages, or phone calls. This section discusses how to restrict access to personal information.

Monkey Business Images/Shutterstock.com

LEARNING GOALS

After completing this section, you will be able to:
- Describe how firewalls and gateways protect data.
- Identify ways to provide password protection.
- List safe hardware and software practices.
- Discuss how to combat viruses and other malware.
- Explain how to determine if websites are reliable.
- Prevent computer threats from public intrusion.

TERMS

gateway
passphrase
personal firewall
strong password
uninterruptable power
  supply (UPS)

662

Firewalls and Gateways

As discussed in Chapter 14, a firewall is a network device that blocks or allows certain kinds of network traffic. This forms a barrier between trusted and distrusted networks. Regardless of whether it is a software or hardware firewall, its purpose is to ignore data that come from unknown, unsecured, or suspicious locations.

Conventional firewalls protect computer networks. A **personal firewall** controls traffic to an individual machine. This type of firewall may control communication based on preset security instructions for specific software programs. This helps defend against malware trying to install executable programs on the individual machine.

For example, a computer may be protected by a hardware firewall while it is in the office. There it is linked to the Internet through the internal routers and servers. However, if the computer is a laptop taken outside of the office, it will not be protected by the hardware firewall. A personal firewall should be installed to protect the computer when it is used outside of the office, such as in airports and hotels.

Another way to protect a mobile computer is to rely on a hardware firewall that comes as part of a home-based router. This is not very expensive, but it must be activated and configured. It is also only available when you are at home. A separate device can be purchased to attach to the computer while on the road. These tend to be expensive.

A computer **gateway** is a device that joins two networks, as shown in Figure 16-9. For example, a gateway may connect a school's internal network to the Internet. A router is an example of a gateway device. It decides where data packets are to be sent based on an IP address.

Living Online
2.1.4, 5.1.2

If a laptop is connected through a VPN, it will be protected by the network's hardware firewall.

Sorapop Udomsri/Shutterstock.com

Figure 16-9. Routers are gateway devices because they determine where data packets are sent based on the IP addresses.

For small networks, there is little practical difference between a gateway and a firewall. In many cases, the functions of a gateway and a firewall are contained in a single unit. However, there are also dedicated versions of each device for use in large networks.

Most operating systems come with a firewall for protection. However, many computer users choose to install a commercial antivirus and antimalware program that includes a firewall, such as Norton Antivirus or McAfee Personal Firewall. Firewalls are also automatically available in popular routers, such as TP-LINK Archer C7 AC1750 Dual Band Wireless AC Gigabit Router.

GS5 Computing Fundamentals
7.6

Firewall settings can be manually changed. However, more often settings are automatically changed by regular updates to the firewall or OS. If a computer is connected to the Internet, it should never be run without a firewall or with the firewall disabled.

To manually modify the Windows firewall, open the Control Panel. Click the **System and Security** link, and then click the **Windows Firewall** link. The page that is displayed lists the current status of the firewall. To allow a specific program or feature through the firewall, click the "allow" link on the left. On the new page, click the **Change settings** button, and then click the **Allow another app...** button. A window is displayed in which you can browse for the application to allow through the firewall.

The settings for the firewall in a router can also be changed. Consult the owner's manual for the router for specific information on doing so.

Password Protection

GS5 Computing Fundamentals
7.1.2

GS4 Living Online
5.1.1

Never write down a password or leave obvious password hints near the computer. A sticky note with your password in plain site or even hidden under the keyboard or mouse pad is easy to find. Instead, write down a clue that will remind you of the password. A reminder might be something like "shoe" for a shoe size number or "lake" for the name of a favorite recreation spot. However, remember that a password should not be based on easily identifiable information. Also recall that real words should not be used in a password. For example, use b00k instead of book, where zeros take the place of the letter O.

Another level of security is gained by using two passwords, one for the username and one for the account password. For example, if a user banks with Wells Fargo, he or she might want to begin the username with something easy to remember, such as wAg@N or R!deR, and then add several characters others could not easily guess. Once the username is accepted, then an account password needs to be created. That password should be a complex combination of at least nine characters. Use a combination of uppercase and lowercase letters, special characters, and numbers in no obvious order. This approach provides a form of double encryption, one for the username and a second for the account password.

Password Management

In today's world, most people have many passwords to remember, and each password should be unique. Some people create a document file to store all of their passwords. If you choose to do this, do not name the file "Password," "Pass," or "PW." A hacker who gains access to the computer can easily search for such obvious file names. Instead of using a document file to store passwords, dedicated password-management software can be used. This type of software provides more security than a simple document file. Password-management software is readily available and can be quickly located by performing an Internet search.

Strong Passwords

Computing Fundamentals
7.1.2.1

In theory, every password can be cracked if given enough time. The goal is to make the password so difficult to crack that even a dedicated hacker will spend his or her time elsewhere. A **strong password** is one difficult for both humans and computers to crack. A strong password takes much more time to crack than a weak password. Strong passwords do not include real words, consecutive characters (aaa or ##), sequential characters (abc or 678), or common keyboard patterns (@#$% or rdxtfc).

- Develop a mnemonic device for remembering complex passwords.
- Use a combination of letters, numbers, and special characters.
- Use both lowercase and uppercase (capital) letters.
- Use passphrases you can memorize.
- Use different passwords on different systems.
- Do not create passwords based on personal information that can be easily accessed or guessed.
- Do not use words that can be found in a dictionary of any language.

Weak or bad passwords contain real words and names. Do not use a maiden name; the name of a pet, child, sibling, celebrity, or sports team; or the title of a song or film. Bad passwords often relate to an address, phone number, SSN, birthday, anniversary, license plate, bank PIN, or sequences on a keyboard.

There are many websites that check the strength of a password. Use one of these sites to be sure you have created a strong password. However, when using such sites, do not enter a password you actually intend to use. Instead, enter a password that keeps the same structure, but does not have the exact characters. Why? Because you never know for sure whether the site has been spoofed (misdirected) or if a malicious hacker has installed a keystroke logger that is recording the characters being entered.

> **FYI**
>
> Reusing the same password or varying it very little when changing it are frequent errors.

Passphrases

Computing Fundamentals
7.1.2.1

Creating long and complex passwords is standard practice. However, these are often hard to remember. A passphrase that is easy to remember can be used to create a password. A **passphrase** is a phrase composed

STEM

Mathematics

To multiply decimals, place the numbers in a vertical list. Then multiply each digit of the top number by the right-hand bottom number. Multiply each digit of the top number by the bottom number in the tens position. Place the result on a second line and add a zero to the end of the number. Add the total number of decimal places in both numbers you are multiplying. This will be the number of decimal places in your answer.

FYI

Password-protecting a Microsoft Office document does not encrypt the file, which means that hackers may still be able to crack the data.

of real words on which a password is based. For example, consider this passphrase: We often ate fish at 6:00 on Fridays? It does not use the real names of people or pets. It is fairly long and complex, but it is also relatively easy to remember. The password created from this passphrase may be: WeOf8F@60F?. This password is strong, which will take a long time to crack. The goal of creating a password from a passphrase is to make the password very hard to crack, but very easy to remember.

Passwords for Documents

A Microsoft Word document can be protected by using a password. The password is case-sensitive. Also, if you lose or forget a password, Word cannot recover your data. To password-protect a Word 2013 document, use this procedure. The procedure may be different depending on which version of Word you have.

1. Click the **File** tab.
2. Click **Info** on the left-hand side of the backstage view.
3. Click the **Protect Document** button on the right-hand side of the backstage view, and then click **Encrypt with Password** in the drop-down menu that is displayed.
4. In the **Encrypt Document** dialog box, enter a password, and then click the **OK** button, as shown in Figure 16-10.
5. In the **Confirm Password** box, enter the password again, and then click the **OK** button. A message appears in the backstage view indicating that a password is now required to open the document.

Microsoft Excel provides several ways to protect a workbook. The user can require a password to open and view the file, a password to change data in the file, and even a password to add, delete, or hide worksheets. The basic approach to adding a password for the workbook structure in Excel 2013 is as follows. The procedure may be different depending on which version of Excel you have.

1. Click the **File** tab.
2. Click **Info** on the left-hand side of the backstage view.
3. Click the **Protect Document** button on the right-hand side of the backstage view, and then click **Protect Workbook Structure** in the drop-down menu that is displayed.

Enter a password

Figure 16-10. Enter a password to protect the document.

4. In the **Protect Structure and Windows** dialog box, enter a password, check the **Structure** check box, and then click the **OK** button, as shown in Figure 16-11.

5. In the **Confirm Password** box, enter the password again, and then click the **OK** button. Now, worksheets cannot be added, deleted, or moved.

6. Click the **File** tab, and then click **Info** on the left-hand side of the backstage view. A message appears in the backstage view indicating that the structure cannot be changed.

Check to protect the structure

Enter a password

Goodheart-Willcox Publisher

Figure 16-11. When protecting the structure of an Excel workbook, a password can be entered.

Password Use

The way in which passwords are used is as important as how they were created. Even a strong password cannot protect a device if a cyber criminal can easily access it. The following habits will help further protect strong passwords.

- Never disclose or share the password with anyone.
- Do not use the same password for multiple accounts.
- Change passwords on a regular basis.
- Use a very strong password to protect a document that contains a list of other passwords.
- Immediately change *all* of your passwords if you detect suspicious activity on *any* of your accounts.

HANDS-ON EXAMPLE 16.3.1

STRONG PASSWORDS

The first line of defense to protecting data is a strong password. There are many websites that will check the strength of a password, many for free.

1. Launch a browser, and navigate to a search engine.
2. Enter the search phrase Microsoft password checker.
3. Click the link for the Microsoft password checker website. It should be at the top or very near the top of the list. Notice that this is a secure web page.
4. Enter a password to see its strength.
5. Vary the length of the password, the characters used, and position of characters within the password to see how the strength of the password changes.
6. Enter a password based on this passphrase: My teacher is great! One example is m1T3chRisGr8!

Safe Hardware and Software Practices

Simply having good hardware and software is not enough to provide cybersecurity. You are responsible for knowing how to properly use what has been purchased and installed. You are also responsible for remaining alert and acting responsibly whenever connected to the Internet. Regardless of precautions taken, every computer user can expect to end up trying to open a corrupted file. Even worse, you may be faced with trying to work on a computer that has been infected with a virus.

MAii Thitikorn/Shutterstock.com

Figure 16-12. A UPS provides a constant supply of power to the computer in case of a power outage. It protects the computer against power surges and prevents data loss during storms.

UPS, System Restore Backup Points, and Individual File Backups

An **uninterruptable power supply (UPS)** is a device that protects computer systems and files against power surges and outages, as shown in Figure 16-12. Electronic equipment should be unplugged during thunderstorms. A UPS can provide power while the system is unplugged or if the building loses power. A UPS also protects the system if there is an electrical surge. An electrical surge can damage or destroy electronic equipment.

Even when file damage has occurred, all is not lost if a system restore point has been established and back-up files have been created. Backups of document files should be made on a flash drive, an external drive, or a cloud-storage site. This subject is discussed in more detail in Chapter 4.

Maintenance Schedule

The operating system and programs on your computer have many security features. However, these features are exactly what hackers and malware try to crack. Therefore, experts suggest reevaluating a computer's security setup at least twice a year. Pick two dates that are easy to remember, such as New Year's Day and the Fourth of July or when daylight saving time starts and stops.

Regularly review the settings associated with the applications on your computers. Browser software, in particular, has security settings in its list of preferences. Each program is a little different, so look for commands such as **Privacy**, **Safety**, and **Security**. Check the settings for deleting browsing history, accessing trusted sites, and blocking pop-up windows. Set the security level to high and save it.

Offers of Free Software Protection

Most credible firewall and antivirus software solutions come as an annual subscription costing $50 or more. Such software must be legally licensed. However, it is common to see offers of free software of this type when online. Most of these offers are bogus and may, in fact, be spreading malware.

Legitimate Free Software

There is some legitimate free antivirus software. These programs are distributed as shareware, even if they are not called that. The best features are either limited or disabled. The providers hope you will upgrade to the deluxe or professional edition to unlock these features. However, the upgrade is not free. There are some fully functional and completely free antivirus programs. Some of these are open-source software.

Free PC Scans

Many of the offers of free software protection come as "free PC scans." These offers often pop up when you surf the Internet. The popup may announce that your system or files have been corrupted and then offers a free security scan or a free service to speed up your machine. These offers are likely to be scams. One company had to pay a $1 million fine for offering "free spyware scans" that told users their systems had been infected even when the systems were entirely clean. Some "scans" do more than give misleading results. They actually try to install malware on your computer.

Many of these pop-up ads do not have a way to be closed. The only button the user sees is a **Scan** button. Do not click this button. The safest approach is to close the browser window. Pop-up blocker software will prevent many of these ads from appearing.

Combating Viruses and Other Malware

Over 40,000 computer viruses have been identified, and they come in many varieties. Here are some common types:

- Boot sector malware infects only the DOS boot sector.
- Backdoor malware creates a software hole in the computer that can be used by hackers as an open door.
- Trojan horse is a seemingly harmless file that unleashes malicious code to tear down a computer's defenses.
- Rootkit is malware that not only infects a computer, but also fights back by restarting or moving itself when a removal attempt is made.

Antivirus software can block virus transmissions and repair damage caused by viruses. In order for it to be most effective, the software needs to be updated on a regular basis.

Block Virus Transmission

Computer viruses can be transmitted in many ways. They may be loaded via CDs and flash drives. They may be hidden in the subject line or body of e-mail messages, activated by clicking on an object or

GS5 Computing Fundamentals
7.2.1, 7.2.2, 7.2.3, 7.2.4, 7.5.1

GS4 Computing Fundamentals
3.4.4, 4.1.3

Living Online
5.1.2

attachment, and even activated by replying to a message. They can be downloaded from many locations on the Internet.

When a virus is suspected in an e-mail, the best approach is to delete the e-mail. Do not open it. If you have already opened it, do not click on any of the content. Immediately close the message, and then delete it. If you suspect an Internet site of transmitting a virus, immediately close the browser.

Always have your antivirus software running. Most antivirus software will actively try to prevent malware from being transmitted to your computer. Some antivirus software will also prescreen Internet sites for potential dangers. If your antivirus software warns against opening a site, do not open the site. Additionally, most antivirus software can be set to run a scan on a regular basis. If this is an option, schedule a scan at least once a week. If the software does not allow scans to be scheduled, manually run a scan on a regular basis.

Repair Virus Damage

If your computer seems unusually slow or your web browser suddenly looks different, your computer may have a virus. Viruses may make a computer unstable, causing it to crash fairly often. If a virus has infected a file you are trying to open, you may receive a message saying the file has been corrupted and cannot be opened.

The first step in repairing virus damage is to run a scan using your antivirus software. Follow the instructions in the software. In some cases, the malware is severe and the computer will not function. If the computer is not functioning, turn it off and seek expert assistance.

Keep Antivirus Software Updated

Always update your operating system and antivirus software with the latest security patches. Doing so offers excellent protection against any hacker attempts to download or execute code on your computer. Always use a well-established and modern web browser. The most current browsers provide protection against malicious activity and warn of sites known to exhibit malicious behavior. Antivirus software often works with search engines to let the user know of safe and unsafe sites, as shown in Figure 16-13.

Most antivirus software automatically checks for updates every few days when you are connected to the Internet. If you have not been on the Internet for some time, it is a good idea to manually update the antivirus software. Do this before navigating to any Internet sites or checking e-mail. If the software does not automatically check for updates, be sure to manually update it every few days.

GS5 Computing Fundamentals
7.5.2

FYI

Do not expect to increase security by loading more than one antivirus program. Most antivirus software does not work well with other antivirus software.

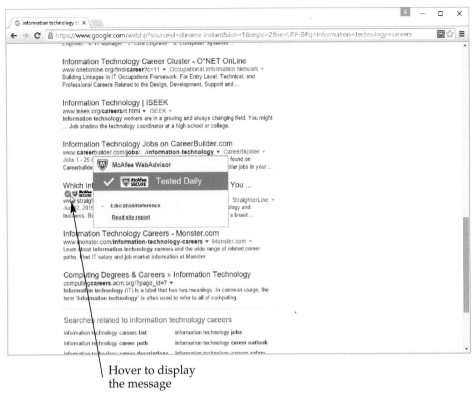

Hover to display
the message

Goodheart-Willcox Publisher

Figure 16-13. Some antivirus software will work with search engines to pre-screen results. In this example, green check marks indicate sites without any reported problems, and hovering the cursor over a check mark displays the message.

HANDS-ON EXAMPLE 16.3.2

ANTIVIRUS SOFTWARE

Antivirus software is an important part of cybersecurity. Before purchasing antivirus software, it is a good idea to research the different programs that are available.

1. Launch a browser, and navigate to a search engine.
2. Enter these keywords: best antivirus software ratings.
3. In the search results, look for a link from a computer magazine such as PC Magazine or PC World that is a review of antivirus software. A link for Consumer's Report that provides a review is also a good choice.
4. Click the link, and review the current ratings and prices. Ratings and prices will vary by source. Most software is usually between $50 and $100 for a one-year subscription. However, some software offers a free version with basic features with premium features available in a subscription version.
5. Select an antivirus software you feel would best meet your needs. Write one paragraph justifying your choice.

GS4 Living Online
5.1.1, 5.1.2

Determining Reliable Websites

How can you know a website can be reliably used without picking up a virus? Unfortunately, there are no iron-clad guarantees. Some of the most famous and secure websites have been hacked. However, there are a number of ways to greatly reduce the risks of downloading a virus.

The safest way to navigate to a site is to manually enter the URL. Clicking a link to the site on another web page could send you to a fake site. If the link is in an e-mail from an unknown sender, delete the e-mail. That is a very common method for getting people to go to virus-infected sites.

Check the domain name to see if it is a typically reliable domain. Governmental (.gov) and educational (.edu) domains are usually safe and reliable. These domains are not available to the general public. However, many educational institutions provide their students with .edu e-mail addresses or web space. Student accounts are often not as closely monitored as the school's main sites. Therefore, they may present the risk of malware.

Look at the structure and appearance of the website. If it is very basic and poorly designed, it may pose a risk. The site may be intentionally passing along malware or it may contain files infected due to carelessness. Look for misspellings and grammar errors, broken links, and elements that overlap or are otherwise improperly formatted. If the site is complex and appears to have been built over many years by dedicated programmers, it is more likely to be a safe site.

Before going to a site, enter the site name into a search engine along with the word "complaint." If there are problems with the site, there will likely be many complaints. For example, compare results from entering "Win 7 Antivirus 2012" or "24x7 help" with results from entering "XP patches." If many Internet users agree a site is unsafe, do not go to the site.

FYI
Many risky websites have a very professional appearance. Just because a site appears well-developed does not mean it is safe.

Safe File Downloads

In the rapidly changing cyber war, any file could be potentially unsafe. However, there are some questions you can ask to help decide if the file is likely safe or unsafe.

- Have you successfully used the site before?
- Is the site a governmental site?
- Does the site name or invitation to download look suspicious?
- Does the site or file have a digital logo or signature?
- Does your antivirus software warn about the site or the file?
- Do you have sufficient time to download the file without interruption?
- Can the file be downloaded to a separate drive and tested there before installing it on your main computer?

Be particularly wary of certain file types, such as those with these file extensions: .bat, .com, .exe, .pif, and .scr. These files are executable files that run programs, which may be malware. Carefully check the source to make sure you trust it before downloading the file. Remember, a file can only have one file name extension. If a file appears to have two file name extensions, such as readme.txt.exe, only the last one is the actual extension. This is an attempt to make the user think the file is safe, but it likely contains malware. Also, most antivirus software will warn of a potentially dangerous download before allowing it, as shown in Figure 16-14.

Consider the topic of the file being downloaded. If the topic of the file appears illegal or suspicious, the file may be dangerous. If the offer seems too good to be true, then there may be a high risk the downloaded file contains malware. However, if the file concerns a bill for cleaning streams in upstate New York, for example, the risk may be low because the audience is limited. Hackers usually focus on areas of high interest, such as offers of free photographs, software, or financial advice.

Goodheart-Willcox Publisher

Figure 16-14. Most antivirus software will warn of a potentially dangerous download and ask the user to block or verify the download.

FYI

Entering the file name into a search engine may return results indicating an unsafe file.

Internet Scams or Fraudulent Websites

Criminals think of clever ways to separate you from hard-earned cash. Check for Internet phishing scams or fraudulent websites. New ones are created daily. Many Internet users turn to Snopes (www.snopes.com) to check out a wide variety of rumors, phishing scams, and websites that mimic or spoof reliable sites. Snopes examines the evidence behind popular Internet and e-mail stories and evaluates whether they are real or fake.

Beware of e-mail about a security concern from your bank or an e-commerce site. Be very cautious of any "urgent" e-mail request to provide or update your personal information. Any link in the e-mail almost certainly goes to a website that is phishing for data or transmitting malware. Never be fooled by e-mail telling sad stories, making unsolicited job offers, or promising lottery winnings. These are almost always Internet scams.

GS4 Living Online
5.1.1

E-commerce Sites

Many people make purchases on e-commerce websites. However, e-commerce sites pose some risks. Since the buyer cannot see or touch the goods offered for sale, there is no way to see if the product is of poor quality. There are many online e-commerce sites that offer prescription medications. Some of these offer medications that are not manufactured under the regulations of the Food and Drug Administration (FDA). These medications may be of poor quality or, in some cases, completely fake. Additionally, a website may be *presented* as an e-commerce site, but its real purpose is to attract people to enter credit card details. Unless shopping on a well-known site with a reputation of providing quality products, do an Internet search to discover comments on the reputation of the site.

Never purchase anything from a spammer. If you did not request information about a service or product, it is almost certainly a scam. If you are interested in the product or service, manually search the Internet for it. Then, go directly to the legitimate source. Do not use the links provided in the spam e-mail.

Pirated Media

Never download pirated media, such as songs, movies, software, or anything else. Not only is doing so illegal, it is a good way to download malware. The idea of viewing a hot new movie or expanding your music library by downloading the current hits for free is appealing. Free file-sharing sites and services are a prime way for a computer to become infected with malware. No movie or song is worth corrupting your machine or the fines and prison time you face by downloading pirated media, as shown in Figure 16-15.

The unauthorized reproduction or distribution of a copyrighted work is illegal. Criminal copyright infringement, including infringement without monetary gain, is investigated by the FBI and is punishable by fines and federal imprisonment.

Goodheart-Willcox Publisher

Figure 16-15. Pirating songs, movies, software, or anything else is illegal and carries a harsh penalty.

Preventing Threats from Public Intrusion

External threats can come from individuals, criminal groups, or foreign governments. The "enemy" may disclose, modify, or destroy your information. Vulnerabilities may be caused by poor software coding or by weak administrative controls.

Peer-to-Peer File Sharing

Do not use peer-to-peer (P2P) file sharing. There is nothing illegal about sharing photographs you take with family and friends. However, many authorities believe that P2P file sharing is mostly used to share illegal content, such as a copyrighted material. Furthermore, becoming part of the P2P network puts your computer at increased risk. Your computer becomes open to viruses, spyware, and other threats.

Public Internet Providers

Conducting any business on shared public Internet providers can be very dangerous. Public Internet providers, or hotspots, are common at airports, hotels, Internet cafés, libraries, and other public places. However, these networks do not provide a secure connection. They are not password-protected. Hackers may be using key-logger software to capture everything entered on the hotspot. Scammers may also be using their cell phone cameras to watch as login, password, or account information is being entered.

Some people have devices that provide their own mobile hotspot. Sometimes these are not password-protected. This allows hackers easy access. Additionally, it may be tempting to take advantage of somebody who has not password-protected his or her hotspot to get free Internet access yourself. However, doing so grants easy access to *your* data.

Access Security

Computer-network connections cannot be guaranteed to be totally secure. Wireless connections are less secure than wired connections. This is because no physical access is required by the hacker. Even wired access does not guarantee security. The network administrator or others can tap into data flowing from individual computers to the router.

Public Wi-Fi hotspots and public-access computers are very convenient. They do not require passwords and there are many tasks that users can feel comfortable performing on open networks. You can browse the web, catch up on news stories, watch online videos, or listen to streaming music. However, these public sites are very vulnerable.

Wireless Security

Computher equipment is commonly connected to the Internet via a wireless router. With wireless connections, security requires some form of data encryption between the computer and the wireless router. However, a wireless router that appears to be protected may be only using the factory-installed user name and password. These are very easy to guess or even to look up on the Internet.

Wireless signals can be easily intercepted. Therefore, it is important to secure the connection by setting a strong password for the router and using a complex router protocol. Whenever the option is available, it is best to use the WAP2 protocol. This requires a passphrase before connecting to the Internet for the first time. The previous router standard (WEP) should not be used. It can be cracked in less than a minute by common hacker software.

Living Online
2.1.3

FYI

When creating a strong password, be sure it offers no hint of the location, your name, or other easily identifiable information.

TITANS OF TECHNOLOGY

Debora A. Plunkett was Information Assurance Director at the National Security Agency (NSA) from 2010 until 2014, when she assumed another position within the NSA. She served as deputy director prior to her appointment as director. While serving as director, she was responsible for all of the national security systems for the United States. Those responsibilities covered vulnerability and threat assessments, cryptography, and spreading information about computer security. In 2007, she was awarded the rank of meritorious executive in the Senior Cryptologic Executive Service by the President of the United States. Beginning her career with the Baltimore City Police Department, Plunkett has used analytical skills developed there to respond to the growing threats of cybersecurity in her role at the national level.

Even if the Wi-Fi network requires a password or certificate to connect, it may still be possible for other people on the network or Internet to access your information unless the connection uses HTTPS. This encrypted connection is often indicated by a lock icon on the link or in the browser's address bar. A VPN can also be used to ensure a more secure, encrypted connection.

The wireless connection to the router within your home may not be secure. Your wireless signal can be "heard" a block or more away. For extra protection, install and use a software firewall on individual computers and devices.

Users of a public hotspot should try to make sure they are connecting to a legitimate hotspot. Hackers sometimes set up pirate routers with familiar names. The name, or identifier, for a wireless connection is known as service set identifiers (SSID).

Public Computers

GS5 Computing Fundamentals
7.4.3.3

Using a public computer, such as those found in libraries, is relatively safe for generalized surfing of the web. However, using one even for a simple task related to personal information, such as checking e-mail, can be quite risky. A hacker may have installed spyware to log keystrokes. It is especially important not to enter credit card information into a public computer.

Social networking sites, web-based mail sites, and e-commerce sites often include automatic log-in features that have been designed to save each user's name and password. If you need to use a public computer to log into one of these accounts, be sure to log out when done. It is not enough just to close the browser window. Even navigating to another site may not log you out of the account. Some browsers have a "private" or "anonymous" mode that allows you to browse the web without leaving a trace. If available, this feature should be used on a public computer.

Even low-tech methods may pose a risk while using a public computer. Someone nearby may be watching. While most password-entry text boxes do not show the actual password as it is entered, somebody could be watching your fingers.

Guidelines

When using public computers or unprotected hotspots, adhere to the following guidelines. Doing so will help increase the level of security.

- Do not opt to save any log-on information while using public computers.
- If you sign into a website, always log out of it.
- Completely log off the computer when finished with the session.
- Disable automatic login features on software or websites so no one can log in as you.
- Do not leave the computer unattended, even if it is your own computer.
- Enable "private" or "anonymous" browsing before entering personal data.

16.3 | SECTION REVIEW

CHECK YOUR UNDERSTANDING

1. What are the characteristics of a strong password?
2. During a thunderstorm, what should be done to the computer?
3. What is the first step in repairing damage caused by a computer virus?
4. Which file types are executable files that can run programs?
5. Which wireless protocol should *not* be used?

IC3 CERTIFICATION PRACTICE

The following question is a sample of the types of questions presented on the IC3 exam.

1. Which of the following is the strongest password?
   A. User123
   B. B00kR3dr
   C. SpotTheDog
   D. 416MainSt

BUILD YOUR VOCABULARY

As you progress through this course, develop a personal IT glossary. This will help you build your vocabulary and prepare you for a career. Write a definition for each of the following terms and add it to your IT glossary.

gateway
passphrase
personal firewall
strong password
uninterruptable power supply (UPS)

16 REVIEW AND ASSESSMENT

Chapter Summary

Section 16.1
Preventing Computer Threats

- Malware is software that intentionally performs actions to disrupt the operation of a computer system, collect private information, or otherwise harm the computer or user. Other computer threats come from phishing, data vandalism, cookies, and computer hacking.

- Internet protocols tell computers, modems, routers, and networks how to communicate with each other. There are several Internet protocols related to security, including TCP/IP, SSH, HTTPS, and others.

- The easiest way to protect information from corruption is by backing up those files in other locations. Data should be cleared from any computer equipment before it is recycled.

Section 16.2
Identity Protection and Ethical Behavior

- Identity theft is an illegal act that involves stealing someone's personal information and using that information to commit theft or fraud. To protect against this, security is important on LANs, WANs, VPNs, and wireless networks.

- Identity theft can occur via e-mail. Check questionable messages, be wary of attachments from unknown sources, do not click links in e-mail, and stay alert for phishing attempts.

- Ethics are the principles of what is right and wrong that help people make decisions. There are legal and ethical responsibilities for everything you do online.

Section 16.3
Restricting Access to Personal Information

- A personal firewall controls traffic to an individual machine, while a computer gateway is a device that joins two networks. A firewall forms a barrier between trusted and distrusted networks.

- A strong password is one difficult for both humans and computers to crack. Never disclose or share the password with anyone, and do not use the same password for multiple accounts.

- An uninterruptable power supply (UPS) is a device that protects computer systems and data files against power surges and outages. Backups should be made and maintenance should be used to further protect against data loss.

- There are thousands of computer viruses, and they can be transmitted in various ways. Keep antivirus software up to date, but if a virus cannot be blocked, its damage must be repaired.

- There are no iron-clad guarantees to ensure a website is safe, but take precautions to see if the site is reliable, such as checking the domain. Do not download any file if you suspect it to be unsafe, and *never* download pirated media.

- External computer threats can come from individuals, criminal groups, or foreign governments. Do not use P2P file sharing sites, and avoid using public Internet providers and unsecured personal hotspots.

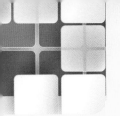

Now that you have finished this chapter, see what you know about information technology by scanning the QR code to take the chapter posttest. If you do not have a smartphone, visit www.g-wlearning.com.

Chapter 16 Test

Multiple Choice

Select the best response.

1. Which of the following is *not* a major computer threat?
   A. hackers
   B. corrupted files
   C. malware
   D. CAPTCHA

2. How can hacking be legitimate?
   A. Hiring a hacker to find security flaws in a competitor's computer system.
   B. Hiring a hacker to find security flaws in your computer system.
   C. Hacking into a social media website to remove your personal data.
   D. Hacking is never legitimate.

3. Which of the following is *not* a safe practice to deter identity theft?
   A. Set social networking profiles to public.
   B. Immediately delete messages from suspicious senders.
   C. Never click any links in unsolicited e-mail.
   D. Ensure that the lock symbol is shown in your browser's status bar.

4. WeOf8F@60F is an example of what?
   A. short password
   B. gateway logon
   C. wireless firewall code
   D. passphrase password

5. What is the function of a firewall in a network?
   A. Join two networks.
   B. Block some network traffic.
   C. Reduce temperature of internal components.
   D. Set port IDs for WANs and LANs.

Completion

Complete the following sentences with the correct word(s).

6. _____ encrypts files or blocks the user's access to programs until the user pays to unlock them.

7. The _____ is a network protocol that secures data communication and remote command execution.

8. Websites that you must join, such as Facebook and Twitter, have _____ that explain what can be posted or shared.

9. A computer _____ is a device that joins two networks.

10. A(n) _____ is a phrase composed of real words on which a password is based.

Matching

Match the correct term with its definition.

A. Trojan horse
B. cookie
C. pharming
D. online piracy
E. strong password

11. Downloading copyrighted material without permission of the copyright holder.

12. Virus or other malware infects the computer and takes control of your web browser.

13. Program that invites the user to run it while concealing malicious code that will be executed.

14. Small text files placed on a computer's hard disk by a website.

15. Difficult for both humans and computers to crack.

Application and Extension of Knowledge

1. Locate three different websites that check the strength of a password. Evaluate each site for validity and relevance. Write one paragraph for each site describing the site, providing the URL, and explaining why you believe the site to be safe.

2. Identify five applications of passwords in your personal life. These may be your cell phone, your computer, online gaming websites, social media sites, or anything that requires a password. Research the password requirements for each. Identify which characters are allowed, if there is a minimum length, and any other requirement. Make a table or chart to compare the requirements.

3. Create five passwords for the applications identified in #2. Be sure each meets the requirements you identified for the application. Also be sure to apply the guidelines provided in this chapter.

4. Using the three websites you identified in #1, check the strength of each password you created in #3. Check each password on each website. If any password does not pass any of the website tests, modify the password until it does pass all three.

5. Create a passphrase and password for a gaming website. Do not create ones you actually want to use. Prepare a presentation for the class identifying the passphrase and password. Explain why you created the passphrase and how you turned it into a password.

Online Activities

Complete the following activities, which will help you learn, practice, and expand your knowledge and skills.

Certification Practice. Complete the certification practice test for this chapter.

Vocabulary. Practice vocabulary for this chapter using the e-flash cards, matching activity, and vocabulary game until you are able to recognize their meanings.

Communication Skills

College and Career Readiness

Writing. Generate ideas that relate to the importance of accurate information. Make a list of reasons you would provide when explaining to a coworker why accurate information is important in each form or communication that is completed in a business situation.

Listening. Hearing is a physical process. Listening combines hearing with evaluation. Effective leaders learn how to listen to their team members. Listen to your instructor as the material of this chapter is presented. Listen carefully and take notes about the main points. Then, organize the key information that you heard. What points would you reiterate if you were presenting the chapter?

Speaking. Participate in a one-on-one communication with a classmate about the benefits of using electronic filing for

personal income tax. Keep in mind that your style of presentation can influence the opinion of the listener.

Internet Research

Internet Security and Ethical Use. Using the Internet, research the laws that relate to Internet security. When were they created? What is their purpose? Next, research laws regulating hacking and browser hijacking. Summarize what you learned about Internet security and ethical conduct.

Teamwork

Learning to work effectively in a team environment will be an asset in your career and personal life. Exhibiting positive interpersonal skills, as well as critical thinking skills, to solve problems or assignments can make you a productive individual. Working with your team, create a list of standards for safety in your classroom as well as personal safety standards for individual well-being. Present your ideas to the class and how these standards can be implemented.

Portfolio Development

College and Career Readiness

Organizing Your Portfolio. You have collected various items for your portfolio and tracked them in your master spreadsheet. Now is the time to organize the contents. Review the items and select the ones you want to include in your final portfolio. There may be documents that you decide not to use. Next, create a flowchart to lay out the organization for your portfolio. Your instructor may have specific guidelines for you to follow.

1. Review the documents you have collected. Select the items you want to include in your portfolio.

2. Check the quality of each item in your folders. Make sure that the documents you scanned are clear. Do a final check of the documents you created to make sure they are high quality in form and format.

3. Create the flowchart. Revise until you have an order that is appropriate for the purpose of the portfolio.

CTSOs

Day of the Event. You have practiced all year for this CTSO competition, and now you are ready. Whether it is for an objective test, written test, report, or presentation, you have done your homework and are ready to shine. To prepare for the day of the event, complete the following activities.

1. Get plenty of sleep the night before the event so that you are rested and ready to go.

2. Use your event checklist before you go into the presentation so that you do not forget any of your materials that are needed for the event.

3. Find the room where the competition will take place and arrive early. If you are late and the door is closed, you will be disqualified.

4. If you are making a presentation before a panel of judges, practice what you are going to say when you are called on. State your name, your school, and any other information that will be requested. Be confident, smile, and make eye contact with the judges.

5. When the event is finished, thank the judges for their time.

17

CAREERS IN IT

CHECK YOUR IT IQ

Before you begin this chapter, see what you already know about information technology by scanning the QR code to take the chapter pretest. If you do not have a smartphone, visit www.g-wlearning.com.

Information technology is an exciting and rapidly changing field in which to consider a career. Few in this field can predict exactly what their jobs will look like in the future. Nonetheless, professionals must make reasonable forecasts about the time ahead to prepare for changing career choices. Many new kinds of jobs are being created as hardware and software innovations expand the functionality of computers.

A good source of data on the future of IT jobs is the United States Department of Labor's Bureau of Labor Statistics (BLS). The BLS examines data and makes projections about many different fields of employment. It reports that two out of the top 15 fastest-growing occupations are in computer technology. The BLS also reports data on average salaries for various careers. This chapter covers some of the common careers in the IT field and what is required to find employment in these careers.

IC3 CERTIFICATION OBJECTIVES

GS4

Key Applications
Domain 1.0 Common application features
   Objective 1.2 Formatting
Living Online
Domain 3.0 Digital communication
   Objective 3.1 E-mail communication

College and Career Readiness

Reading Prep. The summary at the end of the chapter highlights the most important concepts. Read the chapter and write a summary of it in your own words. Then, compare your summary to the summary in the text.

SECTION 17.1

CAREER FIELDS IN INFORMATION TECHNOLOGY

Essential Question

Why is the information technology field an important part of our economy?

The speed with which computer hardware is changing is dramatic. It is happening so fast that it must be represented exponentially, which is described by Moore's law. There are several areas of information technology currently seeing the most growth. These include data storage, the Internet, and supercomputers.

There are many areas of employment affected by changes in the IT field. These include project management, security, networking, mobile applications, and data centers, among many others. Specific jobs in the IT field include software developer, computer systems analyst, security analyst, and a host of others. This section discusses areas of growth in the IT field, areas affected by innovations in IT, and careers in the IT field.

Rommel Canlas/Shutterstock.com

TERMS

chief information officer (CIO)
cloud architects
computer programmer
computer support technician
computer systems analyst
database administrator
IT manager
project management
security analyst
software developer
technical support
virtualization
web developer

LEARNING GOALS

After completing this section, you will be able to:
- Identify areas of growth in the IT field.
- Describe employment areas affected by IT innovations.
- Explain various careers available in the IT field.

Areas of Growth

Four areas in computer science are changing the most rapidly. They are computer forensics, data storage, the Internet, and supercomputers. Because they are experiencing the most growth, many of the careers available in IT will be found in these fields.

Computer Forensics

Computer forensics includes identifying, discovering, preserving, and documenting evidence from computer devices. This evidence is collected to use in court. Devices are obtained by law enforcement officials who have been granted permission in the form of warrants. Then the cybersecurity scientists begin investigating. They preserve the data exactly as they were discovered by making copies. These scientists analyze all data, including hidden files and files that the user may have deleted. They are trained to open encrypted files and to log every step of the process.

Many biometric devices can be used in human identification through fingerprints. They can capture ten prints from a subject and then transmit those prints to an automated fingerprint identification system (AFIS) for near-real-time identity verification. Some devices can perform instantaneous comparisons using a database contained within the device.

The Department of Homeland Security (DHS) recruits many hundreds of cybersecurity professionals each year, as shown in Figure 17-1. The following are the types of careers DHS offers related to computer forensics:

- cyber incident response
- cyber risk and strategic analysis
- vulnerability detection and assessment
- intelligence and investigation
- networks and systems engineering
- digital forensics and forensics analysis
- software assurance

Cybersecurity positions are also available in the Department of Defense and other governmental agencies as well as schools and private companies. For example, the University of Maryland tells prospective cybersecurity students that there are 19,000 openings just in the state of Maryland.

Career Skills

Programmable Logic Controller Programmer
Programmable logic controllers (PLC) originated in the automotive industry to control automated processes in the vehicle assembly line. Now they are used to control a variety of engineering processes, such as offshore oil platforms. These PLCs improve the efficiencies and effectiveness of a technical process. A PLC programmer sets the parameters and monitors the processes that operate the machinery.

Data Storage

The miniaturization of electronic components has progressed dramatically over the past 50 years and will probably continue to do so. This miniaturization has particular application in the field of data storage. The first computer-storage device was manufactured in 1956 by IBM. It had a hard disk drive that weighed over one ton and used fifty 24-inch disks stacked in a closet-like device. The total storage capacity of this device was only about 4.4 MB. In 1973, IBM produced a model with removable disks that could each hold 200 MB. Home PCs with 100 GB

Figure 17-1. Many governmental agencies, such as the Department of Homeland Security, offer careers related to computer forensics.

hard drives were common by 2005, and 1 terabyte (TB) hard drives were common by 2010.

The revolution in data storage occurred with the invention of the floppy disk. As the size of these disks decreased from 8 inches, to 5¼ inches, and eventually to 3.5 inches, the capacity of each version increased. Floppy disks were replaced by CDs, DVDs, Blu-ray discs, and flash drives.

Then came the revolution caused by secure digital (SD) cards. They were first introduced in the early 2000s. These provide storage on a thumbnail-sized unit for digital cameras, cell phones, MP3 players, and other handheld devices. SD cards are three million times lighter and cost over 10,000 times less than an equivalent storage device of 30 years ago.

The future looks exciting for careers in the invention, production, and maintenance of data-storage devices. It may seem that the limit of miniaturizing components has been reached. However, based on history, new formats will be invented that lead to new models and even higher capacities.

Internet

The combination of decreasing cost and exponential improvements in technology have led to the rapid growth in Internet use. It is estimated that by the year 2020 the number of Internet users will reach five billion. To put that in perspective, five billion was the world population in 1987!

A very large number of people in developing countries acquire Internet access every day. This explosive growth is due to the use of mobile telephone technology. The percentages of users in Africa, Asia, and the Middle East are small when compared to North America, as shown in Figure 17-2. This means the estimated increase in Internet usage by 2020 will have two big effects. First, the Internet will reach more and more remote locations. Second, it will need to support more languages and character sets.

The Internet will not just include humans using computers and cell phones. It is expected that by 2020 the number of Internet-connected devices will be greater than the actual number of human users. Internet "users" will include devices, particularly sensors. Most of these devices will be security related. They will be located on buildings and bridges, in airports and train stations, and along highways. These devices will collect high-definition images. Such images require large capacities for storage and transmission. Installation of these devices leads to more jobs in formatting, maintaining, transmitting, and archiving image files.

High-speed data networking technology will see a dramatic increase in use. The Internet is currently becoming wireless. The number of mobile broadband subscribers is rapidly increasing. Asia and Latin America have the highest percentages of wireless subscribers. Meeting the demands of setting up and running data networks will have a significant effect on existing jobs. Many people will be needed to manage the hardware and software necessary to run these networks.

FYI

Developing countries are often seen as areas of great potential investment not only in technology, but many other types of industries.

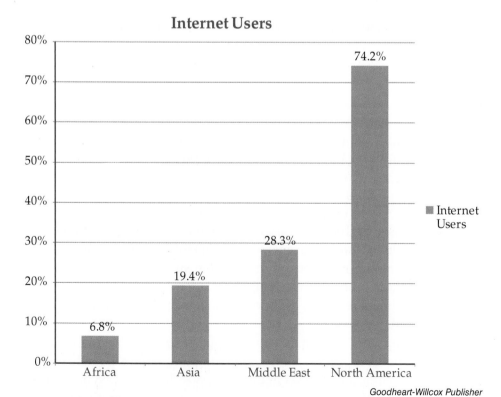

Goodheart-Willcox Publisher

Figure 17-2. The percentage of people using the Internet in North America is very high when compared with the rest of the world.

The Internet architecture currently in use assumes that all users have an "always on" connection. With more users in remote locations and more users depending on wireless communication, that can no longer be taken for granted. Instead, researchers are looking into communication techniques that can handle delays and interruptions of service. They are also investigating new ways of forwarding communication from one user to another.

Hackers are serious threats to the Internet and its users. Experts predict that by 2020 hacker attacks will be more targeted, more sophisticated, and more widespread. That will result in the creation of more jobs in IT to combat and reduce these threats. Computer scientists are now working on redesigning the Internet to improve its security. Unfortunately, security cannot be an add-on feature in a redesign of the existing Internet. A new Internet must be built from the ground up to provide a secure method of communication. More computer scientists will be needed to make the Internet of 2020 a system that is totally safe and private.

HANDS-ON EXAMPLE 17.1.1

WORLDWIDE INTERNET USE

The increase in the number of Internet users is greater than the increase in world population. This can be seen by creating a chart to compare the world population with global Internet usage over a twenty-year span.
1. Launch Microsoft Excel or other spreadsheet software, and begin a new spreadsheet.
2. Enter these data into the spreadsheet.

	Internet Users (billions)	World Population (billions)
2000	.2	6.1
2010	1.6	6.9
2020	5	7.6

3. Use the data to create a 3D area chart. Notice that while the increase in world population is close to a straight line, the increase in Internet users is not a straight line.
4. Change the title of the chart to Internet Growth vs. Population Growth.

Supercomputers

As discussed in Chapter 2, supercomputers have processing power that can handle complex jobs beyond the scope of other computer systems. Supercomputers perform highly intensive calculations. Some examples include problems involving quantum mechanics, weather forecasting, climate research, astronomy, molecular modeling, and physical simulations.

Supercomputers were first developed in the 1960s by Seymour Cray at Control Data Corporation. Cray's own company, Cray Research, took over the supercomputer market in the late 1980s. Today, supercomputers are typically one-of-a-kind designs custom produced by traditional companies such as Cray, IBM, and Hewlett-Packard.

FYI

The computing power of early supercomputers was less than that of most commonly available computers today.

For decades, the increase in supercomputer power has followed a smooth and predictable path. Should this trend continue, it could be that complete simulations of the human brain and all of its neurons will be possible by the year 2025. In the early 2030s, supercomputers could be able to predict weather over a two-week period with 99 percent accuracy. By the 2050s, they may be able to simulate millions of human brains at one time. Along with developments in artificial intelligence and brain-computer interfaces, this could allow creating virtual worlds similar to those seen in today's science fiction movies.

Many new jobs are needed for the development of supercomputers to continue at the current rate. These will be in hardware and software development. Jobs will also be needed to support and maintain supercomputers.

Employment Areas Affected by IT Innovations

All companies have IT needs regardless of the field. Health care, manufacturing, agriculture, entertainment, transportation, governmental administration, and hospitality are some of the fastest growing fields. Companies in these and all other parts of the economy need trained individuals to oversee their computer systems, as shown in Figure 17-3.

Surveys of companies looking to hire IT professionals in the near future show that many of the positions reflect the developments in the IT field. These positions did not exist just a few years ago. There are many areas in non-IT fields that hold promise for IT positions. In many cases, the specific jobs have yet to be defined.

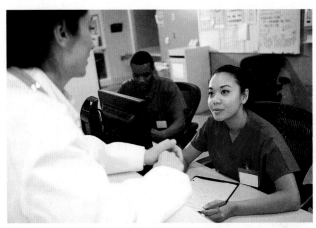

Monkey Business Images/Shutterstock.com

Figure 17-3. The health care field uses computers in many different ways, from tracking patient data and records to computer-assisted surgeries. IT professionals are needed to oversee these systems.

Programming and Application Development

Companies need programming and application development to solve problems that need to be automated. Workers in programming and application development design, create, and modify general computer software or specialized programs. A person in this position must be able to analyze user needs and develop software solutions. He or she may analyze and design databases, working individually or coordinating development as part of a team.

Companies hiring in this area seek to improve productivity, lower costs, and create a better web presence. They need staffers to create new and better technology to do those things. Experience with high-level programming languages, such as Java, J2EE, C++, and Visual Basic.Net, is needed.

Peter Bernik/Shutterstock.com

Figure 17-4. A project manager must apply the available tools and his or her skills to meet the objectives of the project.

Project Management

Project management is applying tools and skills to the tasks in a project in order to meet the objectives of the project, as shown in Figure 17-4. The ongoing need for project management skills correlates with the continuing need for programmers. Both are responses to the demand for new applications that businesses need to have to compete in the economy. If there are more projects, then more project managers are needed. The demand for project managers is strong, in part because projects are becoming more complex.

Successful candidates need to have proven track records of completed projects. They need to be organized, show leadership, know how to follow up, and be attentive to details.

Technical Support

Technical support is providing assistance to others with setting up, running, or fixing technical systems, such as computer systems. Working in technical support is the starting point for many people interested in an IT career. Staffing firms specializing in technical careers report that *help desk technician* is the job title companies most often seek help filling. These jobs are very interactive with users.

Many new systems are being set up and have to be used by employees who are not IT-oriented. For example, a technical support person at a hospital could be working with a new radiology system, genome sequencing, or electronic health record application. Companies are looking not only for people to build and implement the systems, but also for technical support to help employees use them.

Security

Security has long been a concern of IT leaders. IT security ensures a stable, safe computing environment. Businesses are increasingly dependent on computer systems and the Internet. Systems are becoming larger. Hackers are becoming more intrusive. As a result, demand for specialized security is growing.

Candidates for IT security positions must show that they know how a given company does business. They will also have expertise in deploying firewalls, using threat-detection tools, and installing encryption technology. The **chief information officer (CIO)** is the person in charge of data security for a company. He or she has a staff to combat cyber criminals.

The Internet Crime Complaint Center is a partnership between the FBI and the National White Collar Crime Center. It processes more than a quarter of a million complaints related to Internet crime each year.

> ### FYI
>
> Technical support is often referred to as a help desk or simply tech support.

Most complaints deal with fraud. These crimes included nondelivery of ordered items, credit and debit card fraud, and advanced-fee scams.

Business Intelligence and Analytics

As businesses collect more and more data, understanding how to process these data grows in importance. An example is the enormous amount of information collected and transmitted by Twitter. Twitter currently handles about five hundred million tweets per day. Twitter and many other companies analyze all of these tweets to find trends. News media follow social media trends to locate stories. Business intelligence and analytics involves processing data and locating trends.

Hiring staff to evaluate all of the collected data is one of the top priorities for many companies. IT managers have found that getting the right people to analyze all that information is challenging. The best candidates have technical know-how, business knowledge, and a strong background in both statistics and math. This is an uncommon combination of skills to find in one person. As a result, some companies hire statisticians and then teach them about technology and business. If interested in this field, a good background in statistics as well as computer technology is a benefit.

> **FYI**
>
> The vast amount of data collected by businesses and organizations is often called *big data*.

Cloud Computing

Knowledge of cloud computing was not on the list of needs for most companies as recently as 2015. Now cloud computing is a real option for data-storage requirements. Cloud computing also offers many application software solutions. As a result, companies find a need to hire cloud architects.

Cloud architects are experts in establishing cloud-computing solutions for a company, as shown in Figure 17-5. They must be smart businesspeople and know how to economically build a system. In addition, they need to know where the system can be hosted and how it should be configured. Their responsibilities will also include knowing how to negotiate with all of the people responsible for its implementation. Finally, they must make sure all of the company's data are properly backed up.

Syda Productions/Shutterstock.com

Figure 17-5. A cloud architect establishes cloud-computing solutions for a company.

Virtualization

Virtualization is a process that allows multiple operating systems to simultaneously share a processor's resources in a safe and efficient way. It hides the real physical characteristics of a computing platform from users. Instead, it lets them see a simpler, simulated environment. Virtualization allows different operating systems to take turns running the system. This is very helpful in conserving the use of expensive hardware.

A virtualization administrator manages the computer system used for virtualization. The successful candidate for this position must understand the storage and clusters behind the virtual server. Previously, network connections consisted of devices and wires. Now, the CPUs handle virtualization. Therefore, experts in this field must be more knowledgeable in software rather than hardware.

Networking

Computer networking expertise is near the top of most companies' desired employee skills. Networks exist in almost all businesses. They require constant updates and maintenance. The successful candidate will be familiar with wired and wireless hardware components. He or she will also be an expert in the types of networks and their related software. A person who chooses this career path should enjoy troubleshooting and problem-solving. Network administrator is a position often in demand.

Mobile Applications

Mobile technology has created many jobs. Consumers and businesses use smartphones and tablets more and more. Employers need workers who can support these devices. Companies want individuals who can assess business needs and write mobile apps to meet them. This requires expertise in hardware capabilities and skill in the various operating systems of each type of mobile device.

Data Center

A data center houses computer systems and related hardware. Handling the functions of a data center requires core technical skills. Experience in storage and data backup is a concept learned in the early phases of computer hardware courses. These skills still remain in high demand. Database management and administration is the most requested need of companies looking to hire IT professionals.

Careers Available in IT

IT professionals can earn a very good living. They may start out doing technical support with an annual salary of about $40,000. The salary depends on many factors, from where the job is located to the size of the company. From there, an IT technician can be promoted into a variety of positions.

An interesting example of an IT career is the position of Vice President of Trust and Safety at Twitter. Twitter processes over 15 billion tweets each month. About 150,000 of them are dangerous. This vice president has a huge responsibility: to root out risky activity that might put users in harm's way.

There is a wealth of information on the Internet related to careers. Many websites list the education, skills, and experience needed to apply for a job in the field. Create a search string that names the career and includes the keywords of education, skills, experience: "software developer

FYI

The increase in use of mobile devices has been dramatic over the past five years, now exceeding the use of desktop computers.

FYI

After reading about career responsibilities, required training, and predicted salary, begin focusing on mapping out a career plan.

career" education skills experience. Results include a number of websites, many from schools offering education in the career. Sites offer career preparation advice for getting the proper education, developing the needed skills, and gaining experience in the field. Be sure to evaluate each site to see if it is providing reliable information.

Software Developer

A **software developer** writes specifications for programs, applications, and other software, as shown in Figure 17-6. These are the people who make Minecraft entertaining and keep users spelling out Words with Friends on their smartphones. A software developer designs computer software, databases, and games. Or, he or she may be responsible for writing operating systems. Being able to write programs is the most important skill for this position. Testing and debugging the code are also important skills. However, the software developer hands off the project to computer programmers to create the final software.

Growth for both types of software developers will expand. The Bureau of Labor Statistics (BLS) predicts there will be nearly 140,000 new positions created before 2022. It projects 22.8 percent employment growth for software developers between 2012 and 2022. This is much faster growth than average for all occupations. The BLS reports the median salary for software developers is between $90,000 and $95,000 per year.

Ammentorp Photography/Shutterstock.com

Figure 17-6. Software developers write specifications for programs, which are then given to programmers to create the programs.

FYI

The median salary is the salary above which half of the group earned and below which half of the group earned. It is *not* a starting salary.

After software is in operation, developers have to maintain and improve it. If a software developer is working with a business, he or she must know how the company does business. The developer must be able to interview the client and create a list of specifications for a new system. Software developers work with many other people in a company including the managers and other developers. Developers are often natural problem-solvers who possess strong analytical skills and the ability to think outside of the box.

A bachelor degree is usually required for software developer positions. In some cases, practical experience may be enough to land an entry-level job. Developers can enhance their careers by staying up-to-date on the latest programming tools and languages.

Computer Systems Analyst

A **computer systems analyst** makes recommendations to organizations for the best systems to use, as shown in Figure 17-7. He or she must understand not only the software, but the computer hardware, networks, and how they work together. The computer systems analyst

Figure 17-7. A computer systems analyst must understand software, hardware, networks, and how they work together.

has a big responsibility. How these key areas are integrated determines how efficiently the company operates. He or she does not need to know all details of specific technologies, but must understand how the systems interact.

Computer systems analysts are tech-savvy professionals who can visualize the big picture of how a company operates. They must keep the three aspects of an organization working together smoothly: employees, workflow, and computer systems. With employees and priorities constantly changing, a computer systems analyst must be in a problem-solving mode at all times.

Businesses increasingly rely on IT. Therefore, the demand for computer systems analysts is predicted to escalate at a steady pace. The BLS predicts 24.5 percent employment growth for this job by 2022, faster than the average of all occupations. About 127,000 new jobs will be created by then. The BLS reports the median salary for a computer systems analyst is about $80,000 per year.

Web Developer

A **web developer** is responsible for creating websites, as shown in Figure 17-8. This involves developing the website's color scheme, layout, text, images, and user experience. A web developer must work with the client to set the objectives for the website and then meet those objectives. Websites should be functional and visually appealing with user-friendly navigation.

Web developers have to be artistic as well as technical. Knowledge of software programs, web applications, and programming languages such as HTML and Java are essential. They must also have a solid understanding of design principles.

This type of position offers much freedom for an employee. Work environments for web developers vary widely, from large corporations or governmental agencies to small businesses. Developers may be full- or part-time employees. Many work on a contract basis as freelancers, while many others are self-employed.

About 28,500 new jobs will need to be filled by 2022 in an industry that already has roughly 140,000 positions. Increased use of mobile technology will stimulate the industry's employment growth, particularly with new opportunities to create websites for mobile devices. The BLS considers this another example of a fast-growing profession. It estimates employment should

Figure 17-8. A web developer must create a website's color scheme, layout, text, images, and user experience.

increase at a rate of about 20 percent by 2022. The BLS also reports the median salary for web developers as between $60,000 and $65,000.

Security Analyst

The stories of security breaches at retailers and governmental agencies fill the news. With the rise in cyber attacks, there is a greater need to keep personal, corporate, and top-secret information safe. A **security analyst** is responsible for protecting the computer networks of a company, organization, or governmental agency, as shown in Figure 17-9. He or she works hard to stay ahead of cyber attackers. Candidates for this field need strong problem-solving and analytical skills. They also need to understand computer systems. Some information security analysts must be familiar with security regulations and standards.

Security analysts focus on three main areas:
- risk assessment, which is identifying problems an organization might face
- vulnerability, which is determining an organization's weaknesses
- defense planning, which is installing protections such as firewalls and data encryption programs

An entry-level position in this field may involve operating software to monitor and analyze information. A senior-level job may require investigative work to determine whether a security breach has occurred.

There is a high demand for someone with the right skills to protect data and information. The Washington, D.C., area has a high employment level for this occupation, likely due to the needs of governmental agencies that require security clearances. The BLS estimates 27,400 new jobs

STEM

Engineering
According to the Americans with Disabilities Act (ADA), wheelchair ramp slopes should be between 1:16 and 1:20. The ramp should be at least 36 inches wide, and level landings must be provided at both ends. The landings must be at least as wide as the ramp and a minimum of 60 inches long. All businesses must comply with accessible-design standards when constructing or altering facilities.

erwinova/Shutterstock.com

Figure 17-9. A security analyst works hard to stay ahead of cyber attackers and must have strong problem-solving and analytical skills.

with 36.5 percent employment growth for this profession by 2022. This is the highest growth rate among technology jobs. Information security analysts earn a median annual salary of between $85,000 and $90,000.

Database Administrator

Data have become the most valuable assets that companies must protect. A **database administrator** sets up databases to track a company's information and maintains those operations, as shown in Figure 17-10. This is a very fast-growing profession.

Database administrators are viewed as the guardians of data. They have to set up the security procedures to ensure sensitive data do not fall into the wrong hands. At the same time, they have to make the data available to those who need it. Along with problem-solving skills, the job involves resolving complex issues and attention to detail. Many companies run on a schedule that is 24 hours a day and seven days a week. That means many database administrators work more than 40 hours a week.

The successful candidate for this position will have previous IT experience. Most employers require a bachelor degree in a computer-related field, such as computer science or management information systems. Certification on specific database platforms is a plus, if not a requirement. MySQL, Oracle, and Microsoft Certified Database Administrator are examples of certification.

The BLS predicts this field will add 17,900 new positions with 15.1 percent employment growth by 2022. It reports the median salary for a database administrator is between $75,000 and $80,000.

Jean-Philippe WALLET/Shustterstock.com

Figure 17-10. A database administrator must set up the security procedures to ensure sensitive data do not fall into the wrong hands.

IT Manager

An **IT manager** coordinates technology-related matters, plans upgrades of existing software or hardware, and negotiates with service providers, as shown in Figure 17-11. He or she must be technically competent, but will spend most time dealing with management, vendors, users, and other IT professionals. The IT manager must know the short- and long-term needs of the company's technology.

Almost all organizations need IT managers. Financial and insurance companies, manufacturing firms, health care facilities, and federal, state, and local governments all have particular needs for IT managers. In a medium-sized company, the IT manager generally reports to the CIO.

IT managers typically need a bachelor degree in computer or information science. This should include courses in computer

Figure 17-11. Almost all organizations need IT managers. IT managers must be technically competent, but will spend most time dealing with management, vendors, users, and other IT professionals.

programming, software development, and mathematics. Many organizations also require their IT managers to have a graduate degree, such as a Master of Business Administration. Most candidates spend five to 10 years in an IT job before being promoted to IT manager.

The BLS predicts strong employment growth of 15.3 percent and an estimated 50,900 new positions to be filled by 2022. IT managers earn a median salary of about $120,000.

Computer Programmer

Substantial knowledge of programming languages and enjoying solving puzzles is essential for those interested in computer programming. A **computer programmer** writes, rewrites, debugs, maintains, and tests the software essential to key computer functions, as shown in Figure 17-12. He or she encodes instructions provided by software developers. The programmer refines the ideas and solves problems while converting the directions into code to create a final software application.

Computer programmers write instructions in one of the many computer languages. The most commonly used languages are C++ and Python. Other popular languages are C, Perl, Java, Ruby, and VB.Net. Programmers must be able to learn on the job. The programming language you know today may change tomorrow. Programmers must

Figure 17-12. A computer programmer encodes instructions provided by software developers.

stay current on the languages they currently know as well as learn the newest languages.

Many computer programmer jobs require at least a bachelor degree. In some cases, a two-year degree or certificate may be enough to gain an entry-level position. Large computer and consulting firms often train new employees in intensive, company-based programs. Students interested in computer programming can improve their employment outlooks with internships.

The BLS predicts 28,400 new jobs with growth of 8 percent by 2022. This is considered about average growth. The median salary for a computer programmer is about $75,000.

Computer Support Technician

The primary goal of a **computer support technician** is to quickly diagnose and solve computer issues for others in a friendly and effective manner, as shown in Figure 17-13. Tasks may include assistance with log-in difficulties, operating system problems, and a variety of software malfunctions. This assistance may be provided by phone, e-mail, and online chat. On-site meetings may be required. Some computer support technicians specialize in network matters.

Computer support technicians may work in traditional offices or call centers. Candidates for this position must display excellent communication skills. A bachelor degree is usually required along with familiarity with the company's basic hardware and software. Sometimes, a two-year degree or certificate may be enough, especially if the candidate continues to work on a higher-level degree.

The BLS projects 123,000 new jobs will be created with 17 percent employment growth for computer support specialists by 2022. The industry already numbers close to three-quarters of a million workers. Computer support specialists earn a median salary of about $50,000.

Potstock/Shutterstock.com

Figure 17-13. A computer support technician may work in a call center to provide assistance for a variety of computer problems for customers.

HANDS-ON EXAMPLE 17.1.2

EXPLORING IT CAREERS

The Bureau of Labor Statistics website provides data related to many different careers, including the IT field. The site provides statistics on the current number of jobs, projected growth, and median salaries.

1. Launch a browser, and navigate to the BLS website (www.bls.gov).
2. Click the **Students** menu at the top, and click **Student Resources** in the drop-down menu.
3. Click **Career Exploration** on the new page that is displayed.
4. On the Career Exploration page, click **Computers** to expand it, as shown.

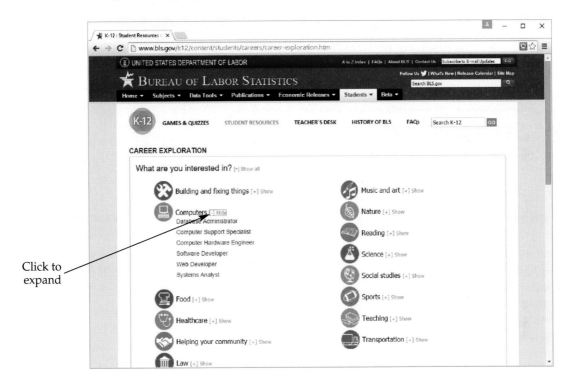

5. Click one of the careers displayed. The summary page of the Occupational Outlook Handbook for the career is displayed.
6. Click the **Work Environment** link.
7. What industries generally need employees in this career?
8. Click the browser's **Back** button to return to the Career Exploration page, select a different computer career, and find out what industries generally need employees in the career.

TITANS OF TECHNOLOGY

Jeffrey C. Taylor is the founder of the online career site Monster.com. It was created in the early days of the World Wide Web. It was the 454th registered domain on the web. Monster.com quickly became one of the first well-known dot-com companies. Taylor's "monster idea" was to revolutionize the way in which people look for employment. He shifted searches from the "want ads" in the backs of newspapers to the web.

Monster.com was the first publically accessible employment search engine on the web. It is now one of the world's leading online career site. Taylor left Monster.com in 2005 to pursue other interests. He founded and was the CEO of Eons.com. This website connected adults in an online community, but is no longer active. He is also the founder and chairman of Tributes.com. This website is a source for national and local obituaries.

17.1   SECTION REVIEW

 ### CHECK YOUR UNDERSTANDING

1. Which four areas of computer science are changing the most rapidly?
2. What are the duties and tasks of a chief information officer?
3. What would be a good search string to use when researching the job opportunities for a web developer?
4. Which IT career involves writing the code to create programs, applications, and other software?
5. What does a database administrator do?

IC3 CERTIFICATION PRACTICE

The following question is a sample of the types of questions presented on the IC3 exam.

1. Which of the following is the program used to create and send an e-mail message?
   A. e-mail server
   B. message header
   C. e-mail client
   D. ISP

BUILD YOUR VOCABULARY

As you progress through this course, develop a personal IT glossary. This will help you build your vocabulary and prepare you for a career. Write a definition for each of the following terms and add it to your IT glossary.

chief information officer (CIO)
cloud architects
computer programmer
computer support technician
computer systems analyst

database administrator
IT manager
project management
security analyst
software developer
technical support
virtualization
web developer

Goodluz/Shutterstock.com

Preparation for a career in IT requires knowledge in a specific set of skills. A candidate for this field must have formal training. Certifications from various technical exams can also command respect for the job-seeker. For example, Microsoft A+ certification in networking is a measure of success.

Essential Question

How has the digital revolution changed the way in which jobs are found?

Most employers require a college degree, some sort of technical certification, or some related experience. Some will require a combination of all three. However, when asked, most employers say personal-success skills are among the most important qualities in a potential employee.

LEARNING GOALS

After completing this section, you will be able to:

- Identify personal-success skills.
- Research a career.
- Describe the education, certification, training, and experience needed for a career.
- Create a résumé and portfolio.

TERMS

529 plan
career and technical
  student organizations
  (CTSOs)
career plan
certification
formal education
Gantt chart
goal
informational
  interviewing

networking
portfolio
postsecondary education
résumé
scholarship
self-assessment
SMART goals
storyboarding

Personal-Success Skills

Employers are looking for employees with the personal skills needed to be successful in the workplace. These skills are commonly called *soft skills*. Good communication skills are required: writing, speaking, and listening. Beyond that, employers expect employees to have good attendance and to be at work at the assigned time. Employees should follow the dress code established by the employer, keep their work areas neat and clean, and take pride in their work. Employees should be able to solve problems by analyzing a situation and finding the best resolution.

Time-Management and Team Skills

Time-management skills are critical in 21st century jobs. The ability to determine how much time a task will take and then completing it on time is a skill everyone must master. Closely related to this is project management. When called on to work on multiple projects, the successful employee must be able to manage the tasks for each project to keep all projects on schedule. Storyboarding projects is a way to help manage them. **Storyboarding** is breaking a project down into its tasks and then arranging the tasks in an order that allows the project to stay on schedule. A storyboard can be used along with a Gantt chart. A **Gantt chart** is like a bar graph that tracks tasks, which tasks are dependent on others, and the completion percentages of each task, as shown in Figure 17-14. Time lines, deadlines, resource allocation, time management, delegation of tasks, and collaboration are all important aspects of time management and project management.

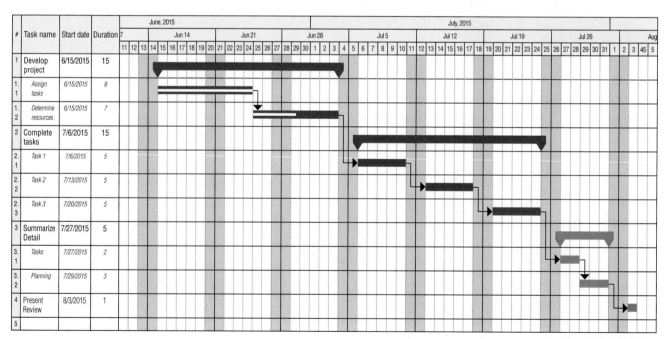

Figure 17-14. A Gantt chart shows how long each task will take and which tasks must be completed before other tasks.

When managing a project, it is important to first plan the project. With planning complete, the project can be started (initiated) and placed in process (executed). While the project is in process, be sure to monitor it to ensure it stays on time and within its scope. Once the project is complete, close it by writing any needed follow-up reports or announcements. Also review the project to see if it met the goals set by the plan.

Employees should be flexible and be able to work with others in a team, responding to multiple priorities. All managers are looking to diversify their workplaces and encourage an atmosphere of acceptance and sensitivity. They want people with good moral fiber who are honest, hardworking, loyal, dependable, and responsible. Employers want happy, productive, life-long learners who will grow with new skills in the 21st century.

Constructive Criticism and Conflict Management

When working with others, it is important to be able to accept constructive criticism. Constructive criticism is feedback provided to you by others with the intent of improving your work. Be understanding while receiving the feedback. Always thank the person for the feedback. When responding to constructive criticism, try not to act on your first impulse. It is natural to be defensive about your work, but the person is trying to help by providing feedback. Take a few seconds or minutes to evaluate the feedback. Determine if the feedback identifies something that should be changed. If you need an explanation, ask for more information.

Even in the best of situations, a conflict may arise. If this happens, be sure to apply appropriate strategies to manage and resolve the conflict. Start by talking to the person. Focus on what happened, not what the *person* did. Be respectful of what the person has to say. Listen without interrupting and wait for a pause in the conversation to respond. When he or she has finished speaking, summarize or restate what was said. If anything is not clear to you, ask follow-up questions. Identify areas where you agree with the person and areas where you disagree. Be sure to ask if the other person agrees these are the areas of agreement and disagreement. Then that work with the person to decide which areas are the most important, and address those areas first. Create a plan that both agree on to resolve the issue. Be sure to follow through with the plan. Meet with the person again as needed to ensure a successful resolution to the conflict.

Verbal and Nonverbal Communication

Verbal communication is speaking words to communicate. It is also known as oral communication. In the course of a workday, most people spend at least some portion of time talking with coworkers, supervisors, managers, or customers. *Nonverbal communication* is an action, behavior, or attitude that sends a message to the receiver. It may send a message that is different from what you speak.

Interpersonal Skills

Interpersonal skills are those skills that help people communicate and work well with each other. The business or organization you will work for expects you to have good interpersonal skills. These skills are necessary to complete the job duties and ensure a positive working environment. The ability to communicate well, showing respect for others, and teamwork are skills all employers want in their employees.

Giving and receiving information efficiently is the key to effective communication. Time is limited in the workplace, and all employees have many duties and responsibilities. Others appreciate it when a person gets to the point quickly and in a positive manner. Being able to state your needs or intentions clearly to others can be learned through practice.

Careful listening and responding are also hallmarks of good communication. If you do not understand what someone wants, ask the person to clarify the request. Make sure to carefully follow directions. Always ask questions when you do not understand how to do a certain task. As in every part of life, communicating in a positive manner gets better results than communicating negatively or with a bad attitude.

Respect is the feeling that someone or something is good, valuable, and important. Respect coworkers. A smile and a few minutes of friendly conversation are good ways to promote good working relationships.

Work environments are usually diverse. There will be people of many different cultures, beliefs, and ages. Regardless of personal differences, show respect to your supervisors, coworkers, and anyone else you interact with on the job. Make sure to remember the golden rule: treat others as you would like to be treated.

Skills for the Workplace

Employers look for potential employees who can help make their companies successful. There are many criteria used to sort through the hundreds of résumés submitted for open positions. Finding a potential employee with the required educational background and experience are usually the first criteria employers use when screening applications. For example, an employer looking to fill a position in cybersecurity will confirm the candidate is truly qualified for the position. The applicant's education and work experience will be reviewed to confirm the individual has job-specific skills. A *skill* is something an individual does well. *Job-specific*

michaeljung/Shutterstock.com

Your working environment will likely be diverse. It is important to be respectful of the beliefs and cultural backgrounds of your coworkers.

skills are critical skills necessary to perform the required work-related tasks of a position. Job-specific skills are acquired through work experience and education or training. Without them, the individual would be unlikely to successfully perform the job.

When applying for a position, the employer will ask questions related to your employability skills. *Employability skills* are applicable skills used to help an individual find a job, perform in the workplace, and gain success in a job or career. Employability skills are also known as foundational or transferrable skills. You have already acquired many of these skills in school. However, some of these skills are gained through life experience, such as working at a job or interacting with others in social situations. These skills are not specific to one career, but rather transferrable to any position.

Finding a candidate with employability skills is crucial in today's workplace. Employability skills can be categorized as basic skills, thinking skills, people skills, and personal qualities.

Basic Skills

Basic skills are the fundamental skills necessary to effectively function in society. These skills include:

- reading;
- writing;
- speaking;
- listening;
- applying mathematics; and
- applying technology skills.

Reading involves acquiring meaning from written words and symbols and evaluating their accuracy and validity. Reading skills allow you to comprehend and locate information in various forms, including in books, on the Internet, and in pictures such as graphs. Reading also helps you evaluate material to ensure understanding and form judgments.

Writing is using written words to express your ideas and opinions. Writing skills enable you to communicate effectively on paper or through electronic means. Writing requires you to edit and revise the message for accuracy, emphasis, and the audience. Effective business writing is required in the workplace.

Speaking is verbally communicating ideas. Speaking skills enable you to verbally present information in a clear manner, maximize word choices, control your tone of voice, and adjust the message for the audience.

Listening is hearing what others say and evaluating their messages for information. When you use listening skills, you pay attention to what other people are saying and understand the points being made.

Mathematics is the study of numbers and their relationships. Mathematical skills enable you to use numbers to evaluate information and detect patterns so that decisions can be made.

Technology skills include how to use social media, software, and basic computer systems. Using technology skills is necessary to be productive in the workplace.

Thinking Skills

Thinking skills are those skills that help people solve problems. Even if you are unable to find a solution, thinking skills help you assess a situation and identify the options. Examples of thinking skills include:

- decision-making;
- creative thinking;
- problem solving;
- visualization; and
- reasoning.

Decision-making is the process of analyzing a situation and evaluating possible outcomes in order to choose the best solution. Decision-making skills enable you to weigh pros and cons in order to solve problems.

Creative thinking involves developing or designing unusual and clever ideas about a given topic or situation. When you use creative-thinking skills, you develop unique or different ways to solve a problem.

Problem solving is identifying a solution and implementing it in the most efficient manner. Problem-solving skills help you carry out a plan or implement new processes to achieve a desired outcome.

Visualization is the ability to form mental images. Visualization skills allow you to imagine how something will function or appear prior to an actual process.

Reasoning is the ability to combine pieces of information or apply general rules to specific problems. Reasoning skills enable you to reach conclusions based on what you already know.

People Skills

People skills are the skills that enable people to develop and maintain working relationships with others. These skills have a significant impact on your relationships with others in the workplace. Examples of people skills include:

- social perceptiveness;
- negotiation;
- leadership;
- teamwork; and
- cultural competence.

Social perceptiveness is being aware of the feelings of others and understanding why others may act a certain way. Socially perceptive people exhibit kindness and understanding. They take an interest in their coworkers and who they are. However, it is important to balance social perceptiveness with the ability to assert yourself in a polite and professional manner when appropriate.

goodluz/Shutterstock.com

Having good people skills is important to success in the workplace. Many jobs require communicating with customers, but even communicating with coworkers requires good people skills.

Negotiation is discussing various positions of an issue and working out the differences of opinion. The key to negotiating is being able to pinpoint the common goals among each position. This prepares everyone to argue the facts from his or her point of view and reach a compromise.

Leadership is the ability to influence or inspire other people. In the workplace, leaders encourage others and coordinate activities to reach goals.

Teamwork is working cooperatively with other people. Important aspects of teamwork include encouraging each other, building mutual trust and respect, and cooperating with team members.

Cultural competence is respecting all people regardless of age, national origin, gender, ability, or other differences. Being culturally competent enables you to effectively interact with all people in the workplace.

Personal Qualities

Personal qualities are the characteristics that make up an individual's personality. Examples of personal qualities include self-esteem, self-management, and responsibility. Having self-esteem is having confidence in yourself and your abilities. Self-management is the ability to work independently without supervision. Responsibility is being trusted to complete duties or tasks.

Employers look for employees who are flexible and can adjust in a positive manner to work situations as they change. This includes being professional, having a positive attitude, and, above all, being ethical. Positive ethics are an important work quality that all employers expect their employees to possess.

HANDS-ON EXAMPLE 17.2.1
IDENTIFYING PERSONAL-SUCCESS SKILLS

To be successful in your chosen career, you will need to have knowledge and skills related to the field. However, you will also need to have certain personal-success skills.
1. Launch a browser, and navigate to a search engine.
2. Enter the search phrase personal success skills employers seek.
3. Visit several of the sites in the search result. Be sure to evaluate each site for validity of information.
4. Collect ten soft skills that an employer wants in a prospective employee.
5. Bring your list to class for a discussion. Be prepared to explain each skill and why you believe the skill is important or why not.

Researching a Career

It is important to know how to find information about career opportunities. You will need to know what education, skills, and experiences are needed to be successful. However, before beginning research, think about yourself and what types of work you might enjoy. Then, develop a career plan.

Career Plan

Planning for your career can be exciting. Your career choice will direct many other decisions in life. It will affect decisions about your education and even where you will live. To determine the careers that will be enjoyable for you, you must first learn about yourself.

A **career plan** is a list of steps on a time line to reach each of your career goals. It is also known as a *postsecondary plan.* A career plan should include options for education. Options include four-year colleges, two-year colleges, and technical schools. It should also address current job opportunities in your career of interest.

There is no set format for writing a career plan. Many free career plan templates can be found on the Internet. Figure 17-15 illustrates action items for a career plan. To create a career plan, you should first conduct a self-assessment and then set SMART goals. SMART goals are discussed later in this chapter. You will continue revising the career plan as you achieve your goals and set new ones.

A **self-assessment** is an evaluation of your aptitudes, abilities, values, and interests. By conducting a self-assessment, you can focus your energy on what is necessary for you to become a successful in a career. Some self-assessment techniques are thinking or writing exercises. Others are in the

Action Items for a Career Plan: IT Specialist			
	Extracurricular and Volunteer Activities	Work Experience	Education and Training
During Middle School	• Help nonprofit groups and local youth groups with information technology needs • Prepare IT components and electronics for fairs and competitive events	Choose a part-time job or volunteer position that allows application of information technology skills	• Participate in a CTSO • For optional or extra credit work, select topics and projects related to computer service, maintenance, repair, or design
During High School	• Volunteer in school IT lab or seek out co-op opportunities • Perform computer service and repair for nonprofit organizations	Work as an intern at a local electronics or computer repair business	Take classes in information technology along with required coursework
During College	Help student, nonprofit, or local groups identify the best solutions for their computing and electronic needs	Work as a part-time service technician for an electronics or computer repair business	Follow the bachelor degree path for information technology
After College	• Obtain certification in your specialized area • Attend local information technology professionals and chamber of commerce events	Work as a technician	• Participate in appropriate professional development opportunities • Consider obtaining a master degree in computer science

Goodheart-Willcox Publisher

Figure 17-15. This is an example of a career plan.

form of tests, such as a personality test. Your career counselor can help you conduct a self-assessment.

Consider what you like to do and what you do well. This can give you clues to aid your self-assessment. If you are very organized and can handle several projects at once, you may find success as a manager. On the other hand, if you do not do well in math class, computer programmer may not be a good career for you. Instead, consider an IT career that has a lesser math requirement. Identifying a career that you will enjoy begins with finding out what you like to do.

What is your work style? Some individuals prefer to work independently. Others need constant direction to accomplish a task. Mornings are more productive for some workers, whereas others perform better in the afternoons. Casual dress influences one person to perform well. Business dress makes others more effective on the job.

Aptitudes

An *aptitude* is a characteristic that an individual has naturally developed. Aptitudes are also called *talents*. When a person naturally excels at a task without practicing or studying, he or she has an aptitude for it. For example, a person with an aptitude for music may be very good at accurately humming a tune or keeping a beat, even if he or she

FYI

When taking a self-assessment, strive to identify your aptitudes, abilities, values, and interests. Learning this information can reveal careers for which you are well suited.

has never studied music. Knowing your aptitudes can lead to job success. Some examples of aptitudes are:

- mathematics;
- drawing;
- writing; and
- art.

Abilities

Ability is a mastery of a skill or the capacity to do something. Having aptitudes and skills are supported or limited by your abilities. For instance, a student who has musical aptitude and skill might not have the ability to perform under pressure in musical concerts.

While aptitudes are something a person is born with, abilities can be acquired. Often, it is easier to develop abilities that match your natural aptitudes. For example, someone with an aptitude for acquiring languages may have the ability to speak French. A person without an aptitude for acquiring language can also learn to speak French. However, it will be more difficult.

Aptitudes and abilities do not always match. Someone with an aptitude for repairing machines may not enjoy doing this type of work and never develop the ability. Examples of abilities include:

- teaching others;
- multitasking;
- thinking logically; and
- speaking multiple languages.

Values

The principles and beliefs that you consider important are your *values.* They are beliefs about the things that matter most to an individual. Values are developed as you mature and learn. Your values will affect your life in many ways. They influence how you relate to other people and make decisions about your education and career.

Your work values can provide great insight into what kind of career will appeal to you. For some individuals, work values include job security. For others, the number of vacation days is important. Everyone has a set of work values that are taken into consideration when choosing a career path. For example, a person who values the environment may want to pursue a career in green energy or conservation, as shown in Figure 17-16. Examples of values include:

- perfection;
- equality;
- harmony; and
- status.

Closely related to values are family responsibilities and personal priorities. These can have a direct impact on career choice. For example,

Goodluz/Shutterstock.com

Figure 17-16. If you wish to pursue an IT career related to green technology, you may consider working with the control systems for solar power installations.

if you expect to have a large family, you may decide that time is a family responsibility. You may want to spend as much time as possible with your children as they grow. This may mean choosing a career that does not typically require travel or working long hours. On the other hand, it may be important to you to live in an expensive house and drive an expensive car. This personal priority will require you to enter a career with an income level that will support these choices.

Interests

An *interest* is a feeling of wanting to learn more about a topic or to be involved in an activity. Your interests might include a subject, such as history. You may be interested in local politics or cars. Your interests can also include hobbies, such as biking or cooking. Since all types of companies need IT professionals, there is a good chance you can find a career that would allow you to be around your interests.

Your interests may change over time. You may find new hobbies or topics that interest you. Try to determine if there is a uniting theme to your interests. When considering your interests, look at the "big picture." For example, you may enjoy working on cars right now. In a few years, a career as an IT professional for a car manufacturer or dealer may suit you because you enjoy cars. Examples of interests include:

- art and creativity;
- woodworking;
- sports and adventure; and
- collecting.

Researching Career Information

There are several resources to help in researching a career. A good thing to keep in mind is that a career is rarely one job you have for 30 or 40 years. Especially in the IT field, job requirements rapidly change. There is almost always the opportunity for a better job through advancement or lateral movement. Better jobs often have more responsibility, more opportunity to impact the final result, and, generally, larger salaries.

Internet Research

The Internet is a good place to start when researching your future career. Researching various professions, employment trends, industries, and prospective employers provides insight to careers that may interest you. Many postsecondary schools have websites that provide career information.

The Occupational Information Network (O*NET) is a valuable resource for career information. O*NET Online (www.onetonline.org) is the most comprehensive database of occupational information. It was created by the US Department of Labor and is regularly updated. This website contains data on salary, growth, openings, education requirements, skills and abilities, work tasks, and related occupations for more than 1,000 careers. The database can be searched by career cluster. IT careers are found in the information technology career cluster.

Another way to explore careers online is through employment websites. Examples of these are Monster.com and Dice.com. Other sites that focus on technical careers include ComputerWork.com, CareerBuilder.com, ComputerJobs.com, and TechCareers.com, as shown in Figure 17-17. Governmental jobs are found on USA.gov. It is a good idea to visit these sites to see what the overall requirements are for jobs in the geographic area being sought.

Career Handbooks

Career handbooks offer a great place to begin researching specific careers, their industries, and areas of the country or world in which these industries thrive. The US Bureau of Labor Statistics publishes the *Occupational Outlook Handbook* and the *Career Guide to Industries*. These handbooks describe the training and education needed for various jobs. They provide up-to-date information about careers, industries, employment trends, and even salary outlooks.

The information technology industry is considered a nature of business. Nature of business is a general category of operations. The business can be organized as proprietorships, partnerships, or corporations.

A *proprietorship* is a business that has a sole owner. This person is responsible for every aspect of the business including making money or losing money.

A *partnership* is comprised of two or more people working toward a joint purpose. Individual partners bring many attributes to a business,

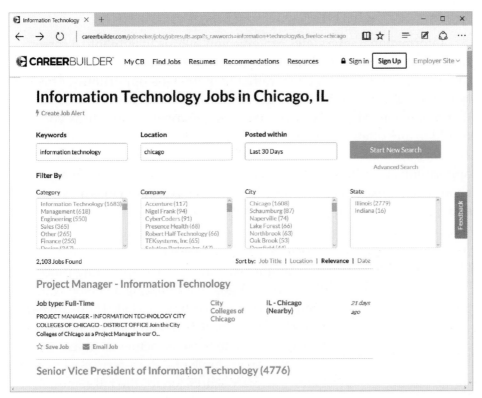

Goodheart-Willcox Publisher

Figure 17-17. CareerBuilder.com is one of the many employment websites that can be used to research and locate career positions.

such as money, talent, and time. All are responsible for the business, including making money or losing money.

A *corporation* is a type of business that is recognized as a separate legal entity from its owners. A corporation is defined by the US Supreme Court as "an artificial being, invisible, intangible, and existing only in contemplation of the law." It is a form of ownership in which owners are not personally liable for the business.

Networking

Eighty percent of new jobs are found by networking. Some open jobs are never even advertised. **Networking** means talking with people you know and making new contacts. Most employers would much rather hire someone who comes recommended by someone they already know. Asking family and friends for contacts in the field is a good way to start. Then it is possible to contact these professionals and ask if they know of any open jobs or employers who are hiring.

Many professional organizations have student chapters. These can be great places to network with others in your chosen career field. When you begin looking for your first job, let other members know. The more contacts you make, the greater your opportunities for finding career ideas.

Green Tech

Green Job Search
Technology has made finding and applying for jobs more eco-friendly than ever before. Job seekers can now locate and apply for job positions online by electronically uploading their résumé in response to a job posting. Many websites allow job seekers to complete their applications online. Searching and applying for jobs electronically saves time and money.

Informational Interviews

Informational interviews can give you unique insight into a career. **Informational interviewing** is a strategy used to interview a professional to ask for advice and direction, rather than for a job opportunity. This type of interview will help you get a sense of what it is like to work in that profession. At the interview, be as professional and polite as you would in any other interview situation.

An informational interview can also be a valuable networking opportunity. By talking with someone in the field, you can learn more about what is expected. You can also learn what types of jobs are available and other information about an industry.

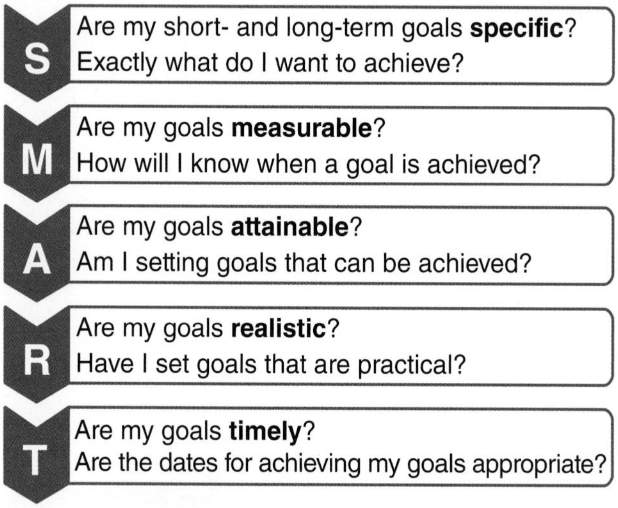

S — Are my short- and long-term goals **specific**? Exactly what do I want to achieve?

M — Are my goals **measurable**? How will I know when a goal is achieved?

A — Are my goals **attainable**? Am I setting goals that can be achieved?

R — Are my goals **realistic**? Have I set goals that are practical?

T — Are my goals **timely**? Are the dates for achieving my goals appropriate?

Goodheart-Willcox Publisher

Figure 17-18. Well-defined career goals follow the SMART goal model.

Setting SMART Goals

Another step in the career-planning process is to set goals. A **goal** is something a person wants to achieve in a specified time period. There are two types of goals: short term and long term. A *short-term goal* is one that can be achieved in less than one year. An example of a short-term goal may be getting an after-school job for the fall semester. A *long-term goal* is one that will take a longer period of time to achieve, usually more than one year. An example of a long-term goal is to attend college to earn a four-year degree.

Goal setting is the process of deciding what a person wants to achieve. Your goals must be based on what you want for your life. Well-defined career goals follow the SMART goal model. **SMART goals** are specific, measurable, attainable, realistic, and timely, as illustrated in Figure 17-18.

Specific. A career goal should be specific and straightforward. For example, "I want to have a career" is not a specific goal. Instead, you might say, "I want to have a career as a security analyst." When the goal is specific, it is easier to track your progress.

Measurable. It is important to be able to measure progress so you know when you have reached your goal. For example, "I want to earn a bachelor degree in information technology." This goal can be measured. When you earn the degree, you will know your goal has been reached.

Attainable. Goals need to be attainable. For example, "I want to be an IT manager at IBM when I graduate from college." This is not reasonable for that point in a person's career. Gaining work experience is necessary before obtaining a management position. For a large corporation, you may need ten or more years of experience to become a manager. This goal becomes more attainable when coupled with a plan to gain the necessary aptitudes, skills, and experience.

Realistic. Goals must be realistic. Obtaining a position as an IT manager may be practical with proper planning. It is not realistic for a new college graduate. Finding an entry-level IT position in the company and working your way up to IT manager over a number of years make this a realistic goal.

Timely. A goal should have a starting point and an ending point. Setting a time frame to achieve a goal is the step most often overlooked. An end date can help you stay on track. For example, you may want to be an IT manager by the time you are 35 years old. Aiming to get the experience and education to achieve this position by a specific age will help you remain motivated to reach your goal on time.

Education, Certification, Training, and Experience

There are many steps you will take as you plan your career. Your educational needs will depend on your career interests and goals. Some careers require a high school diploma followed by technical training or a bachelor degree. Others require graduate work, such as a master degree. Still other careers require professional certification. Early career planning can help you make decisions about your education.

Education

Formal education is the education received in a school, college, or university. Most IT careers require a college degree. This is called postsecondary education. Jobs higher on the career ladder often require additional formal education. This is called graduate, postgraduate, or continuing education.

Two- and four-year colleges have programs set up to offer a degree in information technology. Sometimes the programs are found in the computer science or management information systems (MIS) departments. There are also licensed technical schools whose coursework concentrates on a particular IT career. Some may focus on system networking, while others may offer web development. These schools grant certificates rather than diplomas.

Postsecondary Education

Postsecondary education is any education achieved after high school. This includes all two- and four-year colleges and universities. Common postsecondary degrees are an associate degree and a bachelor degree. An associate degree is a two-year degree. A bachelor degree is a four-year degree.

Students in postsecondary schools choose an area of study that suits an interest or meets a career goal. This is referred to as a *major*. For example, a student who wants a career in the IT field will likely major in computer science, information technology, or management information systems. When considering a major, be sure to look at the earnings

FYI

Academic certificates are professional endorsements that often require fewer classes than a degree. They are usually considered less rigorous than a two-year degree.

potential and the number of jobs available in the area, both for new graduates and for those with experience.

In addition to major area of studies, postsecondary students are typically required to take a wide variety of classes in other subjects. These courses are referred to as *general education courses*. They cover many of the same subject areas as high school courses. They also cover subjects not often offered at the high school level.

A postsecondary school may be either a not-for-profit school or a for-profit school. A *not-for-profit school* is one that returns the money it earns back into the school. These schools receive funding from student tuition and fees, donations, and governmental programs. A not-for-profit school is what most people think of in terms of "college," as shown in Figure 17-19. It may be public, such as a state university. Others may be private, such as a private college or a community college. Not-for-profit schools tend to encourage academic exploration and personal growth beyond the specific requirements of a student's major.

michaeljung/Shutterstock.com

Figure 17-19. What most people think of as "college" is a not-for-profit school. For-profit schools are alternatives for many students.

A *for-profit school* is one that is set up to earn money for investors. It provides a product, which is education. In return for providing education, a for-profit school receives money from its customers, which are students. For-profit schools are also known as *proprietary schools*. They tend to focus on specific skills and do not require general education courses. A trade school is an example of a for-profit school. These schools typically offer a two-year degree specialized in a field of trade, such as information technology technician. Some for-profit schools offer bachelor degree programs.

When considering a college or university, be aware of what is needed to apply. Requirements may include:

- official transcripts;
- college exam test scores;
- essays; and
- interviews.

For all requirements, be sure to know the deadlines for completing and submitting the information. Missing a deadline can mean not being accepted to the school.

The costs of a postsecondary education must be considered. In addition to tuition, there are fees for many classes. As an IT major, you may need to take many laboratory classes. These classes can have more fees than other courses. Living expenses must also be considered as part of the cost of a postsecondary education.

Graduate and Postgraduate Education

Education received after an individual has earned a bachelor degree is *graduate education.* Master degrees are graduate degrees. Education beyond a master degree is called *postgraduate education.* Doctorate degrees are postgraduate degrees.

Graduate and postgraduate study often build on the same subject area or a closely related subject in which the bachelor degree was earned. For example, a student who earned a Bachelor of Science degree in computer programming may pursue a Master of Science degree in information technology.

Continuing Education

Some careers that have professional licenses require *continuing education* classes. These classes are completed to maintain the license. Completing these classes earns the student *continuing education units (CEUs).*

Career and Technical Student Organizations

Career and technical student organizations (CTSOs) are national student organizations with local school chapters that are related to career and technical education (CTE) courses. CTSO programs are tied to various course areas. Internships and other cooperative work experiences may be a part of the CTSO experience. CTSOs can help prepare high school graduates for their next step, whether it is college or a job. The goal of CTSOs is to help students acquire knowledge and skills in different career and technical areas.

Competitive events are a main feature of most CTSOs. Competing in various events enables students to show mastery of specific content. Events also measure the use of decision-making, problem-solving, and leadership skills. Students may receive recognition awards for participation in events. In some cases, scholarships may be awarded if they win at state- and national-level competitions.

Professional Certification

There are many types of certification available. **Certification** is a professional status earned by an individual after passing an exam focused on a specific body of knowledge. When cerfitication is achieved, the person receives a certificate. The individual usually prepares for the exam by taking classes and studying content that will be tested. The exam is often given online.

Certification programs are helpful to employers who are looking for a standardized way to assess a candidate's skill level. Certificates might give the candidate an extra advantage to gaining an interview, such as demonstrating computer literacy with IC3 cerficiation. However, a certificate is not an alternative to a college degree.

FYI

Employees who earn certificates generally make more money than those who do not.

Some certifications must be renewed on a regular basis. For example, many certifications sponsored by Microsoft are only valid for the specific version of software. When the next version is released, another exam must be taken to be certified for the update. Other certifications require regular continuing education classes to ensure individuals are current with up-to-date information in the profession.

HANDS-ON EXAMPLE 17.2.2

INVESTIGATING PROFESSIONAL CERTIFICATION

Software and hardware vendors and professional organizations often offer certification. Becoming certified in an area related to your career can be beneficial.

1. Launch a browser, and navigate to www.microsoft.com.
2. Use the search function and the keywords IT certification MCP to locate articles on certification.
3. Read several of the articles to investigate what types of certifications are available.
4. Navigate to www.cisco.com.
5. Use the search function and the keywords IT certification to locate articles on certification. Cisco offers five levels of network certification.
6. Investigate each of the five levels of certification to see what is needed to do to pass the exam.
7. Navigate to www.comptia.org. The Computing Technology Industry Association (CompTIA) is a professional organization.
8. Click the **Certifications** link. Review the information provided on certification, training, testing, careers, and continuing education.

Training and Experience

Most employers want candidates who have some real-world work experience. Taking advantage of internships or part-time paid positions in the IT field is a good way to start. Many colleges hire students to handle technical support for their call centers. Others allow IT students to assist IT instructors in setting up and maintaining the computer labs. There are many options for career training, including occupational training, internships, apprenticeships, and military service.

Leadership and Mentoring

Leadership is the process of influencing others or making things better. Certain traits such as honesty, competence, self-confidence, communication skills, problem-solving skills, and dependability are examples of leadership characteristics. The ability to set goals, follow through on tasks, and be forward-thinking are also important leadership abilities. A leader has to be able to take responsibility, make decisions, and inspire members to accomplish tasks. Leaders must be able to work with different personalities and motivate the group to accomplish its goals. Each leader has his or her style or may develop a style based on the personalities of the team. Three common leadership styles are democratic, autocratic, and laissez-faire, as shown in Figure 17-20.

Common Leadership Styles	
Leadership Style	**Characteristics**
Democratic	• Open and collegial • Invited participation from team • Shares decision making with team members
Autocratic	• Maintains power within the group • Keeps close control over the members of the team • Makes all decisions for the group
Laissez-faire	• Hands-off approach • Little to no direction is provided • Makes decisions only if requested by the team

Goodheart-Willcox Publisher

Figure 17-20. Every leader has his or her own leadership style. These are three common leadership styles.

A *mentor* is someone with experience who trains or guides a less-experienced person. When you start your first professional job, you will likely be paired with a mentor who will teach you how to apply the skills you learned in school. As you gain experience and move up to higher positions, you may be called on to be a mentor yourself. Mentorship is an important part of most careers. It is a way to pass along information that may be specific to the company. It is also important as a way to help those who have just completed their education to make the transition into the world of work. Often, mentorships extend outside of the workplace and into the community. This is a way for companies and individuals to improve the communities in which they work and live.

Occupational Training

Training for a specific career can be an option for many technical, trade, and technology fields. *Occupational training* is education that prepares you for a specific type of work. This type of training typically costs less than a traditional college education. It can also be completed in less time. A computer repair technician, for example, may receive occupational training, as shown in Figure 17-21.

Internships

An *internship* is a short-term position with a sponsoring organization that gives the intern an opportunity to gain on-the-job experience in a certain field of study or occupation. Internships can be paid or unpaid. Often, high schools, colleges, and universities offer school credit for completing internships. Internships are an opportunity to gain work experience while completing an education.

Figure 17-21. Many career positions will involve occupational training from a mentor.

Apprenticeships

An *apprenticeship* is a combination of on-the-job training, work experience, and classroom instruction. Apprenticeships are typically available to those who want to learn a trade or a technical skill. The apprentice works on mastering the skills required to work in the trade or field under the supervision of a skilled tradesperson. The IT field generally does not have apprenticeship programs.

Military Service

Service in the military can provide opportunities to receive skilled training, often in highly specialized technical areas. In addition to receiving this training, often it can be translated into college credit or professional credentials. After completing military service, there are many benefits available to veterans. For example, the *GI Bill* is a law that provides financial assistance for veterans pursuing education or training. Other forms of tuition assistance are also available.

Some people choose to enter the armed forces through the Reserve Officers Training Corp (ROTC). Each branch of the military has an ROTC program at selected colleges and universities. Some high schools have Junior ROTC programs. The purpose of the ROTC program is to train commissioned officers for the armed forces. It can provide tuition assistance in exchange for a commitment to military service. Students enrolled in this program take classes just like other college students. The program is considered an elective. However, students also receive basic military and officer training. Information is available on the Military Career Guide Online at www.todaysmilitary.com. Also, opportunities available in the armed forces are outlined in the Occupational Outlook Handbook.

Funding Your Education

As you are making decisions on your education, you will need to create a financial plan for paying for your education. You will need to figure out which sources are available to you and which ones fit your needs. Once you have an idea of how much it will cost to go to college, you need to figure out how you will pay for it. Figure 17-22 shows potential sources of funding for your education.

Someone in your family may have established a 529 plan to fund your college education. A **529 plan** is a savings plan for education operated by a state or educational institution. These plans are tax-advantaged savings plans and encourage families to set aside college funds for their children. Each state now has at least one 529 plan available. Make sure you

Potential Sources of Funding a College Education

Source	Brief Description	Repayment
529 Plan	Tax-advantage savings plan designed to encourage saving for future college costs. Plans are sponsored by states, state agencies, and educational institutions.	No repayment.
Grants	Money to pay for college provided by government agencies, corporations, states, and other organizations. Most grants are based on need and some have other requirements.	No repayment.
Scholarships	Money to pay for college based on specific qualifications including academics, sports, music, leadership, and service. Criteria for scholarships vary widely.	No repayment.
Work-study	Paid part-time jobs for students with financial need. Work-study programs are typically backed by government agencies.	No repayment.
Need-based awards	Aid for students who demonstrate financial need.	No repayment.
Government education loans	Loans made to students to help pay for college. Interest rates are lower than bank loans.	Repayment is required. Repayment may be postponed until you begin your career.
Private education loans	Loans made to students to help pay for college. Interest rates are higher than government education loans.	Repayment is required.
Internships	Career-based work experience. Some internships are paid and some are not. In addition to experience, you will likely earn college credit.	No repayment.
Military benefits	The US Military offers several ways to help pay for education. It provides education and training opportunities while serving and also provides access to funding for veterans. The US Reserve Officers' Training Corps (ROTC) programs and the military service academies are other options to consider.	No repayment, however a service commitment is required.

Goodheart-Willcox Publisher

Figure 17-22. There are many ways with which to fund a college education.

understand how the plan works. You will be penalized if you use money invested in a 529 plan for anything other than college expenses.

More than half of the students attending college get some form of financial aid. Financial aid is available from the federal government as well as from nonfederal agencies. There are more than $100 billion in grants, scholarships, work-study, need-based awards, and loans available each year.

A *grant* is a financial award that does not have to be repaid and is typically provided by a nonprofit organization. Grants are generally need-based and are usually tax exempt. A Federal Pell Grant is an example of a governmental grant.

A **scholarship** is financial aid that may be based on financial need or some type of merit or accomplishment. There are scholarships based on standardized test scores, grades, extracurricular activities, and athletics. There are also scholarships available for leadership; service; and other interests, abilities, and talents.

Work-study programs are part-time jobs on a college campus. They are often subsidized by the government. Wages earned at a work-study job go toward paying for tuition and other college expenses.

Need-based awards are financial-aid awards available for students and families who meet certain economic requirements. Income and other demographics determine if a student qualifies for this assistance.

The *Free Application for Federal Student Aid (FAFSA)* is the application form used to determine your eligibility for federal financial aid. Many institutions require the FAFSA form if you are applying for any type of financial aid. You can file your application online at the Federal Student Aid website, which is an office of the US Department of Education. In addition to the financial aid application, the FAFSA website has resources to help you plan for college.

Résumé and Portfolio

When seeking professional employment, it is almost always necessary to compose a résumé. The first impression most employers will have of you is your résumé. As a result, it must be well written and error free. In many cases, you will also need to have a portfolio to showcase your work.

When creating a résumé, use proper formatting. Create styles as needed to help with formatting. Use an appropriate typeface, font size, and formatting such as bold and italic. Look for examples of résumés in books and online. Use these examples to format your résumé. It should reflect your personal tastes, but should also follow similar formatting that other résumés have.

Creating a Résumé

A **résumé** highlights a person's career goals, education, work history, and professional accomplishments. The purpose of the résumé is to show you have the needed skills and qualifications and to influence the reader into requesting an interview. A sample résumé is shown in Figure 17-23.

GS4 Key Applications
1.2.1, 1.2.2

Robert Jefferies
123 Eastwood Terrace
Saratoga Springs, NY 60123
123-555-9715
rjefferies@e-mail.edu

OBJECTIVE
A mature and responsible high school student seeks an entry-level job as a
computer repair technician.

EXPERIENCE
Saratoga Springs City Online Newspaper, Saratoga Springs, NY
September 2016 to present
Computer Support
- Maintained various computers for the newspaper.
- Assisted with network setup.
- Set up new computer stations.
- Installed new software as needed.

Hunter High School, Saratoga Springs, NY
September 2015 to September 2016
Student Volunteer
- Monitored the computer lab.
- Performed troubleshooting on lab computers.
- Installed software updates as needed.
- Performed routine software maintenance.

EDUCATION
Hunter High School, Saratoga Springs, NY
Expected graduation date: May 2017
Relevant coursework: Principles of Information Technology

HONORS
- Hunter High School Honor Roll, 8 quarters
- Winner: Student Troubleshooting Contest, 2014–2016

PUBLICATIONS
- Saratoga Springs City Online Newspaper
- Saratoga Springs City Calendar 2015

Goodheart-Willcox Publisher

Figure 17-23. This is a sample of a properly formatted résumé.

A potential employer will only spend 15 seconds reading the résumé before a decision is made whether or not to set up an interview. Therefore, a résumé should be neat and professional in appearance. It should begin with your contact information followed by an objective. The contact information should include your name, address, phone number, and e-mail address. It is okay to omit the street address, but do not omit the city and state. Make sure the e-mail address is appropriate and professional.

Next, include work and volunteer experience. Follow this with educational experience and certifications with dates. The last part of the résumé is a list of professional accomplishments. If you are experienced with many professional accomplishments, you may choose to place this list immediately after the objective.

Once the résumé is written, proofread it several times. Ask others to read it for errors as well. Potential employers may have to review hundreds of résumés for a single position. Be the one they remember for your skills and qualifications, not for the misspellings or grammatical mistakes you made.

Objective

The objective states what kind of position you are seeking. Use some of the specific terms that appear in the employer's job description. This shows the employer you are looking for that specific position, not just randomly sending out résumés. This section may be labeled Objective, Career Objective, or Career Goal.

Figure 17-24 shows an example of an objective section for someone seeking an IT position. Notice that background qualifications are mentioned, including IT subjects and the skills mastered. The candidate also states that he or she wants to contribute to the profitability of the company. It is a good idea to use the company's name.

Work History

The work history lists all places where you have worked. For someone just beginning in the IT field, this will be short. Include volunteer jobs as well as paid positions. Jobs that are not professional in nature, such as lifeguard or restaurant server, are often omitted unless somehow relevant experience was gained. Be prepared to explain any gaps in your work history. This section may be labeled Work History,

GS4 Living Online 3.1.1

FYI

Some people choose to include a summary before the objective to highlight key points or skills included later in the résumé.

OBJECTIVE

Seeking a challenging position in information technology where broad knowledge of software applications, operating systems, hardware, and networks and a degree in applied information technology can be combined with skills in communication, customer relations, troubleshooting, and attention-to-detail to make the XYZ Company profitable.

Goodheart-Willcox Publisher

Figure 17-24. This is an example of an objective statement for a résumé.

Work Experience, or Experience. Figure 17-25 shows an example of a work history section.

Education and Certification

The education and certification section lists degrees, where they were obtained, and the areas of concentration. Also include any certificates you have and the organizations that granted them. List any awards received in school or from the community, although these may be listed in a separate section. An inventory of various hardware and software expertise should also appear here. Figure 17-26 shows an example of an education and certification section.

Professional Accomplishments

The professional accomplishments section lists specific things you have done. These may be projects you completed, papers you published, or awards you received. Think about your work and educational experience in terms of small successes. These accomplishments should have a beginning and an end. They should be projects or activities where you had a measurable role.

Begin each statement with an active verb. Figure 17-27 shows some examples that might be included on the résumé for a recent college graduate. Notice how this person has chosen to set the action verbs in bold to make them stand out.

Ethics

Applications and Résumés

When applying for a job, to a college, or for a volunteer position, it is important to be truthful in your application and résumé. Fabricating experience or education is unethical and could cost you the opportunity to be a part of that school or company. Always tell the truth about your skills, experience, and education.

WORK HISTORY
University of Baltimore, Baltimore, MD (10/2015 to 8/2017)
Help Desk Analyst: Duties included building positive relations with faculty and students; solving hardware, Microsoft Office, PeopleSoft, and Internet problems.

Goodheart-Willcox Publisher

Figure 17-25. This is an example of a Work History or Experience section for a résumé.

EDUCATION AND CERTIFICATIONS
B.S., University of Baltimore, Baltimore, MD, Applied Information Technology, 2014

Eagle Scout Award, Boy Scouts of America, Baltimore Area Council, 2010

- PC Software: Visual Basic.NET, Java, C++, Cold Fusion, HTML, Microsoft Access, Excel, PeopleSoft, SQL, Windows Server
- Operating Systems: Windows 7, Windows 8, Linux

Goodheart-Willcox Publisher

Figure 17-26. This is an example of an Education and Certifications section for a résumé.

PROFESSIONAL ACCOMPLISHMENTS

Built a computer from individual components. Results: Gained hands-on knowledge of hardware and problem solving; began small, profitable business in computer repair.

Mastered coding in Visual Basic.NET, Java, and C++ as well as database software. Results: Became proficient in programming and database usage.

Goodheart-Willcox Publisher

Figure 17-27. This is an example of a Professional Accomplishments section for a résumé.

HANDS-ON EXAMPLE 17.2.3

SUBMITTING A RÉSUMÉ

Many open positions are posted on online job boards. Other than networking, the Internet is the primary way most people find jobs.

1. Launch a browser, and navigate to www.monster.com.
2. Search for computer support technician jobs in your area.
3. Read a few of the postings, and assess what the job requirements are.
4. Investigate how to upload a résumé and apply for one of the jobs.
5. Write a brief paragraph explaining how to upload a résumé.

FYI

A portfolio provides a quick insight into many facets of your personality and skills.

Creating a Portfolio

A **portfolio** is a collection of examples organized to show what you have accomplished and finished. It shows qualifications, skills, and talents to support a career or personal goal. Artists and other creative professionals have historically presented portfolios of their work when seeking jobs or admission to educational institutions. However, portfolios are now used in many professions and for many educational areas.

If you have created web pages or video games, these should be included in a portfolio. If creating a paper portfolio, include hard copy, color representations of these projects. If creating an electronic portfolio, include the fully functional digital versions. If you have completed any programming projects, these should be included in a portfolio. Include screen captures and documentation. If practical, include functional versions in an electronic portfolio.

Bring your portfolio to the interview. Do not submit it with your résumé and application unless specifically requested to do so.

17.2 | SECTION REVIEW

CHECK YOUR UNDERSTANDING

1. What are the three parts of good communication skills?
2. Why is it important to conduct a self-assessment when researching a career?
3. What is graduate education?
4. What is the purpose of a résumé?
5. What contains visual representations of your work that may be presented in a job interview?

IC3 CERTIFICATION PRACTICE

The following question is a sample of the types of questions presented on the IC3 exam.

1. What should be created to help with formatting a résumé?
   A. documents
   B. graphics
   C. styles
   D. portfolios

BUILD YOUR VOCABULARY

As you progress through this course, develop a personal IT glossary. This will help you build your vocabulary and prepare you for a career. Write a definition for each of the following terms and add it to your IT glossary.

529 plan
career and technical
  student organizations
  (CTSOs)
career plan
certification
formal education
Gantt chart
goal

informational interviewing
networking
portfolio
postsecondary education
résumé
scholarship
self-assessment
SMART goals
storyboarding

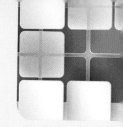

Chapter 17 Summary

Section 17.1
Career Fields in Information Technology

- The four areas of computer science that are changing the most rapidly are computer forensics, data storage, the Internet, and supercomputers. Due to this growth, many IT careers will be in these fields.

- All companies have IT needs regardless of the field. Areas affected by innovations in the IT field include programming and application development, project management, technical support, security, business intelligence and analytics, cloud computing, virtualization, networking, mobile applications, and data centers.

- IT professionals can earn a very good living, and there are many careers available. IT careers include software developer, computer systems analyst, web developer, security analyst, database administrator, IT manager, computer programmer, and computer support technician.

Section 17.2
Starting a Career in IT

- Employers are looking for employees with the personal skills needed to be successful in the workplace. These skills include good communication, time management ability, team skills, ability to receive and provide constructive criticism, and conflict management skills.

- Create a career plan to list the steps on a time line to reach each of your career goals. Research career information and conduct a self-assessment to see what you need to develop.

- Most IT careers require a college degree, and some may require graduate or postgraduate education. There are many options for funding your education, and there are many ways to gain career-related experience.

- A résumé should show you have the needed skills and qualifications for a position and should influence the reader into requesting an interview. A portfolio is a collection of examples organized to show what you have accomplished and finished and should show qualifications, skills, and talents to support a career or personal goal.

Now that you have finished this chapter, see what you know about information technology by scanning the QR code to take the chapter posttest. If you do not have a smartphone, visit www.g-wlearning.com.

Chapter 17 Test

Multiple Choice
Select the best response.

1. What does computer forensics involve?
   A. The miniaturization of electronic components.
   B. Identifying, discovering, preserving, and documenting evidence from computer devices.
   C. Applying tools and skills to the tasks in a project in order to meet the objectives of the project.
   D. Providing assistance to others with setting up, running, or fixing technical systems.

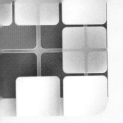

2. Which of the following skills do project managers need to have?
   A. Experience with high-level programming languages.
   B. Ability to install encryption technology.
   C. Background in statistics.
   D. Time management.

3. What should a career plan include?
   A. Your e-mail address.
   B. Examples of your work.
   C. Salary you want.
   D. Steps on a time line to achieve career goals.

4. What is an ability?
   A. Mastery of a skill or the capacity to do something.
   B. A characteristic you have naturally developed.
   C. Principles and beliefs that you consider important.
   D. A feeling of wanting to learn more about a topic or to be involved in an activity.

5. Which of the following describes a for-profit school?
   A. It is set up to earn money for investors.
   B. It returns the money it earns back into the school.
   C. It provides education during high school.
   D. It requires many general education courses.

Completion

Complete the following sentences with the correct word(s).

6. _____ is a process that allows multiple operating systems to simultaneously share a processor's resources in a safe and efficient way.

7. A(n) _____ encodes instructions provided by software developers.

8. A(n) _____ is like a bar graph that tracks tasks, which tasks are dependent on others, and the completion percentages of each task.

9. To create a career plan, you should first conduct a self-assessment and then set _____ goals.

10. A(n) _____ is someone with experience who trains or guides a less-experienced person.

Matching

Match the correct term with its definition.

A. software developer
B. computer systems analyst
C. web developer
D. security analyst
E. database administrator

11. Makes recommendations to the organization for the best systems to use.

12. Designs computer software, databases, games, or operating systems.

13. Viewed as the guardian of data.

14. Involves developing a color scheme, layout, text, images, and user experience.

15. Responsible for protecting the computer networks of a company.

Application and Extension of Knowledge

1. Using the Bureau of Labor Statistics website (www.bls.gov), investigate several careers in the IT field and note the median salary of each. Enter the data into a spreadsheet, and create a chart that shows the relationship of each career and its salary.

REVIEW AND ASSESSMENT

2. Choose an IT career that interests you. Find a position for this on Monster.com or any other career site. Create a résumé using the guidelines in this chapter. For education and certifications you have not earned yet, use future dates for when you think you will secure them.

3. Using the career you selected in #2, investigate the educational requirements for the position. Create an education plan that will lead you to the career. Include at least two options for schools. Be sure to include estimates on the cost of completing your education.

4. Select an advanced position in the IT field that you might like to have after ten years in the field. Create a career plan to meet this goal. Include the behaviors and qualities expected for the position. Follow the guidelines in this chapter.

5. Identify the steps needed to replace a hard drive, reformat it, and install an operating system. You will be the project manager in this simulated work-based project with at least two other members on your team to complete the work. Identify the skills, behaviors, and qualities needed by these workers. Then, create a plan to complete this project. Use a spreadsheet or other software to create a simple Gantt chart to track the tasks. In a word-processing document, describe your plan. Be sure to include how you plan to execute, monitor and control, and close the project. Assume you will have to explain to a customer what was done.

Online Activities

Complete the following activities, which will help you learn, practice, and expand your knowledge and skills.

Certification Practice. Complete the certification practice test for this chapter.

Vocabulary. Practice vocabulary for this chapter using the e-flash cards, matching activity, and vocabulary game until you are able to recognize their meanings.

Communication Skills

College and Career Readiness

Speaking. Select three of your classmates to participate in a discussion panel. Acting as the team leader, name each person to a specific task such as time-keeper, recorder, etc. Discuss the topic of the future of IT careers. Keep the panel on task and promote democratic discussion. The recorder should make notes of important information that was discussed. The notes should be edited and a final document created for distribution to the class.

Reading. Select several chapters of this textbook. Identify two generic features that are used in each chapter. Compare and contrast how each feature is used. Why do you think the author chose those particular features to apply in multiple chapters?

Writing. Personal-technology devices, such as smartphones, tablets, fitness trackers, and similar devices, can be found everywhere. These devices offer many benefits. However, overuse of these devices can result in problems, such as distracted walking or driving and lack of socialization. Write a three- to five-page paper outlining the benefits of personal-technology devices as well as problems that may result from overuse. Describe why limiting your own use of these devices may be beneficial.

Internet Research

Mock Interview. Research mock interviews using various Internet resources. Create two sets of guidelines: one for selecting a person

to conduct the mock interview and another for how the interview candidate should behave during the mock interview. Share your guidelines with the class.

Teamwork

Work in pairs or teams as assigned by your teacher. Take turns interviewing each other. Research typical interview questions, but come up with your own questions as well. When all interviews are completed, write a brief summary evaluating how you performed in the interview. Describe what you could do better in the future.

Portfolio Development

College and Career Readiness

Presenting Your Portfolio. You have organized the components of the portfolio. Now, you will create the final product. Start with a flowchart to create the order of your documents. After you have sorted through the documents that you want to include, print a copy of each. Next, prepare a table of contents for the items. This will help the person reviewing the portfolio.

Your instructor may have examples of print and digital portfolios you can review for ideas. There may be an occasion where a print portfolio is required rather than a digital one. The organization processes are similar. Search the Internet for articles about how to organize a print or digital portfolio.

1. Review the documents you have collected. Select the items you want to include in your portfolio. Make copies of certificates, diplomas, and other important documents. Keep the originals in a safe place.

2. Create the slide show, web pages, or other medium for presenting your e-portfolio.

3. View the completed e-portfolio to check the appearance.

4. Place the items in a binder, folder, or other container.

5. Present the portfolio to your instructor, counselor, or other person who can give constructive feedback.

6. Review the feedback you received. Make necessary adjustments and revisions.

CTSOs

Job Interview. Job interviewing is an event you might enter with your CTSO. By participating in the job interview, you will be able to showcase your presentation skills, communication talents, and ability to actively listen to the questions asked by the interviewers. For this event, you will be expected to write a letter of application, create a résumé, and complete a job application. You will also be interviewed by an individual or panel. To prepare for a job interview event, complete the following activities.

1. Use the Internet or textbooks to research the job application process and interviewing techniques.

2. Write your letter of application and résumé, and complete the application form (if provided for this event). You may be required to submit this before the event or present the information at the event.

3. Make certain that each piece of communication is complete and free of errors.

4. Solicit feedback from your peers, instructor, and parents.

GLOSSARY

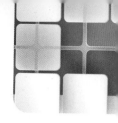

529 plan. Savings plan for education operated by a state or educational institution. (17)

A

absolute cell address. Indicates the formula will refer to the specified cell no matter where the formula is moved or copied. (10)

accessibility options. Used to assist users with vision, mobility, or hearing impairment. (3)

access key. Keyboard key or key combination used instead of the mouse to activate a command. Also called *keyboard shortcut*. (6)

active cell. Currently selected cell, which is indicated by an outline around the cell. (10)

active window. Current window where any command that is entered will be applied. (6)

address book. Contains the e-mail addresses of contacts and may contain other information for each. (15)

adware. Software that creates advertisements designed to drive the user to another website. (16)

alignment. Placing elements in relation to key points in other elements. (13)

all-in-one computer. Computer in which all of the hardware are contained in a single unit. (5)

American Standard Code for Information Interchange (ASCII). Standard for representing text that most computers support. (3)

analog. Continuous signal that can vary over an infinite range. (14)

analytical report. Contains both information and analysis of the data. (8)

animating. Process of adding motion to an object. (9)

antipiracy technology. Technology that has been developed that makes it very difficult for someone to use pirated software. (8)

antivirus software. Cyber-defense software that detects and removes malicious software from a computer. (16)

application software. Allows the user to perform specific activities, such as writing term papers, sending e-mail, paying taxes, editing photos, playing games, and taking online courses. (3)

archiving. Consists of storing e-mail messages in a place where they will not load every time the e-mail client is launched, but can be accessed if needed. (15)

argument. Value the function needs for the calculation. (11)

arithmetic/logic unit (ALU). Temporarily holds data that are being processed and handles all arithmetic operations such as addition and subtraction. (2)

ascending order. When the lowest value is at the top of the list. Also called *A to Z order*. (6, 10)

assembly language. Similar to machine language, but the CPU cannot directly understand it. Also called *assembly*. (3)

attention grabber. Something to arouse the interest of the audience. (9)

audio-input device. Converts sounds into data that can be used by the computer. (2)

audio-output device. Converts data in the computer into sounds. (2)

augmented printing. Form of augmented reality. (1)

augmented reality (AR). View of the live world that has been enhanced with computerized graphics, sounds, or other outputs. (1)

authentication. Refers to providing varying levels of access to information. (14)

auto-respond option. Sends a set reply to every e-mail message received. (15)

B

background image. Overall image that appears behind all other elements on the slide. (9)

backstage view. View that is displayed when saving a file for the first time. (6)

backup. Copy of a file that can be safely retrieved if anything unfortunate happens to the most recent version of the file. (4)

bandwidth. Measure of the amount of data that can travel on a communication system. (1, 14)

bar chart. Best chart type for comparing individual values across categories. Also called a *column chart* in Microsoft Excel. (11)

bit. Basic building block for communication in an electronic computer. (3)

block-style letter. Formatted so all lines are flush with the left-hand page margin. (8)

blog. Type of website that allows people to express their opinions on topics that interest them. (15)

Bluetooth. Radio wave–based wireless connection technology that provides communication between devices within a short range of each other. (14)

body. Message of a letter. (8)

Boolean operator. Defines the relationship between words in the search string. Also called *logical operator*. (13)

booting. Describes the use of a small program to get the computer running and the OS loaded. Also called *bootstrapping*. (2)

bot. Software application that automatically performs Internet-based activities. (16)

browser. Computer program that retrieves hypertext documents via the HTTP protocol and displays them on the computer monitor. (13)

bugs. Programming errors. (3)

bulleted list. Consists of separate lines of text with a small graphic such as a dot in front of the line. Also called an *unordered list*. (6)

bus topology. Network topology in which each node on the network is connected to a single main transmission cable. (14)

byte. Equivalent of eight bits. (3)

bytecode. Set of instructions composed of compact numeric codes, constants, and references that can be efficiently processed by an interpreter. (3)

C

cache. Location on the local hard drive of content files from websites; designed to improve browsing speed. (16)

calculated field. Field that performs a calculation based on data within the same table. (12)

CamelCase. Naming convention in which the beginning of each word in the name is capitalized. (4)

career and technical student organization (CTSO). National student organization with local school chapters that are related to career and technical education (CTE) courses. (17)

career plan. List of steps on a timeline to reach each of your career goals. Also called a *postsecondary plan*. (17)

carrier. Cell phone service provider. (15)

cascading style sheet (CSS). Provides formatting information for a web page. (13)

cell. Individual box where a row and column intersect. (6, 10, 15)

cellular technology. Based on the principle of wireless transmissions distributed over groups of geographic areas. (15)

censorship. Act of limiting access to information or removing information to prevent the information from being seen. (16)

central processing unit (CPU). Device that fetches coded instructions, decodes them, and then runs or executes them. Also called a *microprocessor* or *chip*. (2)

certification. Professional status earned by an individual after passing an exam focused on a specific body of knowledge. (17)

character style. Defines the text formatting for individual characters. (6)

chart. Illustrates data in a picture-like format. Also called a *graph*. (9, 11)

check box. Interface control that looks like a small square. (3)

chief information officer (CIO). Person in charge of data security for a company. (17)

citation. Includes the author, publication date, source document, URL, and other relevant information for material that is referenced or paraphrased within the document. (8)

client. Computer connected to and served by the host. (14)

clincher. Statement to finish a presentation that will make an impact on the audience. (9)

clock speed. Speed rating of a CPU. (2)

closing. Removing a file or application from RAM. (6)

cloud architects. Experts in establishing cloud-computing solutions for a company. (17)

cloud computing. Involves storing and retrieving data from Internet-based spaces. (1)

code. Result of encoding. (3)

collaboration. Working together on a project with at least one other person. (15)

collate. Arrange multiple copies of a document so all pages are in the correct order. (6)

columns. Spaces between the vertical grid lines. (10)

comma-separated values (CSV) file. Contains only the data from a spreadsheet with commas to denote the beginning and end of each datum in a row. (11)

comment. Note inserted into the document. (15)

common knowledge. Consists of notions and factual information that can be found in a variety of places. (8)

compiler. Converts the programmer's code into code the CPU can understand. (3)

completely automated public Turing test to tell computers and humans apart (CAPTCHA). Brief online test to determine whether the request for access comes from a computer or a human. (16)

complimentary close. Sign-off for a letter. (8)

computer. Device that handles input, processes data, stores data, and produces usable output according to sets of stored instructions. (1)

computer algorithm. Series of steps used to perform an action. (3)

computer model. Form a computer takes. (5)

computer programmer. Person who writes, rewrites, debugs, maintains, and tests the software essential to key computer functions. (17)

computer support technician. Person who quickly diagnoses and solves computer issues for others in a friendly and effective manner. (17)

computer system. Computer with its attached devices. (2)

computer systems analyst. Person who makes recommendations to organizations for the best systems to use. (17)

computer virus. Consists of computer code carried in another program that can replicate itself in order to corrupt or otherwise harm either data files or the software used to processes these files. (16)

computer worm. Similar to a virus, but is a stand-alone computer program that replicates itself in order to spread to other computers. (16)

conclusion. Writer's summary of what the audience should take away from the report. (8)

conditional formatting. Changes the appearance of a cell's value based on parameters set by the user. (11)

contact group. Named collection of e-mail addresses from the address book. (15)

contrast. Degree of difference between elements in a design. (13)

control unit. Fetches each instruction from the list directed by the program being run. (2)

cookies. Small text files that websites put on the computer hard disk drive when a user visits the websites. (16)

copy. Exact duplicate of the original at the time the copy was made. (4, 6)

copy notation. Needed when others are being sent a copy of the letter. (8)

copyright. Ownership of a work and specifies that only the owner has the right to sell the work, use it, or give permission for someone else to sell or use it. (8)

Creative Commons (CC) license. Specialized copyright license that allows free distribution of copyrighted work. (8)

credential. Record that saves the authentication criteria required to connect to a service. (15)

criteria. Qualifiers on a query. (12)

crop. Trim the outer portion of an image. (6)

cut. Remove content from a document and place it on the system clipboard. (6)

cyberbullying. Harassment that takes place using electronic technology. (15)

cybersecurity. Branch of IT that protects computer systems. (1)

D

daisy chain topology. Network topology in which devices are added to the network at the end of the line. (14)

data. Pieces of information gathered through research. (8)

database. Structured collection of related information organized for easily locating and retrieving the data. (12)

database administrator. Person who sets up databases to track a company's information and maintains those operations. (17)

database management system (DBMS). Program that handles the collection, storage, sorting, reporting, and organization of data. (12)

data mining. Method of searching through huge amounts of data to find patterns. (1)

data projector. Output device that collects video data from a computer or other media player and projects the images onto a separate screen. (2)

datasheet view. Displays data in table form. (12)

data type. Description of values or information that can be accepted. (3)

data vandalism. Manipulation or destruction of data found in cyberspace. (16)

descending order. When the highest value is at the top of the list. Also called *Z to A order*. (6, 10)

design view. View that allows developers of the database to set up fields. (12)

desktop publishing (DTP). Process of using a computer to typeset text and place illustrations to create, edit, and publish documents. (3, 7)

desktop theme. Sets the colors used for window borders, the desktop background, and other visual qualities. (3)

destination. Folder to where a file or folder is being transferred. (4)

device driver. Special software program that provides instructions to the operating system for how to use a specific peripheral. (3)

device firmware upgrade (DFU) mode. Provides the ability to upgrade or downgrade the firmware. (5)

dialog box launcher. Small arrow in the lower-right corner of groups on the ribbon. (6)

digital. Signal composed of discrete or segmented chunks of data. (14)

digital citizenship. Standard appropriate behavior when using technology to communicate. (15)

digital divide. Most commonly defined as the gap between those individuals, communities, and countries having access to the information technologies that transform life and those who do not have this access. (1)

digital footprint. Data record of all of an individual's online activities. (15)

digital middle class. Group of people who extensively use digital devices and embrace the newest digital technologies. (1)

digital revolution. Ever-expanding progression of technical, economic, and cultural changes brought about by computers. (1)

digital wellness. Area of study to discuss and remedy excessive use of screen time, online addictions, and smartphone addictions. (13)

disk cleanup. Automated process of removing unneeded files. (5)

document template. Document preformatted for a specific use and may contain placeholder text or images the user replaces with actual content. (6)

download. Occurs when a user is retrieving a document from the server to the computer. (13)

drag and drop. Procedure in which an item is selected in one location, moved with the mouse, and placed in another location. (4, 6)

drop-down menu. Interface control that presents command choices in a list once displayed. (3)

E

editing. Make changes to the text, format, layout, or other aspects of the content. (6)

Electronic User's Bill of Rights. Details the rights and responsibilities of both individuals and institutions regarding the treatment of digital information. (8)

e-mail. Communication sent to a computer address where the message is stored to be read at a later time by the recipient. Also called *electronic mail*. (1)

e-mail client. Program used to create and send a message. (15)

e-mail filters. Used to automatically route incoming e-mail to a specified inbox folder. Also called *rules*. (16)

e-mail server. Handles the storing and delivery of the message. (15)

embedded computer. Small digital computer found inside of other devices. (1)

embedding. Form of copying and pasting. (11)

emerging technologies. Innovations that represent significantly new fields or technologies. (1)

emoticon. Combination of keyboard characters used to represent a facial expression. (15)

enclosure notation. Alerts the reader to materials that are included in the mailing along with the letter. (8)

encoding. Process of converting human-readable data and computer programs into a computer-readable format. (3)

encryption. Software process that encodes the file to make it unreadable unless the correct key is entered. (14)

end user license agreement (EULA). Contract outlining the set of rules that every user must agree to before using the software. (3)

endnote. Similar to footnote, but appears at the end of document. Also called the *bibliography*. (8)

ergonomics. Science concerned with designing and arranging things people use so that they can interact with them both efficiently and safely. (13)

Ethernet. Data transmission technology that creates a wired connection between modems or routers and computers. (14)

ethics. Principles of what is right and wrong that help people make decisions. (16)

external audience. Audience that will probably need more background information about your topic. (9)

external style. Similar to internal styles, but contained in a separate CSS file. (13)

extracting. Term given by Windows to the process of taking a file out of a ZIP file. (4)

extranet. Remote devices or remote network of networks. (14)

F

factory-default settings. Original settings that the device had when it was new before the user made any changes. (5)

fair use doctrine. Allows individuals to use copyrighted works without permission in limited situations under very strict guidelines. (8)

field. Contains information about specific characteristics of the entry described in a record. (12)

file association. Process in which Windows links a file name extension to a software program. (4)

file attribute. Characteristic of a file about the display, archiving, and save status of the file. (4)

file compression. Process of compacting the data in a file or group of files to reduce the overall size. (4)

file format. Indicates the manner in which the data a file contains are stored on the disk. (3)

file management. Working with files on the hard disk or other storage medium. (4)

file name. Label that identifies a unique file on a computer system. (4)

file name extension. Tells the Windows operating system which software to use to open the file. (4)

file path. Drive and folder location of a file plus its file name. (4)

file properties. All information about the file, but not the data contained within the file. (4)

file tree. List of available drives and folders shown in the navigation pane; can be expanded to display subfolders and the files contained within them. (4)

filtering. Allows some data to be hidden from view. (10)

firewall. Technology that creates a barrier between computers. (14)

firmware. Circuitry and software that hold instructions for initializing the hardware and loading the main OS. (2)

flaming. Posting in a negative or ill-mannered way. (15)

flash drive. Removable peripheral device and most recognized example of SSD. Also known as a *thumb* or *jump drive*. (2)

floating point operations per second (FLOPS). Measurement of the speed of supercomputers. (2)

folder. Container in which files are stored. (4)

folder name. Label that identifies a unique folder on a computer system. (4)

folio. Page number placed outside of the body copy. (8)

font. Set of characters of a typeface in one specific style and size. (7)

footnote. Numbered annotation that appears once at the bottom of a page. (8)

foreign key. Primary key from another table. (12)

form. Database object used to display only certain data one record at a time. (12)

formal education. Education received in a school, college, or university. (17)

format painter. Copies the formatting applied to selected text and then applies that formatting to a second text selection. (6)

formatting. Changing the appearance of characters. (6)

formula. Equation in Microsoft Excel. (10)

for-purchase software. Software one must buy to use, although one can often download a timed or limited-use demo. (3)

forum. Platform for holding discussions and asking and responding to questions. (15)

fraction. Number of parts of a whole. (10)

freeware. Fully functional software that can be used forever without purchasing it. (3)

function. Preprogrammed formula in spreadsheet software. (11)

G

Gantt chart. Similar to a bar graph that tracks tasks, which tasks are dependent on others, and the completion percentages of each task. (17)

gateway. Device that joins two networks. (16)

goal. Something a person wants to achieve in a specified time period. (17)

graphic. Illustration, photograph, and drawing shape. (9)

H

hacking. Activity by computer programmers to break into the e-mails, websites, computer systems, and files of other computer users. (16)

handles. Used to change the size of the image. (6)

handout. Printed material that is distributed to an audience. Also called a *leave-behind*. (9)

hard disk drive. Sealed unit that contains a stack of individual disks, or platters, which are magnetic media that rotate at a very high speed. Also called a *hard drive*. (2)

hard reboot. Powering down the system and then restarting it. Also called a *cold reboot*. (5)

hard stop. Occurs when the computer completely ceases to function. (5)

hardware. Physical components of the computer. (2)

hardware maintenance. Process of keeping the computer hardware in good working order. (5)

heading. Words and phrases that introduce a section of text. (8)

help. Resource to assist the user in learning how to use a feature of the program. (4)

hibernation. Power state that saves all settings and running programs to the hard disk drive. (3)

high-level programming language. Contains instructions that are far removed from the instructions the computer CPU uses. (3)

host. One computer dedicated to managing the communication tasks. (14)

hotspot. Any LAN that is accessible to connection by roaming users. (14)

hub. Common connection point for devices in a network. (14)

human-computer interaction (HCI). Describes how computer users communicate with the computer. (13)

hyperlink. Electronic link between a marked place in a document to another place in the document or to another document, file, or web page. (9)

hypertext markup language (HTML). Language used to create documents that tell browsers how to assemble text, images, and other content to display as a web page. (13)

I

identity theft. Illegal act that involves stealing someone's personal information and using that information to commit theft or fraud. (16)

image-input device. Used to digitize images so they can be used by the computer. (2)

informational interviewing. Strategy used to interview a professional to ask for advice and direction, rather than for a job opportunity. (17)

informational report. Contains facts, data, or other types of information. (8)

information technology (IT). Includes all of the work done with computers, from the design and installation of hardware and software to the maintenance of these systems. (1)

inline style. Embedded into the HTML file within the element being formatted. (13)

input. Function that translates data from the human world into computer data. (2)

input device. Device that makes it possible for the user to provide communication to the computer. (2)

inserting. Adding a media file to a document. Also called *attaching*. (6)

insertion point. Location where text or images will be placed within the document. (6)

inside address. Name, title, and address of the recipient. (8)

instant messaging (IM). Texting technology that uses the Internet to transfer messages. (15)

integrated development environment (IDE). Provides editing capability to write and correct program codes, compilers to convert the code into machine language, and linkers to make executable files. (3)

intellectual property. Something that comes from a person's mind. (8)

interactive book. Enhanced e-book that contains integrated multimedia features such as audio, video, pop-up graphics, 3D images, and animations. (1)

internal audience. Has a specific background and experience. (9)

internal style. Defined in the head section of the HTML file. (13)

Internet area network (IAN). Builds on the concept of the computing cloud to connect computers. (14)

Internet message access protocol (IMAP). Describes how to store and retrieve e-mail messages. (15)

Internet service provider (ISP). Company or organization that provides access to the Internet. (13)

interpreter. Converts instructions to code the CPU can understand as the program is executing. (3)

intranet. Locally confined network of networks. (14)

introduction. Discusses the purpose of a report and the benefits of the ideas or recommendations one is presenting. (8)

IT manager. Person who coordinates technology-related matters, plans upgrades of existing software or hardware, and negotiates with service providers. (17)

J

JavaScript. Object-oriented programming language most often used in web development. (13)

junk e-mail. Unsolicited e-mail messages. (15)

justification. Technical term for paragraph alignment. (7)

K

kerning. Amount of space between two letters. (7)

key tip badges. Little boxes that appear over each command in the **Quick Access** toolbar and the ribbon tabs. (6)

keyboard. Device for inputting textual and numeric data. (2)

killer app. Software application so compelling that people buy a computer just to be able to use it. (10)

L

landscape. Layout or orientation is when the long edge is on the top and bottom. (6)

language pack. Downloaded from Microsoft and installed to change the language of the OS interface. (3)

leading. Technical term for vertical spacing between lines of text and paragraphs. (7)

learning management system (LMS). Platform for managing digital content, students, and records as well as providing collaboration features. (15)

letterhead. Information about an organization. (8)

libel. Publishing a false statement about someone that causes others to have a bad opinion of him or her. (15)

library. Collection of similar files and folders that are displayed together, but that may be stored in different locations. (4)

licensing agreement. Contract that gives one party permission to market, produce, or use the product or service owned by another party. (8)

line chart. Used to display trends over time. (11)

line spacing. Amount of space between lines of text. (7)

linking. Similar to embedding, but a connection is maintained between the copy and the original source. (11)

local area network (LAN). Consists of a group of computers and their devices that are locally assembled in a limited area. (14)

logical function. Function that tests for true or false. (11)

low-level programming language. Language that is very close to the instruction set used by the CPU. (3)

M

machine language. Low-level language composed of the 0s and 1s the computer CPU uses. Also called *machine code*. (3)

magnetic media. Made of iron oxide–coated disks that can be selectively magnetized to store on-off signals. (2)

mainframe computer. Provides centralized storage, processing, and overall management of large amounts of data. (2)

malware. Software that intentionally performs actions to disrupt the operation of a computer system, collect private information, or otherwise harm the computer or user. Short for *malicious software*. (16)

margins. Points at the top, bottom, left, and right of the page beyond which text is not placed. (7)

master page. Defines the page size, recurring areas for type and graphics, and placement of recurring element. Also called the *master*. (7)

maximized. Describes a window that fills the entire screen. (6)

memory. Part of the computer that stores information for immediate processing. (2)

merge. Combine multiple cells into a single cell. (10)

mesh topology. Network topology in which each node in the network carries a signal to all other nodes until the message is received at its destination. (14)

message header. Contains a variety of information necessary to ensure the proper delivery of the message. (15)

metadata. Details about a file that describe or identify it. (6)

metropolitan area network (MAN). Consists of a group of computers that are not in the same room or building, but in the same city or small geographical area. (14)

millions of instructions per second (MIPS). Measurement of the speed of mainframes. (2)

minimized. Describes a window that is still running, but hidden from view except for the button on the taskbar corresponding to the application. (6)

mixed punctuation. Style in which a colon is placed after the salutation and a comma after the complimentary close. (8)

modem. Device that delivers the data channel for Internet transmissions. (13)

modified-block-style letter. Places the date, complimentary close, and signature to the right of the center point of the letter. (8)

monitor. Device that provides a display output. (2)

motherboard. Connects all of the hardware in the computer. (2)

mouse. Device with one or more buttons that can be moved on a flat surface to control the cursor. (2)

move. Remove a file from a source folder and place it in a destination folder. (4)

move. Remove content from a source location and place it in a destination location. (6)

multimedia messaging service (MMS). Standard for sending messages that include multimedia between mobile devices. (15)

N

naming convention. Pattern that is followed whenever a file name is created. (4)

needs assessment. Process of examining the current condition or state and determining how it differs from the desired condition or state. (5)

nested. Describes a subfolder within the parent folder. (4)

netiquette. Set of guidelines for appropriate behavior on the Internet. Short for *Internet etiquette*. (15)

network adapter. Provides the interface between the computer and the network. (14)

networking. Talking with people and making new contacts. (17)

network topology. Arrangement of the components of the network. (14)

numbered list. Consists of separate lines of text with numbers in sequential order in front of the text. Also called an *ordered list*. (6)

numbers. Floating point number data type. (10)

O

object-oriented language. Contains data structures and actions that can be performed on those structures. (3)

on-demand tab. Tab that is displayed depending on what is selected in the program document. (6)

one-to-many relationship. Occurs when a single piece of data is related to several other pieces of data. (12)

online piracy. Downloading copyrighted material without permission of the copyright holder. (16)

online presence. How you represent yourself through social media, websites, blogs, and other Internet-based media. (15)

online status. How other users will see your availability for immediate interaction. (15)

open punctuation. Style in which there is no punctuation after the salutation or complimentary close. (8)

open source. Applies to software that has had its source code made available to the public at no charge and with no restrictions on use or modification. (8)

open-source software. Software that has no licensing restrictions. (3)

Open Systems Interconnection (OSI) model. Separates the functions of networking into layers that keep the same functions together for all networks. (14)

opening. Placing a file's content into RAM so the content can be used. (6)

operating system (OS). Software that manages all of the devices, as well as locates and provides instructions to the CPU. (2)

optical-character recognition (OCR). Software that can be used with image scanners to digitize text so the computer understands it as text characters. (2)

optical storage. Involves saving data as tiny pits in foil on a plastic disc and reading the data with a laser. (2)

orphan. First line of a paragraph that falls immediately *before* a page break. (7)

out-of-office message. Auto-response message generated once for each user who sends e-mail to the address. (15)

P

output. Data provided to the user. (2)

output device. Makes it possible for the user to receive communication from the computer. (2)

packet. Small file fragments on which the routing mechanism is based. (13)

page break. Where the document changes from one page to another. (7)

page layout. Refers to how the type is placed on the page. (7)

paragraph style. Defines the formatting for a paragraph. (6)

paraphrasing. Expressing an idea using different words. (8)

passphrase. Phrase composed of real words on which a password is based. (16)

password. Code that must be entered to allow access to something. (14)

paste. Occurs when content from the system clipboard is added to the document at the insertion point. (6)

patent. Gives a person or company the right to be the sole producer of a product for a defined period of time. (8)

peer-to-peer (P2P) topology. Network topology in which all devices act like both servers and clients. (14)

percentage. Fraction of 100. (10)

peripheral device. Attached device that is not critical to computer operation. Also called *peripheral*. (2)

personal computer. Processing device designed to meet the needs of an individual user, whether in the home, a business, or a school. (2)

personal firewall. Controls traffic to an individual machine. (16)

pharming. Occurs when a virus or other malware infects the computer and takes control of your web browser. (16)

phishing. Attempt to get sensitive information by appearing as a harmless request. (16)

PHP hypertext preprocessor. Enhances interactions and supplies database support using structured query language (SQL). (13)

pie chart. Chart that displays the relative size of each fractional part of a whole. (11)

piracy. Unethical and illegal copying or downloading of software, files, or other protected material. (8)

plagiarism. Claiming another person's material as your own. (8)

platform. Combination of the operating system and the processor. (3)

plug-in. Helper file that extends the capability of a software application. (13)

podcasting. Distribution of audio files over the Internet via automated or subscribed downloads. (3)

pointing device. Allows the user to control the movement of the cursor, or pointer, on the screen. (2)

point-to-point topology. Network topology that consists of a permanent connection between two nodes. (14)

pop-up. Message or window that appears on top of or under the web page you are viewing. (16)

port. Application- or process-specific software communication endpoint in a computer's operating system. (14)

port. Point of interface between the motherboard and external devices. (2)

portfolio. Collection of examples organized to show what you have accomplished and finished. (17)

portrait. Layout or orientation is when the long edge of the paper is on the sides. (6)

post office protocol (POP). Application-layer protocol that describes how to store and retrieve e-mail messages. (15)

postscript. Information included after the signature. (8)

postsecondary education. Any education achieved after high school. (17)

power down. Occurs when the computer is idle for a period of time. (3)

power options. Manages how the computer uses electricity. (3)

power state. Controls how much power is consumed by the CPU. (3)

presentation. Contains individual slides used to communicate information to an audience. Also, a speech, address, or demonstration given to a group. (6, 9)

presentation notes. Notes used to keep the speaker on topic. Also called *speaker notes*. (9)

primary key. Field that will be used by the DBMS to keep track of records. (12)

primary research. First-hand research conducted by the writer in preparation for writing a report. (8)

principal. Amount of a loan. (11)

print preview. Shows the document exactly how it will look when printed. (6)

printer. Peripheral device that transforms computer information into a physical form. (2)

printing. Outputting the content of a file. (6)

procedural language. Computer programming language in which instructions are gathered into collections. (3)

processing. Transformation of input data and acting on those data. (2)

programs. Sets of instructions that carry out the tasks of the user. (3)

project management. Applying tools and skills to the tasks in a project in order to meet the objectives of the project. (17)

proofing. Process of checking the document for errors. (7)

proposal. Typically contains an idea and attempts to persuade the reader to take a certain course of action. (8)

proprietary software. Owned by the creator and cannot be sold, copied, or modified by the user without permission from the creator. Also called *closed software*. (3)

protected view. View in which most or all of the editing functions have been locked. (6)

proximity. How closely elements are placed to each other. (13)

public domain. Refers to material that is not owned by anybody and can be used without permission. (8)

public switched network. Makes use of packet switching to transfer information and is available to the general public. (13)

Q

qualitative data. Information that provides insight into how people think about a particular topic. (8)

quantitative data. Facts and figures from which conclusions can be drawn. (8)

query. Includes not only searching, but also finding and organizing the related details of records that meet certain search conditions. (12)

quick response (QR) code. Two-dimensional bar code that typically contains an encoded web or e-mail address. (1)

quotation. Exact repeat of a passage of another author's work. (8)

R

radio button. Interface control that looks like a small circle next to a selection choice. (3)

random-access memory (RAM). Memory that can be changed. (2)

range. Selection of more than one cell. (10)

ransomware. Software that encrypts files or blocks the user's access to programs until the user pays to unlock them. (16)

raster-based software. Creates graphics composed of dots or pixels. (3)

readability. Measure of how easy it is for the reader to understand and locate information within a document. (7)

read-only. Means the file can be opened and viewed, but cannot be changed. (6)

read-only memory (ROM). Memory that cannot be changed. (2)

really simple syndication (RSS). Method of subscribing to automatic delivery of web content. (15)

rebooting. Restarting the system. (5)

recommendation. Action the writer believes the reader should take. (8)

record. Contains information related to the entry in the first column of the record. (12)

recycle bin. Special folder used as a collection point for all files and folders that have been deleted. (4)

reference initials. Indicate the person who keyed the letter. (8)

relational database. Collection of tables that have been joined. (12)

relative cell address. Specified as the number of rows and columns that the second cell is from the first cell. (10)

repair function. Allows the current installation to be corrected without completely uninstalling and reinstalling the software. (5)

repetition. When an element occurs more than once. Also called a *pattern*. (13)

report. Output of the database of specific information requested by the user. (12)

reserved symbols. Characters that Windows uses for special meaning. (4)

restore point. Copy of the system files in their state at the earlier date or time. (5)

restoring. Displaying a minimized window. (6)

résumé. Document that highlights a person's career goals, education, work history, and professional accomplishments. (17)

ribbon. Main command interface for the Microsoft Office suite of software. (6)

ring topology. Network topology in which computers and devices are connected one to another so that a circle can be drawn. (14)

ripping. Process of extracting audio from a CD, DVD, or video file. (2)

root. Top folder in a folder hierarchy. (4)

router. Sends data packets between computer networks and is generally used for Internet applications. (14)

rows. Spaces between the horizontal grid lines. (10)

S

safe mode. Windows boot setting in which the computer starts up with the minimum of functions necessary to run. (5)

salutation. Greeting in a letter and always begins with *Dear*. (8)

sampling. Process of taking measurements along the analog signal to convert it into a digital signal. (14)

scareware. Software designed to cause enough anxiety so the computer user leaps at the chance to opt for a poor choice. (16)

scholarship. Financial aid that may be based on financial need or some type of merit or accomplishment. (17)

scope. Guideline of how much information will be included. (9)

search engine. Software program that looks through massive databases of links and information to try to identify the best matches for the search request. (13)

searching. Method to find a particular value among a set of values. (12)

secondary research. Data and information already assembled and recorded by someone else. (8)

sector. Location on a hard drive where files are stored. (5)

security analyst. Responsible for protecting the computer networks of a company, organization, or governmental agency. (17)

self-assessment. Evaluation of your aptitudes, abilities, values, and interests. (17)

semantic tag. Tag in which the purpose of the tag is clear from the tag name. (13)

serif. Small mark that extends from the end strokes of a character. (7)

server. Stores data and responds when requested by other computers in the network. (2)

service mark. Similar to a trademark, but it identifies a service rather than a product. (8)

shareware. Software that can be installed and used, then purchased if you decide to continue using it. (3)

short messaging service (SMS). Protocol for exchanging messages on a wireless network. (15)

shortcut menu. Point-of-use menu displayed by right-clicking. (4)

signature block. Writer's name and title. Also called the *signature*. (8)

simple mail transfer protocol (SMTP). Used to transfer mail from one e-mail system to another over the Internet. (15)

slander. Speaking a false statement about someone that causes others to have a bad opinion of him or her. (15)

sleep. Saves all settings and running programs in memory using just a small amount of power. (3)

slide master. Predefined slide on which the position and formatting of text boxes and graphics is specified. (9)

SMART goal. Goal that is specific, measurable, attainable, realistic, and timely. (17)

smartphone. Handheld computer that contains a telephone, software applications commonly called apps, and the ability to quickly connect to the Internet. (1)

social engineering. Involves manipulative techniques designed to lure unwary computer users into launching an infected file or opening a link to an infected website. (16)

social media. Involves creating, sharing, or exchanging information through websites and applications that promote interaction among people. (15)

soft reboot. Using the restart function of the operating system. Also called a *warm reboot*. (5)

software as a service (SaaS). Software that resides in the cloud and is accessed by users without downloading or installing it on their local computers. (1)

software-defined storage. Cloud-based file storage. (1)

software developer. Writes specifications for programs, applications, and other software. (17)

software maintenance. Keeping the software in good working order. (5)

solid-state drive (SSD). Similar to RAM, but has an integrated circuit to store data as involatile memory rather than volatile memory. (2)

sorting. Arranging a list in either ascending or descending order. (4, 6, 10)

source. Folder where the file or folder being transferred is originally located. (4)

spam. One unwanted e-mail message sent to a large number of users or multiple identical unwanted messages sent to a single e-mail address. (15)

spreadsheet. Special type of document in which data are organized in columns and rows. (6, 10)

spyware. Software that secretly collects a user's data and behavior. (16)

standard capitalization. Involves using uppercase only for the first letter of the first word in a sentence and the first letter of all proper nouns. (15)

star topology. Network topology in which the main node is in the center and all other nodes are connected to the main node. (14)

statistical field. Provides summary information related to other data within a table. (12)

storage. Where data are kept by the computer so the information can be viewed, played, or otherwise used. (2)

storyboarding. Breaking a project down into its tasks and then arranging the tasks in an order that allows the project to stay on schedule. (17)

streaming. Technology that allows a multimedia file to begin playing before it is fully downloaded. (15)

strong password. Password that is difficult for both humans and computers to crack. (16)

style. Group of formatting settings that can be applied in one step. (6)

style sheet. Desktop publishing file that saves the attributes of every font that will be used in a project. (7)

stylus. Pen-like pointer, but without ink. (2)

subfolder. Folder contained within another folder. (4)

subject line. Helps the reader know the content of the message before reading. (8)

supercomputer. Has processing power that can handle complex jobs beyond the scope of other computer systems. (2)

switch. Network transmission device that checks and forwards packets between parts of the network. (14)

system clipboard. Virtual container for storing data. (6)

system image. Backup that is an exact duplicate of all data on the drive, including the drives required for Windows to run, your system settings, programs, and document files. (4)

system requirements. Specifications for the processor speed, RAM, hard drive space, and any additional hardware or software needed to run the software. (3)

system software. Includes four types of software: the operating system, utility programs, device drivers, and programs. (3)

T

table. Contains information arranged in horizontal rows and vertical columns. (12)

table of contents. Lists the major sections and subsections within a report with page numbers. (8)

tabs. Preset horizontal locations across the page in a document. (7)

tag. Code enclosed in chevrons that tells the browser how to format or display the content. (13)

task manager. Analyzes what is going on in the system and reports the results. (5)

technical support. Providing assistance to others with setting up, running, or fixing technical systems, such as computer systems. (17)

telecommuting. Working for a company from home using information technologies. (1)

telepresence. Refers to technology that helps a person feel as if he or she is present with other people in a meeting or gathering in a different location. (15)

template. Formatting and organizational suggestions that can help the user create a professional-looking document. (3)

term. Number of periods it will take to repay a loan. (11)

text. String data type that may consist of any letters, numbers, or other keyboard characters. (10)

text-input device. Image-input device used with software to convert the image to text that can be used by the computer. (2)

theme. Set of specified colors, fonts, and effects. (9)

touch screen. Device that senses applied pressure and sends signals to the CPU. (2)

touch system. When user does not look at the keyboard when entering information, rather has memorized the location of keys based on hand position. (7)

tracked changes. Feature for logging markups. (7).

trademark. Protects taglines, slogans, names, symbols, or any unique method to identify a product or company. (8)

transition. Method of shifting from one slide to the next. (9)

transmission rate. Number of bits per second that can be sent from one device to another. (14)

tree topology. Network topology that connects smaller star topology networks via a bus topology. (14)

Trojan horse. Program that invites the user to run it while concealing malicious code that will be executed. (16)

troubleshooting. Systematically analyzing a problem to find a solution. (5)

typeface. Design of characters. (6, 7)

U

unicode. System for encoding text characters in which two bytes are assigned to each character. (3)

uniform resource locator (URL). Address that points to a specific document or other resource on a computer network. (13)

uninterruptable power supply (UPS). Device that protects computer systems against power surges and outages. (16)

universal serial bus (USB). Industry standard for communication between devices and the computer. (2)

upload. User at one computer sending a document to a server. (13)

user account. Set of privileges for allowed actions. (3)

user interface (UI). Means by which the user enters data and receives feedback. (2)

username. Online identity of the account holder. (15)

utility programs. Assist in managing and optimizing a computer's performance. (3)

V

validation. Process of checking the code to ensure it contains no errors of syntax or usage. (13)

vector-based software. Creates graphics composed of lines, curves, and fills based on mathematical formulas. (3)

videoconferencing. Conducting a meeting with both audial and visual interaction between people in different locations. (15)

virtual printer. Outputs a file instead of a physical hardcopy. (6)

virtual private network (VPN). Uses the Internet as an extension of a LAN or other smaller network. (14)

virtualization. Process that allows multiple operating systems to simultaneously share a processor's resources in a safe and efficient way. (17)

visual design. Arrangement of the visual and artistic elements used to accomplish a goal or communicate an idea. (7)

Voice over Internet Protocol (VoIP). Set of technologies that supports voice and multimedia transmission over the Internet. (15)

volume label. Name of the device itself. Also known as the *volume name.* (2)

W

web developer. Person who is responsible for creating websites. (17)

webcam. Image-input device that can be mounted on top of a monitor or may be built into a laptop computer. (2)

what-if analysis. When a parameter in a data model is changed to see how the outcome will be altered. (10)

wide area network (WAN). Consists of a group of computers within a large geographic area. (14)

widow. Last line of a paragraph that falls immediately *after* a page break. (7)

Wi-Fi. Describes when a wireless router is placed between the modem and the computer and transmissions are sent though the air to the computers with a Wi-Fi receiver. (14)

Wi-Fi Protected Access (WPA). Security algorithm that has replaced WEP in most wireless networks to make them more secure. (14)

wildcard. Used in the search box to represent an unknown character. (4)

windowed. Window that is visible, but does not fill the entire screen. (6)

Wired Equivalent Privacy (WEP). Security algorithm for wireless networks designed to protect data. (14)

workbook. Excel file. (10)

worker productivity. How efficiently and quickly a person completes tasks. (1)

worksheet. Grid of vertical and horizontal lines where work is done in a spreadsheet. (10)

wrap text. Allows a new line within the cell to be automatically started when the length of the text exceeds the width of the cell. (10)

Z

zooming. Changing the magnification of the view. (6)

INDEX

output devices for users with
disabilities, 67–68
pointing devices, 52–54
printers, 63–65
projectors, 62–63
text-input devices, 56–57
touch screens, 54
input device, 41
inserting, 238
insertion point, 217
inside address, 308
Instagram, 621
instant messaging (IM), 610
instruction set, 44
integrated development environment
(IDE), 123
intellectual property, 335
interaction design, 526
interactive books, 15
interactivity, 526
internal audience, 350
internal style, 543
Internet, 511–526
breadcrumbs, 520
browsers, 518–520
career field, 686–688
definition, 511
digital wellness, 526–527
downloads, 515, 521–523
ethical use, 531–532
HTML and Web 2.0, 524–526
hyperlinks, 516
Internet service provider, 512
mouse actions, 521
other protocols, 514–515
programming languages, 546–549
protocol, 512–514
scroll bars, 520
top-level domains, 513
uniform resource locator (URL),
516–518
upload, 515
using search engines, 527–531
World Wide Web, 515–523
Internet and the World Wide Web,
510–532
creating for the Web, 533–549
Internet area network (IAN), 567
Internet etiquette. *See* netiquette.
Internet message access protocol
(IMAP), 590
Internet protocol suite, definition, 514
Internet providers, or hotspots,
674–675
Internet research, career preparation,
712
Internet scams or fraudulent
websites, 673

Internet security protocols, 644–647
HTTPS, 646
other protocols, 646
security measures, 646–647
SSH, 645
TCP/IP, 645
Internet service provider (ISP), 512
interpersonal skills, 704
interpreter, 90
intranet, 520, 567
introduction, 320
IT manager, 696–697
IT professionals. *See* career fields.
IT security positions, 690–691

J

JavaScript, 524, 547
junk e-mail, 601
justification, 274

K

kerning, 295
key applications,
advanced spreadsheet uses, 434–461
common office application
features, 212–263
database software, 462–505
formal documents, 302–345
presentation software, 346–397
spreadsheet software, 398–433
word-processing software, 264–301
key tip badges, 218
keyboard navigation, 218–219
keyboards, 50–52
actions, 50
definition, 50
Dvorak keyboard, 51
factors in evaluating, 52
types, 50–52
virtual, 51
keyboard shortcuts, 218
killer app, 401
knowledge bases, 530

L

land-line technology, 606
landscape, 229
language packs, 101
laptop computers, 39
launching applications, 215–216
Microsoft Excel, 216
Microsoft PowerPoint, 216
Microsoft Word, 215–216
layout, 287
leading, 274
learning management system (LMS),
630

leave-behinds. *See* handouts.
letterhead, 305
libel, 622
library, 142
licensing agreement, 337
line chart, 451
line spacing, 274
LinkedIn, 620, 644
linking, 453
living online,
careers, 682–731
communication networks, 554–585
electronic communication and
collaboration, 586–635
Internet and the World Wide Web,
508–553
security, privacy, and safety,
636–681
local area network (LAN), 567
logical functions, 444
low-level programming language, 90

M

machine language, 90
magnetic media, 71
mainframe computers, 37
maintenance, 185–189
keyboard, 186
monitor, 186–187
software maintenance, 187
ventilation, 186
malware, 639
man-in-the-middle attacks, 646
margins, 272
master page, 286
maximized, 220
media files,
cropping an image, 239
image location and size, 238–239
inserting, 238–241
reversing errors, 241–242
rotating an image, 239–241
searching for text, 243–244
media reader devices, 150
media sharing, 620
memory, 42
merge, 416
mesh topology, 569
message header, 589
metadata, 254
metropolitan area network (MAN),
567
microprocessor, 44
Microsoft Outlook, 591
millions of instructions per second
(MIPS), 38
minimized, 221
mixed punctuation, 308

U

unicode, 89
uniform resource locator (URL), 516
uninterruptable power supply (UPS), 668
universal serial bus (USB), 45
unordered list. *See* bulleted list.
unsecured, 575
upload, 515
user accounts, 100
user interface (UI), 50
username, 590
users with disabilities,
    accessible input devices for, 59–60
    output devices for, 67–68
utility programs, 104

V

validation, 546
validity, 529
vector-based software, 119
verbal and nonverbal
        communication, 703
videoconferencing, 611
viewing angle, 62
virtualization, 691–692
virtual keyboards, 51
virtual printer, 228
virtual private network (VPN), 568
virus and malware scans, 189
virus damage, repair, 670
viruses and other malware,
    block virus transmission, 669–670
    combating, 669–671
    keep antivirus software updated, 670–671
    repair virus damage, 670
virus transmission, block, 669–670
visual appearance, 295
visual design, 285
visual enhancements of data, 447–457
    charts, 450–453
    comma-separated values files, 456–457
    conditional formatting, 448–450
    spreadsheet charts in text
        documents, 453–455
    tables, 456
voice mail messages, 627–628

Voice over Internet Protocol (VoIP), 611
volume label, 73

W

W3C validation site, 546
Web 2.0, 525–526
    human-computer interaction (HCI), 526
    interaction design, 526
    interactivity, 526
    new media, 526
web-based conferencing, 612–613
web-based e-mail, 591–593
web browsers, 518
webcam, 55
web design, 533–549
    alignment, 535
    contrast, 534
    CSS, 542–544
    HTML, 537–541
    HTML5, 541–542
    proximity, 535–537
    repetition, 534
    validation, 546
    web widgets, 544
web developer, 694–695
    career field, 694–695
websites,
    determining reliability, 672–674
    e-commerce sites, 673–674
    Internet scams or fraudulent
        websites, 673
    pirated media, 674
    safe file downloads, 672–673
what-if analysis, 407
wide area network (WAN), 567
widow, 287
Wi-Fi, 512, 558
    network, 9, 676
Wi-Fi Protected Access (WPA), 575
wikis, 620
wildcards, 151
windowed, 220
Windows 7 startup programs, 203–204
Windows file and folder names, 135–140
    file name extensions, 138–139

legal names, 135–137
meaningful names, 137
naming group of related files, 139–140
Windows File Explorer, 140–147
    displaying file name extensions, 143–145
    folders, 141–142
    libraries, 142–143
    renaming files and folders, 146–147
Wired Equivalent Privacy (WEP), 575
wireless network protection, 651–652
wireless network security types, 575–576
    unsecured, 575
    WEP, 575
    WPA and WPA2, 575
wireless security, 675–676
word processing, common terms
        related to (chart), 267
word-processing software, 264–301
    creating a document, 266–288
    proofing text, 289–297
workbook, 401
worker productivity, 21
workplace, 20–24
    advanced medical research, 23
    automotive industry, 23
    changing tools, 21
    computer use, 20–24
    current employment, 22–23
    eliminating distance, 21–22
    finance, 23
    future employment, 23
    green collar jobs, 24
    home health care, 24
    skills, 704–708
    technical knowledge, 22
    worker productivity, 21
worksheet, 401
World Wide Web (WWW), 9
wrap text, 410

Y

YouTube, 621, 644

Z

ZIP file type, 170
zooming, 253